To Rudolph
all my love,
Adolph

MY NEW ORDER

ADOLF HITLER

MY NEW ORDER

Edited with Commentary

by Raoul de Roussy de Sales

With an Introduction

by Raymond Gram Swing

Reynal & Hitchcock

New York

Published August, 1941
Second Printing, August, 1941

PRINTED IN THE UNITED STATES OF AMERICA
BY THE CORNWALL PRESS, CORNWALL, N. Y.

CONTENTS

NOTE

The editor has used italics throughout the text of the speeches in this book to emphasize some of the most significant statements of Hitler. The Fuehrer's own words appear in quotation marks.

INTRODUCTION

by

Raymond Gram Swing

INTRODUCTION

My New Order, a collection of Hitler's speeches set in a running commentary, is a sequel to *Mein Kampf.* Though *Mein Kampf* rates as a written work, indeed as Hitler's only written work, it is not prose but rhetoric, and his speeches follow upon it logically as of the same fabric. The understanding of Hitler, his origin, development and techniques, entails an analysis of his oratory. The analysis is not easy. Hitler has been one of the most prolific orators of his time. He is a special kind of orator, not of the classic school, but of a unique and modern category. It is oratory for the masses, and the masses were never accessible until twentieth-century inventions made it possible for one man to be heard by millions. It is soapbox oratory heard in all corners of the nation, and at times in all corners of the world. Soapbox oratory is based on what an intellectual scorns as an emotional appeal to the baser passions. In the listener it stirs hatred and feeds self-vindication, and whether on paper it bears inspection for consistency, logic or soundness is immaterial. Yet Hitler's oratory contains all there is of Hitler's mind. It may even be questioned whether in his private moments he thinks unoratorically, or can for long discourse with those about him without stepping onto a soapbox. So the analysis of Hitler's oratory is the one revelation of Hitler's thought. Since his thought has engendered, first a party, then a regime, and now a power which spreads over Europe and may reach out to dominate the world, the analyst must approach his oratory with the keenest excitement of search.

He finds present even in the early speeches of the party

leader fighting for local power the elements of the doctrines which by now have shaken the foundations of the world. He finds, too, that the doctrines, recently more clearly developed, are still delivered with the vulgarity and turgid emotionalism of the young party leader. He comes to recognize, not the political plans, but the themes, like musical themes, that run through Hitler's output of words. Hitler is not only a philosophical Wagnerian, he composes his oratory with recourse to Wagnerian *leitmotivs,* which recur insistently, not as statements of political wisdom underlying his plans for government, but as detached concepts to be called upon for repeated reference and modulation. They may contradict other concepts, but that is only an ultimate contradiction, since the themes are not played at the same moment. They are brought forward, then omitted. But as in music, one discovers that they all are woven together into the final structure of the composition.

Since Hitler has been an indefatigable orator, the compilation of a sequel to *Mein Kampf* involves severe editing of a prodigious output. Millions of words have had to be eliminated, so as to retain only such speeches, or parts of speeches, as make a readable and instructive book. Elimination on such a wholesale scale cannot be a scientific task, for the true Hitler is expressed not only by the clear concepts to be identified, but by the very contrast between these concepts and the verbal profusion in which they were set. So this volume is not quite right proportionally, though it is an approximation whose inaccuracy is all in Hitler's favor, in that it helps a reader to grasp more firmly the nature of Hitler's thought than if he had to find his way through Hitler's tempestuous reiterations and perplexing inconsistencies without the editor's aid.

The editor of this volume has made his choices and presented his material so that an American reader can follow the course of Adolf Hitler from his status as No. 7 of the German Workers' Party to his mastery of Europe and his bid for the domination of the world. His comments will depict Hitler's evolution. He will not attempt to answer the question whether Hitler knowingly and from the outset willed to become the supreme leader of Germany and ultimately the ruler of the world, or whether he is a Man of Destiny. The evolution is there, and the facts which reveal it are pointed out. The editor reveals the Hitlerian methods, which are fairly constant, though his immediate objectives changed with a dazzling confusion.

Only a first-rate political journalist is competent for such an editing task. The political journalist is imbued with a sense of history-in-the-making not to be expected of the historian. Indeed the true historian gathers his authority from the backward, not the contemporary look. Perspective and data are his handmaidens. The political journalist must labor without either. He must perceive in the present both the past and the future.

The craftsman of this sequel to *Mein Kampf* is one of the few first-rate political journalists in this country. He is a Frenchman, but he is unique in that the greater part of his journalistic career has been lived in this country as a foreign correspondent. And the foreign correspondent is probably the most objectively trained of all those who write about politics. He sees partisanships as parts, and his real study is the whole.

Raoul de Roussy de Sales was New York correspondent for the *Paris-Soir,* and political correspondent for the Havas agency in the pre-Vichy days. Unlike most correspondents, he entered his profession at the top, and cannot be reckoned a product of the Paris journalistic school. He is a journalist who has matured in the United States, so that his powers are an unusual combination of French civilization and American political observation and experience. His French roots are deep, as he is a descendant of two old French aristocratic families, the de Sales and the de Roussys. In his veins flows the blood of St. Francis de Sales, who was made the patron saint of journalists by the late Pope. Though he had an American and Spanish grandmother, and an education both in France and in England, he is as representative of French culture and refinement as any man of his race I have known. But beyond that, he is a citizen of the world, a political thinker of profundity and detachment, and a superb craftsman. His writings both in France and this country have been recognized and honored. He won the Strassburger Prize for the best Franco-American journalism, and was made a Knight of the Legion of Honor, and among his colleagues in New York he served two years as president of the Association of Foreign Correspondents. These biographical tidbits are not mentioned to add to his stature, which is measured in his professional work, as for example his writings in the *Atlantic Monthly* about this country and France. I know of no American who could write with more valid judgment about this country, and none who could write as authentically about France, and certainly no one equipped to write about both countries with so much sensitivity and wisdom. Only a mind of this clarity is capable of bearing the responsibility of editing the sequel to *Mein Kampf*. That M. de Sales helped in the preparation of the American edition of *Mein Kampf* adds to the logic of his selection to prepare this volume.

Raymond Gram Swing

FOREWORD

ADOLF HITLER is one of the most prolific orators of all time. Approximately 400 to 500 of his speeches have been published in various forms but the total to date is well over 1500. During the period 1933-36, when he was already much absorbed by the duties of Chancellor of the Reich, he nevertheless found time to deliver about 600 speeches. But besides speaking frequently, Hitler also speaks abundantly. Most of his speeches are very long. From one and a half to two hours is normal length. There are several speeches of three and even four hours' duration.

From this mass of verbiage this volume seeks to eliminate the non-essential and to present what is significant and important to an understanding of Hitler's strategy. Many speeches have been eliminated and most have been cut. Admirers or critics of Hitler may deplore certain omissions. The reason for the editorial policy is that the only way to make the speeches of Hitler at all accessible to the public is to sacrifice a very large portion of them.

Care has been taken, however, to preserve such speeches and such fragments as will enable the reader to have a complete picture of Hitler's doctrine and to follow his rise to power and the expansion of his domination over Europe. In view of the fact that Hitler is extremely repetitious, only the most striking and clearest version of each of his ideas has been selected. This does not mean that all repetitions have been eliminated. To use constantly and untiringly the same arguments, and to pound into the heads of his listeners the same formulas, is part of Hitler's oratorical technique. But whatever repetitions are found in this volume, the reader should bear in mind that they are but an infinitesimal sample of Hitler's prodigious capacity for reiteration.

In order to facilitate the reading of the speeches, they have been presented in chronological order and divided into chapters or phases which correspond to the historical development of the last twenty years.

This procedure has not been chosen arbitrarily, but is justified, I believe, by the fact that Hitler being at once a propagandist, a leader of men and a conqueror, it was important to show how he used the platform and the microphone firstly to gain power in Germany and secondly to extend his domination over Europe.

Hitler's speeches are weapons, as much a part of his strategy of conquest as more direct instruments of warfare. Hitler is past master at throwing up verbal smoke screens to conceal his intended moves. He knows equally well the effectiveness of massive oratorical assaults that shake the nerves of his victims or opponents and break down their resistance. He knows how to give pledges, that will be broken later, but will serve temporarily to divide and confuse and to create the illusion of security. He uses insults and lies in the same manner as his generals use Stuka planes and tanks, to break through the respectable but often weak front of his adversaries. He contradicts himself constantly, but his contradictions often produce the effect of a psychological pincer-movement which crushes the best defenses of logic and ordinary morality.

Each chapter is preceded by an explanatory comment intended to bring out the salient aspect of each particular phase, and, furthermore, a running chronology of world events places each speech against its proper background.

Most speeches are followed by comments from the world press to give an idea of the reaction of public opinion at the time. In the early phases, quotations from the liberal German newspapers have been selected, in order to show the frequent similarity between the attitude of the German opposition to Hitler while he rose to power and that of the outside world later on.

To establish the English text of the speeches, several sources have been utilized, among them the *London Times,* the *New York Times,* the *Associated Press* or the official German version. We acknowledge particularly the courtesy of *The New York Times* and the *Associated Press* in permitting the use of their dispatches. But special mention should be made of the important translation prepared by the *Royal Institute of International Affairs* of London, under the editorship of Professor Norman Baynes, which gives substantial excerpts of Hitler's speeches from 1922 to September, 1939. Thanks to the Institute and to the Oxford University Press of London and New York, which is later publishing this translation in America in two volumes, it has been possible to utilize this valuable documentation for this volume.

In many cases, however, special translations have had to be made, either because no English text could be found or because those available did not appear satisfactory.

It should be noted that no translation into English can give a true impression of the original German. Hitler's style reflects the incompleteness of his early education. His grammar is incorrect; his sentences often confused to the point of obscurity. His crudity frequently borders on downright vulgarity. Any translation, however clumsy, is more readable than the original.

I wish to thank the many persons who have helped me in this work, but more particularly the nine research workers—most of them journalists—who have collected the material for this book. My deepest gratitude goes to my friend and former collaborator on *Paris-Soir,* Curt Riess, without whose help, advice, and untiring zeal this work could not have been completed.

It is the purpose of the publishers of this book to keep future editions up to date by adding to them further speeches and comments in order to follow Hitler's progress in the establishment of his New Order, or to register his failure.

R.R.S.

PHASE I

The Rise to Power

1918 — January 30, 1933

COMMENT

THE speeches of Adolf Hitler are the most complete expression of his personality. More than any other ruler, it is through the spoken word that he can best be judged. He is essentially a speechmaker, and although today it is his deeds and his conquests that most impress the world it should not be forgotten that he started as a soap-box orator and spoke his way to power.

His career as an orator began at the end of the World War when his commander sent him around to the various camps to keep up the morale of the soldiers. But his real career as a professional speaker started when he joined the German Workers' party which was later to become the National Socialist party.

The Party, then little more than a *Verein,* had no program as yet. The members knew only that they were against the Republic and against the Jews, two ideas which they held in common with about twenty other little parties.

On the advice of his friend, Dietrich Eckart, a former Berlin newspaper editor who had sensed Hitler's oratorical talent, he asked for the post of Chief of Propaganda in the new Party. The first public meeting of the Party with Hitler as the main speaker took place in Munich on February 24, 1920, before an audience of 107 people. Curiously enough, Hitler nearly lost his chance to speak at this meeting because the other Party members considered him too nervous and excitable and distrusted his bourgeois leanings. He was finally allowed to speak for twenty minutes. The audience applauded. No doubt he was effective, but on the following day no Munich newspaper even mentioned his name.

From then on the building of the Party was achieved entirely through meetings at which Hitler spoke.

The increasing size of his audiences measures his growing influence: On February 3, 1921, speaking for the first time at the Zirkus Krone, the largest hall in Munich, he had an audience of 5,600. On November 4, 1921, at a meeting in a Munich Bräuhaus, there occurred the first brawls between Hitler's Storm Troopers, then called "Order Troops," and the opposition speakers. On November 30, 1922, five mass meetings were held in Munich with 14,000 participants. On December 13, 1922, ten mass meetings were held in the same town with an audience of 20,000.

The movement was now well under way; Hitler was established as a leader who could influence the masses. He was no longer the Chief of Propaganda but the Fuehrer of the Party.

No one knew better than Hitler himself that his real power was his voice. To increase his effectiveness he took elocution lessons from a Munich actor called Basil. To arouse his public he resorted to means which were in strange contrast to the hard and even Spartan spirit of the Party. He did not hesitate to weep before his audience and implore it in a choked voice to follow his leadership.

In these early days Hitler was not taken very seriously by the inner circles of the Party. They spoke of him as "our puppet" and found him singularly incompetent in matters of serious organization. He not only refused to work regularly in the Party office but whenever he appeared there he made scenes, ranted at everybody, and threw himself into fits of rage or hysterics.

But Hitler's apparent lack of self-control and his outbursts of violence were to be among the strong points of his technique. His first premature attempt to seize power, the Putsch of November 9, 1923, was not the result of prolonged consideration and conferences but was born almost spontaneously during a meeting in the Bräuhaus. While the meeting was already in full swing, Hitler was still undecided as to whether he dared make the attempt, and even his most intimate friends were bewildered when he suddenly took the floor and announced the Putsch as a *fait accompli*. Thus his first bid for power was an orator's effort to extend his influence beyond the walls of the hall.

A born orator seldom misses an opportunity to make himself heard and Hitler even utilized the chances which defeat offered. During his trials he made two speeches in which he appealed beyond the Court to the whole of Germany and to the world. Perhaps the real reason he wrote *Mein Kampf* was because he was a prisoner in Landsberg.

After his release he found the Party in a state of collapse, but this does not seem to have disturbed him half as much as the fact that he was forbidden to speak anywhere in Germany. He spared no effort to get the ban lifted. His future and that of Germany depended on it.

Hitler's speeches are no models of oratory. His German is sloppy and often full of grammatical errors. The sentences are long, full of clichés and bourgeois smugness. His voice is not pleasant and he often shouts himself hoarse. The substance of his speeches is usually confused and repetitious. Especially in his early years, his method consisted in repeating and rehashing indefinitely the same theories, in hurling the same accusations at his opponents, and in drowning his audience under an avalanche of words. In no other country but Germany, where orators are rare, could Hitlerian eloquence be tolerated by an average audience, with an average taste and an average endurance.

But Hitler's appeal to the masses was undeniable, and, from the earliest days, he showed that he had the gift and the power to stir the German people and to restore their self-confidence. His energy, his daring, his fanatical faith in his own mission were inspiring. To a country humiliated by defeat, impoverished by postwar inflation, and profoundly demoralized by the sense of its own weakness and impotence, Hitler spoke of hope for the future, of conquest, wealth, and power. He told the Germans that they had not lost the war, but had been betrayed, and that, provided they had faith in themselves and in him, all the glorious dreams of the past would come true—that they would be strong and proud again, and masters of the world.

To defy the Treaty of Versailles, the Weimar Republic, the "November criminals," and all the established powers—if only in words—was sweet music to the ears of Hitler's listeners. No one had spoken such words to them in years, nor held such promises of revenge. No one had told them that they were still a great people, that the sword was nobler than the plow, that they were innocent of all guilt, and that they were right—right in the eyes of God, right in the eyes of history, always and absolutely right, merely because they were Germans. Hitler told his listeners that they belonged to a superior race, but also that they were victims. He told them that what was wrong with the war was not the war itself, but that they had lost it. He told them that the whole world was arrayed against them and wanted the destruction of Germany. He showed them that the Weimar Republic was allied with their enemies because it was a democracy, and therefore international and Jewish. He told them that they had a mission: to regenerate Germany, and to achieve this end, they must be brutal, intolerant and ruthless. He preached violence and hatred to people whom anxiety and despair had made meek and spiritless. Small wonder that Hitler, the ex-soldier, who owned nothing, as he said himself, but a zinc plate with his name on it, should be hailed as a savior when he exclaimed: "Our task is to give to the dictator when he comes a people that is ripe for him. German people, awake! It draws near today!"

The program of the Party, as expressed in Hitler's speeches, was never very coherent or very stable. It changed with circumstances and contained ideas and promises which were mutually exclusive. He promised everything to everybody and offered to fulfill all wishes and hopes. He told the peasants that they would get land, and he promised the Junkers that they would lose no property. He made pledges to the workers that they would get higher wages, and to the employers he promised that labor costs would be reduced.

But these irrelevancies were of no importance, either to Hitler or to his followers. His technique has always been to overlook contradictions and to answer criticism by violent counter attacks. In fact lies and slander were hurled at the Republic in such a way as to give the impression that Hitler was acting in self-defense and that his patience was constantly being tried beyond human endurance. These tactics were to become part of the Hitlerian system of strategy and he made ample use of them when, having assured his power in Germany, he defied Europe. They were to be used before he annexed Austria and before he conquered Czechoslovakia and Poland.

More important, in these early days, is the development of what might be termed the technique of the *leitmotiv:*

Hitler does not seem to have had much interest in practical politics. His object was not to propose concrete reforms but to implant in the consciousness of his followers a certain number of ideas which—through endless repetition and emphasis—would assume the character of obsessions.

The name of Wagner has often been mentioned in connection with Hitler, not only on account of his passionate admiration for that musician, but because the world has sensed that there was a deep affinity between the conceptions of the two men. Without going into the philosophical aspect of this affinity, it can be said, however, that Hitler's method of presenting his ideas and of conveying impressions can indeed be compared to Wagner's use of musical themes, which through their recurrence and development serve to identify certain characters and certain concepts.

The main difference between Wagner and Hitler, in this respect, is that whereas the former is an artist, the latter has no sense of proportion or construction. When Hitler develops an idea—one of his three or four basic *leitmotivs*—there actually seems to be no limit to his resourcefulness and imagination. To make a point, he is bound neither by logic, nor plausibility, nor historic accuracy. His method is to assert as gospel truth both truths and lies and never to concede that he might possibly be in the wrong or even that a doubt could exist.

Hitler uses words as weapons, and his ideas or *leitmotivs,* although fairly consistent, are modified according to the circumstances and the immediate effect which he wishes to obtain. But the technique is always the same: whatever resistance opposes him must finally be broken down by the sheer accumulation of words.

In his early days, Hitler made use of two fundamental themes: anti-Semitism and the denunciation of the Versailles Treaty.

To make the Jew a scapegoat has always been an easy trick for a certain type of demagogue. The relative defenselessness of the Jewish minorities in each country has made them a convenient and safe target all through history. But in the case of Hitler, the Jew has been elevated, so to speak, to a degree of evilness which he had never attained before. In Hitler's conception of the world, the Jew becomes positively demonic and everything to which the qualification "Jewish" can be attached is automatically foul, destructive, and beyond redemption. The Jew has become the symbol of all impurity, and, by extension, all forms of impurity are more or less caused by the influence of the Jews.

By arousing latent anti-Semitic prejudices in his followers and by denouncing as Jewish everything which opposed him, Hitler succeeded in giving to his doctrine a queer mystical unity. He created a new notion of Sin and Evil, a new rallying point for a modern crusade the aim of which is to destroy everything which he denounced as Jewish.

Thanks to Hitler's imagination, he demonstrated to his followers that such words as internationalism, socialism, democracy, capitalism, art, intellectuals, etc., could be made into symbols of evil by the simple process of affixing to them the epithet "Jewish." Communism and Bolshevism were of course the most obvious manifestations of "Jewish" corruption and he made no distinction between Marxism as a political and economic theory and its applications in Russia or elsewhere. To rid Germany of Bolshevism was indeed the first aim which Hitler proposed to his followers. He was later to amplify it and to propose a universal crusade against it to save civilization and Christianity.

As an antithesis to the evilness of the Jews, Hitler opposed the purity, sanctity, and transcendental virtue of the Aryan or Nordic race. To establish the primacy of this "race," Hitler appealed to legends, superstitions, and vague beliefs which lay dormant in the soul of his German followers. Such mystic and barbaric ideas as the doctrine of "Blood and Soil," based on ancient cults, were revived and somewhat modernized and bolstered up with dubious "scientific" references. German science, pan-Germanic teaching, and barbaric atavism were blended into one great revelation—the Hitlerian myth.

Hitler's ideas concerning foreign policy were neither clear nor co-ordinated in these early days. They were in fact determined by considerations of internal politics. He repeated many times that there can be no such thing as a foreign policy for a nation as long as that nation has not proved its internal strength and unity of purpose. His first task was therefore to create that unity. Before Germany could have a foreign policy, there must first of all be a Germany, Hitler's Germany.

Nevertheless, as *Mein Kampf* shows, and as confirmed by

his speeches, there were a few definite points firmly fixed in Hitler's mind.

The first was that the Versailles Treaty was not only unfair but criminal. Its purpose, according to Hitler, was not to make peace but to destroy Germany or to keep her enslaved forever. Moreover, it was not the result of a defeat of the German armies. The German armies, asserted Hitler, had never been defeated; they had been betrayed, stabbed in the back by Bolshevism, Jews, and the "November criminals" (the Weimar Republic). The duty of the German people was therefore clear: they had to repair this monstrous injustice, and to do this nothing should stand in their way. Treaties, signatures, pledges, international contracts were nothing more than instruments of the oppression that Germany had the right to disregard and violate.

A second point in Hitler's program was the reunion of all Germans into one community. This he justified on the principle of the right of self-determination—a principle established by Woodrow Wilson, but which, in the case of Germany, had been shamelessly violated.

The third idea was that Germany should seek no alliance, except perhaps with Italy and England. England, in Hitler's estimation, could be considered as a member of the Nordic race. As for Italy, her alliance should be sought, first of all because Mussolini had originated Fascism, and secondly because it would help to destroy France, the eternal and arch-enemy.

It is not possible to determine how much of Hitler's program seemed to him susceptible of practical achievement, in these early days, and how much was merely intended to stimulate the ardor of his followers. It should be noted, however, that he has but slightly varied from his fundamental objectives, and that the strategy which he employed to seize power in Germany was to be used again, with very little variation, when he undertook to become master of Europe.

There is little doubt that Hitler could have been stopped inside Germany if his opponents had been sufficiently aware of his growing power and of the necessity for uniting against him. But their whole attitude was a prefiguration of the divisions and weaknesses which were to seal the doom of so many European nations at a later date.

In fact, the opposition to Hitler in Germany went through a series of phases which correspond roughly to the same phases, projected in the field of foreign conquest and expansion.

At first the opposition tried to ignore Hitler. Up to the Putsch of 1923, his name hardly appeared in the Berlin press. He was then considered as a purely local, Munich phenomenon.

In the second phase, when he could no longer be ignored, there was a concerted refusal to take him seriously. The democratic newspapers ridiculed his program and were content to prove his lack of logic and his inconsistencies.

The third period was that of appeasement. It follows the fall of Chancellor Bruening, when von Papen had taken over the government. Von Papen wanted to govern without Hitler, but needed the votes of the Nazis in the Reichstag. He succeeded in obtaining them for a while but soon learned, as other appeasers were to learn later, that one can keep Hitler appeased only as long as Hitler himself wants to be appeased.

Then followed an internal "war of nerves," a phase during which opposition parties tried to create a defensive block against the Nazis. General Schleicher attempted to form a coalition against the Nazis embracing the conservatives, the Reichswehr, the labor unions and the Strasser wing.

By then it was too late to stop Hitler. And a fifth phase began: the opposition tried to make treaties with Hitler. Those who had helped Hitler to power, wealthy industrialists like Thyssen, members of the Reichswehr, Junkers, and conservatives, convinced President Hindenburg to make a deal with Hitler. He was offered the post of Chancellor and it was argued that he would be useful in crushing the Communists and liberating Germany from the Versailles *Diktat.* The Nazis were to have only two other posts in the Cabinet. Moreover Hitler had given his promise to Hindenburg that he would collaborate loyally with his conservative colleagues.

Five months later the leader of the Conservative party, Hugenberg, and all his colleagues were out of the government and their party was effectively dissolved. Seven years later Thyssen fled the country as an exile.

The death of President Hindenburg lifted the last restraint on Hitler's absolute power over Germany. It had been a long road from the day he first addressed 107 people in a small room in Munich to the supreme position of President and Chancellor of the Reich. Hitler had said: "The domestic battle must come before the battle with the world without. . . ."

This first battle he had won by the sheer power of his voice. To win the next he needed more than words. Germany had to be armed.

•

SPEECH OF APRIL 12, 1922

Munich

Background

1918

March 7—Meeting of 26 "independently organized" factory workers to form a "Labor Committee for a Good Peace"—the predecessor of the National Socialist party.

October—First public meeting of the group.

1919

January 5—Formation of German Workers party.

July 10—Treaty of Versailles ratified by the German National Assembly (by British Parliament, July 25).

September 19—Hitler becomes the seventh member of the German Workers party in Munich.

1920

January 10—The League of Nations automatically comes into being under the terms of the Versailles Treaty.

February 25—The program of the National Socialist German Workers party is proclaimed in a mass meeting in Munich.

November 2—Bavaria is requested by the Interallied Control Commission at Munich to disband its militia.

1921

January 16—Aristide Briand forms a liberal cabinet in France.

February 20—The first local branches of the National Socialist party are established.

March 20—In Upper Silesia, a plebiscite is held.

April 29—Italian Fascists seize Fiume.

July 23—The Bavarian national guards deliver to the Allies more than half of their 250,000 rifles.

July 26—General strike in Rome. Conflict between Communists and Fascists.

July 29—Hitler is elected to the leadership of the National Socialist German Workers' party.

August 26—Mathias Erzberger, former Vice Chancellor and during the war head of the Kaiser's foreign propaganda, is assassinated by extreme nationalists.

September 30—The Reichstag ratifies the American Peace Treaty.

October 22—Karl of the House of Habsburg tries to regain

the Hungarian throne by flying from Switzerland with his wife Zita, but fails.

December 6—Proclamation of the "Irish Free State."

1922

January 12—French Premier Briand resigns, and is succeeded by Raymond Poincaré.

January 29—First public meeting of the National Socialist party in Munich.

March 28—Reich Chancellor Wirth denounces the Reparations Commission to the Reichstag, saying it is impossible to meet the demand of a tax levy of 60,000,000 marks before May 31.

March—In the Bavarian Assembly, Minister of State Schweyer says, ". . . The expulsion of Hitler is being considered."

April 3—General staffs of Germany and Russia sign a military agreement at Berlin.

The Speech

AFTER the War production had begun again and it was thought that better times were coming. Frederick the Great after the Seven Years War had, as the result of superhuman efforts, left Prussia without a penny of debt: at the end of the World War Germany was burdened with her own debt of some 7 or 8 milliards of marks and beyond that was faced with the debts of "the rest of the world"—"the so-called reparations." The product of Germany's work thus belonged, not to the nation, but to her foreign creditors: "it was carried endlessly in trains for territories beyond our frontiers." Every worker had to support another worker, the product of whose labor was commandeered by the foreigner. "The German people after twenty-five or thirty years, in consequence of the fact that it will never be able to pay all that is demanded of it, will have so gigantic a sum still owing that practically it will be forced to produce more than it does today." What will the end be? and the answer to that question is "Pledging of our land, enslavement of our labor-strength. Therefore, in the economic sphere, November 1918 was in truth no achievement, but it was the beginning of our collapse." And in the political sphere we lost first our military prerogatives, and with that loss went the real sovereignty of our State, and then our financial independence, for there remained always the Reparations Commission so that "practically we have no longer a politically independent German Reich, we are already a colony of the outside world. We have contributed to this because so far as possible we humiliated ourselves morally, we positively destroyed our own honor and helped to befoul, to besmirch, and to deny everything which we previously held as sacred." If it be objected that the Revolution has won for us gains in social life: "they must be extraordinarily secret, these social gains—so secret that one never sees them in practical life—they must just run like a fluid through our German atmosphere. Some one may say 'Well, there is the eight-hour day!' And was a collapse necessary to gain that? And will the eight-hour day be rendered any more secure through our becoming practically the bailiff and the drudge of the other peoples?" One of these days France will say: "You cannot meet your obligations, you must work more." So this achievement of the Revolution is put in question first of all by the Revolution.

"Then some one has said: 'Since the Revolution the people has gained "Rights." The people governs!' Strange! The people has now been ruling three years and no one has in practice once asked its opinion. Treaties were signed which will hold us down for centuries: and who has signed the treaties? The people? No! Governments which one fine day presented themselves as Governments. And at their election the people had nothing to do save to consider the question: there they are already, whether I elect them or not. If we elect them, then they are there through our election. But since we are a self-governing people, we must elect the folk in order that they may be elected to govern us.

"Then it was said, 'Freedom has come to us through the Revolution.' Another of those things that one cannot see very easily! It is of course true that one can walk down the street, the individual can go into his workshop and he can go out again: here and there he can go to a meeting. In a word, the individual has liberties. But in general, if he is wise, he will keep his mouth shut. For if in former times extraordinary care was taken that no one should let slip anything which could be treated as *lèse-majesté*, now a man must take much greater care that he doesn't say anything which might represent an insult to the majesty of a member of Parliament."

And if we ask who was responsible for our misfortune, then we must inquire who profited by our collapse. And the answer to that question is that "Banks and Stock Exchanges are more flourishing than ever before." We were told that capitalism would be destroyed, and when we ventured to remind one or other of these "famous statesmen" and said "Don't forget that Jews too have capital," then the answer was: "What are you worrying about? Capitalism as a whole will now be destroyed, the whole people will now be free. We are not fighting Jewish or Christian capitalism, we are fighting every capitalism: we are making the people completely free."

"Christian capitalism" is already as good as destroyed, the international Jewish Stock Exchange capital gains in proportion as the other loses ground. It is only the international Stock Exchange and loan-capital, the so-called "supra-state capital," which has profited from the collapse of our economic life, "the capital which receives its character from the single supra-state nation which is itself national to the core, which fancies itself to be above all other nations, which places itself above other nations and which already rules over them.

"The international Stock Exchange capital would be unthinkable, it would never have come, without its founders the supra-national, because intensely national, Jews. . . ."

"The Jew has not grown poorer: he gradually gets bloated, and, if you don't believe me, I would ask you to go to one of our health-resorts; there you will find two sorts of visitors: the German who goes there, perhaps for the first time for a long while, to breathe a little fresh air and to recover his health, and the Jew who goes there to lose his fat. And if you go out to our mountains, whom do you find there in fine brand-new yellow boots with splendid rucksacks in which there is generally nothing that would really be of any use? And why are they there? They go up to the hotel, usually no further than the train can take them: where the train stops, they stop too. And then they sit about somewhere within a mile from the hotel, like blow-flies round a corpse.

"These are not, you may be sure, our working classes: neither those working with the mind, nor with the body. With their worn clothes they leave the hotel on one side and go on climbing: they would not feel comfortable coming into this perfumed atmosphere in suits which date from 1913 or 1914. No, assuredly the Jew has suffered no privations! . . ."

"While now in Soviet Russia the millions are ruined and are dying, Chicherin—and with him a staff of over 200 Soviet Jews—travels by express train through Europe, visits the cabarets, watches naked dancers perform for his pleasure, lives in the finest hotels, and does himself better than the millions whom once you thought you must fight as 'bourgeois.' The 400 Soviet Commissars of Jewish nationality—they do not suffer; the thousands upon thousands of sub-Commissars —they do not suffer. No! all the treasures which the 'proletarian' in his madness took from the 'bourgeoise' in order to fight so-called capitalism—they have all gone into their hands. Once the worker appropriated the purse of the landed proprietor who gave him work, he took the rings, the diamonds and rejoiced that he had now got the treasures which before only the 'bourgeoisie' possessed. But in his hands they are dead things—they are veritable death-gold. They are no profit to him. He is banished into his wilderness and one cannot feed oneself on diamonds. For a morsel of bread he gives millions in objects of value. But the bread is in the hands of the State Central Organization and this is in the hands of the Jews: so everything, everything that the common man thought that he was winning for himself, flows back again to his seducers.

"And now, my dear fellow-countrymen, do you believe that these men, who with us are going the same way, will end the Revolution? They do not wish the end of the Revolution, for they do not need it. For them the Revolution is milk and honey.

"And further they cannot end the Revolution. For if one or another amongst the leaders were really not seducer but seduced, and today, driven by the inner voice of horror at his crime, were to step before the masses and make his declaration: 'We have all deceived ourselves: we believed that we could lead you out of misery, but we have in fact led you into a misery which your children and your children's children must still bear'—he cannot say that, he dare not say that, he would on the public square or in the public meeting be torn in pieces."

But amongst the masses there begins to flow a new stream—a stream of opposition. "It is the recognition of the facts which is already in pursuit of this system, it already is hunting the system down; it will one day scourge the masses into action and carry the masses along with it. And these leaders, they see that behind them the anti-Semitic wave grows and grows; and when the masses once recognize the facts, that is the end of these leaders."

And thus the Left is forced more and more to turn to Bolshevism. "In Bolshevism they see today the sole, the last possibility of preserving the present state of affairs. They realize quite accurately that the people is beaten so long as Brain and Hand can be kept apart. For alone neither Brain nor

Hand can really oppose them. So long therefore as the Socialist idea is coined only by men who see in it a means for disintegrating a nation, so long can they rest in peace."

"But it will be a sorry day for them when this Socialist idea is grasped by a Movement which unites it with the highest Nationalist pride, with Nationalist defiance, and thus places the Nation's Brain, its intellectual workers, on this ground. Then this system will break up, and there would remain only one single means of salvation for its supporters: viz. to bring the catastrophe upon us before their own ruin, to destroy the Nation's Brain, to bring it to the scaffold—to introduce Bolshevism."

"So the Left neither can nor will help. On the contrary, their first lie compels them constantly to resort to new lies. There remains then the Right. And this party of the Right meant well, but it cannot do what it would because up to the present time it has failed to recognize a whole series of elementary principles.

"In the first place the Right still fails to recognize the danger. These gentlemen still persist in believing that it is a question of being elected to a Landtag or of posts as ministers or secretaries. They think that the decision of a people's destiny would mean at worst nothing more than some damage to their so-called bourgeois-economic existence. They have never grasped the fact that this decision threatens their heads. They have never yet understood that it is not necessary to be an enemy of the Jew for him to drag you one day on the Russian model to the scaffold. They do not see that it is quite enough to have a head on your shoulders and *not to be a Jew*: that will secure the scaffold for you.

"In consequence their whole action today is so petty, so limited, so hesitating and pusillanimous. They would like to —but they can never decide on any great deed, because they fail to realize the greatness of the whole period.

"And then there is another fundamental error: they have never got it clear in their own minds that there is a difference or how great a difference there is between the conception 'National' and the word 'dynastic' or 'monarchistic.' They do not understand that today it is more than ever necessary in our thoughts as Nationalists to avoid anything which might perhaps cause the individual to think that the National Idea was identical with petty everyday political views. They ought day by day to din into the ears of the masses: 'We want to bury all the petty differences and to bring out into the light the big things, the things we have in common which bind us to one another. That should weld and fuse together those who have still a German heart and a love for their people in the fight against the common hereditary foe of all Aryans. How afterward we divide up this State, friends—we have no wish to dispute over that! The form of a State results from the essential character of a people, results from necessities which are so elementary and powerful that in time every individual will realize them without any disputation when once all Germany is united and free.'

"And finally they all fail to understand that we must on principle free ourselves from any class standpoint. It is of course very easy to call out to those on the Left, 'You must not be proletarians, leave your class-madness,' while you yourselves continue to call yourself 'bourgeois.' They should learn that in a single State there is only one supreme citizen-right, one supreme citizen-honor, and that is the right and the honor of honest work. They should further learn that the social idea must be the essential foundation for any State, otherwise no State can permanently endure.

"Certainly a government needs power, it needs strength. It must, I might almost say, with brutal ruthlessness press through the ideas which it has recognized to be right, trusting to the actual authority of its strength in the State. But even with the most ruthless brutality it can ultimately prevail only if what it seeks to restore does truly correspond to the welfare of a whole people.

"That the so-called enlightened absolutism of a Frederick

the Great was possible depended solely on the fact that, though this man could undoubtedly have decided 'arbitrarily' the destiny—for good or ill—of his so-called 'subjects,' he did not do so, but made his decisions influenced and supported by one thought alone, the welfare of his Prussian people. It was this fact only that led the people to tolerate willingly, nay joyfully, the dictatorship of the great king.

"*And the Right has further completely forgotten that democracy is fundamentally not German: it is Jewish.* It has completely forgotten that this Jewish democracy with its majority decisions has always been without exception only a means towards the destruction of any existing Aryan leadership. The Right does not understand that directly every small question of profit or loss is regularly put before so-called 'public opinion,' he who knows how most skilfully to make this 'public opinion' serve his own interests becomes forthwith master in the State. And that can be achieved by the man who can lie most artfully, most infamously; and in the last resort he is not the German, he is, in Schopenhauer's words, 'the great master in the art of lying'—the Jew.

"And finally it has been forgotten that the condition which must precede every act is the will and the courage to speak the truth—and that we do not see today either in the Right or in the Left.

"There are only two possibilities in Germany; do not imagine that the people will forever go with the middle party, the party of compromises; one day it will turn to those who have most consistently foretold the coming ruin and have sought to dissociate themselves from it. And that party is either the Left: and then God help us! for it will lead us to complete destruction—to Bolshevism, or else it is a party of the Right which at the last, when the people is in utter despair, when it has lost all its spirit and has no longer any faith in anything, is determined for its part ruthlessly to seize the reins of power—that is the beginning of resistance of which I spoke a few minutes ago. Here, too, there can be no compromise—there are only two possibilities: either victory of the Aryan or annihilation of the Aryan and the victory of the Jew.

"It is from the recognition of this fact, from recognizing it, I would say, in utter, dead earnestness, that there resulted the formation of our Movement. There are two principles which, when we founded the Movement, we engraved upon our hearts: first, to base it on the most sober recognition of the facts and second, to proclaim these facts with the most ruthless sincerity.

"And this recognition of the facts discloses at once a whole series of the most important fundamental principles which must guide this young Movement which, we hope, is destined one day for greatness:

"1. *'National' and 'social' are two identical conceptions.* It was only the Jew who succeeded, through falsifying the social idea and turning it into Marxism, not only in divorcing the social idea from the national, but in actually representing them as utterly contradictory. That aim he has in fact achieved. At the founding of this Movement we formed the decision that we would give expression to this idea of ours of the identity of the two conceptions: despite all warnings, on the basis of what we had come to believe, on the basis of the sincerity of our will, we christened it 'National Socialist.' We said to ourselves that to be 'national' means above everything to act with a boundless and all-embracing love for the people and, if necessary, even to die for it. And similarly to be 'social' means so to build up the State and the community of the people that every individual acts in the interest of the community of the people and must be to such an extent convinced of the goodness, of the honorable straightforwardness of this community of the people as to be ready to die for it.

"2. And then we said to ourselves: *there are no such things as classes: they cannot be.* Class means caste and caste means race. If there are castes in India, well and good; there it is possible, for there there were formerly Aryans and dark aborigines. So it was in Egypt and in Rome. But with us in Germany where everyone who is a German at all has the same blood, has the same eyes, and speaks the same language, here there can be no class, here there can be only a single people and beyond that nothing else. Certainly we recognize, just as anyone must recognize, that there are different 'occupations' and 'professions' [*Stände*]—there is the *Stand* of the watchmakers, the *Stand* of the common laborers, the *Stand* of the painters or technicians, the *Stand* of the engineers, officials, etc. *Stände* there can be. But in the struggles which these *Stände* have amongst themselves for the equalization of their economic conditions, the conflict and the division must never be so great as to sunder the ties of race.

"And if you say 'But there must after all be a difference between the honest creators and those who do nothing at all'—certainly there must! That is the difference which lies in the performance of the conscientious work of the individual. Work must be the great connecting link, but at the same time the great factor which separates one man from another. The drone is the foe of us all. But the creators—it matters not whether they are brain workers or workers with the hand—they are the nobility of our State, they are the German people!

"We understand under the term 'work' exclusively that activity which not only profits the individual but in no way harms the community, nay rather which contributes to form the community.

"3. And in the third place *it was clear to us that this particular view is based on an impulse which springs from our race and from our blood.* We said to ourselves that race differs from race and, further, that each race in accordance with its fundamental demands shows externally certain specific tendencies, and these tendencies can perhaps be most clearly traced in their relation to the conception of work. The Aryan regards work as the foundation for the maintenance of the community of the people amongst its members. The Jew regards work as the means to the exploitation of other peoples. The Jew never works as a productive creator without the great aim of becoming the master. He works unproductively, using and enjoying other people's work. And thus we understand the iron sentence which Mommsen once uttered: 'The Jew is the ferment of decomposition in peoples,' that means that the Jew destroys and must destroy because he completely lacks the conception of an activity which builds up the life of the community. And therefore it is beside the point whether the individual Jew is 'decent' or not. In himself he carries those characteristics which Nature has given him, and he cannot ever rid himself of those characteristics. And to us he is harmful. Whether he harms us consciously or unconsciously, that is not our affair. We have consciously to concern ourselves for the welfare of our own people.

"4. And fourthly *we were further persuaded that economic prosperity is inseparable from political freedom and that therefore that house of lies, 'Internationalism,' must immediately collapse.* We recognized that freedom can eternally be only a consequence of power and that the source of power is the will. Consequently the will to power must be strengthened in a people with passionate ardor. And thus we realized, fifthly that

"5. *We as National Socialists* and members of the German Workers party—a Party pledged to work—*must be on principle the most fanatical Nationalists.* We realized that the State can be for our people a paradise only if the people can hold sway therein freely as in a paradise: we realized that a slave state will never be a paradise, but only—always and for all time—a hell or a colony.

"6. And then sixthly we grasped the fact *that power in the last resort is possible only where there is strength,* and that strength lies not in the dead weight of numbers but solely in energy. Even the smallest minority can achieve a mighty result if it is inspired by the most fiery, the most passionate will to act. World history has always been made by minorities. And lastly

"7. If one has realized a truth, that truth is valueless so long as there is lacking the indomitable will to turn this realization into action!

"These were the foundations of our Movement—the truths on which it was based and which demonstrated its necessity.

"For three years we have sought to realize these fundamental ideas. And of course a fight is and remains a fight. Stroking in very truth will not carry one far. Today the German people has been beaten by a quite other world, while in its domestic life it has lost all spirit; no longer has it any faith. But how will you give this people once more firm ground beneath its feet save by the passionate insistence on one definite, great, clear goal?

"Thus we were the first to declare that this peace treaty was a crime. Then folk abused us as 'agitators.' We were the first to protest against the failure to present this treaty to the people before it was signed. Again we were called 'agitators.' We were the first to summon men to resistance against being reduced to a continuing state of defenselessness. Once more we were 'agitators.' At that time we called on the masses of the people not to surrender their arms, for the surrender of one's arms would be nothing less than the beginning of enslavement. We were called, no, we were cried down as, 'agitators.' We were the first to say that this meant the loss of Upper Silesia. So it was, and still they called us 'agitators.' We declared at that time that compliance in the question of Upper Silesia *must* have as its consequence the awakening of a passionate greed which would demand the occupation of the Ruhr. We were cried down ceaselessly, again and again. And because we opposed the mad financial policy which today will lead to our collapse, what was it that we were called repeatedly once more? 'Agitators.' And today?

"And finally we were also the first to point the people on

any large scale to a danger which insinuated itself into our midst—a danger which millions failed to realize and which will nonetheless lead us all into ruin—the Jewish danger. And today people are saying yet again that we were 'agitators.'

"I would like here to appeal to a greater than I, Count Lerchenfeld. He said in the last session of the Landtag that his feeling 'as a man and a Christian' prevented him from being an anti-Semite. *I say: my feeling as a Christian points me to my Lord and Saviour as a fighter. It points me to the man who once in loneliness, surrounded only by a few followers, recognized these Jews for what they were and summoned men to the fight against them and who, God's truth! was greatest not as sufferer but as fighter.* In boundless love as a Christian and as a man I read through the passage which tells us how the Lord at last rose in His might and seized the scourge to drive out of the Temple the brood of vipers and of adders. How terrific was His fight for the world against the Jewish poison. Today, after two thousand years, with deepest emotion I recognize more profoundly than ever before the fact that it was for this that He had to shed His blood upon the Cross. As a Christian I have no duty to allow myself to be cheated, but I have the duty to be a fighter for truth and justice. And as a man I have the duty to see to it that human society does not suffer the same catastrophic collapse as did the civilization of the ancient world some two thousand years ago—a civilization which was driven to its ruin through this same Jewish people.

"Then indeed when Rome collapsed there were endless streams of new German bands flowing into the Empire from the North; but, if Germany collapses today, who is there to come after us? German blood upon this earth is on the way to gradual exhaustion unless we pull ourselves together and make ourselves free!

"And if there is anything which could demonstrate that we are acting rightly, it is the distress which daily grows. For as a Christian I have also a duty to my own people. And when I look on my people I see it work and work and toil and labor, and at the end of the week it has only for its wage wretchedness and misery. When I go out in the morning and see these men standing in their queues and look into their pinched faces, then I believe I would be no Christian, but a very devil, if I felt no pity for them, if I did not, as did our Lord two thousand years ago, turn against those by whom today this poor people is plundered and exploited.

"And through the distress there is no doubt that the people has been aroused. Externally perhaps apathetic, but within there is ferment. And many may say, 'It is an accursed crime to stir up passions in the people.' And then I say to myself: Passion is already stirred through the rising tide of distress, and one day this passion will break out in one way or another: *and now I would ask those who today call us 'agitators': 'What then have you to give to the people as a faith to which it might cling?'*

"Nothing at all, for you yourselves have no faith in your own prescriptions.

"That is the mightiest thing which our Movement must create: for these widespread, seeking and straying masses a new Faith which will not fail them in this hour of confusion, to which they can pledge themselves, on which they can build so that they may at least find once again a place which may bring calm to their hearts."

Press

No comments in the leading German newspapers.

SPEECH OF JULY 28, 1922

Munich

Background

1922

June 24—Walther Rathenau is assassinated by a nationalist gang.

The Speech

". . . IT IS a battle which began nearly 120 years ago, at the moment when the Jew was granted citizen rights in the European States. The political emancipation of the Jews was the beginning of an attack of delirium. For thereby there were given full citizen rights and equality to a people which was much more clearly and definitely a race apart than all others, that has always formed and will form a State within the State. That did not happen perhaps at one blow, but it came about as things come about today and always do come about: first a little finger, then a second and a third, and so bit by bit until at last a people that in the eighteenth century still appeared completely alien had won equal citizen-rights with ourselves.

"And it was precisely the same in the economic sphere. The vast process of the industrialization of the peoples meant the confluence of great masses of workmen in the towns. Thus great hordes of people arose, and these, more's the pity, were not properly dealt with by those whose moral duty it was to concern themselves for their welfare. Parallel with this was a gradual 'moneyfication' of the whole of the nation's labor-strength. 'Share-capital' was in the ascendant, and thus bit by bit the Stock Exchange came to control the whole national economy. The directors of these institutions were, and are without exception, Jews. I say 'without exception,' for the few non-Jews who had a share in them are in the last resort nothing but screens, shop-window Christians, whom one needs in order, for the sake of the masses, to keep up the appearance that these institutions were after all founded as a natural outcome of the needs and the economic life of all peoples alike, and were not, as was the fact, institutions which correspond only with the essential characteristics of the Jewish people and are the outcome of those characteristics.

"Then Europe stood at the parting of the ways. Europe began to divide into two halves, into West Europe and Central and Eastern Europe. At first Western Europe took the lead in the process of industrialization. Especially in England crowds of farm laborers, sons of farmers, or even ruined farmers themselves, streamed into the towns and there formed a new fourth estate. But here one fact is of more importance than we are accustomed to admit: this England, like France, had relatively few Jews. And the consequence of that was that the great masses, concentrated in the towns, did not come into immediate contact with this alien nation, and thus feelings of aversion which must otherwise necessarily have arisen did not find sufficient nourishment for their development. In the end the fifty or sixty thousand Jews in England—there was hardly that number in England then—with supreme ease were able so to 'Europeanize' themselves that they remained hidden from the primitive eye of the ordinary member of the public and as 'Captains of Industry,' and especially as representatives of capital on a large scale, they could appear no longer as foreigners but themselves became Englishmen. This accounts for the fact that anti-Semitism in these States could never attain to any native vigor; for the same is true of France. And precisely for this reason in these countries it was possible to introduce the system which we have to represent to ourselves under the concept of 'Democracy.' There it was possible to create a State-form whose meaning could only be the mastery of the herd over the intelligentsia, the mastery over true energy through the dead weight of massed numbers. In other words: it must be supremely easy for the Jewish intelligentsia, small in numbers and therefore completely hidden in the body of the British people, so to work upon the masses that the latter, quite unconscious of whom they were obeying, in the end did but serve the purposes of this small stratum of society. Through the press propaganda, through the use of the organs of information, it was possible in England to found the great model parties. Already in those early days they saw to it shrewdly that there were always two or three groups apparently hostile to each other, but in fact all hanging on a gold thread, the whole designed to take account of a human characteristic—that the longer a man possesses an object, the more readily he grows tired of it. He craves something new: therefore one needs two parties. The one is in office, the other in opposition. When the one has played itself out, then the opposition party comes into power, and the party which has had its day is now in its turn the opposition. After twenty years the new party itself has once more played itself out and the game begins afresh. In truth this is a highly ingenious mill in which the interests of a nation are ground very small. As everyone knows, this system is given some such name as 'Self-Government of a People.'

"Besides this we always find two great catchwords, 'Freedom' and 'Democracy,' used, I might say, as signboards. 'Freedom': under that term is understood, at least amongst those in authority who in fact carry on the Government, the possibility of an unchecked plundering of the masses of the people to which no resistance can be offered. The masses themselves naturally believe that under the term 'freedom' they possess the right to a quite peculiar freedom of motion—freedom to move the tongue and to say what they choose, freedom to move about the streets, etc. A bitter deception!

"And the same is true of democracy. In general even in the early days both England and France had already been bound with the fetters of slavery. With, I might say, a brazen security these States are fettered with Jewish chains. . . ."

"In consequence of this widespread aversion it was more difficult for the Jew to spread infection in the political sphere, and especially so since traditionally loyalty was centered in a person: the form of the State was a monarchy, and power did not lie with an irresponsible majority. Thus the Jew saw that here it was possible for an enlightened despotism to arise based upon the army, the bureaucracy, and the masses of the people still unaffected by the Jewish poison. The intelligentsia at that time was almost exclusively German, big business and the new industries were in German hands, while the last reservoir of a people's strength, the peasantry, was throughout healthy. In such conditions if, as industry grew, a fourth estate was formed in the towns, there was the danger that this fourth estate might ally itself with the monarchy, and thus with its support there might arise a popular monarchy [*Volkskönig*] or a popular 'Kaisertum' which would be ready and willing to give a mortal blow to those powers of international supra-State finance which were at that time beginning to grow in influence. This was not impossible: in the history of Germany princes had from time to time found themselves forced, as in Brandenburg, to turn against the nobility and seek popular support. . . ."

But this possibility constituted a grave danger for Jewry. If the great masses of the new industrialized workmen "had come into Nationalist hands and like a true social leaven had penetrated the whole nation, if the liberation of the different estates [*Stände*] had followed step by step in an organic development and the State had later looked to them for support, then there would have been created what many hoped for in November, 1918, viz., a national social State. For Socialism in itself is anything but an international creation. As a noble conception it has indeed grown up exclusively in Aryan hearts: it owes its intellectual glories only to Aryan brains. It is entirely alien to the Jew. The Jew will always be the born champion of private capital in its worst form, that of unchecked exploitation. . . . Voltaire, as well as Rousseau, together with our German Fichte and many another—they are all without exception united in their recognition that the Jew is not only a foreign element differing in his essential character, which is utterly harmful to the nature of the Aryan, but that the Jewish people in itself stands against us as our deadly foe and so will stand against us always and for all time."

The master-stroke of the Jew was to claim the leadership of the fourth estate: he founded the Movement both of the Social Democrats and the Communists. His policy was twofold: he had his "apostles" in both political camps. Amongst the parties of the Right he encouraged those features which were most repugnant to the people—the passion for money, unscrupulous methods in trade which were employed so ruthlessly as to give rise to the proverb "Business, too, marches over corpses." And the Jew attacked the parties of the Right. Jews wormed their way into the families of the upper classes: it was from the Jews that the latter took their wives. "The result was that in a short time it was precisely the ruling class which became in its character completely estranged from its own people."

And this fact gave the Jew his opportunity with the parties of the Left. Here he played the part of the common demagogue. Two means enabled him to drive away in disgust the whole intelligentsia of the nation from the leadership of the workers. First: his international attitude, "for the native intelligence of the country is prepared to make sacrifices, it will do anything for the life of the people, but it cannot believe in the mad view that through the denial of that national life, through a refusal to defend the rights of one's own people, through the breaking down of the national resistance to the foreigner, it is possible to raise up a people and make it happy. That it cannot do, and so it remained at a distance. And the Jew's second instrument was the Marxist theory in and for itself. For directly one went on to assert that property as such is theft, directly one deserted the obvious formula that only the natural wealth of a country can and should be common property, but that that which a man creates or gains through his honest labor is his own, immediately the economic intelligentsia with its nationalist outlook could, here too, no longer co-operate: for this intelligentsia was bound to say to itself that this theory meant the collapse of any human civilization whatever. Thus the Jew succeeded in isolating this new movement of the workers from all the nationalist elements. . . ."

"More and more so to influence the masses that he persuaded those of the Right that the faults of the Left were the faults of the German workman, and similarly he made it appear to those of the Left that the faults of the Right were simply the faults of the so-called 'Bourgeois,' and neither side noticed that on both sides the faults were the result of a scheme planned by alien devilish agitators. And only so is it possible to explain how this dirty joke of world history could come to be that Stock Exchange Jews should become the leaders of a Workers Movement. It is a gigantic fraud: world history has seldom seen its like.

"And then we must ask ourselves: what are the final aims of this development?"

So soon as millions of men have had it hammered into them that they are so oppressed and enslaved that it matters not what their personal attitude may be to their people, their State, or economic life, then a kind of passive resistance must result which sooner or later will do fatal damage to the national economy. Through the preaching of the Marxist economic theory the national economy must go to ruin. We see the results in Russia: the end of the whole economic life of the State: the handing over of the community to the international world of finance. And the process is furthered through the organization of the "political strike." Often there are no adequate economic grounds for a strike, but there are always political grounds and plenty of them. And to this must be added the practical political sabotage of the State, since the thought of the individual is concentrated on the idea of international solidarity. It is clear that a nation's economic life depends upon the strength of a national State: it does not live on such phrases as "Appeasement of the peoples" or "Freedom of the Peoples."

"At the moment when no people supports the economic life of a nation, ready to give it its protection, at that moment economic life collapses. The breaking in pieces of a nation's strength is the end of a nation's prosperity, the national existence must cease altogether."

And one can see constantly how wonderfully the Stock Exchange Jew and the leader of the workers, how the Stock Exchange organ and the journal of the workers, co-operate. They both pursue one common policy and a single aim. Moses Kohn on the one side encourages his association to refuse the workers' demands, while his brother Isaac in the factory incites the masses and shouts, "Look at them! they only want to oppress you! Shake off your fetters. . . ." His brother takes care that the fetters are well and truly forged. The Stock Exchange organ seeks without intermission to encourage fevered speculation and unparalleled corners in grain and in the food of the people, while the workmen's newspaper lets off all its guns on the masses, telling them that bread is dearer and this, that, and the other is dearer: up Proletarians! endure it no longer—down with . . .

How long can this process last? It means the utter destruction not only of economic life, but of the people. It is clear that all these apostles who talk their tongues out of their heads, but who spend the night in the Hotel Excelsior, travel in express trains, and spend their leave for their health in Nice—these people do not exert their energies for love of the people. No, the people is not to profit, it shall merely be brought into dependence on these men. The backbone of its independence, its own economic life, is to be destroyed, that it may the more surely relapse into the golden fetters of the perpetual interest-slavery of the Jewish race. And this process will end when suddenly out of the masses someone arises who seizes the leadership, finds other comrades and fans into flame the passions which have been held in check and looses them against the deceivers.

"That is the lurking danger, and the Jew can meet it in one way only—by destroying the hostile national intelligentsia. That is the inevitable ultimate goal of the Jew in his revolution. And this aim he must pursue; he knows well enough his economics brings no blessing: his is no master-people: he is an exploiter: the Jews are a people of robbers. He has never founded any civilization, though he has destroyed civilizations by the hundred. He possesses nothing of his own creation to which he can point. Everything that he has is stolen. Foreign peoples, foreign workmen build him his temples, it is foreigners who create and work for him: it is foreigners who shed their blood for him. He knows no 'people's army': he has only hired mercenaries who are ready to go to death on his behalf. He has no art of his own: bit by bit he has stolen it all from the other peoples or has watched them at work and then made his copy. He does not even know how merely to preserve the precious things which others have created: as he turns the treasures over in his hand they are transformed into dirt and dung. He knows that he cannot maintain any State for long. That is one of the differences between him and the Aryan. True, the Aryan also has dominated other peoples. But how? He entered on the land, he cleared the forests; out of wildernesses he has created civilizations, and he has not used the others for his own interests, he has, so far as their capacities permitted, incorporated them into his State and through him art and science were brought to flower. In the last resort it was the Aryan and the Aryan alone who could form States and could set them on their path to future greatness.

"All that the Jew cannot do. And because he cannot do it,

therefore all his revolutions must be 'international.' They must spread as a pestilence spreads. He can build no State and say 'See here! Here stands the State, a model for all. Now copy us!' He must take care that the plague does not die, that it is not limited to one place, or else in a short time this plague-hearth would burn itself out. So he is forced to bring every mortal thing to an international expansion. For how long? Until the whole world sinks in ruins and brings him down with it in the midst of the ruins.

"That process today in Russia is practically complete. The whole of present-day Russia has nothing to show beyond a ruined civilization, a colony ripe for development through alien capital, and even this capital in order to supply resources in labor for its practical work must introduce Aryan intellects, since for this again the Jew is useless. Here, too, he is all rapacity, never satisfied. He knows no ordered economy, he knows no ordered body of administrators. Over there in Russia he is laying his hands on everything. They take the noble's diamonds to help 'the People.' The diamonds then stray into foreign societies and are no more seen. He seizes to himself the treasures of the churches, but not to feed the people: oh no! Everything wanders away and leaves not a trace behind. In his greed he has become quite senseless: he can keep hold of nothing: he has only within him the instinct for destruction, and so he himself collapses with the treasure that he has destroyed."

It is a tragic fate: we have often grown excited over the death of a criminal: if an anarchist is shot in Spain we raise a mighty howl over "the sacrifice of valuable human blood . . . and here in the East thirty million human beings are being slowly martyred—done to death, some on the scaffold, some by machine guns . . . millions upon millions through starvation. . . . A whole people is dying, and now we can perhaps understand how it was possible that formerly all the civilizations of Mesopotamia disappeared without a trace so that one can only with difficulty find in the desert sand the remains of these cities. We see how in our own day whole countries die out under this scourge of God, and we see how this scourge is threatening Germany, too, and how with us our own people in mad infatuation is contributing to bring upon itself the same yoke, the same misery.

"We know that the Revolution which began in 1918 has covered perhaps but the first third of its course. Two things, however, there are which must scourge it forward upon its way: economic causes and political causes." On the economic side, the ever-growing distress, and in the political sphere, "are not nearly all Germans in their hearts—let each one admit it—in despair when they consider the situation which leaves us quite defenseless in face of a Europe which is so hostile to Germany? *And why is Europe hostile? We see how over there in this other Europe it is not the peoples which agitate against us, it is the secret power of the organized press which ceaselessly pours new poison into the hearts of these peoples.*

"And who are then these bandits of the press? The brothers and the relatives of the publishers of our own newspapers. And the capital source which provides the energy which here —and there—drives them forward is the Jewish dream of World Supremacy."

Today the idea of international solidarity has lost its force, one can still bring men out of the factories, but only by means of terrorism. If you ask for an honest answer the worker will confess that he no longer believes in this international solidarity. And the belief in the so-called reasonableness of the other peoples has gone too. "How often have we been told that reason will lead them not to be too hard with us: true, reason should have moved them thus, but what did move them had nothing to do with reason. For here there is no question of the thought of reasonable peoples: it is the thought of a wild beast, tearing, raging in its unreason, that drives all of them to the same ruin as that to which we ourselves are driven.

"So the masses of the people in Germany are becoming, in the political sphere, completely lost. Yet here and there people are beginning to get some practice in criticism. Slowly, cautiously, and yet with a certain accuracy the finger is being placed on the real wound of our people. And thus one comes to realize: if only this development goes on for a time, it might be possible that from Germany the light should come which is destined to light both Germany and the world to their salvation. And at that point the everlasting lie begins to work against us with every means in its power...."

"It is said, if one criticizes the state of affairs to which we have been brought today, that one is a reactionary, a monarchist, a pan-German. I ask you what would probably have been the state of Germany today if during these three years there had been no criticism at all? I believe that in fact there has been far, far too little criticism. *Our people unfortunately is much too uncritical, or otherwise it would long ago have not only seen through many things, but would have swept them away with its fist!* The crisis is developing towards its culmination. The day is not far distant when, for the reasons which I have stated, the German Revolution must be carried forward another step. The leaders know all too well that things cannot always go on as they are going today. One may raise prices ten times by 100 per cent, but it is doubtful if in the end even a German will accept a milliard of marks for his day's wage if in the last resort with his milliard-wage he must still starve. It is a question whether one will be able to keep up this great fraud upon the nation. There will come a day when this must stop—and therefore one must build for that day, before it comes.

"And so now Germany is reaching that stage which Russia has drunk to the lees. Now in one last stupendous assault they will finally crush all criticism, all opposition, no, rather whatever honesty is still left to us, and that they will do the more rapidly the more clearly they see that the masses are beginning to understand one thing—National Socialist teaching.

"Whether for the moment it comes to them under that name or under another, the fact is that everywhere more and more it is making headway. Today all these folk cannot yet belong to a single party, but, wherever you go, in Germany, yes almost in the whole world, you find already millions of thinking men who know that a State can be built only on a social foundation and they know also that the deadly foe of every social conception is the international Jew.

"Every truly national idea is in the last resort social, i.e., he who is prepared so completely to adopt the cause of his people that he really knows no higher ideal than the prosperity of this—his own—people, he who has so taken to heart the meaning of our great song *'Deutschland, Deutschland über alles,'* that nothing in this world stands for him higher than this Germany, people and land, land and people, he is a Socialist! And he who in this people sympathizes with the poorest of its citizens, who in this people sees in every individual a valuable member of the whole community, and who recognizes that this community can flourish only when it is formed not of rulers and oppressed but when all according to their capacities fulfill their duty to their Fatherland and the community of the people and are valued accordingly, he who seeks to preserve the native vigor, the strength, and the youthful energy of the millions of working men, and who above all is concerned that our precious possession, our youth, should not before its time be used up in unhealthy harmful work—he is not merely a Socialist, but he is also National in the highest sense of that word.

"It is the teaching of these facts which appears to the Jews as leaders of the Revolution today to constitute a threatening danger. And it is precisely this which more than anything else makes the Jew wish to get in his blow as soon as possible. For one thing he knows quite well: in the last resort there is only one danger which he has to fear—and that danger is this young Movement.

"He knows the old parties. They are easily satisfied. Only endow them with a few seats as ministers or with similar posts and they are ready to go along with you. And in especial he knows one thing: they are so innocently stupid. In their case the truth of the old saying is proved afresh every day: 'Those whom the gods wish to destroy, they first strike with blindness.' They have been struck with blindness: therefore it follows that the gods wish to destroy them. Only look at these parties and their leaders, Stresemann and the rest of them. They are indeed not dangerous. They never go to the roots of the evil: they all still think that with forbearance, with humanity, with accommodation they can fight a battle which has not its equal in this world. Through gentleness they think that they must demonstrate to the enemy of the Left that they are ready for appeasement so as to stay the deadly cancerous ulcer through a policy of moderation.

"No! A thousand times No! Here there are only two possibilities: either victory or defeat!

"What today is the meaning of these great preparations for the decisive battle on the part of bolshevist Judaism?—

"To make the nation defenseless in arms and to make the people defenseless in spirit.

"Two great aims!

"Abroad Germany is already humiliated. The State trembles before every French Negro-captain, the nation is no longer dangerous. And within Germany they have seen to it that arms should be taken away from the decent elements of the people and that in their stead Russian-Jewish-bolshevist bands should be armed. Only one thing remains still to do: viz., the muzzling of the spirit, above all the arrest of the evil 'agitators'—that is the name they give to those who dare to tell the people the truth. Not only are their organizations to be known to all, but the masses are to be incited against their persons. Just as the Jew could once incite the mob of

Jerusalem against Christ, so today he must succeed in inciting folk who have been duped into madness to attack those who, God's truth! seek to deal with this people in utter honesty and sincerity. And so he begins to intimidate them, and he knows that this pressure in itself is enough to shut the mouths of hundreds, yes, of thousands. For they think, if I only hold my tongue, then I shall be safe in case they come into power. No, my friend. The only difference will be that I may hang perhaps still talking, while you will hang—in silence. Here, too, Russia can give us countless examples, and with us it will be the same story.

"We know that the so-called 'Law for the Protection of the Republic' which comes from Berlin today is nothing else than a means for reducing all criticism to silence. We know, too, that no effort will be spared so that the last outstanding personalities—those who within Germany foresee the coming of disaster—shall in good time—disappear. And to that end the population of North Germany will be scourged into opposition to Bavaria with every lie and every misrepresentation that comes to hand. Up there they have the feeling that in one corner of the Reich the spirit of the German people is not yet broken. And that is the point to which we National Socialists have to grapple ourselves. We National Socialists are, God's truth! perhaps the most loyal, the most devoted of all men to our German Fatherland. For three years we have waged a war, often against death and devil, but always only for our German Fatherland. We got so far that at the last, as crown of all our labors, we had to land in prison. But in spite of everything there is one thing we would say: We do make a distinction between a Government and the German Fatherland. When today here in the Landtag or in the Reichstag at Berlin some lousy half-Asiatic youth casts in our teeth the charge that we have no loyalty to the Reich, I beg you do not distress yourselves. The Bavarian people has sealed its loyalty to the Reich with its countless regiments which fought for the Reich and often sank under the earth two or three times. We are convinced, and that in the last resort is our one great faith, that out of this bitterest distress and this utter misery the German Reich will rise again, but not as now, not as the offspring of wretchedness and misery—we shall possess once again a true German Reich of freedom and of honor, a real Fatherland of the whole German people and not an asylum for alien swindlers. There is today constant talk about 'Federalism,' etc. I beg you not to abuse the Prussians while at the same time you grovel before the Jews, but show yourselves stiff-necked against the folk of Berlin. And if you do that, then you will have on your side in the whole of Germany millions and millions of Germans, whether they be Prussians or men of Baden, Württembergers, men of Saxony, or Germans of Austria. Now is the hour to stand stiff-necked and resist to the last!

"We National Socialists who for three years have done nothing but preach—abused and insulted by all, by some mocked and scorned, by others traduced and slandered—we cannot retreat! For us there is only one path which leads straight ahead. We know that the fight which now is blazing will be a hard struggle. It will not be fought out in the court of the Reich at Leipzig, it will not be fought out in a cabinet at Berlin, it will be fought out through those factors which in their hard reality have ever up to the present time made world history. I heard recently in the speech of a minister that the rights of a State cannot be set aside through simple majority decisions, but only through treaties. *Bismarck once used different language on this subject: he thought that the destinies of peoples could be determined neither through majority decisions nor through treaties, but only through blood and iron.*

"On one point there should be no doubt: we will not let the Jews slit our gullets and not defend ourselves. Today in Berlin they may already be arranging their festival-dinners with the Jewish hangmen of Soviet Russia—that they will never do here. They may today begin to set up the Cheka—

the Extraordinary Commission—in Germany, they may give it free scope, we surrender to such a Jewish Commission never! We have the conviction, firm as a rock, that, if in this State seven million men are determined to stand by their 'No' to the very last, the evil specter will collapse into nothingness in the rest of the Reich. For what Germany needs today, what Germany longs for ardently, is a symbol of power, and strength.

"So as I come to the end of my speech I want to ask something of those among you who are young. And for that there is a very special reason. The old parties train their youth in the gift of the gab, we prefer to train them to use their bodily strength. For I tell you: the young man who does not find his way to the place where in the last resort the destiny of his people is most truly represented, only studies philosophy and in a time like this buries himself behind his books or sits at home by the fire, he is no German youth! I call upon you! Join our Storm Divisions! And however many insults and slanders you may hear if you do join, you all know that the Storm Divisions have been formed for our protection, for your protection, and at the same time not merely for the protection of the Movement, but for the protection of a Germany that is to be. If you are reviled and insulted, good luck to you, my boys! You have the good fortune already at eighteen or nineteen years of age to be hated by the greatest of scoundrels. What others can win only after a lifetime of toil, this highest gift of distinguishing between the honest man and the brigand, falls as a piece of luck into your lap while you are but youths. You can be assured that the more they revile you, the more we respect you. We know that if you were not there, none of us would make another speech. We know, we see clearly that our Movement would be cudgelled down if you did not protect it! You are the defense of a Movement that is called one day to remodel Germany in revolutionary fashion from its very foundations in order that there may come to birth what perhaps so many expected on the ninth of November: a German Reich and a Germanic and, so far as in us lies, a German Republic.

"Every battle must be fought to the end—better that it come early than late. And he ever stands most securely who from the first goes to the fight with the greatest confidence. And this highest confidence we can carry with us in our hearts. For he who on our side is today the leader of the German people, God's truth! he has nothing to win but perhaps only everything to lose. He who today fights on our side cannot win great laurels, far less can he win great material goods—it is more likely that he will end up in jail. He who today is leader must be an idealist, if only for the reason that he leads those against whom it would seem that everything has conspired.

"But in that very fact there lies an inexhaustible source of strength. The conviction that our Movement is not sustained by money or the lust for gold, but only by our love for the people, that must ever give us fresh heart, that must ever fill us with courage for the fray.

"And as my last word, take with you this assurance: if this battle should not come, never would Germany win peace. Germany would decay and at the best would sink to ruin like a rotting corpse. But that is not our destiny. We do not believe that this misfortune which today our God sends over Germany has no meaning: it is surely the scourge which should and shall drive us to a new greatness, to a new power and glory, to a Germany which for the first time shall fulfill that which in their hearts millions of the best of our fellow-countrymen have hoped for through the centuries and the millennia, to the Germany of the German people!"

Press

No comment in the leading German newspapers.

SPEECH OF SEPTEMBER 18, 1922

Munich

". . . ECONOMICS is a secondary matter. World history teaches us that no people became great through economics: it was economics that brought them to their ruin. A people died when its race was disintegrated. Germany, too, did not become great through economics.

"A people that in its own life [*völkisch*] has lost honor becomes politically defenseless, and then becomes enslaved also in the economic sphere.

"Internationalization today means only Judaization. We in Germany have come to this: that a sixty-million people sees its destiny to lie at the will of a few dozen Jewish bankers. This was possible only because our civilization had first been Judaized. The undermining of the German conception of personality by catchwords had begun long before. Ideas such as 'Democracy,' 'Majority,' 'Conscience of the World,' 'World Solidarity,' 'World Peace,' 'Internationality of Art,' etc., disintegrate our race-consciousness, breed cowardice, and so today we are bound to say that the simple Turk is more man than we are.

"No salvation is possible until the bearer of disunion, the Jew, has been rendered powerless to harm.

"1. We must call to account the November criminals of 1918. It cannot be that two million Germans should have fallen in vain and that afterwards one should sit down as friends at the same table with traitors. No, we do not pardon, we demand—Vengeance!

"2. The dishonoring of the nation must cease. For betrayers of their Fatherland and informers the gallows is the proper place. Our streets and squares shall once more bear the names of our heroes; they shall not be named after Jews. In the Question of Guilt we must proclaim the truth.

"3. The administration of the State must be cleared of the rabble which is fattened at the stall of the parties.

"4. The present laxity in the fight against usury must be abandoned. Here the fitting punishment is the same as that for the betrayers of their Fatherland.

"5. *We must demand a great enlightenment on the subject of the Peace Treaty. With thoughts of love? No! but in holy hatred against those who have ruined us.*

"6. The lies which would veil from us our misfortunes must cease. The fraud of the present money-madness must be shown up. That will stiffen the necks of us all.

"7. *As foundation for a new currency the property of those who are not of our blood must do service.* If families who have lived in Germany for a thousand years are now expropriated, we must do the same to the Jewish usurers.

"8. *We demand immediate expulsion of all Jews who have entered Germany since 1914,* and of all those, too, who through trickery on the Stock Exchange or through other shady transactions have gained their wealth.

"9. The housing scarcity must be relieved through energetic action; houses must be granted to those who deserve them. Eisner said in 1918 that we had no right to demand the return of our prisoners—he was only saying openly what all Jews were thinking. People who so think must feel how life tastes in a concentration camp!

"Extremes must be fought by extremes. Against the infection of materialism, against the Jewish pestilence we must hold aloft a flaming ideal. And if others speak of the World and Humanity we say the Fatherland—and only the Fatherland!"

Press

No comments in the leading German newspapers.

SPEECH OF APRIL 10, 1923

Munich

Background

1922

November 25—The Italian Chamber gives Mussolini *carte blanche* to make reforms by decree until December 31, 1923.

December 12—Moscow Disarmament Conference between Russia and Poland breaks up owing to Russian refusal to sign non-aggression treaty.

1923

January 10—Occupation of the Ruhr by French troops.

January 15—The Lithuanians occupy the neutral port of Memel.

January 27-28—Party Convention of the National Socialist party in Munich, originally planned as "putsch day."

February 2—German authorities call for civil disobedience in the occupied Ruhr district.

The Speech

". . . IN THE Bible we find the text, 'That which is neither hot nor cold will I spew out of my mouth.' This utterance of the great Nazarene has kept its profound validity until the present day. He who would pursue the golden mean must surrender the hope of achieving the great and the greatest aims. Until the present day the half-hearted and the lukewarm have remained the curse of Germany. . . ."

"To the half-heartedness and weakness of the parties in Parliament was added the half-heartedness of Governments. . . . Everything stood under the sign of half-heartedness and lukewarmness, even the fight for existence in the World War and still more the conclusion of peace. And now the continuation of the half-hearted policy of those days holds the field. The people, inwardly united in the hard struggle—in the trenches there were neither parties nor Confessions—has been torn asunder through the economics of profiteers and knaves. Appeasement and the settlement of differences would certainly soon be there if only one were to hang the whole crew. But profiteers and knaves are, of course, 'Citizens of the State,' and what is more important still, they are adherents of the religion which is hallowed by the Talmud.

"*Even today we are the least loved people on earth.* A world of foes is ranged against us and the German must still today make up his mind whether he intends to be a free soldier or a white slave. *The only possible conditions under which a German State can develop at all must therefore be: the unification of all Germans in Europe,* education towards a national consciousness, and readiness to place the whole national strength without exception in the service of the nation. . . ."

"*No economic policy is possible without a sword,* no industrialization without power. Today we have no longer any sword grasped in our fist—how can we have a successful economic policy? England has fully recognized this primary maxim in the healthy life of States; for centuries England has acted on the principle of converting economic strength into political power, while conversely political power in its turn must protect economic life. The instinct of self-preservation can build up economics, but we sought to preserve World Peace instead of the interests of the nation, instead of defending the economic life of the nation with the sword and of ruthlessly championing those conditions which were essential for the life of the people.

"Three years ago I declared in this same room that the collapse of the German national consciousness must carry with it into the abyss the economic life of Germany as well.

For liberation something more is necessary than an economic policy, something more than industry: *if a people is to become free it needs pride and will-power, defiance, hate, hate, and once again hate. . . .*"

"The spirit comes not down from above, that spirit which is to purify Germany, which with its iron besom is to purify the great sty of democracy. To do that is the task of our Movement. The Movement must not rust away in Parliament, it must not spend itself in superfluous battles of words, but the banner with the white circle and the black Swastika will be hoisted over the whole of Germany on the day which shall mark the liberation of our whole people."

Press

No comments in the leading German newspapers.

•

SPEECH OF APRIL 13, 1923

Munich

". . . IN OUR view the times when there was no 'League of Nations' were far more honorable and more humane. . . . We ask: 'Must there be wars?' The pacifist answers 'No!' He proceeds to explain that disputes in the life of peoples are only the expression of the fact that a class has been oppressed by the ruling bourgeoisie. When there are in fact differences of opinion between peoples, then these should be brought before a 'Peace Court' for its decision. But he does not answer the question whether the judges of this court of arbitration would have the power to bring the parties before the bar of the court. I believe that an accused ordinarily only appears 'voluntarily' before a court because, if he did not, he would be fetched there. I should like to see the nation which would allow itself to be brought before this League of Nations Court in the case of a disagreement without external force. In the life of nations, what in the last resort decides questions is a kind of Judgment Court of God. It may even happen that in case of a dispute between two peoples—both may be in the right. Thus Austria, a people of fifty millions, had most certainly the right to an outlet to the sea. But since in the strip of territory in question the Italian element of the population was in the majority, Italy claimed for herself the 'right of self-determination.' Who yields voluntarily? No one! So the strength which each people possesses decides the day. *Always before God and the world the stronger has the right to carry through what he wills.* History proves: He who has not the strength—him the 'right in itself' profits not a whit. A world court without a world police would be a joke. And from what nations of the present League of Nations would then this force be recruited? Perhaps from the ranks of the old German Army? *The whole world of Nature is a mighty struggle between strength and weakness—an eternal victory of the strong over the weak.* There would be nothing but decay in the whole of Nature if this were not so. States which should offend against the elementary law would fall into decay. You need not seek for long to find an example of such mortal decay: you can see it in the Reich of today. . . ."

". . . Before the war two States, Germany and France, had to live side by side but only under arms. It is true that the War of 1870-1 meant for Germany the close of an enmity which had endured for centuries, but in France a passionate hatred against Germany was fostered by every means by propaganda in the press, in school textbooks, in theaters, in the cinemas." . . . All the Jewish papers throughout France agitated against Berlin. "Here again to seek and to exploit grounds for a conflict is the clearly recognizable effort of world Jewry.

"The conflict of interests between Germany and England lay in the economic sphere. Up till 1850 England's position as a World Power was undisputed. British engineers, British trade conquer the world. Germany, owing to greater industry and increased capacity, begins to be a dangerous rival. In a short time those firms which in Germany were in English hands pass into the possession of German industrialists. German industry expands vastly and the products of that industry even in the London market drive out British goods. The protective measure, the stamp 'Made in Germany,' has the opposite effect from that desired: this 'protective stamp' becomes a highly effective advertisement. The German economic success was not created in Essen alone but by a man who knew that behind economics must stand power, for power alone makes an economic position secure. This power was born upon the battlefields of 1870-71, not in the atmosphere of parliamentary chatter. Forty thousand dead have rendered possible the life of forty millions. When England, in the face of such a Germany as this, threatened to be brought to her knees, then she bethought herself of the last weapon in the armory of international rivalry—violence. A press propaganda on an imposing scale was started as a preparatory measure. But who is the chief of the whole British press concerned with world trade? One name crystallizes itself out of the rest: Northcliffe—a Jew! . . . A campaign of provocation is carried on with assertions, libels, and promises such as only a Jew can devise, such as only Jewish newspapers would have the effrontery to put before an Aryan people. And then at last 1914: they egg people on: 'Ah, poor violated Belgium! Up! To the rescue of the small nations—for the honor of humanity!' The same lies, the same provocation throughout the entire world! And the success of that provocation the German people can trace grievously enough!

"What cause finally had America to enter the war against Germany? With the outbreak of the World War, which Judah had desired so passionately and so long, all the large

Jewish firms of the United States began supplying ammunitions. They supplied the European 'war-market' to an extent which perhaps even they themselves had never dreamed of —a gigantic harvest! Yet nothing satisfied the insatiable greed of the Jew. And so the venal press which depended upon the Stock Exchange kings began an unparalleled propaganda campaign. *A gigantic organization for newspaper lying was built up. And once more it is a Jewish concern, the Hearst press, which set the tone of the agitation against Germany.* The hatred of these 'Americans' was not directed solely against commercial Germany or against military Germany. It was directed specially against social Germany, because this Germany had up to that time kept itself outside of the principles which governed the world trusts. The old Reich had at least made an honorable attempt to be socially-minded. We had to show for ourselves such an initiative in social institutions as no other country in the wide world could boast. . . . This explains why, even in Germany itself, the 'comrades' under Jewish leadership fought against their own vital interests. This explains the agitation carried on throughout the world under the same watchword. For this reason the Jewish-democratic press of America had to accomplish its masterpiece—that is to say, it had to drive into the most horrible of all wars a great peace-loving people which was as little concerned in European struggles as it was in the North Pole: America was to intervene 'in defense of civilization,' and the Americans were persuaded so to do by an atrocity propaganda conducted in the name of civilization which from A to Z was a scandalous invention the like of which has never yet been seen—a farrago of lies and forgeries. Because this last State in the world where social aims were being realized had to be destroyed, therefore twenty-six peoples were incited one against the other by this press which is exclusively in the possession of one and the same world people, of one and the same race, and that race on principle the deadly foe of all national States."

Who could have prevented the World War? Not the *Kultursolidarität,* the "solidarity of civilization," in whose name the Jews carried on their propaganda: not the so-called World Pacifism—again an exclusively Jewish invention. Could the so-called "Solidarity of the Proletariat?" . . . "All the wheels stand silent, still, If that be your strong arm's will. . . . The German wheel on November 9, 1918, was indeed brought to a standstill. The Social Democratic party in its principal organ, *Vorwärts,* declared in so many words that it was not in the interest of the workers that Germany should win the war. . . ."

"Could the Freemasons perhaps stop the war?—this most noble of philanthropic institutions who foretold the good fortune of the people louder than anyone and who at the same time was the principal leader in promoting the war. Who, after all, are the Freemasons? You have to distinguish two grades. To the lower grade in Germany belong the ordinary citizens who through the claptrap which is served up to them can feel themselves to be 'somebodies,' but the responsible authorities are those many-sided folk who can stand any climate, those 300 Rathenaus who all know each other, who guide the history of the world over the heads of Kings and Presidents, those who will undertake any office without scruples, who know how brutally to enslave all peoples—once more the Jews!

"Why have the Jews been against Germany? That is made quite clear today—proved by countless facts. They use the age-old tactics of the hyena—when fighters are tired out, then go for them! Then make your harvest! In war and revolutions the Jew attained the unattainable. Hundreds of thousands of escaped Orientals become modern 'Europeans.' Times of unrest produce miracles. Before 1914 how long would it have taken, for instance, in Bavaria before a Galician Jew became—Prime Minister?—Or in Russia before an anarchist from the New York Ghetto, Bronstein (Trotsky), became—Dictator? Only a few wars and revolutions—that was enough to put the Jewish people into possession of the red gold and thereby to make them masters of the world.

"Before 1914 there were two States above all, Germany and Russia, which prevented the Jew from reaching his goal —the mastery of the world. Here not everything which they already possessed in the Western democracies had fallen to the Jews. Here they were not the sole lords alike in the intellectual and economic life. Here, too, the Parliaments were not yet exclusively instruments of Jewish capital and of the will of the Jew. The German and the genuine Russian had still preserved a certain aloofness from the Jew. In both peoples there still lived the healthy instinct of scorn for the Jew, and there was a real danger that in these monarchies there might one day arise a Frederick the Great, a William I, and that democracy and a parliamentry regime might be sent to the devil. So the Jews became revolutionaries! The Republic should bring them to wealth and to power. This aim they disguised: they cried 'Down with the monarchies!' 'Enthrone the "sovereign" people!' I do not know whether today one could venture to call the German or the Russian people 'sovereign.' At least one cannot see any trace of it! What the German people can trace, however, what every day stands in the most crass form before its eyes, is debauchery, gluttony, speculation ruling unchecked, the open mockery of the Jew. . . ."

"So Russia and Germany had to be overthrown in order that the ancient prophecy might be fulfilled. So the whole world was lashed into fury. So every lie and propaganda agency was brutally set in action against the State of the last —the German—idealists! *And thus it was that Judah won the World War. Or would you wish to maintain that the French, the English, or the American 'people' won the war? They, one and all, victors and vanquished are alike defeated:* one thing raises itself above them all: the World Stock Exchange which has become the master of the people.

"What guilt had Germany herself for the outbreak of the

war? Her guilt consisted in this: that at the moment when the ring closed about her existence Germany neglected to organize her defense with such vigor that through this demonstration of her power either the others, despite their abominable purposes, would have been robbed of their will to strike or else the victory of the Reich would have been assured. The guilt of the German people lies in this: that when in 1912 a criminal Reichstag in its unfathomable baseness and folly had refused to allow the raising of three army corps the people did not create for itself those army corps in the Reichstag's despite. With these additional 120,000 men the Battle of the Marne would have been won and the issue of the war decided. Two million fewer German heroes would have sunk into their graves. Who was it who in 1912 as in 1918 struck its weapons from the hands of the German people? Who was it that in 1912, as in the last year of the war, infatuated the German people with his theory that if Germany throws down her arms the whole world will follow her example—who?—the democratic-Marxist Jew who at the same hour incited and still today incites the others to—arm and to subjugate 'barbarous' Germany.

"But someone may perhaps yet raise the question whether it is expedient today to talk about the guilt for the war. Most assuredly we have the duty to talk about it! For the murderers of our Fatherland who all the years through have betrayed and sold Germany, they are the same men who, as the November criminals, have plunged us into the depths of misfortune. We have the duty to speak since in the near future, when we have gained power, we shall have the further duty of taking these creators of ruin, these clouts, these traitors to their State and of hanging them on the gallows to which they belong. Only let no one think that in them there has come a change of heart. On the contrary, these November scoundrels who still are free to go as they will in our midst, they are, even today, going against us. From the recognition of the facts comes the will to rise again. Two millions have remained on the field of battle. They, too, have their rights and not we, the survivors, alone. There are millions of orphans, of cripples, of widows in our midst. They, too, have rights. For the Germany of today not one of them died, not one of them became a cripple, an orphan, or a widow. We owe it to these millions that we build a new Germany!"

Press

Frankfurter Zeitung, April 15, 1923—[First mention of Hitler in a leading German newspaper]

At a meeting yesterday, Hitler made it known that indictments were pending against Editor Eher of the *Voelkischer Beobachter,* against the president of the *Oberland Bund,* and against himself, and he added: "I ask you to be sticky as burrs and hard as steel in standing by our movement. We will not talk . . ."

. . . The right radical press, from the *Muenchen-Augsburger Abendzeitung* to the *Muenchener Zeitung* is decisively rejecting the National Socialists and their friends.

These papers declare that they reject the struggle with illegal means and the creation of conflicts which, in view of the imminent decisions of world-historic importance, cannot but seem grotesque, and they point out that the laws for the security of the State were adopted legally, have been expressly recognized by Bavaria, and must be enforced!

•

SPEECH OF APRIL 24, 1923

Munich

". . . I REJECT the word 'Proletariat.' The Jew who coined the word meant by 'Proletariat,' not the oppressed, but those who work with their hands. And those who work with their intellects are stigmatized bluntly as 'Bourgeois.' It is not the character of a man's life which forms the basis of this classification, it is simply the occupation—whether a man works with his brain or with his body. And in this turbulent mass of the hand-workers the Jew recognized a new power which might perhaps be his instrument for the gaining of that which is his ultimate goal: World supremacy, the destruction of the national States.

"And while the Jew 'organizes' these masses, he organizes business, too, at the same time. Business was depersonalized, i.e., Judaized. Business lost the Aryan character of work: it became an object of speculation. Master and man were torn asunder . . . and he who created this class division was the same person who led the masses in their opposition to this class division, led them not against his Jewish brethren, but against the last remnants of independent national economic life.

"And these remnants, the bourgeoisie which also was already Judaized, resisted the great masses who were knocking at the door and demanding better conditions of life. And so the Jewish leaders succeeded in hammering into the minds of the masses the Marxist propaganda: 'Your deadly foe is the bourgeoisie; if he were not there, you would be free.' If it had not been for the boundless blindness and stupidity of our bourgeoisie the Jew would never have become the leader of the German working-classes. And the ally of this stupidity was the pride of the 'better stratum' of society which thought it would degrade itself if it condescended to stoop to the level of the 'Plebs.' The millions of our German fellow-countrymen would never have been alienated from their people if the leading strata of society had shown any care for their welfare.

"You must say farewell to the hope that you can expect any action from the parties of the Right on behalf of the freedom of the German people. The most elementary factor is lacking: the will, the courage, the energy. Where then can any strength still be found within the German people? It is to be found, as always, in the great masses: *there energy is slumbering and it only awaits the man who will summon it from its present slumber and will hurl it into the great battle for the destiny of the German race.*

"The battle which alone can liberate Germany will be fought out with the forces which well up from the great masses. Without the help of the German workingman you will never regain a German Reich. Not in our political salons lies the strength of the nation, but in the hand, in the brain, and in the will of the great masses. Now as ever: Liberation does not come down from above, it will spring up from below. . . . If we today make the highest demands upon everyone, that is only in order that we may give back to him and to his child the highest gift: Freedom and the respect of the rest of the world. . . ."

The parties of the Right have lost all energy: they see the flood coming, but their one longing is just for once in their lives to form a Government. "Unspeakably incapable, utterly lacking in energy, cowards all—such are all these bourgeois parties and that at the moment when the nation needs heroes —not chatterers."

In the Left there is somewhat more energy, but it is used for the ruin of Germany. "The Communists on principle reject the discipline imposed by the State: in its stead they preach party discipline: they reject the administration of the State as a bureaucracy, while they fall on their knees before the bureaucracy of their own Movement. There is arising a State within the State which stands in deadly enmity against the State which we know, the State of the community of the people. This new State ultimately produces men who reject with fanaticism their own people so that in the end Foreign Powers find in them their allies. Such is the result of Marxist teaching. . . ."

"What we want is not a State of drones but a State which

gives to everyone that to which on the basis of his own activity he has a right. He who refuses to do honest work shall not be a citizen of the State. The State is not a plantation where the interests of foreign capital are supreme. Capital is not the master of the State, but its servant. Therefore the State must not be brought into dependence on international loan capital. And if anyone believes that that cannot be avoided, then do not let him be surprised that no one is ready to give his life for this State. Further, that greatest injustice must be corrected which today still weighs heavily upon our people and upon almost all peoples. If in a State only he who does honest work is a citizen, then everyone has the right to demand that in his old age he shall be kept free from care and want. That would mean the realization of the greatest social achievement."

Press

No comments in the leading German newspapers.

•

SPEECH OF APRIL 27, 1923

Munich

"... WHAT we need if we are to have a real People's State is a land reform. . . . We do not believe that the mere dividing up of the land can by itself bring any alleviation. The conditions of a nation's life can in the last resort be bettered only through the political will to expansion. Therein lies the essential characteristic of a sound reform.

"And land [*Grund und Boden*], we must insist, cannot be made an object for speculation. Private property can be only that which a man has gained for himself, has won through his work. A natural product is not private property, that is national property. Land is thus no object for bargaining.

"Further, there must be a reform in our law. Our present law regards only the rights of the individual. It does not regard the protection of the race, the protection of the community of the people. It permits the befouling of the nation's honor and of the greatness of the nation. A law which is so far removed from the conception of the community of the people is in need of reform.

"Further, changes are needed in our system of education. *We suffer today from an excess of culture* [*Ueberbildung*]. Only knowledge is valued. But wiseacres are the enemies of action. What we need is instinct and will. Most people have lost both through their 'culture.' We have, it is true, a highly intellectual class, but it is lacking in energy. If, through our overvaluation of mechanical knowledge, we had not so far removed ourselves from popular sentiment, the Jew would never have found his way to our people so easily as he has done. What we need is the possibility of a continuous succession of intellectual leaders drawn from the people itself.

"Clear away the Jews! Our own people has genius enough —we need no Hebrews. If we were to put in their place intelligences drawn from the great body of our people, then we should have recovered the bridge which leads to the community of the people.

"Again, we need a reform of the German press.

"A press which is on principle anti-national cannot be tolerated in Germany. Whoever denies the nation can have no part in it. We must demand that the press shall become the instrument of the national self-education.

"Finally we need a reform in the sphere of art, literature, and the theater. The Government must see to it that its people is not poisoned. There is a higher right which is based on the recognition of that which harms a people, and that which harms a people must be done away with.

"And after this reform we shall come to recognize the duty of self-preservation. A man who says: 'I deny that I have a right to defend my personal life' has thereby denied his right to exist. *To be a pacifist argues a lack of conviction, a lack of character.* For the pacifist is indeed ready enough to claim the help of others, but himself declines to defend himself. It is precisely the same with a people. A people which is not prepared to protect itself is a people without character. We must recover for our people as one of its most elementary principles the recognition of the fact that a man is truly man only if he defends and protects himself, that a people deserves that name only if in case of necessity it is prepared as a people to enter the lists. That is not militarism, that is self-preservation.

"*Therefore we National Socialists stand for compulsory military service for every man.* If a State is not worth that—then away with it! Then you must not complain if you are enslaved. But if you believe that you must be free, then you must learn to recognize that no one gives you freedom save only your own sword. What our people needs is not leaders in Parliament, but those who are determined to carry through what they see to be right before God, before the world, and before their own consciences—and to carry that through, if need be, in the teeth of majorities. And if we succeed in raising such leaders from the body of our people, then around them once again a nation will crystallize itself. . . . It is the pride of our Movement to be the force which shall awake the Germany of fighters which yet shall be."

Press

Frankfurter Zeitung— . . . The Bavarian People's party [Bavarian branch of the Center party] issues a warning to the "Fatherland Leagues" to break with the Nazis. The letter reads: "People there are very much blinded by Hitler's outward successes and overestimate the inner strength of the

National Socialist movement. People mistake a lot of noise for real spirit."

•

SPEECH OF MAY 1, 1923

Munich

"... IF THE first of May is to be transferred in accordance with its true meaning from the life of Nature to the life of peoples, then it must symbolize the renewal of the body of a people which has fallen into senility. And in the life of peoples senility means internationalism. What is born of senility? Nothing, nothing at all. Whatever in human civilization has real value, that arose not out of internationalism; it sprang from the soul of a single people. When peoples have lost their creative vigor, then they become international. Everywhere, wherever intellectual incapacity rules in the life of peoples, there internationalism appears. And it is no chance that the promoter of this cast of thought is a people which itself can boast of no real creative force—the Jewish people. ..."

"So the first of May can be only a glorification of the national creative will over against the conception of international disintegration, of the liberation of the nation's spirit and of its economic outlook from the infection of internationalism. That is in the last resort the question of the restoration to health of peoples ... and the question arises: Is the German oak ever destined to see another springtime? And that is where the mission of our Movement begins. We have the strength to conquer that which the autumn has brought upon us. Our will is to be National Socialists—not national in the current sense of the word—not national by halves. We are National Socialist fanatics, not dancers on the tight-rope of moderation!

"There are three words which many use without a thought which for us are no catch-phrases: Love, Faith, and Hope. We National Socialists wish to love our Fatherland, we wish to learn to love it, to learn to love it jealously, to love it alone and to suffer no other idol to stand by its side. We know only one interest and that is the interest of our people.

"We are fanatical in our love for our people, and we are anxious that so-called 'national governments' should be conscious of that fact. We can go as loyally as a dog with those who share our sincerity, but we will pursue with fanatical hatred the man who believes that he can play tricks with this love of ours. We cannot go with governments who look two ways at once, who squint both towards the Right and towards the Left. We are straightforward: it must be either love or hate.

"We have faith in the rights of our people, the rights which have existed time out of mind. We protest against the view that every other nation should have rights—and we have none. We must learn to make our own this blind faith in the rights of our people, in the necessity of devoting ourselves to the service of these rights; we must make our own the faith that gradually victory must be granted us if only we are fanatical enough. And from this love and from this faith there emerges for us the idea of hope. When others doubt and hesitate for the future of Germany—we have no doubts. We have both the hope and the faith that Germany will and must once more become great and mighty.

"We have both the hope and the faith that the day will come on which Germany shall stretch from Königsberg to Strassburg, and from Hamburg to Vienna.

"We have faith that one day Heaven will bring the Germans back into a Reich over which there shall be no Soviet star, no Jewish star of David, but above that Reich there shall be the symbol of German labor—the Swastika. And that will mean that the first of May has truly come."

Press

Berliner Tageblatt, May 2—National Socialist Fiasco in Munich: . . . The National Socialist storm troops did assemble as commanded, about 7000 to 8000 strong, around their Fuehrer, Hitler, on the Oberwiesenfeld, and there awaited further commands. But their rhetorically skillful "dictator" was nonplussed by the firm stand of the authorities. He complained whimperingly that he felt himself "encircled and betrayed," whereupon his disappointed followers gradually vanished. After today's fiasco, Hitler can be considered politically and financially through in Munich. . . .

•

SPEECH OF AUGUST 1, 1923

Munich

". . . THERE are two things which can unite men: common ideals and common criminality. We have inscribed upon our banner the great Germanic ideal and for that ideal we will fight to the last drop of our blood. We National Socialists have realized that from the international cesspool of infamy, from the Berlin of today, nothing can come to save the Fatherland. We know that two things alone will save us: first, the end of internal corruption, the cleansing out of all those who owe their existence simply to the protection of their party comrades. Through the most brutal ruthlessness

New York Herald Tribune, May 20, 1923, published first American interview with Hitler.

towards all party officials we must restore our finances. It must be proved that the official is not a party man, but a specialist! The body of German officials must once more become what once it was. But the second and the most important point is that *the day must come when a German government shall summon up the courage to declare to the Foreign Powers: 'The Treaty of Versailles is founded on a monstrous lie. We refuse to carry out its terms any longer. Do what you will! If you wish for war, go and get it! Then we shall see whether you can turn seventy million Germans into serfs and slaves!'*

"If cowards cry out: 'But we have no arms!' that is neither here nor there! When the whole German people knows one will and one will only—to be free—in that hour we shall have the instrument with which to win our freedom. It matters not whether these weapons of ours are humane: if they gain us our freedom, they are justified before our conscience and before our God. When the eyes of German children look questioning into ours, when we see the suffering and distress of millions of our fellow-countrymen who without any fault of theirs have fallen into this frightful misfortune, then we laugh at the curses of the whole world, if from these curses there issues the freedom of our race.

"But since we know that today the German people consists for one-third of heroes, for another third of cowards, while the rest are traitors, as a condition of our freedom in respect of the outside world we would first cleanse our domestic life. The present 'United Front' has failed in that task. The day of another 'United Front' will come. But before that there must be a day of reckoning for those who for four and a half years have led us on their criminal ways. *The domestic battle must come before the battle with the world without*—the final decision between those who say 'We are Germans and proud of the fact' and those who do not wish to be Germans or who are not Germans at all. Our Movement is opposed with the cry 'The Republic is in danger!' Your Republic of the Ninth of November? In very truth it is: the November-Republic is in danger! How long, think you, you can maintain this 'State'? . . ."

"Our Movement was not formed with any election in view, but in order to spring to the rescue of this people as its last help in the hour of greatest need, at the moment when in fear and despair it sees the approach of the Red Monster. The task of our Movement is still today not to prepare ourselves for any coming election but to prepare for the coming collapse of the Reich, so that when the old trunk falls the young fir-tree may be already standing. The *Via dolorosa* of Germany from Wirth, by way of Cuno to Stresemann, will end in the dictatorship of a Jewish lord of finance. . . . *We want to be the supporters of the dictatorship of national reason, of national energy, of national–brutality and resolution. Germany can be saved only through action, when through* our talking here the bandage has been torn from the eyes of the last of the befooled. It is from our Movement that redemption will come–that today is the feeling of millions. That has become almost a new religious faith! And there will be only two possibilities: either Berlin marches and ends up in Munich, or Munich marches and ends up in Berlin! A bolshevist North Germany and a nationalist Bavaria cannot exist side by side, and the greatest influence upon the fortunes of the German Reich will be his who shall restore the Reich. . . . Either Germany sinks, and we through our despicable cowardice sink with it, or else we dare to enter on the fight against death and devil and rise up against the fate that has been planned for us. Then we shall see which is the stronger: the spirit of international Jewry or the will of Germany."

Press

No comments in the leading German newspapers.

SPEECH OF SEPTEMBER 12, 1923

Munich

Background

1923

August 8—Chancellor Dr. Carl Cuno, in order to meet the drop of the mark to 5,500,000 to the dollar, proposes an unlimited gold loan, a gold tax, and a general tax to finance the passive resistance in the Ruhr.

August 14—Chancellor Stresemann outlines his program to the German Reichstag; the end of passive resistance and the enforced taxation of war and postwar profiteers.

The Speech

". . . THE Republic was founded to be a milk-cow for its founders—for the whole parliamentary gang. It was never intended to be a State for the German people, but a feeding-ground, as pleasant and as rich a feeding-ground as possible. There never was any thought of giving to the German people a free State: the object was to provide a mob of the lowest scoundrels with an obliging object for their exploitation. The fruit of the honest work of other folk has been stolen by those who themselves have never worked. And if *we* refuse to grasp the facts, the outside world knows better. The outside world despises the representatives of this November-Republic! Neither in society nor in the meetings of diplomats are they regarded as equals, much less as men of character. Think of Lloyd George—this man with the single fanatical idea—that England must be led to victory. There comes up to him one of the 'November men' of whom he knows: 'My people would have been defeated if your people by you had not been——.' How will Lloyd George receive him? Surely with unspeakable contempt! For *he* knows what *we* can only guess, how in the war the millions of gold poured into Germany, how they began to take effect, how great associations of traitors were formed through foreign gold—through *his* gold. And now he sees face to face the man to whom before he paid out the Judas-wage. What do you think Lloyd George will do? He can only spit at the sight. Never can any one of the 'November criminals' represent Germany before the world! . . ."

"The Republic, by God! is worthy of its fathers. For hardly was the first deed of shame committed when there followed the second—one dishonor after another! One can scarcely believe any longer that there was once a time when one could speak of the Germans as the first people in the world.

"The essential character of the November-Republic is to be seen in the comings and goings to London, to Spa, to Paris and Genoa. Subserviency towards the enemy, surrender of the human dignity of the German, pacifist cowardice, tolerance of every indignity, readiness to agree to everything until nothing more remains. This November Republic bore the stamp of the men who made it. The name 'November criminals' will cling to these folk throughout the centuries. . . ."

"How are States founded? Through the personality of brilliant leaders and through a people which deserves to have the crown of laurel bound about its brows. Compare with them the 'heroes' of this Republic! Shirkers, Deserters, and Pacifists: these are its founders and their heroic acts consisted in leaving in the lurch the soldiers at the front, in stopping reinforcements, in withholding from them munitions, while at home against old men and half-starved children they carried through a revolutionary coup d'état. They have quite simply got together their November State by theft! In the face of the armies returning wearied from the front these thieves have still posed as the saviours of the Fatherland! They declared the Pacifist-Democratic Republic. On the other hand I ask: What can be the only meaning of loyalty to the State? The loyalty of heroes! This Revolution has dishonored the old heroes on whom the whole earth had looked with wonder; it allowed the scum of the streets to tear off their decorations and to hurl into the mire all that was sacred to the heroes of the front line. And how does the Republic honor now the new heroes? Schlageter? By warrants for his arrest.

"Pacifism as the idea of the State, international law instead of power—all means are good enough to unman the people. They hold India up to us as a model and what is called 'passive resistance.' True, they want to make an India of Germany, a folk of dreams which turns away its face from realities, in order that they can oppress it for all eternity, that they may span it body and soul to the yoke of slavery. . . ."

"In the economic sphere this Revolution has proved to be an immense misfortune. The districts which were most important for the feeding of our people were lost and districts which are the condition for the feeding of the nation have been treasonably alienated. And what did the Revolution not prophesy for us in the political sphere? One heard of the right of Self-Determination of Peoples, of the League of Nations, of Self-Government of the People. And what was the result? A World Peace, but a World Peace over a Germany which was but a field of corpses. Disarmament, but only the disarmament of Germany, with Germany looting its own resources. Self-determination, yes, but self-determination for every Negro tribe: and Germany does not count as a Negro tribe. League of Nations, yes: but a League of Nations which serves only as the guarantor for the fulfillment of the Peace Treaty, not for a better world order which is to come. And government by the people—for five years past no one has asked the people what it thinks of the act of November of the year 1918: at the head of the Reich there stands a President who is rejected by the overwhelming majority of the people and who has not been chosen by the people. Seventeen million Germans are in misery under foreign rule. Hardly ever in five years has so much been torn away from the German nation as in these years of the so-called successful Revolution. We have been rendered defenseless: we are without rights: we have become the pariahs of the world. What are our organs of government today but organs for executing the will of foreign tyrants? . . ."

"We were given a Free State which never deserved the name of 'free.' Then they called it a 'People's State.' But think you that bankers can form a government which befits a 'People's State'?

"In fact the Revolution made three changes in our State: it internationalized the German State, the economic life of Germany, and the German people itself. Thereby Germany has been turned into a colony of the outside world. Those who were fed with the ideal of the International were in fact placed under the 'Diktat' of the International. They have their international State: today international finance is king. . . ."

"While the masses were still told lies about 'socialization,' the economic life of Germany was in fact socialized, not by the German people, but by the outside world. . . ."

"Through the internationalization of the nation itself in the end a people ceases to be master of its own fate: it becomes the puppet of alien forces.

"Is that, now, a People's Revolution? Is such a construction a People's State? No, it is the Jews' Paradise."

Press

No comments in the leading German newspapers.

SPEECH OF FEBRUARY 26, 1924

Before the Munich Court

Background

1923

September 26—The German Government formally proclaims the end of passive resistance in the Ruhr. State of siege declared in Germany and the *Voelkischer Beobachter* banned for the first time.

October 18—Bavaria, backed by Wuerttemberg and Saxony, breaks diplomatic relations with Berlin. The local Bavarian Reichswehr revolts against the Reich.

October 24—During a Communist insurrection in Hamburg, 14 policemen killed and 100 wounded.

October 27—The Chancellor demands the resignation of the Communist Government in Saxony and the restoration of the authority of the Reich in Bavaria.

November 8—Hitler and Ludendorff attempt to seize power in Munich.

November 9—National Socialist party dissolved and its property seized.

November 29—Dr. Stresemann is succeeded by Dr. Marx as German Chancellor.

1924

January 18—A plot on the part of the Executive Committee of the Communist International forces Leon Trotsky, Commissioner of the People for the Red Army, to retire.

January 21—Death of Lenin.

January 22—MacDonald forms the first Labor Government in Britain.

February 26—The trial of General Ludendorff, Adolf Hitler and others begins in Munich.

The Speech

"IT SEEMS strange to me that a man who, as a soldier, was for six years accustomed to blind obedience, should suddenly come into conflict with the State and its Constitution. The reasons for this stem from the days of my youth. When I was seventeen I came to Vienna, and there I learned to study and observe three important problems: *the social question, the race problem,* and, finally, *the Marxist movement. I left Vienna a confirmed anti-Semite, a deadly foe of the whole Marxist world outlook, and pan-German in my political principles.* And since I knew that the German destiny of German-Austria would not be fought out in the Austrian Army alone, but in the German *and* Austrian Army, I enlisted in the German Army. . . ."

"When, on November 7, [1918] it was announced that the Revolution had broken out in Munich, I at first could not believe it. At that time there arose in me the determination to devote myself to politics. I went through the period of the Soviets, and as a result of my opposition to them I came in contact with the National Socialist German Workers Movement, which at that time numbered six members. *I was the seventh.* I attached myself to this party, and not to one of the great political parties where my prospects would have been better, because none of the other parties understood or even recognized the decisive, fundamental problem.

"By Marxism I understand a doctrine which in principle rejects the idea of the worth of personality, which replaces individual energy by the masses and thereby works the destruction of our whole cultural life. This movement has utilized monstrously effective methods and exercised tremendous influence on the masses, which in the course of three or four decades could have no other result than that the individual has become his own brother's foe, while at the same time calling a Frenchman, an Englishman, or a Zulu his brother. This movement is distinguished by incredible terror, which is based on a knowledge of mass psychology. . . ."

"The German Revolution is a revolution, and therefore successful high treason; it is well known that such treason is never punished. . . ."

"For us it was a filthy crime against the German people, *a stab in the back of the German nation.* The middle class could not take up arms against it because the middle class did not understand the whole revolution. It was necessary to start a new struggle and to incite against the Marxist despoilers of the people *who did not even belong to the German race*—which is where the Marxist problem is linked with the race problem, forming one of the most difficult and profound questions of our time. . . ."

"Personally, at the beginning I held a lost position. Nevertheless, in the course of a few years there has grown from a little band of six men a movement which today embraces millions and which, above all, has once made the broad masses nationalistic. . . ."

"In 1923 came the great and bitter scandal. As early as 1922 we had seen that the Ruhr was about to be lost. France's aim was not merely to weaken Germany, to keep her from obtaining supremacy, but to break her up into small states so that she [France] would be able to hold the Rhine frontier. After all the Government's reiterations of our weakness, we knew that on top of the Saar and Upper Silesia we would lose our third coal region, the Ruhr; each loss brought on the next one. . . ."

"Only *burning, ruthless, brutal fanaticism* could have saved the situation. The Reich Government should have let the hundreds of thousands of young men who were pouring out of the Ruhr into the Reich under the old colors of black-white-red flow together in a mighty national wave. Instead, these young people were sent back home. The resistance that was organized was for wages; the national resistance was degraded to a paid general strike. It was forgotten that a foe like France cannot be prayed away, still less can he be idled away. . . ."

"Our youth has—and may this be heard in Paris—but one thought: that the day may come when we shall again be free. . . . My attitude is this: I would rather that Germany go Bolshevist and I be hanged than that she should be destroyed by the French rule of the sword. . . . It turned out that the back-stabbers were stronger than ever. . . . With pride I admit that our men were the only ones to really resist in the Ruhr. We intended to hold fourteen meetings and introduce a propaganda campaign throughout Germany with the slogan: *Down with the Ruhr traitors!* But we were surprised by the banning of these mass meetings. I had met Herr von Kahr in 1920. Kahr had impressed me as being an honest official. I asked him why the fourteen mass meetings had been banned. The reason he gave me simply would not hold water. *The real reason was something that could not be revealed. . . ."*

"From the very first day the watchword was: *unlimited struggle against Berlin. . . ."*

"The struggle against Berlin, as Dr. von Kahr would lead it, is a crime; one must have the courage to be logical and see that the struggle must be incorporated in the German national uprising. I said that all that had been made of this struggle was a Bavarian rejection of Berlin's requests. But the people expected something other than a reduction in the price of beer, regulation of the price of milk and confiscation of butter tubs and other such impossible economic proposals—proposals which make you want to ask: who is the genius that is advising them? Every failure could only further enrage the masses, and I pointed out that while the people were now only laughing at Kahr's measures, later on they would rise up against them. I said: 'Either you finish the job—and there is only the political and military struggle left. When you cross the Rubicon, you must march on Rome. Or else you do not want to struggle; then only capitulation is left. . . .' "

"The struggle had to turn toward the North; it could not be led by a purely Bavarian organization . . . I said: 'The only man to head it is Ludendorff.'

"I had first seen Ludendorff in 1918, in the field. In 1920 I first spoke personally with him. I saw that he was not only the outstanding general, but that he had now learned the lesson and understood what had brought the German nation to ruin. That Ludendorff was talked down by the others was one more reason for me to come closer to him. I therefore proposed Ludendorff, and Lossow and Seisser had no objections.

"I further explained to Lossow that right now nothing could be accomplished by petty economic measures. The fight was against Marxism. To solve this problem, not administrators were needed but firebrands who would be in a position to inflame the national spirit to the extreme. Kahr could not do that, I pointed out; the youth were not behind him. I declared that I could join them only on the condition that the political struggle was put into my hands alone. This was not impudence or immodesty; I believe that when a man knows he can do a job, he must not be modest. . . ."

"One thing was certain: Lossow, Kahr, and Seisser had the same goal that we had: to get rid of the Reich Government with its present international and parliamentary position, and to replace it by an anti-parliamentary government. If our undertaking was actually high treason, then during this whole period Lossow, Seisser, and Kahr must have been committing high treason along with us—for during all those months we talked of nothing but the aims of which we now stand accused. . . ."

"How could we have called for a new government if we had not known that the gentlemen in power were altogether on our side? How else could we, two days before, have given such orders as: at 8:30 o'clock such and such a government will be proclaimed. . . ."

"Lossow talked of a coup d'état. Kahr quite openly declared that he would give the word to strike. The only possible interpretation of this talk is that these men wanted to strike, but each time lost their nerve. Our last conversation, on November 6, was for me the absolute confirmation of my belief that these men wanted to, but—!. . . ."

"My total impression of the meeting of November 6 was the following: Kahr, Lossow, and Seisser can no longer retreat; they will have to fight or capitulate. It is unthinkable that the present situation in Bavaria can last much longer. For whenever I asked about the relations between Kahr and the Bavarian Diet, Seisser and Lossow always assured me: '*The Diet no longer has anything to say. . . .*' "

"On November 6, Lossow declared: 'Under certain conditions I am ready to go ahead with the coup d'état.' Now it is obvious that when a man cannot summon up enough courage to make the break, he cannot tell others to make it. We could not help seeing that the gentlemen were waiting for someone to set things going. . . . Therefore, the only remaining possibility was to set things going ourselves. . . . I immediately perceived that only a very few should be given knowledge of the plan. I had no fear that later I would be reproached for not informing the people beforehand, for all the gentlemen expected nothing else. Hour after hour they hoped the problem would be solved. We did not inform all the elderly gentlemen with families. When I discussed the question of whether Ludendorff should be informed, I was told: No, as an officer Ludendorff must know nothing about it, though it was clear what his position would be when we struck. . . ."

"The actual events of November 8 were, briefly, as follows: At eight o'clock I went to the Buergerbraeukeller. I noticed that there were such crowds standing about the place that one might think our intention had come to the ears of the police. The hall was packed and we tried to get Kahr, Lossow, and Seisser to come out. The circumstances seemed to indicate that we might run into difficulties and therefore I went into the vestibule and told Scheubner to go to Ludendorff immediately and inform him. Then I asked a policeman to clear the street because there might be trouble in the hall. At 8:34 I entered the hall with three men, my permanent bodyguard. We held pistols in our hands, for it was not impossible that someone might shoot at us from behind. . . ."

"I entered and obtained quiet by firing a pistol shot. It was in the nature of the whole affair that I had to fire this shot, and only someone who mouths the words of others could fail to understand this. I then asked Kahr, Lossow, and Seisser to come out. . . . Kahr, Lossow, and Seisser were immediately given assurance that they would be quite safe. I was just as much in command of my senses that day as I am every other day. . . ."

"The few sentences of our conversation in the adjoining room have partly been falsified, partly torn out of content. We did not threaten. I reminded these gentlemen of what we talked about all the time and asked them to act upon their beliefs now. I said there was no turning back. We would be ruined if we did. For I foresaw that if the cause was lost, they would go to prison with us, an opinion which, however, I have had to correct today. I told them that I was ready to go into the hall and propose that he take over these offices. I wanted to ask the people their opinion on these proposals. Let them decide for themselves whether they were satisfied with our solution. In the hall tremendous applause arose. I left the hall again and told Kahr about it. I said: 'You needn't be ashamed when you go in; they will carry you on their shoulders.'

"Ludendorff came. He asked me whether the others had been told that he was coming. Then he declared he was surprised at the others; but now the only possible decision must be made.

"He made it clear that this was only possible with Kahr,

Lossow, and Seisser. *All were deeply moved; Kahr, Lossow, and Seisser had tears in their eyes.* Lossow said to Ludendorff: 'Excellency, your wish is my command.' He held out his hand, everyone was quiet for a moment.

"Seisser, also deeply moved, shook hands with Ludendorff. The two spoke with Kahr again.

"Then Kahr said: *'Good! But all of us here are monarchists. I can take over the administration only as representative of the monarchy. . . .'* "

"Certain people have presented this situation as though I oscillated between the pistol and the beer-mug. *I am almost an anti-alcoholic* and it is only because of the dryness of my voice that I occasionally take a drink of water and beer. It is shameless to put such a filthy interpretation on that. . . ."

"At that moment I trusted Kahr like a brother. It seemed to me unthinkable that a man who talks about a thing for months, agrees to it, who says, we are with you, should suddenly declare: I quit. For Ludendorff it would have been unheard-of to break the word given under such circumstances—and not only to break it but even to interpret it as a kind of blackmail. . . ."

"I went out with Weber. . . . When we came back, Lossow, Seisser, and Kahr had left. Ludendorff was not at all disturbed; he had full confidence in Kahr's word of honor. My idea at the time was that the three had fallen into the hands of traitors around them; whereas with us they had been perfectly safe, they might really be in danger now. . . ."

"On our side it was certain that a struggle against the Reichswehr and the police would be ruinous, for these were the two factors which were primarily to bring about the change. Without these two factors the whole affair was purposeless. Moreover, as long as we were not absolutely certain that Lossow, Seisser, and Kahr . . . would *not* go along with us, it was our duty to carry out our part honestly. It was, therefore, not foolishness that we stuck to our purpose. The people backed us up—even as they are backing us up today.

The prisons to which our comrades are being sent will be places of honor for German youth.

"But even when morning came, we still had no news that would completely clarify things. Nor did we have any news by twelve noon. There were only two possibilities: Either launch our appeal beyond Munich, or remain in Munich and depend once more on public opinion. . . . *Ludendorff himself accordingly said: 'We will enter the city.'* To win public opinion, to see how public opinion reacts, and then to see how Messrs. Kahr, Lossow, and Seisser react to public opinion. For they could not be so foolish as to turn machine guns on the aroused people.

"And so the march on the city was decided. We marched at the head; for we do not behave like the Communists who look for cover when the others are climbing the barricades. I was asked to tell Ludendorff that we might be fired upon. I did so, but Ludendorff merely answered: 'We are marching! . . .' "

"At the Ludwigsbruecke the police met us with loaded guns; but as we marched on this police cordon broke up. They were not disarmed by us. Then men were deeply moved; there were some from whose eyes tears were streaming. If these men were disarmed after we passed, we knew nothing about it. To be sure, civilians were crying: 'Strike them down!' But I said they should not be harmed, for they had not actually done anything against us. We marched to the Marienplatz, where we were greeted jubilantly by the enormous crowd. This crowd was demanding a reckoning with the men who five years ago committed such a monstrous crime. At the Palace we were held up by a stronger cordon of police. We were in civilian clothes and none of us had so much as a pistol in his hand. Then there came a rifle shot, and then a salvo. Scheubner fell, and pulled me down; I felt as though I had received a flesh wound. I tried to get up. Then the shooting stopped. All around me I saw nothing but dead men. On the ground lay a tall man with a black coat that was covered with blood, and at the moment I felt sure it was Ludendorff. Later I learned that Ludendorff still lived. . . ."

"I alone bear the responsibility. But I am not a criminal because of that. If today I stand here as a revolutionary, it is as a revolutionary against the Revolution.

"It is impossible for me to have committed high treason; for the treason could not consist in the events of November 8, but in all our activities and our state of mind in the preceding months, and then I wonder why those who did exactly the same thing are not sitting here beside me.

"If we committed high treason, then countless others did the same. I deny all guilt so long as I do not find added to our little company those gentlemen who helped even in the pettiest details of the preparation of the affair, as I shall prove in the closed hearings.

"I feel myself the best of Germans, who wanted the best for the German people."

Press

Koelnische Zeitung— . . . We had expected a great deal, but in his truly moving oratory Hitler exceeded all that the most lively imagination expected. It seemed to have a tremendous effect upon the audience when Hitler described as a simple soldier he saw the leaders of the army standing on a hill—those men who have been worshiped as incorporating the greatness of Germany; and how to work with these men toward the same goal had always seemed to him, Hitler, the highest ideal. . . .

Frankfurter Zeitung— . . . Read Hitler's defense speech. Is that the way a man speaks who is filled with the noble, clearly-visioned mission of saving Germany? He rants—rants in fearfully exaggerated terms at the Marxists, with ugly distortions of history at the "November criminals," with incredible lack of sympathy at the fighters in the Ruhr. Where do we find one positive idea? We do not doubt that he would have been capable of executing a few of the "November criminals"—and at the same time the French would have bitten off a few more fragments of German territory and once more united the world against us. When will it be seen that these men live in hatred alone, that their so-called "forcefulness," which is worshiped by so many Germans, is nothing more than an attempt to free themselves of the vexation which the disappointments of our hard life in Germany have imposed on them—and that they only succeed in increasing the misery of our country? . . .

London Times— . . . Beginning almost nervously, the little Austrian sign-painter soon recovered himself, and his speech was reminiscent of many that he had made in the beer halls of Munich. There was no applause, but it was evident that the sympathies of a very large proportion of those who were in the Court were with the speaker, when, with emphatic gesture, he declared that it was not himself or his associates who were on trial, but his Excellency Herr von Kahr, the Dictator, and that 'but for the Dictator's treachery a National Government which could have saved Germany would now have been in power. . . .

New York Times— . . . The friendly atmosphere in which the trial began was noticeable. Hitler and Ludendorff chatted animatedly together, while the other accused men seemed not to take the trial seriously. . . .

•

SPEECH OF MARCH 27, 1924

Before the Munich Court

"WHEN did the ruin of Germany begin? You know the watchword of the old German system in its foreign policy: it ran—maintenance of world peace, economic conquest of the world. With both these principles one cannot govern a people. The maintenance of world peace cannot be the purpose and aim of the policy of a State. The increase and maintenance of a people—that alone can be the aim. If you are going to conquer the world by an economic policy, other peoples will not fail to see their danger.

"What is the State? Today the State is an economic organization, an association of persons, formed, it would seem, for the sole purpose that all should co-operate in securing each other's daily bread. *The State, however, is not an economic organization, it is a 'volkic' organism.* The purpose, the aim of the State is to provide the people with its food-supply and with the position of power in the world which is its due. Germany occupies in Europe perhaps the most bitter situation of any people. Militarily, politically, and geographically it is surrounded by none but rivals: *it can maintain itself only when it places a power-policy (Machtpolitik) ruthlessly in the foreground.*

"Two Powers are in a position to determine the future development of Europe: England and France. England's aim remains eternally the same: to balkanize Europe and to establish a balance of power in Europe so that her position in the world will not be threatened. *England is not on principle an enemy of Germany, it is the Power which seeks to gain the first place in Europe. The declared enemy of Germany is France.* Just as England needs the balkanization of Europe, so France needs the balkanization of Germany in order to gain hegemony in Europe. After four and a half years of bitter struggle at last through the Revolution the scale of victory turned in favor of the coalition of these two Powers, with the following result: France was faced with the question: Was she to realize her eternal war-aim or not? That means: Could France destroy Germany and deprive it of all the sources whereby its people was fed? Today France watches the ripening to fulfillment of her age-old plan: it matters not what Government will be at the helm in France: the supreme aim will remain—the annihilation of Germany, the extermination of twenty million Germans, and the dissolution of Germany into separate States. . . ."

"The army which we have formed grows from day to day; from hour to hour it grows more rapidly. *Even now I have the proud hope that one day the hour is coming when these untrained bands will become battalions, when the battalions will become regiments and the regiments divisions,* when the old cockade will be raised from the mire, when the old banners will once again wave before us: and then reconciliation will come in that eternal last Court of Judgment—the Court of God—before which we are ready to take our stand. Then from our bones, from our graves will sound the voice of that tribunal which alone has the right to sit in judgment upon us. For, gentlemen, it is not you who pronounce judgment upon us, it is the eternal Court of History which will make its pronouncement upon the charge which is brought against us. The judgment that you will pass, that I know. But that Court will not ask of us: 'Have you committed high treason or not?' That Court will judge us . . . who as Germans have wished the best for their people and their Fatherland, who wished to fight and to die. You may declare us guilty a thousand times, but the Goddess who presides over the Eternal Court of History will with a smile tear in pieces the charge of the Public Prosecutor and the judgment of the Court: for she declares us guiltless."

Press

Berliner Tageblatt ("Bankrupt Justice" by Ernst Feder)— . . . In full publicity, the bench of the Bavarian People's Court must be destroyed. For the verdict that was passed down today in the Infantry School in Munich, and which exceeded the direst expectations of skeptical critics, is tantamount to a declaration of the bankruptcy of Bavarian justice. It is a verdict without example in a time when so many errors of justice are being committed daily in political trials. . . .

Roehm, Frick, Brueckner, Pernet, and Wagner have been released and can go on planning their putsches. Hitler, Poehner, Kriebel and Weber may be released after six months. . . . Never before has a Court more openly denied the foundation upon which it rests and upon which every modern state is built. . . .

Frankfurter Zeitung— . . . The verdict can only be explained on the basis of the principle that high treason, if born out of "national" aspirations, is a venial, minor crime. Nothing is more symptomatic than that the court calls the minimum punishment of five years imprisonment, which dates from the pre-revolutionary period, "a very considerable term." Once upon a time high treason was a serious crime in Germany. . . .

Germania (Catholic party organ), *Berlin*— . . . Not only from the juridical standpoint, but also from the point of view of national needs, the Munich verdict must be deeply regretted. For it means practically a verdict of not guilty, and an invitation to high treason. . . .

Le Temps— . . . This verdict can be criticized point by point. The crime is obvious: these men have attempted to seize power in Germany; they sought to corrupt the Reichswehr and march on Berlin. . . .

New York Times— . . . Plotting the overthrow of the Republic is not a hazardous occupation in Germany. If the practitioner of treason is a towering figure like Ludendorff, he is acquitted on the ground of "innocent" complicity. . . .

London Times— . . . The trial has at any rate proved that to plot against the Constitution of the Reich is not considered a serious crime in Bavaria. . . .

SPEECH OF NOVEMBER 23, 1926

Essen, Party Convention

Background

1924

April 1—Verdict in the Hitler trial. Ludendorff acquitted, Hitler, Weber, Kriebel, and Poehner condemned to five years' imprisonment.

August 16—Former Allies and Germany reach agreement in London on the Dawes Reparation Plan.

August 18—French troops begin evacuation of the Ruhr.

November 4—Coolidge elected as President of the United States. British Prime Minister MacDonald resigns and is succeeded by Stanley Baldwin.

December 22—Reports of the Supreme Interallied Military Commission show that Germany has not disarmed in accordance with the terms of the Versailles Treaty.

1925

January—Bavarian Government lifts the ban on the old National Socialist party. Hitler is pardoned but is forbidden to make public speeches.

February 27—Hitler's first speech in private in the Bürgerbräu Keller.

February 28—Friedrich Ebert, first President of the German Republic, dies.

March 29—April 26—Election of Hindenburg as President of Germany.

July 31—The French complete the evacuation of the Ruhr.

August 6—The Reichstag ratifies the Dawes Plan.

November 22—Meeting of the "North German Districts" of the Nazi party in Hannover, convoked and led by Gregor Strasser. Rust, the Gauleiter for Hannover, declares that the

North Germans do not want to be ruled by Hitler. A split in the Party is threatened.

November 27—The Reichstag ratifies the Locarno treaties and authorizes the entrance of the Reich into the League of Nations.

December 1—British and Belgian troops evacuate Cologne and Crefeld.

1926

Beginning of the year—National Socialist party announces membership of 30,000.

January—Foundation of the SS. Function: to be Hitler's bodyguard.

February 2—Four members of the German terrorist organization, the Feme of the illegal Black Reichswehr, are sentenced to death. In subsequent trials the German War Office suppresses evidence.

February 12—The League of Nations prepares to admit Germany in accordance with the Locarno Treaty.

May 13—Coup d'état of Marshal Pilsudski in Poland.

May 22—General membership meeting of the National Socialist party in Munich. New Party articles provide for unlimited power of the "Fuehrer." The Party program is established as unchangeable.

September 2-14—Council of the League of Nations offers Germany a permanent seat.

October 26—Appointment of Dr. Josef Goebbels as the Nationalist Socialist party's Gauleiter in Berlin. He is given extraordinary powers.

The Speech

". . . I WAS always particularly anxious to secure that *Parteitag* should on principle never be used for the settlement of personal disputes. Such disputes must certainly be settled in one way or another, but just as certainly the *Partei-*

tag, which once in the year should unite the whole Movement, is not the fitting day for such a settlement. Neither is it the place at which to seek to clarify unripe and uncertain ideas. Neither the length of time available at such a gathering nor its nature admits of giving to it the character of a Council. And it must never be forgotten that in all such cases or those similar to them great decisions have not been made at such Councils: on the contrary, for the most part, world-history pursues its course without paying any attention to them. *World-history, like all events of historical significance, is the result of the activity of single individuals—* it is not the fruit of majority decisions. . . ."

Press

No comments in the leading German newspapers.

•

SPEECH OF SEPTEMBER 16, 1930

Munich

Background

1927

Early March—Bavarian Government lifts the ban on Hitler's speaking.

May 21—Lindbergh transatlantic flight.

August 21—Nazi party convention in Nuremberg. Parade of 20,000 SA-men.

September 5—At the League of Nations at Geneva, compulsory arbitration is accepted by Germany.

1928

January 16—Leon Trotzky is exiled from European Russia.

April 13—Secretary of State Kellogg sends draft of treaty renouncing war as a national policy to Great Britain, Germany, Italy and Japan.

May 20—General elections in Germany result in gains for the Socialist party and losses for the Nationalists and Monarchists.

May 31—Removal of the ban on the Nazi party in Berlin.

June 12—In Germany, a government of the Socialist leader, Hermann Mueller-Franken, succeeds that of Chancellor Marx.

June 23—Kellogg submits to fourteen nations a new draft of the treaty outlawing war as a national policy, with a preamble intended to meet French objections.

July—Removal of the prohibition against Hitler's speaking in Prussia.

August 9—The Nazi party decides against the formation of National Socialist labor unions.

October 1—Soviet Union inaugurates the Five-Year Plan.

1929

January 17—President Coolidge signs the Kellogg Pact.

February 6—The German Reichstag ratifies the Kellogg Pact.

July—National Socialist party claims 120,000 members.

October 18—In Germany, President von Hindenburg condemns the Nationalist referendum which would express disapproval of officials pledged to the Young Plan.

October—Beginning of the stock market crash in New York.

1930

January 15—Communist riots in German industrial centers on account of two million unemployed.

March 7—Declaring that Germany cannot meet the Young

Plan, Hjalmar Schacht resigns as president of the Reichsbank.

March—Nazi party claims 210,000 members. Co-operation of Hitler and Hugenberg in the "Reich committee for a German popular referendum against the Young Plan and the warguilt lie."

March 13—President von Hindenburg signs the Young Plan.

March 28—Dr. Heinrich Bruening forms a government which will support the Young Plan.

April 22—London Naval Conference: U.S.A., England, Japan, France and Italy agree to build no capital ships for six years.

September 14—In the general election Hitler receives 6,406,000 votes, raises Nazi representation in the Reichstag from 12 to 107.

September—Trial against the Nazi Lieutenant Scheringer for high treason. As a witness Hitler takes the oath that in the future he will stick to strict legality and act under the Weimar Constitution. The reaction in the SA is one of sharp disapproval, especially in Prussia.

The Speech

"... THIS election means that the circle is now complete. And the question at this time is: what are the aims of this opposition and its leaders?

"It is a fight for an idea—a *Weltanschauung:* and in the forefront stands a fundamental principle: Men do not exist for the State, the State exists for men. First and far above all else stands the idea of the people: the State is a form of organization of this people, and the meaning and the purpose of the State are through this form of organization to assure the life of the people. And from this there arises a new mode of thought and thus necessarily a new political method.

"We say: a new mode of thought. Today our whole official

political outlook is rooted in the view that the State must be maintained because the State in itself is the essential thing; we, on the other hand, maintain that the State in its form has a definite purpose to fulfill and the moment that it fails to fulfil its purpose the form stands condemned. Above everything stands the purpose to maintain the nation's life —that is the essential thing—and one should not speak of a law for the protection of the State but for the protection of the nation: it is of this protection that one must think. . . . In the place of this rigid formal organization—the State—must be set the living organism—the people. Then all action is given a new untrammelled freedom: all the formal fetters which can today be imposed on men become immoral directly they fail to maintain the people, because *that* is the highest purpose in life and the aim of all reasonable thought and action.

"If today our action employs among its different weapons that of Parliament, that is not to say that parliamentary parties exist only for parliamentary ends. For us Parliament is not an end in itself, but merely a means to an end . . . we are not on principle a parliamentary party—that would be a contradiction of our whole outlook—*we are a parliamentary party by compulsion, under constraint, and that compulsion is the Constitution.* The Constitution compels us to use this means. It does not compel us to wish for a particular goal, it only prescribes a way—a method, and, I repeat, we follow this way legally, in accordance with the Constitution: by the way laid down through the Constitution we advance towards the purposes which we have set before us.

"Never can Constitutions determine for all time the content of a purpose, especially when this content is not identical with the vital rights of a people. If today the Constitution admits for its protection laws which are headed, 'Laws for the Protection of the Republic,' then it is demonstrated that the most which our present Constitution can prescribe is nothing but the protection and the maintenance of a form, and that does not touch the maintenance of the nation, of a people. This purpose is therefore free: this is the goal which we proclaim and to which we shall attain. . . ."

"From blood, authority of personality, and a fighting spirit springs that value which alone entitles a people to look around with glad hope, and that alone is also the condition for the life which men then desire. And when that is realized, then that too is realized for which today the political parties strive: prosperity, happiness of the individual, family-life, etc. First will come honor and then freedom, and from both of these happiness, prosperity, life: in a word, that state of things will return which we Germans perhaps dimly saw before the War when individuals can once more live with joy in their hearts because life has a meaning and a purpose, because the close of life is then not in itself the end, since there will be an endless chain of generations to follow: man will know that what we create will not sink into Orcus but will pass to his children and to his children's children. And so this victory which we have just won is nothing else than the winning of a new weapon for our fight. . . . *It is not for seats in Parliament that we fight, but we win seats in Parliament in order that one day we may be able to liberate the German people. . . .*"

"Do not write on your banners the word 'Victory': today that word shall be uttered for the last time. Strike through the word 'Victory' and write once more in its place the word which suits us better—the word 'Fight.' "

Press

Le Temps, September 20—. . . In order to maintain itself, Hitler's party will naturally be led to continue in this course, to exaggerate its demands and to conform in general terms to the aspirations of all those malcontents who are the most enlightened among his adherents. Hitler has expressly declared that the goal of his party is not a coup d'état but "the revolution of the German soul." But while waiting for this, he prepares his moral revolution by the use of force. . . .

London Times, September 19—In his (Hitler's) speech at Munich . . . after disclaiming any intention of obtaining power by armed revolt, he made some interesting observations about the uses of Parliament as the Nazis see them. For them, Herr Hitler explained, Parliament was not the objective itself, but a means of reaching the objective, not the goal, but a way to the goal. They were not a Parliamentary party by principle but by compulsion, and the compulsion was the Constitution. . . .

•

SPEECH OF JANUARY 27, 1932

Duesseldorf, Industry Club

Background

1931

September 21—In London the House of Commons passes a bill abandoning the gold standard.

October 11—Meeting in Harzburg of the Nazis and Nationalists—Hugenberg-Hitler alliance. Demand that Bruening resign. But even at the meeting Hitler makes his independence clear by reading a proclamation of his own to his own Nazi party members.

Mid-October—Hindenburg receives Hitler.

1932

January—Conversation between Bruening and Hitler. Bruening suggests that Hitler agree to a continuance of Hindenburg's term of office as President of the Reich. In return, Bruening would resign—after a year—and propose Hitler as

Chancellor. Party circles, led by Roehm, strongly oppose this proposal. Hitler thereupon declares that he could only agree to a continuance of Hindenburg's term of office if Bruening were dismissed.

January 15—Approximately six million unemployed in the Reich.

January 23—Russia concludes a non-aggression pact with Finland.

The Speech

". . . IF TODAY the National Socialist Movement is regarded amongst widespread circles in Germany as being hostile to our business life, I believe the reason for this view is to be found in the fact that we adopted towards the events which determined the development leading to our present position an attitude which differed from that of all the other organizations which are of any importance in our public life. Even now our outlook differs in many points from that of our opponents. . . ."

"I regard it as of the first importance to break once and for all with the view that our destiny is conditioned by world-events. It is not true that our distress has its final cause in a world crisis, in a world catastrophe: the true view is that we have reached a state of general crisis, because from the first certain mistakes were made. I must not say 'According to the general view the Peace Treaty of Versailles is the cause of our misfortune.' What is the Peace Treaty of Versailles but the work of men? It is not a burden which has been imposed or laid upon us by Providence. It is the work of men for which, it goes without saying, once again men with their merits or their failings must be held responsible. If this were not so, how should men ever be able to set aside this work at all? I am of the opinion that there is nothing which has been produced by the will of man which cannot in its turn be altered by another human will.

"Both the Peace Treaty of Versailles together with all the

consequences of that Treaty have been the result of a policy which perhaps fifteen, fourteen, or thirteen years ago was regarded as the right policy, at least in the enemy States, but which from our point of view was bound to be regarded as fatal when ten or less years ago its true character was disclosed to millions of Germans and now today stands revealed in its utter impossibility. I am bound therefore to assert that there must of necessity have been in Germany, too, some responsibility for these happenings if I am to have any belief that the German people can exercise some influence towards changing these conditions.

"*It is also in my view false to say that life in Germany today is solely determined by considerations of foreign policy,* that the primacy of foreign policy governs today the whole of our domestic life. Certainly a people can reach the point when foreign relations influence and determine completely its domestic life. But let no one say that such a condition is from the first either natural or desirable. Rather the important thing is that a people should create the conditions for a change in this state of affairs.

"If anyone says to me that its foreign politics is primarily decisive for the life of a people, then I must first ask: what then is the meaning of the term 'Politics'? There is a whole series of definitions. Frederick the Great said: 'Politics is the art of serving one's State with every means.' Bismarck's explanation was that 'Politics is the art of the Possible,' starting from the conception that advantage should be taken of every possibility to serve the State—and, in the later transformation of the idea of the State into the idea of nationalities, the Nation. Another considers that this service rendered to the people can be effected by military as well as peaceful action: for Clausewitz says that war is the continuation of politics though with different means. Conversely, Clémenceau considers that today peace is nothing but the continuation of war and the pursuing of the war-aim, though again with other means. To put it briefly: politics is nothing else and can be nothing else than the safeguarding of a people's vital interests and the practical waging of its life-battle with every means. Thus it is quite clear that this life-battle from the first has its starting-point in the people itself and that at the same time the people is the object—the real thing of value—which has to be preserved. All functions of this body formed by the people must in the last resort fulfill only one purpose—to secure in the future the maintenance of this body which is the people. I can therefore say neither that foreign policy nor economic policy is of primary significance. Of course, a people needs the business world in order to live. But business is but one of the functions of this body-politic whereby its existence is assured. But primarily the essential thing is the starting-point and that is the people itself. . . ."

"It is therefore false to say that foreign politics shapes a people: rather, peoples order their relations to the world about them in correspondence with their inborn forces and according to the measure in which their education enables them to bring those forces into play. We may be quite convinced that if in the place of the Germany of today there had stood a different Germany, the attitude towards the rest of the world would also have been different, and then presumably the influences exercised by the rest of the world would have taken a different form. To deny this would mean that Germany's destiny can no longer be changed no matter what Government rules in Germany. . . ."

"And as against this conception I am the champion of another standpoint: three factors, I hold, essentially determine a people's political life:

"First, the inner value of a people which as an inherited sum and possession is transmitted again and again through the generations, a value which suffers any change when the people, the custodian of this inherited possession, changes itself in its inner blood-conditioned composition. It is beyond question that certain traits of character, certain virtues, and certain vices always recur in peoples so long as their inner nature—their blood-conditioned composition—has not essentially altered. I can already trace the virtues and the vices of our German people in the writers of Rome just as clearly as I see them today. This inner value which determines the life of a people can be destroyed by nothing save only through a change in the blood causing a change in substance. Temporarily an illogical form of organization of life or unintelligent education may prejudice it. But in that case, though its effective action may be hindered, the fundamental value in itself is still present as it was before. And it is this value which is the great source of all hopes for a people's revival, it is this which justifies the belief that a people which in the course of thousands of years has furnished countless examples of the highest inner value cannot suddenly have lost overnight this inborn inherited value, but that one day this people will once again bring this value into action. If this were not the case, then the faith of millions of men in a better future—the mystic hope for a new Germany—would be incomprehensible. It would be incomprehensible how it was that this German people, at the end of the Thirty Years War, when its population had shrunk from eighteen to thirteen and one-half millions, could ever have once more formed the hope through work, through industry, and capacity to rise again, how in this completely crushed people hundreds of thousands and finally millions should have been seized with the longing for a re-formation of their State. . . ."

"I said that this value can be destroyed. There are indeed in especial two other closely related factors which we can time and again trace in periods of national decline: the one is that for the conception of the value of personality there is substituted a levelling idea of the supremacy of mere numbers—democracy—and the other is the negation of the value of a people, the denial of any difference in the inborn capacity, the achievement, etc., of individual peoples. Thus both factors condition one another or at least influence each other in the course of their development. Internationalism and democracy are inseparable conceptions. It is but logical that democracy, which within a people denies the special value of the individual and puts in its place a value which represents the sum of all individualities—a purely numerical value—should proceed in precisely the same way in the life of peoples and should in that sphere result in internationalism. Broadly it is maintained: peoples have no inborn values, but, at the most, there can be admitted perhaps temporary differences in education. Between Negroes, Aryans, Mongolians, and Redskins there is no essential difference in value. This view which forms the basis of the whole of the international thought-world of today and in its effects is carried to such lengths that in the end a Negro can sit as president in the sessions of the League of Nations leads necessarily as a further consequence to the point that in a similar way within a people differences in value between the individual members of this people are denied. And thus naturally every special capacity, every fundamental value of a people, can practically be made of no effect. For the greatness of a people is the result not of the sum of all its achievements but in the last resort of the sum of its outstanding achievements. Let no one say that the picture produced as a first impression of human civilization is the impression of its achievement as a whole. This whole edifice of civilization is in its foundations and in all its stones nothing else than the result of the creative capacity, the achievement, the intelligence, the industry, of individuals: in its greatest triumphs it represents the great crowning achievement of individual God-favored geniuses, in its average accomplishment the achievement of men of average capacity, and in its sum doubtless the result of the use of human labor-force in order to turn to account the creations of genius and of talent. So it is only natural that when the capable intelligences of a nation, which are always in a minority, are regarded only as of the same value as all the rest, then genius, capacity, the value of personality are slowly subjected to the majority and this process is then falsely named the rule of the people. For this is not rule of the people, but in reality the rule of stupidity, of mediocrity, of half-heartedness, of cowardice, of weakness, and of inadequacy. . . ."

"Thus democracy will in practice lead to the destruction of a people's true values. And this also serves to explain how it is that peoples with a great past from the time when they surrender themselves to the unlimited, democratic rule of the masses slowly lose their former position; for the outstanding achievements of individuals which they still possess or which could be produced in all spheres of life are now rendered practically ineffective through the oppression of mere numbers. And thus in these conditions a people will gradually lose its importance not merely in the cultural and economic spheres but altogether; in a comparatively short time it will no longer, within the setting of the other peoples of the world, maintain its former value. . . ."

"And to this there must be added a third factor: namely, the view that life in this world, after the denial of the value of personality and of the special value of a people, is not to be maintained through conflict. That is a conception which could perhaps be disregarded if it fixed itself only in the heads of individuals, but yet has appalling consequences because it slowly poisons an entire people. And it is not as if such general changes in men's outlook on the world remained only on the surface or were confined to their effects on men's minds. No, in course of time they exercise a profound influence and affect all expressions of a people's life.

"I may cite an example: you maintain, gentlemen, that German business life must be constructed on a basis of private property. Now such a conception as that of private property you can defend only if in some way or another it appears to have a logical foundation. This conception must deduce its ethical justification from an insight into the necessity which Nature dictates. It cannot simply be upheld by saying: 'It has always been so and therefore it must continue to be so.' For in periods of great upheavals within States, of movements of peoples and changes in thought, institutions and systems cannot remain untouched because they have previously been preserved without change. It is the characteristic feature of all really great revolutionary epochs in the history of mankind that they pay astonishingly little regard for forms which are hallowed only by age or which are apparently only so consecrated. It is thus necessary to give such foundations to traditional forms which are to be preserved that they can be regarded as absolutely essential, as logical and right. And then I am bound to say that private property can be morally and ethically justified only if I admit that men's achievements are different. Only on that basis can I assert: since men's achievements are different, the results of those achievements are also different. But if the results of those achievements are different, then it is reasonable to leave to men the administration of those results to a corresponding degree. It would not be logical to entrust the administration of the result of an achievement which was bound up with a personality either to the next best but less capable person or to a community which, through the mere fact that it had not performed the achievement, has proved that it is not capable of administering the result of that achievement. Thus it must be admitted that in the economic sphere, from the start, in all branches men are not of equal value or of equal importance. And once this is admitted it is madness to say: in the economic sphere there are undoubtedly differences in value, but that is not true in the political sphere. *It is absurd to build up economic life on the conceptions of achievement, of the value of personality, and therefore in practice on the authority of personality, but in the political sphere to deny the authority of personality and to thrust into its place the law of the greater number—democracy.* In that case there must slowly arise a cleavage between the economic and the political point of view, and to bridge that cleavage an attempt will be made to assimilate the former to the latter—indeed the attempt has been made, for this cleavage has not remained bare, pale theory. The conception of the equality of values has already, not only in politics but in economics also, been raised to a system, and that not merely in abstract theory: no! this economic system is alive in gigantic organizations and it has already today inspired a State which rules over immense areas.

"But I cannot regard it as possible that the life of a people should in the long run be based upon two fundamental conceptions. If the view is right that there are differences in human achievement, then it must also be true that the value of men in respect of the production of certain achievements is different. It is then absurd to allow this principle to hold good only in one sphere—the sphere of economic life and its leadership—and to refuse to acknowledge its validity in the sphere of the whole life-struggle of a people—the sphere of politics. Rather the logical course is that if I recognize without qualification in the economic sphere the fact of special achievements as forming the condition of all higher culture, then in the same way I should recognize special achievement in the sphere of politics and that means that I am bound to put in the forefront the authority of personality. If, on the contrary, it is asserted—and that, too, by those engaged in business—that in the political sphere special capacities are not necessary but that here an absolute equality in achievement reigns, then one day this same theory will be transferred from politics and applied to economic life. But in the economic sphere communism is analogous to democracy in the political sphere. We find ourselves today in a period in which these two fundamental principles are at grips in all spheres which come into contact with each other; already they are invading economics.

"To take an example: Life in practical activity is founded on the importance of personality: but now gradually it is threatened by the supremacy of mere numbers. But in the State there is an organization—the army—which cannot in any way be democratized without surrendering its very existence. But if a *Weltanschauung* cannot be applied to every sphere of a people's life, that fact in itself is sufficient proof of its weakness. In other words: the army can exist only if it maintains the absolutely undemocratic principle of unconditional authority proceeding downwards and absolute responsibility proceeding upwards, while, in contradistinction to this, democracy means in practice complete dependence proceeding downwards and authority proceeding upwards. But the result is that in a State in which the whole political life—beginning with the parish and ending with the Reichstag—is built up on the conception of democracy, the army is bound gradually to become an alien body and an alien body which must necessarily be felt to be such. It is for democracy an alien world of ideas, an alien *Weltanschauung* which inspires the life of this body. An internal conflict between the representatives of the democratic principle and the representatives of the principle of authority must be the inevitable consequence, and this conflict we are actually experiencing in Germany. . . ."

"So in the same way the education to pacifism must of necessity have its effect right through life until it reaches the humblest individual lives. The conception of pacifism is logical if I once admit a general equality amongst peoples and human beings. For in that case what sense is there in conflict? The conception of pacifism translated into practice and applied to all spheres must gradually lead to the destruction of the competitive instinct, to the destruction of the ambition for outstanding achievement. I cannot say: in politics we will be pacifists, we reject the idea of the necessity for life to safeguard itself through conflict—but in economics we want to remain keenly competitive. If I reject the idea of conflict as such, it is of no importance that for the time being that idea is still applied in some single spheres. In the last resort political decisions are decisive and determine achievement in the single sphere. . . ."

"To sum up the argument: *I see two diametrically opposed principles: the principle of democracy which, wherever it is allowed practical effect, is the principle of destruction: and the principle of the authority of personality which I would call the principle of achievement,* because whatever man in the past has achieved—all human civilizations—is conceivable only if the supremacy of this principle is admitted.

"The worth of a people, the character of its internal organization through which this worth of a people may produce its effect, and the character of a people's education—these are the starting-points for political action: these are the foundations for the success of that action. . . ."

"That the evidences of a crisis should today spread over almost the entire world is comprehensible when one considers that the world has been opened up and mutual relations have been strengthened to an extent which fifty, eighty, or a hundred years ago appeared scarcely possible. And yet, despite this fact, one must not believe that such a state of affairs is conceivable only now, in the year 1932. No, similar conditions have been experienced more than once in the history of the world. Always when relations between peoples produced conditions such as these, the malady affecting these peoples was bound to spread and to influence the position of all.

"It is, of course, easy to say: we prefer to wait until there is a change in the general position, but that is impossible. For the position which faces you today is not the consequence of a revelation of God's will, but the result of human weaknesses, of human mistakes, of men's false judgments. It is but natural that there must first be a change in these causes, that men must first be inwardly transformed, before one can count on any alteration in the position.

"That conclusion is forced upon us if we look at the world today: we have a number of nations which through their inborn outstanding worth have fashioned for themselves a mode of life which stands in no relation to the life-space—

the *Lebensraum*—which in their thickly populated settlements they inhabit. We have the so-called white race which, since the collapse of ancient civilization, in the course of some thousand years has created for itself a privileged position in the world. But I am quite unable to understand this privileged position, this economic supremacy, of the white race over the rest of the world if I do not bring it into close connection with a political conception of supremacy which has been peculiar to the white race for many centuries and has been regarded as in the nature of things: this conception it has maintained in its dealings with other peoples. Take any single area you like, take for example India. England did not conquer India by the way of justice and of law: she conquered India without regard to the wishes, to the views of the natives, or to their formulations of justice, and, when necessary, she has upheld this supremacy with the most brutal ruthlessness. Just in the same way Cortez or Pizarro annexed Central America and the northern states of South America, not on the basis of any claim of right, but from the absolute inborn feeling of the superiority of the white race. The settlement of the North American continent is just as little the consequence of any claim of superior right in any democratic or international sense; it was the consequence of a consciousness of right which was rooted solely in the conviction of the superiority and therefore of the right of the white race. If I think away this attitude of mind which in the course of the last three or four centuries has won the world for the white race, then the destiny of this race would in fact have been no different from that, say, of the Chinese: an immensely congested mass of human beings crowded upon an extraordinarily narrow territory, an over-population with all its unavoidable consequences. If Fate allowed the white race to take a different path, that is only because this white race was convinced that it had the right to organize the rest of the world. It matters not what superficial disguises in individual cases this right may have assumed, in practice it was the exercise of an extraordinarily brutal right to dominate others *(Herrenrechtes)*, and from this political conception was developed the basis for the economic annexation of that world which was not inhabited by the white race. . . ."

"Today we are faced with a world-condition which is for the white race in any way comprehensible only if one recognizes as unconditionally valid that marriage of the spirit of domination in political will and the same spirit of domination in economic activity—a wonderful concord which has impressed its stamp upon the whole of the last century and through the consequences of which a part of the white peoples has enjoyed a remarkable development: instead of expanding in space, instead of exporting men, they have exported goods and have built up an economic world-system which finds its characteristic expression in the fact that—presupposing different standards of living on the earth—in Europe and, in most recent times, in America also, gigantic world-central-factories have come into existence while the rest of the world provides enormous markets for the disposal of goods and enormous sources of raw materials. The white race, however, can in practice maintain its position only so long as the difference in the standard of living in different parts of the world continues to exist. If you today give to our so-called export-markets the same standard of living as we ourselves possess, you will find that it will be impossible for the white race to maintain that position of superiority which finds expression not merely in the political power of the nation but also in the economic fortune of the individual.

"The different nations, further, have safeguarded this position of superiority in different ways—in accordance with their individual characteristics—most brilliantly of all perhaps England who has always opened up for herself new markets and immediately anchored them through political dominance, so that it is without doubt conceivable that Great Britain, always supposing that her mental outlook remains unchanged, should build up for herself an economic life of her own, more or less independent of the rest of the world. Other peoples have not attained this goal because they consumed their mental powers in internal conflicts between differing outlooks on the world and formerly in religious struggles. During the great period of the partitioning of the world they doubtless inwardly developed their capacities in these intellectual disputes. Later they sought also to take their part in world-economics, but they did not themselves create export-markets nor did they completely safeguard their control over those markets.

"When Germany, for instance, began to found colonies then the inner conception, this quite cool, sober English conception, of the foundation of colonies had already given place to more or less romantic ideas: the transmission of German culture to the world and the spread of German civilization—things which were utterly remote from the thought of the Englishman in the colonization period. Thus it was that the practical results of our efforts did not come up to our expectations, quite apart from the fact that the objects of our concern were in part unable to fulfill our high romantic hopes. . . ."

"The world-situation today can be briefly stated: Germany, England, France, and further—but not by reason of compulsion—the American Union, together with a whole series of small States, are industrial nations dependent on export. After the close of the War all these peoples were faced with a world-market comparatively emptied of commodities. Methods in industry and in factories had been improved, especially on the scientific and theoretical sides, with vast ingenuity on account of the War, and armed with these new methods men rushed into this great void, began to remodel their works, to invest capital and under the compulsion of this invested capital sought to raise production to the highest possible extent. This process could continue with success for two, three, four, or five years. It could be continued successfully for a further period if new possibilities for export could be created which should correspond to the rapid increase and improvements in production and its methods. This was a problem of primary importance, for the rationalization of business which began in the sphere of agriculture leads to a reduction in the number of men engaged in work, a reduction which is useful only if the men thus turned out of employment can be easily in their turn transferred into new branches of economic activity. *But we see that since the World War there was no further important extension of export-markets: on the contrary, we see that relatively those export-markets contracted, that the number of exporting nations gradually increased, and that a great many former export-markets became themselves industrialized, while finally a new wholesale exporter, the American Union—which perhaps today is not yet all-powerful in all spheres, but certainly in individual cases—can reckon on advantages in production which we in Europe assuredly do not and cannot possess.*

"And as the last momentous feature we regard the fact that, parallel with the gradual growth of confusion in the thought of the white race in Europe, a *Weltanschauung* has seized on part of Europe and a great part of Asia which threatens to tear this continent out of the framework of international economic relations altogether—a portent which today German statesmen still appear to neglect with an astonishing levity. When, for instance, I hear a speech which stresses the necessity for the German people to stand together, then I cannot but raise the question: Does one really believe that this standing together is any longer merely a question of political good will? Cannot people see that in our midst already a cleavage has opened up, a cleavage which is not merely a fancy born in the heads of a few persons but whose spiritual exponent forms today the foundation of one of the greatest world-powers? Can they not see that Bolshevism today is not merely a mob storming about in some of our streets in Germany but is a conception of the world which is in the act of subjecting to itself the entire Asiatic continent, and which today in the form of a State stretches almost from our eastern frontier to Vladivostock?

"With us the situation is represented as if here it was merely a question of purely theoretical problems, of views held by a few visionaries or evil-disposed individuals. No! A *Weltanschauung* has won over to itself a State, and starting from this State it will gradually shatter the whole world and bring it down in ruins. *Bolshevism, if its advance is not interrupted, will transform the world as completely as in times past did Christianity.* In 300 years people will no longer say that it is a question of a new idea in production. In 300 years perhaps people will already realize that it is a question almost of a new religion, though its basis is not that of Christianity. In 300 years, if this movement develops further, people will see in Lenin not merely a revolutionary of the year 1917 but the founder of a new world-doctrine, honored perhaps as is Buddha. It is not as if this gigantic phenomenon could simply be thought away from the modern world. It is a reality and must of necessity destroy and overthrow one of the conditions for our continued existence as a white race. We see the stages of this process: first the lowering of the level of civilization and thereby the capacity to welcome civilizing influences; lowering of the whole level of human society and therewith the sundering of all relations towards other nations, then the construction of an independent system of production, with the help of crutches borrowed from capitalist economics; and then as the final stage its own production to the complete exclusion of other countries, which naturally in those districts near its frontiers will one day find in it the most serious economic rival.

"I know very well that gentlemen of the Reichsministry and gentlemen representing German industry will object: 'We do not believe that the Soviets will ever be able to build up an industry which can really be capable of competing with us.' *Gentlemen, they could never build up such an industry if they were confined to the national resources of Bol-*

shevist Russia. But this industry will be built up by elements of value drawn from the white peoples themselves. It is nonsense to say that it is impossible to build up industry in Russia through forces supplied by other peoples. . . ."

"And if it be further stated: The methods of production will never be able to keep pace with our own—*do not forget that a lower standard of living will fully compensate for any advantage which we perhaps possess in our method of production.*

"In any event—if European and American modes of thought remain in the future as they are today—we shall find that Bolshevism will gradually spread over Asia. Thirty or fifty years, when it is a question of *Weltanschauungen,* count for nothing . . . *Weltanschauungen* of this fundamental character can still five hundred years after their rise display their absolute capacity for conquest if they are not at the outset broken by the natural instinct of self-preservation of other peoples. But if this process continues only for another thirty, forty, or fifty years and our outlook still remains unchanged, it will not then, gentlemen, be possible to say 'How does that concern our economic life?'!

"Gentlemen, the development is clear for all to see: the crisis is very serious. It forces us to cut down expenses in every sphere. The most natural way of economizing is always to save in human labor-power. Industries will continuously be forced to ever greater rationalization, that means increase in achievement and reduction in the number of workmen employed. But if these workmen can no longer be given a place in newly started occupations, in newly developed industries, then that means that gradually three national banking accounts must be opened: the first account is called agriculture: from this national basic account men were formerly economized to constitute the second account. This second account was hand-work and later industrial production. Now an economy in man-power is being practised on this second account and the men saved from this account are driven over into the third account—unemployment. With this word unemployment one is but shamefacedly seeking to put a better appearance upon hard facts: for the proper term is not 'workless' but 'existence-less' and therefore in truth 'superfluous.' It is the characteristic feature of our European nations that gradually a certain percentage of the population is proved statistically to be superfluous.

"It is now quite clear that the necessity for supporting this third account thus falls upon the other two. That increases the pressure of taxation, and the consequence of that will be an enforced further rationalization of the method of production, further economy, and a still greater increase in the third account.

"And to this must be added the fact that the fight which today all European nations wage for the world export-market results naturally in a rise of prices which in its reaction compels men to practise further economies. The final result which today can hardly be foreseen will in any event prove decisive for the future or for the downfall of the white race, and in especial of those peoples which in their narrow living space can establish economic autarchy only with very great difficulty. The further consequence will be that, for instance, England will carry through a reorganization with an eye to her internal market and for its protection will raise tariff barriers, high today and tomorrow still higher, and all other peoples, so far as they are in any way able to do so, will follow suit.

"So far all those are in the right who regard the melancholy position of Germany as calling for special attention when considering our present distress, but they are wrong in seeking the cause of our distress in externals, for this position is certainly the result not merely of the external development but of our internal, I might almost say, aberration of spirit, our internal division, our internal collapse. . . ."

"Gentlemen, we know from our own experience that, through a mental aberration whose consequences you can in practice trace on every hand, Germany lost the War. Do you believe that when seven or eight million men have found themselves for ten or twenty years excluded from the national process of production that for these masses Bolshevism could appear as anything else than the logical theoretical complement of their actual, practical, economic situation? Do you really believe that the purely spiritual side of this catastrophe can be overlooked and that one day it will not transform itself into bitter reality—the evil curse following on the evil deed? . . ."

"The essential thing is to realize that at the present moment we find ourselves in a condition which has occurred several times before in the history of the world: already there have been times when the volume of certain products in the world exceeded the demand. Today we are experiencing the same thing on the largest possible scale: if all the motor-factories in the world today were employed a hundred per cent and worked a hundred per cent, then one could replace the world's entire stocks of motors in four and a half or five years. If all the locomotive-factories were employed a hundred per cent they could easily renew the entire locomotive material in the world in eight years. If all the rail-factories and rolling-mills of the world were employed a hundred per cent perhaps in ten to fifteen years one could put the whole system of railway-lines at present in existence once more round the world. And that holds good for nearly all industries. There has arisen such an increase in productive capacity that the present possible consumption market stands in no relation to this increased capacity. But if Bolshevism as a world-idea tears the Asiatic continent out of the human economic community, then the conditions for the employment of these industries which have delevoped on so gigantic a scale will be no longer even approximately realized. . . . When a politician or economist objects: that was, it is true, the case between Rome and Carthage, between England and Holland, or between England and France, but today the business world decides the matter, then I can only reply: that is not the spirit which formerly opened up the world for the white race, which for us Germans, too, opened the way into the economic life of the world. For it was not German business which conquered the world and then came the development of German power, but in our case, too, it was the power-State (*Machtstaat*) which created for the business world the general conditions for its subsequent prosperity. *In my view it is to put the cart before the horse when today people believe that by business methods they can, for instance, recover Germany's power-position instead of realizing that the power-position is also the condition for the improvement of the economic situation.* That does not mean that one should not forthwith try to oppose the malady which has seized upon our economic life, although one cannot immediately attack the source of the malady. But it does mean that every such external solution ignores the kernel of the problem, since it fails to recognize that there is only one fundamental solution. That solution rests upon the realization that economic systems in collapse have always as their forerunner the collapse of the State and not vice versa—that there can be no flourishing economic life which has not before it and behind it the flourishing powerful State as its protection—that there was no Carthaginian economic life without the fleet of Carthage, and no Carthaginian trade without the army of Carthage—that it goes without saying that also in modern times—when blow is met by blow and the interests of peoples clash—*there can be no economic life unless behind this economic life there stands the determined political will of the nation absolutely ready to strike—and to strike hard.*

"And here I would enter a protest against those who would simply sweep these facts aside by asserting that the Peace Treaty of Versailles is 'according to the almost universal view' the cause of our misfortune. No, certainly not 'according to the almost universal view' but rather only according to the view of those who share in the guilt of having concluded that treaty.

"The Peace Treaty of Versailles is itself only the consequence of our own slow inner confusion and aberration of mind. We find ourselves—no one can doubt it—in a period in which the world is faced by extraordinarily difficult mental conflicts which must profoundly disturb it. I cannot escape these conflicts by simply regretting them, by shrugging my shoulders and—without making clear to myself their causes—by saying 'What we want is unity.' These struggles are not caused merely by the ill-will of a few men; they have in the last resort their deepest roots in the facts of race.

"If Bolshevism is spreading today in Russia this Bolshevism is for Russia fundamentally just as logical as was the Czardom formerly. It is a brutal régime over a people which cannot be held together as a State except through a brutal Government. But if this view of the world gains a hold on us, too, then we must not forget that our people also is composed racially of the most varied elements and that therefore we have to see in the watchword 'Proletarians of all countries, unite!' much more than a mere political battle-cry. It is in reality the expression of the will of men who in their essential character have in fact a certain kinship with analogous peoples on a low level of civilization. Our people and our State, too, were formerly built up only through the exercise of the absolute right of the lord and through the sense of lordship of the so-called Nordic men: it is the work of those sections belonging to the Aryan race which we still possess in our people. Accordingly it is only a question of the regeneration of the German body-politic in accordance with the laws of an iron logic: this must determine whether we shall find our way back to new political strength or not. . . ."

" 'The Government will endeavor to improve the morals of the German people.' But on what moral code, gentlemen? Morals, too, must have a root. What to you appears to be moral appears to others immoral, and what to you seems immoral is for others a new morality. The State, for instance, says: The thief must be punished. But many citizens of the nation reply: The property owner must be punished, for the ownership of property is in itself theft. The thief is glorified, not condemned. The one half of the nation says: The traitor must be punished: the other half considers treason to be a duty. The one half says: The nation must be defended with courage: the other half regards courage as idiotic. The one half says: The basis of our morality is the religious life and the other half answers with scorn: The conception of a God has no basis in reality. Religions are but opium for the people.

"I beg you not to think, when a people has once come under the sway of these conflicts of *Weltanschauungen,* that one can circumvent them by the simple method of emergency decrees or to imagine that it is unnecessary to adopt any attitude towards these conflicts because they are matters which do not concern economics, the life of the administration or cultural life. Gentlemen, these conflicts strike at the power and strength of the nation as a whole. How is a people still to count for anything abroad when in the last resort fifty per cent are inclined to bolshevism and fifty per cent are Nationalists or anti-Bolshevists. It is quite conceivable to turn Germany into a bolshevist State—it would be a catastrophe, but is it conceivable. It is also conceivable to build up Germany as a national State. *But it is inconceivable that one should create a strong and sound Germany if fifty per cent of its citizens are Bolshevist and fifty per cent nationally minded.* From the solution of this problem we cannot escape!

"When the present Government says, 'We are after all industrious, we work, this last emergency regulation has cost us sessions lasting so many hundred hours,' I do not doubt it. But for all that the nation is no whit stronger or more united; the process of internal dissolution goes on just the same. And the goal to which this path must ultimately lead you can only determine by a really great effort of careful thought. Germany possessed once—as the first condition for the organization of our people on a large scale—a *weltanschauliche* basis in our religion—Christianity. When this basis was shattered we see how the strength of the nation turned from external affairs to internal conflicts, since the nature of man from an inner necessity compels him at the moment when the common *weltanschauliche* basis is lost or is attacked to seek for a new common basis. These were the great periods of the civil wars, of the wars of religion, etc., struggles and confusions during which either a nation finds a new *weltanschauliche* platform and on this can build itself up anew and then it can turn its force outwards, or else a people is split in two and falls into chaos. In Germany this process ran its course in a truly classical form. The religious struggles meant that the whole force of Germany withdrew inwards—an absorption and exhaustion of this force internally—while at the same time there ensued automatically a slowly increasing failure to react to great events of world-wide significance outside of Germany: to these events the people remains completely unresponsive because of its own internal tensions which press for a solution.

"It is a mistake to say that world-politics, the world-situation alone determined Germany's fate in the sixteenth century. *No, our own internal condition at that time contributed to form that picture of the world which later caused us so much suffering—the partition of the world without Germany.*

"And once more in an historical example on an immense scale this same experience is repeated: in place of the lost religious unity—for the two Confessions are now ice-bound and neither can overcome the other—a new platform is discovered: the new conception of the State, first in a legitimist form and later slowly passing into the age of the principle of nationality and colored by it. On this new platform Germany once more unites her forces and bit by bit through the consolidation of a Reich which had fallen into decline in the period of the old confusions Germany automatically and permanently recovers her strength in foreign politics. This increase in strength leads to those August days of 1914, an experience which we ourselves had the proud good fortune to share. A nation which seems to have no domestic differences and therefore can turn its united strength towards the world beyond its frontier! and scarcely four and a half years later we see the process once more take its backward course. . . ."

"At this point I can today establish one fact: no matter what the legislature undertakes—especially by way of decrees and above all by way of emergency decrees—unless Germany can master this internal division in *Weltanschauungen,* no measures of the legislature can stop the decline of the German nation. . . ."

"And if the system objects: there is no time for that now—it is true, gentlemen, that far too much time has been wasted in useless work, far too much time has been already lost. One might have begun the process of regeneration in 1919 and then during the past eleven years Germany's external development would have taken a different course. For if the Peace Treaty could be presented in the form in which it was imposed upon us, that was only because Germany at the time when the Treaty was composed had ceased to be a factor which could exercise any influence whatever. And if this Peace Treaty in its application assumed the forms which we know and which we experienced, then that again is only because in all these years Germany had no definite will of her own which could make itself felt. We therefore are not the victims of the treaties, but the treaties are the consequences of our own mistakes; and if I wish in any way to better the situation, then I must first change the value of the nation: *I must above all recognize that it is not the primacy of foreign politics which can determine our action in the domestic sphere, rather, the character of our action in the domestic sphere is decisive for the character of the success of our foreign policy—nay more—it must determine the success of all the aims which we set before us.*

"I take to illustrate my contention two examples from history: firstly, Bismarck's idea of a conflict between Prussia and the House of Habsburg, the construction of a new Reich from which Austria was to be excluded. That idea could never have been realized unless, before one sought to transform the idea into action, one had created the instrument with which one could in practice realize one's political purpose. It was not the political situation which forced Prussia to undertake a reorganization of her army; but it was the reorganization of the Prussian army which Bismarck, looking into the future, carried through in the teeth of the madness of Parliament, which first rendered possible the political situation which found its end at Königgratz and which at Versailles founded the Reich that, since gradually it came to stand upon changed foundations, was later in the same chamber once more broken up and partitioned.

"And conversely: if a German Government today, applying Bismarckian ideas, tries to tread the road which Germany trod then and perhaps as the first step towards a policy of the unification of Germany seeks to establish a new Zollverein, a Customs Union, then the essential thing is not that one should formulate this aim, what is essential is what preparations are made beforehand to render possible the execution of the project. *I cannot formulate an aim which, supported by a Press campaign in one's own papers, is regarded in the whole world as a political aim of outstanding importance if I fail to secure the political means which are absolutely necessary for the execution of such a plan. And the political means—I cannot today put them any lower than this—lie only in the reorganization of an army.* For whether Germany possesses an army of 100,000 men or of 200,000 or 300,000 is in the last resort completely beside the point: *the essential thing is whether Germany possesses eight million reservists whom she can transfer into her army without any fear of falling into the same* weltanschauliche *catastrophe as that of 1918. . . .*"

"If anyone today wishes to hurl against me as a National Socialist the gravest possible accusation he says: 'You want to force a decision in Germany by violence and it is against this that we are bound to protest. You want one day in Germany to annihilate your political opponents. We on the other hand take our stand on the ground of the Constitution, and we are bound to guarantee to all parties the right to exist.' And to that I have only one reply: translated into practice that means: you have a company: you have to lead that company against the enemy. Within the company there is complete liberty to form a coalition. Fifty per cent of the company have formed a coalition on the basis of love of the Fatherland and of protection of the Fatherland: the other fifty per cent have formed a coalition on the basis of pacifism; they reject war on principle, they demand that freedom of conscience should be inviolate and declare that to be the highest, the sole good which we possess today. Still it comes to a fight, and then all desire to stand firmly together. But if a man, relying on freedom of conscience, should desert to the enemy, then there would come the peculiar moment when they would have to arrest and punish him as a deserter, entirely forgetful of the fact that they really had no right to punish him. A State which—under license from the State—permits the spread of the view that treason to the Fatherland is a duty, which allows great organizations calmly to declare: Our task in the event of war will be simply to put a stop to all military activity—with what right does such a State punish a traitor? It is but a side issue that such a State through the madness of this standpoint is reduced *ad absurdum,* for the man who would otherwise be branded as a criminal now becomes for one-half of the nation a martyr. Why? Because the same State, which on the one hand declares the theory of treason to the country to be ethical and moral and protects it, on the other hand has the presumption to imprison a man who seeks to translate this view from the sphere of theory into practice.

"Gentlemen, all that is impossible, absolutely impossible, if one believes at all that a people in order to survive must turn its strength outwards. But consider the present situation: seven or eight millions employed in agriculture, seven or eight millions employed in industry, six or seven millions unemployed. Consider that, so far as man can see, in this state of affairs there will be no change, and then you must admit that Germany as a whole in the long run cannot continue to exist—unless indeed we find our way back to a quite extraordinary, newly created political force working from within which alone may enable us once more to exercise effective influence abroad.

"For it matters not which problem of our life as a people we wish to attempt to solve: if we wish to support our export trade, always the day will come in this sphere, too, when the political will of the nation as a whole must speak a word of warning in order that we may not be thrust on one side by the interests of other peoples. If we want to build up a new internal market, if we want to solve the problem of our living space once again we shall need the collective political strength of the nation. Yes, when it is merely a question of our value as allies, always we must first make of Germany once more a political power-factor. And that can never be achieved by bringing before the Reichstag a proposal that—through negotiations—we should procure a few heavy batteries, eight or ten tanks, twelve aircraft or, if you will, a few squadrons—that is entirely beside the point. In the lives of peoples the technique of arms has continually changed: but what had to remain unchangeable was the formation of the will. That is the constant factor, the condition for everything else. If that fails, no weapons are of any service. On the contrary, if you were to summon the German people to a *levée en masse* and for this purpose supply it with arms, tomorrow the result would be a civil war, not an attack on the foreign foe. *With the body-politic as it is today one cannot any longer conduct any practical foreign policy.* Or do you believe that with the Germany of today Bismarck would have been able to fulfill his historic mission, that the German Reich could have arisen from a constitution inspired by the spirit which animates our own? . . ."

"When I returned from the Front in 1918 I found at home a state of affairs which, like all the others, I might simply have accepted as an accomplished fact. I am firmly convinced that a great part of the German nation in these November and December days of 1918 and even in 1919 were absolutely of the opinion that if Germany continued in her domestic politics on this path she must in foreign policy hasten to a rapid end. They held therefore the same view as I did. There was only one difference. I said to myself at that time: It is not enough to realize that we are ruined: it is also necessary to understand why! And even that is not enough, but it is necessary to declare war on this destructive development, and for that war to create the indispensable instrument. . . ."

"In the year 1918, as I considered the position with cool and considered judgment, I was bound to confess: it is an appallingly difficult course to come before the people at such a time and to form for myself a new organization. It is naturally much easier to join one of the existing formations and thence to seek to overcome the inner division of the nation. But is that at all possible when one starts from the existing organizations? Has not every organization in the last resort the spirit, the men who can find satisfaction in its program and in its struggle? If an organization has continually given way before Marxism and at length one day simply capitulated like a coward, has it not during sixty years been completely filled with a spirit and with men who neither understand the other way nor wish to pursue it? On the contrary, at a period of such confusion, will not the future lie with those who are prepared once more to pass through a sieve the body-politic which has fallen into such disorder so that from out the people a new political leadership can crystallize, which knows how to take the mass of the nation in hand and can avoid the mistakes which led to downfall in the past? *I was naturally forced to say to myself that it would mean an appalling struggle, for I was not so fortunate as to possess an outstanding name; I was only a nameless German soldier, with a very small zinc identification number on my breast.* But I came to realize that if a beginning was not made with the smallest cell, if a new body-politic was not thus formed within the nation, a body-politic which could overcome the existing 'ferments of decomposition,' then the nation itself as a whole could never rise again. . . ."

"And today that Movement cannot be destroyed: it is there: people must reckon with it, whether they like it or not. And I am convinced that for all those who still believe in a future for Germany it is clear what their attitude must be. For here they see before them an organization which does not preach as mere theory the views which earlier in my speech I characterized as essential, but puts them into practice, an organization inspired to the highest degree by national sentiment, constructed on the conception of an absolute authority in the leadership in all spheres, at every stage—the solitary party which amongst its members has completely overcome not only the conception of internationalism but also the idea of democracy, which in its entire organization acknowledges only the principles of Responsibility, Command and Obedience, and which besides all this for the first time has introduced into the political life of Germany a body numbering millions which is built up on the principle of achievement. Here is an organization which is filled with an indomitable aggressive spirit, an organization which when a political opponent says 'your behavior we regard as a provocation' for the first time does not see fit immediately to retire from the scene but brutally enforces its own will and hurls against the opponent the retort 'We fight today! We fight tomorrow!

And if you regard our meeting today as a provocation we shall hold yet another next week—until you have learned that it is no provocation when *German* Germany also professes its belief!' And when you say 'You must not come into the street' we go into the street in spite of you. And when you say 'Then we shall kill you,' however many sacrifices you force upon us, this young Germany will always continue its marches, and one day it will completely reconquer for the Germans the German street. And when people cast in our teeth our intolerance, we proudly acknowledge it—yes, we have formed the inexorable decision to destroy Marxism in Germany down to its very last root. And this decision we formed not from any love of brawling: I could easily imagine a life which in itself was fairer than to be hunted through Germany, to be persecuted by countless Government regulations, to stand constantly with one foot in jail, and to have in the State no right which one can call one's own. I could imagine for myself a fairer destiny than that of fighting a battle which at least at the outset was regarded by all as an insane chimera. Finally I believe that I have the capacity to occupy some post or other in the Social Democratic party: and one thing is certain: if I had turned my capacity to *this* service, I should today presumably be fit even to enter the Government. But for me it was a greater decision to choose a way on which I was guided by nothing save my own faith, my indestructible confidence in the natural forces—still assuredly present—of our people, and in its importance which with good leadership would one day necessarily reappear.

"And now behind us there lie twelve years of fighting. That fight has not been waged in theory only and in the party alone turned into practice: we are also ready to wage that fight on the larger scale. I cast my mind back to the time when with six other unknown men I founded this association, when I spoke before eleven, twelve, thirteen, fourteen, twenty, thirty, and fifty persons; when I recall how after a year I had won sixty-four members for the Movement, how our small circle kept on growing, I must confess that that which has today been created, when a stream of millions of our German fellow-countrymen is flowing into our Movement, represents something which is unique in German history. The *bourgeois* parties have had seventy years to work in; where, I ask you, is the organization which could be compared with ours? Where is the organization which can boast, as ours can, that, at need, it can summon 400,000 men into the street, men who are schooled to blind obedience and are ready to execute any order—provided that it does not violate the law? Where is the organization that in seventy years has achieved what we have achieved in barely twelve years?—and achieved with means which were of so improvised a character that one can hardly avoid a feeling of shame when one confesses to an opponent how poverty-stricken the birth and the growth of this great Movement were in the early days.

"Today we stand at the turning-point of Germany's destiny. If the present development continues, Germany will one day of necessity land in Bolshevist chaos, but if this development is broken, then our people must be taken into a school of iron discipline and gradually freed from the prejudices of both camps. A hard schooling, but one we cannot escape! . . ."

"People say to me so often: 'You are only the drummer of national Germany.' And supposing that I were only the drummer? It would today be a far more statesmanlike achievement to drum once more into this German people a new faith than gradually to squander the only faith they have. Take the case of a fortress, imagine that it is reduced to extreme privations: as long as the garrison sees a possible salvation, believes in it, hopes for it, so long they can bear the reduced ration. But take from the hearts of men their last belief in the possibility of salvation, in a better future—take that completely from them, and you will see how these men suddenly regard their reduced rations as the most important thing in life. The more you bring it home to their consciousness that they are only objects for men to bargain with, that they are only prisoners of world-politics, the more will they, like all prisoners, concentrate their thoughts on purely material interests. On the other hand, the more you bring back the people into the sphere of faith, of ideals, the more will it cease to regard material distress as the one and only thing which counts. And the weightiest evidence for the truth of that statement is our own German people. We would not ever forget that the German people waged wars of religion for 150 years with prodigious devotion, that hundreds of thousands of men once left their plot of land, their property, and their belongings simply for an ideal, simply for a conviction. We would never forget that during those 150 years there was no trace of even an ounce of material interests. Then you will understand how mighty is the force of an idea, of an ideal. Only so can you comprehend how it is that in our Movement today hundreds of thousands of young men are prepared at the risk of their lives to withstand our opponents. I know quite well, gentlemen, that when National Socialists march through the streets and suddenly in the evening there arise a tumult and commotion, then the *bourgeois* draws back the window-curtain, looks out, and says: Once more my night's rest disturbed: no more sleep for me. Why must the Nazis always be so provocative and run about the place at night? Gentlemen, if everyone thought like that, then no one's sleep at nights would be disturbed, it is true, but then the *bourgeois* today could not venture into the street. If everyone thought in that way, if these young folk had no ideal to move them and drive them forward, then certainly they would gladly be rid of these nocturnal fights. But remember that it means sacrifice when today many hundred thousands of SA and SS men of the National Socialist Movement every day have to mount on their lorries, protect meetings, undertake marches, sacrifice themselves night after night and then come back in the gray dawn either to workshop and factory or as unemployed to take the pittance of the dole: it means sacrifice when from the little which they possess they have further to buy their uniforms, their shirts, their badges, yes, and even pay their own fares. Believe me, there is already in all this the force of an ideal—a great ideal! And if the whole German nation today had the same faith in its vocation as these hundred thousands, if the whole nation possessed this idealism, Germany would stand in the eyes of the world otherwise than she stands now! For our situation in the world in its fatal effects is but the result of our own underestimate of German strength. Only when we have once more changed this fatal valuation of ourselves can Germany take advantage of the political possibilities which, if we look far enough into the future, can place German life once more upon a natural and secure basis—and that means either new living-space *(Lebensraum)* and the development of a great internal market or protection of German economic life against the world without and utilization of all the concentrated strength of Germany. The labor resources of our people, the capacities, we have them already: no one can deny that we are industrious. . . ."

"And so in contrast to our own official Government I cannot see any hope for the resurrection of Germany if we regard the foreign politics of Germany as the primary factor: the primary necessity is the restoration of a sound national German body-politic armed to strike. In order to realize this end I founded thirteen years ago the National Socialist Movement: that Movement I have led during the last twelve years, *and I hope that one day it will accomplish this task and that, as the fairest result of its struggle, it will leave behind it a German body-politic completely renewed internally, intolerant of anyone who sins against the nation and its interests, intolerant against anyone who will not ackowledge its vital interests or who opposes them, intolerant and pitiless against anyone who shall attempt once more to destroy or disintegrate this body-politic, and yet ready for friendship and peace with anyone who has a wish for peace and friendship."*

Press

No comments. The speech was delivered before a private audience of financiers and big business men who financed Hitler.

PHASE II

Arming Germany

January 30, 1933 — March, 1936

COMMENT

FROM the moment President Hindenburg appointed Adolf Hitler Chancellor of the Reich, on January 30, 1933, the National Socialist Revolution had to be recognized as an accomplished fact. Whatever might have been the calculations of those who helped Hitler to power and their hopes of controlling him, they were soon to discover that Germany was now ruled by a man whose fanaticism was stronger than political combinations and whose methods of government had no relation whatsoever to the civilized forms of society as they were supposed to exist in the Twentieth Century, but were definitely reminiscent of the brutality, cunning, and ruthlessness of medieval times.

For ten years Hitler had been the prophet of Revolution. The seizure of power did not mean the realization of his ambition, but the opening of a new era during which the whole complexion of Germany was to be transformed. From Hitler's point of view, his work had hardly begun. The Chancellorship was only a stepping stone, a convenient position from which he could now undertake to make good his word, reshape the destiny of Germany and, if possible, that of the world.

What Hitler intended to do had been clearly explained by him in the innumerable speeches he delivered in the ten years preceding his advent to power. There could be no surprise. Nevertheless all his moves to extend his authority over the whole of the German people and over all forms of German life were like so many shocks of increasing intensity which spread surprise and alarm in the ranks of the German opposition and in the outside world.

The fundamental doctrine of National Socialism was based on the unification of all Germans. Only when all opposition had been crushed, and all political parties eliminated, could Germany expect—according to Hitler—to regain her place as a world power.

Leaving aside the ideological aspect of National Socialism, the first objective of Hitler, as soon as he seized power, was to transform the whole of the German nation into one solid monolithic system directed by one will, his own, and governed by one small group of efficient, thoroughly ruthless, and faithful executives—the Nazi leadership.

To gain this end, it was not sufficient for Hitler to have become Chancellor of the Reich. The Chancellor had to be the absolute ruler of the German nation, the undisputed master of all men and all things, the primitive Chief of the tribe.

This was achieved in less than eighteen months. By the time Hindenburg died, on August 2, 1934, Hitler had reached most of his objectives inside Germany. His position of supreme authority had been established. There was no other master of Germany, no opposition left, no resistance possible. Adolf Hitler was indeed the Fuehrer.

During those eighteen months Hitler's dictatorship had been assured through the following steps:

1. After the fire which destroyed the Reichstag, an act was passed adjourning it for four years and giving Hitler full powers. This meant, of course, the final disappearance of even the fiction of parliamentary system in Germany. From then on, the Reichstag was to be nothing but an organized cheering chorus, convoked from time to time to give the superfluous support of its approbation to whatever the Fuehrer had to say.

2. The Communists were banned, which meant that it was possible from then on to persecute or put into concen-

tration camps anyone who could possibly be accused of not being a loyal Nazi.

3. Workers' unions were dissolved and merged into one huge Labor Front organized and controlled by Robert Ley. This was a major accomplishment from the point of view of the National Socialist doctrine. It put an end very effectively to the Marxian notion of class struggle. The German workers were from then on regimented and—to all intents and purposes—mobilized for the duration of Hitlerism.

4. A Four-Year Plan was proclaimed. This was a Russian invention, and in those years (1933-34) it might be said that long-range economic planning was a fashionable idea among economists, sociologists, and brain-trusters all over the world. In the case of Germany, however, the Four-Year Plan had a definite purpose: it enabled Hitler to co-ordinate and place under Nazi control the whole of German industry. Goering was made director of the Four-Year Plan, and it was immediately apparent that his program was to direct the entire effort of Germany toward building up a war machine.

5. The SS and the SA were enlarged and given greater power. Through these faithful legions, the Nazi party was assured of absolute control over the population. The extraordinary "purge" of June 30, 1934, during which Roehm, the head of the SA, was murdered together with an untold number of other extremists and enemies of the Revolution, showed that Hitler was able to accomplish the most difficult feat of all: crush a conspiracy and a possible revolt in the ranks of his own followers.

Several other measures, such as the adoption of the racial laws, the burning of books which did not conform with the Nazi doctrine, the creation of the "Strength Through Joy" organization, the persecution of the Christian churches, the institution of a new cultural dogma, and other attempts to remold the soul of every German according to the views of their Messiah were successfully enforced, and with considerably less resistance, on the whole, than a wishful outside world could have anticipated.

In fact, it was not through brute force, cruelty, terrorism, and cunning alone that Hitler succeeded, in such a relatively short time, in defeating all opposition and establishing himself as the supreme master and living incarnation of the German people.

The secret of his success must be sought elsewhere.

That secret is to be found in the ten years that preceded Hitler's advent to power. His whole life during those ten years was what he himself called a struggle, the struggle of an unknown, down-trodden ex-soldier, profoundly humiliated by defeat, exasperated by what he thought to be the injustices of the world, blinded by the desire for revenge, and, like all those who are weak, dreaming of nothing but force and power.

In many of his speeches Hitler has said that his own story was that of Germany itself. And the very fact that he believed it and offered himself as a kind of symbol to the millions of Germans who felt the bitterness of defeat aggravated in the German people their national tendency to consider themselves as the victims of an unfair destiny.

Hitler could now fulfill the promises he had made to his followers during these ten years, provided he could always keep alive in the minds of the German people the dual conviction that their lot was unjust and that only through a formidable effort to become strong again could they ever hope to regain their self-respect and the respect of the outside world. His entire movement had been built on a demonic principle: everything Hitler stood for was good for Germany, everything else was evil and should be destroyed.

This is why there is no lack of continuity between the speeches delivered before 1933 and those he made as Chancellor of the Reich. Nor was there to be much change in the future. At all times Hitler had to appeal to the same basic German emotions: the sense of humiliation, the revolt against the "crime" of Versailles, the promise of power, and the comforting assurance that there was only one measuring rod of what was right or wrong—Hitler's own judgment.

"I have no conscience," said Goering after the Reichstag fire. "My conscience is Hitler." This was not a mere verbal apology from the man who knew too well who was guilty of the Reichstag fire. It was the recognition of one of the most real sources of Hitler's strength: his identification with the conscience of seventy million Germans.

Besides having promised his followers that Germany would become strong again, Hitler had also promised to cure all the evils of the postwar period, and first of all unemployment.

Now that he was in power, it was not only natural but predetermined that these two promises should be fulfilled at once and merged into one single objective.

It was always to be one of Hitler's greatest boasts that of all civilized countries Germany had been the only one to find a cure for this world evil, unemployment. Naturally he gave credit for this achievement to the transformation of society by the National Socialist Revolution. Unemployment was cured, according to him, as soon as the concept that the wealth of a country was not its gold nor its capital, but its powers of production and its labor, was accepted. Germany having no gold and being, in fact, financially bankrupt, the problem had to be solved by unorthodox methods. And there is no disputing the fact that the system evolved by the German economists and financiers under the pressure of necessity did succeed in producing an apparent recovery which baffled the world. In a very short time after Hitler's advent to power, not only was unemployment wiped out, but a shortage of labor began to appear. The problem of capital was also solved by the simple process of a disguised, but nonetheless real, centralization of control in the hands of the government. Employers and industrialists became, in fact, mere managers, operating under the direction of the State.

They were not free to determine their own production nor to dispose of their profits. They were integrated in one single gigantic system of procurement.

Hitler had frequently said that one of the greatest causes of the world's social and economic unrest was the priority given to economics over politics. By reversing the process, that is by subordinating economics to politics, he pretended that he had been able to perform the greatest miracle of modern times.

But if it looked like a miracle, there was no mystery about it. What Hitler did was to place the whole of German economy on a war footing in the midst of peace. As early as 1934 Germany was totally mobilized, and therefore practically immunized against the maladjustments and the ups and downs of a peace economy. Other nations, including the western democracies, were to find out later that they too could perform the miracle of solving unemployment by going to war or putting themselves on the basis of a war economy. But having started this process five or six years earlier, Hitler benefited by the prestige which derived from the contrast between Germany functioning efficiently on a war basis as one single economic unit, and all other countries which were still clinging to peace methods, with all their advantages from the point of view of individual freedom and all their drawbacks as far as co-ordinated efficiency was concerned.

Hitler was quick to exploit to its limits the propaganda value of this situation and his speeches seldom failed to point out in striking terms the prodigious achievement of the National Socialist regime in giving work, security, and a purpose to all. He proclaimed that he had succeeded in creating at last a perfect Socialist paradise.

The application of Hitler's program was bound to stir up opposition in various circles. But this opposition was uncoordinated and scattered. Hitler had little difficulty, on the whole, in nullifying it, either by force, by trickery, or by offering temporary advantages which were promptly removed afterward.

The easiest obstacle to remove was the opposition of various non-Nazi groups such as the Communists, the Democrats, and liberals of all kinds. The engineering of the Reichstag fire gave the needed pretext to abolish the parliamentary system altogether. By lumping together in his accusations the Bolsheviks, the democrats, the liberals, and the Jews, and by advertising himself untiringly as the great Purifier of all forms of corruption, Hitler created the necessary popular psychosis to enable him to institute the most brutal and shameless methods of repression as a normal means of government.

The second form of opposition which caused a schism in his own following was more dangerous. As early as 1934, disgruntled party members of a particularly violent and immoral kind began to conspire against Hitler himself. They were led by one of Hitler's most intimate friends, Roehm, the leader of the SA. Their general complaint was that Hitler had not gone far enough in his reforms and that a "second revolution" was in order. Hitler tried vainly to placate this group, not only on grounds of political disagreement but because the Army, whose support was essential to Hitler, had made it clear that no such extremism could be tolerated. When all entreaties had failed, Hitler struck with a ruthlessness and a rapidity which sickened the outside world, not yet inured to seeing the head of a state himself supervising the murder of his friends. The purge of June 30, 1934, had a double effect: it recreated unity in the Nazi ranks and sealed the alliance between Hitler and the Army. From then on most of the Army leaders—even if they did not share the popular fanatic trust in Hitler—recognized him for what he was: the man under whose leadership the military strength of Germany would be rebuilt. It is not by accident that Hitler began at that time to compare himself more and more frequently with Frederick the Great and Bismarck and to claim that he was their true heir. Nothing could appeal more strongly to the spirit and tradition of the German Army. He had no princely blood; he was not even a Junker; but prejudices fell before a man who obviously had the good of the Army at heart.

The third form of opposition was religious. Both the Catholic and the Protestant churches rebelled against Hitler's efforts to subordinate the Church to the State and the divinity of God to his own. The latent paganism of the Nazi doctrine came to the surface in many forms, such as various attempts to revive the barbaric cults of the ancient Germanic tribes as more fitting, in their emphasis on warlike virtues and sanguinary mysticism, than Christianity. The churches fought relentlessly, but Hitler retaliated with his usual methods. He sent von Papen to Rome to negotiate a concordat with the Vatican while at the same time cooking up infamous trials against priests and monks. Pastor Niemoeller, who refused to praise Hitler in his church, was thrown into jail.

The conservative elements were, on the whole, easier to handle than any other form of opposition. They had helped Hitler to power by persuading Hindenburg that they could control him even if he was given the post of Chancellor. They rallied around the old hero of Tannenberg as their last bulwark and defender. But Hindenburg was a prisoner on his own estate from the moment Hitler actually assumed power until his death. He could not prevent Hitler from forcing the resignation of Hugenberg, the leader of the Conservative party. Hindenburg left a testament which, according to many, was never published in its original form. Hitler had forged part of it—that part which enabled him to claim the succession of the Marshal. When Hitler arranged that the Reichswehr should take a personal oath of allegiance to him, he ended all possible dissension from these quarters. Moreover he prepared the way for his future elevation as Supreme Commander of the German Armies.

As soon as Hitler became Chancellor of the Reich, the explosive pressure of the new Germany began to be felt in the outside world. But it should be noted that Hitler's foreign policy during those years was less the product of an organized plan of expansion than the natural consequence of Germany's growing strength. Such moves as the withdrawal from the League of Nations, for instance, were dictated primarily by considerations of internal politics. After campaigning for so many years against the Treaty of Versailles and denouncing the League as an instrument for the oppression of Germany, it was necessary for Hitler's own prestige to show that he had at least the courage to liberate himself from the tutelage of Geneva. "I had to do it," he told Hermann Rauschning. "A big understandable action was necessary. Nobody would have understood if we had continued what the Weimar parties did for ten years—debate and nothing but debate."

It was for the same motive that Hitler walked out on the disarmament conference and refused to sign the "Eastern European Locarno Pact." Such steps could not possibly bring about a war, for which Germany was far from being prepared at that time. But it showed the German people and the outside world that the foreign policy of the Third Reich was now being conducted by a man who was ready to make good his promises to place the "Right and Honor" of Germany above all treaties and to impose his will by force if necessary.

Not that Hitler talked of war, as yet. On the contrary, his whole justification for rearming Germany was that there was no other way of re-establishing Germany's equality among nations, and therefore of maintaining peace. One of Hitler's fundamental points of doctrine had always been to establish some sort of mystic link between the power of the sword and the scales of justice. The mightier Germany became under the Nazi rule, the louder did Hitler assert that Germany was right and the more scorn did he heap on those who spoke of any other *rights* than those of the German people.

All through this period, the speeches of Hitler and his actions in the field of foreign policy show increasing defiance of the kind of order that had existed in Europe up to his advent to power. Uneasiness was fast spreading throughout Europe and many cries of alarm were raised, but democratic diplomacy was already showing the signs of timidity, incoherence, and weakness which were to form the basis of the so-called policy of appeasement.

Already, too, Hitler was giving proof of his remarkable insight into the psychology of his opponents, an insight which may be Hitler's only real claim to superiority over other statesmen of his time. This faculty, which a French diplomat described as *"le sens du possible"* (the feeling of what is possible), enabled Hitler—from the earliest days of his dictatorship—to establish a kind of undefinable, but nonetheless real, control over the minds and actions of his opponents. In 1934 or 1936, Hitler was far from being the master of Europe. The road to conquest was not opened as yet. But that he was already dominating the European scene and maneuvering his opponents and outguessing them at every turn was obvious.

A good instance of the manner in which Hitler's insight or instinct functioned was given at the time of the assassination of Chancellor Dollfuss of Austria. This murder had been engineered by the Nazis and was to be followed by a putsch which would have resulted in the annexation of Austria. But the putsch was not followed through when Hitler sensed that the other powers, and especially Italy, might move to prevent it. Four years later, the time was ripe. Hitler's troops marched into Austria without any opposition.

The Saar plebiscite offers another illustration of the same soundness of instinct and sense of timing. It was preceded by a series of speeches in which Hitler implied that the Saar would come back to the Reich whatever might be the result of the plebiscite. There was no doubt that the great majority of the population would vote for a return to the Reich, but the effect of this superfluous threat was to create an exaggerated sense of relief when the plebiscite was over—as if the fact that the foregone result had indeed taken place was a cause to rejoice and a guarantee of peace. Hitler further exploited the psychological advantage thus gained by assuring France that he had no other territorial claims against her—a promise which was greeted as a true sign of generosity and peaceful intentions from Hitler.

During the first three years of his dictatorship, Hitler took great pains to show the German people and the outside world that he did not rule by force but by the quasi-unanimous consent of his people. This was done through a series of elections, or plebiscites, intended to give a kind of popular ratification to Hitler's most important acts (such as the elections of November 12, 1933, to approve the withdrawal from the League of Nations). Although these elections showed returns which were usually close to 100 per cent favorable and were carried on under threat to the voters and trickery of the ballots, they enabled Hitler to increase his prestige as unifier of the German people and torchbearer of their destiny.

A similar effect was produced by the yearly National Socialist Convention held at Nuremberg in September, during which the Nazi leaders and Hitler himself pursued their work of propaganda by imparting to huge and enthusiastic crowds the blessings of the new doctrine.

These meetings, like those of the Reichstag, were used by Hitler as sounding boards. The pageantry, the flags, the ritual of Hitler's appearance in public, the disciplined frenzy of the crowds were all intended to impress not only the German people themselves but also the outside world with a physical sense of awe.

Month by month, year by year, a peaceful and easygoing Europe was getting conditioned to the presence of something brutal, cynical, and defiant in its midst. With incredible speed the whole of Germany was being molded by the voice of its new master. Hitler still said that the National Socialist Revolution was not for export. But that it had been thoroughly established in Germany and that he now was the absolute ruler of a solid mass of seventy million Germans was not disputed.

Neither could it be questioned that Hitler had indeed performed a miracle. Germany, which according to Hitler had been marked for destruction by the victors of the last war, was fast transforming itself into the greatest force for destruction that Europe had known in modern times. With a mixture of anxiety and wishful thinking, the neighbors of Germany watched the growth of the monster, never quite deciding whether it could best be tamed with soft words or with righteous indignation and veiled threats. There was fear in Europe from the very day Hitler assumed power, fear and nervousness and also fatal weakness. But Hitler, as yet, had done nothing irreparable.

By the middle of March, 1935, compulsory military service was re-established in Germany. It was the first open violation of Germany's obligations under the Versailles Treaty.

More daring and threatening ones were to follow soon.

Background

1932

February—Hitler becomes German citizen. This was necessary because of his candidacy for the presidency of the Reich.

March 13—First Ballot in the Presidential Election:

Von Hinderburg, 18.6 million, *i.e.,* 49.6 per cent of the votes; Hitler, 11.3 million, *i.e.,* 30.0 per cent of the votes.

April 10—Second Ballot in the German Presidential Election:

Hindenburg, 19.3 million, *i.e.,* 53 per cent of the votes; Hitler, 13.4 million, *i.e.,* 36 per cent of the votes.

April 14—SA and SS banned.

April 24—The Nazis increase their seats in the Prussian Diet from 6 to 162.

May 30—President von Hindenburg ousts Chancellor Bruening and his Cabinet. Franz von Papen becomes Chancellor.

June 4—Reichstag dissolved.

June 13—Bavaria and Württemberg object to the proposed removal of the ban against the SA and SS.

June 14—Ban on SA and SS lifted.

July 9—The Lausanne Reparations Conference agrees that Germany can settle in full for $714,000,000.

July 20—State of Emergency declared in Germany.

July 31—Reichstag elections:

Nazi party, 13,722,413 votes, 229 seats; Socialists, 7,949,883 votes, 132 seats; Communists, 5,276,887 votes, 88 seats.

August 13—Repeated conferences between Hitler, von Hindenburg, von Papen. Hitler is offered the Vice-Chancellorship and the post of Prussian Minister of the Interior. Hitler demands "the post that Mussolini had after his march on Rome." He requests also "three days in which the streets will be thrown open to the SA." Hindenburg refuses.

September 12—Von Papen dissolves the Reichstag.

November 6—Another general election reduces the 229 seats of Hitler to 195, while the Communists increase theirs from 88 to 100.

November 18—Von Papen resigns.

December 2—Sixteen-day Cabinet crisis ends with Hindenburg's appointing General von Schleicher as Chancellor.

1933

January 5—Calvin Coolidge dies.

Reich-Chancellor von Schleicher wants the Nazis to enter the Government.

January 28—President von Hindenburg refuses to allow von Schleicher to dissolve the Reichstag.

January 29—Von Schleicher Government falls.

January 30—Hindenburg asks Hitler to become Chancellor in a Nazi-Conservative coalition Government.

•

PROCLAMATION TO THE GERMAN NATION, FEBRUARY 1, 1933

Berlin

Background

January 30—Answering Hindenburg's call, Adolf Hitler becomes Chancellor of the Reich. Von Papen is Vice-Chancellor.

The Speech

"MORE than fourteen years have passed since the unhappy day when the German people, blinded by promises from foes at home and abroad, lost touch with honor and freedom, thereby losing all. Since that day of treachery, the Almighty has withheld his blessing from our people. Dissension and hatred descended upon us. With profound distress millions of the best German men and women from all walks of life have seen the unity of the nation vanishing away, dissolving in a confusion of political and personal opinions, economic interests, and ideological differences. Since that day, as so often in the past, Germany has presented a picture of heartbreaking disunity. We never received the equality and fraternity we had been promised, and we lost our liberty to boot. For when our nation lost its political place in the world, it soon lost its unity of spirit and will. . . ."

"We are firmly convinced that the German nation entered the fight in 1914 without the slightest feeling of guilt on its part and filled only with the desire to defend the Fatherland which had been attacked and to preserve the freedom, nay, the very existence, of the German people. This being so, we can only see in the disastrous fate which has overtaken us since those November days of 1918 the result of our collapse at home. But the rest of the world, too, has suffered no less since then from overwhelming crises. The balance of power which had evolved in the course of history, and which formerly played no small part in bringing about the understanding of the necessity for an internal solidarity of the nations, with all its advantages for trade and commerce, has been set on one side. The insane conception of victors and vanquished destroyed the confidence existing between nations, and, at the same time, the industry of the entire world.

"The misery of our people is horrible to behold! Millions of the industrial proletariat are unemployed and starving; the whole of the middle class and the small artisans have been impoverished. When this collapse finally reaches the German peasants, we will be faced with an immeasurable disaster. For then not only shall a nation collapse, but a two-thousand-year-old inheritance, some of the loftiest products of human culture and civilization.

"All about us the warning signs of this collapse are apparent. Communism with its method of madness is making a powerful and insidious attack upon our dismayed and shattered nation. It seeks to poison and disrupt in order to hurl us into an epoch of chaos. . . . This negative, destroying spirit spared nothing of all that is highest and most valuable. Beginning with the family, it has undermined the very foundations of morality and faith and scoffs at culture and business, nation and Fatherland, justice and honor. Fourteen years of Marxism have ruined Germany; one year of bolshevism would destroy her. The richest and fairest territories of the world would be turned into a smoking heap of ruins. Even the sufferings of the last decade and a half could not be compared to the misery of a Europe in the heart of which the red flag of destruction had been hoisted. The thousands of wounded, the hundreds of dead which this inner strife has already cost Germany should be a warning of the storm which would come. . . ."

"In those hours when our hearts were troubled about the life and the future of the German nation, the aged leader of the World War appealed to us. He called to those of us in nationalist parties and leagues to struggle under him once more, in unity and loyalty, for the salvation of the German nation. This time the front lines are at home. The venerable Reichspräsident has allied himself with us in this noble endeavor. And as leaders of the nation and the national Government we vow to God, to our conscience, and to our people that we will faithfully and resolutely fulfill the task conferred upon us.

"The inheritance which has fallen to us is a terrible one. The task with which we are faced is the hardest which has fallen to German statesmen within the memory of man. But we are all filled with unbounded confidence for we believe in our people and their imperishable virtues. Every class and every individual must help us to found the new Reich.

"The National Government will regard it as its first and foremost duty to revive in the nation the spirit of unity and co-operation. It will preserve and defend those basic principles on which our nation has been built. It regards Christianity as the foundation of our national morality, and the family as the basis of national life. . . ."

"Turbulent instincts must be replaced by a national discipline as the guiding principle of our national life. All those institutions which are the strongholds of the energy and vitality of our nation will be taken under the special care of the Government.

"The National Government intends to solve the problem of the reorganization of trade and commerce with two four-year plans:

"The German farmer must be rescued in order that the nation may be supplied with the necessities of life. . . ."

"A concerted and all-embracing attack must be made on unemployment in order that the German working class may be saved from ruin. . . ."

"The November parties have ruined the German peasantry in fourteen years.

"In fourteen years they have created an army of millions of unemployed. The National Government will, with iron determination and unshakable steadfastness of purpose, put through the following plan:

"Within four years the German peasant must be rescued from the quagmire into which he has fallen.

"Within four years unemployment must be finally overcome. At the same time the conditions necessary for a revival in trade and commerce are provided.

"The National Government will couple with this tremendous task of reorganizing business life a reorganization of the administrative and fiscal systems of the Reich, of the Federal States, and the Communes.

"Only when this has been done can the idea of a continued federal existence of the entire Reich be fully realized. . . ."

"Compulsory labor-service and the back-to-the-land policy are two of the basic principles of this program.

"The securing of the necessities of life will include the performance of social duties to the sick and aged.

"In economical administration, the promotion of employment, the preservation of the farmer, as well as in the exploitation of individual initiative, the Government sees the best guarantee for the avoidance of any experiments which would endanger the currency. . . ."

"As regards its foreign policy the National Government

considers its highest mission to be the securing of the right to live and the restoration of freedom to our nation. Its determination to bring to an end the chaotic state of affairs in Germany will assist in restoring to the community of nations a State of equal value and, above all, a State which must have equal rights. It is impressed with the importance of its duty to use this nation of equal rights as an instrument for the securing and maintenance of that peace which the world requires today more than ever before.

"May the good will of all others assist in the fulfillment of this our earnest wish for the welfare of Europe and of the whole world.

"Great as is our love for our Army as the bearer of our arms and the symbol of our great past, we should be happy if the world, by reducing its armaments, would see to it that we need never increase our own.

"If, however, Germany is to experience this political and economic revival and conscientiously fulfill her duties toward the other nations, one decisive step is absolutely necessary first: the overcoming of the destroying menace of communism in Germany. We of this Government feel responsible for the restoration of orderly life in the nation and for the final elimination of class madness and class struggle. We recognize no classes, we see only the German people, millions of peasants, bourgeois, and workers who will either overcome together the difficulties of these times or be overcome by them. We are firmly resolved and we have taken our oath. *Since the present Reichstag is incapable of lending support to this work, we ask the German people whom we represent to perform the task themselves.*

"Reichspräsident von Hindenburg has called upon us to bring about the revival of the German nation. Unity is our tool. Therefore we now appeal to the German people to support this reconciliation. The National Government wishes to work and it will work. It did not ruin the German nation for fourteen years, but now it will lead the nation back to health. It is determined to make well in four years the ills of fourteen years. But the National Government cannot make the work of reconstruction dependent upon the approval of those who wrought destruction. The Marxist parties and their lackeys have had fourteen years to show what they can do. The result is a heap of ruins.

"Now, people of Germany, give us four years and then pass judgment upon us. In accordance with Field Marshal von Hindenburg's command we shall begin now. May God Almighty give our work His blessing, strengthen our purpose, and endow us with wisdom and the trust of our people, for we are fighting not for ourselves but for Germany."

Press

Le Temps, February 3—The Fuehrer, in his emotional and vague phraseology, busied himself with hurling accusations against Marxism, which he said might have ruined Germany, and against communism, which still had not attained any power, but was threatening to ruin Germany. . . . He announced one of the rare positive points of the National Socialist program, namely, compulsory labor service. In regard to foreign politics he spoke cautiously, but with veiled threats.

New York Times, February 3—Although Herr Hitler's radio address was ostensibly a government declaration approved and countersigned by the entire Cabinet, the opposition views it more as an electioneering stunt and soft soap for his own following and as otherwise destitute of practical meaning.

London Times, February 3—Herr Hitler's election speech on the radio is admittedly only a call to come and vote. He did not go into any details on his statement that the Labor Service was one of the cornerstones of his program. . . . Herr Hitler's radio address was repeated three times during the day by all German broadcasting stations. Although it is generally considered obvious that, in view of the divergent doctrines among the Nazi allies, all definite commitments will be avoided during the election campaign, and the appeal made strictly to the emotions, the Right is nevertheless disappointed at the lack of all positive elements in his speech.

•

SPEECH OF FEBRUARY 15, 1933

Stuttgart

The Speech

". . . IN FOURTEEN years the system which has now been overthrown has piled mistake upon mistake, illusion upon illusion. And that is also true for our foreign policy. Only since the time when through our Movement the world has been shown that a new Germany of resolution and resistance is arising—only since then are we once more regarded with other eyes. If today in Geneva a people fights side by side with us for the freedom of Europe, it is *we* who have first formed this friendship and not the representatives of the former system.

"And now Staatspräsident Bolz says that Christianity and the Catholic faith are threatened by us. And to that charge I can answer: In the first place it is Christians and not international atheists who now stand at the head of Germany. I do not merely *talk* of Christianity, no, I also profess that I will never ally myself with the parties which destroy Christianity. If many wish today to take threatened Christianity under their protection, where, I would ask, was Christianity for them in these fourteen years when they went arm in arm with atheism? No, never and at no time was greater internal damage done to Christianity than in these fourteen years when a party, theoretically Christian, sat with those who denied God in one and the same Government.

"I would ask whether the economic policy of this now superseded system was a Christian policy. Was the inflation an undertaking for which Christians could answer, or has the destruction of German life, of the German peasant as well as of the middles classes, been Christian? . . . When these parties now say: we want to govern for a few more years in order that we can improve the situation, then we say:

"No! now it is too late for that! Besides you had your fourteen years and you have failed. In fourteen years you have proved your incapacity—from the Treaty of Versailles by way of the various agreements down to the Dawes and Young plans. Herr Bolz, too, has given his support to the Young Plan while I have always opposed it.

"If today we are told that we have no program, then I answer that for the last two years this other Germany has lived only by making inroads on our thought-world. All these plans for the creation of work, for labor service, etc.—they are not the work of Staatspräsident Bolz, they come from our program of reconstruction from which they have taken them over imperfectly and incompletely.

"We are convinced that the restoration to health of our people must start from the restoration to health of the body politic itself, and we are persuaded of the truth that the future of our people, as in the past so now, lies first of all in the German peasant. If he perishes, our end has come; if he survives, then Germany will never go under. There lie the strength and the source of our people's life, the source of our renewal. The towns would not exist at all, if the peasant did not fill them with his blood. The dweller in our countryside may be primitve, but he is healthy.

". . . We want, too, to restore to the German intelligentsia the freedom of which it has been robbed by the system which has hitherto ruled. In parliamentarianism they did not possess this freedom. We want to liberate Germany from the fetters of an impossible parliamentary democracy—not because we are terrorists, not because we intend to gag the free spirit. On the contrary, the spirit has never had more violence done to it than when mere numbers made themselves its master.

"No, our wish is that responsible folk should once more be brought together so that every class and every individual should be given that authority over those below and that responsibility towards those above which are essential if one is to build up the life of a community. We do not want so to educate the nation that it lives for ideas and artificial constructions; we want to test all ideas and constructions to discover how far they are capable of serving the nation's life.

"I will not build myself a villa in Switzerland, nor will I lay claim to any fund with which to fight criminality in this election campaign. Then after four years people shall judge whether the policy of ruining Germany has come to an end, whether Germany is rising once again."

Press

New York Times, February 16—Opening the election campaign in South Germany tonight, Chancellor Hitler stated unequivocally that the forthcoming election would be the last one in Germany for four years.

London Times, February 18—At a Nazi election meeting at Stuttgart on Wednesday, Herr Hitler repeated the hint which he gave in his national broadcast last week that the Government does not contemplate resigning in the event of a defeat at the polls.

Le Temps, February 17—Hitler expressed surprise that he was accused of destroying liberty. He had only imitated them (his enemies) and made a law for the defense of the National State based on the model of the law for the defense of the Republic.

SPEECH OF MARCH 23, 1933

Berlin, Reichstag

Background

February 22—At Geneva, the German Delegation leaves the conference when Mr. Henderson, President of the Disarmament Conference, refuses to accept a German amendment to the French draft resolution on standardization.

February 27—Reichstag Fire.

March 2—Outbreak of the war between Japan and Manchuria.

March 5—In the Reichstag election, the Nazis and their conservative allies win 330 seats out of a total of 647.

March 9—Nazi troops occupy the Bavarian Government Building.

March 13—Goebbels made Minister of Propaganda. A pact of European mutual assistance is discussed in Geneva. Fourteen states approve it, among them France and Poland; five against, among them Germany and Italy; others withhold their votes, among them England and Russia.

March 21—Anglo-Italian and Anglo-French meeting in Geneva on the maintenance of peace in Europe. The British plan contains following proposals:

1. Duration of the pact—five years.

2. Reduction of arms production and prohibition of rearmament.

3. International control to see that each signatory fulfills the conditions.

4. Creation of a permanent organization to seek new methods of limiting armaments.

5. Establishment of fundamental political co-operation among the Great Powers on the basis of a growing mutual trust.

March 23—The German Reichstag passes an act giving all authority to the Hitler Government for four years, and adjourns *sine die*.

The Speech

"IN NOVEMBER, 1918, Marxist organizations seized the executive power by means of a revolution. The monarchs were dethroned, the authorities of the Reich and of the States removed from office, and thereby a breach of the Constitution was committed. The success of the revolution in a material sense protected the guilty parties from the hands of the law. They sought to justify it morally by asserting that Germany or its Government bore the guilt for the outbreak of the War.

"This assertion was deliberately and actually untrue. In consequence, however, these untrue accusations in the interest of our former enemies led to the severest oppression of the entire German nation and to the breach of the assurances given to us in Wilson's fourteen points, and so for Germany, that is to say the working classes of the German people, to a time of infinite misfortune. . . ."

"The splitting up of the nation into groups with irreconcilable views, systematically brought about by the false doctrines of Marxism, means the destruction of the basis of a possible communal life. . . . It is only the creation of a real national community, rising above the interests and differences of rank and class, that can permanently remove the source of nourishment of these aberrations of the human mind. The establishment of such a solidarity of views in the German body corporate is all the more important, for it is only thereby that the possibility is provided of maintaining friendly relations with foreign Powers without regard to the tendencies or general principles by which they are dominated, *for the elimination of communism in Germany is a purely domestic German affair.*

"Simultaneously with this political purification of our public life, the Government of the Reich will undertake a thorough moral purging of the body corporate of the nation. *The entire educational system, the theater, the cinema, literature, the Press, and the wireless—all these will be used as means to this end and valued accordingly.* They must all serve for the maintenance of the eternal values present in the essential character of our people. Art will always remain the expression and the reflection of the longings and the realities of an era. The neutral international attitude of aloofness is rapidly disappearing. Heroism is coming forward passionately and will in future shape and lead political destiny. It is the task of art to be the expression of this determining spirit of the age. Blood and race will once more become the source of artistic intuition. . . ."

"Our legal institutions must serve above all for the maintenance of this national community. The irremovableness of the judges must ensure a sense of responsibility and the exercise of discretion in their judgments in the interests of society. Not the individual but the nation as a whole alone can be the center of legislative solicitude. High treason and treachery to the nation will be ruthlessly eradicated in the future. The foundations of the existence of justice cannot be other than the foundations of the existence of the nation.

"The Government, being resolved to undertake the political and moral purification of our public life, is creating and securing the conditions necessary for a really profound revival of religious life.

"The advantages of a personal and political nature that might arise from compromising with atheistic organizations would not outweigh the consequences which would become apparent in the destruction of general moral basic values. The national Government regards the two Christian confessions as the weightiest factors for the maintenance of our nationality. It will respect the agreements concluded between it and the federal States. Their rights are not to be infringed. But the Government hopes and expects that the work on the national and moral regeneration of our nation which it has made its task will, on the other hand, be treated with the same respect. . . ."

"Great are the tasks of the national Government in the sphere of economic life.

"Here all action must be governed by one law: *the people does not live for business and business does not exist for capital, but capital serves business and business serves the people.* In principle the Government will not protect the economic interests of the German people by the circuitous method of an economic bureaucracy to be organized by the State, but by the utmost furtherance of private initiative and by the recognition of the rights of property. . . ."

"The Government will systematically avoid currency experiments. We are faced above all by two economic tasks of the first magnitude. The salvation of the German farmer must be achieved at all costs. . . ."

"Furthermore, it is perfectly clear to the national Government that the final removal of the distress both in agricultural business and in that of the towns depends on the absorption of the army of the unemployed in the process of production. This constitutes the second of the great economic tasks. It can only be solved by a general appeasement, in applying sound natural economic principles and all measures necessary, even if, at the time, they cannot reckon with any degree of popularity. The providing of work and the compulsory labor service are, in this connection, only individual measures within the scope of the entire action proposed. . . ."

"We are aware that the geographic position of Germany, with her lack of raw materials, does not fully permit of economic self-sufficiency for the Reich. It cannot be too often emphasized that nothing is further from the thoughts of the Government of the Reich than hostility to exporting. We are fully aware that we have need of the connection with the outside world, and that the marketing of German commodities in the world provides a livelihood for many millions of our fellow-countrymen.

"We also know what are the conditions necessary for a sound exchange of services between the nations of the world. For Germany has been compelled for years to perform services without receiving an equivalent, with the result that the task of maintaining Germany as an active partner in the exchange of commodities is not so much one of commercial as of financial policy. So long as we are not accorded a reasonable settlement of our foreign debts corresponding to our economic capacity, we are unfortunately compelled to maintain our foreign-exchange control. The Government of the Reich is, for that reason, also compelled to maintain the restrictions on the efflux of capital across the frontiers of Germany. . . ."

"The protection of the frontiers of the Reich and thereby of the lives of our people and the existence of our business is now in the hands of the Reichswehr, which, in accordance with the terms imposed upon us by the Treaty of Versailles, is to be regarded as the only really disarmed army in the world. In spite of its enforced smallness and entirely insufficient armament, the German people may regard their Reichswehr with proud satisfaction. This little instrument of our national self-defence has come into being under the most difficult conditions. The spirit imbuing it is that of our best military traditions. The German nation has thus fulfilled with painful conscientiousness the obligations imposed upon it by the Peace Treaty, indeed, even the replacement of ships for our fleet then sanctioned has, I may perhaps be allowed to say, unfortunately, only been carried out to a small extent.

"For years Germany has been waiting in vain for the fulfillment of the promise of disarmament made to her by the others. It is the sincere desire of the national Government to be able to refrain from increasing our army and our weapons, insofar as the rest of the world is now also ready to fulfill its obligations in the matter of radical disarmament. For Germany desires nothing except an equal right to live and equal freedom.

"In any case the national Government will educate the German people in this spirit of a desire for freedom. The national honor, the honor of our army and the ideal of freedom must once more become sacred to the German people!

"The German nation wishes to live in peace with the rest of the world. But it is for this very reason that the Government of the Reich will employ every means to obtain the final removal of the division of the nations of the world into two categories. The keeping open of this wound leads to distrust on the one side and hatred on the other, and thus to a general feeling of insecurity. The national Government is ready to extend a hand in sincere understanding to every nation that is ready finally to make an end of the tragic past. The international economic distress can only disappear when the basis has been provided by stable political relations and when the nations have regained confidence in each other.

"For the overcoming of the economic catastrophe three things are necessary:

"1. Absolutely authoritative leadership in internal affairs, in order to create confidence in the stability of conditions.

"2. The securing of peace by the great nations for a long time to come, with a view to restoring the confidence of the nations in each other.

"3. The final victory of the principles of common sense in the organization and conduct of business, and also a general release from reparations and impossible liabilities for debts and interest.

"We are unfortunately faced by the fact that the Geneva Conference, in spite of lengthy negotiations, has so far reached no practical result. The decision regarding the securing of a real measure of disarmament has been constantly delayed by the raising of questions of technical detail and by the introduction of problems that have nothing to do with disarmament. This procedure is useless.

"The illegal state of one-sided disarmament and the resulting national insecurity of Germany cannot continue any longer.

"We recognize it as a sign of the feeling of responsibility and of the good will of the British Government that they have endeavored, by means of their disarmament proposal, to cause the Conference finally to arrive at speedy decisions. The Government of the Reich will support every endeavor aimed at really carrying out general disarmament and securing the fulfillment of Germany's long-overdue claim for disarmament. *For fourteen years we have been disarmed, and for fourteen months we have been waiting for the results of the Disarmament Conference.* Even more far-reaching is the plan of the head of the Italian Government, which makes a broad-minded and far-seeing attempt to secure a peaceful and consistent development of the whole of European policy. *We attach the greatest weight to this plan, and we are ready to co-operate with absolute sincerity on the basis it provides, in order to unite the four Great Powers, England, France, Italy, and Germany,* in friendly co-operation in attacking with courage and determination the problems upon the solution of which the fate of Europe depends.

"It is for this reason that we are particularly grateful for the appreciative heartiness with which the national renaissance of Germany has been greeted in Italy. . . ."

"In the same way, the Government of the Reich, which regards Christianity as the unshakable foundation of the morals and moral code of the nation, attaches the greatest value to friendly relations with the Holy See, and is endeavoring to develop them. We feel sympathy for our brother nation in Austria in its trouble and distress. In all their doings the Government of the Reich is conscious of the connection between the destiny of all German races. Their attitude toward the other foreign Powers may be gathered from what has already been said. But even in cases where our mutual relations are encumbered with difficulties, we shall endeavor to arrive at a settlement. But in any case the basis for an understanding can never be the distinction between victor and vanquished.

"*We are convinced that such a settlement is possible in our relations with France,* if the Governments will attack the problems affecting them on both sides in a really broad-minded way. *The Government of the Reich is ready to cultivate with the Soviet Union friendly relations profitable to both parties.* It is above all the Government of the National Revolution which feels itself in a position to adopt such a positive policy with regard to Soviet Russia. The fight against communism in Germany is our internal affair in which we will never permit interference from outside. . . ."

"We have particularly at heart the fate of the Germans living beyond the frontiers of Germany who are allied with us in speech, culture, and customs and have to make a hard fight to retain these values. The national Government is resolved to use all the means at its disposal to support the rights internationally guaranteed to the German minorities.

"We welcome the plan for a World Economic Conference and approve of its meeting at an early date. The Government of the Reich is ready to take part in this Conference, in order to arrive at positive results at last. . . ."

Press

Le Temps, March 24—Hitler's speech produced no surprises. He spoke very moderately, in order to wipe out the bad impression that his former methods had created abroad. He declared that he would enter the Four Power Pact and come to a compromise with France. It remains to be seen how these promises will be acted upon. With Hitler's speeches one must always seek what is hidden between the lines.

London Times, March 24—As to the main lines of German foreign policy, there can be clearly traced between the lines of his speech, which implied that Soviet Russia would not regard with more than the most cynical interest the suppression of German Communists, that his government looked for increasingly close relations with Italy, that they valued the spirit prompting British mediatory efforts.

•

SPEECH OF APRIL 8, 1933

Berlin, Sportpalast

"THE great epoch which for fourteen years we awaited has now begun. Germany is awake now. . . ."

"I can say with pride, comrades of the SA and SS, that if the whole German people now was possessed of the spirit which is in us and in you, then Germany would be indestructible. Even without arms, Germany would represent an unheard-of strength through this inner will tempered like steel. It is true that this equality which is realized in you was realized only at the cost of that freedom of which others spoke. We have, too, adopted the principle of leadership, the conception of authority. That was a heavy sacrifice at a time when the whole people was running after the illusion of democracy and parliamentarianism, when millions believed that the majority was the source of a right decision. It was at this time that we began resolutely to build up an organization in which there was not one dictator but ten thousand. *When our opponents say: 'It is easy for you: you are a dictator'—we answer them, 'No, gentlemen, you are wrong; there is no single dictator, but ten thousand, each in his own place.'* And even the highest authority in the hierarchy has itself only one wish, never to transgress against the supreme authority to which it, too, is responsible. We have in our Movement developed this loyalty in following the leader, this blind obedience of which all the others know nothing and which gave to us the power to surmount everything. For fourteen years we were assailed; the attempt was made to bend and break us by cunning, chicanery, and violence, by malice and terror, by everything imaginable. But this instrument of blind obedience remained unbroken, remained steadfast. All we endured was but tests from which we emerged stronger than ever.

"In addition we have fostered the virtue of bravery. Today millions are pouring into our ranks. But the greater part of them must learn now what this brown army has practiced for years; they must all learn to face what tens of thousands of our comrades have faced, and have paid for with their blood, their lives.

"We have succeeded out of our own free wills in once more inculcating in our people the courage which dares to attempt a task in the face of a world of foes.

"Were the discipline of this Movement not so firm, those who today complain of the sacrifices demanded of them would have even more of which to complain. For what we fighters have gained does not compare to the amount of persecution we suffered. Let the bellyachers realize that, wherever they are. The Movement trains itself in this perfect discipline for the sake of Germany, to save our people from being cast down in the eyes of the world to the level of their opponents.

"We have also utilized the virtue of persistence, of unwearying patience. . . ."

"It was this virtue which made you, and therefore us, unconquerable, and which saved the nation. Fourteen years of struggle. It seems as though fate had saved up so terribly many victims especially for the last year of the struggle. Our Brown Shirts prohibited, the members tortured, terror heaped upon terror, and in the end the dissolution of the organization. It was a terribly sad time, and I know how hard it was for many to keep their faith that after all the hour would come at last. We almost doubted justice and providence. Then came the turning point, and battle after battle. Once more many doubted, and some even were beaten down by their doubt. And then came the time when we had to say 'No,' when for the first time it seemed that the way to power was opening before us, tempting us: and yet despite this we had to remain hard and say 'No, it is not possible in that way.' And for a second time the doors seemed to open and for the second time we had to say 'No, impossible.' And then at the third time the hour came and that was given to us which we could not but desire, which we had a right to desire, and at last the National Socialist Movement entered into the great period of its historic action. . . ."

"We have now won power in Germany, and it is up to us to win the German people, to incorporate the people within the power. We must build the millions of our working men of all classes into a close community. This is a struggle which will again take years; but it is necessary if the 600,000 men of today are some day to be the six, eight, ten millions we need. Here, too, we know that if we rest, we rust, that if we stand still, we will retreat. . . ."

"If in the future you continue to stand behind me as one man, in loyalty and obedience, no power in the world will be able to destroy this Movement. It will continue its victorious course. If you preserve the same discipline, the same obedience, the same comradeship and the same unbounded loyalty in the future—then nothing will ever extinguish this Movement in Germany. This is the request I make of you, for myself and in the name of all the comrades who are no longer among us. . . ."

"Our National Socialist Movement, the SA and SS: Sieg Heil, Sieg Heil, Sieg Heil!"

Press

New York Times, April 10—Herr Hitler contended that it was not dictatorship that he was offering Germany. "In our movement it is not one who dictates but tens of thousands—each in his place."

•

SPEECH OF MAY 10, 1933

Berlin, Congress of the German Work Front

Background

March 31—The Communist party is banned in Germany. All the Communist mandates in Parliament are revoked. Law for the "co-ordination" of the Reich and the provinces is passed.

April 1—In retaliation for censorious demonstrations held in New York, London, and Paris, the new German Government begins a planned campaign of anti-Semitic persecution. Boycott of the Jews. Issuance of the first Aryan laws.

May 2—Unions incorporated in the National Socialist party's "Labor Front," founded by Robert Ley.

May 10—Burning of books in the campaign against un-German culture.

The Speech

". . . . AMIDST all the crises under which we suffer and which do but present a single connected picture, perhaps that which the people feels most acutely is the economic crisis. The political crisis, the moral crisis, are only very rarely felt by the individual. The average man sees in the experiences of his day not that which affects the community as a whole but for the most part only that which strikes himself. Therefore the present has only very rarely any consciousness of political or moral collapse so long as this collapse does not extend in one way or another into economic life. For when this happens it is no longer a question of some abstract problem that can perhaps be observed or studied in its effect on others, but one day the individual himself will be caught hold of by this question, and the more intimately such a crisis begins to influence his own life, the more clearly does he come to recognize that existing conditions cannot remain as they are. Then all of a sudden people talk of economic distress, of economic misery, and then, starting from this distress, one can awaken an understanding for that other distress which otherwise is wont to remain for a long time hidden from the individual man.

"It is not enough to say that the German economic distress is a phenomenon resulting from a world crisis, from a general economic distress, since, of course, exactly in the same way every other people could plead the same excuse, could adduce the same reason. It is clear that even so this distress cannot have its roots all over the world, those roots must always be found within the life of peoples. And though only one thing is probably true—that these roots are perhaps the same in the case of many peoples—yet one cannot hope to master this distress by the mere statement that the presence of a certain distress is a feature of the age; rather it is clearly a necessity to disclose these roots in the internal life of a single people and to cure the distress there where one can really effect a cure.

"Unfortunately it is precisely the German who is only too inclined at such times, instead of looking at his own internal life, to let his gaze range into the far distance. Our people has been so long falsely taught to think in international terms that even in such a distress as the present it tends to treat this problem, too, from international points of view. And the result is that many of us simply cannot believe that perhaps it might be possible to remedy such a misfortune in some other way than by international methods. And yet that is an error. It is natural that international infirmities which afflict all peoples in one way or another must be removed by the peoples who suffer from them, but that in no way alters the fact that every people must wage this battle on its own behalf, and above all that no single people can be liberated from this distress by international methods if it does not for its own part take the necessary measures. These measures can, of course, find their place within the framework of international measures, but one's own action must not be made dependent upon the action of others.

"The crisis in German economics is not merely a crisis which is expressed by our economic statistics, but it is above all a crisis which can also be traced in the internal course of our economic life, in the character of its organization, etc. And here we can indeed speak of a crisis which has hit our people more severely than other peoples. It is the crisis which we see in the relations between capital, economics, and people. This crisis is particularly obvious in the relations between our workmen and the employers. Here the crisis has been more acute than in any other country in the world. . . ."

"The first cause lies in the alteration in the form of business organization which determined the character of our economics. That cause may be traced throughout the world precisely as in Germany. . . ."

"The gradual alienation of classes which we in Germany experienced led to the appearance on the one side of the special interests of the employers and on the other side the special interests of the employed. This was the beginning of our unhappy economic development. When one had once started on this road, of necessity the two sides became ever more widely separated. Here a law governs human affairs: when one has once chosen the wrong road this road always leads one further from reason. . . ."

"On the contrary, the road led necessarily to further alienation and this tendency, as I said, was favored by the depersonalization of property. And I might almost say that this process was apparently still further encouraged and strengthened on scientific grounds. There gradually arose an ideology which believed that it could permanently support the conception of property even though those who derived any practical profit from the conception no longer represented more than a minimal percentage of the nation. And on the other hand there arose the view that, since there was now only so small a percentage of those who enjoyed property, the conception of private property as such should be abandoned. . . ."

"When one has once started on this course, then logically the employers will in turn form their organization. And as a matter of course these two organizations will not pursue their own ends in mutual toleration, but they will maintain their apparently separate interests with those weapons which are given them: viz. lockouts and strikes. In this warfare sometimes one and sometimes the other side will conquer. But in either case it is the whole nation which will have to pay the cost of this warfare and suffer the damage. And the final result of this development is that these organizations as they build themselves up, considering the passion of the German for bureaucratization, will continuously become more unwieldy and their personnel will grow constantly larger. And at length the organization will no longer serve the interests of its creators, but these will be subservient to the organization, so that the warfare is continued in order that the existence of the organization may be justified, even though at times reason suddenly comes and says: 'The whole affair is madness; the gain when compared with the sacrifices is positively ludicrous. If you reckon up the sacrifices which we make for the organization they are far greater than any possible profit.' Then the organizations in their turn will have to prove how necessary they are by stirring up the parties to fight each other. And then it may even be that the two organizations come to an understanding, when once they have realized the situation.

"The second reason is the rise of Marxism. Marxism, as a conception of the world with disintegration for its aim, saw with keen insight that the trade-union movement offered it the possibility in the future of conducting its attack against the State and against human society with an absolutely annihilating weapon. Not with any idea of helping the worker —what is the worker of any country to these apostles of internationalism? Nothing at all! They never see him! They themselves are no workers: they are alien litterateurs, an alien gang! . . ."

"One had to inoculate the trade union with the idea: You are an instrument of the class war and that war in the last resort can find its political leaders only in Marxism. What is then more comprehensible than that one should also pay one's tribute to the leadership? And the tribute was exacted in full measure. These gentlemen have not been content with a tithe: they demanded a considerably higher rate of interest.

"This class war leads to the proclamation of the trade union as simply an instrument for the representation of the economic interests of the working classes and therewith for the purposes of the general strike. Thus the general strike appears for the first time as a means for exercising political power and shows what Marxism really hoped to gain from this weapon—not a means for the salvation of the worker, but on the contrary only an instrument of war for the destruction of the State which opposed Marxism. To prove to what lengths this whole madness could go we Germans have an unprecedented example, as frightful as it is instructive, in the War.

"We can add only one remark: Had the German trade unions been in our hands during the War, if they had been in my hands and had they been trained with the same false end in view as was in fact the case, then we National Socialists would have placed the whole of this gigantic organization at the service of the Fatherland. We should have declared: We recognize, of course, the sacrifices entailed; we are ready ourselves to make those sacrifices; we do not wish to escape, we want to fight with you on the same terms; we give our destiny and our life into the hand of Almighty Providence just as the others must do. That we should have done as a matter of course. For, German workmen, we should have said, you must realize: It is not the fate of the German State which is now to be decided, not of the Empire as a constitutional form, not of the monarchy; it is not a question of capitalism or militarism; it is the existence of our people which is at stake and we German workmen make up seventy per cent of this people. It is our fate which is to be decided!

"That is what should have been known then, and it could have been known. We should have known it. . . ."

"It was a crime that this was not done. It was not done because it would have violated the inner meaning of Marxism, for Marxism wanted only the destruction of Germany. . . . For since the days of November, 1918, millions of Germans have held the view that it was the fault of the German workingman which caused the country's collapse. He who himself had made such unspeakable sacrifices, he who had filled our regiments with the millions of their riflemen—he as a class was suddenly made collectively liable for the act of the perjured, lying, degenerate destroyers of the Fatherland. That was the worst that could have happened, for at that moment for many millions in Germany the community of the people was shattered. . . ."

"The third cause of this fatal development lay in the State itself. There might have been something which could perhaps have opposed these millions and that something would have been the State had it not been that this State had sunk so low that it had become the plaything of groups of interested parties. It is no mere chance that this whole development runs parallel with the democratization of our public life. This democratization tended to bring the State directly into the hands of certain strata of society which identified themselves with property as such, with big business as such. The masses increasingly got the impression that the State itself was no objective institution standing above parties, that in particular it was no longer the incorporation of any objective authority, but that it was itself the mouthpiece of the economic will and of the economic interests of certain groups within the nation, and that even the leadership of the State justified such an assumption. The victory of the political *bourgeoisie* was nothing else than the victory of a stratum of society which had arisen as the result of economic laws. . . ."

"While it is natural that amongst soldiers he only can be a leader who has been trained for that post, it was by no means a matter of course that only he should be a political leader who had been trained in that sphere and had besides proved his capacity; gradually the view gained ground that membership of a certain class which had arisen as the result of economic laws carried with it the capacity to govern a people. We have come to realize the consequences of this error. The stratum of society which claimed for itself the leadership has failed us in every hour of crisis and in the nation's hour of supreme difficulty it collapsed miserably. . . . Let no one say to me: 'No other course was possible.' It was only for these leaders that no other course was possible. . . ."

"We must penetrate to the inner causes of the collapse with the resolution that these inner causes shall be removed. I believe that immediately we must begin at the point where in the last resort a beginning must today be made—we must begin with the State itself. *A new authority must be set up, and this authority must be independent of momentary currents of contemporary opinion, especially of those currents which flow from a narrow and limited economic egoism. There must be constituted a leadership of the State which represents a real authority,* an authority independent of any one stratum of society. A leadership must arise in which every citizen can have confidence, assured that its sole aim is the happiness, the welfare, of the German people, a leadership which can with justice say of itself that it is on every side completely independent. People have talked so much of the past Age of Absolutism, of the absolutism of Frederick the Great, and of the Age of Popular Democracy, our Parliamentary Epoch. Regarded from the standpoint of the people the earlier period was the more objective: it could really more objectively safeguard the interests of the nation, while the later period continuously descended more and more to the representation merely of the interests of individual classes.

"Nothing can prove that more clearly than the mere conception of a class war—the slogan that the rule of the *bourgeoisie* must be replaced by the rule of the proletariat. That means that the whole question becomes one of a change in a class dictatorship, while our aim is the dictatorship of the people, i.e., the dictatorship of the whole people, the community.

"And further it is essential that one should sweep away all those forces which consciously abuse human weaknesses in order with their help to carry into execution their deadly schemes. When fourteen or fifteen years ago and over and over again since then I declared before the German nation that I saw my task before the bar of German history to lie in the destruction of Marxism, that was for me no empty phrase, that was a sacred oath which I will keep so long as I draw breath. This confession of faith, the confession of faith of an individual, through my effort has become the confession of faith of a mighty organization. . . ."

"We must accordingly wage our battle without any compromise whatsoever against the force which has eaten at the heart of our German people during the last seventeen years, which has inflicted on us such fearful injuries and which, if it had not been conquered, would have destroyed Germany. Bismarck once declared that liberalism was the pacemaker for social democracy. And I do not need in this place to say that social democracy is the pacemaker for communism. But communism is the pacemaker for death—the death of a people—downfall. *We have begun the fight against communism and we shall wage it to the end.* As so often in German history, it will once more be proved that the greater the distress, the greater is the power of the German people to find its way upwards and forwards. This time, too, it will find the way; indeed, I am convinced that it has already found it.

"Thus the unification of the German Workmen's Movement has a great moral significance. When we complete the reconstruction of the State which must be the result of very great concessions on both sides, we want to have two parties to the contract facing each other who both are in their hearts on principle nationally minded, who both look only to their people, and who both on principle are ready to subordinate everything else in order to serve the common weal. Only if that is possible from the first can I believe in the success of our efforts. It is the spirit from which efforts spring that helps to decide the issue. There must be no conquerors and no conquered; our people must be the only conqueror—conqueror over classes and castes, and conqueror over the interests of these single groups in our people! And thereby we shall come naturally to a nobler conception of work. . . . But the Movement which I and my fellow-fighters represent will, nothing daunted, exalt the word 'Worker' till it becomes the great title of honor of the German nation. . . ."

"Personally, I am against all honorary titles, and I do not think that anyone has much to accuse me of on this score. What is not absolutely necessary for me to do, that I do not do. I should never care to have visiting cards printed with the titles which in this earthly world of ours are given with such ceremony. *I do not want anything on my gravestone but my name.* All the same, owing to the peculiar circumstances of my life, I am perhaps more capable than anyone else of understanding and realizing the nature and the whole life of the various German castes. Not because I have been able to look down on this life from above but because I have participated in it, because I stood in the midst of this life, because fate in a moment of caprice or perhaps fulfilling the designs of providence, cast me into the great mass of the people, amongst common folk. Because I myself was a laboring man for years in the building trade and had to earn my own bread. And because for a second time I took my place once again as an ordinary soldier amongst the masses and because then life raised me into other strata of our people so that I know these, too, better than countless others who were born in these strata. So fate has perhaps fitted me more than any other to be the broker—I think I may say—the honest broker for both sides alike. Here I am not personally interested; I am not dependent upon the State or on any public office; I am not dependent upon business or industry or any trade union. I am an independent man, and I have set before myself no other goal than to serve, to the best of my power and ability, the German people, and above all to serve the millions who, thanks to their simple trust and ignorance and thanks to the baseness of their former leaders, have perhaps suffered more than any other class.

"I have always professed that there is nothing finer than to be the advocate of those who cannot easily defend themselves. I know the masses of my people, and there is only one thing which I should always wish to say to our intellectuals: Every Reich that is founded only on the classes which represent intellect and intelligence has weak foundations. I know this intellect, always so subtle, always inquiring, but also always uncertain, always hesitating, vacillating from side to side—never steadfast! He who would construct a Reich on these intellectual classes alone will find his building insecure. It is no chance that religions are more stable than constitutional forms. Generally they tend to sink their roots deeper into the soil; they would be unthinkable in the absence of the masses of the people. I know that the intellectual classes fall all too easily a victim to that arrogance which measures the people according to the standards of its knowledge and of its so-called intelligence; and yet there are things in the people which very often the intelligence of the 'intelligent' does not see because it cannot see them. The masses are certainly often dull, in many respects they are certainly backward, they are not so nimble, so witty, or intellectual; but they have something to their credit—they have loyalty, constancy, stability. . . ."

"Because I know this people better than any other, and at the same time know the rest of the people, I am not only ready in this case to undertake the role of an honest broker but I am glad that destiny can cast me for the part. I shall never in my life have any greater reason for pride than when at the end of my days I can say: I have won the German workingman for the German Reich."

Press

New York Times, May 11—His long and in part striking speech contained not a single specific statement.

•

SPEECH OF MAY 17, 1933

Berlin, Reichstag

Background

May 10—In Geneva, at the disarmament conference, the German representatives speak for the maintenance of long-term military service. General von Blomberg declares to the Wolff Telegraph Bureau (news agency) that there is room for negotiation on this question, but that Germany is unwilling to accept any kind of ultimatum.

The 1926 trade pact between Germany and Russia is renewed.

May 17—Reichstag summoned.

The Speech

". . . ALL the problems which are causing such unrest today lie in the deficiencies of the Treaty of Peace which did not succeed in solving in a clear and reasonable way the questions of the most decisive importance for the future. Neither national nor economic—to say nothing of legal—problems and demands of the nations were settled by this Treaty in such a way as to stand the criticism of reason in the future. It is therefore natural that the idea of revision is not only one of the constant accompaniments of the effects of this Treaty, but that it was actually foreseen as necessary by the authors of the Treaty and therefore given a legal foundation in the Treaty itself.

"If I deal briefly with the problems which the Versailles Treaty ought to have settled, I do so because its failure in this respect has inevitably given rise to the later situations under which the political and economic relations of States have since then been suffering.

"For many centuries European States and their frontiers developed from conceptions which were only concerned with the State as such. With the triumph of the national conception and of the principle of nationality in the course of the last century, the seed of many conflicts was sown by the failure of States, which had come into existence under other conditions, to take into account these new ideas and ideals. At the end of the World War there could have been no nobler task for a real peace conference than to undertake—in the clear recognition of this fact—a territorial and political reorganization of the European States which should in the highest degree possible do justice to this principle. The more such a settlement succeeded in making the frontiers between peoples coincide with the frontiers between States, the more it would have eliminated a whole series of future possibilities of conflict. . . ."

"As it was, through ignorance, passion, and hatred, decisions were taken which, in their injustice and lack of logic, bore the seeds of fresh conflicts.

"The main characteristics of the present economic situation of Europe are the overcrowding of the west of Europe and the poverty of its soil in certain raw materials which are essential to the standard of life which has grown up in those territories with their ancient culture. If the statesmen at Versailles wanted to bring lasting peace to Europe, they should have recognized and followed, instead of the dangerous and sterile conceptions of expiation, punishment, and reparation, the profound truth that the lack of the necessities of life has always been a source of conflict between peoples. Instead of preaching the idea of extermination, they should have embarked upon a reorganization of international political and economic relationships, so as to do justice, to the fullest possible extent, to the vital needs of each nation.

"It is not wise to deprive a people of the economic resources necessary for its existence without taking into consideration the fact that the population dependent on them are bound to the soil and will have to be fed. The idea that the economic extermination of a nation of sixty-five millions would be of service to other nations is absurd. Any people inclined to follow such a line of thought would, under the law of cause and effect, soon experience that the doom which they were preparing for another nation would swiftly overtake them. The very idea of reparations and the way in which they were enforced will become a classic example in the history of the nations of how seriously international welfare can be damaged by hasty and unconsidered action. . . ."

"The Treaty of Versailles is to blame for having inaugurated a period in which financial calculations appear to destroy economic reason. Germany has faithfully fulfilled the obligations imposed upon her, in spite of their intrinsic lack of reason and the obviously suicidal consequences of this fulfillment.

"The international economic crisis is the indisputable proof of the correctness of this statement.

"The chances of restoring a general international legal sentiment have also been no less destroyed by the Treaty. For, in order to justify all the measures of this edict, Germany had to be branded as the guilty party. This procedure is, indeed, just as simple as it is, however, inadmissible. In any future cases of conflict the vanquished will always be the guilty party, because the victor can establish this fact in the easiest manner possible.

"This procedure therefore assumes a terrible significance, because it gave at the same time an excuse for the conversion of the power ratio existing at the end of the war into a permanent legal status. The conception of conqueror and conquered thus literally became the foundation of a new international legal and social order.

"The degradation of a great people to a second-class nation was proclaimed at the same moment as a League of Nations came into being.

"This treatment of Germany could not lead to the pacification of the world. The disarmed state and defenselessness of the conquered parties which was thus considered necessary—an unheard of procedure in the history of the European nations—was still less calculated to diminish the general dangers and conflicts, but merely led to that condition of constant menaces, demands, and sanctions which, by the unrest and insecurity which they give rise to, threaten to undermine the entire economic structure of the world. If no consideration is given by the nations to the danger of certain actions, reason may easily be overcome by unreason. At any rate, up to the present, the League of Nations has been unable to grant any appreciable assistance to the weak and unarmed in such cases. Treaties concluded for the pacification of the nations only possess an inner meaning when they are based on real and honest equality of rights for all. This is the main reason for the state of unrest which has been weighing on the world for a number of years.

"It is, however, in the interests of all that present-day problems should be solved in a reasonable and final manner. *No new European war could improve the unsatisfactory conditions of the present day.*

"On the contrary, the application of violence of any kind in Europe could have no favorable effect upon the political or economic position which exists today. *Even if a fresh European act of violence had a decisive result, the ultimate effect would be to increase the disturbance of European equilibrium and thus, in one manner or another, to sow the seed of further conflicts and complications.*

"The result would be fresh wars, fresh uncertainty, and fresh economic distress. *The outbreak of such infinite madness, however, would necessarily cause the collapse of the present social and political order.* A Europe sinking into communistic chaos would bring about a crisis, the extent and duration of which could not be foreseen.

"It is the earnest desire of the national Government of the German Reich to prevent such a disturbing development by means of its honest and active co-operation.

"Speaking deliberately as a German National Socialist, *I desire to declare in the name of the national Government, and of the whole movement of national regeneration, that we in this new Germany are filled with deep understanding for the same feelings and opinions and for the rightful claims to life of the other nations.* The present generation of this new Germany, which, so far, has only known in its life the poverty, misery, and distress of its own people, has suffered too deeply from the madness of our time to be able to contemplate treating others in the same way.

"Our boundless love for and loyalty to our own national traditions makes us respect the national claims of others and makes us desire from the bottom of our hearts to live with them in peace and friendship.

"*We therefore have no use for the idea of Germanization.* The mentality of the past century which made people believe that they could make Germans out of Poles and Frenchmen is completely foreign to us; the more so as we are passionately opposed to any attempt on the part of others to alienate us from our German tradition. We look at the European nations objectively. The French, the Poles, etc., are our neighbors, and we know that through no possible development of history can this reality be altered.

"It would have been better for the world if in Germany's case these realities had been appreciated in the Treaty of Versailles. For the object of a really lasting treaty should be not to cause new wounds and keep old ones open, but to close wounds and heal them. A thoughtful treatment of European problems at that time could certainly have found a settlement in the East which would have met both the reasonable claims of Poland and the natural rights of Germany. The Treaty of Versailles did not provide this solution. *Nevertheless no German Government will of its own accord break an agreement which cannot be removed without being replaced by a better one.*

"But the legal character of such a treaty must be acknowledged by *all*. Not only the conqueror but also the conquered party can claim the rights accorded in the Treaty. And the right to demand a revision of the Treaty finds its foundation in the Treaty itself. The German Government, in stating the reasons for and the extent of its claims, wishes for nothing more than the existing results of previous experience and the incontestable consequences of critical and logical reasoning show to be necessary and just. The experience of the last fourteen years, however, is unambiguous from a political and economic point of view.

"The misery of the nations has not been relieved but has increased. The deepest roots of this misery, however, lie in the division of the world into conquerors and conquered, which seems to be intended to form a permanent basis of all treaties and all future order. The worst effect of this order lies in the compulsory defenselessness of one nation as against the excessive armaments of the others. If Germany has continued for years to demand the disarmament of all, it is for the following reasons:

"1. The demand for equality of rights expressed in actual facts is a demand of morality, right and reason; it is a demand which is recognized in the Peace Treaty itself and the fulfillment of which is indissolubly bound up with the demand for German disarmament, as the prelude to world disarmament.

"2. On the other hand the disqualification of a great people cannot be permanently maintained, but must at some time be brought to an end. How long is it thought possible that such an injustice can be imposed on a great nation? What is the advantage of a moment as compared with the permanent development through centuries? The German nation will continue to exist exactly in the same way as the French nation and, as history has proved, the Polish nation.

"Of what value is the temporary oppression of a nation of sixty-five millions as compared with the force of this incontrovertible fact? *No State can possess a greater understanding for the young, newly created European national States than the new Germany which has risen out of the national revolution which was inspired by the same impulses.* Germany wants nothing for herself which she is not prepared to give to others.

"Germany, in demanding at present actual equality of rights such as can only be achieved by the disarmament of other nations, has a moral right to do so since she has herself carried out the provisions of the treaties. For Germany has disarmed and has carried out this disarmament under the strictest international supervision. . . ."

"The Rhineland was demilitarized, the German fortresses were dismantled, our ships surrendered, our airplanes destroyed, our system of military service abandoned and the training of reserves thus prevented. Even the most indispensable weapons of defense were denied us.

"If, in the face of these indisputable facts, anyone should attempt to come forward and declare with truly wretched excuses and pretexts that Germany has not fulfilled the treaties or has even rearmed, as German Chancellor speaking in the Reichstag I must repudiate such views which are as untrue as they are unfair.

"Equally untrue are the statements that Germany has not complied with the provisions of the Treaty in respect of personnel. The statement that the SA and SS of the National Socialist party are connected in any way with the Reichswehr, in the sense that they represent formations with military training or army reserves, is untrue! . . ."

"In actual fact, the Storm Sections [SA] and Storm Troops [SS] of the National Socialist party came into being without any help or financial support from the governments of the Federal States, the Reich, or from the Army, without any military training or equipment, but purely out of the political needs and considerations of the times. Their object was and is exclusively the removal of the communist danger; their development took place without any connection with the Army, purely for purposes of propaganda and national enlightenment, psychological mass effect and the breaking down of the communist terror. They form an institution for creating a true team spirit, for overcoming former class differences and for removing economic distress.

"When, however, at the same time the trained annual contingents of the other armies of the world, in contradistinction to these men who are entirely without military training, are not included, when the armed reserves of other countries are deliberately overlooked, while the unarmed members of the political associations are in our case included, this constitutes a procedure against which I must categorically protest. If the world wishes to destroy confidence in right and justice, these are the best means for the purpose.

"On behalf of the German people and the German Government, I have to make the following statement: *Germany has disarmed. She has complied with all obligations imposed upon her in the Peace Treaty to an extent far beyond the limits of equity and reason. Her army consists of 100,000 men.* The strength and the character of her police are internationally regulated.

"*Germany has thus a fully justified moral claim to the fulfillment by the other Powers of their obligations under the Treaty of Versailles.* The equality of status accorded to Germany in December has not yet been given practical expression. With regard to the contention, repeated by France again and again, that the safety of France must be secured to the same extent as the equality of Germany, I would like to ask two questions:

"1. Germany has so far accepted all the obligations with regard to security arising from the signing of the Versailles Treaty, the Kellogg Pact, the Treaties of Arbitration, the Pact of Non-Aggression, etc. What other concrete assurances are left for Germany to give?

"2. On the other hand, how much security has Germany? According to the figures published by the League, France alone has 3,046 airplanes in service, Belgium 350, Poland 700, Czechoslovakia 670. In addition to these numbers there are innumerable reserve airplanes, thousand of tanks, thousands of heavy guns and all the necessary technical equipment for chemical warfare. Has not Germany, in her state of defenselessness and disarmament, greater justification in demanding security than the overarmed States bound together in military alliances?

"Nevertheless Germany is at any time willing to undertake further obligations in regard to international security, if all the other nations are ready on their side to do the same, and if this security is also to benefit Germany. Germany would also be perfectly ready to disband her entire military establishment and destroy the small amount of arms remaining to her, if the neighboring countries will do the same thing with equal thoroughness. But if these countries are not willing to carry out the disarmament measures to which they are also bound by the Treaty of Versailles, Germany must at least maintain her demand for equality.

"The German Government sees in the British plan a possible basis for the solution of this question, but they must demand that the defense force existing in Germany shall not be abolished unless at least qualitative equality be accorded to Germany. . . ."

"Germany agrees in principle to a transitional period of five years during which to build up her national security, in the expectation that at the end of this period she will really be put on a footing of equality with the other States. She is also entirely ready to renounce all offensive weapons of every sort if the armed nations, on their side, will destroy their offensive weapons within a specified period, and if their use is forbidden by an international convention. Germany has only one desire: to be able to preserve her independence and defend her frontiers.

"According to a statement made by the French Minister of War in February, 1932, a large portion of the French colored troops can be immediately used on the French mainland. He therefore expressly includes them in the forces of the home country.

"It is therefore only just that the colored troops should also be considered by the Disarmament Conference as forming part of the French Army. While this is not being done, it is proposed that associations and organizations of a purely educational or sporting character which have no military training whatsoever should be reckoned as forming part of the Army in the case of Germany. In the case of other countries, however, there is no question of such organizations being counted as military effectives. Such a procedure is, of course, quite impossible. Germany would declare herself willing at any time, in the event of a mutual international supervision of armaments and of equal readiness on the part of other States, to subject these associations to such supervision in order to prove beyond doubt to the whole world that they are of an entirely unmilitary character.

"Moreover the German Government will not reject *any* prohibition of arms as being too drastic if it is applied in the same manner to all other States. . . ."

"These demands do not imply rearmament but only a desire for the disarmament of the other States. In this connection *I again welcome on behalf of the German Government the apt and far-sighted plan of the head of the Italian Government to create, by means of a special pact, close relations of confidence and co-operation between the four great European Powers, the United Kingdom, France, Italy, and Germany*. The German Government is in whole-hearted agreement with Mussolini's view that this would facilitate a permanent understanding, and will show the greatest good will, provided the other nations are prepared really to overcome any difficulties which may arise.

"The proposal made by President Roosevelt, of which I learned last night, has therefore earned the warmest thanks of the German Government. It is prepared to agree to this method of overcoming the international crisis, for they are also of the opinion that no permanent economic reconstruction is possible unless the disarmament question is solved. . . ."

"I am obliged to state that the reason for the present armaments of France or Poland can under no circumstances be the fear of those nations of a German invasion, for such fear would be only justified by the possession by Germany of modern offensive weapons. Germany, however, does not possess such modern offensive weapons at all; she has neither heavy artillery nor tanks nor bombing airplanes nor poisonous gases.

"The only nation therefore which might justifiably fear invasion is the German nation, which not only may not possess offensive weapons but is also restricted in its right to defensive weapons and is even forbidden to erect frontier fortifications.

"Germany is at all times prepared to renounce offensive weapons if the rest of the world does the same. *Germany is prepared to agree to any solemn pact of nonaggression because she does not think of attacking but only of acquiring security.*

"She would welcome the possibility suggested in President Roosevelt's proposal of bringing the United States into European relations as a guarantor of peace. The President's proposal is a ray of comfort for all who wish to co-operate sincerely in the maintenance of peace. . . ."

"The German Government and the German people will under no circumstances allow themselves to be forced to sign what would mean a perpetuation of the degradation of Germany. . . ."

"The attempt has been made in newspaper articles and in regrettable speeches to threaten Germany with sanctions, but such a monstrous step could only be considered as a punishment meted out to Germany for having pressed for the carrying out of the treaties by her demand for disarmament. Such a measure could only lead to the definite moral and effective invalidation of the treaties. Germany, however, even in this case, would never renounce her peaceful claims. The political and economic consequences, the chaos which such an attempt would bring on Europe would be the responsibility of those who used such means against a people which is doing the world no harm.

"Any such attempt or any attempt to do violence to Germany by means of a simple majority vote, contrary to the clear meaning of the treaties, could only be dictated by the intention of excluding us from the conferences. The German people, however, today possesses sufficient character in such a case not to impose its co-operation on other nations but, though with a heavy heart, to draw the only possible consequence.

"It would be difficult for us as a constantly defamed nation to continue to belong to the League of Nations.

"The German Government and the German nation are only too fully aware of the crisis of the present time. For many years Germany has given warnings regarding the methods which would and did inevitably lead to these political and economic results. If the present direction and the present methods are continued, there can be no doubt as to the ultimate result. After apparent political successes of individual nations, the resultant economic and political disasters for all will be all the more severe. We regard it as our first and most important task to avoid these results. . . ."

Press

Le Temps, May 19—Chancellor Hitler has completely changed his tune. . . . It remains to be seen of what value are Chancellor Hitler's declarations on the question which at present is being fought out in Geneva.

New York Times, May 18—Throughout Germany tonight the comment on the Chancellor's declaration is wholly of endorsement and acclamation.

London Times, May 18—This speech was earnestly but moderately worded; most of it might have been spoken by any of his recent predecessory. The case of united Germany in brief is that now, fifteen years after the war, the country expects to be treated on a footing of complete equality with other great powers. This claim is in principle irrefutable.

SPEECH OF JULY 22, 1933

Radio broadcast from Bayreuth

Background

1933

May 20—Election in Danzig gives great Nazi majority.

June 1—Announcement of the German "Four-Year Plan."

June 7—Mussolini makes the first announcement of the signing of the Four-Power Treaty—Germany, France, Great Britain, and Italy. Its object is to establish a ten-year collaboration between the signatories for a revision of the Paris Peace Treaties, as provided for in the League Covenant, and to take up the problem of disarmament, if the Geneva Conference comes to naught.

June 22—The Nazis in Austria are banned.

Social Democratic party dissolved in Germany. Its members are driven from the civil services.

June 27—Leader of the German National party, Hugenberg, resigns from the Reich Government.

July 8—Pacelli, Papal Nuncio, and von Papen sign a concordat.

July 14—Law is passed against the formation of new parties in Germany.

The Speech

"IF I take up any position towards the elections in the Evangelical Church I do this solely from the standpoint of the political leader, that is to say that I am not moved to do so by questions of faith, dogmatics, or doctrine. These are purely internal church affairs. But over and above these questions there are problems which compel the politician and the responsible leader of a people publicly to make known his position. They embrace 'volkic' and State interests in their relation to the Confessions.

"National Socialism has always affirmed that it is determined to take the Christian Churches under the protection of the State. For their part the churches cannot for a second doubt that they need the protection of the State, and that only through the State can they be enabled to fulfill their religious mission. Indeed, the churches demand this protection from the State. On the other hand, in consideration for this protection, the State must require from the churches that they in their turn should render to it that support which it needs to secure its permanence. Churches which fail to render to the State any positive support in this sense are for the State just as worthless as is for a church the State which is incapable of fulfilling its duties to the Church. The decisive factor which can justify the existence alike of church and State is the maintenance of men's spiritual and bodily health, for if that health were destroyed it would mean the end of the State and also the end of the Church. Therefore the State cannot afford to be indifferent to the religious affairs of its day and neither can, on the other hand, the churches be indifferent to the 'volkic'-political events and changes. Just as formerly Christianity and later the Reformation had their gigantic political effects, so will every political-'volkic' upheaval affect also the destiny of the churches. Only a fool can imagine that, for example, the victory of bolshevism could be irrelevant for the Catholic or the Evangelical Church and that therefore it would not disturb or even prevent the former activities of bishops or superintendents. The assertion that such dangers could be overcome through the action of the churches alone is untenable; it is contradicted by the facts. Neither the Catholic Church nor the Evangelical, nor the Russian-Uniate Church has been able or would be able to stay the advance of bolshevism. Wherever there has not been created 'volkic'-political defense to counter that advance, there the victory of communism is already won, or at least the battle is still undecided.

"It is thus clear that the churches themselves must take up a definite position towards such 'volkic'-political revolutionary movements. This the Roman Church in the Lateran Treaties has done for the first time in a clear and unequivocal form toward fascism. The German Concordat which has now been signed is the second equally clear step in this sphere. It is my sincere hope that thereby for Germany, too, through free agreement there has been produced a final clarification of spheres in the functions of the State and of one Church. As a National Socialist I have the most earnest wish that it may be possible to reach with the Evangelical Church also a no less clear settlement.

"But this presupposes that, if it is at all possible, the place of the many Evangelical Churches should be taken by a united Reichskirche. The State has no interest in negotiating with twenty-five or thirty churches, all the more since it is convinced that in face of the gigantic tasks of the present time here, too, it is only a concentration of all forces which can be regarded as effective. The powerful State can only wish to extend its protection to such religious organizations as can in their turn become of use to it.

"And in fact amongst the congregations of the Evangelical Confessions there has arisen in the 'German Christians' a Movement which is filled with the determination to do justice to the great tasks of the day and has aimed at a union of the Evangelical Churches of the German States and at a union of Confessions. If this question is now really on the way toward solution, in the judgment of history no false or stupid objections will be able to dispute the fact that this service was rendered by the 'volkic'-political revolution in Germany and by the Movement within the Evangelical Confessions which clearly and unequivocally professed its allegiance to this national and 'volkic' Movement at a time when unfortunately, just as in the Roman Church, many pastors and superintendents without reason opposed the national uprising in the most violent, indeed often in a fanatical, way.

"In the interest of the recovery of the German nation which I regard as indissolubly bound up with the National Socialist Movement I naturally wish that the new church elections should in their result support our new policy for People and State."

Press

Le Temps, July 24—Referring to the Protestant elections which had taken place the day before, the Chancellor openly took the side of the "German Christians" who had consistently supported the National Socialist State.

New York Times, July 23—In a radio address from this town (Bayreuth) late tonight, Chancellor Hitler upheld the Nazi German Christians "as a movement imbued by the will to rise equal to the great tasks of the present"—one that unequivocally espoused the national popular movement at a time when, just as within the Catholic Church, many Protestant clerics even fanatically opposed the national resurgence.

London Times, July 23—The speech broadcast by Herr Hitler last night inevitably imparted a political element into the campaign. Although Herr Hitler may not have meant it, this speech and a letter to Pastor Mueller, his adviser in Church matters, were exploited by the "German Christians" to give the impression that to vote against them would be to vote against him.

SPEECH OF AUGUST 27, 1933

Tannenberg

"Field Marshal von Hindenburg! Sir!

"Nineteen years have passed since the great day when the German people after centuries once more heard the thenceforth glorious name of Tannenberg. At that time an uncertain destiny hung menacingly over the people and the Reich. Through no fault of their own, the men of our nation had to defend Germany with their lives against an overwhelmingly superior force. With incomparable courage the armies of the West advanced and the few divisions in the East held. Nevertheless, crushing all beneath its heel, the overwhelming numbers of the Russian enemy drove deep into German territory. Large parts of East Prussia were a prey to destruction. Overcome with anxiety, the prayers of millions rose to the Almighty.

"Tannenberg meant our salvation. For not only was a battle won here, but the fortunes of Germany took a decisive turn; East Prussia was freed, and Germany was saved. From that day on there began those tremendous victories in the East which destroyed Russia as a fighting opponent, covered the German armies with immortal glory, and rendered the German nation eternally indebted and grateful to you, Sir, our Field Marshal.

"For no matter how Germany's heroic struggle ended, the Great War will always call forth in our people pride in the immortal sacrifices they laid at the altar of the freedom and life of the Fatherland. But in times to come history will be unable to understand that a nation, having lost a war it never wanted to wage, should be unworthily oppressed and shamelessly mistreated simply because it would not give up its freedom without a struggle, and with unimaginable suffering and unheard-of sacrifices tried to defend its right to live and its independence.

"At that time, Herr Field Marshal, fate was kind enough to allow me to share in the fight for our people's freedom as a simple soldier in the ranks of my brothers and comrades. Today I feel with deep emotion that it is a gracious gift of providence that I should stand here, on the soil of this glorious battlefield of the Great War, and speak in the name of the united German nation. And I am happy in the name of the nation to express once more, Herr Field Marshal, the gratitude and the deep reverence we feel for you.

"We are fortunate that we may celebrate this day of glory of the German nation together with him who made it glorious.

"The German Reich Government speaks in the name of the German nation when it expresses the fervent wish that your name may live forever in the nation's memory, and not for this deed alone. Not only the stone of this memorial shall cherish your memory, but generations of living witnesses will speak of their great ancestor in connection with this sacred soil which they will call their own.

"The German Reich Government as representative of the national honor and in fulfillment of the national debt of gratitude has therefore decided and made law that the soil of this province which today, Herr Field Marshal, is connected with your name, shall be free of the public imposts of the Reich and separate States so long as there is a male heir with the name of Hindenburg associated with it."

Press

Le Temps, August 28—The Chancellor declared among other things: "History will never understand why a blameless nation was given such shameful treatment merely because it had sought to defend its liberty."

London Times, August 28—It was at the opening of this

[Tannenberg] memorial in September, 1927, that President von Hindenburg repudiated responsibility for the war. Today Herr Hitler, in phrases no less decisive, repeated this repudiation.

•

SPEECH OF SEPTEMBER 1, 1933

Nuremberg, Festhalle of the Luitpoldhain

Background

1933

August 7—England and France protest against the Reich's anti-Austrian agitation.

August 27—Hitler declares that Germany will never surrender the Saar, no matter what the plebiscite decides.

The Speech

"WHEN in the year 1919 the National Socialist Movement came into being in order to create a new Reich in place of the Marxist-democratic Republic, such an enterprise seemed hopeless and foolish. Above all, the caviling intellectuals with their superficial historical education had no more than a pitying smile for such an undertaking. Most of them very well knew that Germany would fall on evil times. The greater part of the so-called intelligentsia understood very well that the rulers of the November Republic were either too evil or too incompetent to lead our people. But they did not recognize that this new regime could not be overcome by those forces which for fifty years have steadily retreated before the attacks of Marxism, finally, in the hour of greatest emergency, to capitulate miserably. Perhaps part of the reason for this was that the political leaders of the nation were aging, outdated. They could not or would not recognize the time necessary for the restoration of the strength of a nation.

"Strength cannot be found in an organization which has none. It was therefore an error when in 1919 and 1920 the men who recognized the distress of the Fatherland thought that a change in the leadership of the bourgeois parties would suddenly give them the strength to annihilate the inner enemy . . ."

"When one has glorified a false democracy for seventy years, one cannot attempt a dictatorship in the seventy-first year. It leads to ridiculous experiments.

"With few exceptions, age destroys the mental as well as the physical powers of generation. Because each man wishes to see for himself the growth and the fruits of his struggle, he seeks for easier, that is, quicker ways to transform his ideas into realities. The rootless intellectual, lacking all understanding of organic development, tries to evade the law of growth by hasty experiments. Nationalism, on the other hand, was ready from the very first to undertake the long and painful task of building up anew the structure which would later destroy Marxism. *But because this way was not understood by the superficial intelligence of our politicalized bourgeoisie, the new Movement could at first develop only among those groups who were not miseducated, who were uncomplicated and therefore closer to nature.*

"What the intellect of the intellectual could not see was grasped immediately by the soul, the heart, the instinct of this simple, primitive, but healthy man. It is another one of the tasks of the future to re-establish the unity between feeling and intellect; that is, to educate an unspoiled generation which will perceive with clear understanding the eternal law of development and at the same time will consciously return to the primitive instinct.

"National Socialism directed its appeal for the formation

of a new Movement to the broad masses of the people. Its first task was to inspire by suggestion those few whom it had first won over with the belief that they would one day be the saviors of their Fatherland. This problem of educating men to believe and have faith in themselves was as necessary as it was difficult. Men who socially and economically belonged to subordinate, and frequently oppressed groups, had to be given the political conviction that some day they would represent the leadership of the nation.

"While the former leaders of the bourgeois world talked about 'quiet progress' and declaimed profound treatises at tea parties, National Socialism began its march into the heart of the people. We held hundreds of thousands of demonstrations. A hundred and a hundred thousand times our speakers spoke in meeting halls, in small, smoky taverns, and in great sports arenas. And each demonstration not only won us new adherents, but above all made the others firm in their belief and filled them by suggestion with the kind of self-confidence without which success is not possible. The others talked about democracy and kept away from the people. National Socialism talked about authority, but it fought and wrestled with the people as no movement in Germany had ever done.

"For all time to come this city shall be the place where our Movement will hold its Party Congress, for it was here that for the first time we proclaimed the new will of Germany.

"It is for this reason that you have been convoked here for the Fifth Party Congress of the N.S.D.A.P., the first in the new German Reich. A miracle has taken place in Germany. . . ."

"The National Socialist Revolution has overthrown the republic of treason and perjury, and in its place has created once more a Reich of honor, loyalty, and decency. It is our great good fortune that we did not have to bring about this Revolution as leaders of the 'historic minority' against the majority of the German nation. We rejoice that at the end of our struggle but before the final turn in our destiny, the overwhelming majority of the German people had already declared itself for our principles. Thus it was possible to accomplish one of the greatest revolutions in history with hardly any bloodshed. As a result of the splendid organization of the movement which brought about this Revolution, at no moment did we lose control of it.

"Aside from the Fascist Revolution in Italy, no similar historic action is comparable in discipline and order with the National Socialist uprising. It is particularly pleasing that today the great majority of the German people stand loyal and united behind the new regime. . . ."

"Our perilous political situation was accompanied by a no less dangerous economic situation. The rapid decline of the past winter seemed to be leading to a complete collapse. The great historian, Mommsen, once characterized the Jews in the life of nations as a 'ferment of decomposition.' In Germany this decomposition had already made great progress. National Socialism opposed with fierce resoluteness this creeping 'decline of the West,' because we were convinced that those inner values which are natural to the civilized nations of Europe, and to our own German nation in particular, had not yet been completely destroyed. . . ."

"As sole possessor of State power, the Party must recognize that it bears the entire responsibility for the course of German history. The work of education which the Movement must carry on is tremendous. For it is not enough to organize the State in accordance with pacific principles; it is necessary to educate the people inwardly. Only if the people has an intimate sympathy with the principles and methods which inspire and move the organization of its State, will there grow up a living organism instead of a dead, because purely formal and mechanistic, organization.

"Among the tasks we face, the most important is the question of eliminating unemployment. The danger in unemployment is not only a material one. It is neither logical, nor moral, nor just, to continue taking away from those who are able to work a part of the fruits of their industry in order to maintain those unable to work—no matter for what reasons they are unable. It is more logical to distribute the work itself instead of distributing wages. No one has a moral right to demand that others should work for him so that he will not have to work himself. Each has a right to demand that the political organization of his nation, the State, find ways and means to give work to all.

"We are following paths for which there is hardly any model in history. It is thus at any time possible that one or another measure that we take today may prove unworkable. It is thus all the more necessary to put a stop to that carping criticism which tends only towards disintegration. It is no matter whether a thousand critics live or die, what does matter is whether a people shall be conquered and ruined and in consequence as a community lose its life. All those who since November, 1918, through their mad or criminal action hurled our people into their present misfortunes, those who proclaimed such phrases as 'Freedom,' 'Brotherliness,' and 'Equality,' as the *leit-motiv* of their action—they do not share today the fate and the sufferings of the victims of their policy! Millions of our German fellow-countrymen through them have been given over to the hardest stress imaginable. Need, misery, hunger, do violence to their existence. Those who misled them indeed enjoy abroad the freedom to slander their own people for foreign gold, the liberty to deliver them up to the hatred of their neighbors: they would, if they could, see them attacked and shot down, defenseless, on the battlefield. . . ."

"The rise and the astonishing final victory of the National Socialist Movement would never have happened if the Party had ever formulated the principle that in our ranks everyone can do as he likes. This watchword of democratic freedom led only to insecurity, indiscipline, and at length to the downfall and destruction of all authority. *Our opponents' objection that we, too, once made use of these rights, will not hold water; for we made use of an unreasonable right, which was part and parcel of an unreasonable system, in order to overthrow the unreason of this system.* No fruit falls which is not ripe for falling. When old Germany fell, it betrayed its inner weakness, just as the November Republic has revealed its weakness to everyone by now.

"By its political education, therefore, the Party will have to fortify the mind of the German people against any tendency to regression. While we deny the parliamentary-democratic principle, we champion most definitely the right of the people itself to determine its own life. In the parliamentary system we do not recognize any true expression of the will of the people, but we see in it a perversion, if not a violation, of that will. The will of a people to maintain its existence appears first and in its most useful form in its best brains.

"The greater the tasks with which we are faced, the greater must be the authority of those who must accomplish these tasks. It is important that the self-assurance of the leaders of the whole organization in their decisions should arouse in the members and followers of the Party an untroubled confidence. For the people will justifiably never understand it if they are suddenly asked to discuss problems which their leaders cannot cope with. It is conceivable that even wise men should not in questions of special difficulty be able to reach complete clarity. But it means a capitulation of all leadership if it hands over precisely those questions to public discussion and allows the public to state its views. For the leaders thereby imply that the masses have more judgment than they themselves have. This cannot be the attitude of the National Socialist party. The Party must be convinced that it will be able to cope with all problems, that because it has chosen its human material in living struggle, its leaders are politically the most competent men in Germany.

"Our Party must follow the same law that it wishes to see the masses of the nation follow. It must, therefore, constantly educate itself to recognize authority, to submit voluntarily to the highest discipline, so that it will be able to educate the followers of the Party to do the same. And in doing this the Party must be hard and logical. . . ."

"Power and the brutal application of power can accomplish much. But in the long run no state of affairs is secure unless it is firmly rooted in logic. Above all: The National Socialist Movement must profess its faith in that heroism which is content to face all opposition and every trial rather than for a moment to be false to the principles which it has recognized to be right. The Movement must be filled with one fear alone—the fear lest the time should ever come when it could be charged with dishonesty or thoughtlessness.

"To save a nation one must think heroically. But the heroic thinker must always be willing to renounce the approval of his contemporaries where truth is at stake.

"May the very manner of this demonstration renew our understanding that the Government of the nation must never harden into a purely bureaucratic machine: it must ever remain a living leadership, a leadership which does not view the people as an object of its activity, but which lives within the people, feels with the people and fights for the people. Forms and organizations can pass, but what does and must remain is the living substance of flesh and blood. All of us desire that the German people shall remain forever upon this earth, and we believe that by our struggle we are but carrying out the will of the Creator, who imbued all creatures with the instinct for self-preservation. Long live our nation. Long live the National Socialist party!"

Press

Le Temps, September 2—The Chancellor has made a final accounting with liberalism which, he says, leads to insecurity in intellectual life. Both in art and in politics, he says, Marxism is the same as nihilism.

London Times, September 2—The proclamation contained a vehement attack on the Jews and also condemned the democratic system. Our own good sense and our determination, the proclamation said, will prevent our people for all time from abandoning the inner unity of thought and desire for the sake of the slogan, "The right of free criticism."

•

SPEECH OF SEPTEMBER 3, 1933

Nuremberg

The Speech

". . . IN ORDER to understand the diseases from which a people suffers, it is first necessary to understand how a people is built up. Almost all the peoples of the world are composed today of different racial primary elements. These original elements are each characterized by different capacities. Only in the primitive functions of life can men be considered as precisely like each other. Beyond these primitive functions they immediately begin to be differentiated in their characters, their dispositions, and capacities. The differences between the individual races, both in part externally and, of course, also in their inner natures, can be quite enormous and in fact are so. The gulf between the lowest creature which can still be styled man and our highest races is greater than that between the lowest type of man and the highest ape.

"If on this earth there were not some races which today determine its cultural appearance, it would hardly be possible to speak of any such thing as human civilization. For this neither climate nor education can be regarded as responsible, but only man himself who was endowed by providence with this capacity.

"But if this cultural capacity is fundamentally inherent in certain races, its full effect is realized only under certain favorable circumstances. Man as an individual, whatever powers he may have in himself, will be incapable of higher achievements unless he can place the powers of many in the service of a single idea, a single conception, a single will, and can unite them for a single action.

"A glance at Nature shows us that creatures belonging to a pure race, not merely corporeally but in character and capacities, are more or less of equal value. This equality is the greatest hindrance in the way of the formation of any community in work; for since every higher civilization receives its stamp through achievements which are possible only through uniting the forces of human labor, it is thus essential that a number of individuals must sacrifice a part of their individual freedom and must subject themselves to a single will. However much reason may counsel such a course, in reality it would be difficult amongst those who are complete equals to demonstrate the reasons why in the last resort one must be in a position to assert his will as against that of the others.

"The two conceptions—Command and Obedience—however, exercise quite another and more compelling force when folk of *different* value come into conflict or association with each other, and then through the action of the stronger section are bound together in pursuit of a common purpose.

"The most primitive form of association for a common purpose can already be traced at the moment when man forces his supremacy upon the animals, tears them from the freedom of their former life, and builds them into his own life-process without troubling himself whether his animal-helper consents thereto or not.

"But long ago man has proceeded in the same way with his fellow-man. The higher race—at first 'higher' in the sense of possessing a greater gift for organization—subjects to itself a lower race and thus constitutes a relationship which now embraces races of unequal value. *Thus there results the subjection of a number of people under the will often of only a few persons, a subjection based simply on the right of the stronger, a right which, as we see it in Nature, can be regarded as the sole conceivable right because founded on reason.* The wild mustang does not take upon itself the yoke imposed by man either voluntarily or joyfully; neither does one people welcome the violence of another.

"But, despite this, in the course of a long development this compulsion has very often been converted into a blessing for all parties. Thus were formed those communities which created the essential features of human organization through the welding together of different races. And this organization always demands the subjection of the will and the activity of many under the will and the energy of a single individual. As men come to discover the astonishing results of this concentration of their capacity and labor-force they begin to recognize not merely the expediency but also the necessity of such action. And thus it is that a great and significant Aryan civilization did not arise where Aryans alone were living in racial purity, but always where they formed a vital association with races otherwise constituted, an association founded not on mixture of blood but on the basis of an organic community of purpose. And what was at first undoubtedly felt by the conquered as bitter compulsion, later became in spite of this even for them a blessing. Unconsciously in the master-people there grew up ever more clearly and vitally a recognition of the ethical demand that their supremacy must be no arbitrary rule but must be controlled by a noble reasonableness. The capacity to subdue others was not given to them by providence in order to make the subjects feel that the lordship of their conqueror was a meaningless tyranny, a mere oppression: *that capacity was given that through the union of the conqueror's genius with the strength of the conquered they might create for both alike an existence which because it was useful was not degrading to man.*

"However this process of the formation of a people and a State was begun, its beginning signified the close of humanity's communistic age. For communism is not a higher stage of development: rather it is the most primitive form of life—the starting-point.

"Men of completely similar characteristics, men who are precisely like each other and endowed with the same capacities, will be of necessity also alike in their achievement. This condition is realized in the case of peoples who are throughout of one and the same race. Where these conditions are realized, the individual result of the activity of each will correspond only with the general average of all. . . . In this case it can be a question only of quite primitive values, and the condition for any clear definition of the idea of property is lacking because of the absence of any differentiation in achievement which is essential for the rise of such a concept. . . ."

"In such a state communism is therefore a natural and morally comprehensible ordering of society. But when men of very different values have met together the result of their achievements will also be different, that is to say that the race which stands higher in the scale of quality will contribute more to the sum total of common work than the race which is lower in the qualitative scale. And in particular men's capacities will lie on different levels. The primitive capacity of the one race will from the first produce values other than those higher developed or otherwise constituted values produced by the other partner in the common life. As a consequence the administration of the labor-product will necessarily lead to a division which proceeds from a consideration of the character of the achievement, in other words:

that which has been created will be administered as property on the same basis as that of its origin. The conception of private property is thus inseparably connected with the conviction that the capacities of men are different alike in character and in value and thus, further, that men themselves are different in character and value.

"But one cannot in one sphere of life accept this difference in value—which I will now call difference in talent—as giving rise to a moral claim on the result produced by this superiority and then go on to deny that difference in another sphere. That would be to act illogically. . . . One cannot in fact proceed to maintain that all alike have the same capacity for politics, that is for the most important sphere in the entire conduct of life.

"While it is denied that everyone in a nation is capable of administering a court or a factory or of appointing its administration, yet that they are all capable of administering the State or of appointing its administrators is solemnly certified in the name of democracy.

"But here is a direct contradiction: either because of equal capacity all men are equally capable of administering a State, and then the maintenance of the concept of property is not only unjust but simply stupid, or men are in truth not in a position to take into their common administration as common property that sum-total of material and cultural treasure which the nation as a whole has created, and then in that case they are far less in a position to govern the State in common. . . . *The State does not owe its existence to all but only to a definite section—the section which formerly created the State and which still supports and maintains it.* This view is not unjust or hard: it is simply a statement of the truth. . . . The German people arose in no other way than did almost all of the truly creative civilized peoples in the world of which we have any knowledge. A race, though small in numbers yet with capacities for organization and possessing a creative gift in the sphere of culture, in the course of many centuries spread itself over other peoples, absorbing some, adapting itself to others. All the different elements of which our people is composed naturally brought with them into this alliance their special capacities; but the alliance itself was created solely by a single core which fashioned both people and State. This core-people caused its language to prevail not, of course, without borrowings from its subjects, and in the end it subdued all for such a length of time to a common destiny that the life of the people which controlled the State became indissolubly united with the life of the other parts which were gradually fused into and on to it. Thus in course of time out of the conquerors and the conquered there was long since created a single community. And that community is our German people of today, and as it is today we love it and cling to it. In the course of its thousand years of history all its very varied characteristics, each of them so different from the others, have become familiar and dear. So great is this community of which we all form a part that we rejoice at every contribution which adds to our wealth. . . ."

"For one cannot only infer from the fact of race that certain capacities will be present, one can also start from the capacities and infer the race. That means, for instance, that it is not necessary first to discover musically gifted persons through the fact of their race in order to entrust to them the encouragement of music, but Music discloses the Race by discovering the capacity.

"The sole interest of a people must be that this voice of inherited talent should always be given a hearing. For this voice gives to the people, not men under the violence of compulsion since they were never inwardly born for such an activity, but men filled with a passion and therefore devoted to their task.

"And just as in all spheres of life we cannot feel any jealousy when those who are specially born thereto, i.e., endowed from the outset, exercise decisive influence, so it is in the sphere of the political safeguarding of that which in the course of the millennia has become for us a people. Just as the unmusical person will not feel himself injured or insulted because he does not compose music or conduct an orchestra like one who is musically gifted, so in every other sphere the appointment of qualified persons cannot be regarded as a slight by those who have no capacities in that field. And in fact this does not occur; only a conscious perversion could breed such madness.

"Starting from the fact that any created thing can be maintained only by the same force which created it, it follows that the body of a people can be maintained only by those forces which called it into being and which through their capacity for organization welded it together and solidified it. Thus all who love their people and wish for its maintenance must therefore see to it that that part of the people can bring its political capacities into play which formerly was responsible for the political formation and development of this community. . . ."

"Since the bourgeoisie, as a new class, claimed and received the political leadership of the nation, the reasonable organic evolution was interrupted in the most important sphere of all. The German bourgeoisie as a social body was the product of a selection which was based essentially less upon political than upon economic functions. The Liberalistic age through the introduction of money and property as the standard of valuation in the bourgeoisie produced a social class which corresponded with its own essential character. That many members of this social class did produce outstanding achievements in many spheres not concerned with material interests is not really connected with any valuation based upon the bourgeois idea, but rather with those fundamental racial values which survived in them. But in themselves these have no relation to the concept of the bourgeoisie; for membership of this social class all that was necessary was talent in the economic sphere which was evidenced by good fortune, and a talent in the mental or cultural sphere which similarly could be turned into some form of economic success. In no case for determining membership of this class were such characteristics as valor or heroism the decisive test. On the contrary: since economic life has for the most part more unheroic than heroic features, the German bourgeoisie had very little heroic about it: it was rather 'economic.' And the bourgeois parties were a true reflection of this cast of soul—associations of hucksters, void of any capacity for a real leadership of the people.

"And the people felt that. For that is the remarkable thing. Since from different racial cores a people came into being, each part learned gradually to tolerate the other—so long as it remained within its own sphere. Thus the people tolerates music only when it is good music, that is when it is practised by that part of the people which is born for music. It tolerates those engineers only who understand the law of their craft and, thank God! it tolerates only those politicians whose calling is written on their brows. . . ."

"But with the claim of the German bourgeoisie to lead the nation a class of society presented itself to the people as leaders which was never born to the task.

"And this serves also to explain how it was that a bourgeoisie which was not in the least destined for political leadership sought to transfer to the political sphere the methods and usages of economic life. For with the anonymous share in a limited liability company corresponds the anonymous voting-paper, and with the majority of shareholders corresponds the parliamentary coalition!

"And it was clear that with either of these it was impossible to find any logical, ethical, or moral foundation for the conception of private property. And the farther the age lapsed into these internal contradictions, the easier it was for an alien race, consistently pursuing its purpose, to foster the people's mistrust in its political leadership—a mistrust that had already instinctively arisen—and to shatter completely all confidence in that leadership. For the same reason it is also quite natural that this bourgeoisie, being a completely inorganic political leadership and possessing no native talent or capacity for its task, must break down in face of the attack of Marxism while there could be no thought of bringing about a change in the situation through the bourgeoisie or by means of its political organizations. . . . And thus the question which arose after the collapse of the year 1918 was only this: first, whether there yet remained in our people a sufficiently large core of that part of the race which formerly had begun and effected the creation of our people and which therefore can alone be capable of leading and sustaining the people in the future, and secondly whether one could discover this part and entrust it with the leadership.

"And it was further clear that since the new formation of our society had developed out of economic functions, the capacity for political leadership could in no way be presumed to be necessarily identifiable with the social position of the individual German, that is to say, that men drawn from lower economic or social classes might be well fitted to lead the people just as on the other hand members of the highest social classes, especially those who represented economic or financial interests, would have to be rejected. The native talent necessary for our purpose—that alone must be decisive; our task was to discover these men out of all the different towns, callings, and classes.

"This was in truth a socialistic action, for insofar as I seek, for every function in life, to find from my people the man who was born for this task in order to hand over to him in this sphere full responsibility without considering to what economic or social class he belongs. . . ."

"And thus it was that in the year 1919 I set forth a program, I defined a tendency which was consciously a blow in the face of the pacifist-democratic world. If there were still in our people men of the kind we needed, then victory was certain. For this fanaticism in decision and in action was bound to draw to itself men of kindred nature. Wherever those who possessed these characteristics might be, they were bound one day to hear the voice which was that of their blood, and willy-nilly they would follow the Movement which was the expression of their own inmost being. That might take five, ten, or twenty years, but gradually there grew up within the State of Democracy the State of Authority, within the Reich of lamentable absurdity a core of fanatical devotion and ruthless determination. There was only one possible danger which might oppose this development—that the opponent might understand the principle, might clearly grasp these ideas and then avoid all opposition, or on the other hand that he might with the last extreme of brutality annihilate the new association at the very beginning and nip it in the bud. . . ."

"And so I was able to wait for fourteen years, ever more and more assured that our hour must come. For in these years just as a magnet draws to itself the steel splinters so did our Movement gather together from all classes and callings and walks of life the forces in the German people which can form and also maintain States.

"Once more it was proved that one may well be able to control a great business and yet be incapable of leading even a group of eight men. And on the other hand it was shown that from peasants' rooms and workmen's huts came the born leaders, for that was the wonderful thing in this period when we were propagating our idea that its waves spread over the whole country and drew man after man, woman after woman under its spell. While bourgeois politicians were asking questions about our program they never dreamed that hundreds of thousands were devoting themselves to this Movement simply because their inner receiver was adjusted to the wavelength of this idea. . . . And therein lies the Movement's mighty mission of reconciliation between the classes. A new valuation of men begins—not according to the standards of Liberalistic thought but according to the measures which

Nature has determined. And the more the opponent believed that he could check the development through terrorism applied only in such doses as his character allowed him to use, the more he encouraged it. Nietzsche's word that a blow which does not fell a strong man only strengthens him found its verification a thousandfold. Every blow increased our defiance, every persecution increased our resolution, and that which did fall away proved in its falling away to be the greatest good fortune for the Movement. . . ."

"Out of forty-five million adult men three million fighters have organized themselves: they represent the political leadership of the nation. . . . Into their hands the people in full confidence has placed its destiny. But thereby the organization has undertaken a solemn obligation: it must see to it that this core whose mission it is to safeguard the stability of the political leadership in Germany must be preserved for all time.

"The task of the Movement is to secure that through a skillful method in the choice of recruits only those are received into membership who will never change the inmost character of these forces which sustain our nation. It must realize that it is not the number of members of this core which counts but only its inner worth and thus its inner homogeneity. The Movement must make it clear that the selection of members in the future must proceed according to the same rigorous principles which a stern fate has imposed upon us in the past. . . ."

"Insofar then as we devote ourselves to the care of our own blood—that blood which has been entrusted to us by destiny—we are at the same time doing our best to help to safeguard other peoples from diseases which spring from race to race, from people to people. If in West or Central Europe but one single people were to fall a victim to bolshevism, this poison would continue its ravages, it would devastate the oldest, the fairest civilization which can today be found upon this earth.

"Germany by taking upon itself this conflict does but ful-

fill, as so often before in her history, a truly European mission."

Press

Le Temps, September 5—The Fuehrer wants to establish an aristocracy of leaders who will be chosen from the people. He has advanced the same reasons as Napoleon: "Every private has a marshal's baton in his pack." But there is a great difference between conquest and government. The Fuehrer must now prove that he can place his moral force at the service of the true interests of his country and build its political life with the same skill and good fortune with which he built his own Party."

•

SPEECH OF OCTOBER 14, 1933

Berlin, Reichstag

Background

1933

September 21—Beginning of the Reichstag Fire Trial.

October 3—Attempted assassination of Dollfuss in the Parliament Building in Vienna.

October 13—American Federation of Labor declares a boycott against Nazi goods.

October 14—Germany withdraws from the League of Nations and the Disarmament Conference. At the request of Hitler, Hindenburg dissolves the Reichstag. New elections will be held on November 12.

The Speech

"IN NOVEMBER, 1918, in trustful faith in the assurances laid down in President Wilson's fourteen points, the German people lowered their arms in the unholy struggle that had reached an end; for which, perchance, individual statesmen but certainly not the peoples could be made responsible. . . ."

"If in those months the world had in a fair manner stretched out a hand to a prostrate opponent, much suffering and endless disappointments would have been spared humanity. The German people suffered the worst possible disappointment. Never before has the vanquished so honestly endeavored to assist in healing the wounds of its opponents as had the German people during the long years, fulfilling dictates loaded upon them. If all of these sacrifices could not lead to real pacification of peoples, this was due solely to the nature of the Treaty, which, in its attempt to render eternal the concepts of the victor over the vanquished, also had to eternalize the hatred of the enemy. . . ."

"The German people destroyed their weapons. Relying upon the good faith of their former enemies, they, themselves, fulfilled the obligation of the treaties with really fanatical fidelity. Unmeasureable quantities of naval, aerial, and land war material were dismantled, destroyed, or scrapped. According to the wish of the dictating powers, a small professional army inadequately armed replaced the former army of millions.

"Political leadership of the nation, however, at this time lay in the hands of people who were spiritually rooted in a world of the victor States. The German people could rightly expect for this reason alone that the rest of the world would redeem its promise in the same manner as the German people, who in the sweat of their labor amid thousandfold distress and unspeakable privations were engaged in redeeming their treaty obligations.

"No war can become the permanent condition of mankind. No peace can be the perpetuation of war. Some time victors and vanquished must find the way back into the community of mutual understanding and confidence. For a decade and a half the German people have hoped and waited for the time when the end of war would at last become the end of hatred and enmity. The purpose of the Versailles Treaty, however, did not seem to be the one to give mankind the final peace, but rather to keep it in a state of perpetual hatred. The consequences were unavoidable. When right definitely yields to might, a lasting uncertainty will derange and arrest all normal functions of national life.

"In concluding this Treaty, it was completely forgotten that the reconstruction of the world cannot be vouchsafed by the slave labor of the violated nation, but solely through trustful co-operation of all, and that for this co-operative effort the elimination of war psychosis is the foremost pre-condition. It was also forgotten that the problematical question of responsibility for war cannot be cleared up historically by having the victor compel the vanquished, as the introduction to the peace treaty, to sign his confession of guilt.

"The German people is most deeply convinced of its guiltlessness for the war. Other participants in this tragic misfortune may, as far as we are concerned, have the same conviction. . . ."

"What sense, if any, did the World War have if its consequences, not only for the vanquished but also for the victors, manifest themselves only in an endless chain of economic catastrophes? The welfare of nations is not any greater, and their political happiness and their human contentment have not really become deeper. Armies of unemployed have developed into a new class of society. And precisely as the nations' economic foundations have been shaken, so now also are their social foundations beginning to weaken.

"Germany had suffered most from these consequences of the peace treaties and the general instability arising therefrom. The number of unemployed mounted to one-third of the number normally employed in the nation's productive life. That means, however, that in Germany some 20,000,000 human beings, counting in the members of families, out of 65,000,000 were without the possibility of existence and found a hopeless future staring them in the face.

"It was merely a question of time when this army, economically disinherited, had become an army of fanatics who politically and socially were estranged to the world. One of the oldest lands of culture in present-day civilized humanity stood with more than 6,000,000 Communists at the brink of a catastrophe which only conceited ignorance could overlook. . . ."

"If Red insurrection had overswept Germany like a firebrand, certainly Western Europe's lands of culture would have realized that it is not immaterial whether on the Rhine and on the North Sea the outposts of the spiritually and revolutionary expansive Asiatic world empire stood watch or the peaceful German peasants and workers, who, in honest feeling of comradeship with other nations of our European culture, desire to earn their bread by honest labor. When the National Socialist Movement tore Germany back from the brink of this threatening catastrophe, it not only saved the German people but also rendered a historical service to the rest of Europe. . . ."

"We owe Providence humble thanks for not withholding success from our fight against the distress of unemployment and for saving the German peasant. In the course of executing the program, the successful conclusion of which we predicted four years ago, two and a quarter million out of six million unemployed have, in scarcely eight months, again been led into useful production.

"The best witness for this tremendous achievement is the German nation itself. It shall prove to the world that it is guided by a regime which knows no aim but with peaceful labor and civilized culture to assist in the reconstruction of a world which today could hardly be called happy. This world, however, which we do no harm and only wish it would let us work peaceably, has been persecuting us for months with a flood of lies and slander.

"While in Germany a revolution occurred—not like the French and the Russian with their catacomb butcheries and the murdered hostages; not like the communards of Paris or the Red revolutionaries of Bavaria and Hungary who destroyed culturally valuable buildings and art works with petroleum but contrarily smashed not a single show window, looted no store, damaged no house—unscrupulous agitators spread a flood of atrocity tales only comparable to the lies fabricated by the same elements at the beginning of the war.

"Tens of thousands of Americans, Englishmen and Frenchmen during these months visited Germany and could with their own eyes make observations that there was no land on earth with more law and more order than present-day Germany, that in no land in the world was a person's property more highly respected than in Germany, but that perhaps, also, to be sure, in no land in the world is there a sharper combat against those who, as criminal elements, believe they may freely let their low instincts vent themselves at the expense of their fellow-humans. It is these and their communistic accomplices who today are attempting to set honest and decent nations at loggerheads.

"The German nation has no reason to envy the rest of the world for this gain. We are convinced that a few years will suffice thoroughly to open the eyes of honor-loving citizens of other nations concerning the real value of those worthy elements, who, traveling under the effective flag of political fugitives, cleared out of the scenes of their more or less extensive economic consciencelessness.

"But what would this world say about Germany if we permitted a mock trial to be held in favor of a creature who attempted to set fire to the British Parliament, a mock trial whose only meaning could be that of placing British justice and its judges on a lower level than such a scoundrel? As a

German and National Socialist I would have no interest in exerting myself in Germany on behalf of a foreigner who in England tries to undermine the State and the laws effective there or even attacks with fire the architectural symbol of the British Constitution.

"And even if this subject—from which disgrace we hope God may spare us—were a German, we would not back him, but rather would deeply regret that such a misfortune had struck us, and we would harbor but only one wish, namely, that British justice might mercilessly liberate humanity from such a menace. Collaterally, however, we also possess honor enough to be filled with indignation at the spectacle which, instigated by obscure elements, is intended but to shame and dishonor Germany's highest court.

"We are extremely sad at the thought that by such methods nations are set at loggerheads and estranged, of whom we know that in their hearts they stand infinitely above these elements—nations whom we desire to respect and with whom we are anxious to live together in honest friendship. These noxious low-class fellows succeeded in starting the world psychosis whose inner morbid hysterical conflict may be branded as classic.

"The same elements which on one hand lament 'oppression' and 'tyrannization' of the poor German people by Nazi potentates, declare on the other hand, with brazen unconcern, that the Germans' pacific professions are valueless because they are uttered only by a few Nazi Ministers or the Chancellor, whereas in the nation a wild war spirit is raging. Thus the German people are represented at one time as piteously unhappy and oppressed, at another time as brutally aggressive—as the case may call for. I regard it as a sign of a nobler sense of justice that French Premier Daladier, in his last speech, found words to indicate the spirit of conciliatory understanding for which untold millions of Germans are grateful at heart.

"National Socialist Germany has no other wish than to direct the competition of European people again to those fields of endeavor upon which they have given to all humanity through the noblest mutual rivalry those magnificent boons to civilization, culture, and art which today enrich and beautify the picture of the world. Similarly, we take cognizance, with hopeful emotion, of the assurance that the French Government, under its present chief, does not intend to wound the feelings of or humiliate the German people.

"We are touched by the reference to the unfortunately but too sad truth that these two great peoples so often in history have sacrificed the blood of their best youths and men on the battlefields. I speak in the name of the entire German people when I solemnly declare that we all are imbued with the sincere wish to wipe out an enmity that, as regards its sacrifices, is all out of proportion to any possible gain.

"The German people are convinced that its martial honor in thousands of battles and skirmishes has remained clean and without blemish, exactly as we also see in the French soldier our old glory-bedecked opponent.

"We and the entire German people would all be happy at the thought of sparing to the children and to the children's children of our people what we ourselves as honorable men in bitter long years have had to witness and what we ourselves have endured in the way of misery and pain. The history of the last 150 years, through all their vicissitudes, ought to have taught both peoples one thing, namely, that the essential changes of lasting duration are no longer possible no matter how much blood is sacrificed.

"As a National Socialist I, together with all my followers, decline on the very basis of our nationalistic principles to conquer the people of a strange nation who will not love us anyway by sacrificing the blood and lives of those who are dear and precious to us. It would be a tremendous event for all humanity if the two peoples could once and for all ban force from their common life.

"The German people are ready for this. While we frankly

claim the rights granted to us by the treaty itself, I will say just as frankly that, beyond this, *there are no more territorial conflicts as far as Germany is concerned. After the return of the Saar to the Reich only a madman could believe in the possibility of war between the two States*—for which, as we see it, no moral or reasonably justifiable ground exists. Nobody can wish that millions of young lives be annihilated for the sake of a boundary correction of doubtful extent and of doubtful value.

"When, however, the French Premier asks why the German youth is marching and falling in line, I reply it is not to demonstrate against France, but to evince that political determination, and give visible evidence thereof, that was necessary for throwing down communism and that will be necessary to hold it down. There is in Germany but one arms-bearer, and that is the Army. There exists for National Socialist organizations but one enemy, and that is communism.

"The world, however, must accept the fact that the German people, for their internal organization and to preserve our people from this danger, will choose those forms which alone can guarantee success. If the rest of the world digs itself in behind indestructible fortresses, builds tremendous aerial squadrons, constructs giant tanks and molds enormous cannon, it cannot talk of being threatened because German National Socialists, totally unarmed, are marching in columns of four and thereby are giving visible expression of effective protection to the German community of citizens.

"If, furthermore, French Premier Daladier raises the question as to why, forsooth, Germany demands weapons which must later be destroyed anyway, he is in error—the German people and the German Government have not demanded weapons at all, but equality.

"If the world decides that all weapons, including the last machine gun, are to be destroyed, we are ready immediately to join such a convention. If the world decides that certain categories of weapons are to be destroyed we are ready to renounce them from the beginning. If, however, the world concedes certain weapons to every nation we are not ready to permit ourselves, in principle, to be excluded therefrom as a nation of minor rank.

"If, in accordance with our convictions, we defend this viewpoint honorably we are more decent partners for other nations than if we were ready, in contravention of this conviction, to accept humiliating dishonorable conditions. Our signature binds the whole nation, whereas a dishonorable, characterless negotiator is only disavowed by his own people. When we wish to make treaties with the English, French or Poles, we want from the start to make them only with men who think and act 100 per cent English, French or Polish, for we do not want pacts with negotiators but with nations. . . ."

"The German people has fulfilled its disarmament obligations to more than the full measure. The turn would seem to have come for armed nations to do no less than meet their analogous obligations. The German Government is not participating in this conference in order to barter for a single cannon or machine gun for the German people, but as a factor with equal rights to help in the general pacification of the world. Germany's security constitutes no inferior right to the security of the other nations.

"If British Acting-Premier Baldwin regards it as self-evident that England understands disarmament to mean nothing but disarmament of the more highly armed nations concomitantly with England's increasing armaments to a common level, then will it be an unfair reproach upon Germany, when, finally, as a member with equal rights in this conference, it claims the same interpretation for itself?

"In this demand by Germany there cannot possibly be any threat to the rest of the Powers, for the defensive armament of other peoples is constructed to ward off the heaviest weapons of attack, while Germany demands no weapons of attack, but only those defensive arms which in the future are not to be forbidden, but permitted to all nations. Here, too, Germany is ready at once to content itself numerically with the minimum that is all out of proportion to the gigantic armaments of attack and defense of our former enemies.

"The deliberate relegation of our people to an inferior class, in that every nation of the world is conceded the self-evident right which is denied us, we feel, is the perpetuation of a discrimination unbearable to us. In my peace speech of last May I said that under such conditions we would regretfully no longer be able to belong to the League or to participate in international conferences. . . ."

"We cling with exactly the same boundless love to our people as we, out of this love, wish for understanding with other nations and try, whenever we can, to achieve it. It is, however, impossible for us, as representatives of an honorable nation and of an honest conscience, to participate in institutions under conditions that would be bearable only for the dishonorable. As far as we are concerned, there may once have been men who may have believed they could participate in international conferences, even though thus weighed down. It is futile to seek to establish whether they themselves were the best part of our nation, but it is certain that the best part of the nation never backed them. . . ."

"Having gathered from the declarations of the official representatives of the Great Powers that they are not thinking of genuine equality for Germany at the moment, it is thus not possible at present for Germany, so placed in a dishonorable position, to intrude itself upon other nations.

"Threats of force, if carried out, could only be breaches of law. The German Government is most deeply convinced that her appeal to the whole German nation will prove to the world that the Government's love of peace as well as its conception of honor are also those of the whole nation. To give this claim documentary form, I decided to beg the Reich President to dissolve the Reichstag and give the German people opportunity for making a historic affirmation by means of new elections, coupled with a plebiscite not only for the purpose of approving the Government's basic principles but also for testifying to their unreserved unity with them. May the world, from such an affirmation, gain the conviction that the German people, in this battle for equality and honor, declares itself completely at one with the Government, but also that both are animated at heart by no other desire than to help end the human epoch of tragic aberrations, regrettable quarrels and fights between those who, as inhabitants of the culturally most important continent, have to fulfill the common mission before all mankind.

"May this tremendous manifestation of our people for peace with honor succeed, creating in the interrelationships of European States such conditions as are requisite for termination not only of centuries-old discord and strife but also for rebuilding a better community through the recognition of a higher common duty springing from common equal rights."

Press

Le Temps, October 16—The Chancellor made a comparison between the German Revolution—"where not a windowpane was broken"—and the French and Russian Revolutions. In the realm of foreign policy, it is clear that M. Hitler and his government have not desired to break windows. The speech is proof of this.

New York Times, October 14—It is apparently the plan of the Nazi government of Germany to defy the former Allies which defeated her in the World War and to face the consequences. In the European capitals the German decision is regarded with much gravity. At the Quai d'Orsay the news from Berlin was characterized as "the gravest news in twenty years."

SPEECH OF OCTOBER 17, 1933

Berlin

The Speech

"IN THE field of foreign policy, the struggle for equality of rights which is now entering on its decisive stage is inseparably bound up with the fight for economic revival, with the fight for bread which the German people has now been consistently waging for the last eight months. The political pacification of the world is the condition of any economic recovery. Until equality of rights is granted, it will be purposeless for Germany to take part in any international conferences. My predecessors in the Government suffered, so to speak, from the 'Geneva sickness.' That made them pessimists concerning the nation, optimists concerning the League. I, on the other hand, am an optimist concerning my people but a pessimist concerning Geneva and the League of Nations. Germany never loved peace so much until she turned her back upon the none-too-pleasant atmosphere of that city. The entire German people stands behind the Government's reply to humiliating imputations: We want peace, but we will not allow ourselves to be treated as a second-rate nation.

"Germany will be inflexible in her demands for her rights; she will hold to her claim of equality with the kind of unflinching determination which the National Socialist Movement exercised in its fourteen-year struggle for power in Germany. Honor is no more a vain delusion than is loyalty; without them it is impossible to live in this world. Germany wants peace and nothing but peace, but Germany is determined in the future to enter no conference, no league, no agreement, determined to sign nothing, until she is treated as a Power with equal rights. Somewhere or other there must be a limit below which one cannot go—otherwise one is not worthy to lead a people.

"Our propaganda in this election campaign must be marked by a profound earnestness, for this is one election that carries no moral taint and the campaign is being waged for the nation's right to live. National Socialist Germany, perhaps more than any other people, desires peace, since the National Socialist idea is directed inwards toward the *volkic* conception of a leadership which is bound by the tie of common blood and consequently does not know of any imperialistic policy of conquest directed against the world without.

"Yet, while we thus reject any policy of violence, we are resolutely determined to preserve our rights. The propaganda of the Party must be viewed in this framework and avoiding inessentials must be concentrated on these great questions. A deep and holy seriousness must mark the people in these weeks; there must be no superficial jingoism, but a profound inner realization of the consciousness of its right. This attitude rests on trust in their leaders, who are now approaching their tasks with the highest sense of responsibility.

"The work of the Party in the weeks to come must be inspired by the belief that strength is proved not in small matters but in concentration upon the major problems. The inner freedom and unity of the movement must become more apparent than ever. The great work of the reconciliation of our people, which was begun by National Socialism, must now be completed. Our former political opponents within Germany, in view of this struggle of the whole nation, we would meet halfway and we would extend to them our hand if they prove that they are prepared to defend German honor and share the people's love of peace. . . ."

"If we carry on this struggle with the feeling of our great responsibility, I am sure we will carry it to a successful issue. He who fights bravely for his rights, will win it in the end.

If we all do our duty to the best of our ability, the people will recognize it and on November 12 will show its trust in us. For the people is too decent to refuse to trust those who deserve trust."

Press

New York Times, October 20—Chancellor Hitler today reiterated his demand that equal rights be accorded to Germany, said she wanted only peace and declared she had heavy domestic burdens.

London Times, October 19—Berlin, Oct. 18, 1933—At a conference of Nazi leaders . . . yesterday . . . Herr Hitler made a speech in which, in addition to reaffirming his foreign policy, he made a rather cryptic reference to reconciliation with opponents at home.

Herr Hitler said that the foreign political situation was closely bound up with the home political work of the next few weeks. Germany's struggle for equality of status, upon the decisive stage of which the nation had just entered, was inseparably bound up with struggle for economic recovery, the struggle for bread.

Le Temps, October 20—Mr. Hitler delivered a long speech on the political situation and the significance of the election campaign which was about to begin. He emphasized the necessity of an election campaign which would demonstrate the liberty and the unity of the National Socialist Movement. He ended by a stern call for discipline.

SPEECH OF OCTOBER 30, 1933

Frankfurt

The Speech

"AS ON March 5, 1933, the German people had to decide upon domestic policy, so on November 12 it must decide on foreign policy. It must make a clear decision whether it is its will that the honor of the nation and its equality of rights shall in future be championed freely and openly before the world. It must decide for a way which in the first moment may perhaps be difficult but which, we are convinced, will alone be able in the long run to maintain a great nation in its greatness. . . ."

"We have a feeling for the honor of the nation, because personally we have our own honor. I have not become Chancellor of the Reich in order now to maintain other moral principles than those which I have previously maintained. In my eyes the honor of a nation is composed of the honor, the feeling for honor, the claim to honor of its individual citizens. I believe that the honor of a government is the honor of a people and that a people's honor must be the honor of the government. We want no war, but the right for our people to fashion its own life: and that is no concern of the rest of the world. If all talk of security, although they are not threatened, then to us, who can rightly feel threatened, they must at least grant the same security. If they do not wish to disarm, let them say so; if they do not wish to give us equality of rights, again, let them say so. But there is only one thing to be said, and said once more: never will we take part in any agreements where we are not on a footing of completely equal rights: We may be isolated, but dishonored, never! I would prefer not to enter into agreements which I must purchase at the price of my honor: and when they say 'But then you will be isolated,' then I declare I would rather be isolated with honor, than be tolerated without honor. I believe that the German people has too much character to think otherwise than its Government: I believe that in this hour, this historic hour, it cannot decide otherwise than with the word 'Yes.' There remains no other way. I have no cannons. I have only you, my fellow-countrymen. With you I must fight for this right for Germany. You must stand behind me. We must hold together. We can wage this struggle only if we are a single army."

Press

London Times, October 31—Berlin.—At Frankfurt yesterday Herr Hitler said that Germany would never take part in conventions in which she was not a fully equal partner.

Le Temps, October 31—The Fuehrer repeated that Germany would never participate in conferences which did not afford her full equality of rights; the German people had not only disarmed in a technical, military sense—they were morally disarmed.

•

SPEECH OF NOVEMBER 10, 1933

Siemensstadt

The Speech

"I HAVE grown up from amongst yourselves; once I myself was a workman; for four and a half years I served amongst you in the War; I speak now to you to whom I belong, with whom I still feel myself to be united and for whom in the last resort I fight. . . . I wage that fight for the millions of our honest, industrious, working, creative people. . . . I was in my youth a worker as you are; through industry, through learning, and, I may say, also through hunger I slowly worked my way up. But in my innermost being I have always remained that which I once was. . . ."

"The organizations defending class interests naturally resisted their own dissolution: but one cannot let a people go to ruin because these organizations wish to live. For a people does not live for theories, for programs or for organizations, but all these have to serve a nation's life. Similarly today we see that the struggle between peoples is fostered by folk with definite interests to promote. It is an uprooted international clique which incites the peoples one against another. They are folk who are at home everywhere and nowhere: they have no soil of their own on which they have grown up: today they are living in Berlin, tomorrow they may be in Brussels, the day after in Paris, and then again in Prague or Vienna or London—everywhere they feel themselves at home. Everywhere they can carry on their business, but the people cannot follow them: the people is chained to its soil, is tied to its homeland, tied to the possibilities of life of its State, its nation. The peasant cannot leave his soil, the workman depends upon his factory. If his factory is ruined, where will he find help? What is today the meaning of international class solidarity? That is mere theory at a time in which on every hand distress cries aloud and peoples have to fight hard for their existence. The strength of all of us lies—not in this international phantom, it lies in our homeland. My aim has always been to arouse and to reinforce this strength. . . ."

"I believe that all problems in life, when more than one party is concerned, can be solved only when the parties are on a footing of equality. It is exactly the same in the economic sphere: when one party, be he employer or workman, has all the law and all the power on his side and the other has no rights, you know yourselves that no tolerable contract, no tolerable conditions are possible. The same is true in the life of peoples: there, too, it should not be that one people should have all the rights and another none at all. . . . I should be a liar to the German people if I were to promise it an improvement in its economic position without at the same time demanding for it a recognition of its equal rights in the world. The one is impossible without the other. . . ."

"If the world wishes to issue its *Diktat,* it will do so without my signature. If the world says we are compelled to act thus, because we cannot trust you, how so? Has the German people ever broken its word? It has unfortunately generally kept its word only too resolutely, all too loyally! If we had not stood by our allies so obstinately, so loyally in the World War, then perhaps Germany might have fared better. . . ."

"For many centuries foreign countries have always reckoned on having allies in Germany. First it was princes—men without character who, cold as ice, betrayed their peoples; then it was parties, *Weltanschauungen.* Always they have had their allies. Now I want to show our opponents that they have no longer any allies in Germany. That which feels itself allied is the German people—allied with itself. For centuries the people has made trial of its destiny in disunion and it has reaped a dire harvest. Now I intend that we should make trial of our destiny in unity: that we should now attempt to fashion our destiny in a community of the people which nothing shall break. I am the guarantor in Germany that this community shall not result in the favoring of one section of our people. You can look upon me as the man who does not belong to any class, who belongs to no rank, who stands above all that. I have nothing but the ties which bind me to the German people. Here for me every German is on a complete equality. What interest have I in the intellectuals, in the bourgeoisie, in the proletariat? I am interested only in the German people. To the people alone I belong and for the people I spend my energies."

Press

New York Times, November 11—The wheels of industry and business were stopped for a full hour throughout Germany today and rail and street traffic everywhere halted for a minute—a "minute of silence"—ordained to put Germany's millions of workers of "the brow and the fist" into an appropriately solemn and receptive mood for hearing Chancellor Adolf Hitler's concluding election appeal. The minute's pause and the 45-minute speech by the Chancellor were pre-eminently dedicated to the working men and women of Germany. It was a tribute to labor, rendered under the slogan "Honor and Equality."

London Times, November 11—"The Leader's" speech, delivered with Herr Hitler's characteristic vigor of voice and gesture, was one of his most eloquent. . . .

Editorial (same date)—The machinery for peace has been injured, yet the desire for peace is unshaken. Herr Hitler's own election speeches have placed peace in the forefront of his program.

Le Temps, November 12—The Chancellor returned to the problems of international policy. He denied that Germany was bent on war. The Chancellor stated that Germany was ready to co-operate in any international arrangement, but that the German delegates would sit down to a mediation table only on condition that Germany was treated as equal to the other Powers.

SPEECH OF DECEMBER 11, 1933

Berlin

Background

1933

November 10—MacDonald requests Germany to return to Geneva.

November 11—Hindenburg urges "100 per cent vote" for Hitler.

November 12—Plebiscite about the withdrawal from the League of Nations: Eligible voters: 45,142,000; Cast votes: 43,452,000; Yea votes: 40,602,000; Nay votes: 2,100,000; Invalid votes: 750,000.

Reichstag Election: Eligible voters: 45,142,000; Cast votes: 42,988,000; For NSDAP: 39,639,000; Invalid votes: 3,349,-000.

November 15—Hitler proposes non-aggression agreement to Polish Ambassador in Berlin.

November 17—German "Strength Through Joy" organization founded by Dr. Ley.

December 1—Law is passed relating to the equality of State and Party in Germany. Hess and Roehm given ministries in Cabinet as representatives of the Nazi party.

The Speech

"THE Government which prepared the way for Marxism, the anti-national democracy, has been overthrown and now no power in Germany can destroy the true 'People's State' *(Volksstaat)* which has been established through the National Socialist Movement. The essence of leadership as conceived by the National Socialist State is the capacity to form rapid decisions. . . ."

"The entire German people proved to the world on November 12 that it stood firmly behind the desires of its Government. On November 12 the German people won a victory unique in the history of the nations. On that day we proved we were a decent people, healthy to the core. What other people could have accomplished so profound and decisive a change within a few months after a political upheaval? In place of weapons which we lacked, November 12 gave us this unique picture of the strength of a united people. . . ."

"The people gave its approval not only to the Government, but also to the Party in power. Fate had given all power into the hands of a single Movement. The NSDAP had reached the goal for which it had fought for fourteen years. Upon the Party there now rested an enormous responsibility before the bar of history: today upon the Party rested the fate of the whole German nation: they had now to fulfill what centuries had wished and longed for. . . ."

"Each of us will pass, but Germany must live, and in order for her to live all questions of the day must be overridden and certain pre-conditions established. . . ."

"Traditions of the past which were not valuable for the people's future cannot be regarded by us as binding: the Movement must feel itself to be the founder of a new tradition in our people's life. This vote imposes upon you the duty of creating the conditions for a rebuilding of the nation which shall last for centuries. . . ."

"This Movement must tower above all pettiness and petty ideas. The possibilities which are ours today may perhaps not return for hundreds of years. We shall all one day be together weighed in the balance and together we shall be judged. Either we shall together stand this test or history will condemn us together. History must one day be able to speak of us as a generation of men who, bold, courageous, resolute, and tough, thought only of their people. . . ."

"The new Reichstag has the duty of supporting with its authority the great work of reconstruction undertaken by the National Socialist Government and, through the Party, to form the living link with the people.

"A people which is given noble and honorable leadership will in the long run show its noblest and most honorable virtues. The people must realize through its leaders that the Government in power is of one mind and of one piece: that in all questions of principle it is a single sworn community. The leaders of the Party must be in everything a model for the people. . . ."

"The authority upon which the new State rests is not founded on superficial qualities; it is based in the forty millions we have behind us. . . ."

"If this Reichstag does its duty, then in four years' time we can with assurance and confidence appeal once more to the people. I am convinced that then it will give us a new and still more complete vote of confidence.

"From time to time I shall appeal to the people if only in order that the Movement may remain as elastic as it has been in the past, and that it may recognize in good time any failings which may inadvertently slip in. The Reichstag is a youthful Reichstag, and through this recurrent appeal to the people care will be taken that youth should never die out from its ranks. Of this new Reichstag it must one day be said that it was the youngest, the most courageous, and the boldest, and that it solved the great problems set by history, the problems on which the centuries had suffered shipwreck. . . ."

"From every one of us it must be expected that he should be a fighter—brave, forthright, daring, and true—true to his last breath. As I have kept true to the Movement so I ask of everyone that he should keep true to me. Then we shall go forward into history as a community of sworn men who leave the history of the present to enter the history of the future."

Press

New York Times, December 12—The Chancellor, addressing the Deputies, acclaimed the Nazi election victory of November 12 which produced an all-Nazi Reichstag. He concluded: "No power in Germany will ever be able to overthrow this true people's state."

Le Temps, December 12—Mr. Hitler referred to the principles underlying the National Socialist Party, which were a complete departure from anything in the past. Also he promised to hold a new election after four years to secure a vote of confidence even more unanimous than that of November 12.

•

SPEECH OF JANUARY 30, 1934

Berlin, Reichstag

Background

1933

December 23—Reichstag Fire Trial ends.

December 27—General Kurt von Hammerstein-Equard resigns as head of the Reichswehr.

1934

January 8—Suicide or murder of Stavisky in France.

January 15—Execution of van der Lubbe, accused of Reichstag Fire.

January 26—Germany signs ten-year peace treaty with Poland.

January 30—On the anniversary of the Hitler regime the Reichstag legislates the Reichsrat and the State Legislatures out of existence.

The Speech

"... WHEN the President of the Reich entrusted me on January 30, 1933, with the leadership of the new Government, I, and with me not only the members of the Cabinet but also the entire German people, were moved solely by the ardent desire that Almighty God would permit us to win back for the German people its honor and equality of rights in the eyes of the world. As honest adherents of a real policy of reconciliation, we believed that this was the best way in which we could contribute to a genuine peace among the nations. We have adopted this idea as the principle governing the whole of our foreign policy. The German Reich solemnly proclaimed to all nations and States that it was animated solely by the wish to live with them in peace and friendship. We were convinced that it must be possible once more in this world to discuss differences in international life without always at once thinking of having recourse to arms.

"For fourteen years the German people have endeavored by means of a really suicidal policy of fulfillment to propitiate irreconcilable enemies, and to contribute to the establishment of a new European community of States. The results were profoundly tragic. A reference to the alleviations in the reparations policy does not prove the contrary. For it was only after the ruin not only of German economy but also to a large extent of world economy that it was decided to put an end by agreement to a procedure which as a matter of fact had in any case already come to an end for lack of any kind of assets in Germany.

"While the new German Government was determined to fight for German equality in the political sphere as well, they were convinced that it was only thus that they could really provide a contribution to the recovery of world economic relations. For unless the political relations between the nations have been regulated and the political atmosphere thus cleared co-operation, even in economic matters, is impossible.

But co-operation will be necessary if in the coming years a serious attempt is to be made to master the great problems arising out of the shifting and alteration of the world's markets on the one hand and the fact that certain nations must still maintain their exports on the other.

"In principle, the German Government starts with the assumption that, as regards the form of our relations with other countries, it is obviously a matter of indifference what kind of constitution and form of government the nations may be pleased to adopt for themselves. It is an absolutely private matter for each nation to determine the form of its internal life in accordance with its own estimation of its requirements. Hence the selection of the spiritual content and the constructive form of the organization and government of Germany according to the German people's own conception is also a private affair which concerns no one except the German people themselves.

"For many months we have been painfully aware that the difference between our philosophy and that of other nations has been seized upon not only as an opportunity of heaping numerous unjustified reproaches on the German people and the German Reich, but also as an excuse for regarding it with a mistrust for which there are no grounds whatever.

"We have not done the same. During the last twelve months we made a really honest endeavor to cultivate the relations between the German Reich and all other States in a spirit of reconciliation and readiness to come to an understanding, even in cases in which there were great and even irreconcilable differences between the ideas of government held in these countries and ours. Both in the case of the States with a democratic form of government as well as in that of those with an anti-democratic tendency we aimed at finding ways and means for adjusting differences and for international co-operation.

"This is the only explanation of why, in spite of the great difference of the two prevailing forms of philosophy, the

German Reich continued to endeavor in this year to cultivate friendly relations with Russia. *As M. Stalin in his last great speech expressed the fear that forces hostile to the Soviet might be active in Germany, I must correct this opinion insofar by stating here that communistic tendencies or even propaganda would be no more tolerated in Germany than German National Socialistic tendencies would be tolerated in Russia.* The more clearly and unambiguously this fact becomes evident and is respected by both parties, the easier will be the cultivation of the interests common to both countries. Hence we greet the effort to stabilize relations in the East of Europe by a system of pacts, if the leading idea of this activity is the strengthening of peace rather than tactical and political aims.

"For this reason and with these intentions *the German Government has endeavored in its first year to secure a new and better relationship with the Polish State.*

"When I took over the government on January 30, the relations between the two countries seemed to me more than unsatisfactory. There was a danger that the existing differences, which were due to the territorial clauses of the Treaty of Versailles and the mutual tension resulting therefrom, would gradually crystallize into a state of hostility which if persisted in might only too easily acquire the character of a dangerous traditional enmity. Apart from its latent dangers such a development would constitute a permanent obstacle to the profitable co-operation of the two peoples. *Germans and Poles will have to learn to accept the fact of each other's existence.* Hence it is more sensible to regulate this state of affairs which the last thousand years has not been able to remove and the next thousand will not be able to remove either, in such a way that the highest possible profit will accrue from it for both nations. . . ."

"Further, it seemed to me right in such a case to attempt to deal with the problems affecting both countries by means of a frank and open exchange of views between the two parties rather than to go on entrusting third and fourth parties with this task. *Moreover, whatever the differences between the two countries in the future may be, the catastrophic effects of the attempt to remove them through warlike actions would far outweigh any possible advantage gained.*

"Thus the German Government was fortunate in finding the same generous attitude in the leader of the present Polish State, Marshal Pilsudski, and in being able to incorporate this mutual recognition of the situation in a treaty which will not only be of equal advantage to the Polish and German peoples, but which also represents an important contribution to the maintenance of world peace.

"In the spirit of this treaty the German Government is willing and prepared to cultivate economic relations with Poland in such a way that here, too, the state of unprofitable suspicion can be succeeded by a period of useful co-operation.

"It is a matter of particular satisfaction to us that in this same year the National Socialist Government of Danzig has been enabled to effect a similar clarification of its relations with its Polish neighbor.

"It is on the other hand a matter of great regret to the German Government that *the relations of the Reich to the present Austrian Government are by no means satisfactory.* The fault does not lie with us. *The assertion that it is the intention of the German Reich to coerce the Austrian State is absurd, and cannot be substantiated or proved.*

"It is, however, a matter of course that an idea which has permeated the whole German nation and moved it to the depths will not pause before the boundary stones of a country whose people are not only German, but whose history shows it, the Eastern March of Germany, to have been for many centuries an integral part of the German Reich, and whose capital had for half a millennium long the honor of being the seat of the German Emperors, and whose soldiers marched side by side with the German regiments and divisions in the Great War.

"But even apart from this there is nothing peculiar in this fact when one considers that almost all revolutionary ideas in Europe hitherto have penetrated beyond the frontiers of the land of origin. Thus the ideas of the French Revolution permeated the whole of Europe, just as the ideas of National Socialism have been taken up by the Germans in Austria from a natural intellectual and spiritual communion with the entire German people.

"If the present Austrian Government considers it necessary to suppress this movement with all the means in its power, that is of course its own affair. *But in that case it must take over the responsibility for the consequences of its own policy.* Not until German citizens living in or visiting Austria were affected by it did the German Government take action against the measures of the Austrian Government against National Socialism. It cannot be expected of the German Government that it is going to send its citizens as guests into a country whose Government has made it unmistakably clear that the National Socialist as such is considered an undesirable element. Just as we should be unable to count on Americans and Englishmen visiting Germany, if their national emblems and flags were forcibly removed, so the German Government cannot consent to the subjecting of German subjects who travel as visitors in another land, and that a German land, to this ignominious treatment. For the national emblems and the Swastika flag are symbols of the modern German Reich, and Germans who travel abroad today are, apart from the emigrants, always National Socialists.

"The Austrian Government complains that Germany prevents its citizens from traveling to a country whose Government adopts this hostile attitude toward even the individual adherent of the political philosophy which obtains here. But it should reflect that the measures taken by the German Government have prevented a state of affairs which would be frankly intolerable. For since the modern German citizen is too proud and independent to allow his national emblems to be torn from him, we have no alternative but to spare such a country the pleasure of our presence.

"I must emphatically reject the further assertion of the Austrian Government that an attack on the part of the Reich against the Austrian State will be undertaken or even planned. If the tens of thousands of political refugees from Austria now in Germany take a warm interest in what happens in their native land, that may be regrettable in some of its effects; but it is all the more difficult for the Reich to prevent this in that the rest of the world has not yet succeeded in suppressing the activities of German emigrants abroad against the developments in Germany.

"If the Austrian Government complains of political propaganda carried on from Germany against Austria, then the German Government could with more justice complain of the political propaganda carried on against Germany by emigrants living in other countries. The fact that the German press appears in the German language and can thus be read by the Austrian Government is perhaps regrettable for the present Austrian Government, but it is not in the power of the German Government to alter it. But when in non-German countries German newspapers with million sales are printed and forwarded to Germany, then the German Government has a real ground for protest; for it is difficult to explain why Berlin papers, for instance, should have to appear in Prague or Paris.

"How difficult it is to suppress the action of emigrants against their mother country is seen most clearly from the fact that even where the League of Nations itself takes charge of a country the activities of these emigrants cannot be stopped. Only a few days ago the German police arrested sixteen Communists on the Saar frontier, who were attempting to smuggle large quantities of treasonable propaganda material from this domain of the League into Germany. But if this is possible under the eyes of the League then it is difficult to reproach the German Reich for alleged happenings of a similar nature.

"Without wishing to meddle in the slightest degree in the internal affairs of other nations I feel I must say one thing: In the long run no government can last by force alone. Thus it will always be a first care of the National Socialist Government of the Reich to ascertain anew how far the will of the nation is incorporated in its Government. And in this sense we 'savages' are really the better democrats.

"And further, as a proud son of the Austrian brotherland, my home and the home of my fathers, I must protest against the idea that the German temperament of the Austrian people is in need of any stimulus from the Reich. I believe I still know my native land and its people well enough to realize that the same enthusiasm which fills 66 million Germans in the Reich moves *their* hearts too. May providence decree that a way out of this unsatisfactory state of affairs may be found to a really conciliatory settlement. The German Reich is always ready to hold out a hand for a real understanding with full respect for the free will of Austrian Germans.

"In this review of foreign policy I cannot refrain from expressing my lively satisfaction at the fact that this year has seen a further and many-sided strengthening of the traditional friendship to Fascist Italy, which has always been cultivated by National Socialism. The great leader of this people has always been held by us in high honor. The German people gratefully recognizes the many proofs of the statesmanlike and objective sense of justice which marked the Italian attitude in its dealings with them in the Geneva negotiations and afterwards.

"Just as the National Socialist Government of the Reich has in this year striven to come to an understanding with Poland, so it has been our earnest endeavor to lessen the differences between France and Germany and if possible to find the way to a final understanding by means of a general clearing up of the outstanding problems.

"The struggle for German equality of rights, a struggle for the honor of our people which we can never renounce, could in my opinion find no better end than a reconciliation between the two great nations, who have so often shed the blood of their finest sons on the battlefields of the last centuries, without changing anything essential in the final circumstances.

"Thus I believe that this problem should not be seen exclusively through the spectacles of the cold professional politicians and diplomats, but will only finally be settled by the warm-hearted decision of those who formerly perhaps stood facing each other as foes, but who should be able to find a bridge to the future in the respect based on the gallantry displayed by both sides. For a repetition of our past troubles will have to be avoided in the future if Europe is not to plunge into the abyss.

"*France fears for her security. No one in Germany wants to threaten it, and we are ready to do everything to prove that.* Germany demands her equality of rights. No one in the world has the right to refuse this to a great nation, and no one will have the strength to withhold it indefinitely. But for us who were living witnesses of the horrors of the Great War nothing is further than the thought of bringing these feelings and demands, intelligible on both sides, into any sort of connection with any wish for a fresh trial of strength on the battlefield between the two peoples, which would inevitably lead to an international catastrophe.

"Guided by such reflections, and in the spirit of co-operation so necessary and desirable between the two nations, I have attempted to find a solution for those questions which are otherwise only too liable to lead to fresh conflicts.

"My proposal that Germany and France should now settle the Saar question together sprang from the following considerations:

"1. *This is the only territorial question which is still open between the two countries. After it has been settled the Ger-*

man Government is ready to accept not only the letter but also the spirit of the Locarno Pact, as there will then be no other territorial question at stake between France and Germany.

"2. The German Government fears that, although the plebiscite will give an unparalleled majority for Germany, a fresh incitement to national passions—fanned by irresponsible emigrant circles—will take place during the preparations for the plebiscite, which, in view of the certain result, is unnecessary and therefore to be regretted.

"3. Whatever the result of the plebiscite, it will in either case leave one nation with a sense of defeat. And even though fires of rejoicing would then burn in Germany, from the point of view of reconciliation between the two countries we would prefer that a solution equally satisfactory to both sides should be found beforehand.

"4. We are convinced that if France and Germany regulated and decided this question previously in a common treaty, the entire Saar population would joyfully vote for such a regulation by an overwhelming majority. And the result would be that the population would have been enabled to record its vote, without either of the interested nations having to consider the result of the plebiscite as a victory or defeat; thus the possibility of a fresh disturbance of the mutual understanding beginning between the German and French peoples would have been avoided.

"I still regret that the French Government has not found it possible to act on this suggestion. But I have not given up the hope that the will to a true reconciliation in the two nations and for a final burying of the hatchet will grow ever stronger and finally triumph.

"If this succeeds, Germany's unalterable demand for equality of rights will no longer be felt by France to be an attack on the security of the French nation, but will be regarded as the obvious right of a great people, which has so very many economic interests in common with her, and with whom friendly political relations are maintained.

"We welcome the efforts of the British Government to help to pave the way to this understanding. The outline of the new disarmament proposals handed to me yesterday by the British Ambassador will be examined by us in the friendly spirit which I described in my speech in May as inspiring German foreign policy.

"The German Government's decision to leave the Disarmament Conference and the League of Nations was taken only because the treatment of the question of the granting of our equality of rights in relation to an international scale of armaments, which was a question of vital import to Germany, was no longer compatible with what I declared in May to be the unalterable basic claim not only for the security of the German Reich but also for the national honor of our people.

"I can only once again repeat to the world at this moment that no threat and no force will ever move the German people to give up those rights which cannot be denied to a sovereign nation. I can, however, also give the assurance that this sovereign nation has no other wish than eagerly to apply the strength and weight of her political, moral, and economic resources not only to the healing of the wounds which the past has inflicted on humanity, but also toward the co-operation of those cultured and civilized nations which—as an English statesman has justly said—make life in this world really fine and worth having by their labors and spiritual achievements."

Press

Le Temps, February 2—The Chancellor . . . solemnly affirmed once again his desire for peace, reconciliation and co-operation with the other nations. He hailed the Polish-German pact as an attempt at stabilization in Eastern Europe, and he repeated his offer of a pact with France. He stated that Germany had not the least intention of violating the independence of Austria.

New York Times, January 30—In a speech charged with confidence as well as with defiance, Chancellor Hitler tonight spread before the Reichstag the balance sheet of National Socialism's first year in office. It was the anniversary of his elevation to the Chancellorship and he spoke as the tribune and leader of the German people. Its keynote was a bold asseveration of faith in the cause he led, combined with a warning to foes at home and the outside world that National Socialism was the master and would remain the master of the new Germany, but otherwise he held out a friendly hand to other nations.

London Times, January 31—In his speech before the Reichstag yesterday Herr Hitler dealt with the National Socialist achievements. He laid emphasis on the racial unity of the German people, thanked the British Government for their new disarmament proposals, declared that National Socialism could not halt at the frontier of Austria.

•

SPEECH OF MARCH 19, 1934

Munich

Background

1934

January 31—England and Germany study proposals for the rearming of Germany and the disarmament of the other powers. The Italian plan envisages an army of 300,000 men for Germany, on condition that Germany re-enter the League of Nations.

February 6—Riots in Paris. Fascist leagues try to overthrow the Government.

February 7—Daladier, Prime Minister, resigns.

February 9—Gaston Doumergue, ex-President of the Republic, forms a government of "national union" comprising among others Edouard Herriot, Louis Barthou, Etienne Flandin, Pierre Laval, and Marshal Pétain (Minister of War).

February 12-15—In Austria, Chancellor Dollfuss strikes at the Social Democrats. Socialist workers, entrenched in the municipal houses, put up a violent fight. They are subdued with artillery.

The Speech

" . . . THE March revolution of the year 1933 was in truth the spring revolution of the German people. A spring has now once more begun for us—in this spring we all live and in this spring we all are happy.

"There is no romance in world history more wonderful than the development of our Party. . . ."

"History will never be able to lay to our charge that we wrought blind havoc. I believe that no revolution in the history of the world has proceeded and been conducted with more caution and skill than ours. Everything had been considered ten times over and we have taken not one step too many. No one in Germany should complain. If our enemies of the Red Flag had come to power, then in Germany as elsewhere we should have seen only a heap of smoking ruins. But today we see in Germany vigorous life. . . ."

"We fight for an independent German people. If God created the German tribes, they will remain. If anyone says, 'What then of the single States? After all God made them too.' No! Men made the States. State forms have always been transitory. Look back a hundred years, two hundred, three hundred years, and study the map and the changes marked on it. And if anyone says to me, 'But from now on things must remain as they are,' I can only answer: 'Sir, if you have grown sterile, our German people is anything but sterile.' The people is still living: it feels its way open towards its goal and strives towards it, *and therefore the map of our Reich will change in the future and in it there will be further alterations. . . .*"

"Every German belongs to a tribe. But where would we as Germans be, where would our people be, if we saw in that fact a license to fight no more for our people as a whole? No! That can never be! When I went to Berlin, one who was by descent a Bavarian became for the first time Chancellor of the Reich. Then I set before myself as my aim to see to it that the period of my Chancellorship should one day be marked with honor in the history of Germany. From this city you have sent a tribune of the people to Berlin, and it is my determination that my name shall be able to take an honorable place amongst the Chancellors of the German Reich. I went to the North as a man from the South with a program of which I can say: 'Test it all of you! It is a German program!'. . ."

"Whatever the attitude of the individual may be towards this or that detail which does not please him, yet I would have everyone say to himself: We have experienced a miracle, something unique, something the like of which there has hardly been in the history of the world. God first allowed our people to be victorious for four and a half years, then He abased us, laid upon us a period of shamelessness; but now after a struggle of fourteen years he has permitted us to bring that period to a close. It is a miracle which has been wrought upon the German people, and we would not fall into the fault which possessed the German people at the end of the war years: we would not be ungrateful. What has come to pass during the last year is so unheard of that it must constrain us to profound humility. It shows us that the Almighty has not deserted our people, that He received it into favor at the moment when it rediscovered itself. And that our people shall never again lose itself, that must be our vow so long as we shall live and so long as the Lord gives us the strength to carry on the fight."

Press

Le Temps, March 22—The Chancellor declared that the 1933 revolution was another springtime of the German people. M. Hitler referred to the inner boundaries between the German "lands," which had in the course of centuries often been altered, and which would be altered once again.

London Times, March 21—Herr Hitler declared . . . that the revolution had to be carried further until the final goal was reached. The map of Germany had to be altered until the unification of the German people was complete.

•

SPEECH OF MARCH 21, 1934

Unterhaching

Background

1934

March 20—Regent Horthy of Hungary and Chancellor Dollfuss of Austria meet with Mussolini. They agree to work for maintenance of European peace and the revival of economic life.

The Speech

"I DO not believe that any government ever took over a worse inheritance than we did on January 30, 1933. . . ."

"What was one now to do and *how* must one make a beginning? My fellow-countrymen, how many there were at that time who warned the German people of the danger of National Socialism, maintaining that, worst of all, we had in our ranks no 'heads': that our victory could mean nothing else than the complete annihilation of German economic life.

"But now when at the beginning of the second year of our attack upon the economic distress of Germany we come before the nation, despite all our critics, despite all those who knew so much better, we can point to achievements which even they themselves declared to be impossible.

"But how did that become possible? The considerations which at that time determined our action, and the decisions which we then took and resolved to realize, were the following:

"1. If in a period of such sinister general collapse, especially in the economic sphere, there was to be a revolution in the State, that revolution must in no circumstances lead to chaos. We wished to make a revolution, and a revolution was in fact made. But it is only the meanest spirit which can regard the essence of a revolution as consisting merely in destruction. We, on the contrary, regarded it as consisting in a gigantic work of reconstruction.

"If today we dare to look with some confidence into the future, that is only because, thanks to the discipline of the National Socialist party, of its fighters and adherents, we were able to carry through one of the greatest revolutionary changes in the history of the world in orderly fashion and according to plan.

"2. The greatness of the distress compelled us to make really great decisions. But great decisions must be long-term decisions: their realization demands time, as indeed do all great things in this world. So it was essential to give to the new Government an unexampled stability, since only governments which are stable, which are assured of their existence and of the permanence of that existence are in a position to rise to the making of really fundamental and far-reaching decisions.

"3. The internal stability of a regime always becomes a source of a people's trust and confidence. When the masses in their millions see that above them there stands a government which is sure of itself, part of this certainty is transferred to the masses. Only in this way the boldness of a government's plans is matched by a like boldness in the readiness of the people to execute and carry into effect these plans. But trust and confidence are the fundamental conditions for the success of any economic revival.

"4. Further, one must make up one's mind not merely to act with judgment, but if necessary to take stern measures. We were prepared to do everything that man could do. We want to do everything which we can—with a good conscience and so far as our knowledge goes. We are therefore not prepared or willing to allow any scoundrel, any conscienceless domestic foe of our people, to continue his destructive activity.

"To be able to criticize one must oneself have learned something; but what one has learned is demonstrated through action.

"To those men who came before us Fate gave fourteen years—time enough to prove through acts their real capacity. But one who through fourteen years failed as miserably as these men have done, one who brought to such ruin a healthy people and drove it into misery and despair, he has no right suddenly in the fifteenth year to play the part of a critic of those who wish to improve things and have also in fact improved things. For fourteen years they had opportunity enough for action. Today we do not intend to give them any longer the opportunity for chattering.

"5. And, further, we cannot do so, for the great work can succeed only if we all co-operate; it is a mistake to believe that any government unaided can achieve the miracle of a restoration. It must succeed in winning over the people to serve its mission. The eternal pessimists and those who carp on principle have never yet saved any people, though they have destroyed many a people, many a State and Empire. We therefore determined not to trouble our heads about them, but rather to count on those who, undismayed, were ready to undertake with us the fight for the resurrection of Germany and to wage that fight to the end.

"6. And that resurrection could come only through fighting. For there can be no miracle—whether it comes from above or from without—which gives to man anything which he has not himself earned.

"7. We were convinced that the salvation of the German people must take its start from the salvation of the agricultural class. For if anyone else is compelled to leave his post or himself loses his business, he can one day find once more a new position or through industry and efficiency found a new undertaking: the farmer who has once lost his farm is generally lost forever.

"8. The fight for the salvation of the middle class is primarily also a fight against unemployment. Unemployment is the gigantic problem which is set before us for solution: in face of that problem everything else must take second place. From the very day when we assumed power we were convinced that we had to master this evil, and we were determined ruthlessly to subordinate everything else to the fight against this evil.

"The German people of the future shall not give to any of its citizens doles for doing nothing at all; rather it will give to everyone the possibility, through honest work, of earning his own bread and thus of contributing towards and co-operating in the raising of the standard of life of all. For no one can consume that which others have not with him first created.

"But our wish is that our people in all its various ranks should rise in its standard of living, and we must accordingly see to it that the conditions for this should be realized in our production.

"I am happy to know that, despite rates of wages which in part are positively impossible, the German workman has understood our action, but it is a melancholy fact that many employers have failed to show any comprehension of problems such as these; they would seem to believe that expression should be given to the present epoch of German economic revival through an extraordinary rise in dividends. Henceforth we shall oppose by all means and with the greatest determination every attempt thus to increase the rate of dividends.

"Such then were the principles which in the past year served to guide our action. They marked out for us the path which we in fact followed.

"At the outset we had done with all theories. It is very interesting when doctors amuse themselves by discussing the possible ways to cure an illness, but for the patient the immediate—the most important—thing is that he should get well again. And the theory which restores him to health is not only the most important, it is also the right theory.

"We therefore began on the one hand to free economic life from theories, and on the other to liberate it from the chaos of oppressive regulations and of restrictive measures on the merits or demerits of which it is idle to dispute, since, whether they were right or wrong, they were in any event only stifling economic life. We further sought to free production step by step from those burdens which in the shape of unreasonable taxation-decrees were strangling economic life. . . ."

"Again we were determined on principle not to distribute any further presents to the business world but to use all our available resources solely for the practical and positive aim of creating work. The intelligent, efficient, and methodical businessman will have a free field for his activity, the lazy and unintelligent—to say nothing of the disreputable and dishonest—must go to ruin. The decisive point is that the means which the State can mobilize should not be distributed as a present but should be employed in order practically to stimulate production and thus be usefully invested.

"This to a large extent we have done with striking success. The initiative thus taken by the State had always solely as its aim and purpose to awake private economic initiative, and thus slowly to set economic life once more on its own feet. . . ."

"But beyond this we have endeavored to introduce a better social order: thus amongst other measures through State aid we have made possible a vast increase in the number of new marriages; thereby we took countless young women out of economic production and brought them back into the family and the home. . . ."

"In the year which lies before us we must wage the campaign against unemployment with still greater fanaticism, with still greater determination than in the year which is past. With ruthless severity we must repel everyone who offends against this idea and its realization. I would have everyone in Germany understand that only through a truly socialistic view of this problem which faces the community will it be possible to find its solution. I would have everyone rise above his egoism and triumph over his personal interests. . . ."

"Wages and dividends must take second place, however regrettable it may be in the case of wages, before the paramount realization that we must first create the goods which when they are created we may hope to consume.

"Above all I would have every employer understand that the accomplishment of the economic tasks which are set us is possible only if all place themselves in the service of this task, subordinating to it their egoistic desire for personal gain. And further I would have them realize that a failure in this task would not merely produce some fresh millions of unemployed, but would mean the end and the collapse of our economic life, and thus perhaps the end of the German people.

"Only a madman can therefore be so indecent as to offend, in the pursuit of his personal advantage, against this common distress and its alleviation. But if personal advantage does not win the day, then we can with complete confidence look to the future, for the gigantic program of this nationwide creation of work which we planned and laid down last year must in part take many months before the project can ripen into realization.

"Conditions essential to our effort must first be created before at last we can begin the work itself, and that is a vast undertaking. We have an example of that in the new motor roads of the Reich: for the mere planning of these one needs a whole army of surveyors and engineers, of draughtsmen and of workers. But with ever-increasing speed the construction of one stretch of road after another will be undertaken. . . ."

"The program of the Government which is already worked out in detail will be the greatest program for the creation of work which Germany has ever known, and it will also mean a great alleviation of the burdens which oppress our economic life. At the same time it will provide for the ordering of our whole financial life. For however huge the sums demanded for this program may be, they will not be produced by printing more notes: an inflation on the model of the November Government is for us unthinkable. All current outgoings will be met from the ordinary income of the State, while permanent improvements will at the proper time be financed through loans.

"To procure these means the people's confidence and the help of the people's savings are the essential condition. We are able to state with satisfaction that in the past year the savings deposits alone in Germany have increased by about a milliard marks. . . .

"We shall continue in the future also to alleviate debt

burdens and to favor the formation of capital, and in so doing we shall not make use of any means which could in any way prejudice respect for property or for contractual rights. . . ."

"Would that at last the intelligence of the other peoples and their statesmen might come to realize that the wish and the will of the German people and its Government seek nothing else than, in freedom and in peace, to co-operate in the building up of a better world.

"And so with this great achievement of the community we begin the new battle for work of the year 1934.

"Our goal is set! German workmen, carry on!"

Press

New York Times, March 21—The government radio carried the speech to every town and village throughout the Reich, and whole settlements stopped work to listen, making it a holiday. . . . They all heard Hitler promise those things all Germany craves—the end of unemployment and the beginning of a new era of prosperity and plenty, of lower taxes and abundance for all. . . .

Le Temps, March 22—The Chancellor's speech disappointed those who expected a new, definite program for the fight against unemployment.

SPEECH OF JULY 13, 1934

Berlin, Reichstag

Background

1934

April 30—Austrian Parliament ratifies new constitution and dissolves.

May 16—Roosevelt informs the countries of Europe that America is willing to accept token payments of the war debts due on June 15.

June 14—Goebbels visits Pilsudski in Warsaw and Hitler meets Mussolini in Venice.

June 25—Hess in Cologne makes speech against a "second revolution."

June 30—The Roehm purge in Germany.

The Speech

"COMMISSIONED thereto by the Government the President of the Reichstag, Hermann Goering, has called you together today to give me the possibility of explaining before this best-qualified Forum of the Nation events which may well remain for all time in our history as a memory alike of sorrow and of warning. Out of a sum of material causes and personal guilt, from human inadequacy and human defects, there arose for our young Reich a crisis which only too easily might for an incalculable period have produced consequences completely disastrous. To make clear to you and thereby to the nation how this crisis arose and how it was overcome is the aim of my speech. The content of this speech will be of ruthless frankness. Only in its scope do I feel bound to impose upon myself some limitation, and that limitation is on the one side conditioned by the interests of the

Reich and on the other side by bounds which are set by the sentiment of shame.

"When on January 30, 1933, Field Marshal and President of the Reich von Hindenburg entrusted me with the leadership of the newly formed German Government, the National Socialist party took over a State which both politically and economically was in complete decline. All political forces of the former state of affairs which had just been brought to a close had their share in this decline, and consequently a share in guilt. Since the abdication of the Kaiser and the German princes the German people had been delivered into the hands of men who, as the representatives of our past world of parties, had either consciously induced this decline or had weakly suffered it to continue. Beginning with the Marxist revolutionaries and proceeding by way of the Center till one reached the Bourgeois Nationalists—all parties and their leaders were given an opportunity to prove their capacity to govern Germany. Endless coalitions allowed them to put to the test their political arts and their economic skill. They have all failed miserably. January 30 [1933] was therefore not the day when our Government formally took over responsibility from the hands of another Government, it was rather the final liquidation, long desired by the nation, of an intolerable state of affairs.

"It is essential that this should be clearly stated since, as subsequent events have proved, some individuals would seem to have forgotten that previously they were given full opportunity for demonstrating their political capacities. There is no one in Germany who could have any ground, even did he so wish, to charge the National Socialist Movement with having obstructed or even blocked the way to political forces which offered any hope of success. Fate, for reasons which we cannot fathom, condemned our people for fifteen years to serve as the field on which these politicians could make their experiments—as the rabbit in the hands of the vivisector.

"It may have been interesting and pleasurable for the outside world—especially for the world that is ill-disposed toward us—to follow these experiments; for the German people they were as painful as they were humiliating. Look back on this period and before your eyes let all those figures pass who succeeded each other as Chancellors of the Reich. In what land were the scales of providence more often brought into use, and where more frequently was the verdict passed that the object weighed had fallen short of the due weight? No! We National Socialists have the right to refuse to be counted as members of this line. On January 30, 1933, it was not a case of a new government being formed as had happened times without number before, but a new regime had superseded an old and sick age.

"This historic act of the liquidation of that most melancholy period in our nation's life which now lies behind us was legalized by the German people itself. For we have not seized possession of power as usurpers, as did the men of November 1918; we have received power constitutionally and legally. We have not made a revolution as uprooted anarchists, but, as executing the nation's will, we have set aside a regime born of rebellion, and we have seen our task to lie not in maintaining power at the point of the bayonet, but in finding that power in the heart of our people, and anchoring it there.

"When today I read in a certain foreign newspaper that at the present time I am filled with profound anxieties, and at this moment in particular with economic anxieties, I have only one answer for these scribblers: assuredly that is true, but it is not merely today that anxiety tortures me; it has done so for a long time past. If it was formerly the anxiety for our people which led us to protect our people in the war which, despite its innocence, had been forced upon it, after the collapse it was the far greater anxiety for the future which turned us into revolutionaries. And when after fifteen years of struggle at last we received the leadership of the nation, this torturing anxiety not only did not loosen its hold upon us, but on the contrary did but embrace us the more closely. I may be believed when I assure you that never yet in my life have I allowed myself to be anxious for my own personal fate. But I confess that from the day when the confidence of the Field Marshal appointed for me my place I have borne the burden of that heavy anxiety which the present and the future of our people lays upon us all. . . ."

"When I as Chancellor of the Reich came into the Wilhelmstrasse, the authority of the Reich had become a worthless phantom. The spirit of revolt and insubordination dominated the German States and communes. The shadows of the most melancholy political past of the German people rose alarmingly before us. Particularism and Separatism insolently proclaimed themselves as the new German conception of the State. From the internal weakness of the Reich sprang its undignified attitude toward the world without. It had once more become a humiliation to confess publicly that one was a German. The spirit of insubordination and of internal revolt within a few months we exterminated and destroyed. While fully respecting the essential character of our German tribes we have strengthened the authority of the Reich as the expression of the common will of our people's life and have made it supreme. The German Reich is today no longer a merely geographical conception: it has become a political unity. We have directed our people's development on to lines which only two years ago were regarded as unattainable. And just as within the Reich we firmly secured the unity and therewith the future of the German people, so in the sphere of foreign policy we have resolutely championed the rights of our people. . . ."

"The features which marked our former political confusion have not been set aside because we destroyed them, but because the German people removed them from its heart. And I must—today and in this place—confess that assuredly our work would have been utterly vain, and must have been vain, had not the German people given us its confidence and its loyal cooperation in so large a measure. Our success is due to the 41½ million men and women from all walks of life who gave us no merely superficial 'Yes,' but devoted themselves with all their hearts to the new regime.

"To them our success is mainly due. Without their confiding trust, without their patient forbearance, without their devotion and readiness for sacrifice, the work of German recovery would never have succeeded. They are, as the supporters of the people's rebirth, at the same time the best representatives of the people. They are in truth the German people. . . ."

"And over against this positive world of the German spirit, the incorporation of the true values of our people, there stands also, it is true, a small negative world. They take no part in their hearts in the work of German recovery and restoration. First there is the small body of those international disintegrators of a people who as apostles of the *Weltanschauung* of communism alike in the political and economic sphere systematically incite the peoples, break up established order, and endeavor to produce chaos. We see evidence of the activity of these international conspirators all about us. Up and down the countries the flames of revolt run over the peoples. Street riots, fights at the barricades, mass terrorism, and the individualistic propaganda of disintegration disturb today nearly all the countries of the world. Even in Germany some single fools and criminals of this type still again and again seek to exercise their destructive activity. Since the destruction of the Communist party we experience one attempt after another, though growing ever weaker as time passes, to found and to sustain the work of communistic organizations of a more or less anarchistic character. Their method is always the same. . . ."

"The second group of the discontented consists of those political leaders who feel that their political future has been closed since January 30, but yet are still unable to accept the irrevocability of this fact. The more time veils with the gracious mantle of forgetfulness their own incapacity, the more do they think themselves entitled gradually to bring themselves back into the people's memory. But since their incapacity was not formerly limited to any special period but was born in them by nature, they are today, too, unable to prove their value in any positive and useful work, but they see the fulfillment of their life's task to lie in a criticism which is as treacherous as it is mendacious. With them, too, the people has no sympathy. The National Socialist State can neither be seriously threatened by them nor in any way damaged.

"A third group of destructive elements is formed of those revolutionaries whose former relation to the State was shattered by the events of 1918; they became uprooted and thereby lost altogether all sympathy with any ordered human society. They became revolutionaries who favored revolution for its own sake and desired to see revolution established as a permanent condition. We all formerly suffered under the frightful tragedy that we, as disciplined and loyal soldiers, were suddenly faced with a revolt of mutineers who managed to seize possession of the State. Each of us had been brought up to respect the laws and to reverence authority, we had been trained in obedience to the commands and regulations issued by the authorities, in a subordination of our wills in face of the State's representatives. Now the revolution of deserters and mutineers forced upon us in our thought the abandonment of these conceptions. . . ."

"Amongst the numberless documents which during the last week it was my duty to read, I have discovered a diary with the notes of a man who, in 1918, was thrown into the path of resistance to the laws and who now lives in a world in which law in itself seems to be a provocation to resistance. It is an unnerving document—an unbroken tale of conspiracy and continual plotting: it gives one an insight into the mentality of men who, without realizing it, have found in nihilism their final confession of faith. Incapable of any true co-operation, with a desire to oppose all order, filled with hatred against every authority, their unrest and disquietude can find satisfaction only in some conspiratorial activity of the mind perpetually plotting the disintegration of whatever at any moment may exist. Many of them in the early days of our struggle have together with us fulminated against the State which is now no more, but their inner lack of discipline led most of them, even during the course of the struggle, away from the disciplined National Socialist Movement.

"The last remnant appeared to have separated itself from us after January 30. The link with the National Socialist Movement was severed at the moment when the Movement itself, now representing the State, became the object of their pathological aversion. They are on principle enemies of every authority, and therefore there can be no hope at all of their conversion. . . ."

"This third group of pathological enemies of the State is dangerous because they represent a reservoir of those ready to co-operate in every attempt at a revolt, at least just for so long as a new order does not begin to crystallize out of the state of chaotic confusion.

"I must now mention the fourth group, which often perhaps even against its own will does in fact carry on a truly destructive activity. The group is composed of those persons who belong to a comparatively small section of society and who, having nothing to do, find time and opportunity to report orally everything that has happened in order thus to bring some interesting and important variety into their otherwise completely purposeless lives. For while the overwhelming majority of the nation has to earn its daily bread in toilsome work, in certain strata of life there are still folk whose sole activity it is to do nothing, only to need afterwards a rest-cure from doing nothing. The more paltry is the life of such a drone, the more eagerly will he seize upon anything which may give some interesting content to the vacuity of his mind. Personal and political gossip is eagerly swallowed and even more eagerly handed on. Since these men as a result of doing nothing do not possess any living relation to the millions which form the mass of the nation, their life is confined in its range to the circle within which they move. Every bit of gossip which strays into this circle reverberates backwards and forwards like figures reflected in two distorting mirrors. Because their whole ego is full of nothingness, and since they find a similar nothingness amongst their like, they look upon the whole world as equally empty; they come to think that the outlook of their own circle is the outlook of everyone. Their anxieties, they imagine, form the cares of the whole nation. In reality this little cloud of drones is but a State within the State; it has no contact with the life, the sentiments, the hopes and cares of the rest of the people. They are, however, dangerous because they are veritable bacillus-carriers of unrest and uncertainty, of rumors, assertions, lies and suspicions, of slanders and fears, and thus they contribute to produce gradually a state of nervousness which spreads amongst the people so that in the end it is hard to find or recognize where its influence stops. . . ."

"The first idle talk which one heard here and there of a new revolution, of a new upheaval, of a new revolt, gradually grew in intensity to such an extent that only an irresponsible statesmanship could afford to ignore it. One could no longer simply dismiss as silly chatter all the information which came to us in hundreds and at last in thousands of reports both orally and in writing. Only three months ago the leaders of the Party were still convinced that it was simply the irresponsible gossip of political reactionaries, of Marxist anarchists, or of all sorts of idlers with which they had to deal—gossip which had no support in fact.

"In the middle of March I took steps to have preparations made for a new wave of propaganda which was to render the German people immune from any attempt to spread fresh poison. At the same time I gave orders to certain departments of the Party administration to trace the rumors of a new revolution which were continually cropping up and to find out, if possible, the sources from which they came. The result was that certain tendencies appeared in the ranks of some of the higher leaders of the SA which were bound to cause the gravest anxiety. At first it was a case of general symptoms, the inner connections of which were not at once clear:

"1. Against my express order, and in despite of declarations made to me through the Chief of Staff, Roehm, there had been such an increase in the numbers of the SA that the internal homogeneity of this unique organization must be endangered.

"2. Education in the National Socialist *Weltanschauung* in the above-mentioned sections of individual higher SA authorities had been more and more neglected.

"3. The natural relationship between the Party and the SA began slowly to be weakened. We were able to establish that efforts were being made, as it seemed systematically, to withdraw the SA more and more from the mission appointed for it by me and to use it in the service of other tasks or other interests.

"4. Promotions to posts of leadership in the SA when they were tested showed that a completely one-sided valuation had been set on purely external skill or often only on a supposed intellectual capacity. The great body of the oldest and most loyal SA men was always more and more neglected when appointments to the post of leader were made or when vacancies had to be filled, while a quite incomprehensible preference was shown for those who had been enlisted in the year 1933 who were not specially highly respected in the Movement. Often only a few months' membership in the Party or even only in the SA was enough to secure promotion to a high position in the SA which the old SA leader could not reach after years of service.

"5. The behavior of these individual SA leaders who had for the greater part not grown up with the Movement at all was false to National Socialist standards and often positively revolting. It could not be overlooked that it was precisely in these circles that one source of the unrest in the Movement was discovered, in that their incomplete practical National Socialism sought to veil itself in very unseemly demands for a new revolution.

"I drew the attention of the Chief of Staff, Roehm, to these abuses and to a number of others without meeting with any appreciable help in their removal, indeed without any recognizable concurrence on his part with my objections.

"In the months of April and May there was a constant increase in these complaints, and it was then that I received for the first time reports, confirmed by official documents, of conversations which had been held by individual higher leaders of the SA and which can only be described as 'gross impropriety.' For the first time in some official documents we obtained irrefutable evidence that in these conversations references had been made to the necessity for a new revolution and that leaders had received instructions to prepare themselves both materially and in spirit for such a new revolution. The Chief of Staff, Roehm, endeavored to maintain that these conversations had not in fact been held and that the reports were to be explained as veiled attacks upon the SA.

"The confirmation of some of these cases through the statements of those who had been present led to the most serious ill-treatment of these witnesses who for the most part came from the ranks of the old SA. Already by the end of April the leaders of the Party and a number of State institutions concerned in the matter were convinced that a certain group of the higher SA leaders was consciously contributing toward the alienation of the SA from the Party as well as from the other institutions of the State, or at least was not opposing this alienation. The attempt to remedy this state of affairs through the normal official channels always remained unsuccessful. The Chief of Staff, Roehm, promised me personally over and over again that he would inquire into these cases and that he would remove or punish the guilty parties. But no visible change in the situation resulted.

"In the month of May numerous charges of offenses committed by SA leaders, both those of high rank and of intermediate position, were received by officials of the Party and of the State; these offenses were supported by official documents and could not be denied. Provocative speeches led directly to intolerable excesses. The Minister-President Goering had already previously endeavored, so far as Prussia was concerned, to maintain the authority of the will of the National Socialist State over the self-will of individual elements. In some other German States, meanwhile, the authorities of the Party and the officials had been compelled to oppose single intolerable excesses. Some of the responsible parties were taken into custody. I have before this always stressed the fact that an authoritarian regime is under special obligations. When one demands of a people that it should put blind confidence in its leaders, then for their part these leaders must deserve this confidence through their achievement and through specially good behavior. Mistakes and errors may in individual cases slip in, but they are to be eradicated. Bad behavior, drunken excesses, the molestation of peaceful decent folk—these are unworthy of a leader, they are not National Socialist, and they are in the highest degree detestable.

"I have for this reason always insisted that in their conduct and behavior higher demands should be made of National Socialist leaders than of the rest of the people. He who desires to receive higher respect than others must meet this demand by a higher achievement. The most elementary demand that can be made of him is that in his life he should not give a shameful example to those about him. I do not desire, therefore, that National Socialists guilty of such offenses should be judged and punished more leniently than are other fellow-countrymen of theirs; rather, I expect that a leader who forgets himself in this way should be punished with greater rigor than would be an unknown man in a like case.

And here I would make no distinction between leaders of the political organizations and leaders of the formations of our SA, SS, Hitler Youth, etc.

"The resolution of the National Socialist Government to put an end to such excesses of individual unworthy elements which did but cover with shame the Party and the SA led to a very violent counter-activity on the part of the Chief of Staff. National Socialist fighters of the earliest days, some of whom had striven for nearly fifteen years for the victory of the Movement and now as high State officials in leading positions in our State represented the Movement, were called to account for the action which they had taken against such unworthy elements: that is to say, that through Courts of Honor, composed in part of some of the youngest members of the Party or even at times of those who were not members of the Party at all, the Chief of Staff, Roehm, sought to secure the punishment of these oldest Party combatants.

"These disagreements led to very serious exchanges of views between the Chief of Staff and myself, and it was in these interviews that for the first time doubts of the loyalty of this man began to rise in my mind. Though for many months I had rejected every such idea, though previously through the years I had protected this man with my person in unswerving loyalty and comradeship, now gradually warnings which I received—especially from my deputy in the leadership of the Party, Rudolf Hess—began to induce suspicions which even with the best of will I was not able to stifle.

"After the month of May there could be no further doubt that the Chief of Staff, Roehm, was busied with ambitious schemes which, if they were realized, could lead only to the most violent disturbances.

"If during these months I hesitated again and again before taking a final decision that was due to two considerations:

"1. I could not lightly persuade myself to believe that a

relation which I thought to be founded on loyalty could be only a lie.

"2. I still always cherished the secret hope that I might be able to spare the Movement and my SA the shame of such a disagreement, and that it might be possible to remove the mischief without severe conflicts. It must be confessed that the last days of May continuously brought to light more and more disquieting facts.

"The Chief of Staff now began to alienate himself from the Party not only in spirit but also in his whole external manner of life. All the principles through which we had grown to greatness lost their validity. The life which the Chief of Staff and with him a certain circle began to lead was from any National Socialist point of view intolerable. It was not only terrible that he himself and the circle of those who were devoted to him should violate all laws of decency and modest behavior, it was still worse that now this poison began to spread in ever wider circles. The worst of all was that gradually out of a certain common disposition of character there began to be formed within the SA a party which became the kernel of a conspiracy directed not only against the normal views of a healthy people but also against the security of the State. The review which took place in the month of May of promotions in certain SA districts led to the horrible realization that men without regard to services rendered to the National Socialist party or to the SA had been promoted to positions in the SA solely because they belonged to the circle of those possessing this special disposition. Individual cases with which you are familiar, such, for example, as that of the Standard-Leader Schmidt in Breslau, disclosed a picture of conditions which could only be regarded as intolerable. My order to proceed against the offenders was followed in theory, but in fact it was sabotaged.

"Gradually from amongst the leaders of the SA there emerged three groups: a small group of elements which were held together through a like disposition, men who were ready for any action and who had given themselves blindly into the hands of the Chief of Staff, Roehm. The principal members of this group were the SA leaders Ernst from Berlin, Heines in Silesia, Hayn in Saxony, and Heydebreck in Pomerania. Besides these there was a second group of SA leaders who did not belong to the former group in spirit but felt themselves bound to obey the Chief of Staff, Roehm, solely from a simple conception of a soldier's duty. Over against these stood a third group of leaders who made no secret of their inner disgust and reprobation and were in consequence in part removed from responsible posts, in part thrust aside, and in many respects left out of account.

"At the head of this group of SA leaders, who because of their fundamental decency had been hardly treated, stood the present Chief of Staff, Lutze, and the leader of the SS, Himmler.

"Without ever informing me, and when at first I never dreamt of any such action, the Chief of Staff, Roehm, through the agency of an utterly corrupt swindler—a certain Herr von A—, entered into relations with General Schleicher. General Schleicher was the man who gave external expression to the secret wish of the Chief of Staff, Roehm. He it was who defined the latter's views in concrete form and maintained that:

"1. The present regime in Germany cannot be supported.

"2. Above all the Army and all national associations must be united in a single band.

"3. The only man who could be considered for such a position was the Chief of Staff, Roehm.

"4. Herr von Papen must be removed and he himself would be ready to take the position of Vice-Chancellor, and that in addition further important changes must be made in the Cabinet of the Reich.

"As always happens in such cases there now began the search after the men for the new Government, always under the view that I myself should at least for the present be left in the position which I now hold.

"The execution of these proposals of General von Schleicher was bound, as soon as Point 2 was reached, to come up against my unalterable opposition. Both from a consideration of the facts and from a consideration of personal character it would never have been possible for me to consent to a change in the Reich Ministry of War and to the appointment of the Chief of Staff, Roehm, to that Ministry.

"Firstly: the consideration of the facts: for fourteen years I have stated consistently that the fighting organizations of the Party are political institutions and that they have nothing to do with the army. On the facts of the case it would be, in my opinion, to disavow this view of mine and my fourteen years of political life if I were now to summon to the head of the army the leader of the SA. In November, 1923, I proposed that an officer should lead the army and not the man who was then the leader of my SA., Captain Goering.

"Secondly: the consideration of human character. On this point it would have been impossible for me ever to concur in the proposal of General von Schleicher. When these plans became known to me my picture of the value of the character of the Chief of Staff, Roehm, was already such that before my conscience and for the sake of the honor of the army I could no longer under any circumstances contemplate admitting him to this post: above all, the supreme head of the army is the Field Marshal and President of the Reich. As Chancellor I gave my oath into his keeping. His person is for us all inviolate. The promise which I gave him that I would preserve the army as a non-political instrument of the Reich is for me binding, both from my inmost conviction and also from the word which I have given. But further, any such act would have been impossible for me on the human side in the face of the War Minister of the Reich. Both I myself and all of us are happy to be able to see in him a man of honor from the crown of his head to the soles of his feet. He reconciled the army with those who were once revolutionaries and has linked it up with their Government today and he has done this from the deepest convictions of his heart. He has made his own in truest loyalty the principle for which I myself will stand to my last breath.

"In the State there is only one bearer of arms, and that is the army; there is only one bearer of the political will, and that is the National Socialist party. Any thought of consenting to the plans of General von Schleicher would be, so far as I am concerned, not only disloyalty to the Field Marshal and the War Minister, but also disloyalty to the army. For just as General von Blomberg as War Minister in the National Socialist State fulfills his duty in the highest sense of the word, so do, also, the other officers and the soldiers. I cannot demand from them that as individuals each of them should take up a definite position towards our Movement, but not one of them has lost the true position of loyal service to the National Socialist State. And, further, I could not without the most compelling cause have permitted the removal of men who as a united body on January 30 gave me their promise to co-operate in the salvation of the Reich and of the people. . . ."

"Since the Chief of Staff, Roehm, was himself uncertain whether any attempt on the lines which I have described might not well meet with resistance from me, the first plan was devised in order to achieve the desired result by compulsion. Extensive preparations were made, in the first place:

"1. Psychological conditions which should favor the outbreak of a second revolution were to be systematically created. For this end by means of the SA propaganda authorities themselves the assertion was spread through the ranks of the SA that the army intended to disband the SA, and it was later added that unfortunately I myself had been won over to the support of this plan. A wretched and infamous lie!

"2. The SA must forthwith anticipate this attack, and in a second revolution must remove the reactionary elements on the one hand and the opposition of the Party on the other. Authority in the State must be entrusted to the leaders of the SA.

"3. To this end the SA should make as rapidly as possible all the necessary material preparations. Through different pretexts, e.g. by the lying statement that he was anxious to carry through a scheme of social relief for the benefit of the SA, the Chief of Staff, Roehm, succeeded in collecting contributions running into millions of marks. Twelve million marks were raised for these objects.

"4. In order to be in a position to deliver ruthlessly the most decisive blows there were formed under the title of 'Staff-Guards' groups of terrorists specially sworn in for the purpose. The old SA man had for more than a decade gone starving in the service of the Movement; now these new formations were paid troops, and the personal character and the purpose for which they were enlisted cannot be more clearly shown than by the truly fearful list of the punishments which they had previously incurred; indeed the old, true SA leader and SA man now very quickly were thrust into the background in favor of those elements which had enjoyed no political training but were better qualified for the kind of work for which they were intended. At certain gatherings of leaders as well as on holiday-trips gradually the SA leaders concerned in the plan were brought together and dealt with individually, that is to say, that while the members of the inner circle systematically prepared the main action, the second and larger circle of SA leaders was only given general information to the effect that a second revolution was on the way, that this second revolution had no other object than to restore to me personally my freedom of action, and that therefore the new—and this time bloody—rising—'The Night of the Long Knives' was their ghastly name for it—was exactly what I myself desired. The necessity for the initiative of the SA was explained by reference to my own inability to come to any decision: that disability would be removed only when I was faced with an accomplished fact. Presumably it was by means of these untrue pretexts that the preparation for the scheme so far as foreign policy was concerned was given to Herr von Detten. General von Schleicher saw to this aspect of the scheme in part personally, but left the practical side of the negotiations to his intermediary General von Bredow. Gregor Strasser was brought in.

"At the beginning of June I made a last attempt and had yet another talk with Roehm, which lasted nearly five hours and was prolonged until midnight. I informed him that from numberless rumors and from numerous assurances and statements of old, loyal comrades and SA leaders I had gained the impression that by certain unscrupulous elements a national-bolshevist rising was being prepared which could only bring untold misery upon Germany. . . . The Chief of Staff left this interview after assuring me that the reports were partly untrue and partly exaggerated, and that moreover he would for the future do everything in his power to set things to rights.

"The result of the interview, however, was that the Chief of Staff, Roehm, recognizing that for the undertaking which he was planning he could in no circumstances count on my personal support, now prepared to remove me personally from the scene. To this end it was explained to the larger circle of SA leaders who had been drawn into the plot that I myself was in thorough agreement with the proposed undertaking, but that I personally must know nothing about it or else that I wished on the outbreak of the rising immediately to be arrested and kept in custody for some twenty-four or forty-eight hours in order thus through the *fait accompli* to be relieved from an awkward responsibility which must otherwise arise for me in the sphere of our foreign relations. This explanation is conclusively illustrated by the fact that meanwhile care had been taken to bribe the man whose task it was later to carry through my removal. Standard-leader

Uhl, a few hours before his death, confessed that he had been ready to execute such an order.

"The first plan for the revolution was founded on the idea of granting leave to the SA. During this period of leave, since any plausible excuse was lacking, inexplicable riots were to break out similar to the conditions in August, 1932. These would compel me to summon the Chief of Staff, who alone would be in a position to restore order; for this purpose I should have to entrust him with full executive authority. But when meanwhile it had been clearly shown that in no circumstances could my willingness to give such an order be relied upon, this plan was abandoned and direct action was now contemplated.

"That action was to begin by a blow struck without any warning in Berlin: there was to be an assault upon the Government building, I myself was to be taken into custody so that further steps, as though ordered by me, could follow without any hindrance. The conspirators calculated that commands given in my name to the SA would immediately call into action the SA throughout the Reich, and also that thereby there would result automatically a division in all the other forces of the State ranged in opposition to the rising.

"The Chief of Staff, Roehm, the Gruppenführer (Group-Leader) Ernst, the Obergruppenführer Heines, Hayn, and a number of others declared in the presence of witnesses that immediately there was to follow a conflict of the bloodiest kind, lasting several days, with their opponents. The economic side of such a development was dismissed with positively insane irresponsibility: bloody terrorism in one way or another was to provide the necessary means. Here I must deal with the view that every successful revolution provides in itself its own justification. The Chief of Staff, Roehm, and his followers declared their revolution to be a necessity because only so could the victory of pure National Socialism receive its full justification. But at this point I must assert, both in the interest of the present and of posterity, that these men no longer had any right at all to appeal to National Socialism as their *Weltanschauung*. Their lives had become as evil as the lives of those whom we defeated in 1933 and whose places we took. The behavior of these men made it impossible for me to ask them to my house or, even if it were once only, to enter the house of the Chief of Staff in Berlin. It is difficult to conceive what would have become of Germany if these people had won the day. The greatness of the danger could not be fully realized until we received the communications which now reached Germany from abroad. English and French papers began with increasing frequency to speak of an upheaval which would shortly take place in Germany, and from the ever-growing stream of communications it was clear that the conspirators had systematically sought to foster the view in foreign countries that the revolution of the genuine National Socialists was at hand and that the existing regime was now incapable of action. General von Bredow, who as political agent in foreign affairs for General von Schleicher looked after these connections, worked in sympathy with those reactionary circles who—though not perhaps standing in any direct connection with this conspiracy—yet readily allowed themselves to be misused as subterranean purveyors of information for foreign Powers.

"Thus at the end of June I had made up my mind to put an end to this impossible development, and that, too, before the blood of ten thousand innocent folk should seal the catastrophe. . . . I decided that on Saturday, June 30, I would deprive the Chief of Staff of his office and for the time being keep him in custody and would arrest a number of SA leaders whose crimes were unquestioned. Since it was doubtful, when things had reached so threatening a climax, whether the Chief of Staff, Roehm, would have come to Berlin at all, or indeed anywhere else, I decided to go in person to a discussion amongst SA leaders which had been announced to be held at Wiessee. Relying on the authority of my own personality and on my power of decision which had never failed me in the hour of need, I determined that there at twelve o'clock midday I would deprive the Chief of Staff of his office, I would arrest those SA leaders who were principally responsible, and in an earnest appeal to the others I would recall them to their duty. However, in the course of June 29, I received such threatening intelligence concerning the last preparations for action that I was forced at midday to interrupt an inspection of a workers' camp in Westphalia in order to hold myself in readiness for all emergencies. At one o'clock in the night I received from Berlin and Munich two urgent messages concerning alarm-summonses: firstly that for Berlin an alarm-muster had been ordered for four o'clock in the afternoon, that for the transport of the regular shock-formations the requisition of lorries had been ordered, and that this requisition was now proceeding, and that promptly at five o'clock action was to begin with a surprise attack: the Government building was to be occupied. Gruppenführer Ernst with this end in view had not after all gone to Wiessee but had remained behind in Berlin to undertake the conduct of operations there.

"Secondly: in Munich the alarm-summons had already been given to the SA; they had been ordered to assemble at nine o'clock in the evening. The SA formations had not been dismissed to their homes, they were already stationed in their alarm-quarters. That is mutiny! I and no one else am the commander of the SA!

"In these circumstances I could make but one decision. If disaster was to be prevented at all, action must be taken with lightning speed. Only a ruthless and bloody intervention might still perhaps stifle the spread of the revolt. And then there could be no question that it was better that a hundred mutineers, plotters, and conspirators should be destroyed than that ten thousand innocent SA men should be allowed to shed their blood. For if once criminal activity was set in motion in Berlin, then the consequences were indeed unthinkable. The effect which had been produced by the fact that the conspirators purported to act in my name was proved by the distressing fact that, for instance, these mutineers in Berlin had succeeded through citing my authority in securing for their plot four armored cars from unsuspecting police-officers and further by the fact that the plotters Heines and Hayn in Saxony and Silesia through their appeals had made police-officers doubtful which side they should support in the coming conflict between the SA and the enemies of Hitler. It was at last clear to me that only one man could oppose and must oppose the Chief of Staff. It was to me that he had pledged his loyalty and broken that pledge, and for that I alone must call him to account!

"At one o'clock in the night I received the last dispatches telling me of the alarm-summonses; at two o'clock in the morning I flew to Munich. Meanwhile Minister-President Goering had previously received from me the commission that if I proceeded to apply a purge he was to take similar measures at once in Berlin and in Prussia. With an iron fist he beat down the attack on the National Socialist State before it could develop. The necessity for acting with lightning speed meant that in this decisive hour I had very few men with me. In the presence of the Minister Goebbels and of the new Chief of Staff the action of which you are already informed was executed and brought to a close in Munich. Although only a few days before I had been prepared to exercise clemency, at this hour there was no place for any such consideration. Mutinies are suppressed in accordance with laws of iron which are eternally the same. *If anyone reproaches me and asks why I did not resort to the regular courts of justice for conviction of the offenders, then all that I can say to him is this: in this hour I was responsible for the fate of the German people, and thereby I became the supreme Justiciar of the German people!*

"Mutinous divisions have in all periods been recalled to order by decimation. Only one State has failed to make any use of its Articles of War and this State paid for that failure by collapse—Germany. I did not wish to deliver up the young Reich to the fate of the old Reich. I gave the order to shoot those who were the ringleaders in this treason, and I further gave the order to burn out down to the raw flesh the ulcers of this poisoning of the wells in our domestic life and of the poisoning of the outside world. And I further ordered that if any of the mutineers should attempt to resist arrest, they were immediately to be struck down with armed force. The nation must know that its existence—and that is guaranteed through its internal order and security—can be threatened by no one with impunity! And everyone must know for all future time that if he raises his hand to strike the State, then certain death is his lot. And every National Socialist must know that no rank and no position can protect him from his personal responsibility and therefore from his punishment. I have prosecuted thousands of our former opponents on account of their corruption. I should in my own mind reproach myself if I were now to tolerate similar offences in our own ranks. No people and no Government can help it if creatures arise such as we once knew in Germany, a Kutisker for example, such as France came to know in a Stavisky, or such as we today have once more experienced —men whose aim is to sin against a nation's interests. But every people is itself guilty if it does not find the strength to destroy such noxious creatures. If people bring against me the objection that only a judicial procedure could precisely weigh the measure of the guilt and of its expiation, then against this view I lodge my most solemn protest. He who rises against Germany is a traitor to his country: and the traitor to his country is not to be punished according to the range and the extent of his act, but according to the purpose which that act has revealed. He who in his heart purposes to raise a mutiny and thereby breaks loyalty, breaks faith, breaks sacred pledges, he can expect nothing else than that he himself will be the first sacrifice. I have no intention to have the little culprits shot and to spare the great criminals. It is not my duty to inquire whether it was too hard a lot which was inflicted on these conspirators, these agitators and destroyers, these poisoners of the well-springs of German public opinion and in a wider sense of world opinion: it is not mine to consider which of them suffered too severely: I have only to see to it that Germany's lot should not be intolerable. A foreign journalist, who enjoys the privileges of a guest in our midst, protests in the name of the wives and children of those who have been shot and awaits the day when from their ranks there will come vengeance. To this gentleman I can say only one thing in answer: women and children have ever been the innocent victims of the criminal acts of men. I, too, have pity for them, but I believe that the suffering inflicted on them through the guilt of these men is but a minute fraction in comparison with the suffering that perhaps ten thousand German women would have had to endure if this act had been successful. A foreign diplomat explains that the meeting with Schleicher and Roehm was of course of an entirely harmless character. That matter I need not discuss with anyone. In the political sphere conceptions of what is harmless and what is not will never coincide. But when three traitors in Germany arrange and effect a meeting with a foreign statesman which they themselves characterize as 'serviceable,' when they effect this meeting after excluding every member of their staff, when they give strict orders that no word of this meeting shall reach me, then I shall have such men shot dead even when it should prove true that at a consultation which was thus kept secret from me they talked of nothing save the weather, old coins, and like topics.

"*The penalty for these crimes was hard and severe. Nineteen higher SA leaders, thirty-one leaders and members of the SA, were shot, and further, for complicity in the plot, three leaders of the SS, while thirteen SA leaders and civilians who attempted to resist arrest lost their lives. Three more committed suicide. Five who did not belong to the*

SA but were members of the Party were shot for taking part in the plot. Finally there were also shot three members of the SS who had been guilty of scandalous ill-treatment of those who had been taken into protective custody.

"In order to prevent political passion and exasperation venting itself in lynch justice on further offenders when the danger was removed and the revolt could be regarded as suppressed, still on Sunday, July 1, strictest orders were given that all further retribution should cease. Thereby from the night of Sunday, July 1, the normal state of affairs was reestablished. A number of acts of violence which do not stand in any connection with the plot will be brought before the ordinary courts for judgment.

"These sacrifices may indeed be heavy, but they will not be vain if from them once and for all results the conviction that every attempt at treason will be broken down without respect of person. If at some hour or another fate should summon me from my place, then I confidently hope that my successor will not act otherwise, and if he too must give place to another, that the third after us will be ready to protect the security of people and of nation with no less resolution.

"If in the two weeks that now lie behind us a part of the foreign press in place of any objective and just report of events has flooded the world with untrue and incorrect assertions and communications, I cannot admit the validity of the excuse that it was impossible to obtain any other information. In most cases it needed only a short telephone call to the authorities concerned in order to show that most of these assertions could not be sustained. When in particular the report was spread that among the victims of the conspiracy there were included even members of the Cabinet of the Reich, it would not have been difficult to establish that the contrary was the case. The assertion that the Vice-Chancellor, von Papen, that the Minister Seldte, or other members of the Cabinet of the Reich had been connected with the mutineers is most strongly contradicted by the fact that one of the first intentions of the mutineers was the murder of these men. Similarly all reports of any complicity in the plot on the part of any one of the German princes or of any pursuit of them is free invention. If finally during the last few days an English paper can report that I was at present suffering from a nervous breakdown, it would have needed only a small inquiry to establish the truth. I can only assure these anxious reporters that neither in the War nor after the War have I ever suffered such a breakdown, but this time I have indeed suffered the severest breakdown of the trust and faith which I had placed in a man for whose protection I had done everything in my power, for whom I had actually sacrificed myself. . . ."

"In these days which have been days of severe trial both for me and for its members the SA has preserved the spirit of loyalty. Thus for the third time the SA has proved that it is mine, just as I will prove at any time that I belong to my SA men. In a few weeks' time the brown shirt will once more dominate the streets of Germany and will give to one and all clear evidence that because it has overcome its grievous distress the life of National Socialist Germany is only the more vigorous. . . ."

Press

Le Temps, July 15-16—The speech of Chancellor Hitler did not live up to expectations. For not only did it fail to throw any new light on Germany's tragic June 30, but also it failed to give any direct or indirect hint as to the direction of the Reich's foreign policy. One can only conclude that the Fuehrer, only yesterday possessing absolute power in Germany, is now on the defensive at home. . . .

New York Times, July 14—It was a new role in which Chancellor Hitler appeared yesterday. Although hailed with frantic acclaim in the streets of Berlin, and sure in advance of the hysterical applause of a slavish Reichstag, he was distinctly on his defense. He spoke as one conscious that he had to justify himself to his own people. Even more significant than that, he was standing before the bar of public opinion throughout the whole world. Perhaps never before did so many foreigners wait eagerly for the speech of a German Chancellor. It is safe to say that never before did they get so little from one. Hitler promised to make his explanations "brutally frank." But for the larger part they were a rather monotonous repetition of what he had said a hundred times before. . . . His own anxieties are all too apparent in his speech.

London Times, July 14—Herr Hitler, the Chancellor, gave his account of the events of June 30, to the Reichstag last night. He declared that Captain Roehm had plotted to bring about a new revolution and he described the plans of the "mutineers." He admitted that seventy-seven people had been killed. The Reichstag unanimously approved the Government's action and thanked Herr Hitler. Herr Hitler bore the sign of strain on his features.

•

SPEECH OF AUGUST 17, 1934

Hamburg

Background

July 25—Assassination of Chancellor Dollfuss in Vienna by the Nazis. The attempted coup d'état fails. Dr. Schuschnigg becomes Chancellor, pledging that he will maintain Austrian independence.

August 2—Marshal Hindenburg, President of the Reich, dies.

August 3—Adolf Hitler assumes the dual functions of President and Chancellor of the Reich and orders a plebiscite to ratify this act. Hitler appoints Dr. Schacht (President of the Reichsbank) to the post of Minister of Economics.

The German Army takes an oath of loyalty to Hitler.

August 15—Publication of Hindenburg's testament.

The Speech

"... THE Field Marshal and President of the Reich was a unique figure and cannot be replaced. His mission as President of the Reich reached its fulfillment in himself. No one in the future shall bear this title any more.

"However logical the union of the two functions is, and though the law of the Government by which the question is settled cannot be challenged on constitutional grounds, yet I must absolutely decline to derive the right to take this most momentous step towards the new formation of the German Reich from any previous mandate. No! The people itself must decide!

"Although I do not desire in any way to anticipate the final form which one day the constitution of the German Reich will assume, I believe that I shall succeed in adding only new honor to the title of Chancellor of the German Reich for the future. The right to express so bold a view I assume on the basis of nearly fifteen years' work which—whether voluntarily or involuntarily—will one day be recognized as having produced a transformation and a development of truly historic magnitude. . . ."

"Millions lived in a world of Socialist conceptions which they might not be able to define in detail but as a whole appeared to them as fixed and necessary. Over against this world of Socialist conceptions there stood the national idea. Here, too, definitions might vary greatly, but here, too, the word 'national' embraced a sum of ideas which led up to a general conception for which millions were ready to give their all. Now the decisive factor was that the qualified representatives of these two views—or those who regarded themselves as such—maintained on principle that between these two worlds not only was any connecting link lacking but that they must of necessity stand opposed to each other in deadly enmity.

"The Socialist world was mainly inhabited by those who worked with the hand, the national world by those who worked with the brain. If these divided worlds were not to lead to the annihilation of Germany, one of the two, within a not too distant future, must emerge as victor, for in the long run a nation cannot survive when its brain workers see in the organized workers with the hand their deadly enemy and vice versa. The worst therefore which threatened us was thus not a victory of Marxism over bourgeois nationalism, but the worst fear was that this state of things should harden into permanency—that the German people should slowly but finally split into two self-sufficing bodies with different outlooks upon the world. The religious division within our people can teach us that such a development is possible.

"This, my fellow-countrymen, was the situation which met me and millions of others at the end of the War. . . . Only a tiny clique of international destroyers which favors strife in the world because it lives on strife could welcome such madness. . . . This struggle was bound at last to end in bolshevist chaos. What that would mean for Germany perhaps even today not everyone can completely realize. When I recognized this I could not at that time enter into a world of political parties which I was convinced could lead the nation only to its ruin. These were the considerations which determined my outlook.

"If the nationalism of our bourgeois world and the socialism of our Marxists could never unite; if, in consequence, the mass of the intelligentsia finally lost all relation to the mass of the people; and if lastly the nation, i.e. the German people, fell in consequence into complete disintegration and weakness, and therefore into economic annihilation, then both these theories could have no value for this people. For theories do not exist to annihilate peoples, but to make them happier. . . ."

"Thus, my fellow-countrymen, when I entered political life it was with the burning vow in my heart that I would root out from Germany this world of the political parties—that I would set in its place a community of the German people.

"And from the first day I saw clearly that this goal could not be reached in weeks or months or even in a few years. I realized the immense work which such a decision entails. Just as surely as an examination of the terms socialism and nationalism leads to a single definition, so certain is it that the realization of such a definition means unending work in educating the people. One can easily state, so far as the mere understanding of the statement goes, that the highest form of Nationalism finds its expression only in an unconditional devotion of the individual to the people. It will never be denied that the purest form of socialism means the conscious elevation of the claims of the people, its life and its interests above the interests and the life of the individual. But it is a task of immeasurable difficulty to translate the recognition of these facts from the world of ideals, from the sphere of abstract thought, into the realm of hard actualities.

"Here one was met by a world of prejudices. Descent, education, culture, profession, income, poverty, and wealth have all raised barriers which are apparently insurmountable. They need not be consciously hostile, these folk, and yet they cannot find the way to each other. The course of a long life which now lies behind them has so filled them with traditions that they seem to themselves—as innocent victims perhaps—to be no longer able to recognize that greater common element which should unite them. If in spite of all this I then attacked this great task with faith in my heart, I, an unknown German soldier of the World War, that was precisely because of the stupendous impression produced upon me by that—the greatest of all experiences. . . ."

"I would like further to deal briefly with those who think, quite wrongly, that they are restricted in their freedom to criticize.

"In my eyes criticism in itself is not an important function in life. The world can live without critics, it cannot live without workmen. I protest against the notion that there should exist a profession whose sole reason for its existence is that its professors, without personal responsibility, should of their superior wisdom continually interrupt those who are working and who do carry responsibilities. In my own life I have fought for thirteen years against a Government, but not with negative criticism but always pointing to that which should be done. I accepted responsibility when it was offered me. And no action will be taken by me which I am not prepared to defend before this people with my head and with my life.

"But at least I can claim before this people the same right which every worker, every peasant, and every employer can also claim for himself. What would a peasant say if while he toils in the sweat of his face someone wanted continuously to stroll round his land and did nothing else in his rounds than carp and criticize and stir up discontent? What would a workman do if while he stands before his machine some-one who can do nothing himself and does nothing were to address him and without stopping carped at his work and criticized it? I know that you would not tolerate the creature for a week but would send him to the Devil. The organiza-tion of the Movement gives to hundreds of thousands of men the possibility of co-operating in a positive way in shaping our national existence. Every helpful suggestion and all real co-operation will be welcomed with gratitude. But men whose sole activity is to express an opinion on the activity of others and to paint it in the darkest colors with-out ever themselves undertaking any practical responsibility —such men I will not tolerate. In this State everyone must in one way or another take his share in the struggle—and create.

In this State there can be no right to carp, but only a right to do the thing better. He who knows how to improve any activity, he who can put better knowledge in the place of worse, he who exposes an abuse and points out the way to mend it, he has every possibility of expressing himself and of employing himself. I have, it is true, in my life seen over and over again that one finds more men who know how a thing should be done than men who can actually put their knowledge into practice. And for every thousand men who are ready to judge a piece of work and give their opinion on it, there are rarely to be found ten who are themselves prepared to take part in the work. Ninety-nine per cent of all the professional criticizers who are ready enough to chatter will say not a word the moment anyone invites them to give proof of their better knowledge through actually putting it into practice and doing the job themselves. . . ."

"Our Government is supported by two organizations: politically by the community of the people organized in the National Socialist Movement, and in the military sphere by the army. . . . On the loyalty of these two organizations to the State rest the strength and the force of the State. In the maintenance of this construction the whole German people must have the greatest interest, for it assures to the German State an indestructible solidity both internally and externally; . . . it gives to the Government stability and permanence and enables it to pursue a long-range policy. . . ."

"There is no one in whose eyes the German Army needs to rehabilitate its fame in arms. *The German Government has no need to seek successes in war,* for its regime is based on a foundation which nothing can shake and it is supported by the confidence of the whole people. The Government of the German Reich needs no such successes in foreign politics to strengthen its domestic position. . . ."

"The vote of August 19 will, I hope, prove to the world afresh the unquestioned stability of the German Reich today, that this State can be relied upon just as much as can the love of peace which inspires both the people and its leaders.

"It is thus clear that the period of the German Revolution is now a closed chapter. . . ."

"Not for my own sake have I asked for this vote, but for the sake of the German people. It is not I who need such a vote of confidence in order to strengthen or maintain my position; it is the German people which needs a Chancellor supported in the eyes of the whole world by such a display of confidence. For I am nothing, my fellow countrymen, but the spokesman on your behalf, and I have no desire to be anything but the representative of your life and the defender of your vital interests. . . ."

"Real mistakes which can be proven against me—for them I will readily answer and accept responsibility. They are all within the limits set for everyone by general human fallibility. But against these mistakes I can set the fact that never in my fight have I taken any action which I was not convinced was for the welfare of the German people. For during my whole political fight I have been dominated, commanded, so help me God! by one thought alone, Germany!"

Press

New York Times, August 17—In this city (Hamburg), whose declining trade was skillfully hidden beneath a mantle of evergreens and swastika banners, and amid enthusiasm fostered by propaganda unimaginable elsewhere, Chancellor Adolf Hitler tonight made his culminating appeal to the German people to endorse next Sunday his grant to himself of unlimited authority over them and their future. . . . Above all, it was a conciliatory speech, evidently designed to dispel the misgivings of the business man and the worker regarding Germany's economic prospects.

Le Temps, August 19—The Fuehrer and Chancellor of the Reich pleaded his case with all his customary fire. He ordered every German to have faith in his government. In the realm of foreign affairs, M. Hitler said only that the world must recognize that the Reich will never sacrifice its honor and its equal rights, and that the German people, now that they had put their internal affairs in order, were ready to defend the security and independence of the Reich against all threats.

London Times, August 18—The Fuehrer's speech tonight contained little that was new. Referring to his action in uniting the Presidency and Chancellorship in his own person first and consulting the nation afterwards, he said that it had been necessary to spare the Reich a leaderless period. He again proclaimed that the German nation would never surrender its honor and reaffirmed its intense desire for a real peace.

•

SPEECH OF SEPTEMBER 8, 1934

Nuremberg

Background

August 19—The plebiscite gives Hitler 88.1% of the votes. He becomes "Reichsfuehrer."

August 20—Beginning of the campaign for the return of the Saar to the Reich.

September 4—Fourth rally of the National Socialist party opens at Nuremberg.

September 4-10—USSR joins the League of Nations.

The Speech

"IF ONE says that man's world is the State, his struggle, his readiness to devote his powers to the service of the community, one might be tempted to say that the world of woman is a smaller world. For her world is her husband, her family, her children, and her house. But where would the greater world be if there were no one to care for the small world? How could the greater world survive if there were none to make the cares of the smaller world the content of their lives? . . . Providence has entrusted to woman the cares of that world which is peculiarly her own, and only on the basis of this smaller world can the man's world be formed and built up. These two worlds are never in conflict. They are complementary to each other, they belong together as man and woman belong together. . . ."

"Every child that a woman brings into the world is a battle, a battle waged for the existence of her people. Man and woman must therefore mutually value and respect each other when they see that each performs the task which Nature and Providence have ordained. And from this separation of the functions of each there will necessarily result this mutual respect. It is not true, as Jewish intellectuals assert, that respect depends upon the overlapping of the spheres of activity of the sexes: this respect demands that neither sex should try to do that which belongs to the other's sphere. Respect lies in the last resort in this: that each knows that the other is doing everything which is necessary to maintain the whole community. . . . Woman is an egoist in the maintenance of her small world so that man may be free to defend the larger world: man is an egoist in maintaining this greater world, for it is indissolubly bound up with the other, smaller world. We would protect ourselves against a corrupted intellectualism which would put asunder that which God hath joined. Woman because she springs from that root which is the prime cause of life is also the most stable element in the maintenance of a people. She it is who in the last resort has the infallible sense for all that is necessary if a race is not to perish, for it will be her children who will be the first victims of that disaster. Man is often far too mentally unstable to find his way immediately to these fundamental truths. But in good time and with good education man will know just as clearly what his task is.

"We National Socialists have for many years protested against bringing woman into political life; that life in our eyes was unworthy of her. A woman said to me once: You must see to it that women go into Parliament; that is the only way to raise the standard of Parliamentary life. I do not believe, I answered, that man should try to raise the level of that which is bad in itself. And the woman who enters into this business of Parliament will not raise it, it will dishonor her. I would not leave to woman what I intend to take away from men. My opponents thought that in that case we would never gain women for our Movement; but in fact we gained more women than all the other parties together, and I know we should have won over the last German woman if she had only had the opportunity to study Parliament and the dishonoring role which women have played there. . . ."

"So our Women's Movement is for us not something which inscribes on its banner as its program the fight *against* man but something which sets on its program the common fight of woman *together with man:* For the new National Socialist community of the people was set on a firm basis precisely because we gained in millions of women our truest, our fanatical fellow-combatants, women who fought for the common life in the service of the common task of maintaining life, who in that combat did not set their gaze on rights which a Jewish intellectualism mirrored before their eyes, but rather on duties which nature imposes on all of us in common. . . ."

"The program of our National Socialist Women's Movement has in truth but one single point, and that point is The Child—that tiny creature which must be born and should grow strong, for in the child alone the whole life-struggle gains its meaning. . . . It is a glorious sight, this golden youth of ours: we know that it is the Germany of the future when we shall be no more. What we create and construct, that youth will maintain. For youth we work; it is that fact which gives its significance to all this effort of ours. And since we recognize this goal which Nature herself has set before us in all its lapidary simplicity, for us the work of both sexes naturally finds its true and logical setting, no longer in conflict, but in the common struggle for the realities of life."

•

SPEECH OF SEPTEMBER 10, 1934

Nuremberg

". . . INDUSTRY, commerce, agriculture, the middle class, shareholders, officials, employees, etc., were dragged into the political game of their own parties with the sole object of being able to stay the ruin of these classes which were incontestably necessary for the life of the nation. . . ."

"The character of this our former world of political parties must be understood if one is to comprehend the meaning of this parliamentary democracy and vice versa: we can thus state:

"1. That in these formations, despite all their talk, there was hardly a trace of a *Weltanschauung;*

"2. That in view of the whole mental content of these parties and their composition they were incapable of ever awakening the interest of the nation for a single great aim or of winning for that aim the nation as a whole;

"3. That they had not the least intention, in the interest of securing for the parties any higher idea or aim, to sacrifice those business possibilities which with their capitalistic skill it was not difficult for them to discover in the political divisions of the body of the people.

"It was, in consequence, to be expected that the tie which connected these parties with the people could only be a loose one, and such in fact it always was. Only in times of crisis did they suddenly recall to mind the poor elector and gave some thought to him in assemblies gathered together with more or less skill or naïveté. For the rest it was the task of the press to maintain the divisions of the people and to see to it that the wounds caused by these divisions were kept open. For *Parteitage* this mass of humanity was of no use. For at these gatherings there was no word about the party's *Weltanschauung:* it was only party tactics that were discussed, i.e. it was debated and decided how far compromise transactions could be concluded with the mass of the electors who were already committed to their differing outlooks on the world. So in the party gatherings, with their programs, of course, carefully determined beforehand, there were frequent moments of tension when amongst the illustrious political leaders no unanimous decision could be reached on the assignment of duties or when some felt it prudent to adopt the pretense of opposition in order not to lose those electors who were showing threatening signs of discontent. Nothing but imposture! . . ."

"When the National Socialist party appealed for the first time to the German people it resolutely refused to pledge itself to champion the cause of any separate group which was committed to the support either of religious or economic interests within the nation: its appeal was from the first directed to the heroic instincts of the people. It did not set its hopes upon those who always consider only the advantage of their own business or keep in view the members of the group associated with them; the National Socialist party looked to those idealists whom others so often mock as visionaries who without regard to their own interests, with faith in their hearts, cling to their people and their Reich and are ready if necessary to sacrifice their own existence to the eternal life of people and of Reich. . . ."

"Thus a new Party was formed, that is true; its membership was limited, but its leaders and its fighters were not to be measured by any economic standards: they possessed the essential quality of leadership. But the people which before then had grown hesitant, since it had been continuously betrayed by its own parties representing class, economic, and other interests, now turned with a sure instinct to those who, disregarding all economic limitations, simply on the ground of the value of their innermost conviction could rightly raise a claim to general leadership. And not only the people felt this instinctive attraction, but in the end the leaders and heads of this old party-world themselves shared that feeling. Unable to crush us, for half a decade they lived, now in the hope of a miracle, and now in fear of their own destruction. The only lucid intervals in their lives were those in which a dazed recognition of the danger of the National Socialist party began to dawn upon them. Their artificial scorn of the Movement was but the attempt to stifle with mockery and laughter that recognition which held them by the throat. . . ."

"Thus the minority of the National Socialist Movement as a Party cannot be compared with the former minorities of our opponents. . . . As a Party we were compelled to remain in a minority since we were mobilizing the most valuable elements in the nation—the fighters, those who were ready for sacrifice—and these have always formed not the majority, but the minority. . . ."

"And because we were racially the most valuable section of the German nation, because we proudly valued ourselves as such, because we courageously, boldly demanded that to us should be entrusted the leadership of the Reich and of the people, the people in ever growing numbers joined us and acknowledged our leadership. Its innermost consciousness rightly told it that its better self had found in the National Socialist party its point of concentration and its expression. Thus it was that our movement as an 'historic minority' could grasp supremacy in Germany in understanding with and with the will of the overwhelming majority of the German nation. And as soon as the Government of the Reich was finally united with the leadership of the Party then there happened the miracle which most profoundly shattered the illusions of our foes.

"They all calculated, deceived by their own experiences, that after a few months of National Socialist government the German people would be disillusioned and return to its former party divisions. . . . But the German people after a year and a half has continuously devoted itself only the more completely to the Movement in the heart of which it recovered its best self, its best characteristics. . . ."

"The basis which formed the foundation for our rise and growth in the past is valid also for the future. The following principle must be recognized: always only a part of the people will be composed of really active fighters. They have been in Germany the supporters of the National Socialist struggle: they were the fighters in the National Socialist revolution and it is they who uphold the National Socialist State. From them more is demanded than from the millions of their other fellow-countrymen. For them the mere profession 'I believe' is not enough: their vow must be 'I fight.'

"The Party will for all time form the picked body of the leaders of the German people. It will develop a State of political apostles and combatants who then as obedient officers, true to their duty, will serve the Movement. It will be that great school which attracts to itself the millions of our people, educates them and then sends them out into the world. In it there will develop a tradition in the art of leading a people which will not permit that men of alien spirit should ever again confuse the brain and the heart of the Germans.

"It will be in its teaching unalterable, in its organization hard as steel, in its tactics supple and adaptable, but in its whole appearance it will resemble an Order.

"It is for all time the mustard-seed of the National Socialist idea, the teacher of the art of National Socialist organization, the school of National Socialist propaganda.

"The aim must be that all decent Germans shall be National Socialists: only the best National Socialists shall be members of the Party.

"If these views are not understood especially by the members of the bourgeois class, if we are asked whether the people will in the long run be content to be led by such a minority, then we must answer these inquisitive, anxious folk as follows:

"1. Peoples have never yet been successfully led by a majority but always only by a minority.

"2. This minority is not something outside, alien to the majority and opposed to it, it is composed of the best elements chosen out of the people as a whole. Just as the nation entrusts to a minority the defence of all its individual vital interests and feels no jealousy, so it will without hesitation entrust to a minority also the defence of its most weighty affairs so soon as it realizes that the minority is the most capable authority and, further, represents those from its own ranks best qualified to perform these tasks. . . ."

"It is above all else our task only to admit to the Party as new members those who can offer us guarantees that they do in fact belong to that minority which in the past by virtue of its intrinsic worth has always made history. If formerly the necessary conflict, the demands made and the sacrifices called for secured of themselves a sound selection amongst the candidates for membership and prevented the chaff from mingling with the wheat, in the future by conscientious methods and rigorous tests we must see to it that the same care is taken. For in the early days it was dangerous to become a National Socialist, and for this reason we gained the best fighters. Now it is profitable for folk to 'co-ordinate' themselves with us, and we must therefore be on our guard lest those hasten to join us who under the symbol of our fight and our sacrifices do but wish to do business cheaply. In the early days our opponents took good care that through waves of vetoes and persecutions the Movement should from time to time go through a fresh 'combing out' process and we thus got rid of the light trash that began to find its way into our ranks. Today we ourselves must hold a muster and must reject what has proved itself to be base and which therefore does not in any true sense belong to us. . . ."

"A young generation is growing up and it has never experienced the infection of our poisonous party politics, it has never experienced the corruption of our parliamentary-democratic system: all this is alien to our youth, it is from the outset incomprehensible. Those of advanced years may still have their doubts, but youth is devoted to us: it has joined us in body and in soul. Youth lives in this proud Germany of the swastika, and that symbol it will nevermore be able to tear from its heart. Youth loves the singleness of purpose, the resolution of our leadership, and would not understand if suddenly a mummified past were to come with utterances which even in their language are drawn from an alien period—a language no longer spoken, no longer comprehended. Youth is not growing up in the belief that status, classes, professions are of importance; its faith is in a single German nation. In their hearts there is no room for the prejudices, the conceit, the arrogance which in former generations were the characteristics of some classes of our people. For the young live with one another, they march together, they sing in common the songs of the Movement and of the Fatherland: they believe in a Germany which belongs to them all. In their ranks we shall find the best recruits for the National Socialist party. We see them grow from childhood: we watch them as they develop. We can test the character of each, we can follow their individualities, and at length we can choose from their number those who seem to us the worthiest to take their places in the ranks of the Old Guard. . . ."

"He who breaks his vow of loyalty has no longer any right to demand loyalty from his subordinates. He who refuses to obey has no longer any right to expect obedience. He who ceases to act as a comrade must not be surprised if one day he also finds himself lonely, betrayed, abandoned."

Press

New York Times, September 10—Predictions of startling revelations of party or governmental policies were upset and his concluding speech tonight was largely a repetition of his former indictments of the old Parliamentary regime . . .

Le Temps, September 12—The Fuehrer defined the aims of National Socialism. It had become the only and the universal party. M. Hitler made a discreet allusion to the race-theory: "The Party represents an élite, a natural aristocracy," the Fuehrer said, "which must be preserved by exercising a rigorous choice of its members."

•

SPEECH OF JANUARY 15, 1935

Berchtesgaden

Background

1934

September 10—The "East European Locarno Pact" guaranteeing the status quo of Eastern Europe is rejected by Germany.

October 9—French Foreign Minister Barthou and King Alexander of Yugoslavia assassinated in Marseilles.

November 8—In Paris, Gaston Doumergue resigns after

having failed to bring about a reform of the Constitution. He is succeeded by Etienne Flandin. Pierre Laval takes charge of the Quai d'Orsay.

December 22—International troops occupy the Saar in anticipation of the plebiscite.

1935

January 13—Plebiscite in the Saar territory. Out of a total of 528,005 votes cast, 477,119 (90.5 per cent) were for Germany, and the Saar returned to the Reich.

The Speech

"GERMANS!

"An injustice that has lasted for fifteen years is approaching its end! The suffering of hundreds of thousands of folk-comrades in the Saar during this period was shared by the whole German nation. The whole German nation rejoices at the return of our comrades. It was fated that not reason was to put an end to this senseless and miserable situation, but the provisions of the Treaty which promised to bring peace to the world and brought only endless misery and constant destruction.

"We are therefore all the prouder that after fifteen years of oppression, on January 13, 1935, the voice of the blood spoke out in a mighty declaration of faith!

"There is one thing we all realize, my folk-comrades of the Saar: that we owe our joy to you. Today, a few hours from now, throughout the whole German Reich the bells will ring as an external expression of our pride and joy. We owe this to the unshakable loyalty of you Saar Germans, to your patience and perseverance, as well as to your bravery. Neither force nor temptation made you waver in your faith that you are Germans, as you always have been and always will be! Therefore, as the Fuehrer of the German people and Chancellor of the Reich, in the name of all Germans, I now express the nation's gratitude to you. At this moment when you are once more with us, sons of our people and citizens of the new German Reich; we are filled with rejoicing.

"It is a proud thing to be chosen by providence as representative of a nation. Now and in the weeks to come, you Germans of the Saar are the representatives of the German people and the German Reich. I know that despite the intoxication of victory, you will keep your heads, as you always did in the past under the most difficult circumstances. You will not forget that many of our enemies are still eager to find some fault with you, even now when you have returned to your great Fatherland.

"Therefore you must continue to maintain the firmest discipline.

"The German people is all the more grateful to you because your act has removed one of the key sources of tension in Europe. For we all wish to view this act of January 13 as a first and decisive step toward a gradual reconciliation of those nations which twenty years ago, through fatal alliances and human incompetence, plunged into the most terrible and most ruthless struggle of all time. Your decision, German comrades of the Saar, today gives me the opportunity to make a historic sacrifice, our contribution to the peace which is so necessary to Europe. *The opportunity to declare that after your return the German Reich has no more territorial demands on France*. I believe that this will also be an expression of our appreciation to the powers who together with us and France agreed that the vote should take place and saw to it that it did take place.

"It is the wish of all of us that this German end to a tragic injustice shall contribute to the pacification of Europe. For, although we are unconditionally resolved to win equal rights for Germany, we are also willing to take all measures which will restore true solidarity among the nations and eliminate the present perils and miseries. You, my German folk-comrades of the Saar, have made an important contribution.

Other nations will now recognize the indestructible community of our people and the true inward and outward worth of the German nation and the Third Reich.

"For this millions of overflowing hearts in Germany thank you!

"Welcome to our dear homeland, to our united German Reich!"

Press

London Times, January 16—Herr Hitler delivered a broadcast address in which he renounced any further German territorial claims against France and referred to the prospects of a gradual reconciliation in Europe.

New York Times, January 16—Chancellor Adolf Hitler, his strident voice ringing in triumph, told the Reich, the Saar, and the world today that the plebiscite vote had erased both fifteen years of injustice and Germany's territorial claims on France.

Le Temps, January 17—In the Proclamation of the results, M. Adolf Hitler made some friendly references to our country. . . . Even though such assurances hardly correspond to certain recent acts of the German Front, we must not disclaim their importance. M. Hitler in effect declared that the new strength which Germany has just acquired will be used in the cause of peace. It may possibly be true. But only on the condition that the German power finds on every hand other well-organized powers, which exist not to oppose her or to strangle her but to guard her and collaborate with her.

SPEECH OF MARCH 1, 1935

Saarbruecken

Background

January—Throughout the month of January, conflicts occur between Germany and Lithuania on account of the administration of the Memel territory.

January 17—In Soviet Russia, Kamenev and Zinoviev are imprisoned for counter-revolutionary activities.

February 3—Following a visit to London of the French Ministers, Etienne Flandin and Pierre Laval who met MacDonald and Sir John Simon, an Anglo-French declaration is published containing the following points: 1. Renewal of pledge between England, France, and Italy to consult one another in case the independence and integrity of Austria should be menaced. 2. Offer to free Germany from the clauses of the Versailles Treaty restricting her armaments and substituting a new agreement between all powers on an equal footing. 3. Suggestion that Germany should return to the League. 4. Suggestion of an Eastern pact of mutual security.

February 11—Italian mobilization against Abyssinia.

February 26—Creation of the Luftwaffe with Goering as Commander-in-Chief.

March 1—The Saar Territory is handed over to Frick, German Minister of the Interior, by M. Aloisi, President of the Commission of Three, acting in behalf of the League of Nations.

The Speech

"THIS day is not a day of good fortune for Germany alone. I believe that this day is a fortunate day for the whole of Europe. It was a blessed decision to fix the day [for the plebiscite] and to respect its result—to restore to the German Reich this territory which so easily could have become a permanent apple of discord, this territory which had been torn away against all justice and reason.

"A day of happy fortune for Europe especially, because through this return of the Saar territory there can perhaps be best removed that crisis under which two great nations have had to suffer most. *We hope that through this act of conciliatory justice, through this restoration of natural reason, the relations between Germany and France will be finally improved.* Just as we wish for peace so must we hope that the great neighbor people will be ready and willing to seek this peace with us. It must be possible that two great peoples should unite their hands in order that, working together, they may attack those distresses which threaten to bury Europe beneath their weight.

"And this day shall at the same time be a lesson, a lesson for all those who, in ignorance of an eternal historical truth, imagine that through terrorism or violence they can rob a people of its inmost character, a lesson for those who think they can tear away a part of a nation in order to steal from it its soul. Would that all statesmen from this experience might realize one thing—that it is useless to seek to tear asunder peoples by such methods. In the end blood is stronger than all paper documents. *What ink wrote will one day be blotted out by blood.* This deepest voice will in the end sharply, clearly, drown every other sound. Woe to him who can learn nothing from these facts. He will bring distress and trouble upon men without attaining his purpose. He will for the time being bring suffering and distress upon the peoples, but in the end he will be shamefully defeated."

Press

New York Times, March 3—In an address Herr Hitler declared that the return of the Saar paved the way for Franco-

German reconciliation, and that it was quite possible it had ended the crisis from which the two nations had suffered.

Le Temps, March 3—The significant part of M. Hitler's speech is the passage: "We hope that with the return of the Saar region to Germany the relations between France and Germany will improve more and more. Even as we desire peace, we hope that our great neighbor people is willing to seek peace with us. We hope that we will join hands to this end, upon which the salvation of Europe depends." Let us pray that the acts of the Reich Chancellor will not belie the words of the Fuehrer, and that the restoration of the Saar to Germany will have quite other consequences than those anticipated by certain National Socialist organs across the Rhine, who envisage a future in terms not at all pacific or reassuring.

London Times, March 2—In a speech to an enthusiastic crowd Hitler expressed the hope that the "great historic" event of that day would lead to an improvement in the relations of France and Germany.

•

PROCLAMATION OF MARCH 16, 1935

Radio Broadcast

Background

March 4—The British Government publishes a "White paper" commenting on German re-armament, particularly in the air.

March 15—France adopts an extension of military service from one to two years.

March 16—Germany decrees the re-establishment of universal military service. Hitler thus wipes out the military restrictions of the Versailles Treaty.

The Proclamation

"... The Government of the German Reich of today desires only a single moral and material power—that is the power to be able to safeguard peace for the Reich and thereby for the whole of Europe.

"It has therefore taken all further steps which lay within its power which might serve to advance the cause of peace:

"1. It has for a long time past offered to all neighboring States the conclusion of pacts of non-aggression.

"2. With its neighboring State on the East it has sought and found a treaty arrangement which, thanks to ready understanding on the part of that State, has, the Government hopes for all time, cleared the poisonous and threatening atmosphere which it found in existence when it came into power and which will lead to a permanent understanding and friendship between the two peoples.

"3. Finally it has given to France the solemn assurance that Germany, now that the question of the Saar has been settled, will not make or raise any further territorial claims on France. It believes that thereby, in a form which can have but few parallels in history, it has created the conditions for the termination of a century-long dispute between two great nations, through a heavy political and material sacrifice.

"The German Government must, however, to its regret, observe that for months past there has been taking place a continuous increase in armaments on the part of the rest of the world. *It sees in the creation of a Soviet-Russian army of 101 divisions, i.e. an admitted peace-strength of 960,000 men, an element that could not have been contemplated at the time of the conclusion of the Treaty of Versailles.*

"It sees in the speeding-up of similar measures in other

States further proofs of the rejection of the idea of disarmament which had formerly been proclaimed. The German Government has no intention of wishing to level a reproach against any State: but today it feels bound to put on record that through the introduction, which has now been decreed, in France of a two-year period of military service the conceptions which underlay the creation of short-service defensive armies have been abandoned in favor of a long-service organization.

"But the short-service system was one of the arguments on which was based the claim that Germany should sacrifice her Reichswehr.

"The German Government feels that in these circumstances it is impossible any longer to delay the measures which are necessary for the security of the Reich or indeed to fail to disclose those measures to others.

"If, therefore, the German Government now complies with the wish expressed in the speech of the English Minister Baldwin on November 28, 1934, for information on German intentions it does so:

"1. In order to give to the German people the conviction and to the other States the knowledge that *the safeguarding and security of the German Reich from henceforth will be entrusted to the German nation's own strength*. And

"2. In order that through fixing the extent of the German measures *it may invalidate all insinuations that the German people is seeking to establish a military hegemony in Europe.*

"What the German Government, as protector of the honor and interests of the German nation, desires is to secure such a measure of military force as is necessary not merely for maintaining the integrity of the German Reich but also for assuring international respect and esteem for Germany as coguarantor of general peace.

"For at this hour the German Government renews before the German people and before the entire world the affirmation of its resolve never to go beyond that which the protection of German honor and the freedom of the Reich demand and especially *it affirms that it wishes in the national German armament to create no instrument of military aggression,* but on the contrary to create exclusively an instrument of defense and therefore an instrument for the maintenance of peace.

"The Government of the German Reich further expresses the confident hope that the German people which thus once more finds its way back to its honor may be able in independence and in the enjoyment of equal rights to make its contribution to the pacification of the world in free and frank co-operation with the other nations and their Governments. . . ."

Press

Le Temps, March 18—This is violation of the military, naval, and air clauses of the 1919 Peace Treaty. It is a flagrant, brutal, and coldly premeditated violation. It is also the conclusion of the Reich's policy of camouflaged, clandestine rearmament, which could no longer continue to develop under cover of certain deceptions. . . . What will be the result of this? . . . It is too early to discuss the problem. We can only remark that this act of Germany's has thrown every European capital into confusion and indignation.

London Times, March 17—If Herr Hitler's move is simply a rather crude method of asserting German equality, then no irreparable harm has been done. The negotiations can go forward.

New York Times, March 17—No more ominous word has been spoken to a world that is longing for a period of international peace and good will than that which came from Germany yesterday. . . . The change of outward attitude manifested in the conscription of millions for military training in the years of the immediate future can have but one of two interpretations: one a deliberate, vengeful menace to the peace of Europe and the other a confession of a failure in domestic economic policies. From yesterday will date a new period of anxiety and stress and strain.

•

SPEECH OF MAY 1, 1935

Berlin

Background

1935

March 20—France asks the League of Nations to take up the matter of the new German conscript army of 500,000 men decreed on March 16; on March 18 Great Britain also formally protests against this violation of the Versailles Treaty. On March 21 Italy joins the protest. On March 25, Anglo-German conversations begin at Berlin with Sir John Simon and Anthony Eden.

April—Stresa Conference between the English (MacDonald and Sir John Simon), the French (Flandin and Laval), and the Italians (Mussolini).

The results of the conference are: 1, an Anglo-Italian declaration stating that the two countries will adopt a common line of action in connection with France's appeal to the League of Nations against Germany's violation of the Versailles Treaty; reaffirmation of Austrian independence; 2, a declaration by the three Powers stating their complete agreement in opposing by all practical means any unilateral repudiation of treaties.

This declaration was to be known as forming the basis for the "Stresa Front."

Council of League of Nations condemns unanimously Germany's violation of the military clauses of the Versailles Treaty (Denmark abstaining).

The Speech

" . . . A WRITER has summed up the impressions made on him by this time in a book which he entitled 'The Decline of the West.' Is it then really to be the end of our history and of our peoples? No! we cannot believe it. This age must be called, not the decline of the West, but the resurrection of the peoples of this West of ours! Only that which was old, decayed and evil perishes; and let it die! But new life will spring up. Faith can be found, if the will is there. Our leadership has the will, and faith is with the people. . . ."

"So we have come together on this day to prove symbolically that we are more than a collection of individuals striving one against another, that none of us is too proud, none of us too high, none is too rich, and none too poor, to stand together before the face of the Lord and of the world in this indissoluble, sworn community. And this united nation, we have need of it. When was a leadership at any time faced with a heavier task than our German leadership? Consider, my comrades, what our Germany is, and compare it with other countries. What have we? One hundred and thirty-seven people to the square kilometer; no colonies; no raw materials; no foreign exchange, no capital, no longer any foreign credits; only heavy burdens, sacrifices, taxation, and low wages. What have we, compared with the wealth of other States, the wealth of other countries, the wealth of other peoples, with the possibilities of living that they possess? What have we? One thing only; we have our people. Either it is everything or it is nothing. On it alone can we count. On it alone can we build. Everything that we have created up to the present we owe solely to its goodness of heart, its capacity, its loyalty, its decency, its industry, its sense of order. And if I weigh all this in the balance, it seems to me to be more than all that the rest of the world can offer us. So this, I believe, can be our message to the other peoples on this first of May: '*You need have no fear that we want anything of you. We are proud enough to confess that we ourselves own that treasure, which you certainly could not give us—our people.'* I could, as leader, think of no more glorious, no prouder task in this world than to serve this people. One might give me continents, but I would rather be the poorest citizen among this people. And with this people we must and shall succeed in achieving also the tasks that are still to come.

"What we want lies clear before us: not war and not strife. *Just as we have established peace within our own people, so we want nothing else than peace with the world.* For we all know that our great work can succeed only in a time of peace. But just as the leadership of the nation in the domestic sphere has never sacrificed its honor in its relations with the German people, so it can never surrender the honor of the German people in its dealings with the world.

"We know what we owe to the world. May the world come to understand what she can never deny to a proud people, and above all may she comprehend one thing: the Germany of today is not the Germany of yesterday—just as little as the Germany of yesterday was the Germany of today. The German people of the present time is not the German people of the day before yesterday, but the German people of the two thousand years of German history which lie behind us."

Press

London Times, May 2—Herr Hitler said that May Day is the day of solidarity of a people in work.

New York Times, May 2—In his own twenty-minute speech, which ended in a peroration about "my people" and "God" that recalled some of the speeches by the former Kaiser, Herr Hitler repudiated defeatism that talked about "the decline of the Occident" and appealed for national solidarity and obedience to his will in order to resurrect the

Occidental peoples and win peace—on National Socialist terms.

Le Temps, May 3—He pointed out to "his" people that in Germany the population was 137 to each square kilometer, that the Germans possessed no raw materials, that they had no colonies, that they had only heavy taxes and slender wages. . . . Exactly what is this speech leading up to? It needs some clarification. Perhaps the Chancellor's words imply the condemnation of the whole policy of antagonism and defiance which has led the Reich into that misery and isolation from which she suffers today. On the other hand, perhaps they are intended to inflame the German people into envy of the prosperity of other nations. And we know where such agitation leads to, under the impact of despair. That the situation of the German people is tragic, no one would deny. But it is the very same leaders of Germany who, having created the situation, persist in isolating Germany from the rest of Europe, and deliberately reject any fruitful international co-operation.

•

SPEECH OF MAY 21, 1935

Berlin, Reichstag

Background

Early May—Beginning of agitation in Sudeten Germany, with Henlein as leader.

May 2—Laval goes to Moscow to meet Stalin and confer on the Russo-French mutual assistance pact. On his return Laval meets Goering in Cracow. Pilsudski dies in Poland. Russo-Czech mutual assistance pact is signed.

End of May—Elections in Czechoslovakia. Henlein's Sudeten German "Home Front" becomes the strongest German party and the second strongest party in the country.

The Speech

"FROM Anglo-Saxon countries I often hear expressions of regret that Germany should have departed from just those principles of democratic government which such countries consider as specially sacred. This opinion is based upon a serious error. Germany too has a 'democratic' constitution. The present German Government of the National Socialist State has also been elected by the people and feels itself in the same way responsible to the people. It does not matter how many votes a deputy must have in the individual countries. There are countries which consider 20,000 votes necessary for a deputy, others consider 10,000 or 5,000 sufficient, while in others again the number is 60,000 or more.

"The German people has elected a single deputy as its representative with 38 million votes. This is perhaps one of the most important differences between ours and the conditions existing in other countries. It means that I feel myself just as responsible to the German people as would any Parliament. I act on the trust they have placed in me and I carry out their mandate. The German people therefore have the right to expect that an explanation such as I am about to give today should be the unvarnished truth, and that it should openly discuss those questions which affect not only the rest of the world but also, and at least to the same degree, the German nation itself. And I am glad of this for the following reasons:

"As Fuehrer and Chancellor of the nation and as head of the Government of the Reich, unfortunately I have often to make decisions which are of themselves hard enough to decide upon and which are all the more difficult because it is not possible for me to share the responsibility and even less to shift it to someone else's shoulders. And it is for this reason that I desire at least to be able to give to the nation itself an insight into the ideas on which I act and thus make it easier for them to understand the decisions and measures which arise from these ideas. But the more difficult the decisions, so much the more I as a German should like to make sure that my actions are completely uninfluenced by instincts of weakness or fear and to bring them into harmony with my conscience towards my God and the nation which He permits me to serve. . . ."

"For the German nation the economic consequences of the peace on the one hand and the disadvantages from which Germany suffered in her home and foreign trade and commerce, on the other, must inevitably have compelled any Government, whether it willed or not, to take the actual situation into account. We are all convinced that the complete carrying out of the idea of economic self-sufficiency for all States, which is threatening us today, is, when seen from a higher standpoint, foolish and can only result in harm for all nations. . . ."

"For Europe this development will one day have very unpleasant and evil consequences. But to alter it is unfortunately not within Germany's power. Looked at from the broad economic angle, it is against the dictates of reason. What happens is that insofar as we are deprived of foreign markets for our exports we are forced to restrict our imports. To that extent, so that German productive labor may not stagnate, we must either employ a complicated process for the production of raw materials that we lack internally or else we must use substitutes. This task can be undertaken only by means of a planned economic system. And that is a perilous adventure; for planned economics lead to bureaucratic control and thus to the suppression of individual creative effort. In the interests of our own nation it was not desirable to risk the eventuality of having the productive efficiency of our people reduced, and the standards of living lowered rather than raised by an economic system not far removed from the communist ideal and by the accompanying paralysis of initiative effort. . . ."

"If, despite such knowledge, we have nevertheless taken this path it was only under the hard pressure of necessity. What we have achieved in two and a half years in the way of a planned provision of labor, a planned regulation of the market, a planned control of prices and wages was considered a few years ago to be absolutely impossible. We only succeeded because behind these apparently dead economic measures we had the living energies of the whole nation. . . ."

"We Germans can only regret that the rest of the world still takes so little trouble to study objectively what has been going on in Germany within the last two and a half years and that it does not study the ideals which are solely responsible for these achievements. . . ."

"This new Germany cannot be compared with the Germany of the past. Its ideas are just as new as its actions. The spirit of bourgeois jingoism as a decisive political factor has been just as much overcome as the tendencies of Marxist internationalism. If the present Germany advocates peace, it does so neither owing to weakness nor to cowardice. It advocates peace from another standpoint regarding people and State, namely, the standpoint of National Socialism. For National Socialism regards the forcible amalgamation of one people with another alien people not only as a worthless political aim, but in the long run as a danger to the internal unity and hence the strength of a nation. National Socialism therefore dogmatically rejects the idea of national assimilation. That also disposes of the bourgeois belief in a possible 'Germanization.'

"It is therefore neither our wish nor our intention to deprive alien sections of our population of their nationalism, language, or culture, in order to replace these by something German and foreign to them. We issue no directions for the Germanization of non-German names; on the contrary, we do not wish that. *Our racial theory, therefore, regards every war for the subjection and domination of an alien people as a proceeding which sooner or later changes and weakens the victor internally, and eventually brings about his defeat.* But we do not believe for a moment that in Europe the nations whose nationalism has been completely consolidated could in the era of the principle of nationalities be deprived of their national birthright at all. The last 150 years provide more than enough instructive warnings of this. In no future war will the European national States be able to achieve—apart from the temporary weakening of their opponents—more than petty adjustments of national frontiers, of no consequence in comparison with the sacrifices made.

"But the permanent state of war that will be established between the various peoples by such intentions may perhaps appear advantageous to various political and economic interests. For the nations, however, it merely means burdens and misfortune. The blood shed on the European Continent in the course of the last 300 years bears no proportion to the national result of the events. In the end France has remained France, Germany Germany, Poland Poland, and Italy Italy. What dynastic egoism, political passion, and patriotic blindness have attained in the way of apparently far-reaching political changes by shedding rivers of blood has, as regards national feeling, done no more than touched the skin of the nations. It has not substantially altered their fundamental characters. If these States had applied merely a fraction of their sacrifices to wiser purposes the success would certainly have been greater and more permanent.

"When I, as a National Socialist, advocate this view perfectly frankly, I am also influenced by the following realization. The principal effect of every war is to destroy the flower of the nation. But as there is no longer any unoccupied space in Europe, every victory—without making any difference to the fundamental distress in Europe—can at best result in a quantitative increase in the number of the inhabitants of a country. But if the nations attach so much value to that, they can achieve it without tears in a simpler and more natural way. A sound social policy, by increasing the readiness of a nation to have children, can give its own people more children in a few years than the number of aliens that could be conquered and made subject to that nation by war.

"No! Nationalist Socialist Germany wants peace because of its fundamental convictions. And it wants peace also owing to the realization of the simple primitive fact that no war would be likely essentially to alter the distress in Europe. It would probably increase it. . . ."

"Germany needs peace and desires peace. And when I now hear from the lips of a British statesman that such assurances are nothing, and that the only proof of sincerity is the signature appended to collective pacts, I must ask Mr. Eden to be good enough to remember that it is a question of an 'assurance' in any case. It is sometimes much easier to sign treaties with the mental reservation that one will reconsider one's attitude at the decisive hour than to declare, before an entire nation and with full publicity, one's adherence to a policy which serves the cause of peace because it rejects anything that may lead to war.

"I might have signed ten treaties, but such action would not have been of the same importance as the statement I made to France on the occasion of the Saar plebiscite. When I, as the Fuehrer and representative of the German nation, gave to the world and to my own people the assurance that with the settlement of the Saar question no further territorial demands would be made on France, that was a contribution to peace much greater than many a signature under many a pact. I believe that this solemn declaration really ought to have put an end to a quarrel of long duration between these two nations. We made it in the belief that this conflict and the sacrifices involved were for both nations out of all proportion to the object which has constantly been and would be the cause of so much general suffering and misfortune.

"But if such a declaration only receives the answer that it

has been 'taken cognizance of' then there naturally remains for us nothing else to do but to 'take cognizance of' this reply too. But I must protest here against every attempt to interpret statements differently according to requirements. If the German Government gives an assurance in the name of the German people that they wish nothing but peace, then this declaration is either of exactly the same value as their signature under any specially worded pact, or otherwise this signature could not be of more value than the solemn declaration.

"It is peculiar that in the history of nations inflated formulas frequently occur which would hardly withstand exact examination in the light of reason.

"For some time the world has been suffering, for instance, from a regular mania for collective co-operation, collective security, collective obligations, and so on, all of which seem to have a concrete meaning at the first glance, but which, when regarded more closely, at least allow of manifold interpretations.

"What is meant by collective co-operation?

"Who shall determine what is collective co-operation and what is not? . . ."

"I believe I am right when I say that besides many other rights the victor states of the Versailles Treaty have also arbitrarily assumed the right to decide, without allowing anyone to contradict them, what 'collective co-operation' is and what it is not.

"In allowing myself to criticize this procedure here, I do so because it is the simplest way in which the essential necessity of the latest decisions of the Government of the Reich can be explained and understanding for our real intentions awakened.

"The present idea of collective co-operation among the nations is in essence and fundamentally the intellectual property of President Wilson. The policy of the prewar period was determined rather by the idea of separate alliances of the nations brought together by common interests. Rightly or wrongly, this policy was formerly held responsible for the outbreak of the World War. Its termination—at least as far as Germany is concerned—was hastened by the doctrine of Wilson's fourteen points and the three points that supplemented them later. The essential ideas laid down in them to prevent a similar catastrophe happening again to mankind were as follows:

"The Peace should not be a peace of unilateral rights but of general equality and henceforth of universal justice. It should be a peace of reconciliation, of general disarmament, and thereby of general security. From this resulted as crowning achievement the idea of international collective collaboration of all States and nations within a League of Nations.

"I should like at this juncture to reaffirm that no nation greeted these ideas more eagerly at the end of the War than Germany. Her sufferings and sacrifices were far more severe than those of any other nation which had taken part in the War. It was in reliance upon these promises that the German soldiers laid down their arms.

"When in 1919 the Peace of Versailles was dictated to the German people, a death sentence was thereby pronounced upon collective collaboration of the nations. For where there should have been equality there was division into victors and vanquished. Instead of equal rights there was discrimination between those with rights and those without. Instead of general reconciliation there was punishment of the defeated. Instead of international disarmament, the disarmament of the vanquished. Instead of general security there was security for the victors.

"Yet even in the dictated Peace of Versailles it was expressly provided that the disarmament of Germany should only be carried out first to enable the others to disarm also. Here we are afforded an instance of the extent to which the idea of collective collaboration has been violated by those who are today its loudest protagonists. . . ."

"Germany had disarmed. The other States really could not assert that any danger threatened them from a State which had become completely helpless from a military point of view.

"If, on the other hand, the other nations had disarmed this would have given such a tremendous moral strength to the League of Nations that no State could have dared to have had recourse to violence against a partner in this collective system of general disarmament afterwards.

"Then would have been the best opportunity to convert theoretical doctrines into an actual 'deed.' And this all the more so because:—

"From the political point of view also the necessary conditions had been fulfilled. For Germany was then a democracy such as has never before existed. Everything had been exactly copied and dutifully imitated from the existing great models. It was not National Socialism which ruled in Germany. Even bourgeois nationalism had almost completely disappeared. The world of party politics stretched from Social Democracy by way of the Center Party to the Democratic Party, and not only resembled outwardly in its '*Weltanschauung*' the world around it, but felt itself programmatically bound up with it. What then were they waiting for?

"Could there have been a better opportunity to set up a collective system of co-operation than at the time when in Germany that spirit ruled exclusively which also inspired the world around her? No! The time was ripe, it was there, only the will was not.

"In demonstrating the breaches of the Treaty of Versailles by the other side I will not refer at all to the fact that they had not disarmed. Even if one believes that at that time there may have been valid objections to excuse the breach of the obligation to disarm, it will be hard to give the reasons which led to an ever-increasing rearmament.

"That is the decisive point.

"The other States have not only failed to disarm, but they

have on the contrary supplemented their armaments, improved them, and increased them.

"The reply has been made that there have been to some extent limitations of personnel—but this reply is no valid excuse. These limitations of personnel were more than made up for by the technical and planned improvement of the most modern weapons of warfare. Incidentally they could easily be made good.

"And one must pay especial attention to the following:

"During the course of the disarmament negotiations the attempt was made to divide armament into weapons which were more suitable for defense and those which were more suitable for attack.

"I must here point out that Germany did not possess any of the weapons at all which were designated as suitable for attack. They were all destroyed without exception. And it must further be pointed out that it was these very weapons which were suitable and designed for attack that the partners of the Peace Treaty developed, improved, and increased to the very utmost extent.

"Germany had destroyed all her aircraft. She not only had no active aerial weapons but she did not even have any weapons for warding off attack from the air.

"At the same time, however, the other partners to the Treaty not only failed to destroy their existing aircraft, but on the contrary they developed it to a vast extent. . . ."

"So they did what was absolutely contrary not only to President Wilson's intentions, but also—in the opinion of the most prominent representatives of the other side—contrary to the obligations to which they had subscribed in the Treaty of Versailles.

"If that is not a glaring example of breach of the Treaty and indeed one-sided breach of the Treaty, after the other partner had completely fulfilled his obligations, it will be difficult to see what is the use of signing treaties in future at all.

"No. . . . There is no excuse and no glossing over that fact. For Germany in her completely defenseless and unarmed state was really anything but a danger to the other States. . . ."

"The hope is now frequently expressed that Germany might herself come forward with a constructive plan. I have made such proposals not once but several times. If my constructive plan for an army of 300,000 men had been adopted, then perhaps many a care would have been less and many a burden lighter today. But it is almost useless to present constructive plans when their rejection can be regarded as certain from the start. Nevertheless, I propose once more to give a short survey of our views. This is done solely from the feeling that it is our duty to leave no stone unturned in order to restore the necessary internal security to Europe and the feeling of solidarity to the European nations.

"After the other States had not only failed to fulfill their obligation to disarm, but in addition all proposals for a limitation of armaments had also been declined, I felt myself obliged, as the Fuehrer of the German nation, responsible to God and my own conscience, in face of the growth of new military alliances and after receiving the information that France was introducing a two-year period of service, to restore once more, by virtue of the right to life of the nation itself, the legal equality of Germany, which has been refused her internationally. It was not Germany who broke a contractual obligation which had been laid upon her but those States which had compelled us to adopt this independent action. The introduction of the universal military service and the promulgation of the law for the establishment of the new German Army were nothing else than the restoration to Germany of a status of equal rights which threatens nobody but guarantees Germany security. . . ."

"I should like here to deal just briefly with the reproaches and imputations which have been levelled against the restoration of the German military service.

"It is stated in the first place that Germany is not menaced by anyone and hence, secondly, that it is not comprehensible why Germany should rearm at all.

"This would give rise to the counter-question of why the other side, who in any case could feel less menaced by a disarmed Germany than vice versa, did not stop rearming and finally reduce armaments. But when it is asserted that Germany menaces the other States by rearming, then the increase of the armaments of the other States was at least a much greater menace for a disarmed and defenseless Germany.

"I believe that in this case there is only a choice of one thing or the other. If warlike armaments are a menace to peace, then they are a menace for all States. But if they are not a war menace, then they are not a menace for any State. It will not do for one group to represent their armaments as an olive branch of peace and those of the others as the Devil's wand. A tank is a tank, and a bomb is a bomb. The opinion that it is possible to divide up the world for all time into States with different rights will always be recognized only by the one side. The German nation, in any case, is not prepared to be regarded and treated for all time as a second-class nation or one with inferior rights. Our love of peace is perhaps greater than that of the other nations, for we suffered most from this unhappy war. No one of us means to threaten anybody. It is only that we are all determined to secure and maintain equality for the German people. But this equality is also the primary prerequisite for every form of practical and collective co-operation. . . ."

"The world is living today in the age of conferences. If many of these meetings were completely unsuccessful, then the reason for this disappointment is not infrequently to be found in the way in which the program was drawn up and in the kind of goal which it was desired to achieve. Some cabinet or other feels—like all the others—that it is necessary to do something for the peace of Europe, which is considered to be menaced. But instead of communicating the general idea to all those who it is proposed should co-operate, with the wish to learn the views of the various States and of their Governments regarding the possible ways and means of dealing with and solving this question, a complete program is drawn up between two or three chancelleries. In such cases it is frequently difficult to resist the impression that, in fixing the contents of the resolutions to be adopted, the wish is the father of the thought in mingling the possible with the impossible and thus bringing about certain failure at the cost of those invited to participate later. For, while two or three States agree upon a program laid down in such detail, the party subsequently invited is merely informed of the contents of such a program, with the remark that this program is an inseparable whole, and must either be accepted or rejected in its entirety. As very good ideas may naturally be found in such a program, the State which does not agree to the whole draft is thereby held responsible for the failure of the useful parts as well. The procedure is very reminiscent of the practice of certain film distributors who adopt the principle of always distributing good and bad films together. . . ."

"So far as Germany is concerned, I can only say the following in regard to such attempts:—

"We shall take part in no further conference if we have not had our share in the drawing up of the program from the outset. Because two or three States dish up a draft treaty, we have no wish to be the first to sample it; which is not, however, to say that we do not reserve the right to give our assent and signature subsequently to a treaty because we were not present when it was drafted or at the conferences themselves. Not at all. . . . It is quite possible that in its final shape and form a treaty may satisfy us as being useful although we were present neither when it was drafted nor at the conference in which it was accepted by a number of States. . . ."

"I must, however, again emphasize the fact that to draft

programs for conferences with the heading 'All or Nothing' seems to me to be the wrong method. . . ."

"It seems to me an equally doubtful procedure to misuse the thesis of the indivisibility of peace as an excuse for interpretations which—intentionally or unintentionally—serve the cause of war preparations rather than that of general security. In this respect the World War should serve as a terrible warning. I do not believe that Europe can survive such a catastrophe for a second time without the most frightful upheaval. But such a catastrophe can arise all the more easily when the possibility of localizing smaller conflicts has been rendered less and less by an international network of intersecting obligations, and the danger of numerous States and nations being dragged into the struggle becomes all the greater. So far as Germany is concerned I wish to leave no shadow of doubt in what I am about to say:—

"*Germany has solemnly recognized and guaranteed France her frontiers* as determined after the Saar plebiscite. Without taking the past into account *Germany has concluded a non-aggression pact with Poland*. This is more than a valuable contribution to European peace, and *we shall adhere to it unconditionally*. We dearly wish that it may continue without interruption and that it may tend to still more profound and friendly sincerity in the mutual relationships between our two countries. We did all this although *we thereby finally renounced, for instance, all claims to Alsace-Lorraine,* a land for which we have also fought two great wars. But we did it in particular to spare our own German nation a new and terrible sacrifice of lives. We are convinced that in so doing we are benefiting not only our own people, but also this frontier territory. We are prepared to do everything on our part to arrive at a true peace and a real friendship with the French nation. With the understanding and heartfelt friendship of genuine nationalists, *we recognize Poland as the home of a great and nationally conscious people*. While wishing to spare the German nation further bloodshed even where the renunciation of war implies a certain sacrifice, we certainly have no intention of pledging our blood, without right of choice, for the sake of foreign interests. We do not intend to enable anybody to sell by treaty the people of Germany, her manhood and her sons, in some conflict for which we cannot lay down conditions and which we cannot influence. The German soldier is too valuable and we love our people too well to commit ourselves to mutual assistance pacts where our undertakings are not defined.

"We believe that we can thus serve the cause of peace much better. For it can but enhance the necessary feeling of responsibility on the part of every individual State to know from the beginning that it possesses no mighty and powerful military allies in an eventual conflict.

"Here, too, of course, there are things which are possible and things which are not.

"As an example I should like to deal briefly with the Eastern pact as proposed to us.

"In this pact we find a mutual-assistance clause which in our view may lead to completely unforeseeable consequences. The German Reich—and in particular the present German Government—have no other wish than to live on friendly and peaceful terms with all neighboring States. We entertain these feelings not only toward the larger States, but also toward the neighboring smaller States. Indeed, insofar as they have a really independent existence we welcome them as peaceable neutral factors on our frontiers, which are otherwise from the military standpoint quite open and unprotected. Much as we ourselves love peace, it does not lie in our power to prevent inter-State conflicts from breaking out, especially in the East. In itself it is infinitely difficult in such a case to determine the guilty party. A divinely inspired court, which would be able to discover and pronounce the eternal truth in such a case, does not exist on this earth. As soon as the dogs of war are loosed on the nations, the end begins to justify every means. And then people soon begin to lose all clear sense of right and wrong. More than twenty years have passed since the beginning of the World War, and every nation lives in the sacred conviction that right stood on its side and wrong on the side of the opponents. I am afraid that if such a conflict were to break out again treaty obligations would contribute less to the identification of the aggressor than to the support of that State which served his particular interests. It would perhaps be more serviceable to the cause of peace if the other nations were to withdraw at once from both sides at the outbreak of such a conflict rather than to allow themselves to be involved in this conflict from the outset by treaty obligations.

"But apart from these considerations of principle we have here a special case. Germany today is a National Socialist State. The ideas by which we are governed are diametrically opposed to those of Soviet Russia. National Socialism is a doctrine which applies exclusively to the German people. Bolshevism lays emphasis on its international mission.

"We National Socialists believe that in the long run man can be happy only in his own nation. We live in the belief that the happiness and the achievements of Europe are indissolubly connected with the existence of a system of free, independent national States. Bolshevism preaches the constitution of a world empire and only recognizes sections of a central International. . . ."

"Both we National Socialists and the Bolshevists are convinced that there is a gulf between us which can never be bridged. . . ."

"Insofar as bolshevism can be considered a purely Russian affair we have no interest in it whatever. Every nation must seek its salvation in its own way. So far as bolshevism draws Germany within its range, however, we are its deadliest and most fanatical enemies. . . ."

"Germany has nothing to gain by a European war of any kind. What we want is freedom and independence. For this reason we were ready to conclude pacts of non-aggression with all our neighbors, Lithuania excepted. The sole reason for this exception, however, is not that we wish for a war against that country, but because we cannot make political treaties with a State which ignores the most primitive laws of human society. . . ."

"A few weeks ago I saw the statement made in a great international newspaper that Germany could easily renounce her claim to the Memel Territory because she is big enough already. But the noble humanitarian author of that statement forgot one thing—namely, that 140,000 people have the right to live in their own way and that it is not a question whether Germany wants them or not but whether they themselves want to be Germans or not.

"They are Germans. By a surprise attack in the midst of peaceful conditions they were torn away from Germany and the attack was subsequently sanctioned. As a punishment for still adhering to their German feelings, they were persecuted, tortured, and maltreated in a most barbarous way. What would be said in England or France if members of one of these nations were subjected to a similar tragedy? . . ."

"With this exception, however—an exception which can be removed at any time by the Great Powers who are responsible—we are ready, through pacts and non-aggression undertakings, to give any nation whose frontiers border on ours that assurance which will also be beneficial to ourselves. But we cannot supplement such treaties by giving undertakings to assist other countries in case of war. . . ."

"Moreover, in the concluding of certain assistance pacts which are known to us we see a development that in no way differs from the old type of military alliances. *We regret this in a special way because, as a result of the military alliance between France and Russia, an element of legal insecurity has been brought into the Locarno Pact, which is the most definite and most really valuable treaty of mutual assurance in Europe.* The points that have recently been raised in various quarters as to the legal obligations arising out of these new alliances are presumably the result of similar misgivings and prove, both in the way the questions are put and the manner in which they are answered, how great is the number of possible eventualities which might give rise to corresponding differences of opinion. The German Government would be specially grateful for an authentic interpretation of the retrospective and future effects of the Franco-Russian military alliance on the contractual obligations of the single parties who signed the Locarno Pact. The German Government also does not wish to allow any doubts to arise as to its own belief that these military alliances are contrary to the spirit and letter of the Covenant of the League of Nations.

"The signing of individual non-aggression pacts, as long as it is not clearly defined what this non-aggression means, is just as impossible for us as to undertake the aforementioned unlimited obligations. On our part we Germans would have more reasons to rejoice than any one if finally a way or method could be found to prevent the exercise of influence by outside forces on the inner political life of the nations. Since the end of the War, Germany has been the victim of such interferences continually. Our Communist party was a section of a political movement which had its headquarters abroad and was directed from abroad. All the revolts in Germany were fomented by teaching from abroad and were materially supported from abroad. The rest of the world knows this quite well but has never taken much pains about it.

"An army of emigrants is working against Germany from abroad. In Prague and Paris revolutionary newspapers are still being printed in the German language and are constantly being smuggled into Germany. Public incitements to acts of violence are published not merely in these papers but also in several of the great papers which have a large circulation. What are called 'blackleg' radio stations broadcast appeals which call for murderous activities in Germany.

Other stations make propaganda in the German language for terrorist organizations which are forbidden in Germany. Courts of justice are publicly set up abroad which endeavor to interfere in the German administration of justice. We are interested in seeing all these ways and methods abolished; but besides our own interest we recognize that if such operations are not defined with great exactitude a government which—in its own interior—does not govern by any other right but that of force might attribute any internal revolt to the influence of outside interference and then, in order to maintain its position, demand such military assistance as had been guaranteed contractually.

"The fact that in Europe political frontiers do not correspond to the cultural frontiers is a fact that can be and is very much regretted. Since the rise of Christianity certain ideas have spread in an unbroken tradition throughout Europe. They have formed groups which have had a decided influence on the destiny of Europe. They have bridged across frontiers of States and nations and have created elements of union.

"If, for instance, some foreign cabinet minister should express his regret that certain ideas which are held valid in Western Europe are not recognized today in Germany, then it will be easier to understand how the doctrines of the German Reich cannot be entirely without their influence in one or other of the German countries.

"Germany neither intends nor wishes to interfere in the internal affairs of Austria, to annex Austria, or to conclude an Anschluss. The German people and the German Government have, however, the very comprehensible desire, arising out of a simple feeling of solidarity due to a common national descent, namely, that the right to self-determination should be guaranteed not only to foreign nations but to the German people everywhere. I myself believe that no regime which does not rest on public consent and is not supported by the people can continue permanently. If there are no

such difficulties between Germany and Switzerland, which is to a large extent German, that is due to the fact that the independence and self-reliance of Switzerland is a reality, and because nobody doubts that the Swiss Government represents the real and legal expression of the will of the people.

"We Germans have every reason to be glad that there is on our frontier a State, a large percentage of whose population is German, which is firmly established and possesses a real and actual independence. The German Government regrets the tension which has arisen from the conflict with Austria all the more because it has resulted in disturbing our former good relations toward Italy, a State with whom we otherwise have no conflict of interests.

"Passing from these general considerations to a more precise summing up of the present issues, I hereby declare that the position of the German Government is as follows:

"1. The German Government rejects the Geneva resolution of April 17. It was not Germany which unilaterally broke the Versailles Treaty. The Versailles Dictate was unilaterally broken, and thereby rendered invalid as regards the points at issue, by those Powers who could not decide to carry out in their turn the disarmament which was imposed on Germany and which should have followed in their case by virtue of the Treaty.

"The new discrimination introduced at Geneva makes it impossible for the German Government to return to that institution until the preconditions for a real legal equality of all members has been established. For this purpose the German Government considers it necessary to make a clear separation between the Treaty of Versailles, which was based on a classification of the nations into victors and vanquished, and the League of Nations, which must be constituted on the basis of equal valuation and equality of rights for all the members.

"This equality of rights must be extended to all functions and all property rights in international life.

"2. The German Government, consequent on the failure of the other States to fulfill their disarmament obligations, has on its part renounced those articles of the Versailles Treaty which, because of the one-sided burden this laid on Germany contrary to the provisions of the Treaty, have constituted a discrimination against Germany for an unlimited period of time. It hereby most solemnly declares that these measures relate exclusively to the points which involve moral and material discrimination against the German people and of which notice has been given. The German Government will therefore unconditionally respect the articles concerning the mutual relations of the nations in other respects, including the territorial provisions, and those revisions which shall be rendered necessary in the course of time will be put into effect only by the method of peaceful understandings.

"3. The German Government intends not to sign any treaty which seems to them incapable of fulfillment; but they will scrupulously maintain every treaty voluntarily signed, even though it was concluded before their accession to power and office. *In particular they will uphold and fulfill all obligations arising out of the Locarno Treaty, so long as the other partners are on their side ready to stand by that Pact. In respecting the demilitarized zone the German Government considers its action as a contribution to the appeasement of Europe,* which contribution is of an unheard-of hardness for a sovereign State. But it feels bound to point out that the continual increase of troops on the other side can in no way be regarded as a complement to these endeavors.

"4. The German Government is ready at any time to participate in a system of collective co-operation for safeguarding European peace, but regards it necessary to recognize the law of perpetual evolution by keeping open the way to treaty revision. . . ."

"5. The German Government is of the opinion that the reconstruction of European collaboration cannot be achieved by the method of imposing conditions unilaterally. In view of the fact that the various interests involved are not always concordant, it believes it right to be content with a minimum instead of allowing this collaboration to break down on account of an unalterable maximum of demands. It has the further conviction that this understanding—with a great aim in view—can be brought about only step by step.

"6. The German Government is ready in principle to conclude pacts of non-aggression with its neighbor States and to supplement these pacts with all provisions that aim at isolating the warmaker and localizing the area of the war. In particular it is ready to assume all consequent obligations regarding the supply of material and arms in peace or war where such obligations are also assumed and respected by all the partners.

"7. The German Government is ready to supplement the Locarno Treaty with an air agreement and to enter upon discussions regarding this matter.

"8. The German Government has announced the extent of the expansion of the new German Defence Force. Under no circumstances will it depart from this. It does not regard the fulfillment of its program in the air, on land, or at sea, as constituting a menace to any nation. It is ready at any time to limit its armaments to any degree that is also adopted by the other Powers.

"The German Government has already spontaneously made known the definite limitations of its intentions, thereby giving the best evidence of its good will to avoid an unlimited armaments race. Its limitation of the German air armaments to parity with the individual Great Powers of the West makes it possible at any time to fix a maximum which Germany will be under a binding obligation to observe with the other nations. The limitation of the German Navy is placed at thirty-five per cent of the British Navy, and therewith still at fifteen per cent below the total tonnage of the French Navy. As the opinion has been expressed in various press commentaries that this demand is only a beginning and would increase, particularly with the possession of colonies, the German Government hereby makes the binding declaration: *For Germany this demand is final and abiding.*

"Germany has not the intention or the necessity or the means to participate in any new naval rivalry. The German Government recognizes of itself the overpowering vital importance, and therewith the justification, of a dominating protection for the British Empire on the sea, precisely as we are resolved conversely to do all that is necessary for the protection of our continental existence and freedom. *The German Government has the straightforward intention to find and maintain a relationship with the British people and State which will prevent for all time a repetition of the only struggle there has been between the two nations hitherto.*

"9. The German Government is ready to take an active part in all efforts which may lead to a practical limitation of boundless armaments. It regards a return to the former idea of the Geneva Red Cross Convention as the only possible way to achieve this. It believes that first there will be only the possibility of a gradual abolition and outlawry of weapons and methods of warfare which are essentially contrary to the Geneva Red Cross Convention, which is still valid. . . ."

"The German Government considers as erroneous and ineffective the idea of doing away with airplanes while leaving bombardment free. But they believe it possible to proscribe the use of certain arms as contrary to international law and to excommunicate those nations still using them from the community of mankind—its rights and its laws.

"Here also they believe that gradual progress is the best

way to success. For example, there might be prohibition of the dropping of gas, incendiary, and explosive bombs outside the real battle zone. This limitation could then be extended to complete international outlawry of all bombing. But so long as bombing as such is permitted, any limitation of the number of bombing planes is questionable in view of the possibility of rapid substitution.

"Should bombing as such be branded as an illegal barbarity, the construction of bombing airplanes will soon be abandoned as superfluous and of no purpose. If, through the Geneva Red Cross Convention, it became possible as a matter of fact to prevent the killing of a defenseless wounded man or prisoner, then it ought to be equally possible to forbid, by an analogous convention, and finally to stop, the bombing of equally defenseless civil populations.

"In such a fundamental way of dealing with the problem, Germany sees a greater reassurance and security for the nations than in all pacts of assistance and military conventions.

"10. The German Government is ready to agree to any limitation which leads to abolition of the heaviest arms, especially suited for aggression. Such are, first, the heaviest artillery, and, secondly, the heaviest tanks. In view of the enormous fortifications on the French frontier such international abolition of the heaviest weapons of attack would *ipso facto* give France one hundred per cent security.

"11. Germany declares herself ready to agree to any limitation whatsoever of the caliber strength of artillery, battleships, cruisers, and torpedo boats. In like manner, the German Government is ready to accept any international limitation of the size of warships. And finally it is ready to agree to the limitation of tonnage for submarines, or to their complete abolition in case of international agreement. And it gives the further assurance that it will agree to any international limitation or abolition of arms whatsoever for a uniform space of time.

"12. The German Government is of the opinion that all

attempts to bring about an alleviation of certain strained relations between individual States by means of international or multilateral agreements must be in vain until suitable measures are taken to prevent the poisoning of public opinion among the nations by irresponsible elements orally or in writing, through the theater or the cinema.

"13. The German Government is ready at any time to reach an international agreement which shall effectively prevent all attempts at outside interference in the affairs of other States. It must demand, however, that such a settlement be internationally effective, and work out for the benefit of all States. As there is a danger that in countries where the Government does not rest on the general confidence of the people, internal upheavals may all too easily be ascribed to external interference, it seems necessary that the conception of 'interference' should be subjected to a precise international definition.

"Members of the German Reichstag:

"I have been at pains to give you a picture of the problems which confront us today. However great the difficulties and worries may be in individual questions, I consider that I owe it to my position as Fuehrer and Chancellor of the Reich not to admit a single doubt as to the possibility of maintaining peace. The peoples wish for peace. It must be possible for the Governments to maintain it. *I believe that the restoration of the German defense force will contribute to this peace. Not because we intend to increase it beyond all bounds, but because the simple fact of its existence has got rid of a dangerous vacuum in Europe.* Germany does not intend to increase her armaments beyond all bounds. *We have not got ten thousand bombing planes and we shall not build them. . . ."*

"I cannot better conclude my speech of today to you, my fellow-fighters and trustees of the nation, than by repeating our confession of faith in peace. The nature of our new constitution makes it possible for us in Germany to put a stop to the machinations of war agitators. May the other nations too be able to give bold expression to their real inner longing for peace. *Whoever lights the torch of war in Europe can wish for nothing but chaos.* We, however, live in the firm conviction that in our time will be fulfilled, not the decline but the renaissance of the West. That Germany may make an imperishable contribution to this great work is our proud hope and our unshakable belief."

Press

Le Temps, May 23—There are two things which stand out in the speech of the German Chancellor. First, a doctrinal section wherein the Fuehrer forcefully states his desire for peace and his willingness to co-operate, and attempts to justify the Reich's policy by interpreting according to his own view events, principles, and methods. The other part contains the thirteen points which summarize the attitude of Berlin toward the current major problems of international disputes. . . . Rearmament is a *fait accompli* which Berlin is not going to undo. Now that the Chancellor has, in effect, said this, what means is left for diplomacy to pave the way for a general settlement? Now every government concerned must weigh its responsibilities in the light of the policy Germany has announced and reaffirmed.

London Times, May 22— . . . But the speech turns out to be reasonable, straightforward, and comprehensive. No one who reads it with an impartial mind can doubt that the points of policy laid down by Herr Hitler may fairly constitute the basis of a complete settlement with Germany—a free, equal, and strong Germany instead of the prostrate Germany upon whom peace was imposed sixteen years ago. The conditions on which she is prepared to return to the League of Nations are the same as were stated to Sir John Simon on the occasion of his visit to Berlin. . . . Germany, as he [Hitler] plainly admitted, had broken away from legal obligations; but they were obligations which had never been voluntarily accepted. He declared most solemnly that the German Government would respect unconditionally all the obligations affecting the relations between the German and other Governments that had already been assumed, even if they had been assumed before the advent of the National Socialist regime. In this connection Herr Hitler specifically mentioned the Locarno Pact. . . .

It is to be hoped that the speech will be taken everywhere as a sincere and well-considered utterance, meaning precisely what it says. There are no greater enemies to the peace of Europe than those who would spread an atmosphere of suspicion about an important and long-awaited pronouncement of this kind. . . .

In the present case the mere probability that Herr Hitler's attitude might on the whole be conciliatory and pacific has led in the last few days to a good deal of interested propaganda to the effect that any olive branch from such a quarter must be poisoned and that any pleas from Germany for a respite from competition in armaments can only mean that its author is not yet ready for war. Even if this view were well founded at this moment it will be a crime against peace to make it the basis of a permanent policy.

New York Times, May 22—Herr Hitler's speech on foreign policies holds out a number of fair promises, but they are vitiated by the fact that the speaker is the man who claims the right to annul solemn treaty obligations without the consent of the other side. All through the Reichstag address there sounds this note of unilateralism. . . .

It is strange that Herr Hitler should be so eager to live at peace with his neighbors on the Continent and yet will not try to work out a basis for peace by sitting down with his neighbors in conference or council. He deserts Geneva. When Sir John Simon and Captain Eden visit him in Berlin he fails badly in conveying to them his burning desire for peace. He will not go to Rome and discuss a Danubian settlement. The only people who can really understand him are his own Reichstag, where his performance is a monologue. Is the Fuehrer really qualified for membership in a family of nations? He lacks the first requisite for communal living, and that is the sense of mutuality. He is incurably unilateral. He promises many things, but when the time comes his law of eternal development threatens to end up like that famous necessity which knew no law in Belgium in 1914.

•

SPEECH OF SEPTEMBER 13, 1935

Nuremberg, Reichstag

Background

May 30—In France the Etienne Flandin Cabinet resigns after the Chamber refuses to give him plenary powers to reorganize the finances of the country. Bouisson forms a new cabinet with Joseph Caillaux as Finance Minister.

June 4—The Bouisson Cabinet resigns in France. Pierre Laval forms a cabinet.

June 7—Stanley Baldwin succeeds Ramsay MacDonald as Prime Minister of England.

June 18—Ribbentrop, in London, signs naval pact with England allowing Germany to build up to 35 per cent of the British tonnage.

September 11—The League meets in Geneva to study the Italo-Ethiopian conflict. In a speech Sir Samuel Hoare pledges British support to the League.

September 10–15—The Reichstag meets in Nuremberg.

September 15—The British Home Fleet is sent to the Mediterranean.

The Speech

". . . A COMMANDER without officers and soldiers—could many people make much of that? I will not be the commander without soldiers, but I will remain your Leader. For me you are the political officers of the German nation, bound up with me for better or for worse, even as I am bound up with you for better or for worse. It was not one man who conquered Germany, it was all in common who conquered Germany. One man has won you, and you have won the German people! One man has conquered with his will, and you have conquered with your wills. One man stood at the head as Leader in the Reich, and you stood every one of you at the head and led in the battle whether in a Gau or a District or a local center, and everywhere the National Socialist who stood at the head was better than the foes who stood against him! . . ."

"Is this fight, then, a closed chapter? The conquest of power is a process which is never, never ended, for here, if anywhere, does the principle hold true, 'What you have won, win it ever anew, if you are to possess it!' There is no people in history that has won liberation as a gift, there is no people that will keep its freedom as a gift! Always and forever must this precious possession be guarded without ceasing. And thereto are we National Socialists resolved! . . ."

"So the fight goes on, and now we are coming to the period of our second great task, the continuous education of our people, and the constant watch upon our people. Education to the end that all of us and our German people may be increasingly drawn into the world of the National Socialist idea, and watchfulness in order that continuously we may see to it that nowhere shall there be found retrogression or collapse. The fate which was unleashed upon the world in 1918 shall never strike us. Just as we mean to gather here together, year after year, in answer to this general muster, so we mean to hold continual musters of the German nation. And that is necessary. . . . Hoist the flag of courage, of willingness for sacrifice, of devotion, and mark well who ranges himself under it. Mark those who are drawn by the flag, for it is they who are called to lead a people, and no one else. . . ."

"There are perhaps in Germany certain individuals who either regard this Movement as an incomprehensible phenomenon, or else cannot make at all clear to themselves the reason for its existence, and who comprehend still less clearly the conditions which made its existence a necessity, and why in the future it will never be overthrown. They have not felt one breath of the spirit which governs this Movement; they have experienced nothing of the strength of this ideal; they have remained cold. They imagine that a people and a State are nothing but a lifeless machine, which can be set in action only by considerations of reason. They have not understood that these 68 millions of men could never be governed by commands, as they could by an appeal to their inner instincts, an appeal to their conscience. Where should we stand today if we had not found the way to the soul of our people? . . . The strength of idealism alone has accomplished these acts which have moved the world. Were any yet greater proof needed of the might of idealism, it can be found in this Movement. At its beginning there stood the word idealism; not calculation—we did not reckon up the risks! What could a man who undertook single-handed to take the field against a world of enemies, what could he expect? I made the venture, because I believed that I knew the heartbeat of my people: and I was not deceived.

"You have all felt this in the past, for to every single one of you at some time has occurred the reflection that *it is no subtlety of the intellect, but rather an inner voice that has at some time given its commands to every one of you. Reason must have dissuaded you from coming to me; faith alone gave you the command.* What idealism it was—but what a force lay in that idealism! . . ."

"We are especially happy today to see among us for the first time officers and men of the new army of the German people, that army from which almost all of us once came, and to which the German people will again in the future give its sons, entrusting them to loyal hands, that they may become brave, disciplined, reliable, and trustworthy men, as were our soldiers in the past.

"We know that our army does not educate them for a warlike militarism, any more than we have done. It educates them only to be reliable, decent members of the community, men who in the hour of need and danger will feel themselves united in loyalty with the nation; and should fate confront them with the sternest ordeal, will defend the freedom of their people with bravery and honor. That is the meaning of this recreation of our army. It has been formed not to wage wars of aggression, but to guard and protect our people, so that Germany may not again suffer the tragic fate which we were all forced to endure in this country for fifteen years. It is not to deprive other peoples of their freedom, but to protect our own German freedom: that is why the army is here."

Press

Le Temps, September 15—The Fuehrer's speech was short but forceful. He said that now he wished to make his first task the education of German youth in the spirit of National Socialism. The Chancellor concluded his speech with a tribute to the new army. The German Army will never be put to the service of any militarism; it exists only to defend the liberty of the Fatherland, if that should ever be threatened.

SPEECH OF SEPTEMBER 15, 1935

Nuremberg, Reichstag

"... THIS international unrest in the world would unfortunately seem to have given rise to the view amongst the Jews within Germany that the time has come openly to oppose Jewish interests to those of the German nation. From numerous places vigorous complaints have been received of the provocative action of individuals belonging to this people, and the remarkable frequency of these reports and the similarity of their contents point to a certain system of operations. This attitude actually resulted in demonstrations which in a Berlin cinema were directed against a foreign film by which, though harmless in itself, certain Jewish circles felt themselves to be offended.

"If this proceeding is not to lead to very determined action in its own defense by the outraged population—the consequences of which in any single case cannot be foreseen—the only way to deal with the problem which remains open is that of legislative action. The German Government is in this governed by the thought that through a single secular solution it may be possible still to create a level ground on which the German people may find a tolerable relation toward the Jewish people. Should this hope not be fulfilled and the Jewish agitation both within Germany and in the international sphere should continue, then the position must be examined afresh."

Press

New York Times, September 16—Hitler was, according to advance predictions, to blow a trumpet in his speech at Nuremberg. It turned out to be very like a penny whistle. He scarcely touched upon any of the great issues which are agitating public opinion in Europe. . . . More serious, of course, and more repulsive was Hitler's action in fanning anew the flames of anti-Semitism in Germany. Not able to lead his Nazi troops against a foreign foe, he beckoned them to attack again a weak and inoffensive minority at home.

London Times, September 16—Herr Hitler . . . delivered a short sharp speech and three laws were passed. One declares the swastika flag . . . to be the sole official flag of the German Reich; the second imposes special conditions for full German citizenship which will exclude all Jews; and the third prohibits the marriage of Aryans with Jews and illicit relations between Jews and "Germans" and forbids German girls to serve as domestic servants in Jewish houses. The proceedings were dominated by the militant note of anti-Semitism and anti-communism that has been the most noticeable feature of all the speeches at the rally.

Le Temps, September 17—There is no reason to be surprised that the Fuehrer expanded on the theme of a "purified Germany" in which internal and foreign affairs are to be well regulated. One wonders, however, whether all Germans, especially those who are excluded from the national community, are equally appreciative of their "liberty. . . ." As for the Jews, they have simply been placed outside the law.

•

SPEECH OF SEPTEMBER 16, 1935

Nuremberg, Address to Army

The Speech

". . . THE German was always a good soldier: the service of arms was never for our people an enforced service but at all periods of our history a service of the highest honor. It was thus the more grievous and the more depressing for the decent, honor-loving German not to be allowed to be a soldier—especially when that veto was imposed under dishonoring and humiliating conditions. To what an extent this state of affairs has now been overcome you, my soldiers, are the witness, and today the whole German people can see the evidence of this in this picture of the union of the German as soldier with the armament which is the result of modern technical achievement. Once more every young German man, if the nation considers him worthy of the honor, will take his place in your ranks; once more you will perform your service with the arms that are today employed by the other nations of the world. . . ."

"But what are all these sacrifices which are demanded today from you and from us when compared with the sacrifices which twenty years ago were demanded from us and from our comrades? Let each of you if he should ever feel the service of the soldier a burden consider that eight days' drum-fire demanded more sacrifices from the battalions and regiments of our old army than does a whole year's peacetime service. But that drum-fire did not break the German people in arms. The German people broke only because it had lost its inner freedom, its inner faith in the right of its cause. This faith has today returned, and this faith is not merely the possession of the hundreds of thousands in your own ranks, but millions and millions of our fellow-countrymen wrap you about with this burning faith, this burning confidence, this warm love.

"And if you must bring your personal sacrifice in obedience in performance of duty, in subjection to your superiors, in hardness, endurance, capacity, forget not, my soldiers, that on its side the whole German people brings great sacrifices for you. . . ."

"Before now Germany had a proud and brave army, had heroic fighters. This is but natural for the German soldier. But the army was not merely in war the nation's great defense, it was in peace the splendid school of our people. It is the army which has made men of us all, and when we looked upon the army our faith in the future of our people was always reinforced. And this old glorious army, it is not dead; it only slept, and now it has arisen again in you!

"You, my comrades, bear on the points of your weapons and on your helmets an unequaled legacy. You are not an artificial creation, without tradition, without a past: there is nothing else in the whole of Germany which is so rich in traditions as that which you have to embody and can embody. There is indeed no need for you to win for the German Army a title to fame; that it possesses already. Your task is but to preserve that fame.

"And when we stand here in steel and armor of metal that is not because we feel that we must restore the honor of the German people. So far as this honor was supported by our soldiers, no one in the world has ever yet been able to take it away. Germany has never lost her military honor and least of all in the last war. We need not to recover it. . . ."

Press

Le Temps, September 17—The maneuvers and the review of 16,000 men of all branches of the military made a very handsome demonstration which should interest professional military men as much as the public at large. What was most striking were the regiments and the arms which the Treaty of Versailles had forbidden. . . .

New York Times, September 16—It was as fine a soldiery as to be found anywhere in the world . . . and it seemed to most Germans as though the good old days of the Kaiser were back again even if other war lords now took the salute. But history has moved on and Hitler made this very plain in his oration before the closing session of the party congress. . . .

SPEECH OF JANUARY 15, 1936

Detmold

Background

1935

October 3—Mussolini begins conquest of Abyssinia.

October 19—League agrees to apply economic sanctions to Italy.

November 14—In England, general elections give strong support to the Baldwin Government.

November 18—The League of Nations, supported by 51 members, applies economic sanctions to Italy.

December 9-20—Five Power naval conference in London: U. S., Great Britain, Japan, France, and Italy.

December 9—Publication of the Hoare-Laval plan offering a large slice of Abyssinia to Italy. Violent popular reaction in England.

December 18—Resignation of Sir Samuel Hoare. Anthony Eden succeeds him at the Foreign Office.

The Speech

"TIME has proved that we were right. We saw the battle through and from it we have drawn a lesson for the future. There may yet be difficulties at some time in the future. But you do not know me yet—not by a long way. I see here my people, and I see history, and I recognize its teachings. I have trained up the whole Movement in accordance with my ideals. Our opponents do not understand this, but I cannot help them. National Socialism governs in accordance with its ideals, and these the others must accept. We have no thought of giving up our ideals and adopting different aims. There is yet one more lesson for the future to be drawn from the election campaign of that time: the Movement was then controlled by a single will, which swept everyone along with it. What should we have come to in Germany, if there had been not one Movement, but thirty-six or forty-five? A leadership worthy of the name must have the courage to make its will the will of the nation—or else abdicate. There is only one central power, and it confers authority and sovereignty. But it can recall them instantly in the case of every person and of every thing. We look back on this election campaign in Lippe with deep inward emotion and stirring of the heart. We beat our opponents on their own democratic basis. I am convinced of this, that our opponents of that time would not now be in a position to beat us on *our* basis. Yet that is what they would have to do, and for this reason I look forward with boundless confidence to the future. It is quite hopeless for anyone in Germany to try to alter this regime. If anyone should wish to make the attempt he may rest assured that he will be smashed to pieces like glass. Moreover, the Movement does not rest on one person alone. There is a Government today whose succession is secured, without being bound up with any single person.

"I am prepared to admit that the National Socialist ideal, in its final perfection, stands like a polar star above mankind. But mankind must ever follow a star. If it laid hold of this star, it would see it no more. We are on the right road, and we have the right goal. We shall be reforming the German people for centuries. . . ."

SPEECH OF FEBRUARY 12, 1936

Schwerin

Background

1936

January 26—In Geneva, Eden confirms many instances of infraction of the Constitution of the Free City of Danzig which the High Commissioner of the League for Danzig revealed.

February 4—Nazi leader Gustloff murdered in Switzerland.

The Speech

". . . BEHIND every murder stood the same power which is responsible for this murder; behind these harmless insignificant fellow-countrymen who were instigated and incited to crime stands the hate-filled power of our Jewish foe, a foe to whom we had done no harm, but who none the less sought to subjugate our German people and make of it its slave—the foe who is responsible for all the misfortune that fell upon us in 1918, for all the misfortune which plagued Germany in the years that followed. Those members of the Party and honorable comrades of ours all fell, and the same fate was planned for others: many hundreds survived as cripples or severely wounded, blinded or lamed; more than 40,000 others were injured. And among them were so many loyal folk whom we all knew and who were near and dear to us, of whom we were sure that they could never do any harm to anyone, that they had never done any harm to anyone, whose only crime was that they devoted themselves to the cause of Germany.

"In the ranks of those whose lives were thus sacrificed

there stood also Horst Wessel, the singer who gave to the Movement its song, never dreaming that he would join those spirits who march and have marched with us.

"And now on foreign soil National Socialism has gained its first conscious martyr—a man who did nothing save to enter the lists for Germany which is not only his sacred right but his duty in this world: a man who did nothing save remember his homeland and pledge himself to her in loyalty. He, too, was murdered, just like so many others. Even at the time when on January 30 three years ago we had come into power, precisely the same things happened in Germany, at Frankfort on the Oder, at Köpenick, and again at Brunswick. The procedure was always the same: a few men come and call someone out of his house and then stab or shoot him down.

"That is no chance: it is the same guiding hand which organized these crimes and purposes to do so again. Now for the first time one who is responsible for these acts has appeared in his own person. For the first time he employs no harmless German fellow-countryman. It is a title to fame for Switzerland, as it is for our own Germans in Switzerland, that no one let himself be hired to do this deed so that for the first time the spiritual begetter of the act must himself perform the act. So our comrade has fallen a victim to that power which wages a fanatical warfare not only against our German people but against every free, autonomous, and independent people. We understand the challenge to battle and we take up the gage! My dear comrade! You have not fallen in vain!"

Press

London Times, February 13—The principal funeral oration was delivered by the Fuehrer, who accused the Jews of being responsible for every murder of a German patriot that had taken place since the war.

PHASE III

Scrapping the Treaties

March, 1936 — March, 1938

COMMENT

THE plebiscite which was held in the Saar, on January 13, 1935, and which resulted in the peaceful return of this territory to Germany, may be considered as one of the rare instances in which Hitler consented to work within the legality of international treaties. It was certainly to be the last.

From then on, Hitler showed an increasing disregard for all kinds of international obligations, whether contracted by his predecessors or by himself.

Now that the world has been conditioned—so to speak—to Hitler's technique of violating all engagements and breaking his own pledges with an absolute cynicism, it is difficult to recapture the astonishment and indignation which spread through the prewar world when Hitler first gave proof of his faithlessness. The statesmen of the western countries, and particularly those of England and France, had been educated in a tradition of diplomatic usage which had certainly not prepared them to deal with the unorthodox methods of Adolf Hitler. They played the rules of the game they had learned, and it seemed to them that the real crime of their opponent was his scorn of all rules. What they hated in Hitler was less his deeds than his complete lack of consideration for the trouble he gave them and for the infinite difficulties he created for them in the eyes of their own public opinion.

Ever since Hitler had assumed power in Germany, all his pronouncements on foreign policy could be interpreted as a mere reassertion of his fundamental purpose to awaken the soul of the German people. His denunciations of the Versailles Treaty, his complaints of the injustices to which Germany was subjected, all his most violent tirades against the outside world could be viewed with a certain amount of serenity by the leaders of the neighboring countries. Statesmen and dipomats, versed in history, know that political power cannot be obtained nor maintained without a good deal of demagoguery. The rantings and threats of Hitler were excessive, but it was felt that some allowances should be made for a man whose power was so recently acquired, and whose natural tendency would be to exaggerate this power—at least in his speeches—in order to impress his own people. Such had always been the ways of *parvenus*. No doubt, as absolute ruler of seventy million Germans, he should be treated with politeness and decency, but no doubt, also, nothing would be more foolish than to consider him as a real threat to the peace of Europe. As long as he actually remained within the limits of international law, to show undue alarm could only serve to encourage his recklessness.

The first form of the "appeasement" policy was therefore a mere attempt to preserve the subtleties and complexities of European diplomacy, and to ignore, as long as possible, the fact that both Mussolini and Hitler were determined to take practically any risks in order to break down the postwar peace structure which—in their own estimation—was keeping them down in a state of permanent inferiority.

The period which extends from the Saar plebiscite to the annexation of Austria in March, 1938, can be considered as a preliminary phase during which the two dictators tested the resistance of the democracies and—having found it even weaker than they could have hoped for—were able to undertake their program of geographic expansion.

The first definite violation of the Versailles Treaty by Germany took place on March 16, 1935, when Hitler decreed the re-establishment of universal military service.

The timing of this announcement was well planned. The

day before, France had decided to extend her own military service from one to two years. Hitler's decision therefore could appear as a reply to the French increase in military power.

The shock in the democracies was very great, however. For the first time, they had actually to decide on a positive course of action in the face of an open break of contract by Hitler.

The decision they took was to serve as a model for all the future evasions and half-measures which were to lead them step by step to accept every new show of force on the part of the dictator as a *fait accompli*.

Meeting in Stresa in April, the French and British delegates persuaded Mussolini to join them in lodging a protest with the League of Nations.

This was considered a great diplomatic success. But the truth is that the formation of the so-called Stresa Front was a remarkable example of unrealism. The basic principle of this so-called front was not a show of strength or unity, but the demonstration on the part of the democracies of their belief that the dictators could be bought. It revealed one of the most serious miscalculations of their statesmen. At Stresa they overemphasized the power of Mussolini and underestimated that of Hitler. They believed that they could establish a new balance of power in Europe by taking Mussolini into their camp—thus isolating and paralysing Germany. They believed that the only way to repair the damage done to existing treaties was to make new agreements. To Hitler's first positive action, they merely opposed a vote of the League of Nations condemning Germany for violating a pact which Hitler himself had so often proclaimed he would not keep.

Nothing could serve Hitler better. The Stresa Front showed that the democracies were unable to act according to their own principles. It showed, in fact, that they had no principles. For England and France, in attempting to placate Mussolini, the founder of Fascism, gave proof that some of their statesmen—such men as Pierre Laval and Sir John Simon—were ready to go to any lengths to avoid facing a showdown. They were obviously still confident that bargains, signed agreements, and solemn protests would be enough to keep up the fiction of international law. .

When, a few days later, the same Pierre Laval signed a pact of assistance with Russia—the Franco-Soviet pact—further argument was given to Hitler to denounce the unscrupulousness and duplicity of the democracies.

This pact, it is true, had been engineered by Louis Barthou, who, with King Alexander of Serbia, had been murdered in Marseilles in 1934, and it was certainly not in line with the pro-Fascist policy of Pierre Laval who signed it. Nevertheless, it aggravated a fatal cleavage in the democracies, which for several years to come was to render national unity impossible and to help Hitler at every step.

The short-lived Stresa Front on the one hand, and the signing of the Franco-Soviet pact on the other, were symbolical of the ideological conflicts which were destroying from within the very substance of democracy in the western countries. It showed that while Hitler was pursuing one single objective: the domination of Europe—the democracies could be sidetracked by a fear greater than war: the fear of revolution.

One of Hitler's most persistent themes of propaganda, the crusade against bolshevism, was bearing fruit. Hitler had allies within the democracies themselves—allies who were ready to buy him off at practically any price as long as he promised them peace and left them some hope that if he ever went to war, it would be against Russia.

There can be little doubt today that the desire to see Hitler come to grips with Stalin was the guiding idea of most of the conservative parties in England and France from that time on. However senseless their policy toward Hitler may appear in retrospect, this is the only plausible explanation of the course they followed. From the very moment that Hitler actually began to make his power felt outside of Germany, the illusion that his real purpose was to extend toward the East obsessed the statesmen of the West. It explains also the persistent refusal to disbelieve all proofs of Hitler's real ambition which was, and still is, to establish German domination over the whole world. Being themselves limited in their views and calculations, the democratic statesmen could not conceive that Hitler's ambition knew no bounds, and that for the first time since Napoleon they were dealing with this phenomenon called a conqueror.

All the speeches of Hitler during that period were intended to encourage the belief that his real enemies were the Bolshevists and the Jews, and that he had no warlike intentions in the West. Indeed, according to him, his dream was to establish a solid peace in Europe, a peace which would reunite all people under the anti-communist banner. His chief complaint against the democracies was that they could still tolerate leaders who did not recognize 1) that the whole system of Versailles was unjust, and therefore a permanent threat to peace, and 2) that the salvation of Europe was in his hands, because he alone saw clearly the mortal peril of Jewish bolshevism.

Having restored German pride and German equality, all Hitler wanted was a recognition of his mission by other powers. Certainly he did not want war. War, in modern times, was absurd and could only bring about the ruin of Europe.

This idea was expressed not only by him, but by the heads of the German Army who had rallied around Hitler. Speaking at the Heroes Memorial Day, on March 17, 1935, General von Blomberg said: "We do not want to be dragged into another world war. Europe has become too small for another world-war battlefield. Because all nations have equal means at their disposal for war, the future war would only mean self-mutilation for all. We want peace with equal rights and security for all. We seek no more."

This, at the time, seemed reasonable and convincing enough. If such was the considered opinion of one of Germany's military leaders, who could doubt that Hitler would dare to disregard the moderating influence of his own army?

In fact, the outside world was already indulging in one of the most curious and persistent self-deceits concerning the relations of the Nazi party and the Reichswehr. The prevalent idea was that the German High Command exerted a restraining influence upon Hitler and that it could be counted on to prevent him from committing any irreparable folly.

This was true in part, as proved by numerous clashes between Hitler and his generals. But what was not fully realized abroad was that in all those clashes, Hitler finally came out on top. The very same General Blomberg who showed such moderation in 1935 was to be dismissed in 1938 on the eve of Hitler's invasion of Austria because he thought it unwise.

The real test between Hitler and his generals was to come much sooner, however, on the occasion of Hitler's biggest gamble, which was the reoccupation of the Rhineland.

This event took place on March 7, 1936.

From the point of view of Hitler's long-range strategy, it was by far the most daring and far reaching coup that he had, as yet, undertaken. In making this decision, Hitler was risking not only his whole future, but the fate of his country. At no point during his whole career—not even in the fateful days of the Munich crisis—did he gamble for such high stakes and with so few real trump cards in his hand. This is so true that, in order to convince his generals to let him go forward, he had to promise them that the occupying army would immediately withdraw if the French showed the slightest signs of offering resistance. And if that had happened, there is no doubt today that Hitler's career would have come to an end then. He could not have survived the humiliation of such a failure, and his prestige—however great in Germany—would not have saved him.

That the High Command, the Nazi leaders and Hitler himself lived anxious hours after the fateful order was given has been confirmed by many witnesses and by the Nazis themselves. The tension in Berlin, while Hitler was explaining his coup in a speech at the Reichstag, was tremendous. The conviction of most was that the French would mobilize and march in. But the French did not move. "Hitler has got away with it!" wrote William Shirer in his *Berlin Diary* on March 8. "France is not marching. Instead, it is appealing to the League of Nations! No wonder the faces of Hitler and Göring and von Blomberg and von Fritsch were all smiles this noon while they sat in the royal box at the State Opera and for the second time in two years celebrated in a most military fashion Heroes Memorial Day. . . ."

The reoccupation of the Rhineland was indeed a daring gamble, not only because it could not have been accomplished if the French army had opposed it (it was then infinitely stronger than the feeble contingents that Hitler sent in) but also because the action constituted the most flagrant breach of a treaty that Europe had seen since the armies of the Kaiser invaded Belgium in 1914.

It is true, as we have seen, that Hitler had already violated the Versailles Treaty in re-establishing universal military service a year before, but the democracies had more or less admitted that the *Diktat* was dead and Hitler, anyhow, had never accepted it. But the demilitarization of the Rhineland was inscribed in the Locarno agreements. These agreements had been entered into voluntarily by Germany in 1925, and Hitler had never questioned that fact.

He did not question it even then and his only excuse for tearing up the Locarno agreement was the existence of the Franco-Soviet pact. This pact, according to Hitler, made Locarno invalid and relieved him of the obligation of keeping his own word.

This excuse was obviously mere window-dressing and it does not seem that Hitler himself had much hope that it would be accepted. He was determined to occupy the Rhineland. The pretext mattered little. During an "election" speech delivered a few days later (March 14) Hitler expressed his real thought in the following words: "Germany has no intention of being dragged before any international courts; for no international court has the same responsibility towards the German people as I have."

In other words, Hitler wanted the world to know that he considered himself as the sole judge of what was right or wrong for Germany and that no treaty—even if previously approved by himself—could be allowed to stay once he had decided that it stood in his way.

In the same election campaign, the Gauleiter Wagner was even more explicit. "We have not broken any treaty," he said. "But even if we have, we deny others the right to condemn us. What Hitler declares to be right is and will remain right for all time. What Hitler did on March 7 benefited the German people. Anything that benefits the German people is right; anything that harms the German people is wrong."

Such was the new doctrine which confronted the democracies.

Most observers have agreed that if there ever was a time when Hitler's growing power could have been broken without much cost or danger, it was on the seventh of March, 1936.

France, England, and Germany were cosignatories of the Locarno agreement. The reoccupation of the Rhineland constituted a clear violation of that agreement. France and England were not only entitled to act, they were morally bound to do so if they wished to preserve any vestige of international law and self-respect.

But they did not act. Instead of sending their troops into the Rhineland, the French—after consultation with the English—once more sent a protest to the League of Nations and asked that the matter should be arbitrated by the International Court of Justice of the Hague.

The interesting point about this behavior is not so much

the weakness which it reveals on the part of the democracies, but the proof which it provides concerning the accuracy of Hitler's judgment. Green as he was in matters of foreign policy, his first move in this field showed that his understanding of the real condition of Europe was keener than that of all his experienced opponents. His first stroke was a very daring one, but it had been well prepared and, if it was a gamble, it was not as rash as it appeared on the surface.

To the preparation of this coup, both Hitler and the democracies had contributed. The responsibility for the deterioration of international morality which culminated in this sensational unilateral action on the part of Hitler could be evenly shared. During the previous year, Hitler had watched the pitiful episode of the conquest of Ethiopia by Mussolini, the inability of the League to enforce its own regulations, and the betrayal of the Covenant by its two most important supporters, the English and the French. The scandalous deal embodied in the Hoare-Laval agreement, which delivered Abyssinia to Mussolini, had caused a violent revulsion of feeling in England, and forced the resignation of Sir Samuel Hoare and the fall of the Laval Cabinet. But it had not been sufficient to change the course of events. Mussolini had defied the League. Sanctions had been applied to Italy but the only sanction that could actually stop Mussolini —the embargo on oil—was never applied. Mussolini, in defiance of the whole world, conquered Ethiopia, and the world accepted his conquest.

The experiment of Mussolini was not lost on Hitler. It proved to him that even a weak power like Italy could blackmail successfully the combined forces of England and France. It showed that, in spite of all their appeals to justice and the sanctity of treaties, the democracies were not willing to use force to maintain order. It showed the internal disintegration of the moral position of the democracies. It showed that the threat of war was enough to scare them into accepting practically any *fait accompli.*

Hitler did not have to give any effective help to Mussolini. He merely gave him his moral encouragement in his fight against the League. Hitler was not strong enough then to embark on an adventure which was of no direct interest to Germany. But he could see in Mussolini's action a confirmation of one of the ideas which he had expressed in *Mein Kampf*: that Italy could become an ally of Germany.

The Ethiopian affair also proved to Hitler that the entente between England and France was not as solid as it appeared on the surface. It revealed that there existed in both countries men who were ready to break the entente—Frenchmen who, like Laval, sought a rapprochement with Italy; Englishmen who, like Sir John Simon, Lord Londonderry, Lord Lothian, and many others, felt that Germany should be appeased at all costs.

Hitler exploited this situation with consummate skill. Now that he had attained supreme power in Germany, his efforts were bent on reassuring the outside world. To encourage the appeasers, it was necessary to prove that National Socialism was becoming respectable. Such manifestations as the Olympic Games which were held at Garmisch-Partenkirchen in February, 1936, served to show not only the prowess of the German athletes, but also the hospitality of the new Nazi Germany. No effort was spared to please the visiting foreigners and to make them feel that what they had heard about the brutality of the Nazi regime was nothing but the product of distortion and lies on the part of the democratic journalists.

Simultaneously, Hitler never missed an occasion to cajole and lull to sleep the suspicious critics. In an interview given to a French journalist, Bertrand de Jouvenel, he went so far as to offer a twenty-five-year peace to France and to revise *Mein Kampf* because it contained offensive passages towards France. This interview is sufficiently typical to be quoted here in part:

"I was in prison when I wrote this book *(Mein Kampf),"*

Hitler told Jouvenel. "French troops were occupying the Ruhr. It was the moment of greatest tension between our two countries. Yes, we were enemies. And naturally, with my whole country, I was against yours, as I had been against it in the trenches during four years and a half. I would despise myself if I was not a German above everything else when the conflict comes. But today there is no more reason for a conflict. You would like me to correct my book, like a writer preparing a new edition of his work? But I am not a writer. I am a politician. Corrections? I make them every day in my foreign policy, which is entirely aimed towards friendship with France. If I succeed in my policy of Franco-German rapprochement, as I wish to, it will be a correction worthy of me. My corrections will be written in the great book of History!"

It should be noted that this interview was given out on the eve of the ratification of the Franco-Soviet pact by the French parliament. Hitler's intention was to confuse the French deputies and prevent them, if possible, from sanctioning a measure which Hitler feared would upset his future plans.

A few words will suffice to show the tremendous advantages which Hitler gained by the reoccupation of the Rhineland.

From the purely strategic point of view, he abolished the main protection against a new aggression which France had secured for herself after the war. The German armies were now face to face again with the French. No demilitarized zone separated them any more. This very fact reduced considerably the military value of the Maginot Line. It could still be used as a wall, but not as a basis of offensive operations for the French. Very soon, Hitler was to order the construction of the Siegfried Line, thus achieving the immobilization of the French army, behind its own fortifications.

Another result was to prevent France from bringing any effective help to her Eastern allies in case of need. The Poles saw this clearly when they offered to attack Germany on the seventh of March providing France attacked them too. But nothing was farther from the thought of the French leaders than a preventive war at that time. Rebuffed, the Poles turned toward Germany in the forlorn hope of pacifying Hitler.

The other allies of France, Czechoslovakia, Rumania, Jugoslavia, immediately felt their insecurity. They did not formally cancel their alliances with France, but they knew from then on that France would be unable to help them in case Germany chose to attack them.

Generally speaking, the occupation of the Rhineland by the German armies, enabled Hitler to regain complete liberty of action. The French Army was still much more powerful than his own but it was neutralized. It could neither act promptly in an offensive way, nor feel so sure of being able to repulse an attack.

From the seventh of March, 1936, on, Hitler was potentially the master of the whole of Europe east of the Rhine. The road for annexation and conquest was wide open to him.

But Hitler was not quite ready to act yet, at least directly. Mussolini was not yet his ally and he still threatened to defend Austria's independence by force if Hitler tried to invade it.

The Civil War in Spain which broke out in July, 1936, and which was to last until March, 1939, gave the two dictators the chance to test once again the will of the democracies and at the same time to try out their own weapons in a general dress rehearsal for war. The weakness of Franco-British diplomacy, on this occasion, showed itself in an even more glaring manner than during the Italo-Ethiopian conflict.

Although it was quite obvious that the Republican government in Spain could have crushed the Fascist rebellion of General Franco if they had been able to obtain arms from France, both France and England embarked on the policy of so-called "non-intervention" by which the Spanish Republican government was deprived of all legitimate help, relying mostly on the uncertain support of Soviet Russia.

From the very start of the Franco rebellion, it was known —and lately confirmed—that the whole enterprise had been encouraged and organized by Mussolini with the full approval of Hitler. Both dictators poured troops and material into Spain. Never once did they even pretend to obey the regulations of the Non-Intervention Committee sitting in London. Their trickery and cynicism knew no limits, but once again they got away with it.

This was due not only to the weakness of the democratic statesmen, but to a new factor: Now that Hitler occupied the Rhineland, his power became apparent. Europe realized that he could actually threaten war. Europe was scared.

Mussolini, who up to the time of the seventh of March, 1936, might have reason to doubt the real power of his "pupil" could now make his choice. The Spanish Civil War cemented the alliance between the two dictators. A possible basis for the future New Order in Europe and in the world was laid in the ruins of Spain. That basis was Hitler's oldest theme: the fight against bolshevism.

On November 25, 1936, Germany and Japan signed the Anti-Comintern Pact which Italy joined a year later.

But while the reoccupation of the Rhineland and Hitler's lawlessness were thus bearing fruit in Spain, the Fuehrer was preparing for his next step—the annexation of Austria and the showdown of Munich.

SPEECH OF MARCH 7, 1936

Berlin, Reichstag

Background

January 3—President Roosevelt, addressing Congress, denounces dictatorship and aggression. This is obviously aimed at Mussolini's attack on Abyssinia.

January 21—Death of King George V of England.

January 22—In France, resignation of the Pierre Laval Cabinet. A cabinet, headed by the Radical-Socialist Albert Sarraut succeeds him.

February 4-16—Olympic winter games are held at Garmisch-Partenkirchen in Germany.

February 10-21—Lord Londonderry, notorious "appeaser," visits Hitler and Goering in Berlin.

February 27—French Chamber ratifies the Franco-Soviet pact by large majority. The pact was registered with the League of Nations and its application made conditional to the approval of the signatories of the Locarno agreements.

February 27—League of Nations, before applying oil sanctions against Italy, decides to make a final appeal to Mussolini.

March 7—German Army reoccupies the Rhineland in violation of both the Versailles Treaty and the Locarno agreements.

The Speech

"MEN of the German Reichstag: Reichstag President Goering has called at my order the present session to give you an opportunity to receive a declaration of the Reich Government relative to questions which instinctively are regarded not only by yourselves but also by the whole German people as important, nay, decisive.

"When in the gray November days of 1918 the curtain was lowered on the bloody tragedy of the great war, millions of people throughout the whole world breathed easier again. Like a harbinger of springtime hope spread among the nations not only because one of the saddest wars in the history of mankind had come to an end but also because a period full of errors, therefore a calamitous period, had passed into history.

"Amid the tumult of war, savage threats, accusations, maledictions, and condemnations, the views of the President of the United States had reached the ear of the world. They spoke of new times and a better world.

"In fourteen points, the nations were given an outline such as would make a new order for the peoples of mankind. Whatever faults there might be, or were, found with these points, one thing doubtless is in their favor:

"Recognition that the mechanical restoration of former conditions and institutions and opinions would in a short time lead to like consequences.

"This was the magic of these theses, that they, with uncontestable grandeur, attempted to give new laws to a community of peoples, to fill them with a new spirit through which an institution could grow and flourish to become a League of Nations, not only to weld nations together outwardly but, above all, to bring them inwardly closer together in mutual consideration and mutual understanding.

"No people succumbed more completely to the magic power of this fantasy than the Germans. Germany had the honor of having fought against the whole world and the misfortune to have been defeated in this struggle. As the defeated party, however, she was loaded down with the curse of responsibility for a struggle that the German people had neither foreseen nor desired.

"The German people believed in these theses with the strength of one despairing of himself and the world. Thus Germany was led to her most sorrowful period. . . ."

"We had been dragged into the war, for whose outbreak we were exactly as guiltless, or guilty, as other peoples. But precisely because we sacrificed the most, we also were those who succumbed most easily to a faith in better times. But not only we, the vanquished, but also the victors experienced a transformation of the fanciful image of new times in human development into a pitiful reality.

"Since the statesmen of those times met at Versailles to determine a new order of things, seventeen years have passed. It has been long enough to form a judgment on the general tendency of development. It is unnecessary to search for or to co-ordinate the critical voices from literary or publicist sources to arrive at a final conclusion. . . ."

"That peace, which was intended to be the final stone laid on the cover of the tomb of war, developed into dragons' seed for new struggles. Wherever we have looked since then we have experienced the flaring up of domestic and foreign troubles. . . ."

"One thing more. We are not to blame for this development for it was not in our power after the terrible collapse in the time of our humiliation and defenseless ill-treatment to give ideas to the world, let alone prescribe laws. That was done by the mighty rulers of the world. Germany for fifteen years belonged only to the ruled. . . ."

"Since that time there has existed a discrepancy between a world divided by the peace treaty into the defeated—that is, the people without rights—and the victors—that is, people who alone possess rights—and the only thoretical principle of a League of Nations as a community of free and equal nations.

"From the spiritual atmosphere of this treaty there further ensued short-sighted treatment of numerous political and economic questions of the world. Frontiers were drawn not according to the clear necessities of life and recognition of factual traditions but were dominated by the idea of revenge and retribution, accompanied by feelings of fear and apprehension concerning the spirit of revenge that might result. . . ."

"Worst of all, however, is that the spirit of secrecy inherent in this treaty became part and parcel of the general mentality of the peoples. It began to infect and master public opinion. Because of this spirit of hatred, lack of sense began to triumph and failed to recognize at their worst the most natural problems of life of the peoples; yes, even the most personal interests, and destroyed them with the poison of misspent passion. . . ."

"That the world, for example, will reach no understanding of the causes behind the difficulties of the German people's need for living is lamentable.

"Just as shocking, however, are the daily reports in so many press organs of the satisfaction with which one regards these sorrows which forcibly accompany the life of our people. So far as this concerns unimportant journals the matter can be overlooked. But it is an ugly consideration, however, when statesmen also begin to see joyful moments in regard to judgments of the present situation and the future in growing or waning indications of need and suffering of our people. . . ."

"There was the folly with which, for instance, in the case of Germany, a nation of 60,000,000, all possible vital strands connecting her with the outside world were first cut off with scientific accuracy, all economic connections prevented, all capital invested abroad confiscated, her trade destroyed and then an unfathomable astronomic debt foisted upon this people.

"Finally, to enable Germany to pay off this debt, foreign credits were granted upon which again to draw interest, then an export-at-any-price move encouraged, then markets for foreign sales were walled up. Thus this people was driven into terrible poverty and misery: and now complaint is made about the lack of ability to pay, or about ill-will. That, however, was then called 'wise statesmanship.'

"My deputies! If I always go with so much detail into these psychological problems, it is because I am convinced that without a change of spiritual outlook regarding the development of our international relationships real pacification of the world will never be attained.

"Today's fatal tension in Europe, of which we are witnesses, also owes its existence to this folly with which it is believed the natural interest of nations can be managed. There are politicians today who seem to feel secure only when the living conditions of their neighbors are as bad as possible. The worse off their neighbors are the more triumphant these politicians feel in the belief that it is all due to their farsighted policies. . . ."

"I should, therefore, like to have the German people understand the inner motives underlying the National Socialist foreign policy, which, for instance, is very much pained that the approach of 33,000,000 people to the sea leads over territory formerly belonging to the Reich, which, however, regards it as senseless, because impossible, simply to want to deny so large a State an approach to the sea.

"It cannot be the meaning or purpose of a superior foreign policy to bring about conditions that would of necessity immediately cry for a change. It is no doubt possible, especially by falling back on one's power, for politicians to commit such violations of natural vital interests, but the more this is done, the greater will the pressure be for giving vent to stored-up and violated power and energies. . . ."

"How much anxiety could have been spared humanity, especially the peoples of Europe, if the natural self-evident necessities of life had been respected and taken into account in the political constitution of European space for existence as well as in co-operating along economic lines!

"This, however, seems to me to be an essential if one wants to reach better and more satisfactory results. And this particularly is true for Europe. European peoples represent just one family of this world—often somewhat quarrelsome, but, despite everything, related to one another and not separable spiritually, culturally, or economically. Every attempt to see and treat European problems other than according to the laws of cool, considered reasonableness leads to a reaction which would be inconvenient to everybody. . . ."

"It is wise statesmanship to put a brake on turbulent senselessness, but at the same time to yield to the visible necessities of the time and intelligently aim at a social settlement which avoids one extreme without falling into another.

"For Europe, it can be prophesied today that where this process is not followed intelligently or where it fails, tension is bound to increase, eventually finding an outlet for itself in accordance with the spiritual tendencies of the time.

"It also belongs to the wisdom of constructiveness and the maintenance of the family of nations as we have it in Europe to apply these inner State laws externally. It is not sound judgment to imagine in the space of a restricted house, such as Europe, a community of nations can be kept for long under different principles of law. Any such attempts lead to an accumulation of will and energies by those suffering unrightfully and thereby, of course, again an accumulation of the psychosis of fear among those who are guilty.

"Such a development, however, I deem to be not sensible but, on the contrary, consider it senseless and very dangerous besides. I consider it especially critical if, in addition thereto, spiritual incitation occurs which, originating with shortsighted literateurs and internationally known troublemakers, also mobilizes the passions of confused and excited masses of people.

"If I give expression to these fears, I merely render also what millions of humans are divining, feeling or experiencing without perhaps being able to explain the deeper causes to themselves. I have the right to unfold these viewpoints of mine for you gentlemen, Deputies of the Reichstag, because they furnish the key at the same time to our own political experience and to our work among our people domestically as well as our position in matters abroad.

"If the rest of the world frequently speaks of the 'German question,' then it is necessary to assure one's self with objective clarity regarding the nature of this question. For many the question involves the German administration, in misunderstood differentiation of the German administration in contrast with another administration in the so-called rearmament which generally is felt to be threatening.

"The question for many resides in the noticed desire for war of the German people, in a slumbering intention of making an attack or in a devilish dexterity in outwitting an opponent.

"No, my dear politicians! The German question involves something entirely different.

"Here 67,000,000 persons are living on a very restricted and not everywhere fertile area. That means, roughly, 136 per square kilometer. These people are no less industrious than other European peoples and also no less insistent upon getting what they want.

"They are no less intelligent but also no less insistent upon living. They have exactly as little ambition to be shot dead heroically in pursuit of a shadow as have the French or English.

"But neither are they more cowardly and in no case are they less honorable than the citizens of other European nations. They were once dragged into a war in which they believed as little as did the other Europeans and for which they bore just as little responsibility.

"Today's young German of twenty-five was in the time leading up to the war just one year old. Therefore he was hardly responsible for the world catastrophe. Even the youngest German who might be held responsible was, according to the voting age then, twenty-five years old. So today he would be fifty.

"That means that the overwhelming majority of German

men have simply taken part in war as a matter of course exactly like the last of the surviving members of the French or British peoples. If they were loyal they at that time did their duty exactly as every loyal Frenchman or Englishman did his if he possessed the necessary age. . . ."

"Now the German question consisted in the fact that this people as late as 1935 was supposed to stand, because of a fault which it never committed, for the inferiority of rights, which for the honor of a loving people is unbearable, for an industrious people, fraught with suffering, and for an intelligent people a cause for indignation. . . ."

"For the Germans there is eighteen per cent less ground per capita of population than, for example, for the Russians. It is understandable, therefore, how hard the struggle for existence and for daily bread must be. And without the energy and diligence of the German farmers and the organization capacity of the German people, finding a means of existence for these 67,000,000 would be scarcely thinkable. . . ."

"And here it would be in the interest of the rest of the world to understand the cry for bread among a 40,000,000, 50,000,000 or 60,000,000 population is not a trumped-up piece of maliciousness of a regime or certain regimes but is the natural expression of the necessities of the struggle for existence.

"And to comprehend also that well-fed peoples are more sensible than hungry ones and that governments should not only be interested in feeding their own citizens but also in feeding surrounding peoples and therefore to comprehend that providing for such living maintenance is in the highest sense of the word in the interest of all. . . ."

"The second German question is the following:

"Owing to the fact that, as a consequence of the extraordinarily unhappy general conditions and presuppositions, the economic struggle for existence of the German people is very difficult, while the intelligence, industry, and natural standard of life are very high, exceptional concentration of all energies is necessary to master this first German question.

"This can succeed, however, only if this people also in its relations with other nations possesses a feeling of political equality and with it of political security. It is impossible to deal with or even lead a people possessed of honor and of bravery forever, though it were made up of helots.

"There is no better proof of the innate love of peace of the German people than the fact that despite its ability and its bravery, which I suppose cannot be denied even by opponents, and despite its dense population, it has secured for itself only such a modest share of space for living and the good things of this world. However, precisely, this more and more introspective character of the German nature cannot put up with being deprived of its rights unworthily, nor with violation of its rights. . . ."

"I have determined not to solve this problem according to the signature of the peace treaty of the year 1919. Not because I want to harm France or any other State, but because the German people cannot forever bear the injury done it, should not bear it and will not bear it!

"In the year 1932 Germany stood on the brink of a bolshevistic collapse. What this chaos in so large a State would have meant for Europe perhaps several European statesmen will sometime have an opportunity to study in other places.

"I have, at all events, conquered this approaching crisis of the German people only through the mobilization of the general moral values of the German nation. The man who wanted to save Germany from bolshevism had to bring the question of German equality to a decision and thereby to a solution.

"He had to solve it, not to add to the sorrows of other peoples but just the opposite, to prevent, indeed, a perhaps greater sorrow through the hindering of an outbreak, the extent of which cannot be estimated.

"The re-winning of German equality has caused nothing

painful to the French people. Only the Red uproar and threatened collapse of the German Reich has given a blow to European order and business of whose results most European statesmen unfortunately have no real conception. This fight for German equality which I led for three years is not the setting up of the German problem, but its solution.

"It is truly a tragic misfortune that precisely by the Versailles treaty a situation was created in the preservation of which the French people were believed to be especially interested. The real advantages derived from it by a single Frenchman were small, but the unreal link between the anti-German discrimination of Versailles and French interests seemed all the greater.

"Possibly it was the fault of a character weakness of the German post-war years and of our governments, especially our parties, that the fallacy of these views could not be brought home sufficiently to the French people and to serious French statesmen. For the worse our previous governments were, the more they were bound to shrink from a national awakening of the German people.

"Hence all the greater was the dread of any revival of national consciousness, hence their bowing to the general international defamation of the German people. More, they used these shameful bonds to prop up their own miserable regimes. . . ."

"I shall at some future date be able to demand of history that it will certify that at no hour of my actions in behalf of the German people did I forget the duties which I and all of us owe to the preservation of European culturalized civilization. A prerequisite, however, for the continued existence of this Continent, which is so extraordinary because of the differences of its cultures, is the realization that it is unthinkable without the existence of free and independent national States. Let every European people be convinced it has made the greatest contribution to our Occidental culture. . . ."

"During these years I have tried again and again—unfortunately too often in vain—to construct a bridge of understanding to the French people. The further we become removed from the bitterness of the World War and the years following it, the more human memories forget the unpleasant incidents, and the more beautiful aspects of life, knowledge and experience push into the foreground.

"Those who once faced each other as embittered opponents respect each other today as brave combatants in a past great struggle and meet each other again as bearers and conservators of the great general human treasure of culture. Why, then, should it not be possible to call off the purposeless, century-long quarrel which could not and cannot bring a final decision to either of the two peoples and to substitute for it a recognition of a higher common sense?

"The German people is not interested in having the French people suffer, and vice versa. Where would there be any advantage for France if Germany were to go under in misery? What advantage does the French farmer enjoy if the German farmer has a bad time of it, and vice versa?

"What advantage can the French worker derive from, say, the misery of the German? And what blessing could it bring the German worker, the German middle class or the German people at large if France were to be visited by misfortune?

"I have tried to solve the questions of the hateful class struggle theory within the interior of Germany along the lines of a higher common sense. In this I have succeeded.

"Why should it not be possible to lift the problem of general European differences between nations and States out of the sphere of senselessness and passion and move it under the quieter light of higher reasonableness?

"At any rate, I once swore to myself I would fight doggedly and bravely for German equality and to achieve it in one way or another. I also determined to strengthen the feeling of responsibility for the necessity of European mutual respect for each other and of European co-operation.

"If I am reproached by my international opponents on the grounds that I refuse this co-operation with Russia, then I must explain the following in that connection: I refused and refuse co-operation, not with Russia, but with bolshevism, which has claimed the mastery of the world. . . ."

"I tremble for Europe and the thought of what would happen to our old, overpopulated continent if the chaos of a bolshevistic revolution should be successful through the outbreak of this destructive Asiatic world conception, which strikes at all hitherto recognized values.

"To many European statesmen, I am, perhaps, a fantastic and, at all events, an inconvenient admonisher. That I, however, pass for one of the greatest enemies in the eyes of the bolshevistic international world oppressors is for me a great honor and justification for my dealings before posterity. . . ."

"I see no possibility for making it clear to the German workers the danger, so disturbing to me, of the misery coming from bolshevistic chaos in Germany, if I myself, as leader of the nation, were to bring myself into close relationship with this danger.

"Here, as a statesman and as the people's leader, I will do all that I demand and expect from any single fellow-citizen.

"I do not believe that close contacts with a concept which is detrimental to a people can be useful to a statesman. We have had full opportunity to gather experiences of this sort in Germany's history of the past twenty years.

"The first contact with bolshevism in 1917 brought us revolution one year later. The second contact sufficed to bring Germany a few years later to the brink of communist ruin.

"I have severed these connections and thereby saved Germany from perdition.

"Nothing will move me to go another way but the way

which experience, insight, and foresight tell me to go. I know this conviction has become the deepest realization and the ideal of the whole National Socialist Movement. . . ."

"If I transmute this attitude of principle to the realm of general European politics, their results will mean the division of Europe into two halves:

"That half which is built up of independent, self-sustaining national States of the peoples with whom we are bound a hundredfold through our history and culture, and with whom we should like, for all the future, to remain bound just as with the free and independent nations of other than European continents.

"And in the other half: That which is governed by that intolerant bolshevik doctrine which lays claim to general international rule, a doctrine which preaches destruction even to the most eternal and sacred values of this life and the life hereafter, in order to build up another world, which, to us, appears horrible as regards culture and the appearance of its contents.

"Aside from the necessity of political, economic, and international relations, we do not desire any more intimate contact with it.

"A fathomless tragedy lies in the fact, as a conclusion to our honest endeavor of many years to win the confidence, sympathy, and affection of the French people, a military alliance was born, the beginnings of which we know today but the end of which, will, perhaps, be accompanied by consequences which no one can foresee unless, indeed, providence once again proves more merciful than men deserve.

"I have endeavored for the past three years, slowly but steadily, to create the prerequisites for Franco-German understanding. I have never left a doubt that these prerequisites include absolute equality, equality of the status of the German people and States.

"Intentionally, I have not only seen in this understanding merely a problem capable of solution by means of parleys, but also a problem that first has to be brought near to the two peoples psychologically, as it must be prepared, not only for the intellect but also for the emotion.

"I therefore have also often been subjected to the charge that my offers of friendship contained no concrete proposals. That is not true. Whatever could be proposed at all concretely to improve German and French relations, I have proposed courageously and concretely.

"There was a time when I did not hesitate to support a concrete proposal for the limitation of armaments to 200,000 men. Then, when this proposal was abandoned by the responsible originators themselves, I turned to the French people and the European governments with quite a concrete new proposal. My proposal for 300,000 men also was turned down.

"I have brought a whole array of further concrete proposals for the purification of the public viewpoints in the various States and for cleansing the conduct of war and, in the final analysis, for careful but certain disarmaments.

"Only one of these German proposals has been really considered. The realistic sense of an English administration received my proposal for the restoration of a lasting relation between the German and British fleets which takes into consideration the needs of German security and the enormous overseas interests of a great World Power.

"And I may well explain that until today only this agreement has remained as the single practical existing attempt to eliminate armaments.

"The Reich administration is ready to extend this treaty through a wider qualitative understanding with England.

"I have expressed the very concrete principle that the joint programs of an international pact mania contain just as little prospect of workability as general treaties for world disarmament, which, under such conditions, have been demonstrated to be incapable of fulfillment. I have expressed the opinion, in contrast, that these problems can be approached only step by step and, indeed, in the direction of the least opposition.

"I have developed from this conviction a concrete proposal also for an air pact on the basis of like strength for France, England, and Germany. The result was first a misconception of this proposal and then the introduction of a new Eastern European-Asiatic factor, incalculable in its military extent, into the European equilibrium. . . ."

"I may point out here that it would have been quite possible for me, as a German, to set up the restoration of the 1914 frontiers morally as my program and to proclaim it by publicity and oratory just as the French Ministers and popular leaders did after 1871.

"The critics cannot pretend that I have no capacity for such a thing. It is far more difficult for a nationalist to preach understanding to people than to do the opposite. And it would probably be easier for me to excite popular instincts for revenge than to awaken sentiments for the necessity for European understanding and to make them ever stronger.

"And that is what I have done. I have eliminated from German public opinion a pact of this nature against our neighbors.

"I have removed from the German press all hatred directed against the French people. I have tried to inculcate in our youth an appreciation for the ideal of such an understanding, certainly not without success. . . ."

"This endeavor of mine was doubly difficult because I was compelled at the same time to liberate Germany from the meshes of the treaty which robbed it of its equality but in the continuance of which the French people—whether rightly is secondary—thought they must continue to be interested.

"In that connection I, as a German nationalist, had to bring an additional and especially great sacrifice. Until now, at least in the more modern times, an attempt had never been made after a war to deprive a loser of sovereign rights over large and ancient parts of his territory.

"In the interests of understanding, and for this reason alone, I have made this greatest sacrifice that could be imposed upon us politically and morally, and I was ready to continue to make it merely because I believed I ought to stick to a treaty which might possibly help to take the poison out of the political atmosphere between France, Germany, and England and to spread a feeling of security to all sides.

"Yes, beyond that also, here in this house, I have often taken the position that we were not only ready to make this most heavy contribution to the security of European peace as long as the other partners also live up to their obligations, but that we saw in this treaty the only possible—because concrete—attempt at making Europe secure.

"You, my deputies, know the content and the meaning of this treaty. It was intended for all future to prevent the use of force between Belgium and France on one hand and Germany on the other.

"Through France's treaties of alliance previously concluded there unfortunately arose the first difficulty, although it did not rob this pact of its meaning.

"Germany made her contribution to this pact, for while France supplied her frontier with ore and weapons and studded it with numerous garrisons, we were burdened with a continuous maintenance of complete defenselessness. . . ."

"In contravention of this pact there now exists an arrangement upon which France has entered in the past year with Russia and which it has already signed, while its ratification by the Chamber of Deputies has just taken place.

"For, through this new Franco-Soviet arrangement, there is led into the middle of Europe, via detour of Czechoslovakia, which has entered upon a similar arrangement with Russia, the threatening military power of a gigantic empire.

"The impossible situation which has risen consists of the fact that these two States obligate themselves in this arrangement—without taking into consideration a decision of the League of Nations' Council which either already has been rendered or which is expected to be—in the event of Eastern European entanglements to settle the question of guilt according to their own lights and in accordance therewith to regard the obligation of mutual assistance as existent or nonexistent.

"The idea that in this pact a primary obligation is again affirmed through an added restriction is not understandable. I cannot establish and thereby accept as binding a definite method at a point where there is an explicit break with an otherwise valid obligation in order to determine at another point that there should be no dealings concerning these other obligations. . . ."

"France has not concluded the pact with an old European power. France had, even before the Rhine pact, assistance agreements with Czechoslovakia as well as with Poland. Germany took no exception thereto, not only because these pacts, in contrast to the Franco-Soviet pact, were within the framework of the League of Nations, but also because Czechoslovakia, like Poland, always primarily followed the policy of representing the national interests of these States.

"Germany does not desire to attack these States nor does it believe it will lie in the interests of these States to launch an attack upon Germany. Above all, Poland will remain Poland; France will remain France.

"Soviet Russia, however, is the constitutionally organized exponent of the revolutionary philosophy of life. Its State creed is its confession in favor of world revolution.

"It is impossible to determine whether or not, tomorrow or the day after tomorrow, this creed also will triumph in France. Should, however, such an eventuality occur—and as a German statesman I must make provision for it—then it is certain that this new bolshevik State would become a section of the bolshevik International which means a decision concerning attack or nonattack will then not be arrived at

according to their own objectives and desires, but in accordance with directions given from one place.

"That place would, however, in the event of such a development, no longer be Paris but Moscow.

"*Germany hardly is in a position—if only for purely territorial reasons—to attack Russia, but Russia could at any time, using its advanced positions, start a conflict with Germany.* The determination as to who was the attacker would be certain from the beginning, since that determination would be independent of the League of Nations Council.

"The assertion that France and Russia would do nothing to expose themselves to eventual sanctions—from England or Italy—is immaterial, because it is impossible to gage the kind of sanctions that would be applied against a structure which is so overwhelming. . . ."

"Our serious misgivings in this connection have been met by the argument that the Russian war-machine is not ready, even that it is a clumsy and unwieldable machine, for a European war.

"We have always opposed this view, not because we think the Germans are inferior, but because we all know that numbers have their own weight and importance.

"We are all the more grateful for the explanations given by M. Herriot in the French Chamber regarding Russia's military significance. We know that these explanations were furnished M. Herriot by the Soviet Government itself and we are convinced that the latter cannot have supplied false particulars to inspire in France the desire for the new alliance.

"Neither do we doubt that M. Herriot has passed on all this information correctly.

"According to this information, it is certain, first of all, that the Russian Army has a peace strength of 1,350,000 and that it comprises, secondly, 17,500,000 men in war strength and reserves, and that it is, thirdly, equipped with the largest tank equipment, and that it, fourthly, owns the largest air force in the world.

"The introduction of this most powerful of all military factors, which also, as regards its mobility and leadership, was described as excellent and at all times ready to give an account of itself, into the Central European field of operation, destroys every real European balance of power.

"Besides, it renders impossible any determination as to the necessary weapons for defense on land and in the air as far as the European States concerned are involved, especially as regards the one opponent envisaged, namely Germany.

"This gigantic mobilization of the East against Central Europe stands, not only according to the letter but also according to its meaning, in contravention of the spirit of the Locarno Pact. Not only we as the nation affected feel that way about it. Our feelings are shared by uncounted sensible men among all peoples and are being freely expressed everywhere, as can be evidenced publicly and politically.

"On February 21 a French journalist approached me with the request to grant him an interview. As I was told that he was one of those Frenchmen who, just like ourselves, are trying to find the ways and means for an understanding between the two peoples, I wanted all the less to decline, as such an act would immediately have been interpreted as a sign of my lack of respect for French journalism.

"I gave the desired explanations just as I have expressed them in Germany hundreds of thousands of times, and as I have again tried to turn to the French people with the plea for understanding which we want with all our hearts and which we, so willingly, would like to see in actuality.

"I expressed my deepest sorrow over the development in France, through the formulation of the pact for which no pressing need is visible, but which in the event of its realization must and will produce a new situation.

"This interview was, as you know, on grounds which are unknown to us, withheld, and it appeared first on the day after the ratification in the French Chamber [of the Franco-Soviet pact].

"In accordance with my announcement in this interview, I shall also be ready, and sincerely desirous in the future, to serve this Franco-German understanding because I see in it the necessary element for the security of Europe against unseen danger and because I can promise for both peoples from no other procedure any possible advantage and see without it the most serious general and international danger, so much so that the knowledge of the final conclusion of this pact has forced me now to enter upon the examination of the new situation created and to draw the necessary conclusions.

"These consequences are very serious, they deeply grieve us and me personally. But I am obliged not only to make sacrifices for European understanding but also to obey the interests of my own people.

"So long as the sacrifice meets appreciation and understanding on the other side, I will gladly make it and recommend the same to the German people. But from the moment that it becomes certain that a partner no longer values or appreciates such sacrifices, a one-sided burden is placed on Germany and thereby there is discrimination which is unbearable to us. . . ."

"I want to cheat neither ourselves nor the rest of the world with a people that would then have no value whatever because it lacked the most natural feeling of honor. I believe at the same time that even in the hour of such bitter realizations and difficult decisions, one must not fail, despite everything, to champion European co-operation and to cast about for new methods for making possible the solution of these questions in a manner useful to all concerned.

"I have therefore made further efforts, by concrete proposals, to give expression to the feelings of the German people, who, anxious about their security, and ready, for the sake of freedom, to make every sacrifice, are at all times ready for real, honest, and equal European co-operation.

"After a hard struggle within myself, I have therefore decided in the name of the German Reich Government today to transmit to the French Government and other powers signatory to the Locarno pact a memorandum.

"Men of the German Reichstag! In this historic hour, when in the Reich's western provinces German troops are just entering their future peace garrisons, we all unite in two holy inner confessions:

"First, we swear to yield to no force whatever in the restoration of the honor of our people, and rather to succumb with honor to the severest hardships than capitulate to it;

"Secondly, to confess that now, more than ever, we shall strive for an understanding between European peoples, especially for one with our western neighbor nations.

"After three years, I believe I can today regard the struggle for German equality as over. I believe that the first ground for our one-time withdrawal from European collective co-operation has been removed.

"If we now are again ready to resume this co-operation, it is with a sincere wish that perhaps the present proceedings and a review of these years may help to strengthen an understanding for this co-operation among other European peoples also.

"*We have no territorial demands to make in Europe.* We know above all that the tension resulting either from long territorial provisions or from the wrong relationships between the population living in areas can, in Europe, not be solved by wars.

"We hope, however, that human insight will help to alleviate the painful consequences of such conditions and to remove tension by embarking upon a slow evolutionary development of peaceful co-operation. . . ."

"I cannot terminate this historic period of restitution of the honor and freedom of my people without now asking the German people to give its supplementary approval to me and thereby to all my co-workers and co-fighters, for all that I have had to execute during these years in the way of decisions which seemed to be stern, and for what I had to demand in the way of sacrifices.

"I have therefore decided today to dissolve the German Reichstag so the German people may pass judgment on my leadership and on that of my associates. . . ."

"I now ask the German people to strengthen me in my faith and to give me, through the strength of its will, further individual strength with which to fight always courageously for its honor and freedom and to be able to take care of its economic well-being. And especially to support me in my struggle for a new peace."

Press

London Times, March 8—Herr Hitler's invasion of the Rhineland is a challenge abrupt in form and deliberate in fact, to the voluntary agreement which has maintained the inviolability of the eastern frontiers of France and Belgium for the last eleven years. The age-old clash of suspicions lies behind the story. Is Germany, who has now repudiated a freely negotiated treaty, ever to be trusted? Is France, who has brought Russia to redress the balance of manpower in the West, ever to be satisfied? . . . France and Britain alike have reason for indignation and food for suspicions. But since neither stands alone, they have the more power, even while they are faced with an admitted offense against the law of Europe, to take a steady measure of the undertakings which Germany has offered in extenuation.

New York Times, March 8—That Germany has created a grave situation in Europe is readily apparent. Military occupation of the Rhineland is a clear violation both of the Versailles Treaty and of the Locarno Pact. It is a brusque repudiation of Hitler's many declarations that he had no intention of jeopardizing the safeguards of peace erected on Germany's western frontier . . . Hitler has chosen not to wait for a judicial settlement of the status of the new treaty.

. . . No one can mistake the significance of this latest move.

Le Temps, March 8—The Fuehrer's statement went much further than anyone expected. M. Hitler denounced the Locarno Pact and proclaimed the sovereignty of the Reich in the demilitarized zone. He announced that German troops were going to occupy their garrisons. At the same time he proclaimed that Germany would henceforth consider herself possessing equal rights with other nations. He then declared himself ready to return to the League of Nations.

•

SPEECH OF MARCH 20, 1936

Hamburg

Background

March 8—After a prolonged cabinet meeting and consultations with the French General Staff, the Sarraut Cabinet decides to lodge a protest with the League of Nations against the reoccupation of the Rhineland.

In Warsaw, the French Ambassador is informed that the Polish Army is ready to march if the French Army marches too.

March 9—In a speech, Albert Sarraut says that France will not negotiate under threat of violence and as long as Strasbourg is under the Nazi guns.

The Speech

"I NEED the German people in the struggle that I carry on for its own sake, in the struggle for German equality, in the struggle against the insolence of others who still regard

Germany as an inferior or as enjoying inferior rights or who try to act as if such were the case.

"I need the German people to demonstrate therewith to the whole world that whatever happens we will not retreat one inch from our equal rights—not because we want to disturb European order but because we are convinced, contrary to the opinion of temporary and mortal politicians, that permanent order in Europe is possible only on a foundation of peoples enjoying equal rights.

"The opinion that European order can be founded permanently on the defamation of a people numbering 67,000,000 is lunatic and madness. They do not need to think that the German nation has rebelled simply because a certain man, Adolf Hitler, stands at its head. No, if I were not there, another would have come sooner or later. Germany will live longer than such an opinion will live.

"The German nation in its history has often suffered a bitter fate, as other nations have. It is alone in that it has never been destroyed by such events, as our enemies once believed. When they struck at Germany's heart in 1918 they did not recognize that they had thereby created the deepest basis for a German resurrection. What at that time they regarded as a death-blow was in reality nothing else than the signal for a new and stronger unification of the German nation. . . ."

"I do not desire anything further than that this German nation shall take its place and grow into the unity and co-operation of the European community.

"I am sorry, however, for statesmen who think that such co-operation can best be commenced by new defamation of the German nation. If they would only look a little further than supposed momentary successes, I believe they would be shocked to recognize the inevitable results of such historically false policies.

"In any case, I do not feel myself, as leader of the German people and as its spokesman and responsible administrator, in a position to take even one step that is not in accord with the honor of the German nation. . . ."

Press

London Times, March 21—In his speech at Hamburg tonight Herr Hitler said that the General Election had not been called to decide any home political question, but to let the world know that when he spoke he was speaking for the entire German nation.

New York Times, March 21—Chancellor Adolf Hitler delivered a stormy oration here tonight on the old thesis of German equality which outdid in fury any of his preceding campaign speeches.

•

PROCLAMATION AT PARTY CONVENTION, SEPTEMBER 9, 1936

Nuremberg

Background

March 29—Elections are held in Germany to ratify reoccupation of the Rhineland. Ninety-five per cent approval is recorded.

April 20—Dedication of three monasteries as schools for the future Party members.

Goering is made Commissioner of Raw Materials and Foreign Exchange.

Himmler is made chief of the unified German police.

April 26—May 3—National elections in France. They are won by the Popular Front (a coalition of Radical-Socialists, Socialists, and Communists).

May 2—The Italians enter Addis Ababa. The Negus is in flight.

May 26—First sit-down strikes in France.

June 4—Sarraut Cabinet resigns formally. Léon Blum, head of the Socialist party forms new cabinet.

July 11—Germany and Austria conclude a "cultural pact."

July 17—The Senate of Danzig, dominated by the Nazis, abolishes the Danzig Constitution.

July 18—Civil war breaks out in Spain.

July 30—Two Italian military planes en route for Spain crash in North Africa.

August 1—Olympic games open in Berlin.

Léon Blum issues communiqué stating that no exports of arms to Spain will be authorized.

August 5-6—British and French governments present a convention to all interested powers laying down the plan of the policy of "non-intervention" in Spain.

August 8—The "blockade" of Spain, i.e., embargo on war material from England and France, is decreed.

September 8—Opening of the Nuremberg annual convention of the National Socialist party.

September 9—Hitler announces a Four-Year Plan to make Germany self-sufficient in raw materials. Goering is put in charge of the plan.

Germany, Italy, and Soviet Russia join the non-intervention conference.

The Proclamation

"AS WE open this 'congress of honor,' we are stirred by two emotions, first, one of pride as we look back on the last four years, especially the last year, and, secondly, a feeling of the justification of all our acts as we behold the world about us filled with dissension and instability.

"Elsewhere years, if not decades, in the life of a nation pass without claiming especial consideration except where they involve political and economic collapse, and it is in this connection that we National Socialists proudly assert that the period of Germany's collapse dating from November, 1918, moved at a slower pace than the period that marks the four years of our national recovery.

"Was this miracle a genuine revolution or was it not? Have our achievements justified it in the eyes of the German people and, above all, who else but us could have accomplished this wonder. . . ."

"What, however, has Nazism made of Germany in these four years? Which of our opponents would have the insolence to appear as a complainant against us today?

"What appeared in my proclamation of 1933 to be fantastic and impossible now appears a mere modest announcement of accomplishments that tower above it.

"Our opponents did not believe it possible that time would accomplish that program of 1933, which now looks so small to us. What would they have said, however, if I had presented to them that program which Nazism has genuinely accomplished in the last four years?

"How they would have laughed if I had declared on January 30, 1933, that in four years Germany would have reduced its unemployment from six to one million;

"That the forced sale of peasant holdings would have been brought to an end;

"That the income of German agrarian economy would be higher than in any preceding year in our peace time;

"That the total national income would have risen from 41,000,000,000 marks to 56,000,000,000;

"That the German middle class and the German trades would experience a new period of prosperity;

"That commerce would regain its feet;

"That the German Hanseatic cities would no longer resemble ship cemeteries;

"That in 1936 ships totaling 640,000 tons would be under construction at German wharfs;

"That a multitude of factories would not double but triple and quadruple their employes;

"That many other new factories would appear;

"That the Krupp works would again hear the rumble of machines working for Germany's regeneration;

"That all these undertakings would recognize that their final law was service to the nation and not unscrupulous private profit;

"That inactive automobile factories would not only come to life again but would be greatly increased in size;

"That our production of automobiles of all sorts would increase from 45,000 in 1932 to almost 250,000 now;

"That in these four years the deficits of our cities and provinces would disappear;

"That the Reich would have a tax income increase of about 5,000,000,000 marks yearly;

"That the Reichsbank would finally be made financially sound;

"That its trains would be the fastest in the world;

"That the German Reich would receive roads such as had never been built since human culture existed;

"That of 7,000 kilometers [about 4,350 miles] of roads projected 1,000 would be in use after only four years and 4,000 more would be under construction;

"That tremendous new homestead colonies with hundreds of thousands of houses would appear in the Reich;

"That new buildings would rise which are among the largest in the world;

"That hundreds upon hundreds of new immense bridges would cross valleys and gulleys;

"That German culture in such and like accomplishments would demonstrate its internal character;

"That the German theater would experience a renaissance;

"That the German people would take an active part in the revival of the drama;

"That Germany would experience a great intellectual awakening without a single Jew having a hand in it;

"That the German press would work only in the interests of Germany;

"That new professional ethics would be proclaimed for German business;

"That the German human being would experience a thorough reformation of his modes of activity and his character. . . ."

"What would our opponents have said if four years ago I would have predicted that four years hence the German people would be a united nation with neither Social Democrats, Communists, Centrists nor bourgeois parties left to transgress against the German people or trade unions to scatter dissension among the workers?

"What would they have said had I then predicted that four years hence there would no longer be independent states with their own legislatures and sixteen different flags and traditions, but that the whole nation from the humblest worker up to the soldier would be pledged to one flag?

"But, above all things, what would our opponents have said had I then prophesied that during these four years Germany would have shaken off the chains of the slavery of Versailles, that the Reich would have regained its defense freedom, that, as formerly in peace time, every German would dedicate two years of his life to the freedom of his country, that our coasts and our commerce would be protected by a navy now in the course of construction, that a powerful new air weapon would vouchsafe protection to our cities and factories, and that the Rhineland would again be restored to the sovereignty of the Reich?

"And perchance what would these opponents have said had I predicted that before even four years had elapsed this National Socialist policy for the recovery of our honor and national freedom would receive an affirming endorsement by ninety-nine per cent of the German electorate? . . ."

"But a second miracle, and one which cannot fail to fill us with grim satisfaction, is the realization that our other predictions have proved all too true.

"Unrest, hate, and mistrust fill the world about us. With the exception of one major Power and a few other States, we encounter throughout Europe the convulsions of bolshevistic rioting and revolution.

"My party comrades, did it not strike you as something akin to symbolism that at a time when in other countries hate reigned and ruin spread there could take place in Berlin amid the plaudits of a happy people an Olympic festival dedicated to the noble motives of enlightened humanity?

"Despite all their attempts, it was not possible for even Jewish reporters to distort the truth and misrepresent what millions had seen with their own eyes. . . ."

"But while these Jewish-bolshevistic baiters and revolution mongers talked and showed a preference for applying an incendiary torch to human culture, National Socialist Germany, through heroic efforts and within its own frontiers and the restricted scope of its domestic resources has striven to rehabilitate its national economy, protect the lives of its people, and insure its economic future.

"The worries and disappointments that the government of the German people have encountered in this process in the last four years were probably greater and more acute than those that had confronted other governments in half a century. . . ."

"The problems of our national economic maintenance are infinitely great. First, the 136 persons per square kilometer in Germany cannot find complete sustenance of their own even with the greatest efforts and the most ingenious exploitation of their existing living room.

"What the German peasant has accomplished in these last few years is singular and unique. What the National Socialist State has accomplished in the cultivation of the last heath and the last moor in Germany cannot be surpassed.

"However, in spite of all, there will always remain a deficiency in some fields of our nutrition. To cover this deficiency by import is all the more difficult because unfortunately we also lack in Germany a number of important raw materials.

"German economy is, therefore, compelled to compensate for its lack of foods and raw materials by industrial export, which must likewise take place under all circumstances because of the unavoidability of imports, especially in the case of food.

"It is regrettable that the rest of the world has no understanding for the nature and magnitude of these tasks, thanks to the frivolous as well as stupid and, yes, even spiteful treatment of these problems.

"In order to buy a certain amount of fat for Germany, Germany must export goods to an even greater value. But since questions of food are not, as some foreign statesmen seem to think, matters of malicious intentions but vital tasks, it follows that the exports that are a presupposition of these imports must take place under all circumstances.

"It is therefore a truly deplorable lack of reason to reproach a people with its cheap exports when for lack of self-sustaining economic territory that people absolutely needs exports in order to import the food lacking.

"If, therefore, an English politician declares that Germany does not need colonies because it is free to buy raw materials, then the declaration of this gentleman is about as intelligent as the question of that well-known Bourbon Princess who at the sight of the revolutionary mob roaring for bread remarked in surprise why, if the people did not have bread, they did not eat cake.

"If the German people and the German Reich had not been squeezed for fifteen years and deprived of all their international savings, if they had not lost all their foreign investments and if they still had their own colonies, we could master these problems much easier.

"The objection that colonies would not help us much is

unjustified. The leadership of the State which has produced no longer deniable economic accomplishments under conditions such as faced the German Government would likewise know how to administer colonies with economic usefulness.

"For it was much harder for the German State and economic leadership, for instance, to reduce the number of unemployed from six and one-half to one million within our overpopulated territory and at the same time assure daily bread for all than it was in those countries which at any rate seem to have been unable to solve this question thus far. . . ."

"As National Socialist State leaders we follow a natural but to some foreigners perhaps incomprehensible principle, namely, we are not so much moved by the question whether butter is more or less plentiful at the time or whether eggs get scarcer or not; our first concern is rather to keep the broad masses of our people at work earning wages and thereby save them from sinking back into the ghastly distress of unemployment.

"We are less interested in whether the upper classes get so and so much butter all the year round, but we are greatly concerned to assure cheaper fats for the broad masses and, most of all, to keep them from unemployment.

"The bourgeois governments surrounding us will naturally consider this wholly incomprehensible, but then Germany has no bourgeois but a National Socialist government.

"It is therefore also the great task of our national economy to guide the consuming power of our people in those directions in which we can satisfy it from our own national production.

"Inasmuch as an increase in our agricultural production is possible only to a limited extent, the increase in production must take place in other fields. It is the task of our national leadership and popular education to guide and interest the nation in these fields and increase its requirements in these directions.

"But if foreign critics make German armaments responsible for the German butter shortage, if they reproach us that instead of buying butter we are carrying through Germany's rearmament, then I can only give these notable economists the advice to consider what would happen if the millions of German workers now producing for Germany's domestic requirements and therewith for our armaments should suddenly be put to the production of export goods.

"I am afraid that these clever economists would cry out in even greater despair in view of the then inevitable flooding of the world markets with cheap German export goods.

"Like every healthy national economy German economy has first of all the desire to utilize as far as possible its own economic possibilities for the maintenance of its people, in order to use the secondary consideration and participate with its own healthy economy in world economy.

"Inasmuch as the National Socialist State under no circumstances is willing to restrict the numbers of its population, but is rather determined to increase the natural fertility of the nation, we are forced to consider and weigh the consequences of such a development for the future.

"A substantial increase in production from our soil is impossible and a substantial increase in exports in the near future is improbable.

"It is therefore the task of the National Socialist State economic leadership to investigate thoroughly what essential raw materials, fuel, etc., can be produced within Germany.

"The foreign exchange we can save will serve in the future as an additional safeguard for our food supply and for the purchase of those materials which cannot be found in our territory under any circumstances.

"I therefore announce this today as our new four-year program:

"In four years Germany must be wholly independent of foreign countries in respect to all those materials which can in any way be produced through German capability, through our chemistry, machine, and mining industries. The creation of this great German raw material industry will employ productively those masses freed by the completion of rearmament. We hope thus to increase national production in many fields so as to reserve the proceeds of our exports first of all for food and for raw materials, which we will still lack.

"I have just issued necessary orders for carrying out this mighty German economic plan. Its execution will take place with National Socialist energy and force.

"Independent of this, Germany cannot, however, relinquish her demand for a solution of her colonial demands. The right of the German people to live is just as great as that of the people of other nations.

"I know, my National Socialist racial comrades, that this new program represents a mighty task, but scientifically it is already solved in many fields; the production methods are being already partly tried.

"As National Socialists we never acknowledged the word 'impossible' and we shall not accept it in the future as an enrichment of our vocabulary. In four years we will give an accounting to the nation on this gigantic work and assure its nutrition and with that its life and independence.

"Perhaps we shall hear anew in the mouths of Western democrats the complaint that we deprive business of freedom for its own arbitrary activity and put it in the straight-jacket of our State planning. But you, my racial comrades, will understand that the question here is not democracy or freedom, but being or not being.

"Not the freedom or profit of some industrials is the subject for debate here, but the life and freedom of the German nation. Whoever believes he cannot exist because of the curtailing of freedom has no right to exist in our community. Posterity will not ask us whether in this critical and dangerous period we held high democratic freedom, meaning license, but whether we succeeded in keeping a great people from economic and political collapse. . . ."

"The National Socialist State leadership is so sovereign,

so above all economic ties, that in its eyes the designations 'employe' and 'employer' are immaterial concepts. Before the higher interests of the nation there are neither employer nor employe, but only labor delegates of the entire people. . . ."

"Just as we in Germany can solve the problems before us only if internal peace is preserved, so we are convinced that the European peoples and States can approach a happier future only through the preservation of European peace. It is our grim determination, however, not to let Germany become the unarmed victim of any foreign military power.

"We have learned from the last eighteen years. We know what is the fate of the nation that, without force of its own, depends on foreign justice. We see around us signs of evil times to come. What we preached for years about the greatest world danger of the end of this second thousand years of our Christian era has become a terrible reality.

"Everywhere the undermining work of bolshevist agents has begun. In the period while bourgeois statesmen are discussing non-intervention, the Jewish revolutionary headquarters in Moscow is using the radio and every available financial and other agent to accomplish revolution on this continent.

"Do not tell us that by constantly referring to these dangers to Germany we are creating a fear psychosis. We are National Socialists. We have never been afraid of bolshevism.

"We are not, however, members of that absurd bourgeois guild who sing 'Who's afraid of the big, bad wolf?' on the edge of a catastrophe and then, when its eyes are finally opened, jumps under the bed, teeth chattering.

"We German National Socialists have never been afraid of communism. We only recognized the real character of this shameful Jewish world-destroying doctrine. We studied its abominable methods and warned against its results. . . ."

"We are not afraid today of a bolshevist invasion of Germany, not, however, because we do not expect it but because we are determined to make the nation so strong that it will be able, like National Socialism within our boundaries, to face this doctrine of world hate and resist victoriously every foreign attack.

"This is the explanation of the military measures we have taken. Germany's measures will be larger or smaller in proportion to the dangers surrounding us. It is for us no pleasure to lock up these forces of our people in armaments and barracks. We are simply men enough to look the facts in the face.

"I want to state this proclamation before the whole German people that I am profoundly convinced that it is necessary to preserve Germany's bulwark of peace as I guaranteed its internal peace. I will not avoid any measure calculated to give the nation a sense of security and above all to secure for ourselves the sense that the complete independence of the Reich is guaranteed. . . ."

"I, therefore, after discussions with the Reich War Minister, decreed the immediate introduction of a two-year military service term. I know that the young German, without moving an eyelash, will obey this necessity.

"The present regime in Germany has the right to ask this of Germans, for we all served in the great war, not for two but for four years. We did it for Germany, for the German nation, for our German homeland. The Nazi movement fought fifteen years and required great sacrifices from its followers for the salvation of Germany from the internal bolshevist enemy. . . ."

"The army educated us. We have all come from the army, those of us who became the party Storm Troops and the motor corps. The army gave us the men with whom we created our Storm Company's old guard and movement.

"To the army shall belong for two years the young sons of our people so they will secure the strength and capacity to fight for the independence and freedom of our Fatherland, for the protection of the German nation. Because I am able to make this declaration on the fourth Reich Party Day

I regard with profound joy this proudest accomplishment of the National Socialist Government's military spirit.

"Now generation after generation will make the most noble sacrifice that can be demanded of man.

"The German people have in the year 1936, in the fourth year of the National Socialist regime, ended the period of their historic dishonor."

Press

New York Times, September 11—There is no reason to believe, that he is satisfied or that he has relinquished the determination expressed in *Mein Kampf* not only to absorb Austria but also to expand Germany's frontiers eastward to include within the Reich all Germans "for the safeguarding of the race." This could be achieved only through the dismemberment of Poland and Czechoslovakia—and this means war; or the amputation of a portion of the Ukraine from Soviet Russia—and this means war.

These territorial ambitions help to explain Hitler's violent and uncompromising hatred of Soviet Russia and his wooing of Great Britain. If Western Europe and especially Great Britain can be persuaded that Germany is in fact the bulwark against communism, British pressure may be brought to bear on France and its Eastern European allies to permit German expansion at Russia's expense. There are influential British Conservatives who favor this "solution. . . ."

Hitler's reaffirmation of peaceful intentions may be accepted as sincere. But are his ambitions consistent with a peaceful Europe? Does his denunciation of democracy as the forerunner of anarchy help toward stabilization in a troubled world? Does his extolling of the military spirit strengthen the forces of conciliation? To ask these questions is to answer them. Hitler has shown that Nazi Germany is still on the march. The direction and nature of its future advances may determine the issues of peace or war.

London Times, September 10—. . . The general tone of the proclamation would seem to support the belief that while the Nazi are so much preoccupied with the manipulation of the bolshevist bogey on the stage of foreign affairs there will be a relaxation of the pressure which militant forms of Nazi activity have been exerting at home. Both the Roman Catholic and the Protestant Churches will presumably benefit by this concentration on foreign affairs. Even the Jews may find themselves no worse off for some little time to come, although the wild cheering which greeted a casual but unfavorable reference to Jews in the proclamation today was an indication of the extent to which an announcement of further anti-Jewish legislation would have been welcomed in extremist party circles.

London Times, editorial, September 10, 1936—The claim to colonies which Herr Hitler stated at the opening of the Congress of the National Socialist party at Nuremberg yesterday was only the culmination of a propaganda which has assumed steadily large prominence in Germany during the last six months. . . .

There can at least be an understanding of the German desire to possess colonies on grounds of prestige; and, in spite of considerable pressure in Parliament, the British Government have not specifically bound themselves never to discuss the question with Germany. . . .

SPEECH OF SEPTEMBER 12, 1936

Nuremberg, Labor-Front

"HOW Germany has to work to wrest a few square kilc
meters from the ocean and from the swamps while others ar
swimming in a superfluity of land!

*"If I had the Ural Mountains with their incalculable stor
of treasures in raw materials, Siberia with its vast forests, an
the Ukraine with its tremendous wheat fields, Germany an
the National Socialist leadership would swim in plenty! . . .*

"There was sometimes advanced as an excuse for Russi
that she had been through war and through revolutior
Well, we stood against twenty-six States in the war and w
had a revolution, but I have taken as my fundamental la
not to destroy anything. Had I done so there would hav
been an excuse for rebuilding during another eighteen year

"But that was not our plan. We wanted additional wor
for our unemployed and the use of the volume of thei
increased production to increase every man's share in cor
sumption. Wages are not based on production; productio
itself is the wage.

"If I had wished I could have substituted officials for en
ployers, but nature and reality select best. We do not wis
bureaucratic economics as in Russia, nor do we wish t
establish economic democracy here.

"Yet that does not mean either that we wish to let thing
drift as they please. Our fundamental economic principl
are, first, to unite all the forces existing, and secondly, t
educate our people better in their use.

"This Labor Front is the greatest element in such educ
tion. You are servants of the nation, but you alone are notl
ing. As part of the organic whole you are everything. . . ."

"It is hard to build up a new life out of your poverty, bu

I am not complaining. On the contrary, I find it wonderful to face difficult problems.

"Some people say, 'He has brought out another plan.' When he had completed the first, why couldn't he leave us in peace? Now he is tackling problems that cannot be solved.'

"I say that they can be solved; there is no problem that cannot be, but faith is necessary. Think of the faith I had to have eighteen years ago, a single man on a lonely path. Yet I have come to leadership of the German people. . . ."

"People complain of a shortage of this and that—for instance, of a shortage of cotton. I say that in the next four years we shall produce our own German cloth.

"Others raise the question of rubber. I tell you that factories will spring from the earth and that in four years we shall ride on our own German rubber tires.

"It may then be asked, 'With what motive power will you drive you cars?' I say that we shall take gasoline from our own oil and coal.

"Whenever I see the Labor Front I am impressed by the word 'front.' It signifies one will, one goal of achievement. Life is hard for many, but it is hardest if you are unhappy and have no faith. Have faith. We are not a helpless State.

"Nothing can make me change my own belief. I am convinced that the unworthiest among us is he who cannot master his ill fortune."

Press

New York Times, September 13—. . . There was no expression of a wish to acquire these resources (Russian) and there was distinctly no threat. Yet when the cheers that greeted this passage had died away one was conscious that a thought had been cast into the pool of German mentality and that the ripples created by it might spread far indeed. . . .

To the shop stewards and factory leaders there assembled

Hitler spoke extemporaneously and at length, quite simply, his voice rising at times to passionate earnestness.

London Times, September 14—. . . On his way to the meeting Herr Hitler received an obvious inspiration from the sight of units of the 400 military aircraft summoned for tomorrow's display exercising in formation at a very low altitude over the railway station and the headquarters of the foreign press representatives. . . .

•

SPEECH OF SEPTEMBER 14, 1936

Nuremberg

"I CAN come to no terms with a *Weltanschauung* [bolshevism] which everywhere as its first act after gaining power is—not the liberation of the working people—but the liberation of the scum of humanity, the asocial creatures concentrated in the prisons—and then the letting loose of these wild beasts upon the terrified and helpless world about them. . . ."

"Bolshevism turns flourishing countrysides into sinister wastes of ruins; National Socialism transforms a Reich of destruction and misery into a healthy State and a flourishing economic life. . . ."

"Russia planned a world revolution and German workmen would be used but as cannon-fodder for bolshevist imperialism. But we National Socialists do not wish that our military resources should be employed to impose by force on other peoples what those peoples themselves do not want. Our army does not swear on oath that it will with bloodshed extend the National Socialist idea over other peoples, but that it will with its own blood defend the National Socialist idea and thereby the German Reich, its security and freedom, from the aggression of other peoples. . . . The German people as soldiers is one of the best peoples in the world: It would have become a veritable 'Fight to the Death Brigade' for the bloody purposes of these international disseminators of strife. We have removed this danger, through the National Socialist Revolution, from our own people and from other peoples. . . ."

"These are only some of the grounds for the antagonisms which separate us from communism. I confess: these antagonisms cannot be bridged. *Here are really two worlds which do but grow further apart from each other and can never unite.* When in an English newspaper a Parliamentarian complains that we wish to divide Europe into two parts, then unfortunately we are bound to inform this Robinson Crusoe living on his happy British island that—however unwelcome it may be—this division is already an accomplished fact. . . . That one should refuse to see a thing does not mean that it is not there. For many a year in Germany I have been laughed to scorn as a prophet; for many a year my warnings and my prophecies were regarded as the illusions of a mind diseased. . . ."

"Bolshevism has attacked the foundations of our whole human order, alike in State and society, the foundations of our conception of civilization, of our faith and of our morals: all alike are at stake. If this bolshevism would be content to promote this doctrine in a single land, then other countries might remain unconcerned, but its supreme principle is its internationalism and that means the confession of faith that these views must be carried to triumph throughout the whole world, i.e., that the world as we know it must be turned upside down. That a British headline-writer refuses to recognize this signifies about as much as if in the fifteenth century a humanist in Vienna should have refused to admit the intention of Mohammedanism to extend its influence in Europe and should have objected that this would be to tear the world asunder—to divide it into East and West. Unfortunately I cannot escape the impression that most of those who doubt the danger to the world of bolshevism come themselves from the East. As yet politicians in England have not come to know bolshevism in their own country; we know it already. Since I have fought against these Jewish-Soviet ideas in Germany, since I have conquered and stamped out this peril, I fancy that I possess a better comprehension of its character than do men who have only at best had to deal with it in the field of literature. . . . I have won my successes simply because in the first place I endeavored to see things as they are and not as one would like them to be; secondly, when once I had formed my own opinion I never allowed weaklings to talk me out of it or to cause me to abandon it; and thirdly, because I was always determined in all circumstances to yield to a necessity when once it had been recognized. Today when fate has granted me such great successes I will not be disloyal to these fundamental principles of mine. . . ."

. . . : "It is not necessary for me to strengthen the fame of the National Socialist Movement, far less that of the German Army, through military triumphs. He who is undertaking such great economic and cultural tasks as we are and is so determined to carry them through can find his fairest memorial only in peace. . . . But this bolshevism which as we learned only a few months since intends to equip its army so that it may with violence, if necessary, open the gate to revolution amongst other peoples—this bolshevism should know that before the gate of Germany stands the new German Army. . . . I believe that as a National Socialist I appear in the eyes of many bourgeois democrats as only a wild man. But as a wild man I still believe myself to be a better European, in any event a more sensible one, than they. It is with grave anxiety that I see the possibility in Europe of some such development as this: democracy may continuously disintegrate the European States, may make them internally ever more uncertain in their judgment of the dangers which confront them, may above all cripple all power for resolute resistance. *Democray is the canal through which bolshevism lets its poisons flow into the separate countries and lets them work there long enough for these infections to lead to a crippling of intelligence and of the force of resistance.* I regard it as possible that then—in order to avoid something still worse—coalition governments, masked as Popular Fronts or the like, will be formed and that these will endeavor to destroy—and perhaps will successfully destroy—in these peoples the last forces which remain, either in organization or in mental outlook, which could offer opposition to bolshevism."

"The brutal mass-slaughters of National Socialist fighters, the burning of the wives of National Socialist officers after petrol had been poured over them, the massacre of children and of babies of National Socialist parents, e.g. in Spain, are intended to serve as a warning to forces in other lands which represent views akin to those of National Socialism: such forces are to be intimidated so that in a similar position they offer no resistance. If these methods are successful: if the modern Girondins are succeeded by Jacobins, if Kerensky's Popular Front gives place to the Bolshevists, then Europe will sink into a sea of blood and mourning. . . ."

Press

Le Temps, September 16—The Fuehrer's closing speech at the National Socialist Congress was another manifestation of the prevailing mood at Nuremberg: against bolshevism.

London Times, September 15—As the gathering force of anti-bolshevist invective here had suggested, Herr Hitler's closing speech at the Party Congress tonight was an appeal and a warning to Europe against the bolshevist menace in extremely violent terms. . . .

The nearest Herr Hitler came to this point tonight was when he declared passionately that National Socialist Germany could not enter into any kind of bargain with the bolshevist outlook; they could not negotiate with bolshevism. Rhetorically, to judge by the rousing response, the speech was a fitting climax; what it was diplomatically will become clearer through the course of events. . . .

London Times, September 14—Against a background of marching troops and massed airplanes the fourth official rally of the National Socialist party will be brought to an end at Nuremberg today, and a murmur of relief will surely rise from the lips of all who hope and work for the pacification of Europe. . . . Herr Hitler alternated between invocations of peace and a call to stand fast against the Russian terror, which must bring to many minds the former warnings of the ex-Kaiser against the Yellow peril. . . .

From the Fuehrer himself downwards it has always been a stock theme of Nazi writings and oratory that Germany ought to have more territory to the East in which to hold her cramped population. The alarm of the two countries (France and Russia) and their determination to help each other is therefore wholly understandable. . . .

•

SPEECH OF JANUARY 30, 1937

Berlin, Reichstag

Background

1936

October 3—In Germany, battleship *Scharnhorst* is launched.

November 18—Germany and Italy recognize Franco.

November 28—Germany and Japan sign the anti-Comintern pact.

December 4—England and France propose to extend the non-intervention agreement to so-called "volunteers."

December 8—Battleship *Gneisenau* is launched in Germany.

December 27—First rationing of fats introduced in Germany. Death penalty is decreed for evasion of foreign exchange regulations.

1937

January 7—Marriage of Prince Lippe-Biesterfeld to Princess Juliana of Holland.

January 13—State Department in Washington warns citizens against serving in Spain.

January 19—Opening of the Trials against "Trotskyists" in Moscow. Karl Radek and 16 others are condemned to death in the first trials.

The Speech

"MEN! Deputies of the German Reichstag! The Reichstag has met today on a day momentous for the German people. Four years have passed since the greatest national revolution and reformation that Germany has ever experienced began. These were the four years which I asked for as a trial period. . . ."

"I do not know whether there has ever been such a thorough revolution as ours, which nevertheless left unmolested numerous former political functionaries and allowed them to work in peace and paid pensions to its bitterest enemies.

"But our policy has not been of much use to us as far as other countries are concerned. Only a few months ago honorable British citizens felt they must make a protest to us for detaining in a concentration camp one of the most criminal subjects of Moscow. [Presumably Herr von Ossietzky, winner of the Nobel Peace Prize.] I do not know whether these honorable men have also protested against the slaying and burning of tens of thousands of men, women, and children in Spain. We are assured that the number of people slain in Spain is 170,000. On this basis we would have had the right to murder 400,000 to 500,000 people in the Nazi Revolution!

"The National Socialist program replaces the liberalistic conception of the individual by the conception of a people bound by their blood to the soil. Of all the tasks with which we are confronted, it is the grandest and most sacred task of man to preserve his race. This will not lead to an estrangement of the nations; on the contrary, it will lead for the first time to a mutual understanding. It will also prevent the Jewish people from trying to disintegrate and dominate other people under the mask of an innocent bourgeoisie.

"Within a few weeks the social prejudices of a thousand years were swept away. So great was the Revolution that its spiritual foundations have not been understood even today by a superficial world. They speak of democracies and dictatorships, and have not realized that in this country a Revolution has taken place that can be described as democratic in the highest sense of the word. Does a more glorious socialism or a truer democracy exist than that which enables any German boy to find his way to the head of the nation? The purpose of the Revolution was not to deprive a privileged class of its rights, but to raise a class without rights to equality. . . ."

"There is now only one representative of German sovereignty—the people itself.

"The will of the people finds its expression in the Party as its political organization.

"Therefore there is only one legislative body.

"There is only one executive authority.

"Therefore the people is the basis, and Party, State, Army, industry, justice, etc., are only the means of maintaining the people.

"In a new penal code, justice will be put for all time into the service of maintaining the German race.

"When I took over power there were more than 6,000,000 unemployed and the farmers seemed doomed to decay. Today you must admit that I have fulfilled my promises. . . ."

"The Four-Year Plan will give permanent employment to those workmen who are now being released from the armament industry. It is significant for the gigantic economic development of our people that there is today a lack of trained workmen in many industries. There will be no strikes or lockouts in Germany, because every one has to serve the interests of the entire nation.

"Education of the people will never come to an end, and this education includes the Hitler Youth, the Labor Service, the Party, and the Army, as well as books, newspapers, theaters, and films.

"The restoration of Germany's equality of status was an event which exclusively concerns Germany herself. We have never taken anything from any people or harmed any people. In this sense I will deprive the German railways and the Reichsbank of their former character and place both without reservation under the sovereignty of the Government.

"The time of so-called surprises has thus been ended.

"I solemnly withdraw the German signature from the declaration, extracted by force from a weak Government against its better judgment, that Germany was responsible for the War.

"The restoration of the honor of the German people was the most difficult and the most audacious task and work of my life.

"As an equal State, Germany is conscious of its European task to co-operate loyally in removing the problems which affect us and other nations. My views concerning these problems can perhaps be most suitably stated by referring to the statements recently made by Mr. Eden in the House of Commons. I should like to express my sincere thanks for the opportunity of making a reply offered me by the frank and notable statement of the British Foreign Minister.

"I shall first try to correct what seems to me a most regrettable error—namely, that Germany never had any intention of isolating herself, of passing by the events of the rest of the world without sharing them, or that she does not want to pay any consideration to general necessities. I should like to assure Mr. Eden that we Germans do not in the least want to be isolated and that we do not feel at all that we are isolated. *Our relations with most States are normal, and are very friendly with quite a number. I only call your attention to our agreement with Poland, our agreement with Austria, our excellent relations with Italy, our friendly relations with Hungary, Yugoslavia, Bulgaria, Greece, Portugal, Spain, etc.,* and our no less friendly relations with a whole series of nations outside Europe. *The agreement with Japan for fighting the Comintern is a virile proof of how little the German Government is thinking of isolating itself.*

"Germany, and I solemnly repeat this here, has declared that there can be no humanly conceivable object of dispute whatsoever between Germany and France.

"The German Government has assured Belgium and Holland of its readiness to recognize and guarantee these States as untouchable and neutral regions for all time.

"From the economic point of view there is not the least reason to assert that Germany is giving up international cooperation.

"When I consider the speeches of many statesmen in the last few months, the impression may be obtained that the whole world is waiting to inundate Germany with economic favors, which we refuse to share. The German people have been making commercial treaties to bring about a more lively exchange of goods. German foreign trade has increased since 1932 both in volume and in value.

"I do not believe that there can be durable economic cooperation except on the basis of a new mutual exchange of goods. World economics are not suffering from any refusal of Germany to participate in them. When we got into power the world economic crisis was worse than today.

"I fear that I must interpret Mr. Eden's words as meaning that he sees in the carrying out of the Four-Year Plan a refusal of international relations on the part of Germany. The decision to carry out this plan does not allow of any change. Germany has an enormous number of people who do not only want to work but to eat. I cannot build the future of the German nation on the assurances of a foreign statesman or on any international help, but only on the real facts of production.

"If Europe does not awaken to the danger of bolshevist infection, commerce will decrease in spite of all the good will of individual statesmen. Therefore I am not in a position to judge the economic future of Europe as optimistically as Mr. Eden apparently does. I rejoice at every increase of our foreign trade, but in view of the political situation I shall not regret anything that will guarantee to the German people their existence when other nations have perhaps become the victims of bolshevist infection. The British Foreign Minister offers us theoretical prospects of existence, whereas in reality totally different things are happening—for instance, the revolutionizing of Spain has driven 15,000 Germans from the country and done great harm to our commerce. Should this revolutionizing of Spain spread to other European countries the damage would be increased. . . ."

"The League of Nations has never been a real league of peoples. A number of great nations do not belong to it or have left it, without anybody being able to assert that these countries were in favor of a policy of isolation. I think, therefore, that in this respect Mr. Eden misjudges Germany's intentions and views. I have already tried to bring about a good understanding in Europe, and I have especially assured the British people and Government how ardently we wish for sincere and hearty co-operation with them.

"The division into two parts, not only of Europe but of the rest of the world, is an accomplished fact. It is to be regretted that the British Government did not decide earlier that a division of Europe must be avoided under all circumstances, for then we would not have had a Treaty of Versailles.

"Secondly, division has been brought about by the proclamation of the bolshevist doctrine, the chief feature of which is to enforce itself on all peoples. For Mr. Eden, bolshevism is perhaps a thing which has its seat in Moscow, but for us it is a pestilence against which we have had to struggle at the cost of much bloodshed—a pestilence which tried to make of our country the same desert as Spain. National Socialism has not sought to conquer bolshevism in Russia, but Jewish International Moscow Bolshevists have tried to invade Germany and are still trying to. It is not suitable that National Socialist Germans should ever hope to protect bolshevism or that we should ever accept help from a bolshevist State.

"Three times I have made concrete offers for armament restriction or at least limitation. These offers were rejected. . . ."

"It would be better to mention in the first instance the armaments of that Power which is the basis of the armaments of all the others. Mr. Eden believes that in future all States should have only that armament which is necessary for their defense. I do not know whether Mr. Eden has already got into touch with Moscow about the realization of this fine idea or what assurances he has got there. I must, however, state one thing. It is absolutely clear that the amount of armaments for defense is determined by the degree of dangers which threaten a country. We cannot imagine anyone outside London being competent to estimate the strength necessary for the protection of the British Empire. The estimate of our need for protection is decided exclusively in Berlin. A general recognition of these principles would contribute to a lessening of the tension. Germany is happy to have found

Italy and Japan to be of the same opinion. Nobody welcomed the apparant lessening of the tension in the Mediterranean brought about by the Anglo-Italian agreement more than we.

"Germany has no interest in Spain but the cultivation of those economic relations which Mr. Eden himself has described as so important and profitable.

"Germany has no colonial claims on countries which have taken no colonies away from her. Our sympathies with General Franco and his Government are in the first place of a general nature, but they are also based on the hope that the consolidation of a real National Spain may lead to a strengthening of the European economic system. We are ready to do everything which may lead to a restoration of orderly conditions in Spain.

"During the last 100 years a number of new nations have arisen in Europe which, owing to their incapacity, have been of no economic importance and almost of no political significance. They have brought into the world new tensions. The new Italian State, however, is a reality. The German people and the German Reich are also a reality. The Polish people and State are also a reality.

"The unreasonable division of the world into peoples who have and peoples who have not does not remove or solve problems. If it is to be the task of the League of Nations only to guarantee the existing state of the world and to safeguard it for all time, then we might as well entrust it also with the task of guarding the high tide and the low tide, or of regulating for the future the direction of the Gulf Stream. Its continued existence depends on the extent to which it is realized that necessary reforms which concern the relations of the nations must be considered and put into practice.

"The German people once built up a Colonial Empire, without robbing anyone and without any war. This was taken away from us. It was said that the natives did not want to belong to Germany, that the colonies were not administered properly by the Germans, and that these colonies had no true value. If this is true, this valuelessness would also apply to the other nations, and there is no reason why they should wish to keep them from us. Germany has never demanded colonies for military purposes, but exclusively for economic ones. It is obvious that in times of general prosperity the value of certain territories may shrink, but it is just as clear that in time of distress such value changes. Today Germany lives in a time of fierce struggle for foodstuffs and raw materials. Sufficient imports are only conceivable if there is a continued increase in our exports. *Therefore the demand for colonies for our densely populated country will again and again be raised as a matter of course.*

"I should like to express a few opinions on possible ways of bringing about a genuine pacification of Europe, and beyond:—

"1. It is in the interests of all nations that individual countries should possess stable political and economic conditions. This is the most important condition for lasting and solid economic and political relations between the nations.

"2. The vital interests of the different nations must be frankly recognized.

"3. The League of Nations, to be effective, must be reformed and must become an organ of evolutionary commonsense and not remain an organ of inactivity.

"4. The relations of the nations with one another can only be regulated and solved on a basis of mutual respect and absolute equality.

"5. It is impossible to make one nation responsible for armaments or another responsible for armaments limitation, but it is necessary to see this problem as it really is.

"6. It is impossible to maintain peace so long as an international, irresponsible clique continues its agitation unchecked. I greatly regret that the British Foreign Minister did not state categorically that there was not one word of truth in the calumnies about Morocco spread by these international war agitators. Thanks to the loyalty of a foreign diplomat and his Government, the immediate clearing up of this stirring case was made possible, but is it not conceivable that on another occasion it might not be possible to enable the truth to come to light so quickly, and what would happen then?

"7. It has been proved that European problems can be solved properly only within the limits of the possible. Germany is hoping to have close and friendly relations with Italy. May we succeed in paving the way for such relations with other European countries. The German Reich will watch over its security and honor with its strong Army. On the other hand, convinced that there can be no greater treasure for Europe than peace, it will always be a reasonable supporter of those European ideals of peace, and will be conscious of its responsibilities.

"8. It would be profitable to European peace as a whole if, in the treatment of the nationalities who are forced to live as minorities within other nations, mutual consideration were shown for national honor and consciousness. This would lead to a decisive lessening of tension between the nations who are forced to live side by side and whose State frontiers are not identical with the frontiers of the people.

"In concluding these remarks I should like to deal with the document which the British Government addressed to the German Government on the occasion of the occupation of the Rhineland. We are convinced that the British Government at that time did everything to lessen the tension, and that the document in question was intended to contribute to disentangling the situation. Nevertheless it was not possible for the German Government, for reasons which the British Government will certainly appreciate, to reply to those questions.

"We preferred to settle some of those questions in the most natural way by the practical improvement of our relations with our neighbors. I should like to state now that complete

German sovereignty and equality have been restored, and that Germany will never sign a treaty which is in any way incompatible with the honor of the nation and of the Government which represents it, or which otherwise is incompatible with Germany's vital interests and therefore in the long run cannot be kept. With all my heart I hope that the intelligence and good will of responsible European governments will succeed, in spite of all opposition, in preserving peace for Europe. Peace is our dearest treasure. . . ."

"When I look upon the work of the past four years my first feeling is of gratitude to the Almighty who made it possible, and who has blessed our work and enabled us to pass through all obstacles.

"I have had three unusual friends in my life. In my youth, poverty accompanied me for many years. When the Great War came to an end it was great sorrow that took hold of me and prescribed my path—sorrow at the collapse of our people. Since January 30 four years ago I have made the acquaintance of anxiety as the third friend—anxiety for the people and Reich which have been confided to my leadership. Since that time it has never left me, and in all probability will accompany me to my end. How could a man shoulder the burden of this anxiety if he had not faith in his mission and the consent of Him who stands above us?"

Press

New York Times, February 1—A certain amount of reflection . . . is required to classify, appraise, and digest all the varied implications left by such a speech as that made by Chancellor Adolf Hitler before the Reichstag yesterday.

. . . Germany must choose between co-operation and isolation. . . . But Hitler . . . has not chosen, or if he has, he did not make known his choice yesterday. He merely indicated he was willing to discuss matters before announcing it. . . . The era of German surprises has ended, Hitler said.

That is so much gain and should help soothe European nerves. But he has not surrendered or even modified a single point in his program, although expressing his willingness to talk about all points. This is no surprise. Anyone who has devoted more than casual study to Nazism and its mentality long ago accepted it as an axiom that its program would never voluntarily be modified. . . . As to arms limitation, Hitler definitely refuses to trade German armaments for economic concessions, as it was expected he would. However, if the speech is read correctly, he does leave the door open for an armament agreement without economic ties on the basis of "security." That means security according to the German idea and not the French idea.

London Times, February 1—The part concerned with international affairs was a blend of defense and defiance. The Fuehrer's pronouncements have a way of proving later to have had more significance in unexpected places than they seemed to have. . . . He withdrew—symbolically, of course —Germany's signature from the so-called "War-guilt" paragraph of the treaty. . . .

Le Temps, February 1—The character of the Chancellor's renewed demand for equal rights is obvious. From the first our neighbors across the Rhine have felt that such equality should be unqualified by any preliminary guarantees. On the other hand, the Geneva Resolution, while recognizing in principle Germany's right to equality, required such guarantees. . . . The Fuehrer expressed indignation at England's blindness to the fact that bolshevism was a doctrine of world revolution. . . . He said that now the epoch of "surprises" was over. This, then, amounts to a formal promise of loyal co-operation in the European Order. As for the West, the Fuehrer once more emphasized that there were no possible causes for dispute between Germany and France. The Chancellor also declared that the German Government is willing to recognize Belgium and the Low Countries as neutral territory and to guarantee their inviolability. In reference to Russia and bolshevism, the Fuehrer's most significant statement was that any new pact with Soviet Russia would be utterly worthless to Germany. Obviously this would exclude Soviet Russia from the European commonwealth, and would render extremely difficult any general settlement upon the basis of collective security and mutual assistance. On the question of Spain, the leader of the Reich, while openly admitting his hopes for the victory of the Burgos government, declared that the Germans are ready to do all in their power to re-establish order in that country.

•

SPEECH OF MAY 1, 1937

Berlin

Background

January 31—Germany: Foundation of the National Prize for Arts and Science. Germans are forbidden to accept any Nobel Prize in the future.

February 2—Germany: Gauleiter Bohle is made chief of a new organization, attached to the Foreign Office, to organize the Germans abroad.

February 18—England: Stanley Baldwin announces a program in four points: 1, rearmament; 2, closer collaboration with France; 3, project of a new Locarno treaty; 4, no return of German colonies.

March 30—Reconciliation between Hitler and Ludendorff, estranged since the Munich revolt.

April 19—Germany: Creation of the National Socialist Flying Corps.

April 30—Germany: 1000 Catholic monks are put on trial. Opening of the Four-Year Plan Exhibition.

The Speech

"IF ON this day we celebrate the festival of the community of the German people, then the question arises: What is it which is common to this people? Our blood? Certainly, but that community of blood has never prevented this people from shedding its best blood in civil warfare. Language? Certainly, but community of language has never prevented men who spoke one common language from failing, often for centuries, to understand one another. Is it our common economic interests? But it was precisely over economic differences that conflicts raged most fiercely. Or is it our history? That history we know; it is a tragic chronicle of perpetual wars, of disagreements between brothers. Is it a common religion? No! here too we have fought and striven with each other; for thirty years in our people's life bloodshed ever followed bloodshed and all in the name of religion. And it was not either common custom or common usage. No, it is something other than all these which guides, nay rather forces us to this community. It is, my fellow-countrymen, our common destiny, this compelling common destiny from which none can escape, our life's destiny in this world.

"And it is no easy thing, it is a hard destiny, for the problems which life sets for us are harder than those of other peoples. There are peoples perhaps who can allow themselves the luxury of domestic warfare, they may indulge in quarrels, may smash each other's heads with impunity. Where Nature gives everything to man in superfluity there perhaps folk need not value so highly the necessity for unity of action and of will. But we Germans have been treated by Nature in our life on this earth in a more than stepmotherly fashion. A great people, a people of endless capacity, an industrious people, a people that has the will to live, which has the courage to make demands on life, yet lives in a space which even with the greatest industry is far too small and limited to give it from its own territory the essentials for its existence. When we often hear foreign politicians say, 'For what purpose do you need other wider possibilities of life?' we could turn the question back on them and ask, 'Why do you then set such value on them?' Precisely because this life-struggle with us is much harder than anywhere else we are forced to draw from this fact, which is our fate, conclusions which are peculiar to our own case. We cannot live from phrases, from platitudes and theories, but only from the results of our work, our capacity, and our intelligence. This hard life-struggle of ours is not made any easier by each going his own way, if each man says, 'I do what I will and what seems good to me.' No, we must live one with another. No one can shut himself off from this community, because no one can escape from this common destiny. And from this hard and sober recognition of facts there arises the compelling necessity for our German community of the people. That community is the condition for the practical conduct of our life-struggle. . . ."

". . . We cannot admit that this [the Government's] authority, which is the authority of the German people, shall be attacked by any other instance whatever. That applies also for all churches. So long as they concern themselves with their religious problems the State does not concern itself with them. But so soon as they attempt by any means whatsoever—by letters, Encyclica, or otherwise—to arrogate to themselves rights which belong to the State alone we shall force them back into their proper spiritual, pastoral activity. They have no title to criticize the morals of a State when they have more than enough reason to concern themselves with their own morals. For the morals of the German State and of the German people the leaders of the German State will be responsible—of that we can assure all anxious folk both within and without Germany. For this people must remain sound; with its soundness stands or falls our own existence. It is for the generation now growing up that we live; they are our care and them we will guard and protect in the face of everyone. Many may regret that our youth is not so divided now as it was formerly, that it can no longer be broken up into class organizations, into confessional organizations, and so on. Such times are past! We will see to it that our youth shall be the strong support of Germany's future. . . ."

Press

New York Times, May 2—Chancellor Adolf Hitler, in the name of the Nazi Party and the German State it dominates, flung defiance at protesting church organizations, especially the Catholic Church and the Pope, whom, however, he did not name. . . . He went on later to state uncompromisingly the National Socialist demand for exclusive control over the molding of youth, which is at the bottom of the quarrel with the Catholic Church.

London Times, May 3— . . . the speech was striking for its vehement expression of the Fuehrer's conviction that the German people must be subjected in the interests of national unity to an iron discipline ruthlessly overriding all manifestations of individualism and of the principles of the Christian churches insofar as these are incompatible with the idea of the supreme authority of the State.

•

SPEECH OF JULY 18, 1937

Munich

Background

May 3—Germany: Lord Lothian visits Goering in Berlin.

May 7—Zeppelin *Hindenburg* goes up in flames in Lakehurst.

May 12—England: Coronation of King George VI and Queen Elizabeth.

May 29—Spain: Republican planes bomb German cruiser *Deutschland.*

May 31—In reprisals, German battleships bomb Almeria. In his first speech, the new British Prime Minister Neville Chamberlain pledges conciliation abroad.

June 21—France: Léon Blum's Cabinet falls.

June 25—Germany: The State takes over the financial regulation of the Protestant Church.

June 29—France: Camille Chautemps forms new Popular Front Cabinet with Léon Blum as Vice-President.

July 16—Cordell Hull sends an appeal to thirty-seven nations in favor of peace between Japan and China.

The Speech

". . . WORKS of art that cannot be understood but need a swollen set of instructions to prove their right to exist and find their way to neurotics who are receptive for such stupid or insolent nonsense will no longer find the road whereby they can reach the German nation open.

"Let no one have illusions. National Socialism has set out to purge the German Reich and our people of all those influences threatening its existence and character. . . ."

"If this purge cannot occur in one day, all those taking part in such pollution do not want to forget that sooner or later the hour will strike for their disappearance. With the opening of this exhibition has come the end of artistic lunacy and with it the artistic pollution of our people.

"I can promise you all that cliques of gossips, dilettantes and artistic cheats will be sought out and suppressed. . . ."

"Either these so-called artists really see things in the fashion they represent, and in that case we would merely need to discover whether their visual abnormality is the result of mechanical defects or inheritance, or they do not themselves believe in the reality of such impressions but burden the nation with such humbug for other reasons, in which case such activity is a matter for the police and the criminal court. . . ."

"Like all truly great architecture this building is unparalleled and inimitable. It will remain entrenched in the memory of all seeing it and it is a true monument for this city and all German art. This master work is as great in its beauty as it is practical in its construction.

"The creation of this building is to be the turning point, putting an end to the chaotic and stumbling architecture of the past. It shall be the first new building to take its place in the ranks of the immortal creations of our German artistic life.

"It is the present State alone that has laid the basis for a new and mighty flowering of German art. Not bolshevist art collectors or their literary satellites have created the foundation for the new art, but it is we who have called this State to life and since then have given German art immense means and have, above all, presented German art with new, stupendous undertakings.

"If I had done nothing more for German art than merely to have ordered the construction of this building, I would have done more than all the absurd Jewish scribblers of our former Jewish newspapers.

"I know, however, that the new Reich will call into being an astounding blossoming of German art. For never has art been presented with greater duties and opportunities than in this Reich. Never before has more generous support been measured out than in National Socialist Germany. . . ."

Hitler earlier in his address revealed that he had perfect trust in his own artistic judgment, saying:

"I was always determined if fate ever gave us power not to discuss these matters with anyone, but to make decisions. Understanding for so great affairs is not given to everyone."

SPEECH OF SEPTEMBER 13, 1937

Nuremberg

Background

July 24—Germany: The "Herman Goering" corporation for mining and ironworks is founded.

July 31—Chamberlain and Mussolini exchange personal letters which seem to lead to an Anglo-Italian rapprochement.

September 6—National Socialist party convention opens in Nuremberg.

September 11—England and France agree to guard Mediterranean against attacks of mysterious submarines. Italy refuses to join them.

The Speech

". . . THIS is the greatest crisis in which humanity has ever found itself, the greatest upheaval since the advent of Christianity. It may be unpleasant for democratic statesmen to concern themselves with bolshevism, but it will not matter whether they will want to or not—they will have to deal with it. . . ."

"Germany, like Italy, has become immune from this danger because we have protected ourselves by a new internal order. But while we are thus secure, we believe many other countries surrounding us are unsafe. The world is in a state of growing unrest emanating from the Jewish bolshevist dictatorship in Moscow. If Russia is to be a bridgehead whence other nations are to be invaded, there arises a problem that will be solved only because it has to be solved. . . ."

"In the press of our Western democracies and in the speeches of many politicians, we discern recurring asseverations of the common interests of these Powers in certain spheres. It appears to representatives of these States as self-evident that their interests include every ocean and every State in Europe and even beyond by natural ordination. Conversely we encounter immediate outbreaks of indignation whenever a nation not belonging to this exclusive circle aspires to speak of certain interests lying beyond its own frontiers.

"In the face of this assumption I desire once for all to make the following declaration: We repeatedly hear from Britain and from France that they possess certain interests in Spain. Of what nature are these interests? Are they of a political or an economic nature? In the event they are political, we are unable to comprehend them any more than we would be if someone claimed a political interest in Germany. Who rules in Germany concerns nobody so long as this regime does not contemplate hostilities against another State.

"Exactly as Britain and France do not desire a shift in the European balance of power in favor of Germany or Italy, so equally we do not desire a shift of power in the sense of an accretion of bolshevist influence in Europe. . . ."

"If fascism rules in Italy, that is purely an Italian national affair. It would be stupid to assume that fascist Italy is receiving from the outside instructions or commands. It would be still more stupid to assert that fascist Italy constitutes a component part of a greater international organization that dominates it. On the contrary, it is an integral principle of fascism and National Socialism that they are based on a political principle whose ideology and effectiveness are confined within their national frontiers. It is equally certain that a national Spain will remain Spanish rather than international, as bolshevism consciously is.

"Just as Britain and France profess to be concerned that Spain may be occupied by Italy or Germany, so we are disturbed by the prospect that Spain may be conquered by Soviet Russia. Such a conquest need not be in the nature of an occupation by Russian troops. It would become an accomplished fact the very moment a bolshevized Spain became an intriguing annex of the Moscow bolshevist headquarters, from which it would receive not only political orders but material subventions. . . ."

"Speaking generally, we recognize in every attempt to expand bolshevism to Europe a shift in the European balance of power. Just as Britain is interested in preventing a shift under her own interpretation so we are interested in similar prevention from our viewpoint.

"In that connection we must categorically decline to receive instructions concerning what a shift in power toward bolshevism might mean from statesmen who do not possess the knowledge of it that we have acquired and who furthermore are not in a position to acquire the practical experience forced upon us.

"Of no less importance is the circumstance that a shift of power toward bolshevism would be identical with an economic development that might have catastrophic results in our closely knit European community of States. The first visible result of every bolshevist revolution is not an enhancement of production but the total destruction of prevailing economic values and economic functions in the country affected.

"The world does not live by reason of international economic conferences such as are convoked from time to time, but by the exchange of commodities and their production. If, therefore, through criminal madness the production of commodities is destroyed the results cannot be remedied by further conferences. They will reach into such States as have not secured their frontiers against bolshevism and will deprive them of their international commerce. We have had practical experience of this. . . ."

"In the very moment that bolshevism controls Spain an entire national production will be so endangered that the further exchange of commodities with it will become impossible. If this is countered with the assertion that Britain and France are still doing good business with Spain, we must point out that payment for their goods is being made in gold, which is not a product of bolshevism but of previous Spanish national labor pilfered by bolshevism and sent abroad.

"It may be a matter of indifference to Britain if Spain is converted into an economic desert, but for us Germans, who do not have an opportunity to shift our trade from one continent to another, Europe as it exists today constitutes a prerequisite to our existence. A bolshevized Europe would make our commercial policies impossible because we could no longer find markets.

"If Spain should become bolshevized and the wave should further reach Belgium, France, and Holland it would mean an economic catastrophe to Germany because we are dependent upon a reciprocal exchange of goods with these countries for the existence of the German people. We have therefore a serious interest in preventing the spread of this bolshevist plague. In the community of European nations Jewish world bolshevism is an alien body that does not contribute a single element to our economic or cultural life, but instead creates confusion in it. . . ."

Press

New York Times, September 14—Chancellor Adolf Hitler closed the National Socialist Congress here tonight with a new tirade against bolshevism and a declaration of Germany's relentless opposition to any extension of its influence. . . .

London Times, September 14—Herr Hitler wound up the National Socialist Party Rally of Work tonight with an assertive speech on German foreign policy, which, he again made clear, means in general a campaign against international bolshevism wherever it raises its head.

Le Temps, September 14—The Fuehrer's closing speech at the Nuremberg Congress last night was almost entirely an attack upon bolshevism. The important part of the speech was that devoted to the Spanish problem. M. Hitler objected strenuously that France and England were pretending to fight Franco for the sake of their own interests. . . . In the course of his speech the Fuehrer replied to the widespread opinion abroad that Germany is economically isolated.

•

SPEECH OF SEPTEMBER 28, 1937

Munich

Background

September 22—Germany: First air-raid protection drill in Berlin.

September 25—Mussolini visits Munich and Berlin.

The Speech

". . . WE HAVE just witnessed a historic event, the significance of which has no parallel. More than a million people have gathered here, participating in a demonstration which is being closely followed by the national communities of two countries, numbering one hundred and fifteen millions, besides hundreds of millions more in other parts of the world who were following the proceedings over the radio as more or less interested listeners.

"What moves us the most at this moment is the deep-rooted joy to see in our midst a guest who is one of the lonely men in history who are not put to trial by historic events but determine the history of their country themselves.

"Secondly, we realize that this demonstration is not one of those meetings which we can experience anywhere. It is an avowal of common ideals and common interests. It is the avowal pronounced by two men and it is heard by a million people assembled before us, an avowal which is expected by and is the concern of one hundred and fifteen millions with a burning heart.

"That is why the present demonstration is more than a public meeting. It is a manifestation of nations. The true meaning of this public gathering consists of the sincere desire to guarantee a peace to our two countries which is not the reward for resigned cowardice but the result of a responsible policy safeguarding the racial intellect and physical fitness of the nation as well as its cultural possessions. In doing this we hope to serve the interests of two nations and, more than that, the interests of the European Continent.

"The fact that we are in a position today to hold this meeting reminds us of the changes that have taken place in the period which we have left behind us. There is no nation in the world which longs more for peace than Germany and no country has suffered more from the terrible consequences of misplaced blind confidence than our nation. We recall a period of fifteen years before National Socialism came into power, a time which was marked by oppression, exploitation, the denial of equal rights with other nations, and with unutterable mental torture and material distress.

"The ideals of liberalism and democracy have not preserved the German nation from the worst depression history has ever seen. National Socialism was thus forced to create a new ideal and a more effective one, according all human rights to our people which had been denied the nation for fifteen long years.

"During this time of bitter experience Italy, and fascist Italy especially, refused to take part in the humiliation Germany was subjected to. I must make it a point to say this tonight before the German people and the whole world.

In the course of these years, Italy has shown understanding for the demands of a great nation claiming equal rights with other peoples in the endeavor to provide the means of subsistence and, above all, to save its honor.

"We are only too glad that the hour has come in which we are given the opportunity to recall the past and, I believe, we have remembered our debt of gratitude.

"The common trend of ideas expressed in the fascist and National Socialist Revolutions has developed today into a similar course of action. This will have a salutary influence on the world, in which destruction and deformation are trying to win the upper hand. Fascist Italy has been transformed into a new Imperium Romanum by the ingenious activities of a compelling personality.

"You, Benito Mussolini, will have realized that in these days, due to the National Socialist State, Germany has become a Great Power, thanks to her racial attitude and her military strength. The inherent strength of the two countries is the best guarantee for the preservation of Europe, which is inspired by a sense of responsibility in the discharge of its cultural mission. It is not willing to allow destructive elements to cause its decline and dissolution.

"You who are present at this very hour and those who are listening to us in other parts of the world must acknowledge that two sovereign national regimes have come into contact at a time in which the democratic and Marxist International revels in demonstrations of hatred which must result in dissension. Every attempt to interfere with the understanding between the two nations or to play one up against the other by casting suspicion and by obscuring the real aims in order to dissolve the ideal partnership will be of no avail because of the innermost desire of one hundred and fifteen million people, who are united at the manifestation of this very hour, and because of the determination of the two men who are standing here to address you. . . ."

Press

New York Times, September 29—There was no menace to anybody, although, of course, there were hard things said about bolshevism and its corrosive and disruptive effects upon peaceful peoples. There was no hint of war because, as it appeared, there will not be any need for war, since the whole world is gradually coming around to fascism or Nazism, realizing how good these are for nations presently sweltering in the darkness and confusion of democracy. . . .

•

SPEECH OF FEBRUARY 20, 1938

Berlin, Reichstag

Background

1937

October 7—Roosevelt makes a speech in Chicago suggesting that aggressors be put "in quarantine."

October 22—Fifteen hundred German veterans attend a French veteran meeting in Besançon (France).

November 3—The Nine-Power Conference meets in Brussels to study the Sino-Japanese conflict. Japan declines to appear and the conference brings no results.

November 6—Italy joins the Anti-Comintern Pact.

November 10—Germany warns Austria against alleged infractions to the "cultural pact."

November 16—France: The "Cagoulards," a secret fascist society, is unmasked and their offices and armories raided.

November 26—Germany: Schacht leaves the Cabinet and is succeeded by Walter Funk.

December 1—Big Colonial demonstration in Berlin.

December 11—Mussolini, in a violent speech, announces Italy's withdrawal from the League of Nations.

December 12-26—Strong tension between Washington and Tokyo following the sinking of the gunboat *Panay*.

December 20—Death of Ludendorff.

December 24—Christmas talk of the Pope denouncing German persecutions of the Catholic Church.

1938

February 4—War Minister von Blomberg and Foreign Minister von Neurath resign. Hitler becomes Commander-in-Chief of the Wehrmacht; Keitel, Chief of Staff, Ribbentrop, Foreign Minister.

February 12—Chancellor Schuschnigg of Austria visits Hitler at Berchtesgaden, following which Nazi ministers are introduced in the Austrian Cabinet.

The Speech

"I KNOW you and the German people expected to be called together on the fifth anniversary of the National Socialist State.

"The selection of this date is due to two considerations: first, I thought it right to make certain personal changes beforehand, and second, it was necessary to bring about a clarification in one specific sphere of foreign politics, because such a speech of mine not only deals with the past but also with the future.

"Despite the really exemplary discipline, strength, and restraint which National Socialists preserved in their revolution, we have seen that a certain portion of the foreign press inundated the new Reich with a virtual flood of lies and calumnies. It was a remarkable mixture of arrogance and deplorable ignorance which led them to act as the judges of a people who should be presented as models to these democratic apostles.

"The best proof for showing up these lies is success. For if we had acted during these five years like the democratic world citizens of Soviet Russia, that is, like those of the Jewish race, we would not have succeeded in making out of a Germany, which was in the deepest material collapse, a country of material order. For this very reason we claim the right to surround our work with that protection which renders it impossible for criminal elements or for the insane to disturb it. . . ."

"It was the A B C of our creed to find help in our own strength. The standard of living of the nation is the outcome of its total production; in other words, the value of every wage and salary corresponds to the volume of goods produced as a result of the work performed. This is a very unpopular doctrine in a time resounding with cries such as 'higher wages and less work.'

"Next to the United States, Germany today has become the greatest steel country in the world. I could give many more examples. They are documentary proof of the work such as our people never before achieved. To these successes will be added in a few years the gigantic results of the Four-Year Plan. Is it not a joke of history when those very countries which themselves have only crises think they can criticize us and give us advice?

"We have given the German nation that weapon of steel which presents a wall at our frontiers against the intentions of the malicious international press campaign. . . ."

"The Reich's protection against the outer world, however, is in the hands of the new National Socialist armed forces. The German Army of peace has now a vast air force to protect our homes and a new power on the sea protects our coasts.

"There exists in Germany no problem between the National Socialist State and the National Socialist party, no problem between the National Socialist party and the National Socialist armed forces. In this Reich every one who holds a responsible position is a National Socialist.

"I had to respect the wish of Blomberg [Field Marshal Werner von Blomberg] to spare his health which had been undermined by his first-rate work. In this connection I should like to express the thanks of myself and the German people for the faithful and loyal work of this soldier of the new Reich and its armed forces.

"The same applies to the activity and surpassing achievements of Fritsch and all those who gave up their places in the most noble spirit for the sake of having younger men in the ranks of our political and military leaders.

"If ever international agitation or poisoning of opinion should attempt to rupture the peace of the Reich, then steel and iron would take the German people and German homesteads under their protection. The world would then see, as quick as lightning, to what extent this Reich, people, party, and these armed forces are fanatically inspired with one spirit, one will.

"Furthermore, it is not my intention to protect the honorable corps of officers from the slander of international journalism. That is not necessary, for, although there are two kinds of journalists—those who prove the truth and those who are miserable swindlers and war agitators—there is only one kind of German officer.

"If Great Britain should suddenly dissolve today and England become dependent solely on her own territory, then the people there would, perhaps, have more understanding of the seriousness of the economic tasks which confront us. If a nation which commands no gold reserves, no foreign exchange—not because National Socialism reigns but because a parliamentary, democratic State was exploited for fifteen years by a world hungry after loot; in other words, if a nation which must feed 140 people to the square kilometer and has no colonies, if a nation which lacks numerous raw materials and is not willing to live an illusory life through credits, reduces the number of its unemployed in five years to nil and improves its standard of living, then all those should remain silent who, despite great economic advantages, scarcely succeed in solving their own unemployment problems.

"The claim for German colonial possessions, therefore, will be voiced from year to year with increasing vigor. These possessions, which Germany did not take away from other countries and which today are practically of no value to these Powers, are indispensable for our own people.

"I should like to refute here the hope that such claims can be averted by granting credits. Above all, we do not wish for naïve assurances that we shall be permitted to buy what we need. We reject such statements once and for all. . . ."

"I cannot allow our natural claims to be coupled with political business. Recently rumors have been cropping up, rumors that Germany was about to revise her opinion concerning her return to the League of Nations. I should like again to declare that in 1919 the peace treaty was forced upon some countries. This treaty brought in its train far-reaching inroads upon the lives of the peoples involved. The rape of national and economic destinies and of the communal lives of the nations took place under a cloud of moralizing phrases which, perhaps, tended to salve the uneasy conscience of those who instituted the affair.

"After the revision of the map of the world and of territorial and racial spheres, which was as thorough as it was fundamental, had been effected by means of force, a League of Nations was founded whose task it was to crystallize these crazy, unreasonable proceedings and to co-ordinate its results into an everlasting and unalterable basis of life.

"I notice very often that English politicians would be glad to give back to us our colonies if they were not so disturbed by the thought of the wrong and violence which would thus be done to the native inhabitants.

"All those colonial empires have not come into being through plebiscites. They are today naturally integral parts of the States in question and form, as such, part of that world order which always has been designated to us, especially by democratic policies, as the 'world order of right.'

"That right the League of Nations now has been ordered to protect. I cannot understand why a nation which itself has been robbed by force should join such illustrious company and I cannot permit the conclusion to be drawn that we should not be prepared to fight for the principles of justice just because we are not in the League of Nations. On the contrary, we do not belong to the League of Nations because we believe that it is not an institution of justice but an institution for defending the interests of Versailles.

"A number of material considerations must, however, be added.

"First, we left the League of Nations because—loyal to its origin and obligations—it refused us the right to equal armament and just as equal security.

"Second, we will never re-enter it because we do not intend to allow ourselves to be used anywhere in the world by a majority vote of the League of Nations for the defense of an injustice.

"Third, we believe we will please all those nations who are misled by misfortune to rely on and trust the League of Nations as a factor of genuine help. We should have regarded it as more correct, for instance, in the case of the Ethiopian war, for the League to have shown more understanding for vital Italian needs and less disposition to help the Ethiopians with promises. This would, perhaps, have enabled a more simple and reasonable solution for the whole problem.

"Fourth, on no account will we allow the German nation to become entangled in conflicts in which the nation itself is not interested. We are not willing to stand up for the territorial or economic interests of others without the slightest benefits to Germans being visible. Moreover, we ourselves do not expect such support from others. Germany is determined to impose upon herself wise moderation in her interests and demands. But if German interests should be seriously at stake we shall not expect to receive support from the League of Nations but we shall assume the right from the beginning to shoulder our task ourselves.

"Fifth, we do not intend to allow our attitude to be determined in the future by any international institution which, while excluding official recognition of indisputable facts, resembles less the acts of a man of considered judgment than the habits of a certain type of large bird [evidently the ostrich]. The interests of nations insofar as their existence or nonexistence are ultimately concerned are stronger than formalistic considerations. For in the year 2038 it is possible that new States may have arisen or others disappeared without this new state of affairs having been registered at Geneva.

"Germany will not take part in such unreasonable proceedings by being a member of the League of Nations.

"*Germany will recognize Manchukuo.* I have decided on this step in order to draw the line of finality between the policy of fantastic lack of understanding and the policy of sober respect for the facts of reality. To sum up, I want to explain that Germany no longer thinks of returning to this institution and certainly not since Italy's departure from it.

"That does not mean the refusal to collaborate with other nations. On the contrary it only means the rejection of obligations which in most cases are impossible of fulfillment.

"*With one country alone have we scorned to enter into relations. That State is Soviet Russia.* We see in bolshevism more now than before the incarnation of human destructive forces. We do not blame the Russian people as such for this gruesome ideology of destruction. We know it is a small Jewish intellectual group which led a great nation into this position of madness. If this doctrine would confine itself territorially to Russia maybe one could put up with it. Alas, Jewish international bolshevism attempts to hollow out the nations of the world from its Soviet center.

"Any introduction of bolshevism into a European country means a changing of conditions. For those territories under bolshevik leadership are no longer sovereign nations having a national life but sections of the revolutionary center of Moscow.

"I know Eden [British Foreign Secretary] does not share this view. Stalin shares it and admits it openly, and in my opinion Stalin himself is a more trustworthy expert and interpreter of bolshevik views and intentions than the British Minister. We, therefore, oppose any attempt at spreading bolshevism, wherever it may take place, with disdain, and wherever it threatens us, with hostility.

"From this arises our relationship with Japan. I cannot agree with those politicians who believe they are rendering the European world a service by harming Japan. *I believe a Japanese defeat in the Far East would never be any good to Europe or America, but would exclusively benefit bolshevist Soviet Russia.*

"I do not consider China mentally or materially strong enough to resist any bolshevik attack on it, but I believe even the greatest victory for Japan would be infinitely less dangerous to the culture and general peace of the world than a bolshevik victory would be. Germany has a treaty with Japan to combat Comintern aspirations. It has always been on friendly terms with China. *I believe we may be considered most genuinely as neutral observers of this drama.*

"I do not need to emphasize that we all wished and still wish that relations between those two great Eastern nations will again calm down and become peaceful. We believe that there might have been a peaceful solution in the Far East long ago if certain powers had not, as in the case of Ethiopia, thrown into one scales their advice and, perhaps, promise their moral support.

"But a drowning man clutches at any straw. It would have been better to have called China's attention to the full seriousness of her position instead, as usual, of quoting the League of Nations as a sure guarantee of peace.

"No matter when and how events in the Far East find their final solution, Germany will always consider and value Japan as an element of security in its stand against communism and in its assurance of human culture.

"*Germany has no territorial interest in East Asia.* She has an understandable desire for trade and business. This does not bind us to take sides for one party or the other. It does, however, bind us to the recognition that victory for bolshevism would destroy the last possibility in this sphere. Moreover, Germany once had possessions herself in East Asia. This did not prevent certain nations from combining with yellow races to drive out the Germans. We no longer want an invitation to return there.

"Nor have we any territorial interests connected in any way with the terrible civil war now raging in Spain. There is a situation there similar to one Germany once experienced. An attack on an independent national State carried out with men and materials furnished by Moscow leads to the defense by the national population not willing to be slaughtered. Exactly as in the case of Germany, the democratic international is on the side of the incendiaries.

"The German Government would see the introduction of bolshevism into Spain as not only an element of unrest in Europe but also as upsetting the European balance of power, for if this country were to become a section of the Moscow center there would arise the danger of the further spread of this plague of destruction to which we should under no circumstances be indifferent.

"But we are happy that our anti-bolshevist attitude is shared by a third State.

"The condition in which Italy finds herself is somewhat similar to that of Germany. It was, therefore, only natural that we who suffer from the same overpopulation showed understanding for the actions of a man and a regime not willing to let a nation perish to please the fantastic ideals of the League of Nations but were determined to save it. Also in the Spanish conflict Germany and Italy have adopted the same views and, therefore, the same attitude. It is their goal to secure for national Spain complete independence. German and Italian friendship has gradually developed from certain causes into an element of stabilization for European peace.

"In this connection the two States with Japan represent the most formidable obstacle against the further advance of the Russian bolshevik force.

"As I have more than once stated Germany has in Europe no more territorial demands to make of France. With the return of the Saar we trust the period of Franco-German territorial differences is finally closed.

"Germany also has no quarrel with England apart from her colonial wishes. However, there is no cause for any conceivable conflict. The only thing that has poisoned and thus injured the common life of these two countries is the utterly unendurable press campaign which in these two countries has existed under the motto 'freedom of personal opinion.'

"I do not understand it when I am told by foreign statesmen and diplomats that there is no legal possibility in these countries of putting an end to the lies, for private matters are not at stake. It concerns the problems of the common lives of the peoples and States. We cannot shut our eyes to the consequences of these campaigns for it could so easily come to pass that in certain countries contemptible international lie manufacturers could generate such violent hatred against our country that gradually hostile public opinion would be created against us which the German people would not be able to resist. This is a danger to peace. I am no longer prepared to tolerate unanswered this unbridled slander. From now on we shall answer back and do so with National Socialist thoroughness.

"What has occurred in the last few weeks in the way of utterly mad, stupid, and imprudent statements about Germany is simply unendurable.

"What can we reply when Reuters [British News Agency] discovers attacks on my life? When English newspapers publish outrageous stories of the number of arrests in Germany and the closing of the German frontiers on the Swiss, Belgian and French sides? When other newspapers say that the Crown Prince had fled Germany, that there had been a military putsch in Germany, that German generals had been imprisoned, that German generals had marched with their regiments to the Reich Chancellery, that a quarrel over the Jewish question had broken out between Hitler and Goering and that I, myself, was in a difficult position, that a German general, through intermediaries, had contacted with Daladier [French Defense Minister], that a regiment had mutinied in Skolp, that 2,000 officers had been dismissed from the Army, that the entire German industry had received mobilization orders for war, that between the government and private industry violent differences had arisen, that twenty German officers and three generals had fled to Salzburg, that fourteen generals with the body of Ludendorff had fled to Prague; also that I had lost my voice and that my voice would be imitated by someone else so that I could in the future speak from gramophone records.

"In a recent speech Eden referred warmly to various forms of freedom in his country. There was one very special freedom which had been forgotten, namely, that of allowing journalists to insult other countries, their institutions, their public men, and their government. All this is too stupid to be taken seriously. But in the long run this will prove to be a serious strain on international relations. I gladly state that a section of the foreign press has not taken part in these infamous attacks against the honor of other nations.

"Nevertheless, the damage wrought by such a press campaign is so great that henceforth we will no longer be willing to tolerate it without stern objections. This crime becomes especially evil when it obviously pursues the goal of driving nations into war.

"I need only to point to a few facts. I remind you of how in the past year the lie was suddenly spread that Germany had landed 20,000 men on the Spanish Moroccan coast. It was fortunate that this most infamous falsification could be put right immediately. What, however, would happen if such a rectification could not be brought about in the necessarily short space of time?

"To the series of these felonies belongs also the assertion that Germany and Italy had come to an agreement to divide Spain between themselves, or the very recent infamous falsehood that Germany and Japan had arrived at an agreement to acquire jointly the Dutch colonial possessions.

"The British Government desires the limitation of armaments or the prohibition of bombing. I myself proposed this some time ago. However, I also suggested at the time that the most important thing was to prevent the poisoning of the world's public opinion by infamous press articles. That which strengthened our sympathy with Italy, if this were possible, is the fact that in that country State policy and press policy tread the same road.

"To this chapter of disturbance of international relations belongs the arrogance of writing letters to the head of a foreign State with the request for information about court judgments. I recommend that the British House of Commons worry themselves about the verdicts of the British court-martial in Jerusalem and not about the verdicts of the German peoples' court.

"Interest in German cases we can, perhaps, understand. But it certainly does not contribute to the improvement of relations between Great Britain and Germany. Moreover, let nobody imagine he can exert any influence by such tactless interferences in German courts or on the execution of German verdicts. I should never allow members of the German Reichstag to interfere in matters of English justice.

"The interests of the British Empire certainly are very great and they are recognized by us. Concerning the interests of the German people the German Reichstag decides and as its delegate it is I who decide and not a delegation of British letter writers.

"I think it would not only be useful work to prevent the international dropping of poison, incendiary, and explosive bombs upon populations but above all to abolish the selling of newspapers which have a worse effect upon populations than bombs could ever have.

"Since this press campaign must be considered as an element of danger to the peace of the people I have decided to carry through that strengthening of the German Army which will give us the assurance that these threats of war against Germany will not one day be translated into bloody force.

"These measures have been under way since February 4 and will be carried out rapidly and with determination.

"Under these circumstances it cannot be seen what use there is in conferences and meetings as long as governments in general are not in a position to take decisive steps irrespective of public opinion.

"I believe, therefore, that for the present the procedure of diplomatic exchanges of notes is the only one that can be adopted in order to remove the possibility of excessive misinterpretation on the part of the international press.

"There are more than 10,000,000 Germans in States adjoining Germany which before 1866 were joined to the bulk of the German nation by a national link. Until 1918 they fought in the great war shoulder to shoulder with the German soldiers of the Reich. Against their own free will they were prevented by peace treaties from uniting with the Reich.

"This was painful enough, but there must be no doubt about one thing: Political separation from the Reich may not lead to deprivation of rights, that is the general rights of racial self-determination which were solemnly promised to us in Wilson's fourteen points as a condition for the armistice. We cannot disregard it just because this is a case concerning Germans.

"In the long run it is unbearable for a world power, conscious of herself, to know there are citizens at her side who are constantly being inflicted with the severest sufferings for their sympathy or unity with the total nation, its faith and philosophy.

"We well know there can scarcely be a frontier line in Europe which satisfies all. It should be all the more important to avoid the torture of national minorities in order not to add to the suffering of persecution on account of their belonging to a certain people.

"That it is possible to find ways leading to the lessening of tension has been proved. But he who tries to prevent by force such lessening of tension through creating an equilibrium in Europe will some day inevitably conjure up force among the nations themselves. It cannot be denied that Germany herself, as long as she was powerless and defenseless, was compelled to tolerate many of these continual persecutions of the German people on our frontier.

"But just as England stands up for her interests all over the globe, present-day Germany will know how to guard its more restricted interests. *To these interests of the German Reich belong also the protection of those German peoples who are not in a position to secure along our frontiers their political and philosophical freedom by their own efforts.*

"I may say that since the League of Nations has abandoned its continuous attempts at disturbance in Danzig and since the advent of the new commissioner this most dangerous place for European peace has entirely lost its menace.

"Poland respects the national conditions in the Free City of Danzig and Germany respects Polish rights.

"Now I turn to Austria. It is not only the same people but above all a long communal history and culture which bind together the Reich and Austria.

"Difficulties which emerged in the carrying out of the agreement of July 11, 1936, made essential an attempt to remove misunderstandings and obstacles to final reconciliation. It is clear that whether we wished it or not an intolerable position might have developed that would have contained the seeds of catastrophe. It does not lie in the power of man to stop the rolling stone of fate which through neglect or lack of wisdom has been set moving.

"I am happy to say that these ideas correspond with the viewpoint of the Austrian Chancellor, whom I invited to visit me. The underlying intention was to bring about a détente in our relations which would guarantee to National Socialist sympathizers in Austria within the limits of the law the same rights enjoyed by other citizens.

"In connection with it there was to be an act of conciliation in the form of a general amnesty and better understanding between the two States through closer and friendlier relations in the various spheres of cultural, political, and economic co-operation. All this is a development within the framework of the treaty of July 11.

"I wish to pay tribute to the Austrian Chancellor for his efforts to find together with me a way which is just as much in the interests of both countries as in that of the entire German people whose sons we all are regardless of where we came from. I believe we have thus made a contribution to European peace.

"Our satisfactory relations with other countries are known to all. Above all is to be mentioned our co-operation with those two great powers which, like Germany, have recognized bolshevism as a world danger and are therefore determined to resist the Comintern with a common defense. It is my earnest wish to see this co-operation with Italy and Japan more and more extended.

"We welcome any détente which may arise in the general political situation. For however great the achievements of our people may be, we do not doubt that all would benefit by an improvement in international co-operation.

"The German people is no warlike nation. It is a soldierly one which means it does not want a war but does not fear it. It loves peace but it also loves its honor and freedom. . . ."

Press

Le Temps, February 22—The Chancellor was peculiarly insistent in his emphasis that all German institutions, and especially the Army, were being incorporated into National Socialism. It is noteworthy that the Fuehrer refrained from making any allusion to the religious question. There seemed to be far more substance in his speech when he touched on foreign problems. . . . Special attention should be paid to the passage in which he speaks of the "10,000,000 Germans" who live so close to the borders of the Reich. "We shall know how to defend German interests wherever they are found," the Chancellor said. When we consider the manner in which M. Hitler spoke of that "defense" in the course of his recent interview at Berchtesgaden, we will not be long in doubt as to the interpretation National Socialist diplomacy may choose to put upon that phrase in the future. The Fuehrer congratulated himself on the "spirit of understanding" M. von Schuschnigg evinced and declared that at Berchtesgaden all were working "for peace." What kind of peace can it be that is based on a "Diktat" unmercifully handed down, while behind the scenes the naked bayonets gleam?

London Times, February 21—These passages in the speech, bearing upon the Eastern frontier, will have been awaited with particular interest both in Germany and abroad, and they will be read with as much attention here as in any country. Herr Hitler's comparison between German and British interests and their defense half suggested that Britain had no concern with events in Central and Eastern Europe. Public opinion in some other countries seems to have reached the same conclusion. They have noted, whether with relief or with regret, that the changes effected in the state of Austria in the last ten days have been accepted here with comparative equanimity. But there was never the slightest excuse for supposing that Great Britain would "intervene," if the occasion for intervention had arisen, in what would have been in effect an Austrian civil war, provoked by Germany, but involving a large part of Austria on the German side. That does not mean for a moment that this country, which can never be isolated from Europe, is not deeply concerned with the fortunes of Austria; nor that it has taken anything but warning from the methods by which the Berchtesgaden agreement was apparently brought about. If these methods are pursued to the end in every case where Germany cherishes unsatisfied ambitions, then they can only end in a catastrophic conflict, from which Great Britain would not be able to stand aloof. The temptation to pursue them may grow with success, and the vigilance of other nations is bound to keep pace with it. Our own program of rearmament, for example, cannot be relaxed for a moment so long as Europe is liable to sudden spasms when opportunity provides an opening for a stroke of policy. It is not a time for provocative speaking and writing, least of all for empty threats. But it is emphatically a time when the British Government must be perfectly clear in their own mind about the requirements and limits to a settlement in Europe, and about the point at which they are bound to take a stand against pressure.

THE ANNEXATION OF AUSTRIA

Background

1938

February 20—Anthony Eden resigns as British Foreign Secretary, on grounds of "fundamental differences" between him and Chamberlain concerning foreign policy.

February 26—French Chamber approves government's policy of co-operation with Great Britain, maintenance of the Franco-Soviet pact, and fulfillment of obligations to Czechoslovakia.

February 28—Lord Halifax appointed Foreign Secretary.

March 9—Schuschnigg calls plebiscite for March 13 on the question of maintaining Austria's independence.

March 11—Yielding to Hitler's threat of invasion, Schuschnigg resigns. An Austrian Nazi, Seyss-Inquart, forms a cabinet.

England and France protest to the German Government.

March 12—German troops enter Austria.

March 13—Formal annexation of Austria.

PHASE IV

Bloodless Conquests

March, 1938 — March, 1939

COMMENT

IF ANYONE had any doubts as to what Hitler's next step should be, these doubts were to be dispelled on February 20, 1938, when he told the Reichstag that it was Germany's intention to take into her hands the protection of "over ten million Germans who live in two of the States adjoining our frontiers."

The population of Austria being seven million and the Sudeten Germans of Czechoslovakia three millions, it was clear that these were the two States concerned.

It took exactly twelve months for Hitler to achieve his objectives. By March 13, 1938, the *protection* of the Germans living in Austria had been assured by the radical process of annexing that country to the Reich. And by March 1939, not only the Sudeten Germans but the Czechs and the Slovaks were also brought under the *protection* of the German Fuehrer. Two sovereign countries were wiped off the map in spite of the fact that the independence of both was guaranteed by all the nations of the world, either by formal treaty or by the general spirit of international law and order.

This twelve-month period can be considered as Hitler's first campaign. True enough the conquests were bloodless, but they were no less real. From the strategic point of view, they assured Hitler a solid basis from which to undertake expansion in both the south and the east of Europe. They allowed him to dominate the Balkans, and to establish a common frontier between him and his partner, Mussolini, thus forcing the latter to follow from then on a policy of subservient collaboration. They enabled him, too, to prepare the encirclement of Poland and to create a springboard for the later march into Russia.

Moreover they brought to a climax the long drawn out conflict between the western democracies and the totalitarian dictators—a climax which ended at Munich with the utter defeat of the democracies. It was a bloodless campaign, but it was the first one of World War II. Hitler came out of it the undisputed victor. The moral humiliation suffered by his opponents and the loss of prestige were perhaps greater than their strategic defeat. Returning from Munich, Chamberlain was to say that he was bringing back "peace with honor" and that he believed "it was peace for our time." But what he brought back in fact was a stinging moral defeat and the certainty of war.

The technique of Hitler to achieve his victory was both simple and effective. His speeches of that period reflect it clearly and they present no difficulty of interpretation.

The basic theme was not new: Hitler promised his people to deliver them from the shackles of the Versailles Treaty and to do so against any opposition. The Versailles Treaty was not only unjust to the Germans and intolerable, it was also a perpetual threat for the peace of Europe. Until the wrongs of that treaty were righted, there could be no peace for any nation. It was Hitler's mission to destroy the whole Versailles system and to create a new European peace.

These ideas had been droned into the ears of the world so often that they ceased to produce any reaction. The victors of World War I were by now so convinced of their own guilt that they had lost all power of argument. They did not defend their work. Quite the contrary, they concurred with Hitler that he was right in destroying it. Speaking in Commons on March 24, Chamberlain admitted that his "original belief in the League as an effective instrument for preserving peace has been profoundly shaken."

Versailles and everything that stems from it being wrong and unbearable, it naturally followed, according to Hitler, that the nations born out of the Treaty had no real right to existence. They were artificial and monstrous creations which should be treated accordingly.

This was particularly true of such nations as Austria—which was completely German—and Czechoslovakia—which contained an important German minority.

Although Hitler despised all the principles upon which the Versailles Treaty was founded, he nevertheless claimed, in his Reichstag speech of February 20, that there was such a thing as the Wilsonian "right to self-determination"—as far as the Germans were concerned at any rate—and that the separation of ten million Germans from the Reich was therefore a violation of that right.

This was the more intolerable when these German minorities were persecuted (as in the case of the Sudeten Germans) or unable to express freely their National Socialist convictions (as in the case of Austria).

The theme of the persecution of the Germans was exploited by Hitler with relentless energy first in the case of Austria, then in the case of Czechoslovakia, and finally in Poland.

The method was always the same: news was brought to the German people that their blood-brothers across the border were being discriminated against, persecuted, robbed, tortured, and murdered. Flaming headlines in the papers and stories on the radio told of the most infamous atrocities. On September 19, 1939, during the Sudeten crisis, Berlin newspapers carried the following headlines: "WOMEN AND CHILDREN MOWED DOWN BY CZECH ARMORED CARS," "POISON-GAS ATTACK ON AUSSIG," "EXTORTION PLUNDERING SHOOTING—CZECH TERROR IN SUDETEN GERMAN LAND GROWS WORSE FROM DAY TO DAY," etc. . . .

The next step was usually to single out the political head

of the neighboring country (Schuschnigg in the case of Austria, Benes in the case of Czechoslovakia) and to heap upon their heads all the conceivable—or inconceivable—abuses for allowing such horrors to be perpetrated.

While these propaganda campaigns were going on, Hitler was represented as making superhuman efforts to control his indignation and to settle the conflict by peaceful negotiations. But all his efforts were in vain, either because the neighboring State was too obdurate, or because the government had lost control, or because the big democracies encouraged them in defying Germany—or for all these reasons at once. Finally, Hitler's patience was exhausted. He had to take matters into his own hands and send the Reichswehr across the border to protect the unfortunate Germans, and bring back order.

In the case of Austria and Czechoslovakia—and in order to insure the success of the projected annexation—Hitler also worked from the inside. Nazi parties, whose task was to create violent agitation and call for the Liberator, existed in both these countries. Even before Hitler marched in, such men as Seyss-Inquart in Austria and Henlein in the Sudeten Land served as his official agents and acted openly under his orders. Chancellor Schuschnigg, in fact, sealed the doom of his country the day he was forced by Hitler to take Seyss-Inquart into his government.

Intimidation, terrorization, and even moral torture was inflicted on the leaders of the victimized countries in order to force them into submission. During his visit at Berchtesgaden in mid-February, 1938, Chancellor Schuschnigg was abused by Hitler who called him "dwarf," "Jesuit's spawn," and "murderer." General von Reichenau was called in to explain to the Chancellor of Austria the plan of invasion of his country. During the ordeal which lasted one whole day, Chancellor Schuschnigg was treated to several scenes on the part of Hitler who shouted, wept, stamped on the floor, and all but threatened his guest with physical violence.

A year later, another statesman, Dr. Hacha, President of

Czechoslovakia, was subjected to an even worse treatment when Hitler had him come to Berlin in order to force him to accept the statute of so-called "protectorate" over what was left of his country. Coulondre, French Ambassador to Germany, related the scene in detail: how Dr. Hacha and his minister Chvalkovsky "were literally hunted round the table on which the documents were lying," how Goering, Ribbentrop and other Nazis "were thrusting continually these documents before them, pushing pens into their hands, incessantly repeating that if they continued in their resistance, Prague would lie in ruins from aerial bombardment within two hours . . . ," how "President Hacha was in such a state of exhaustion that he more than once needed medical attention from the doctors," and how finally, "at 4:30 in the morning, Dr. Hacha, in a state of total collapse and kept going only by means of injections, resigned himself, with death in his soul, to give his signature."

Such methods had not been seen in Europe since the Middle Ages, but the scenes during which Hitler displayed with no shame the brutality of his temper, his hysterical emotionalism, and his sadism are too frequent not to lead one to the conclusion that "acting like a madman" had become part of Hitler's technique to terrorize his victims. His frequent references to himself as a "fanatic," which can be found in his speeches, were not figurative. Hitler knew that his fanaticism placed him more or less in the category of the abnormal and that nothing was better calculated to disconcert and scare his adversaries who had been trained to believe that the affairs of the world should be dealt with in an atmosphere of sanity and reasonableness.

But neither fanaticism, nor terror, nor third-degree methods would have been enough to assure the success of Hitler in his progress towards the domination of Europe. In spite of the growing strength of the German war machine and of the strategic advantages which he had gained since the reoccupation of the Rhineland, the potential forces that could be aligned against him were still far greater than his own. A united front comprising all the countries which were to be later on destroyed or threatened by Nazi Germany (and that meant all the European nations, including Russia, plus the Americas)—such a united front would have been well able to stop Hitler at any moment. The only condition for the constitution of such a front was the perception of its necessity and the will to create it.

But the leadership of Europe during those years—and particularly that of England and France—was not confided to men who had that kind of vision and that kind of will. Although very different in temperament, motives, and training, such men as Neville Chamberlain or Lord Halifax in England, Edouard Daladier or Georges Bonnet in France, were united in one common purpose: to avoid war at practically any price.

A great deal has been written about the policy of "appeasement." Various motives, such as selfish interest, reactionary fear of revolution, cowardice, and even collusion with Hitler have been attributed to the "appeasers." But at the root of the policy of appeasement one finds a popular and universal sentiment against the phenomenon of war, so deep and so imperative that it overshadowed all other considerations. The fear of war and the desire to maintain even the most precarious form of peace proved stronger than national honor and faithfulness to signed treaties. They justified, in the eyes of the people, humiliation as well as treachery, any compromise and even the renunciation of future security for the sake of a few more months or weeks of relative tranquillity. This profound horror of war explains why Chamberlain and Daladier, returning from Munich, were greeted as saviors, while one of them, at least, expected to be lynched.

The German people were no less fearful of war than the people of the democracies, but whereas the democratic leaders were compelled to speak more or less in conformity with their actions, and to submit to the control of public opinion, Hitler could talk of peace and take whatever risks he chose, including that of war. For many years there had been no public opinion in Germany. Goebbels manufactured it. The result was that Germany spoke with only one voice—that of Hitler—was governed by only one will—the will of Hitler.

Hitler, in other words, could prepare his plans in secrecy and act with lightning speed. The democratic leaders had to consult their ministers and their parliaments. They had to consult with the leaders of other countries. They followed the orthodox rules of diplomacy while Hitler had initiated gangsterism and the strategy of terror. In fact, while his opponents were clinging to peace and performing the clumsy rites of peace-time diplomacy, Hitler was already at war and moving freely in the realm of pure force.

The "appeasers" therefore were the misguided interpreters of a genuine and deep-rooted popular feeling: the hatred and fear of war. While Hitler, although he pretended to obey a similar sentiment, was at any moment ready to betray it and plunge his country into war.

But these allowances for the fundamental reason of the policy of appeasement and for the natural advantages which Hitler, as an absolute dictator, enjoyed over his democratic opponents, are not sufficient to explain or excuse the methods of the appeasers in dealing with such a situation. If one is to judge them by the result, they failed completely to achieve their purpose: Munich brought no peace to Europe, but only a brief truce. It did not strengthen the position of the democracies; it weakened it to such a point that a few months later, both England and France, realizing the catastrophic plight in which they found themselves, had only one solution left—to arm intensively and to prepare for war.

Moreover, they had to find a new excuse for Munich. The argument that they had hoped to save peace permanently was not acceptable any longer. They were therefore forced to admit that Munich, far from being a triumph for the cause of peace, was a retreat—a retreat made necessary by the fact that England and France were not prepared to meet successfully the new might of Germany. This new line of apology served Hitler well. The spokesmen and the press of the democracies had now become his best propaganda agents. They advertised his military power, and especially his air superiority with a persistency and a masochistic emphasis which could only result in spreading fear and discouragement among their own people. On the other hand, they described their own military position and that of their potential allies (especially Russia) as so feeble and inadequate that the very notion of fighting Hitler appeared as suicidal.

All this was done in order to justify the failure of the appeasers and to enable them to wash their hands of the frightful consequences of their own miscalculations. But it also shows how the so-called policy of appeasement finally led to sheer defeatism. The events which preceded and followed Munich established a pattern which was to serve again at the time of the Polish crisis and later on in America where the isolationists utilized in their campaigns many of the basic arguments which had led Neville Chamberlain and Georges Bonnet to their shameful and useless capitulation to Hitler.

At no time did the speeches of Hitler carry more significance than during that fateful period. At no time did he enjoy a vaster and more responsive audience. The whole world, literally, listened to him and willingly admitted that it waited for his words to know its fate. At no time did one man exert such power over the whole of the human race by the virtue of his unpredictable words and the facilities of the radio. No supremacy was established so thoroughly, no will of man transmitted so far and so instantaneously to millions of other men.

Hitler reached then the highest point of his effectiveness as what might be called a "strategic orator." With consummate skill, he used the platform and the microphone as instruments of torture. The nerve-racking suspense which preceded many of his speeches was greatly instrumental in creating the condition of universal jitters necessary for the development of his plans and for the disintegration of the morale of his opponents. Thanks to the radio, the whole world was subjected to the same third-degree methods which had broken the resistance of Chancellor Schuschnigg and President Hacha—with the difference that Hitler's radio audiences had no doctor at hand to administer stimulants.

Moreover, thanks to the censorship established in Germany, it was always possible for Hitler to speak in such a way as to give the maximum of reassurance to the Germans and the maximum of alarm to the outside listeners. For instance, in his speech of September 26, 1938, at the Sportpalast, he dealt with the Czech problem in such a way that his German listeners could have no idea that the crisis implied more than a localized conflict, at the worst. But Hitler knew, and so did the outside world, that England and France had finally warned Hitler that his actions might force them to go to war. Thus, while the vituperations of Hitler conveyed nothing more to the Germans than the impression of an unpleasant tension with a small neighbor, they meant the possibility of Armaggedon for the rest of Europe.

The two main crises which took place in that period—the Anschluss and the dismemberment of Czechoslovakia—revealed to what extent the civilized world had disintegrated from within. For twenty years the western democracies had oscillated between two possible policies: collective security and the system of balance of power. Neither had been clearly nor consistantly pursued either by England or France, although the firm adherence to one or the other of these formulas offered the only chance to maintain peace. However, up to the moment when Hitler showed his intention to disregard treaties and to break his own pledges—i.e., from the moment he reoccupied the Rhineland—Britain and France's only hope of saving the peace was to compel Hitler, by force if necessary, to return to an observance of the law and international order. And it mattered little, in practice, whether that order assumed the form of collective security, or of a coalition of all the threatened nations.

But at no time between 1936 and 1939 did England or France possess leaders with enough foresight and resolution to enlighten public opinion concerning the reality of the peril. On the contrary, the Anglo-French leaders seemed infinitely more concerned with justifying or concealing their own devious maneuvers and defending themselves against their respective oppositions, than assuring the security of Europe.

It might be said that one of the most disastrous effects of Hitler's methods of duplicity, treachery, brutality, and blackmail was that they were contagious. Hitler's terrorism and cynicism actually demoralized Europe, and in the absence of opponents of sufficient integrity and courage to purify the poisonous atmosphere he had created, the example of Hitler tended to bring out the worse aspects of European diplomacy.

An easy indictment can be drawn against the democratic leaders of those years which would show that, while they were denouncing Hitler for treachery and lawlessness, they themselves gave many proofs of the same immorality and perversions of truth. The refusal to apply effective sanctions against Mussolini when he attacked Ethiopia and the farcical policy of non-intervention in Spain, which covered in fact the violation of an established right for a legal government to receive help from other governments, prefaced the abandonment of Austria and the betrayal of Czechoslovakia.

The world was shocked when Hitler invaded Austria—his first bloodless conquest—but no gesture was made to help the unfortunate Schuschnigg. France and England pretended it was Mussolini's concern, but the *Duce,* by that time, was at once too frightened by the power of his Axis partner and too far committed to support him to do anything that might displease him.

In the case of Czechoslovakia's dismemberment, the behavior of the democratic leaders was considerably worse still. Under the cover of "appeasement," the English and French statesmen were led, step by step, into a jungle of deceit and double dealings more odious perhaps than Hitler's brutality because their actions were veiled with hypocrisy and fallacious good will.

Both the British Cabinet, under the leadership of Neville Chamberlain, and the French Cabinet, under Georges Bonnet and Daladier, carried on their negotiations with Hitler and with the Czechs in an atmosphere of conspiracy and dishonesty which was only surpassed by Hitler himself.

Although as early as May 10, 1938, Chamberlain had confided to a group of American correspondents that he had no intention of upholding the Czechs, and although a few weeks later in Paris, Georges Bonnet said the same thing in the presence of this commentator, both London and Paris proclaimed officially and repeatedly their resolve to abide by their engagements. Up to the very last days of the crisis, the Czechs were made to believe that France would stand by her treaty and that England would stand by France. But at the same time, both Chamberlain and Bonnet were threatening to make Benes responsible for the war if he did not give in to Hitler, of whom they had, by then, become the frightened spokesmen.

The part played by Lord Runciman, Chamberlain's envoy, during these negotiations has never been made completely clear, but although his mission was that of an arbitrator and possible mediator, it soon turned out that his purpose was to "soften up" the Czechs. As Hamilton Fish Armstrong stated it: Lord Runciman's mediation "ended in a series of international ultimata—from Hitler via Henlein (the Sudeten leader) to Benes, then from Hitler to Chamberlain, then from Chamberlain and Daladier to Benes, and finally from Chamberlain, Daladier, Hitler and Mussolini to Benes." The expression "Trojan horse" was not used in those days, but it is no exaggeration to say that Lord Runciman was a forerunner in that respect—the first "Trojan horse" of appeasement sent into the bastion of Czechoslovakia to demoralize its defenders and prepare their surrender.

Many other examples could be given to show how the doctrine of appeasement was used by Hitler to defeat the appeasers themselves and assure his own success. Without impugning the sincerity of Chamberlain and his high-mindedness, the fact remains that Hitler could not have found a better adversary—or collaborator—had he chosen him himself. Even the famous flight of Chamberlain to Berchtesgaden—which the British Prime Minister conceived as a psychological and political master stroke—turned out to be a disastrous mistake. Taking this step could only impress Hitler in one way: whatever respect he might have retained for the dignity and legendary lordliness of a British Prime Minister, he lost that day. The very fact that the aged Chamberlain stepped in a plane for the first time in his life to visit the ex-war corporal in his own eagle's nest convinced the Fuehrer that the game was won, and increased—if it were possible—the high opinion he had of himself as the real ruler of Europe.

It is true that he did not treat him quite as badly as Chancellor Schuschnigg, but the confrontation was a terrible ordeal for Chamberlain. All his dignity and stiffness were of no avail. He did not impress Hitler, but Hitler scared him.

In fact it would appear that Chamberlain never quite recovered from his visits to Berchtesgaden and Godesberg. When he went to Munich a few days later, he had ceased to fight. Both he and Daladier behaved as if they had been vanquished. They let their victors, Hitler and Mussolini, dictate the terms of the capitulation without a word.

England and France, and with them all the democratic world, had indeed suffered a catastrophic defeat. From the purely political point of view, a radical change in the European balance of power had taken place. England and France, who through the Entente Cordiale had effectively controlled the destinies of Europe since 1905, suffered an extraordinary setback. The powers of the Axis, or rather Hitler alone, had won out in one of the most remarkable diplomatic struggles of history.

That this was clearly realized in the outside world was shown by the reaction everywhere, but more particularly in America. The Americans, being separated from the conflict by three thousand miles of ocean, judged the event with the objectivity that comes from security. There were no "appeasers" then in America (appeasers, realists, defeatists, and the like only appear when the danger comes close—as was to be demonstrated in America later on). American public opinion was quick to feel the blow which had been inflicted on the whole moral order of the world and to condemn those responsible for it: Hitler first, but also Chamberlain, Bonnet, the "Cliveden set," etc. America had difficulty in understanding why the "appeasers" who had brought such disaster upon their own countries were still kept in power. At this distance it was difficult to appreciate the extraordinary sense of relief that swept all over Europe—in Berlin as well as in London, in Paris as in Rome—merely because war had been avoided.

In fact, and during a few more months, appeasement far from being discredited in Europe reached new heights. On December 6, Ribbentrop came to Paris to sign a pact of friendship with Georges Bonnet, through which both countries recognized the permanency of their current frontiers. Paris was not cordial to Ribbentrop. His presence in the capital brought home a sense of humiliation and defeat. But the French as well as the English were too tired by the many crises, they were content enough to go about their daily affairs and wait. They were unnerved.

But Hitler was neither unnerved nor tired.

With relentless activity he pressed his advantages. He visited the western frontiers of the Reich and hastened the completion of the Siegfried Line. He negotiated feverishly to extend his influence in the affairs of Bohemia, Slovakia, Yugoslavia, Turkey. He gave moral support to Mussolini in the latter's new defiance to France when the Fascist deputies, assembled in Rome, shouted for the return of Savoy, Corsica, Nice, and Tunis.

Hitler also spoke.

In a speech delivered at Saarbruecken, on October 9, 1938, Hitler made two remarkable and disturbing statements. He revealed that his decision to lead back into the Reich ten million Germans had been taken "at the beginning of this year." This was an admission by Hitler himself that he was lying when he promised so many times during that year that he intended to respect the integrity of Austria and Czechoslovakia. The second statement was a direct warning given to France and England that they could not change their present rulers—the men of Munich—without incurring Germany's displeasure. "In England," said Hitler, "it is merely necessary that instead of Chamberlain, a Duff Cooper or an Eden or a Churchill come into power. We know that the aim of these men would be to start war."

Thus Hitler clearly asserted that he had a right to tell the English and French what kind of government they should have. Even the "appeasers" received a jolt when they heard this and the London press was very alarmed.

A month later, an event of another nature reminded the world that the man with whom they had made their peace in Munich still possessed resources of brutality and cruelty rarely seen in modern history. On November 11, at a given hour and throughout Germany, a wave of anti-Jewish atrocities was let loose by the Nazis in retaliation for the assassination of a German diplomat in Paris by a young Jew. Disgust and revolt shook the world. The American Ambassador in

Berlin was called back to Washington. The English public was struck with horror.

Were those the fruits of Munich? Could this be what Hitler meant by European peace?

Thus it soon became apparent, through both Hitler's speeches and his actions that Munich, far from being a humane settlement and a permanent *understanding,* was to be on the contrary the source of new troubles and more horrors. Munich had not bridged the abyss that separated two worlds.

The reason for this was simple and it was to be found in the profound and irreparable opposition between the mentality of Hitler and that of the democratic leaders. Whereas for Chamberlain and Daladier and for the great majority of the English and French people, Munich meant the extreme limit of possible concessions, it meant for Hitler merely a new springboard from which to jump to new conquests.

Chamberlain came back from Munich believing he had secured "peace for our time." And that would have been true enough if that meant Hitler's peace. But peace to Chamberlain meant order, repose, quiet, the possibility of calm negotiation and of business as usual. It did not mean allowing Hitler to pursue his career of annexation, conquest, plunder and terrorism of the strong and the weak.

The misunderstanding between Hitler and Chamberlain was as complete after Munich as it had been before.

That Chamberlain and the other democratic leaders could not understand what had happened to them, exasperated Hitler. Couldn't they see what had happened to them? Didn't they realize that he was the master of Europe for the simple reason that they had delivered Europe to him? Wasn't that implicit in the Munich agreement and in the new pacts of friendship with England and France? What did friendship mean then?

In the presence of such stubbornness and incomprehension,

Hitler resolved to carry out his program without bothering any longer with Munich, London or Paris.

One year after he had entered Vienna as a conqueror, he entered another European capital, Prague. What was left of Czechoslovakia disappeared from the map.

This was the second and last of his bloodless conquests.

President Roosevelt had said that he was not sure that "peace by fear" was better than "peace by the sword." Hitler, having successfully tried one, was now going to attempt the other.

•

SPEECH OF MARCH 12, 1938

Linz (Austria)

Background

1938

March 11-12—German troops enter Austria.

The Speech

"I THANK you for your words of greeting. Above all I thank all of you assembled here who have borne witness that it is not the will and the wish of some few only to found this great Reich of the German people, but that it is the wish and the will of the German people. Would that on this evening some of our international seekers after truth whom we know so well could not only see the facts but later admit them to be facts. When years ago I went forth from this town, I bore within me precisely the same profession of faith which today fills my heart. Judge of the depth of my emotion when after so many years I have been able to bring that profession of faith to its fulfillment.

"If Providence once called me forth from this town to be the leader of the Reich, it must, in so doing, have given to me a commission, and that commission could be only to restore my dear homeland to the German Reich. I have believed in this commission, I have lived and fought for it, and I believe I have now fulfilled it. You all are witnesses and sureties for that. I know not on what day you will be summoned, I hope it will not be far distant. Then you must make good your pledge with your own confession of faith, and I believe that then before the whole German people I shall be able to point with pride to my own homeland. And this must then prove to the world that every further attempt to tear this people asunder will be in vain.

"And just as then it will be your duty to make your contribution to this German future, so all Germany is ready for its part to make its contribution and it is already making it today. In the German soldiers who now from all the shires of the Reich are marching into Austria you must see those who are ready and willing to make sacrifices in their fight for the unity of the whole great German people, for the power of the Reich, for its greatness and its glory now and evermore—Germany, Sieg Heil!"

Press

London Times, March 13—This, the latest and worst demonstration of the methods of German foreign policy, can only deepen in this country the suspicions and indignation aroused by the manner in which the Berchtesgaden agreement was negotiated. . . . It deals a blow to the policy of appeasement by leaving it more than doubtful whether appeasement is possible in a continent exposed to the visitations of arbitrary force. . . . Inevitably, as Germany and all the world know, and as history warns them, no limit can be set to the consequences of any act which risks a European upheaval.

New York Times, March 13—No event in the recent history of Europe matches in importance Germany's conquest of Austria by force of arms . . . what remains to be seen is whether large developments are not now in the making which may in the end overshadow in importance even the conquest of Austria itself.

•

SPEECH OF MARCH 18, 1938

Berlin, Reichstag

Background

1938

March 13—Léon Blum forms new Cabinet in France.

March 17—Soviet Foreign Minister Litvinov hands out a statement protesting against the Anschluss and reiterating that the USSR will stand by its engagements with Czechoslovakia.

The Speech

"I HAVE summoned you in order to give a report on events the importance of which you all appreciate. Moreover, I must bring to your cognizance decisions that concern the German people and the German Reichstag itself. . . ."

"Innumerable racial enclaves in Europe make it, to a certain degree, simply impossible to find a frontier that would be equally just toward racial State interests. In Europe alone there are national forms that bear in themselves the strong appearance of intentional national injustice. But in the long run their maintenance is only possible by the most brutal force.

"Thus, for instance, the creation of the new, mutilated State of Austria was in a measure brought about by the naked violation of the right to self-determination of 6,500,000 people of German birth. This violation was admitted with cynical frankness. It was of no importance to the well-known discoverer of the rights of self-determination and the freedom of peoples, nor to the other interested, pious rulers of the world who were then so much preoccupied with righteousness on earth, that the free will of 6,500,000 should be strangled by this so-called peace treaty and that they should thus be compelled by force to acquiesce in the violation in their right of self-determination and accept an unnatural separation from the great common motherland.

"Indeed, when it was decided in Austria, despite this, to hold a plebiscite—I should like to remind the democrats in London and Paris particularly of this point—more than 95 per cent of the voters were in favor of incorporation, but the apostles of new rights prevented this action with the help of brutal force.

"At that time neither in Germany nor in Austria did National Socialism exist. The tragedy of this was that the State of Austria represented from the outset a State completely unable to live. The economic distress was correspondingly dreadful and the people's mortality figure rose in the most fearful manner. In Vienna alone last year out of 100,000 births there were 20,000 fatalities. I don't say this because I believe I could impress the self-righteous citizens of the world, for I know they are completely without feeling toward such affairs. They can firmly look on while in Spain 500,000 people are butchered, without being in the slightest moved by it. And without going red in the face they can hypocritically display profound disgust when in Berlin or Vienna a Jewish provocateur is deprived of his business foundation.

"No, I merely mention this in order to state quite coldly

how the crime of a dictated peace treaty pronounced for millions of persons a death sentence that has been gradually executed by creating nations that could not live.

"That persons should be willing to secure for themselves positions in the government at the expense of their people by personally supporting such sham sovereignty organized from the outside does not surprise anyone who has an insight into the moral and spiritual weaknesses of mankind.

"It is little to be wondered at that among the mass of national thinking people affected there began to spread slowly a disgusted bitterness and that there arose the fanatical determination to destroy one day such unnatural and disgusting maltreatment and set up in the place of a lying, democratic violation of the people the more holy rights of the eternal racial life. But as these oppressed people attempted to alter the lot that was forced upon them, an increased power had to be employed against them, for only thus can the most natural of feelings and hopes be suppressed. But he who knows any history can have no doubt that the stamina of racial maintenance is stronger than the efficacy of oppression.

"It, therefore, comes about in the long run that even the most brazen cannot talk about rights when injustice is so horribly obvious; and above all that a proceeding cannot at one moment be characterized as the just foundation of the life of the people and at another as the devilish attempt to destroy the peace of nations. . . ."

"Right must be right even where Germans are concerned. And who will be surprised that the people who have been so obstinately deprived of this right have been compelled to secure it for themselves?

"Nations are the creations of gods of will and are of everlasting duration, but the League of Nations is of the highly dubious construction of human fallibility and human greed and interests. This is certain—just as the nations have lived for innumerable centuries without a League of Nations so there will soon be no more League of Nations. And despite this fact nations will continue to live for centuries. This institution would only have a meaning if its ideas were reconciled with those higher ideas that correspond with the general and equal and thus better notion of justice.

"It is, therefore, clear that a State molded by force, such as Austria, if prevented by force from joining her motherland and already condemned to death economically, can only be maintained by the permanent use of force. So long as Germany lay in the deepest distress its attraction to our millions living outside was limited—although even they desired to unite themselves despite the misery then prevailing in the Reich.

"As the Reich experienced its renaissance and the German people became filled with a new racial faith and became lifted higher by great confidence the eyes of the oppressed and ill-treated comrades outside her frontiers naturally turned with ever-increasing longing toward the great mother country. As Germany's economic recovery began to show from year to year more visible effects the idea of Anschluss grew because of the desire for self-preservation.

"On the other hand disgust also reigned in the Reich the more the continual persecution of Germans living along the frontier was realized. Germany now again has become a world power. But which power of the world would calmly tolerate in the long run that a host of its own members, numbering millions, should be most bitterly ill-treated before its very gates?

"There are moments when it is impossible for a proud nation to look on any longer. I, therefore, decided also for these reasons to bring about the conversations in Berchtesgaden known to you with the former Federal Chancellor Schuschnigg.

"I explained to this man most solemnly that a regime lacking every kind of legality and that fundamentally was only ruled by force must in the long run get into conflict with that expression of public opinion that is diametrically opposed to its tendencies. I, therefore, explained to him that this development must lead, on the one hand, to ever-increasing rejection and, on the other hand, to ever-increasing oppression and that, in view of the revived great power of the German Reich, revolutionary upheavals were bound to take place in the long run. The only consequence, in these circumstances, would be a further increase of the terror. Finally State affairs must arise that would make it impossible for a Great Power with a sense of honor patiently to continue to look on or declare itself disinterested.

"I left Schuschnigg in no doubt on the matter that there was no German-born Austrian with a feeling of national decency and honor who did not, at the bottom of his heart, long for union with the German people and would strive toward it. I begged him, a German Austrian, to spare himself and the German Reich a situation that sooner or later must lead to a grave dispute. I warned Schuschnigg it would be the last attempt undertaken on my part and that I was resolved, in the event of the miscarriage of this attempt, to protect the rights of the German people in my country with those means that alone remained when human understanding declined to listen to the call of justice.

"Not a single decent nation has died for the sake of democratic formalities; moreover people think least about them in these democracies who talk most about them.

"Deputies, men of the German Reichstag, on February 20, in your presence, I stretched out my hand to former Chancellor Schuschnigg. In his first answer he rejected this hand. He began to fulfill the obligations agreed upon with hesitancy. Moreover, we are now in a position to know that part of the lying campaign against Germany was inspired by the press office of Schuschnigg himself. There could no longer be any doubt that Schuschnigg, who possessed no legal right of existence and who violated German Austria with a dwindling minority, was determined to break this agreement.

"The first reports of the planned plebiscite appeared on Tuesday, March 8. They seemed so fantastic that they were thought to be pure rumors. On Wednesday evening we received knowledge through a really astounding speech of the attempted attack not only against the agreement worked out between us but also, and principally, against the majority of the Austrian people.

"In a country in which for years there had been no election, in which there were neither election files nor lists, it was decided there should be an election in exactly three days. The vote in question was put in such a way that a refusal appeared to be punishable, according to laws then in force. There were no voters' lists. It was, therefore, impossible to examine them. Demands for corrections could not be made. Secrecy was neither safeguarded nor desired. The voter who voted 'no' was a marked man right from the beginning. 'Yes' voters were to receive every opportunity for falsifying the results; in other words, Schuschnigg, who well knew there was only a minority of the population back of him, tried by an unexampled election forgery to obtain moral justification for open violation of the agreement that he had entered. He desired a mandate for the further and still more brutal oppression of the overwhelming majority of the German Austrian people.

"This breaking of his word to this extent could only lead to insurgency. Only a crazy, blinded man would believe he could thus close the mouth of a tremendous majority of the people in order to give a legal foundation, in the eyes of the world, to an illegal regime. This insurgence, however, in whose outbreak there could be no doubt and that showed itself immediately, would have led this time to a new and, on this occasion, more terrible shedding of blood.

"I was now determined to put an end to the further oppression of my home country. I therefore immediately gave orders for those measures to be taken that appeared adequate to save Austria from the fate of Spain.

"The ultimatum that suddenly caused the world to complain was nothing but the resolute declaration that Germany would no longer stand for the further suppression of her German-Austrian compatriots and, therefore, it was meant as a warning against taking a course that must have resulted in bloodshed. That this attitude was wise was proved by the fact that within three days my whole country rushed to meet me without a shot being fired and without a single victim, so far as I am aware, although to the sorrow of our international pacifists.

"Perhaps Schuschnigg did not think it possible that I would decide in favor of intervention. He and his supporters may thank God I did so, for probably only my decision saved his life and the lives of thousands of others who had forfeited them through their responsibility in the deaths of countless Austrian victims of the movement. I am happy that I have been the man who carried out this highly historic task. Behind my decision stand 75,000,000 people protected by the German Army.

"It is almost tragic that an event, that cannot but remove what in the long run must have become a point of unrest in Central Europe, was greeted with a complete lack of understanding by our democracies. . . ."

"Their reactions were in part beyond understanding, in part insulting. A number of other States had, it is true, from the first declared that they were not concerned in the matter or had expressed their hearty approval. This was the case not only with most of the smaller European countries, but also with quite a number of large States. I will mention only the dignified and understanding attitude of Poland, the friendly and warm-hearted approval of Hungary, the declarations, inspired by hearty friendship, of Yugoslavia, together with the assurances of sincere neutrality on the part of several other countries. . . ."

"I cannot, however, conclude the enumeration of these friendly voices without alluding more in detail to the attitude of Fascist Italy. I felt obliged to explain to the leader of that great Fascist country, who is such a great friend of mine, in a letter my reasons for my action and to assure him in particular after this event that nothing will change the attitude of Germany toward Italy and that Germany regards—just as in the case of France so also in the case of Italy—the existing frontiers as given frontiers.

"I should like to express to the great Italian statesman in the name of the German people and my own name our warmest thanks. We know what Mussolini's attitude has meant for Germany in these days. If there could have been a strengthening of the relations between Italy and Germany it took place then.

"The ideological unity of our interests has become for us Germans an indissoluble friendship. The land and frontiers of this friend are to us inviolable. I repeat I shall never forget Mussolini's attitude. The Italian people know that the German nation supports my word. Thus on this occasion as before, the axis that connects our two countries proves of the greatest service to the peace of the world.

"For Germany wants only peace. She does not want to add to the sorrows of other nations. She is ready, however, to give her last man for her honor and existence. Let nobody think this is only a phrase. Let it be understood that a great and honorable people cannot stand by inactive while millions of their own blood are oppressed.

"Deputies of the German Reichstag! I believe that in these great historical hours in which, thanks to the National Socialist idea of the new power of the Reich, the eternal dream of the German people has been fulfilled, not just a single part of our people should be called on to confirm by its consent the tremendous events of the foundation of a truly greater German Peoples Reich.

"On April 10, millions of German Austrians will testify before history to greater German unity. They shall not be left alone on this their first action in the new German Reich. From March 13 the path of the Austrians is the same as that of the other men and women of our Reich. Therefore, on April 10 the whole German nation will come forward and declare themselves solemnly for a greater Reich. Not 6,500,000 are to be asked, but 75,000,000.

"And secondly, I now dissolve the Reichstag of the old German Reich and order the election of new representatives of greater Germany. I also order it to be held on April 10. I appeal to the 50,000,000 electors of our people to give me a Reichstag which with the gracious aid of God will enable me to carry out our new tasks.

"In these days the German people should once again examine what I and my colleagues accomplished in the last five years since the Reichstag elections of March, 1933.

"I expect for my people that they will have the understanding and strength to come to such decisions. *German people, give me another four years so that I can now exploit the accomplished union for the benefit of all.*

"After the expiration of this period the new German people's Reichstag must grow into indissoluble unity anchored in the will of its people, politically led by the National Socialist party, protected by its young National Socialist forces and rich in the prosperity of its economic life. . . ."

Press

New York Times, March 19— . . . No National Socialist Reichstag session in the last five years equaled tonight's with respect to the tumultuous ovation showered on Hitler. . . . Hitler literally bristled with furious determination to justify his Austrian adventure before a hostile world. . . . The most significant portion of the . . . speech was that in which he made a cordial acknowledgment of Premier Mussolini's attitude. . . .

•

SPEECH OF MARCH 25, 1938

Königsberg

"GERMANY was to be weakened! She was to be torn asunder so that she might remain powerless as in past times. That was the purpose of this 'sovereignty,' that was the meaning of the veto on the Anschluss. . . . And that is only what one might expect. Today it is only under quite peculiar presuppositions that such small State formations can have a possibility of life. . . ."

"That is what all these international apostles of truth should have seen who today lie about an act of violence and refuse to see the facts because they do not suit their book. The world and the conscience of the world had no understanding for the facts. A foreign paper asks: 'Why could you not have done this "peaceably"? The world would have been ready to grant you all you wanted?' We know better: the conscience of the world, the justice of the world shone forth upon us for the first time from the Peace Treaties. When has more shameless violence been done to peoples than in the period when men began to talk about 'world-conscience' and 'world-justice'? When have economic territorial unities been torn apart with less regard to conscience than since the day when a 'League of Nations' was established with the professed aim of serving the interests of peoples? . . . How often have I made representations, have warned and counseled—but all to no effect? I should only rejoice if now—as perhaps may be deduced from the remarks in this English newspaper—there should be a change of mind. We still have a few injustices to complain of: perhaps now they may be settled by agreement! Up to the present our complaints fell on ears that were stone deaf. . . ."

" . . . and then one day there came the hour when one had to make a decision before one's conscience, before one's own people, and before an eternal God Who had created the peoples. And a fortnight ago I made that decision, and it was the only possible decision. For when men are deaf to every behest of justice, then the individual must assert his rights himself. Then he must turn to that ancient creed: Help yourself and then God will help you. And God has helped us! . . ."

"I said to the Austrian Chancellor: 'Herr Schuschnigg, you are oppressing a country. You have no right to do so. This country is my homeland as much as it is yours. How comes it that you are continually doing violence to it? I am ready to stand with you before the people at an election. Both of us will stand as candidates. The people shall decide.' He objected that that was impossible on constitutional grounds. But I warned him to seek a peaceful way of lessening the tension, as otherwise no one could guarantee that a people's tortured soul would not cry aloud. And besides I could not let there be any doubt that on the frontiers of Germany no more fellow-countrymen could be shot.

"And I tried to make clear to him in all seriousness that this was the last way which perhaps might lead to a peaceful solution of this crisis. I left him in no doubt that, if this way should fail, in one way or another matters would not end there. I begged him to have no doubt that I was serious in my intention to place the help of the Reich at the service of my oppressed fellow-countrymen and not to doubt my resolution if, through deserting this way, a crisis should arise. He did not believe the seriousness of my assurances and for this reason, one may suppose, he broke the agreement.

"Today we have the proofs of that. We have found the letters in which on February 19—one day before my speech in the Reichstag—he writes that on his part the whole affair would be purely a tactical move in order to gain time so that he could wait until the situation abroad should be more favorable. He therefore counted on being able at a more propitious hour to stir up foreign countries against Germany. In order to give a moral foundation to his scheme this man then invented this ridiculous comedy of a plebiscite on which the clearest light is thrown by the fact that we were able to confiscate broad-sheets and placards in which eight days before the plebiscite the figures of the voting were published! It was an unheard-of fraud in a country in which for many years there had been no election, where no one could vote. It was clear that if this new fraud should be a success, then the world, cold as ice, would have declared: 'Now this regime is legitimated!'

"And against this the German people in Austria at last began to rise, it turned against its persecutors. It revolted. And now I had to intervene in its behalf. And so I gave the order to answer the wish of this people: I let the forces march!

"And I did this firstly in order to show the world that I was now in bitter earnest, that the time for any further oppression of Germany was past. . . ."

"I admit openly that at times, in view of the terrible persecutions, the thought might even come to one that it was only right if the people did at last wreak its vengeance on its torturers; but in the end I decided to prevent that. For I saw one thing: amongst our opponents there are men who are so depraved that they must be counted as lost to the community of the German people, but on the other hand there are many blinded and mad folk who have only run with the rest. Perhaps their eyes have been thoroughly opened. And above all, who can guarantee that when once madness has begun private passions will not begin to rage as well, that private scores will not be settled under the watchword of a political act? . . ."

"We will be quit of those of our opponents who are incurable through the normal means of our State. Part of them will without our help go where all the European 'worthies' of this stamp have assembled of recent years. And we are glad that some of them have gone already. I can but hope and expect that the rest of the world which feels so deep a sympathy with these criminals will be at least magnanimous enough to turn this pity into practical assistance. On our side we are quite prepared to put all these criminals aboard luxury ships and let these countries do with them what they will. We have in the overwhelming joy of these days forgotten all desire for vengeance. . . ."

"I wanted to spare this country the horrors of Spain and then I *had* to help: I had been summoned. I could not have borne the responsibility before the history of Germany if I had not given the order to march.

"Certain foreign newspapers have said that we fell on Austria with brutal methods: I can only say: even in death they cannot stop lying. I have in the course of my political battle won much love from my people, but when in these last days I crossed the former frontier of the Reich there met me such a stream of love that I have never experienced a greater. Not as tyrants have we come, but as liberators: an entire people rejoiced. . . ."

"Here not brutal violence, but our Swastika has conquered. As these soldiers marched into Austria, I lived again a song of my youth. I have in days past sung it so often with faith in my heart, this proud battle-song: 'The people arises, the storm breaks loose.' And it was in truth the uprising of a people, and the breaking loose of the storm. Under the force of this impression I decided not to wait until April 10 but to effect the unification forthwith. . . ."

"That which has happened in these last weeks is the result of the triumph of an idea, a triumph of will, but also a triumph of endurance and tenacity and, above all, it is the result of the miracle of faith: for only faith has availed to move these mountains. I once went forth with faith in the German people and began this vast fight. With faith in me first thousands, then hundreds of thousands, and at last millions have followed after me. With faith in Germany and in this idea millions of our fellow-countrymen in the New Ostmark in the south of our Reich have held their banners high and have remained loyal to the Reich and to the life of the German people. And now I have faith in this April 10. I am convinced that on this day for the first time in history in very truth all Germany will be on the march. . . ."

"And on this day I shall be the Leader of the greatest army in the history of the world; for when on this April 10 I cast my voting-paper into the urn then I shall know that behind me come 50 millions and they all know only my watchword: One People and one Reich—Deutschland!"

Press

London Times, March 26— . . . Herr Hitler said he had read in a newspaper that he might have accomplished the Anschluss in a peaceful manner, since the world was ready to agree with it. He had been grateful for the information. An apparent allusion to *Times,* March 19, 1938, editorial: "The stock of confidence": ". . . All over Europe the opinion has steadily gained acceptance that the prohibition of the Anschluss with Austria was a mistake, and if Hitler had set about to achieve it with the consent of both peoples, he had every opportunity to do so with international good will or, at the least, acquiescence."

New York Times, March 26— . . . Hitler delivered his . . . speech . . . in a distinctly threatening tone, warning again that the Reich was going to watch over the fate of Germans on the other side of its frontiers and act again if he thinks it necessary. . . .

SPEECH OF APRIL 9, 1938

Vienna

Background

1938

April 8—Speaking in Birmingham, Chamberlain says he disapproves of dictatorships, but adds: "There they are. You cannot remove them. We have to live with them."

In France, Léon Blum falls. It is the end of the Popular Front Government.

The Speech

"BE ASSURED that this city is in my eyes a pearl. I will bring it into that setting which is worthy of this pearl and I will entrust it to the care of the whole German Reich, the whole German nation. . . ."

"I desire particularly to address those who in this hour do not feel that they can give their approval and confidence to the new Germany or still less to me or who think that they must stand apart in the face of this truly great world-historical decision. I want to speak as a man who is himself completely guiltless of all that which Germany has suffered in the past. . . ."

"For every people there is only one help possible: the help which lies in itself. But for that there is a condition: the people must come together into a single closely united body, for only from such a unity can the strength to win salvation come. . . ."

"I have not relied upon Geneva or Moscow, but on one thing alone, on my people, on Germany. . . ."

"Others have built castles in the clouds, but we build for our German folk an earthly but a decent life. . . ."

"But if that will not suffice I stand here because I pride myself that I can do more than Herr Schuschnigg!

"I believe that it was God's will to send a boy from here into the Reich, to let him grow up, to raise him to be the leader of the nation so as to enable him to lead back his homeland into the Reich.

"There is a higher ordering and we all are nothing else than its agents. When on March 9 Herr Schuschnigg broke his agreement then in that second I felt that now the call of Providence had come to me. And that which then took place in three days was only conceivable as the fulfillment of the wish and the will of this Providence.

"In three days the Lord has smitten them! . . . And to me the grace was given on the day of the betrayal to be able to unite my homeland with the Reich! . . ."

"I would now give thanks to Him who let me return to my homeland in order that I might now lead it into my German Reich! Tomorrow may every German recognize the hour and measure its import and bow in humility before the Almighty who in a few weeks has wrought a miracle upon us!"

Press

Le Temps, April 11—The Fuehrer constantly presents himself as conducting his defense against imaginary critics. He spoke one sentence which is, perhaps, one of the most interesting in the speech, for it throws astounding light upon the psychology of the orator. "March 9, . . . when I learned that Schuschnigg had broken our treaty, I felt at that moment that Providence had summoned me." And so, when news came that M. von Schuschnigg had decided upon a plebiscite, M. Hitler immediately came to his decision; it was a kind of revelation. As a matter of fact, his last speech ends on a religious note. . . .

London Times, April 11—Had the elections in Austria itself been perfectly free, in the sense in which freedom is understood in this country, the result would probably have been a majority in favor of the Anschluss. Herr Hitler has justification for the claim which he made in his last speech, on Saturday, when he said that Austrians are a German people, living in a German country, who wanted to be a part of Greater Germany from the moment that the old Austro-Hungarian Monarchy was broken up. Others must take the responsibility that the union was not effected in a quieter way, which might have given historic Austria a place in a less rigidly centralized system, and on the other hand would not have left so many sore feelings behind. . . .

Almost every one of the Fuehrer's election speeches invites Germans to think of themselves as a people oppressed and ill-used by foreign countries and compelled to win their rights by force alone. Whatever substance there may have been in these charges in the past, they have no relevance in the present or future. Certainly in this country there have been many ready to reckon with Greater Germany—which, whoever likes it or not, is the product of inevitable forces and Herr Hitler's historic accomplishment as one of the sure developments in Europe.

The task of the future is to succeed where the Europe of twenty-four years ago failed in finding a settled basis of relations proof against fundamental disturbance, and, in the new phase now opening, the question is what limit is to be set to the employment of force. Mr. Chamberlain and successive Foreign Ministers have made it perfectly clear for their part that they do not for a moment refuse to deal with any foreign country because its social doctrine differs from our own. Apart from the methods by which it was accomplished, there has never been any public feeling in England against the union of Austria and Germany, nor is it in itself the slightest bar to an understanding between *Grossbritannien* and *Grossdeutschland*. It will no doubt increase the resources and the strength of Germany. Great Britain is also engaged in increasing her strength. But it is perfectly appropriate that negotiations should be conducted from strength by both parties.

New York Times, April 10—Chancellor Hitler closed his campaign for tomorrow's plebiscite with a speech here tonight in which he greeted a huge audience with frequent references to the Deity.

•

SPEECH OF MAY 7, 1938

Rome

Background

1938

April 10—Election, Austrian plebiscite.

April 10—Daladier forms Cabinet with Georges Bonnet as Foreign Minister. Socialists are excluded.

April 16—Anglo-Italian pact signed in Rome. Recognition of Ethiopia and withdrawal of Italian troops from Spain to come into effect after Franco's victory.

April 24—Konrad Henlein, leader of the Sudeten German party, makes a speech at Karlsbad asking for revision of Czech foreign policy which has led the country in the ranks of Germany's enemies.

April 28—Anglo-French agreement signed by Daladier in London. It provides for military consultations and unified command in case of war.

May 7—Hitler visits Rome, assuring Mussolini of inviolability of frontiers.

The Speech

"DUCE, with deep emotion I thank you for the moving words which you have addressed to me in the name both of the Italian Government and of the Italian people. I am happy to be here in Rome in which the powerful manifestations of the young Fascist Italy are united with the evidences of its incomparably venerable past.

"Since the moment when I first set foot on Italian soil I have been conscious everywhere of an atmosphere of friendship and sympathy which fills me with profound pleasure. With the same heartfelt emotion the German people last autumn greeted in your person the creator of Fascist Italy, the founder of a new Imperium and at the same time also the great friend of Germany.

"The National Socialist Movement and the Fascist Revolution have created two new powerful States which today in a world of unrest and disintegration stand as creations of order and healthy progress. Germany and Italy have thus like interests and through sharing in a common *Weltanschauung* are closely bound together. *In this way there has been created in Europe a bloc of 120,000,000 people who are determined to safeguard their eternal vital rights and to defend themselves against all those forces which might venture to oppose their natural development.*

"Out of this fight against a world which rejects and refuses to understand their claims, a fight which Germany and Italy have had to wage shoulder to shoulder, there has gradually grown up a warm friendship between the two peoples. This friendship has proved its strength during the events of the last few years. These events have, further, shown to the world that in one way or another account must be taken of those justified interests which are of vital import to great nations. It is therefore only natural that our two peoples should in the future continue to build up and deepen in constant co-operation this friendship which in recent years has ever proved of increasing value.

"Duce, last autumn on the Maifeld in Berlin, you proclaimed a principle which, as you said, the moral law was sacred both for yourself and for Fascist Italy: 'Speak plainly and frankly, and if you have a friend, march with him right to the end.'

"In the name of National Socialist Germany I, too, profess my allegiance to this law. Today I wish to give you the following answer:

"Two millennia have now passed since Romans and Germans met for the first time in history so far as that history is known to us. Standing here, on this the most venerable soil in our human history, I feel the tragedy of a destiny which formerly failed to draw clear frontier lines between these two highly gifted, valuable races. The consequence of that failure was untold suffering for many generations. Now today after nearly two thousand years, thanks to your historic activity, Benito Mussolini, the Roman State arises from remote traditions to new life, and north of you there arose, formed out of numerous tribes, a new Germanic Reich. Now that we have become immediate neighbors, taught by the experience of two millennia, we both wish to recognize that natural frontier which Providence and history have clearly drawn for our two peoples. *That frontier will then render possible the happiness of a permanent co-operation peacefully secured through the definite separation of the living-spaces of the two nations, but it will also serve as a bridge for mutual help and support.* It is my unalterable will and my bequest to the German people that it shall accordingly regard the frontier of the Alps, raised by Nature between us both, as for ever inviolable. I know that then through this delimitation a great and prosperous future will result both for Rome and Germany.

"Duce, just as you and your people maintained your friendship with Germany in days of crisis, so I and my people will show the like friendship towards Italy in times of difficulty.

"The stupendous impressions I have just received of the youthful strength, the will to work, and the proud spirit of the new Italy will remain for me an imperishable memory. Unforgettable, too, was the sight of your soldiers and Blackshirts covered with the glory of their recent operations [in Abyssinia], of your well-tried fleet, and of the *élan* of your magnificent air force. They give me the certainty that your admirable constructive work which I follow with the sincerest well-wishing will in the future as in the past lead to great successes.

"So I raise my glass and drink to your health, to the good fortune and greatness of the Italian people and to our unchanging friendship. . . . How can I translate the sentiment which I experienced as I stood before the millennial monuments of Rome? How profoundly I regret that I could only see their grandeur far too quickly and then had to pass by. This journey to Italy and my visit here I have experienced not merely as a politician but also as an artist. It has always been against my will and with sorrow that I parted from every room of the splendid palaces which were shown to me. . . ."

Press

London Times, May 9—The speeches of Signor Mussolini and Herr Hitler, delivered on Saturday night after four full days of impressive pageantry on land and sea, were notable for their restraint. They held the language of statesmanship. . . . The meeting in Rome will have been immensely valuable if it has led to any understanding which may help forward a peaceful settlement of the issues raised by Herr Henlein.

New York Times, May 9—Mussolini and Hitler exchanged pledges of continued warm friendship between their countries at a State banquet in Rome last night. The German leader promised the Alpine frontier would remain inviolate.

Le Temps, May 9—The Fuehrer interpreted the natural frontier between Germany and Italy as a sacred pledge, which was confirmed not only by the Alps, but by "Providence and history." He spoke not only of the frontier itself, but of its significance . . . that the frontier between the two countries was inviolable.

In his toast, the Fuehrer spoke of Rome as the most glorious spot in the history of humanity. Is the Germanic myth to bow down before the Roman myth? Are we to think that the German Chancellor accepts the supremacy of the Eternal City and of fascism? Some observers may find that his words have an overtone reminiscent of Canossa.

•

SPEECH OF MAY 26, 1938

Fallersleben

(To inaugurate new automobile plant)

Background

1938

May 12—Henlein, leader of Sudeten party, visits London.

May 19—Henlein visits Hitler.

German troop movements are reported on the Czech frontiers.

May 21—German press starts campaign against Czechs, speaking of "intolerable provocations."

In Paris, Georges Bonnet assures foreign press that France will fulfill all her engagements, if need be.

The Speech

"THE first step towards making Germany motor-minded was to free people from the earlier conception that the motor-vehicle was an article of luxury. That is natural enough, if in a country there are only two, three, or four hundred thousand motor-vehicles on the roads. But in the case of the German people there is a demand not for two to three hundred thousand, but for six or seven million motor-cars! Here the only decisive factor is that the cost of the production and maintenance of this most modern means of transport shall be brought into conformity with the people's income. 'That is impossible!' was the objection raised in 1933. To this I could give only one answer: 'What is possible in other countries shall be possible in Germany as well!' I hate the word 'impossible'; it has always been the mask of the faint-hearted, of men who did not dare to carry out great resolves.

"The motor-car, then, must become the people's means of transport! Since this goal could not be reached with car prices as they were then, I had already determined, before I came into power, that immediately the government fell into our hands I would begin the preliminary work for the production of a car whose price would enable it to become a real means of transport for the great mass of the people. By this means the motor-car would at last cease to be an instrument of class division.

"And there was a further reason which induced me to give special attention to this policy of motorization. If the people of Germany decided to spend wholly on foodstuffs all the money which it received as wages for its work—foodstuffs, which we, with our 140 people to the square kilometer, could not produce in unlimited quantities—this was bound to lead to a catastrophe. So it is necessary for us to guide the purchasing power of the German people into other directions. These, to be sure, are problems about which our former national economists did not worry themselves. But we have to grasp these conditions and to solve the problems which arise from them. And among many other such measures which serve to secure for the purchasing power of the German people an equivalent object for it to spend its money on, the People's Car will also take its place. Here every year hundreds of millions of marks will find investment; and these demands can be satisfactorily met by our own industry and from our own raw materials—our metals, our coal, and so forth.

"The significance of this factory in its wider effects is still today recognized by very few. The People's Car will not be a rival to other automobile manufacturers. . . . It is for the great mass of people that this car has been designed. Its purpose is to answer their needs in transport and it is intended to give them joy."

•

SPEECH OF SEPTEMBER 6, 1938

Nuremberg, Proclamation

Background

1938

May 28—Hitler orders "serious measures" such as increase in air force and extension of fortifications in the West.

Cordell Hull issues statement reminding Germany and Czechoslovakia of their obligations under Briand-Kellogg Pact.

(During the month of June there was a general merger)

July 9—Henlein visits Hitler in Munich.

July 11—German press and radio renew attacks on Czechs, alleging several frontier violations.

July 12—Daladier, in a speech, renews pledges to Czechoslovakia.

July 18—Captain Wiedemann, Hitler's personal aide, visits Lord Halifax in London.

July 19—British sovereigns arrive in Paris for State visit.

July 22—Dedicating a memorial in France, King George says that England and France are bound by "ties that the passing of years can never weaken."

Britain and France reject a German proposal for a four-Power settlement of the Sudeten problem, because Czechoslovakia would be excluded from the discussion.

July 25—British Cabinet suggests sending Lord Runciman to Prague to advise in the settlement of the Sudeten dispute. Prague accepts.

July 29—Speaking in Breslau, Henlein proclaims that all Germans, whatever may be their official nationality, remain citizens of Germany and place themselves under the laws of the Reich.

August 3—Runciman arrives in Prague with Ashton-Gwatkin.

August 5—400,000 labor conscripts are reported working on the West Wall. London hears of further mobilization measures in Germany.

August 12—750,000 reservists are called up in Germany, trucks are requisitioned, doctors and nurses called.

August 15—Hitler attends army maneuvers.

August 18—Runciman confers with Henlein at the Castle of Prince Max of Hohenlohe.

President Roosevelt assures Canada of American protection in case of threat.

August 23—Runciman visits Benes, President of Czechoslovakia.

August 26—Sudeten party gives orders to its members to defend themselves "whenever attacked."

August 28—Hitler visits fortifications on the western frontier.

August 30—The French Cabinet issues a decree authorizing unlimited overtime in national defense industries, and reasserts its determination to assist Czechoslovakia in case of aggression.

September 1—Henlein, in Berchtesgaden, confers with Hitler, Goering, Goebbels, and Hess. It is understood that Hitler has rejected Prague's third plan proposing a reorganization of Czechoslovakia on cantonal basis, like Switzerland.

September 2—Benes has conference with Sudeten leaders.

Henlein is again in conference with Hitler, Ribbentrop, Goebbels, and General Bodenschatz.

September 5—French Cabinet announces "precautionary measures" such as canceling of army leaves.

September 6—Opening of the National Socialist party meeting in Nuremberg.

Benes hands over to the Sudeten leaders a fourth plan embodying further concessions.

The Proclamation

"WE CAME to Nuremberg this year more deeply moved than ever before. For many years the party conventions have not only been a festival of joy and pride but have become one of inner consciousness. Old fighters come here in the joyful hope to see again many old acquaintances of the long struggle for power, and thus they greet one another in this city as fighting comrades of the greatest German revolution.

"This year, for the first time, the circle has been drawn much wider. The National Socialist Reich has absorbed new German fellow-citizens. Many of them are in our midst for the first time in this sacred hour. . . ."

"Perhaps in the future one may speak of a miracle that destiny worked on us. Be that as it may, at the beginning of this miracle stood belief—the belief in the eternal German nation. . . . The creative bearer of this rebirth is the National Socialist party. . . . It had to cleanse Germany of all parasites for whom the distress of the Fatherland and of the people was a source of personal enrichment. It had to recognize the eternal values of blood and soil and raise them to the level of the governing laws of our life. It had to begin to fight against the greatest enemy that threatened to destroy our people: the international Jewish world enemy. Its task was to cleanse the German nation, our race and our culture from this enemy. . . ."

"Several weeks ago an English paper wrote that I had a burning desire to conclude a pact with several States on various subjects, because otherwise it would not have been possible for me to appear before the party convention this year. I never had nor have this intention.

"I come before you, my old party comrades, not with a pact but with seven new German districts of my own homeland. It is a greater Germany that in these days appears for the first time in Nuremberg, as the insignia of the old Reich have returned into this old German city. They were carried here and accompanied by six and a half million Germans who, today, spiritually unite here with all other men and women of our people. Stronger than ever, they are embraced by happy consciousness of membership in a great, indissoluble community. What every man carries within himself, all carry. . . ."

"The return of Austria into the Greater German Reich gives us an additional task for the coming here. Politically, the construction of National Socialism in this territory can be regarded as essentially completed.

"Economically, its [Austria's] incorporation in the large sphere and powerful rhythm of German life will make rapid progress.

"Several months ago I expressed the confident hope that we would succeed in removing unemployment in this section of the Reich in from three to four years. Today I can be more precise about this hope: already at the end of next year the unemployment crisis in Austria will be completely overcome.

"Today we are only suffering from two real economic troubles:

"First, the need of laborers, and especially skilled laborers in industry and, second, the need of farm hands. . . ."

"Through the grace of God, this year we have an abundant harvest. Through the energetic measures of Goering it has been possible in spite of bad harvests in preceding years to enter the new year with large reserves. With these reserves and the rich yields of this year's crops we shall be without food worries for years to come. However, we want to remain frugal. It is our will to store a reserve of bread grain which, under all circumstances, will protect us from every need. . . ."

"In addition, I ask you, my fellow-countrymen, to consider: Whatever the future may bring, one thing is certain—one cannot foretell what world economic relations will be. For if it should occur to other people instead of increasing their production to destroy it, then a shortage of exchange goods will sooner or later ruin this so-called world trade. It is, therefore, more important to keep one's own economy in order, which is, at the same time, the best contribution for possible betterment of world trade. World trade will not be revived through seemingly learned but in reality meaningless phrases of democratic statesmen, but only can be aided through the putting into order of their own slowly dying democratic economic life.

"So long as statesmen, instead of worrying about their production and bringing their own economics to order, prefer to argue with the authoritarian States in general phrases of partly schoolmasterly and partly fault-finding content, they not only do nothing for restoration of the so-called world economy, and especially world trade, but on the contrary harm it.

"Germany in any case can say of itself that thanks to its continued increasing internal production it has become not only an increasing buyer of its own products, but also of foreign products. . . ."

"On the whole, German economy is being so constructed that at any time it can be completely independent from other countries and stand on its own feet. And this is succeeding. *The idea of blockading Germany can even now be buried as an entirely ineffective weapon.* The National Socialist State, with energy that is peculiar to it, has drawn conclusions from the lessons of the World War. And now as before we hold to the fundamental principle that we would rather limit ourselves in this or that field should it become necessary in order to make ourselves independent from foreign countries.

"Above all, the following decision always will stand at the top of our economic actions: security of the nation goes ahead of everything else.

"Its economic existence is, therefore, to be secured materially in its fullest measure with our own standard of life and our own living space. For only then can the German Army be in a position at all times to take the freedom and interests of the Reich under its strong protection. And then Germany will be also of higher value as a friend and ally for anyone. If I say this on the occasion of the tenth party congress, then I do it in contented satisfaction that also politically, as well as economically, the period of German isolation is over. The Reich has great and strong World Powers as friends.

"Party comrades! More threatening than ever, bolshevist danger of the destruction of nations rises above this world. A thousandfold, we see the activities of the Jewish virus in this world pest. . . . I think I can say in my name and yours how deeply happy we are in face of the fact that another great European power, out of its own experience, its own decision and on its own road, shares the same conception and has drawn the most far-reaching conclusions. . . ."

"Whatever the way and developments the Fascist and National Socialist revolutions must take because of their own obvious needs, and however independently the two historical revolutions originated and developed, it is fortunate for all of us that in all great, vital questions of our time we find this mutual spiritual attitude, which in this world of unreason and destruction leaves us more and more humanly together. This new spirit brings the two peoples together according to their inner convictions. . . ."

"We want to give our deepest thanks to the Almighty for the success of the union of old Austria with the new Reich. Through His bounty He has allowed the German nation a great victory without its being necessary to stake the lives or the blood of our people. May Germans never forget that this never would have been possible without the united strength of the entire nation in National Socialism!

"For when on the morning of March 12 the flags of the new Reich were carried over the frontiers they were no longer, as before, the insignia of a conqueror but a symbol of the all-engrossing unity of all Germans. The war flag carried by our young army into the new districts had become the standard of victory in the hard struggle in Austria. This time an idea first conquered and united a nation!

"For us and for all who come after us the country of the Germans will now always be only Greater Germany!"

Press

New York Times, September 7—Amid continuing tension over Czechoslovakia, Chancellor Hitler in his annual Nuremberg proclamation yesterday warned the world that Germany had had a good harvest, that she had stored food reserves and that the idea of an economic blockade "can henceforth be buried." Discussion of Czechoslovakia was absent from the Nazi Party Congress.

London Times, September 7—The opening address of the Fuehrer to his followers at Nuremberg contained nothing about the subject uppermost, probably, in their minds, and certainly uppermost in the minds of the listening outside world. No doubt he left Czechoslovakia for treatment on a subsequent occasion, knowing, like a good showman, that what follows the *pièce de resistance* may easily produce the effect of an anti-climax.

. . . If the Sudetens now ask for more than the Czech Government are apparently ready to give in their latest set of proposals, it can only be inferred that the Germans are going beyond the mere removal of disabilities and do not find themselves at ease within the Czechoslovak Republic. In that case it might be worth while for the Czechoslovak Government to consider whether they should exclude altogether the project, which has found favor in some quarters, of making Czechoslovakia a more homogeneous state by the secession of that fringe of alien populations who are contiguous to the nation with which they are united by race. In any case the wishes of the population concerned would seem to be a decisively important element in any solution that can hope to be regarded as permanent, and the advantages to Czechoslovakia of becoming a homogeneous State might conceivably outweigh the obvious disadvantages of losing the Sudeten German districts of the borderland.

•

SPEECH OF SEPTEMBER 6, 1938

Nuremberg (Kultur-Sagung)

"THE proof of the endowment of a true artist is always to be found in the fact that his work of art expresses the general will of a period. Perhaps that is most clearly shown in architecture. . . . The religious mystical world of the Christian Middle Ages, turning inwards upon itself, found forms of expression which were possible only for that world—for that world alone could they be of service. A Gothic stadium is as unthinkable as a Romanesque railway station or a Byzantine market hall. The way in which the artist of the Middle Ages, of the beginnings of the modern world, found the artistic solution for the buildings which he was commissioned to create is in the highest degree striking and admirable. That way, however, is no evidence that the conception of the content of life held by the folk of his day was in itself either absolutely right or absolutely wrong; it is evidence only that works of art have rightly mirrored the inner mind of a past age. It is therefore quite comprehensible that insofar as the attempt is made to carry on the life of that past age, those who search for solutions of artistic problems can still seek and find there fruitful suggestions. Thus one can easily imagine that, for instance, in the sphere of religion men will always work backwards to the form-language of a period in which Christianity in its view of the world appeared to meet every need. On the other hand, at the present moment the expression of a new view of the world which is determined by the conception of race will return to those ages which in the past have already possessed a similar freedom of the spirit, of the will, and of the mind. Thus, naturally, the manifestation in art of a European conception of the State will not be possible through civilizations, as, for example, the civilization of the Far East, which—because foreign to us—have no message for our day, but will rather be influenced in a thousand ways through the evidences and memories of that mighty imperial Power of antiquity which, although in fact destroyed fifteen hundred years ago, still as an ideal force lives on and works on in the imaginations of men. The more nearly the modern State approaches to the imperial idea of the ancient World-Power, so more and more will the general character of that civilization be manifested in its influence upon the formation of the style of our own day. . . ."

"National Socialism is not a cult-movement—a movement

for worship; it is exclusively a *'volkic'* political doctrine based upon racial principles. In its purpose there is no mystic cult, only the care and leadership of a people defined by a common blood-relationship. *Therefore we have no rooms for worship, but only halls for the people—no open spaces for worship, but spaces for assemblies and parades. We have no religious retreats, but arenas for sports and playing-fields, and the characteristic feature of our places of assembly is not the mystical gloom of a cathedral, but the brightness and light of a room or hall which combines beauty with fitness for its purpose.* In these halls no acts of worship are celebrated, they are exclusively devoted to gatherings of the people of the kind which we have come to know in the course of our long struggle; to such gatherings we have become accustomed and we wish to maintain them. *We will not allow mystically-minded occult folk with a passion for exploring the secrets of the world beyond to steal into our Movement.* Such folk are not National Socialists, but something else—in any case something which has nothing to do with us. At the head of our program there stand no secret surmisings but clear-cut perception and straightforward profession of belief. But since we set as the central point of this perception and of this profession of belief the maintenance and hence the security for the future of a being formed by God, we thus serve the maintenance of a divine work and fulfill a divine will—not in the secret twilight of a new house of worship, but openly before the face of the Lord.

"There were times when a half-light was the necessary condition for the effectiveness of certain teachings: we live in an age when light is for us the fundamental condition of successful action. It will be a sorry day when through the stealing in of obscure mystic elements the Movement or the State itself issues obscure commissions. . . . It is even dangerous to issue any commission for a so-called place of worship, for with the building will arise the necessity for thinking out so-called religious recreations or religious rites, which have nothing to do with National Socialism. *Our worship is exclusively the cultivation of the natural, and for that reason, because natural, therefore God-willed.* Our humility is the unconditional submission before the divine laws of existence so far as they are known to us men: it is to these we pay our respect. Our commandment is the courageous fulfillment of the duties arising from those laws. But for religious rites we are not the authorities, but the churches! If anyone should believe that these tasks of ours are not enough for him, that they do not correspond with his convictions, then it is for him to prove that God desires to use him to change things for the better. In no event can National Socialism or the National Socialist State give to German art other tasks than those which accord with our view of the world.

"The only sphere in which the Jewish international newspapers still today think that they can attack the new Reich is the cultural sphere. Here they attempt, by a constant appeal to the sentimentality—untroubled by any sort of knowledge—of the world-citizens of democracy to bewail the downfall of German culture: in other words, they lament the commercial closing-down of those elements which, as the heralds and exponents of the November Republic, forced their cultural characteristics, as unnatural as they were deplorable, upon the period between the two Empires; and which have now played out their role for good and all. . . ."

"Fortunately, however, despite the short time which the National Socialist leadership has been able to allot to works of culture, positive facts, here too, speak louder than any negative criticism. We Germans can today speak with justice of a new awakening of our cultural life, which finds its confirmation not in mutual compliments and literary phrases, but rather in positive evidences of cultural creative force. German architecture, sculpture, painting, drama, and the rest bring today documentary proof of a creative period in art, which for richness and impetuosity has rarely been matched in the course of human history. And although the

Jewish-democratic press magnates in their effrontery even today seek brazenly to turn these facts upside down, we know that the cultural achievements of Germany will in a few years have won from the world respect and appreciation far more unstinted even than that which they now accord to our work in the material field. The buildings which are arising in the Reich today will speak a language that endures, a language, above all, more compelling than the Yiddish gabblings of the democratic, international judges of our culture. What the fingers of these poor wretches have penned or are penning the world will—perhaps unfortunately—forget, as it has forgotten so much else. But the gigantic works of the Third Reich are a token of its cultural renascence and shall one day belong to the inalienable cultural heritage of the Western world, just as the great cultural achievements of this world in the past belong to us today.

"Moreover, it is naturally not decisive what attitude, if any, foreign peoples take toward our works of culture, for we have no doubt that cultural creative work, since it is the most sensitive expression of a talent conditioned by blood, cannot be understood, far less appreciated, by individuals or races who are not of the same or related blood. Therefore we do not trouble in any way to make German art and culture suit the tastes of international Jewry. . . ."

"The art of Greece is not merely a formal reproduction of the Greek mode of life, of the landscapes and inhabitants of Greece; no, it is a proclamation of the Greek body and of the essential Greek spirit. It does not make propaganda for an individual work, for the subject, or for the artist; it makes propaganda for the Greek world as such, which confronts us in Hellenism. . . ."

"And so art today will in the same way announce and herald that common mental attitude, that common view of life, which governs the present age. It will do this not because this age entrusts commissions to artists, but because the execution of these commissions can meet with understanding only if it reveals in itself the true essence of the spirit of this age. The mysticism of Christianity, at the period of its greatest intensity, demanded for the buildings which it ordered an architectonic form which not only did not contradict the spirit of the age, but rather helped it to attain that mysterious gloom which made men the more ready to submit to renunciation of self. The growing protest against this crushing of the freedom of the soul and of the will, which had lasted for centuries, immediately opened the way to new forms of expression in artistic creation. The mystic narrowness and gloom of the cathedrals began to recede and, to match the free life of the spirit, buildings became spacious and flooded with light. Mystical twilight gave way before increasing brightness. The unsteady, groping transition of the nineteenth century led finally in our days to that crisis which in one way or another had to find its solution. Jewry, with its bolshevist onslaught, might smash the Aryan States and destroy those native strata of the people whose blood destined them for leadership, and in that case the culture which had hitherto sprung from these roots would be brought to the same destruction. . . ."

Press

London Times, September 8—The Fuehrer in his cultural speech tonight gave a passionate interpretation of National Socialist cultural policy, which he considered of more lasting importance than any other phase of the regime.

New York Times, September 8—He set up as a standard for all art its appeal to the sense of the beautiful, the healthy, and the natural. This, he said, was also in direct opposition to Jewish ideas. According to them, he declared, decadent intellectuals alone were entitled to set up standards.

Le Temps, September 9—The Fuehrer blamed Jewish propaganda for the fact that the culture of the Third Reich was little respected abroad. . . . From this, he went on to anti-religious propaganda. He finally admitted that National

Socialism could have no influence upon music and he concluded that in all realms of art, writers and painters must cultivate the wholesome, for what was wholesome was true and beautiful.

•

SPEECH OF SEPTEMBER 12, 1938

Nuremberg

Background

September 7—France calls up reservists to man Maginot Line.

The *London Times* publishes an editorial suggesting that the Czech Government should cede that "fringe of alien populations who are contiguous" to Germany.

The Sudeten party breaks off negotiations with the Czech Government.

September 8—Henlein visits Hitler in Nuremberg.

September 9—President Roosevelt denies that the United States is allied with European democracies in a "Stop Hitler" movement.

September 11—Violent Sudeten riots take place in Czechoslovakia. There is bloodshed.

September 12—Full meeting of the British Cabinet in London and of the French in Paris.

Nazi disorders continue in the Sudetenland.

The Speech

"SINCE the days when we took over the Government the united front around Germany is standing against us. Today we again see plotters, from democrats down to Bolsheviks, fighting against the Nazi State. While we were struggling for power, and particularly in the decisive final struggle, they formed a united bloc against us.

"We are being insulted today, but we thank God that we are in a position to prevent any attempt at plundering Germany or doing her violence. The State that existed before us was plundered for fifteen years. But for this it was praised as being a brave and democratic State.

"But it becomes unbearable for us at a moment when a great German people, apparently defenseless, is delivered to shameless ill-treatment and exposed to threats. I am speaking of Czechoslovakia. This is a democratic State. It was founded on democratic lines by forcing other nationalities, without asking them, into a structure manufactured at Versailles. As good democrats they began to oppress and mishandle the majority of the inhabitants. They tried gradually to enforce on the world their view that the Czech State had a special political and military mission to perform in the world. Former French Air Minister Cot has only recently explained this to us. According to his opinion, the task of Czechoslovakia is in case of war to bombard German towns and industrial works.

"This mission, however, is in direct contrast to the vital interests, to the wishes, and to the conception of life of a majority of the inhabitants of this State. But the majority of the inhabitants had to be quiet, as any protest against their treatment was regarded as an attack on the aims of this State and therefore in conflict with the Constitution. This Constitution, as it was made by democrats, was not rooted in the people but served only the political aims of those who oppressed the majority of the inhabitants. In view of these political aims, it had been found necessary to construct this Constitution in a manner giving the Czechs a predominant position in the State.

"He who opposes such encroachment is an enemy of the State and, according to democratic conceptions of the State, an outlaw. The so-called nation of the Czechs has thus been selected by Providence, which in this case made use of those who once designed Versailles, to see that no one rose against this purpose of the State. Should, however, some one belonging to the majority of the oppressed people of this nation protest against this, the nation may knock him down with force and kill him if it is necessary or desired. If this were a matter foreign to us and one that did not concern us, we would regard this case, as so many others, merely as an interesting illustration of the democratic conception of people's rights and the right of self-determination and simply take note of it.

"But it is something most natural that compels us Germans to take an interest in this problem. Among the majority of nationalities that are being suppressed in this State there are 3,500,000 Germans. That is about as many persons of our race as Denmark has inhabitants. These Germans, too, are creatures of God. The Almighty did not create them that they should be surrendered by a State construction made at Versailles to a foreign power that is hateful to them, and He has not created 7,000,000 Czechs in order that they should supervise 3,500,000 Germans or act as guardians for them and still less to do them violence and torture. The conditions in this nation are unbearable, as is generally known. Politically more than 3,500,000 people were robbed in the name of the right of self-determination of a certain Mr. Wilson of their self-determination and of their right to self-determination. Economically these people were deliberately ruined and afterward handed over to a slow process of extermination.

"These truths cannot be abolished by phrases. They are testified to by deeds. The misery of the Sudeten Germans is without end. They want to annihilate them. They are being oppressed in an inhuman and intolerable manner and treated in an undignified way. When 3,500,000 who belong to a people of almost 80,000,000 are not allowed to sing any song that the Czechs do not like because it does not please the Czechs, or are brutally struck for wearing white stockings because the Czechs do not like it, and do not want to see them, and are terrorized or maltreated because they greet with a form of salutation that is not agreeable to them, although they are greeting not Czechs but one another, and when they are pursued like wild beasts for every expression of their national life, this may be a matter of indifference to several representatives of our democracies or they may possibly even be sympathetic because it concerns only 3,500,000 Germans. I can only say to representatives of the democracies that this is not a matter of indifference to us.

"And I say that if these tortured creatures cannot obtain rights and assistance by themselves, they can obtain both from us. An end must be made of depriving these people of their rights. I have already said this quite clearly in my speech of February 22.

"It was a short-sighted piece of work when the statesmen at Versailles brought the abnormal structure of Czechoslovakia into being. It was possible to violate the demands of millions of another nationality only so long as the brother nation itself was suffering from the consequences of general maltreatment by the world.

"To believe that such a regime could go on sinning without hindrance forever was possible only through a scarcely credible degree of blindness. I declared in my speech of February 22 before the Reichstag that the Reich would not tolerate any further continued oppression of 3,500,000 Germans, and I hope that the foreign statesmen will be convinced that these were no mere words.

"The National Socialist State has consented to very great sacrifices indeed, very great national sacrifices for the sake of European peace; not only has it not cherished so-called thoughts of revenge, but on the contrary it has banished them from all its public and private life.

"In the course of the seventeenth century France took

Alsace and Lorraine from the old German Reich in the midst of peace. In 1870 to 1871, after a hard war that had been forced upon her, Germany demanded these territories back and obtained them. After the World War they were lost again. The minster of Strasbourg meant a great deal to us Germans. When we decided finally to renounce it, it was for the purpose of serving the cause of European peace in the future.

"Nobody could have forced us to give up these ideas of revenge of our own accord if we had not wanted to do so. We have given them up because we wanted once and for all to end this eternal dispute with France. At other frontiers also the Reich ordered that the same determined measures be taken and adopted the same attitude.

"National Socialism advanced, truly supported by the spirit of responsibility. We shouldered voluntarily the greatest sacrifices in the form of claims surrendered in order to preserve peace for Europe in the future and, above all, in order to have on our part a way for a reconciliation of nations. We have acted far more than merely from loyalty. Neither in the press nor in the films nor on the stage was propaganda carried out contrary to these decisions. Not even in literature was an exception tolerated. In this spirit I myself made an offer for a solution of the questions at issue in order to remove tension in Europe. We ourselves voluntarily restricted our power in an important field in a hope never to have to cross swords again with the nation in question.

"This was not done because we could not have built more than 35 per cent of its ships, but it was done in order to make a contribution toward a final lessening of tension, and appeasement in a serious situation. They immediately accepted it and confirmed an agreement that meant for Europe's peace more than all the talk made in Geneva's League of Nations. *Germany had definitely become reconciled to a large number of her frontiers. Germany is determined to accept these frontiers as unalterable and definite, and thereby give Europe a feeling of peace.*

"This self-restriction of Germany is obviously interpreted by many people as a sign of Germany's weakness. I wish to put this view right today. I think it would hardly serve European peace if I left any doubt about the following: Acceptance of these frontiers does not mean that Germany is disinterested in all European problems and particularly that she is indifferent to what is happening to 3,500,000 Germans and that she does not feel with them in their plight. We quite understand that the French and British defend their interests in the whole world. I may assure the statesmen in Paris and London that there are also German interests that we are determined to defend in all circumstances.

"May I remind you of my speech to the Reichstag in 1933, when for the first time I stated before the world that there may be national questions that I would take it upon me to fulfill in spite of all distress and danger that may be connected with them. No European nation has done more for peace than Germany. No nation has made greater sacrifices. But it must be realized that these sacrifices also have their limits and that the National Socialist State must not be confused with the Germany of Bethmann-Hollweg and Hertling.

"If I make this statement here, it is done especially because in the course of this year an event took place that forced us all to subject our attitude to certain correction. In this year, as you know, after endless postponement of any kind of plebiscite had occurred, local elections, at any rate, were to take place in Czechoslovakia. Even in Prague people were convinced of the untenable nature of the Czech situation. They were afraid of Germans joining up with other nationalities. They thought that at last measures must be taken to influence the result of the elections by bringing pressure on the conduct of the elections. The Czech Government discovered the idea that the only effective thing to do was brutal brow-beating. To give effect to this they decided to make a demonstration to the Sudeten Germans of the forces of the Czechoslovak State. Above all, the brute force of the Czechs' power must be displayed to warn them against representing their national interests and to make them vote accordingly. In order to make this demonstration plausible before the election, Dr. Benes and the Czech Government invented the lie that Germany had mobilized troops and was about to invade Czechoslovakia.

"I have the following statement to make on this subject today: There is nothing new about making such lying statements. Last year the press of other countries published the false news that 20,000 German soldiers had landed in Morocco. The Jewish fabricators of these press lies hoped to bring about war by this means. A statement to the French Ambassador sufficed to put an end to this lie. Also the Ambassador of another great power was immediately informed that there was not a word of truth in this Czech statement. This statement was repeated a second time and immediately brought to the notice of the Prague Government. But the Prague Government needed this lie as a pretext for their own monstrous work and terrorist oppression in influencing the elections.

"I can assure you in addition that, first, at that time not a single German soldier more was called up and, second, not a regiment marched to the frontier. At this time there was not one soldier not in his peacetime garrison. On the contrary, an order was given that anything that might appear like pressure on the Czechs on our side was to be avoided. Despite this, this base campaign took place in which the whole of Europe was mobilized with the object of holding elections under military pressure, brow-beating citizens and thus depriving them of their right to vote.

"For this purpose moral justification was needed so that no one should shrink from the unscrupulousness of plunging a great State and Europe into a great war. As Germany had no such intention, and indeed, on the contrary, was convinced that local elections would confirm the rights of the Sudeten Germans, nothing was done by the Reich Government. That, however, was made the occasion for saying, after nothing had happened, that Germany had drawn back in consequence of the agitation of the Czechs and the intervention of Great Britain and France.

"You all understand that a Great Power cannot suddenly submit a second time to such a base attack. In consequence I took the necessary precautions. I am a National Socialist and as such I am parrying every attack. I know exactly that by yielding to such an irreconcilable enemy as Czechoslovakia this enemy could never be reconciled but only incited to a still higher opinion of itself.

"The old German Reich is a warning for us. In its love for peace it went as far as self-sacrifice without thereby being able to prevent war. Conscious of this, I took very serious measures on May 28.

"First, the strengthening of the Army and air force was, on my order, considerably increased forthwith and immediately carried out.

"Second, I ordered an immediate extension of our fortifications in the West.

"I may assure you that since May 28 the most gigantic fortifications that ever existed are under construction there. With the same aim in view, I have entrusted the Inspector General of German Road Constructions, Dr. Todt, with a new task. He has accomplished one of the greatest works of organization of all time. On the construction of the defenses in the West there are now 278,000 workmen in Dr. Todt's army. In addition, there are, further, 84,000 workmen and 100,000 men of the labor service as well as numerous engineer and infantry battalions.

"The German railways are taking to these districts daily 8,000 cars of material apart from the materials transported by motor vehicles.

"The daily consumption of gravel is more than 100,000 tons. Before the beginning of winter, Germany's fortifications in the West will be finished. Their power of defense is already in existence to its full extent. After completion it will comprise 17,000 armored and concrete fortifications. Behind this front of steel and concrete, which is laid out in three and partly in four lines, of a total depth up to fifty kilometers, there stands a German people in arms.

"These most gigantic efforts of all time have been made at my request in the interest of peace. In no circumstances shall I be willing any more to regard with endless tranquillity a continuation of the oppression of German compatriots in Czechoslovakia.

"Herr Benes indulges in tactics and speeches. He is trying to organize negotiations to clear up questions of procedure on the lines of Geneva and to make small concessions. This cannot go on forever. This is not a matter of phrases; it is of right—that is, of violated right.

"What the Germans demand is the right of self-determination, which every other nation also possesses. It is not up to Herr Benes to give the Sudeten Germans gifts. They have the right to claim a life of their own just as much as any other people.

"If the democracies, however, should be convinced that they must in this case protect with all their means the oppressors of Germans, then this will have grave consequences. I believe I am serving peace the more if I do not leave any doubts about this. I did not raise the claim that Germany may oppress 3,500,000 French or then that 3,500,000 English shall be surrendered to Germany for oppression. But I demand that the oppression of 3,500,000 Germans in Czechoslovakia shall cease and be replaced by the free right of self-determination. We would regret it if thereby our relations with other European nations should suffer harm. However, we are not to be blamed. Moreover, it is up to the Czechoslovak Government to discuss matters with the authorized representatives of the Sudeten Germans and bring about an understanding in this or that way.

"My business and the business of us all, however, my comrades, is to see today that right does not become injustice in this case, for German comrades are concerned. Moreover, I am not willing to allow a second Palestine to be created here in the heart of Germany by actions of other statesmen.

"The poor Arabs are defenseless and perhaps deserted. The Germans of Czechoslovakia, however, are neither defenseless nor deserted. I believe I must state this especially at this party convention at which for the first time representatives of our German Austrian legion take part. They know best how much pain it causes to be separated from a mother country. They, too, will first understand the meaning of my statements today. They will also agree with me most enthusiastically if I state before the entire nation that we would not deserve to be Germans if we were not willing to adopt such an attitude and bear the consequences in this or that way arising from it.

"If we remember the exacting demands that in past years even small nations believed they could address to Germany, the only explanation that we can find is that there is scant willingness to see the German Reich as a State that is more than a temporary upstart.

"Standing in Rome in the spring of this year I realized how the history of mankind is viewed and judged in intervals that are too short and therefore inadequate. The history of a millennium comprised only a few successions of generations. What becomes exhausted in the present can rise up again in the same time. The Italy and Germany of today are proof of this. They are rejuvenated nations that one may describe as new in this sense.

"But this youth does not rest on new soil, but on old historic soil. The Roman Empire begins to breathe again; however, though historically and infinitely younger, it is likewise no new creation in its national new form.

"I had the insignia of the old Reich brought to Nuremberg in order to induce not only my own nation but also the whole world to consider that more than a thousand years before the discovery of a new world a mighty Germanic Deutsches Reich existed. Dynasties came and disappeared. Outer forms have changed. The people today have been rejuvenated, but substantially they always remained the same. The German Reich has slumbered a long time and the German people have now awakened and taken their thousand-year-old crown to themselves.

"For us, the historical witnesses of this revival, there is proud joy and a humble sense of gratitude to the Almighty. For the rest of the world it should equally be a suggestion and a lesson that they should study history again from a higher vantage point and a lesson not to fall into their old mistakes again.

"The new Italian Roman Empire and the German Empire are in all truth very old creations. People do not need to love them, but no power in the world can any more remove them. . . ."

Press

Le Temps, September 14—Chancellor Hitler left matters in an indecisive state. He did not close the door against a peaceable solution of the Sudeten German problem, he put no obstacles in the way of continued negotiations within the framework of Lord Runciman's mediation. But he voiced what were but thinly veiled threats for the future, which were not calculated to dispel the uneasiness which now troubles the life of Europe. The vehement tone of his speech is regrettable. It is quite unprecedented, we believe, that the head of one state should express himself publicly about the head of another in the terms which Chancellor Hitler used in speaking of President Benes. The French will keep in mind the Chancellor's declaration that he would like to put an end to all hostility between Germany and France.

London Times, September 13—In his concluding speech to the Nuremberg rally last night, Herr Hitler put forward a firm demand for self-determination on behalf of the Sudeten German subjects of Czechoslovakia. In other respects the speech fell short of expectations. It contained no clear-cut program for a solution of the Central European problem. But at least any temptation to make a coup, which the sight of his surrounding soldiers, airmen, massed storm troopers, and enthusiastic followers might have prompted, has been resisted for the present. The speech in fact, though not altogether reassuring, was not violently disturbing.

New York Times, September 13—Herr Hitler did not declare war in the anxiously awaited speech delivered in Nuremberg yesterday, but no one who listened to that clear, harsh explosive voice coming over the air to the accompaniment of a thunderous undertone of "Sieg Heil!" received any assurance that he meant peace. . . .

•

SPEECH OF SEPTEMBER 26, 1938

Berlin

Background

September 13—Czech Government proclaims martial law. The Sudeten party replies with an ultimatum demanding its repeal.

September 14—Chamberlain offers to go and visit Hitler at any place he chooses for the meeting.

Japanese Foreign Office issues a statement praising Hitler's demands and assuring him that Japan is ever ready to join Germany and Italy against "Red operations" if necessary.

September 15—Chamberlain flies to Berchtesgaden. In his

meeting with Hitler, the latter agrees to refrain from hostilities while Chamberlain consults his Cabinet concerning Hitler's proposal for the return of the Sudetenland to the Reich on the basis of "self-determination."

September 16—Czech Government issues warrant for the arrest of Henlein on charges of high treason.

Chamberlain returns to London.

September 17—Henlein orders the establishment of a *Freikorps* and issues a call to arms.

September 18—Daladier and Bonnet arrive in London.

In Trieste Mussolini calls for a "totalitarian solution" of the problem, i.e., a plebiscite.

In the evening the British and French Ministers agree to tell Czechoslovakia to accept Hitler's demands.

September 21—The Czech Cabinet accepts the ultimatum.

September 22—Chamberlain flies to Godesberg to see Hitler a second time. In Prague, the Hodza Cabinet resigns. General Syrovy takes charge.

September 23—Chamberlain finds that Hitler's demands have stiffened. The interview between them breaks up, but after an exchange of written notes, Chamberlain agrees to transmit Hitler's new propositions, but without any recommendation. Czechs order general mobilization.

England and France speed up their military preparations.

September 24—Speaking in Padua, Mussolini reveals that the memorandum handed to Chamberlain by Hitler has the character of an ultimatum, expiring October 1.

September 25—The Czech Government notifies London and Paris that it cannot accept Hitler's proposals, which, it states, go far beyond the Anglo-French plan previously accepted.

September 26—President Roosevelt sends a personal appeal to Hitler and Benes asking them to settle their controversy by negotiation.

Daladier, Bonnet, and General Gamelin confer with the British Cabinet. Chamberlain gives them the assurance that

England will assist France in case France decides to support Czechoslovakia.

Chamberlain sends a personal letter to Hitler making a last appeal before Hitler speaks in the Sportpalast.

The Speech

"GERMAN fellow-countrymen and fellow-countrywomen, on February 20 before the members of the German Reichstag I expressed for the first time a fundamental demand of an absolute character. At that time the whole nation heard me and it understood me. *One* statesman failed to share in this understanding. He has been removed and the promise which I made at that time has been fulfilled. Then for the second time I spoke on this same demand before the Parteitag of the Reich. And again the nation heard this demand. Today I now come before the nation and for the first time I speak before the people itself, just as I did in the time of our great fight, and you know what that means. For the world there is no longer room for any doubt: now it is not a leader or one man who speaks: now the German people speaks.

"If I am now the spokesman of this German people, then I know: At this second the whole people in its millions agrees word for word with my words, confirms them, and makes them its own oath! Let the other statesmen ask themselves whether that is also true in their case!

"The question which in these last months and weeks has moved us so profoundly has long been familiar to us: *it is not so much Czechoslovakia: it is rather Mr. Benes.* In this name is concentrated all that which today moves millions, which causes them to despair or fills them with a fanatical resolution.

'But why was it that this question could rise to such significance? I wish, my fellow-countrymen, quite briefly to explain to you once again the character and the aims of German foreign policy.

"In contradistinction to the many democratic States, German foreign policy is fixed and conditioned by a *Weltanschauung*. The *Weltanschauung* of this new Reich is directed to maintaining and to securing the existence of our German people. We have no interest in oppressing other peoples. We wish to seek our blessedness after our own fashion: the others can do so in their own way. This view, which in our *Weltanschauung* is racially conditioned, leads to a limitation of our foreign policy: that is to say, the aims of our foreign policy are not unlimited, they are not determined by chance, but they are grounded on the determination to serve the German people alone, to maintain it in our world and to safeguard its existence.

"What is then the position today? You know that formerly under the watchword 'The Right of the Peoples to Self-Determination' the German people, as well as others, was filled with a belief in super-State help and therefore allowed itself to the last extreme to renounce any resort to its own strength. . . . You know that this trust of those days was most shamefully betrayed! The result was the Treaty of Versailles, and of the frightful consequences of this Treaty you are all aware. . . ."

"Although now today through our own efforts we have once more become free and strong, yet we are not moved by any hatred against other nations. We bear no grudge. What happened we know: the peoples are not to be held responsible for that, but only a small conscienceless clique of international profit-makers seeking their business ends, who do not hesitate, if necessary, to let whole nations go to ruin if only their despicable interests are served. Therefore we nurse no hatred against neighboring peoples, and that we have also proved.

"We had hardly begun the restoration of Germany to equality of rights when, as the clearest sign of our renunciation of a policy of '*Revanche*' upon the rest of the world, I proposed a series of agreements which were intended to lead to a limitation of armaments. . . ."

"When thus for two years I had made to the world offer on offer, and these offers always met with rejection and then once more rejection, I gave orders that the German Army should be brought to the best attainable condition. *And now I can proudly admit: we did then certainly complete an armament such as the world has never yet seen.* I have offered disarmament as long as it was possible. But when that was rejected then I formed, I admit, no half-hearted decision. I am a National Socialist and an old German front-line soldier!

"If they do not wish the world to be without arms, good: then, German people, do you, too, now carry your arms!

"I have in fact armed in these five years. I have spent milliards on this armament: that the German people must now know! I have seen to it that a new army should be provided with the most modern armament known. I have given to my friend Goering the order: Make me now an air-arm which can protect Germany in the face of any conceivable attack. Thus we have built up a military force of which today the German people can be proud and which the world will respect if at any time it makes its appearance.

"We have created for our protection the best air-defense, the best tank-defense which is to be found on earth. In these five years, day and night, work has been carried on. Only in one single sphere have I succeeded in bringing about an understanding. To this subject I shall return. But in spite of this I have continued to follow up the ideas of the limitation of armaments and of a policy of disarmament. I have really in these years pursued a practical peace policy. I have approached all the apparently impossible problems with the firm resolve to solve them peacefully even when there was the danger of making more or less serious renunciations on Germany's part. I myself am a front-line soldier and I know how grave a thing war is. I wanted to spare the German people such an evil. Problem after problem I have tackled with the set purpose to make every effort to render possible a peaceful solution.

"The most difficult problem which faced me was the relation between Germany and Poland. There was a danger that the conception of a 'hereditary enmity' might take possession of our people and of the Polish people. That I wanted to prevent. I know quite well that I should not have succeeded if Poland at that time had had a democratic constitution. For these democracies which are overflowing with phrases about peace are the most bloodthirsty instigators of war. But Poland at that time was governed by no democracy but by a *man.* In the course of barely a year it was possible to conclude an agreement which, in the first instance for a period of ten years, on principle removed the danger of a conflict. We are all convinced that this agreement will bring with it a permanent pacification. *We realize that here are two peoples which must live side by side and that neither of them can destroy the other.* A State with a population of thirty-three millions will always strive for an access to the sea. *A way to an understanding had therefore to be found. It has been found and it will be ever further developed.* The decisive point is that both Governments and all reasonable and intelligent folk in both peoples and countries should have the firm determination continuously to improve relations. It was a real achievement in the cause of peace which is of more value than all the chatter in the Palace of the League of Nations at Geneva.

"At this time I have also sought gradually to establish good and lasting relations with the other nations. *We have given guarantees for the States in the West, and to all those States bordering on our frontiers we have given assurances of the inviolability of their territory so far as Germany is concerned. These are no mere words. That is our sacred determination.* We have no interest in breaking the peace.

"These German offers also met with a growing understanding. Gradually ever more peoples are freeing themselves from that insane infatuation of Geneva which, I might say, serves no policy of an obligation to peace but rather a policy of obligation to war. They are freeing themselves, and they begin to see the problems soberly: they are ready for understanding and for peace.

"I went further and offered the hand to England. I have voluntarily renounced the idea of ever again entering upon a competition in fleet-building in order to give to the British Empire the feeling of security. And that I have not done because I was not able to build above the limit fixed: let no one have any illusions on that score: I acted thus solely in order to maintain a lasting peace between the two peoples. But it must be admitted that here one condition must be observed; it will not do that one party should say: *I am determined never again to wage war* and to this end I offer you a voluntary limitation of my armaments at 35 per cent, while the other party declares: If it suits me I shall wage war again from time to time. Such an agreement is morally justified only when both peoples solemnly promise that they are determined never again to wage war with each other. Germany has this determination. We all desire to hope that amongst the English people those who share this determination may gain the upper hand!

"I went further. Directly after the restoration of the Saar territory which was decided by a plebiscite *I declared to France that there were now absolutely no differences outstanding between us. I said that for us the Alsace-Lorraine question no longer existed.* It is a frontier district. The people of this country during the most recent decades has never really been asked for its own opinion. We have the feeling that the inhabitants of this province will be happiest if they are not fought over again. All of us do not wish for any war with France. *We want nothing from France—positively nothing!* And when the Saar territory had returned to the Reich thanks to the loyal execution of the treaties by France—that

I desire to reaffirm in this place—I solemnly declared: for the future all territorial differences between France and Germany have been removed. Today I cannot any longer see any difference between us. Here are two great peoples who both wish to work and live. And they will live their lives best if they work together.

"After this irrevocable renunciation, made once for all, I turned to a further problem which was easier to solve than others because here the common *weltanschaulich* basis forms a favorable condition for a readier mutual understanding—the problem of the relation of Germany to Italy.

"It is true that the solution of this problem is only in part to be put to my credit, in part it is due to the rare genius of that great man whom the Italian people has the good fortune to be able to possess as its leader. This relation has long ago overstepped the sphere of a pure economic or political expediency: it has passed beyond treaties and alliances and has become a true, strong union of hearts. Here an axis has been formed represented by two peoples who both have come to be united, alike in ideology and in politics, in a close indissoluble friendship.

"Here, too, I have taken a final step—once and for all—fully conscious of my responsibility before my fellow-countrymen. I have banished from the world a problem that from henceforth simply does not exist for us. However bitter that may be for the individual, with us in the last resort it is the interest of the people as a whole which stands above everything. And this interest is: to be able to work in peace! This whole work for peace, my fellow-countrymen, is no mere empty phrase, but this work is reinforced through deeds which no lying mouth can destroy.

"Two problems still remained. Here I was bound to make a reservation. Ten million Germans found themselves beyond the frontiers of the Reich in two great closed areas of settlement, Germans who wished to return to their Reich as their homeland. This number—ten millions—is no small affair: here it is a question of a quarter as many people as make up the population of France. And if for over forty years France never gave up her claim to the few millions of the French population of Alsace-Lorraine, then we had a right before God and the world to maintain our claim to these ten million Germans. My fellow-countrymen, there is a point at which concession must cease because otherwise it would become ruinous weakness. I should have no right to take my stand before the history of Germany had I been willing in simple indifference to sacrifice these ten millions. I should then also have no moral right to be the leader of this people. I have taken upon myself sacrifices and renunciations enough: here was the limit beyond which I could not go!

"How true that was has been proved through the plebiscite in Austria. At that time a glowing profession of faith was made, a profession of faith such as the rest of the world had certainly not expected. But we know by experience: a plebiscite for the democracies is superfluous or even harmful the moment it does not lead to the result that they themselves expect. In spite of this, this problem was solved to the satisfaction of the whole great German people.

"And now before us stands the last problem that must be solved and will be solved. It is the last territorial claim which I have to make in Europe, but it is the claim from which I will not recede and which, God willing, I will make good.

"The history of the problem is as follows: in 1918 under the watchword 'The Right of the Peoples to Self-Determination' Central Europe was torn in pieces and was newly formed by certain crazy so-called 'statesmen.' Without regard for the origin of the peoples, without regard for either their wish as a nation or for economic necessities, Central Europe at that time was broken up into atoms and new so-called States were arbitrarily formed. To this procedure Czechoslovakia owes its existence. This Czech State began with a single lie and the father of this lie was named Benes. This Mr. Benes at that time appeared in Versailles and he first of all gave the assurance that there was a Czechoslovak nation. He was forced to invent this lie in order to give to the slender number of his own fellow-countrymen a somewhat greater range and thus a fuller justification. And the Anglo-Saxon statesmen, who were, as always, not very adequately versed in respect of questions of geography or nationality, did not at that time find it necessary to test these assertions of Mr. Benes. Had they done so, they could have established the fact that there is no such thing as a Czechoslovak nation but only Czechs and Slovaks and that the Slovaks did not wish to have anything to do with the Czechs but . . ."

"So in the end, through Mr. Benes, these Czechs annexed Slovakia. Since this State did not seem fitted to live, out of hand three and a half million Germans were taken in violation of their right to self-determination and their wish for self-determination. Since even that did not suffice, over a million Magyars had to be added, then some Carpathian Russians, and at last several hundred thousand Poles.

"That is this State which then later proceeded to call itself Czechoslovakia—in violation of the right of the peoples to self-determination, in violation of the clear wish and will of the nations to which this violence had been done. When I speak to you here it goes without saying that I should sympathize with the fate of all these oppressed peoples, with the fate of Poles, Hungarians, and Ukrainians. I am naturally spokesman only for the fate of my Germans.

"At the time Mr. Benes lied this State into being, he gave a solemn pledge to divide it on the model of the Swiss system into cantons, for amongst the democratic statesmen there were some who still had some twinges of conscience. We all know how Mr. Benes has redeemed his pledge to introduce this cantonal system. He began his reign of terror. Even at that time the Germans already attempted to protest against this arbitrary violence. They were shot down. After that a war of extermination began. In these years of the 'peaceful' development of Czechoslovakia nearly 600,000 Germans had to leave Czechoslovakia. This happened for a very simple reason: otherwise they would have had to starve!

"The whole development from the year 1918 up to 1938 showed one thing clearly: Mr. Benes was determined slowly to exterminate the German element. And this to a certain extent he has achieved. He has hurled countless people into the profoundest misery. He has managed to make millions of people fearful and anxious. Through the continuous employment of his methods of terrorism he has succeeded in reducing to silence these millions, while at the same time it also became clear what were the 'international' duties of this State.

"No longer was any secret made of the fact that this State was intended, if necessary, to be employed against Germany. A French Minister for Air, Pierre Cot, has expressed this wish quite soberly: 'We need the State,' he said, 'because from this State German business life and German industry can be most easily destroyed with bombs.' And then bolshevism uses this State as the gateway through which it can find entry. It is not we who have sought this contact with bolshevism, but bolshevism uses this State in order to possess a canal leading into Central Europe.

"And now the shameless part of this story begins. This State whose Government is in the hands of a minority compels the other nationalities to co-operate in a policy which will oblige them one of these days to shoot at their own brothers. Mr. Benes demands of the German: 'If I wage war against Germany, then you have to shoot against the Germans. And if you refuse to do this, you are a traitor against the State and I will have you yourself shot.' And he makes the same demand of Hungary and Poland. He demands of the Slovaks that they should support aims to which the Slovak people are completely indifferent. For the Slovak people wish to have peace—and not adventures. Mr. Benes thus actually turns these folk either into traitors to their country or traitors to their people. Either they betray their people, are ready to fire on their fellow-countrymen, or Mr. Benes says: 'You are traitors to your country and you will be shot for that by me.' Can there be anything more shameless than to compel folk of another people, in certain circumstances, to fire on their own fellow-countrymen only because a ruinous, evil, and criminal Government so demands it? I can here assert: when we had occupied Austria, my first order was: no Czech needs to serve, rather he must not serve, in the German Army. I have not driven him to a conflict with his conscience.

"But he who opposes Mr. Benes is also sent to his death in the economic sphere. This fact the democratic world apostles cannot lie away. In this State of Mr. Benes the consequences for the nationalities have been appalling. I speak only for the Germans. It is they who have the highest death-rate of all the German tribes, their poverty in children is the highest, their unemployment is the most frightful. How long is such a condition to last? For twenty years the Germans in Czechoslovakia have had to watch these conditions and the German people in the Reich has had to look on these conditions, not because it was at any time prepared to accept this state of affairs but simply because it was powerless and in the world of democracies could not help itself in face of these torturers. Yes, when anywhere a traitor to his country is imprisoned, when a man who from the pulpit hurls down his abuse is taken into custody, then there is excitement in England and indignation in America. But when hundreds of thousands are driven into exile, when tens of thousands come into prison, and thousands are butchered, that does not move these true-blue world democrats in the slightest degree. We have learned much in these years. For them we feel a profound contempt.

"There is but a single Great Power and one man at its head who have understanding for the distress of our people. And that is—I may, I think, give his name—my great friend, Benito Mussolini. What he has done at this time and the attitude taken up by the Italian people—this we shall not forget! And if some time the hour of a similar distress should come for Italy, then I will stand before the German people and call upon it to take the same attitude. And even then it will not be two States which act in self-defense, but a bloc!

"In the Reichstag on February 20 of this year I stated that in the life of the ten million Germans beyond our frontiers there must come a change. Mr. Benes has now taken a different course. He instituted a still more ruthless oppression. He set on foot a still greater terrorism. There began a period of disbanding of associations, of vetos, confiscations, and the like. This continued until at last May 21 came. And you cannot deny, my fellow-countrymen, that we have exhibited a truly unexampled patience. This May 21 was intolerable. I have given its history at the Parteitag of the Reich. In Czechoslovakia at last an election was to take place which could not be postponed any longer. Then Mr. Benes invented a way to intimidate the Germans in Czechoslovakia: the military occupation of the districts.

"This military occupation even now he intends to continue for the future in the hope that no one will venture to oppose him so long as his myrmidons are in the country. It was that insolent lie of May 21—that Germany had mobilized—that now had to serve to cover the Czech mobilization, to excuse it, and to supply a motive. What followed you know: an infamous international world-wide agitation.

"Germany had not called a man to the colors: it never thought for a moment to solve this problem by military intervention. Still I always hoped that the Czechs at the last minute would realize that this tyranny could not be maintained any longer. But Mr. Benes adopted the standpoint that, protected by France and by England, one could do anything with Germany with impunity—nothing could happen to him. And above all: when all other strings failed, behind him stood Soviet Russia.

"And so the answer of this man was now more than before: Shoot down, arrest, imprison—the fate of all those who in any way failed to please him. Thus it was that there came my demand in Nuremberg. This demand was quite clear: for the first time I there expressed the claim that now at last—almost twenty years since the statements of President Wilson—for these three and a half millions the right of self-determination must come into force. And once again Mr. Benes gave his answer: more deaths, more imprisonments, more arrests. The Germans began perforce to flee.

"And then came England. I have told Mr. Chamberlain quite distinctly what we regard now as the sole possibility of a solution. It is the most natural solution that there can be. I know that *all* nationalities no longer wish to remain with Dr. Benes, but I am in the first place spokesman of the Germans, and for these Germans I have now spoken and asserted that I am no longer willing to look on calm and inactive and see how this madman in Prague thinks that he can, undisturbed, ill-treat three and a half million human beings.

"And I have left him in no doubt that now at last German patience has really come to an end: I have left him in no doubt that, though it is a characteristic of our German mentality to bear something for a long time and again and again to raise no protest, yet one day the moment comes when it has to stop! And now England and France have sent to Czechoslovakia the only possible demand—to set free the German area and to surrender it to the Reich.

"We are now accurately informed on the conversations which Dr. Benes conducted at that time. Faced by the declaration of England and of France that they would no longer support Czechoslovakia if at last the fate of these peoples was not changed and the areas liberated, Mr. Benes found a way of escape. He conceded that these districts must be surrendered. That was what he stated, but what did he do? He did not surrender the area but the Germans he now drives out! And that is now the point at which the game comes to an end. Mr. Benes had hardly spoken when he began his military subjugation afresh—only with still greater violence.

We see the appalling figures: on one day 10,000 fugitives, on the next 20,000, a day later, already 37,000, again two days later 41,000, then 62,000, then 78,000: now 90,000, 107,000, 137,000 and today 214,000. Whole stretches of country were depopulated, villages are burned down, attempts are made to smoke out the Germans with hand-grenades and gas. Mr. Benes, however, sits in Prague and is convinced: 'Nothing can happen to me: in the end England and France stand behind me.'

"And now, my fellow-countrymen, I believe that the time has come when one must mince matters no longer. If anyone for twenty years has borne such a shame, such a disgrace, such a misfortune as we have done, then in very truth it cannot be denied that he is a lover of peace. When anyone has the patience which we have shown then in very truth it cannot be said that he is bellicose. For in the last resort Mr. Benes has seven million Czechs, but here there stands a people of over seventy-five millions.

"I have now placed a memorandum containing a last and final German proposal in the hands of the British Government. This memorandum contains nothing save the putting into effect of what Mr. Benes has already promised. The content of this proposal is very simple:

"That area which in its people is German and has the wish to be German comes to Germany and that, too, not only when Mr. Benes has succeeded in driving out perhaps one or two million Germans, but now, and that immediately! I have here chosen that frontier which on the basis of the material which has existed for decades on the division of people and language in Czechoslovakia is the just frontier-line. But in spite of this I am more just than Mr. Benes and I have no wish to exploit the power which we possess. I have therefore laid it down from the outset that this area will be placed under German supremacy because it is essentially settled by Germans. The final delimitation of the frontier, however, I then leave to the vote of our fellow-countrymen themselves who are in the area! I have therefore laid down that in this area there must then be held a plebiscite. And in order that no one can say that the procedure of the plebiscite might be unjust, I have chosen as the basis for this plebiscite the Statute that governed the Saar Plebiscite.

"Now I am and was prepared, so far as I am concerned, to allow a plebiscite to be held throughout the area. But Mr. Benes and his friends objected. They wished that a plebiscite should be allowed only in certain parts of the area. Good, I have yielded the point. I was even prepared to allow the plebiscite to be subject to the inspection of international Commissions of Control.

"I went even further and agreed to leave the delimitation of the frontier to a German-Czech Commission. Mr. Chamberlain suggested: might it not be an international Commission? To this, too, I agreed. I even wished during this period of the plebiscite to withdraw again the troops, and I have today declared my readiness to invite for this period the British Legion, which offered me its services, to go into these districts and there maintain calm and order. And I was further ready to allow the international Commission to fix the final frontier and to hand over all details of procedure to a Commission composed of Germans and Czechs.

"The content of this memorandum is nothing else than the practical execution of what Mr. Benes has already promised, and that, too, under the most complete international guarantees. Mr. Benes now says that this memorandum is 'a new situation.' And in what, in fact, does this 'new situation' consist? It consists in this: that this time—exceptionally—the promise made by Mr. Benes must also be kept! That is for Mr. Benes the 'new situation.' What is there that Mr. Benes has not promised at some time in his life? And no promise has been kept! Now for the first time he has got to keep to something.

"Mr. Benes says: 'We cannot go back from this area.' Mr. Benes has then understood the transfer of this area to mean that the legal title is recognized as belonging to the German Reich but the area is still to be subject to the violence of the Czechs. That is now past!

"I have demanded that now after twenty years Mr. Benes should at last be compelled to come to terms with the truth. *On October 1 he will have to hand over to us this area.*

"Mr. Benes now places his hopes on the world! And he and his diplomats make no secret of the fact. They state: it is our hope that Chamberlain will be overthrown, that Daladier will be removed, that on every hand revolutions are on the way. They place their hope on Soviet Russia. He still thinks then that he will be able to evade the fulfillment of his obligations.

"And then I can say only one thing: now two men stand arrayed one against the other: there is Mr. Benes, and here stand I. We are two men of a different make-up. In the great struggle of the peoples, while Mr. Benes was sneaking about through the world, I as a decent German soldier did my duty. And now today I stand over against this man as the soldier of my people!

"I have only a few statements still to make: I am grateful to Mr. Chamberlain for all his efforts. I have assured him that the German people desires nothing else than peace, but I have also told him that I cannot go back behind the limits set to our patience. *I have further assured him, and I repeat it here, that when this problem is solved there is for Germany no further territorial problem in Europe. And I have further assured him that at the moment when Czechoslovakia solves her problems, that means when the Czechs have come to terms with their other minorities, and that peaceably and not through oppression, then I have no further interest in the Czech State. And that is guaranteed to him! We want no Czechs!*

"But in the same way I desire to state before the German people that with regard to the problem of the Sudeten Germans my patience is now at an end! I have made Mr. Benes an offer which is nothing but the carrying into effect of what he himself has promised. The decision now lies in his hands: Peace or War! He will either accept this offer and now at last give to the Germans their freedom, or we will go and fetch this freedom for ourselves. The world must take note that in four and a half years of war and through the long years of my political life there is one thing which no one could ever cast in my teeth: I have never been a coward!

"Now I go before my people as its first soldier and behind me—that the world should know—there marches a people and a different people from that of 1918!

"If at that time a wandering scholar was able to inject into our people the poison of democratic catchwords—the people of today is no longer the people that it was then. Such catchwords are for us like wasp-stings: they cannot hurt us: we are now immune.

"In this hour the whole German people will unite with me! It will feel my will to be its will. Just as in my eyes it is its future and its fate which give me the commission for my action. And we wish now to make our will as strong as it was in the time of our fight, the time when I, as a simple unknown soldier, went forth to conquer a Reich and never doubted of success and final victory. Then there gathered close about me a band of brave men and brave women, and they went with me. And so I ask you, my German people, take your stand behind me, man by man, and woman by woman.

"In this hour we all wish to form a common will and that will must be stronger than every hardship and every danger. And if this will is stronger than hardship and danger then one day it will break down hardship and danger.

"We are determined!

"Now let Mr. Benes make his choice!"

Press

Le Temps, September 28—The part of the Fuehrer's speech which was most eagerly awaited was that which concerned the present crisis. Leaving aside the confused outpouring of invective against Dr. Benes, and the soft words aimed at Mr. Chamberlain, this part of M. Hitler's speech seems to be fundamentally a justification of the Godesberg memorandum and a reminder to the Czechs that they must choose between peace and war. M. Hitler promised guarantees to the diminished frontier of Czechoslovakia. M. Hitler also declared that after the Sudeten problem there would be no other territorial problems in Europe.

London Times (editorial), September 27—Herr Hitler's speech in Berlin yesterday was a tempestuous and rather offensive statement of what is admitted to be a perfectly reasonable cause—the right of the Sudeten Germans to be united with the Reich. A great part of it was taken up with abuse of Czechoslovakia and vilification of President Benes. The language was violent and unmeasured, but—and this is most important of all—he did not seem absolutely to close the door to negotiation.

New York Times (editorial), September 27—The announcement that Great Britain and Russia will join France in a triple front if Germany invades Czechoslovakia is a clear and momentous answer to Hitler. . . . The last word is now his. He can turn back to his original terms. Or he can use his one-man power to lead his own people to destruction. At last the issue is clearly joined. If as "the first soldier" of the German nation he marches into Czechoslovakia, he will be met by such a coalition of force that only a man lost to all sense of responsibility and all contact with reality would risk the certain disaster that course entails, for himself, for his country, for the world.

SPEECH OF OCTOBER 3, 1938

Eger, Czechoslovakia

Background

September 27—Hitler tells Sir Horace Wilson, Chamberlain's envoy, that German "action" will begin the next day at 2 P.M.

Hitler reviews troops marching through Berlin.

Roosevelt addresses new appeal to Hitler, suggesting a conference of all the nations concerned in the dispute.

The British Fleet is mobilized.

September 28—British Parliament assembles to hear Chamberlain's report on the situation. The Prime Minister interrupts his speech to announce that Hitler has invited him to go to Munich the next day. Parliament adjourns to October 3.

September 29—Hitler, Mussolini, Chamberlain, and Daladier meet in Munich. The Czechs are not invited to the conference.

September 30—At 1 A.M. the Munich agreement is signed.

Before leaving Munich, Chamberlain signs a declaration with Hitler expressing the desire of Germany and England never to go to war with one another.

On his return to London, Chamberlain is greeted by an enthusiastic crowd. Chamberlain says that the Munich settlement means "peace with honor" and "peace for our time."

Similar demonstrations greet Daladier in Paris.

October 1—German troops begin to occupy Zone I in Czechoslovakia.

Duff Cooper, First Lord of the Admiralty, resigns in protest against Munich.

The French demobilize.

October 3—Hitler enters Czechoslovakia while his troops occupy Zones II and III.

The Speech

"THROUGH me the whole German people greets you. . . . This greeting is also a vow: never shall this land in the future be torn from the Reich! Over this Great German Reich lies for protection the German shield, and guarding it the German sword. You yourselves are a part of this protection. From henceforth like all other Germans you will have to bear your part of the burden. For it is the pride of us all that every son of Germany takes his share not only in the joys of Germany but also in our duties, and if necessary in our sacrifices.

"For you the nation was ready to draw the sword. You will be just as ready to do so if ever German soil or German people is threatened. . . ."

"Now begin your march which leads into the great German future. In this hour we wish to render thanks to the Almighty that He has guarded us on our path in the past, and we would implore Him that in the future, too, he would go with us and prosper our way."

●

SPEECH OF OCTOBER 4, 1938

Carlsbad, Czechoslovakia

"IT WAS a hard decision which brought me to this place. Behind this decision stood the will, if necessary, to call force to my aid in order to make you free. We wish to be only the happier and the more thankful that this last and gravest appeal was not necessary to procure for us our rights. . . ."

"I did not know how or by what way I should one day come here. *But that I would stand here one day, that I knew!* If I now stand before you here, it is not only you who have to thank me, but I would also thank you for your loyalty, your affection, and your readiness for sacrifice."

Press

New York Times, October 5—Chancellor Adolf Hitler himself came here this afternoon and made a short speech from a theater balcony to a great crowd filling the square below. . . . Only one dramatic utterance stood out. "I always knew," said Herr Hitler, "that one day I would stand where I am now, but I did not know how it would come about."

•

SPEECH OF OCTOBER 5, 1938

Sportpalast, Berlin

Background

1938

October 4—The French Cabinet decides to recognize Italy's conquest of Ethiopia.

October 5—Eduard Benes resigns as President of Czechoslovakia.

The Speech

"WHEN six years ago I took over the leadership of the Reich one of our so-called 'statesmen' of that day said: 'Now this man has taken the decisive step. Up to now he has been popular, because he has been in opposition. Now he must govern and we shall see in six or eight weeks how his popularity will look'! Six years—not six weeks only—have passed and I believe that they have been the most decisive years for German history. The most characteristic feature of this period is the close unity of the German people. What I have achieved in these six years was possible only because I had standing behind me the *whole* German people. The problems which faced us no single man could solve unaided: only when he could speak and, if necessary, also act in the name of the whole German people could he master these questions. . . ."

"During the last few months and weeks I have had in my foreign policy a great helper and previously, in my last speech in this hall [the *Sportpalast*], I expressed my thanks to the man who took his stand in support of Germany as a true, great friend, Benito Mussolini. He has thrown into the scale of a just solution the entire force not only of his own genius but of the power which stands behind him. I must also thank the two other great statesmen who at the last minute recognized the historical hour, declared themselves ready to give their support to the solution of one of Europe's most burning problems and who thereby made it possible for me, too, to offer the hand towards an understanding. But above all my thanks fly to the German people which in these long months has never deserted me. . . . I am proud of my German people! I hope that in a few days the problem of the Sudeten Germans will be finally solved. By October 10 we shall have occupied all the areas which belong to us. Thus one of Europe's most serious crises will be ended, and all of us, not only in Germany but those far beyond our frontiers, will then in this year for the first time really rejoice at the Christmas festival. It should for us all be a true Festival of Peace. . . ."

"Above us all stands the motto: 'no one in the world will help us if we do not help ourselves.' This programme of self-help is a proud and manly programme. It is a different programme from that of my predecessors who continually ran round through the world, going a-begging now in Versailles, then in Geneva, now in Lausanne or at some conference or other elsewhere. It is a prouder thing that to-day we Germans are determined to solve our own problems and to help ourselves. . . ."

"We have been witnesses of a great turning-point in history. At this moment we must bethink ourselves, too, of those who through twenty years in an apparently hopeless state still nursed a fanatical faith in Germany and never surrendered their *Deutschtum*—their life as Germans. It is so easy here in the heart of the Empire to profess one's belief in Germany. But it is inexpressibly difficult, in the face of an unceasing persecution, not to allow oneself to be drawn away from this faith—to remain fanatically true to it, as though redemption were coming the next day. But now the hour of redemption has come. I have just had my first sight of these areas and what moved me so profoundly was two impressions. First: I have often known the jubilation and the enthusiasm of joy, but here for the first time I have seen hundreds of thousands shedding tears of joy. And secondly I saw appalling distress. When in England a Duff Cooper or a Mr. Eden say that injustice has been done to the Czechs, then these men should just for once see what in reality has happened there. How can one so pervert the truth! I have seen here whole villages undernourished, whole towns reduced to ruin. My fellow-countrymen, you have a great debt of honor to pay! . . . I expect of you that the Winter Help Contribution of 1938-39 shall correspond with the historical greatness of this year.

"In the history of our people the year 1938 will be a great, incomparable, proud year. . . . Later historians will show that the German nation found its way back again to the position of an honourable great nation—that our history has once more become a worthy history. . . ."

Press

London Times, October 6—Herr Hitler returned from the Sudeten German country to Berlin today. . . . He spoke in the Sports Palace, where ten days ago he had told President Benes that the Sudeten German territory would be either surrendered to the Reich by October 1 or be taken by the Reich. . . .

Le Temps, October 7—The Fuehrer's speech, though brief, was eloquent and boastful. He declared that the past six years had been among the most decisive in Germany's history. He extolled the courage of the men and women, the soldiers and workers of Germany. . . . From his trip through the Sudeten districts he gathered two impressions: the tears of joy of the welcoming populace and their wretched conditions.

•

SPEECH OF OCTOBER 9, 1938

Saarbruecken

Background

1938

October 7—Hitler Youth attack the Bishop's Palace in Vienna.

The Speech

"German Folk!

"If in the midst of these great days and their occurrences I have come into your district, then it was done in the conviction that nobody can evince greater appreciation of these last weeks and days than yourself.

"You may, men and women of Saarland, you have experienced for yourselves what it means to be separated from the Reich and you yourselves have gone through the joy of being reunited. You, too, suffered all this woe for two decades, and you, too, were supremely happy when the hour of reunion struck and you could return to the common Reich. Exactly that same thing was experienced and participated in by millions of Germans. The same joy seized them that once stirred you. At the beginning of this year, the twentieth after our collapse, I made a decision to lead back into the Reich 10,000,000 Germans who still stood outside.

"It was perfectly clear to me that this return could be compelled only by our own strength. The rest of the world, for the largest part, had no understanding. It neither saw nor wanted to see that here, 10,000,000 humans, in violation of the so-called right of self-determination of peoples, had been separated from the German people and the Reich and had been maltreated. But it has not understood that these human beings had but one great yearning, namely, to return to the Reich. These international world citizens have compassion, indeed, for every scoundrel who is called to account in Germany, but they are deaf to the sufferings of millions. That world is still filled with the spirit of Versailles. It did not free itself from it. No, Germany has liberated herself from it.

"Even today it still is a mixture of terrible inconsiderateness and appalling ignorance for these countries to overlook justice and give lasting effect to injustice. And so these world democracies remained deaf for twenty years to all the sufferings and demands of 10,000,000 Germans. Accordingly, a hard decision had to be made. Among us, too, there were weak characters who did not understand this. It is self-evident, however, that statesmen conscious of their responsibility made it a point of honor to take responsibility.

"The following were the preconditions for bringing about and carrying through solutions:

"First, internal unity of the nation. I am convinced I am Fuehrer of a manly people. I know what probably many in the rest of the world and even isolated ones in Germany do not seem as yet to know—namely, that the people of the year 1938 are not the people of 1918. Only those who were blind concerning National Socialism could overlook the tremendous work of education that the good philosophy of life has accomplished. There has been created today a community of spirit throughout our people of power and strength such as Germany never before has known. This was the first precondition for the undertaking, and for the success of this task.

"Second was national rearmament, which I sponsored fanatically for six years. I am of the opinion that it is cheaper to prepare one's self before events than to lie prostrate unprepared for events and then pay the foreign country.

"The third thing was rendering secure the Reich, and here you yourselves are witnesses to the tremendous work that is being accomplished in your very neighborhood. I need tell you no details about it. I will give expression, however, to but one conviction: *no power in the world will be able to push through this wall.*

"Fourth, we have gained foreign friends. That axis that people in other countries so often think they can ridicule has, during the last two and a half years, not only proved durable but has proved that even in the worst hours it continues to function. Nevertheless, we are especially happy that this task of the year 1938 of again joining 10,000,000 Germans and about 110,000 square kilometers [42,470 square miles] to the Reich could be accomplished in peace.

"We are all so happy no blood was shed over this despite the hopes of so many international agitators and profiteers. If I mention the help of the rest of the world in bringing about this peaceful solution, I must again and again place at the head of it our only real friend whom we possess today—Benito Mussolini.

"I know, and I know that you know what we owe this man. I should like also to mention two other statesmen who tried hard to find a way to peace and who, together with the great Italian and us have concluded an agreement that secured justice for 10,000,000 Germans and peace for the world. I am happy these millions of Germans are free, that they belong to us and that peace has been secured.

"Nevertheless, the experiences, especially of the last eight months, must strengthen our resolve to be careful and never to leave anything undone that must be done for the protection of the Reich. Opposite us are statesmen who—that, we must believe of them—also want peace. *However, they govern in countries whose internal construction makes it possible for them at any time to be supplanted by others who do not aim at peace. These others are there. In England, it merely is necessary that instead of Chamberlain, a Duff Cooper or an Eden or a Churchill come into power. We know that the aim of these men would be to start war.* They do not attempt to hide it. That obligates us to be on the watch to think of the protection of the Reich.

"We know further that now, as before, there is lurking threateningly that Jewish-international world enemy who has found a living expression in bolshevism. We also know the power of the international press that lives solely on lies and calumniation. In view of this peculiarity of the world about us and of these forces we must be careful about the future. We must at all times have a will for peace but be ready for defense.

"I have, therefore, decided to continue construction of our fortifications in the west with increased energy as already indicated in my Nuremberg speech. Also, I shall include large districts that hitherto lay before our fortifications, namely the Aachen region and Saarbruecken region, in this belt of fortifications. That will be done for the protection of the Reich.

"As for the rest, I am happy now to be able within the next few days to rescind those measures that we have projected or been compelled to introduce during critical months and weeks. I am happy hundreds of thousands of men can go home and reservists can be discharged. I am happy to be able to thank them for doing their duty. I am particularly happy to be able to thank the German people for having conducted itself in so wonderfully manly a manner. Especially do I thank a hundred thousand German workers, engineers and others of whom 10,000 are standing in your midst—men who helped build fortifications. You have helped, my comrades, to secure peace for Germany, and so, as a strong State, we are ready at all times to embark upon a policy of understanding with the world about us. We can do that. We want nothing from others. We have no wishes or demands. We want peace.

"There is only one thing—*this refers to our relations to England: it would be good if in England certain mannerisms held over from the Versailles period were discarded. We just cannot stand for a governess-like guardianship of Germany.*

"Inquiries by British statesmen or Parliamentarians concerning the fate of the Reich's subjects inside Germany are out of order. We do not bother about similar things in England. The rest of the world would sometimes have had reason enough to bother about international happenings—happenings in Palestine. We leave this to those who feel themselves pre-ordained by God to solve these problems. And we observe with amazement how they do solve them. We must, however, give these gentlemen advice to attend even more to the solution of their own problems and to leave us in peace.

"It also is part of the task of securing world peace that responsible statesmen and politicians look after their own affairs and refrain from constantly meddling talk with the problems of other countries and peoples. By such mutual considerateness, preconditions are really created for durable peace, of which no one is more earnestly desirous than the German people.

"We have great tasks facing us, great cultural tasks. Economic problems must be solved. No people can make better use of peace than we. However, no people knows better than we what it means to be weak and be at the mercy of others for better or for worse. . . ."

Press

Le Temps, October 11—The Fuehrer's speech produced an impression which one can at the very least call strange. Perhaps it would be too much to say that it was challenging, but he stressed Germany's most recent victory in a way which France and England could only find disagreeable. The essential point of the speech was the announcement of new fortification projects in the Saar and Aix-la-Chapelle region. Germany desires, as M. Hitler states, to have her western frontier protected by invulnerable armor.

London Times, October 10—At Saarbruecken yesterday Herr Hitler spoke sarcastically of the "governess admonitions" of Englishmen and of their occasional inquiries as to the fate of German citizens in the Reich. There is, of course, not the slightest desire anywhere to interfere in the internal affairs of Germany, and there is no intention of it in comment on German affairs. But comment there must be, just as British domestic politics are the subject of free comment in Germany. Herr Hitler himself yesterday, by no means for the first time, alluded slightingly to British democratic practices; and he made the singularly inept observation that "the rest of the world" would some time have "good ground to concern itself with" events in Palestine. Great Britain administers Palestine as an international mandate, and actually courts the counsel of all the nations which are members of the League of Nations. Nor is there the slightest objection to foreign comment on the admittedly unsatisfactory conditions prevailing in Palestine, so long as it is not deliberately calculated to make them worse.

New York Times, October 10—Those who had hoped that giving in to virtually all of Hitler's demands at Munich would lead to European appeasement would find little consolation in the speech of the Fuehrer at Saarbruecken. The moral that Hitler draws from the events of the past few weeks is that only by military strength and threats of war can Germany get what she wants. . . . Supposing after Chamberlain there came Cooper or Eden or Churchill? They are men who would like to make war, he adds. In other words, Hitler is now declaring in effect that he would regard any one of these three men in the position of Prime Minister as an unfriendly gesture toward Germany. He is beginning to tell the British what sort of Government they must have to meet his approval. Finally, he is initiating the new era of "peace in our time" by promising "to continue construction of our fortifications in the west with increased energy."

SPEECH OF NOVEMBER 6, 1938

Weimar

Background

1938

October 21—Japanese capture Canton in South China.

November 2—German and Italian Ministers draw new boundaries for Slovakia, giving Hungary a large slice of territory.

November 5—Incorporation of the Sudeten German Heimatfront in the National Socialist party.

The Speech

"WHAT seems to us almost a miracle as we look back upon it is nothing else than the reward for infinite and unwearying labor. . . . And now for that labor we have received from Providence our reward, just as the Germany of 1918 received its reward." At that time Germany shared in those blessings which we think of under the collective idea "Democracy." "But Germany has learned that democracy in practice is a different thing from democracy in theory.

"If today at times in foreign countries Parliamentarians or politicians venture to maintain that Germany has not kept her treaties, then we can give as our answer to these men: the greatest breach of a treaty that ever was practised on the German people. Every promise which had been made to Germany in the Fourteen Points—those promises on the faith of which Germany had laid down her arms—was afterwards broken. In 1932 Germany was faced with final collapse. The German Reich and people both seemed lost. And then came the German resurrection. It began with a change of faith. While all the German parties before us believed in forces and ideals which lay outside of the German Reich and outside of our people, we National Socialists have resolutely championed belief in our own people, starting from that watchword of eternal validity: God helps only those who are prepared and determined to help themselves. In the place of all those international factors—Democracy, the Conscience of Peoples, the Conscience of the World, the League of Nations, and the like—we have set a single factor—our own people. . . ."

"We were all convinced that a true community of the people is not produced overnight—it is not attained through theories or programs—but that through many decades, yes, and perhaps always and for all time the individual must be trained for this community. This work of education we have carried through ever since the Party was founded and especially since we came into power. But nothing is perfect in this world and no success can be felt to be finally satisfying. And so, even today, we have no wish to maintain that our achievement is already the realization of our ideal. We have an ideal which floats before our minds and in accordance with that ideal we educate Germans, generation after generation. So National Socialism will continually be transformed from a profession of political faith to a real education of the people. . . ."

"The umbrella-carrying types of our former *bourgeois* world of parties are extinguished and they will never return. . . ."

"From the very first day I have proclaimed as a fundamental principle: 'the German is either the first soldier in the world or he is no soldier at all.' No soldiers at all we cannot be, and we do not wish to be. Therefore we shall be only the first. As one who is a lover of peace I have endeavored to create for the German people such an army and such munitions as are calculated to convince others, too, to seek peace.

"There are, it is true, people who abuse the hedgehog because it has spines. But they have only got to leave the animal in peace. No hedgehog has ever attacked anyone unless he was first threatened. That should be our position, too. Folk must not come too near us. *We* want nothing else than to be left in peace; we want the possibility of going on with our work, we claim for our people the right to live, the same right which others claim for themselves. And that the democratic States above all others should grasp and understand, for they never stop talking about equality of rights. If they keep talking about the rights of small peoples, how can they be outraged if in its turn a great people claims the same right? Our National Socialist Army serves to secure and guarantee this claim of right.

"It is with this in view that in foreign policy also I have initiated a change in our attitude and have drawn closer to those who like us were compelled to stand up for their rights.

"And when today I examine the results of this action of ours, then I am able to say: Judge all of you for yourselves: Have we not gained enormously through acting on these principles?

"But precisely for this reason we do not wish that we should ever forget what has made these successes of ours possible. When certain foreign newspapers write: 'But all that you could have gained by the way of negotiation,' we know very well that Germany before our day did nothing but negotiate continuously. For fifteen years they only negotiated and they lost everything for their pains. I, too, am ready to negotiate but I leave no one in any doubt that neither by way of negotiation nor by any other way will I allow the rights of Germany to be cut down. Never forget, German people, to what it is you owe your successes—to what Movement, to what ideas, and to what principles! And in the second place: always be cautious, be ever on your guard!

"It is very fine to talk of international peace and international disarmament, but I am mistrustful of a disarmament in weapons of war so long as there has been no disarmament of the spirit.

"There has been formed in the world the curious custom of dividing peoples into so-called 'authoritarian' States, that is disciplined States, and democratic States. In the authoritarian, that is, the disciplined States, it goes without saying that one does not abuse foreign peoples, does not lie about them, does not incite to war. But the democratic States are precisely 'democratic,' that is, that all this can happen there. In the authoritarian States a war-agitation is of course impossible, for their Governments are under an obligation to see to it that there is no such thing. In the democracies, on the other hand, the Governments have only one duty: to maintain democracy, and that means the liberty, if necessary, even to incite to war . . .

"Mr. Churchill had stated his view publicly, namely that the present régime in Germany must be overthrown with the aid of forces within Germany which would gladly co-operate. If Mr. Churchill would but spend less of his time in émigré circles, that is with traitors to their country maintained and paid abroad, and more of his time with Germans, then he would realize the utter madness and stupidity of his idle chatter. I can only assure this gentleman, who would appear to be living in the moon, of one thing: there is no such force in Germany which could turn against the present régime.

"I will not refuse to grant to this gentleman that, naturally, we have no right to demand that the other peoples should alter their constitutions. But, as leader of the Germans, I have the duty to consider this constitution of theirs and the possibilities which result from it. When a few days ago in the House of Commons the Deputy Leader of the Opposition declared that he made no secret of the fact that he would welcome the destruction of Germany and Italy, then, of course, I cannot prevent it if perhaps this man on the basis of the democratic rules of the game should in fact with his party in one or two years become the Government. But of one thing I can assure him: I can prevent him from destroying Germany. And just as I am convinced that the German people will take care that the plans of these gentlemen so far as Germany is concerned will never succeed, so in precisely the same way Fascist Italy will, I know, take care for itself!

"I believe that for us all these international hopes can only teach us to stand firm together and to cling to our friends. The more that we in Germany form a single community, the less favorable will be the prospects of these inciters to war, and the closer we unite ourselves in particular with the State which is in a position similar to ours, with Italy, the less desire they will have to pick a quarrel with us! . . ."

"Germany has become greater by the most natural way, by a way which could not be more morally unassailable. . . ."

"When the rest of the world speaks of disarmament, then we too are ready for disarmament, but under one condition: the war-agitation must first be disarmed!

"So long as the others only talk of disarmament, while they infamously continue to incite to war, we must presume that they do but wish to steal from us our arms in order once more to prepare for us the fate of 1918-19. And in that case my only answer to Mr. Churchill and his like must be: That happens once only and it will not be repeated! . . ."

Press

New York Times, November 7—While all German commentators emphasize that Germany achieved her recent diplomatic victories only because she was armed, and because she was ready to employ this force if necessary, Chancellor Hitler, speaking at Weimar today, called on the world to disarm the "war agitators."

Le Temps, November 8—In sum, the Weimar speech leaves us completely in the dark as to what measures can be effectively adopted in the immediate future to obtain any appreciable results.

London Times, November 7—As expected, Hitler touched on foreign affairs, but mainly by way of venting his anger at foreign newspapers and politicians given to what he called "war agitation." To the names of Mr. Churchill, Mr. Eden and Mr. Duff Cooper, he added today that of Mr. Greenwood, on the ground that Mr. Greenwood had said he desired to destroy Germany and Italy.

•

SPEECH OF NOVEMBER 8, 1938

Munich

Background

1938

November 7—Grynzpan, a seventeen-year old Jew, shoots Ernst von Rath, a German diplomat in Paris.

The Speech

"... IT WOULD be very fine if the world would bethink itself and would take a new path, a path of general, peaceful justice. We should be happy if we were to observe any signs of such a change of outlook. But for the moment I see only one thing: on every hand a world of menace and a world which is arming itself. People say: 'We have now found a new basis for a peaceful development: it is for that reason that we must arm.' I personally do not quite understand this solution, although I raise no protest against it. But nowhere must I be misunderstood. When I read every day in the foreign newspapers that our armament profoundly disturbs the world about us, then I can assert one thing only: 'The one thing which would disturb me would be the German nation's failure to arm! The armaments of the others do not disturb me!' But on this point there can be no doubt: if the world clothes itself in armour the German people will not be the only one to wander about the earth armed with nothing but a palm-branch of peace. In that case we shall do everything which is necessary to secure peace for ourselves. When people complain that we give such little credence to their peaceful assurances, then I must revert to my most recent speeches. It is not as though we desired to be presumptuous and to lecture others on the form of their constitutions. I have no desire at all that others should adopt National Socialist principles. Let them keep their democracy and we will keep our National Socialism. But as a German statesman I am myself obliged in the interest of my people to study the measures adopted by the others, to examine the questions arising from such measures, and to consider possible dangers. And here I am not prepared to receive instructions from a member of the British Parliament. When someone says 'We meant always that the dictatorships should be destroyed—not the German or the Italian people,' the only answer which I can give him is: That sort of talk was possible before

November, 1918, but not after. Then the same circles stated that it was only a matter of overthrowing 'Prussian militarism,' only a matter of overthrowing the dynasty, it was only the house of Hohenzollern that was in question and not the German people. After that the German people would be led to its freedom within the framework of international democracy. Then we got to know what this 'freedom' meant. The German people learned its lesson. A collapse such as Germany then experienced through its credulity will not repeat itself in the next thousand years. On that point I can assure all those who believe that they can kindle a war-agitation against the German people. One can no longer delude Germany with phrases such as these. As responsible leader I will direct the attention of the nation to dangers, and I see a danger in the fact that in other countries there is a continuous incitement to war. He who does not wish to believe that has only to look at certain very recent happenings. It is no long time since in the English House of Commons questions of civil aviation were being discussed and a new civil aeroplane was said to be especially useful and serviceable. On that occasion a member of the Opposition called out 'It is to be hoped that it can also carry bombs to Berlin.' We know what that means! Perhaps someone may reply: 'Yes, but that is only a member of the Opposition.' And my answer is: 'According to the constitution of the democracies the Opposition of today may be the Government of tomorrow. In general that is in fact the rule.'

"We are very thankful when in France and England the leading men will have nothing to do with such ideas and wish to live in good relations with Germany. *We have more than once stated that we want nothing from these countries save the return of our former colonies—unjustly taken from us. But I have always affirmed that that is, of course, no occasion for war.* It is, let us say, a question of justice and of a real desire to make it possible for nations to live together. Otherwise we have no demands to make of these countries and we ask nothing from them. We wish only to carry on business with them, that is to say, we wish to trade with them. So when people talk of 'understandings,' we do not know on what we should come to an understanding.

"But there is one thing I must keep in view. In France and England there are certainly men at the helm who wish for peace, but there are others who make no secret of the fact that they want war with Germany. I am compelled to state this quite soberly before the nation and to draw the consequences which arise from that fact. *Tomorrow Mr. Churchill may be Prime Minister.* And when a British leader of the Opposition explains: we do not wish to destroy the German people, only the régime, the two are precisely identical, for nobody can destroy the régime without destroying the German people. When someone declares that he wishes to liberate the German people from the régime, then I would say to him: 'For the German people you are not the competent authority!' If there is anyone at all who is the competent authority for the German people, then, gentlemen of the British Parliament, that person is myself! The régime in Germany is a domestic affair of the German people, and we would beg to be spared every form of schoolmasterly supervision! Besides, I have an idea that we have more achievements to our credit than all these gentlemen, above all, we have set our State in order, which cannot be said of all countries in the world.

"I am therefore compelled to consider also the outlook of those who today are not in the Government, but who may be in the Government tomorrow and who leave no doubt of what they are thinking in their own minds. The German people will understand why I utter this warning and why I myself am determined to take all measures so as to be safeguarded from every attack. And I can further give the assurance: the German people is in no fear that bombs may fall upon it from Mars, let us say, or from the moon. Here, too, as is the way of Germans, we shall keep within limits. But I

am determined to strengthen the defenses of the Reich to the utmost extent, and I know that in this the whole German people will agree with me. That, doubtless, means sacrifices. But it is better that we should accept these sacrifices than that we should one day make them in favor of the outside world in the form of contributions or, as they were called in the past, of reparations. For us there can be only the one decision, that which I expressed at Saarbrücken: at any time we are ready for peace: we have not broken the peace. But also at any time we are ready to defend ourselves and that, too, with manliness and resolution.

"Then if anyone says to me: 'You wish to make history not by the way of right but by the way of force,' I can only say: The Germany of today has not refused to gain its rights by the way of negotiation. Year after year we have sought to attain our rights by the way of negotiation. Especially members of the English Parliament have no reason to doubt that, for it is by the way of negotiation that we concluded a treaty with England. If the others refused to co-operate, we cannot help that. But people must note one fact: National Socialist Germany will never go to Canossa! We have no need to do so. If the rest of the world obstinately bars the way against any attempt to let rights be recognized as rights by the way of negotiation, then there should be no surprise that we secure for ourselves our rights by another way if we cannot gain them by the normal way.

"When these British advocates for world-democracy now declare that in one year we have destroyed two democracies, then I can only ask, What is democracy then after all? Who has the right to speak in the name of democracy? Has the good God handed over to Mr. Churchill and Mr. Duff Cooper the key to democracy? Is this inscribed on tables of the law which are in the possession of the British Opposition? Democracy in our eyes is a régime that is supported by the will of the people. Formerly I became Chancellor in Germany under the rules of Parliamentary democracy—and that, too, as the leader of by far the strongest party. Under the rules of Parliamentary democracy I obtained the absolute majority of votes and today—of course Mr. Churchill can doubt it—I have the unanimous support of the German people. In this year I have not overthrown two democracies but, I might almost say, as Arch-democrat, I have overthrown two dictatorships—the dictatorship of Herr Schuschnigg and the dictatorship of Mr. Benes. I have, it is true, endeavored to persuade these two dictatorships to introduce for their subjects the right of self-determination by the way of democracy. In this endeavor I failed. Only then was the strength of the great German people thrown into the scale in order to establish democracy in these countries, that is to give freedom to the oppressed.

"The gentlemen of the English Parliament can assuredly be quite at home in the British World-Empire, but not in Central Europe. Here they lack all knowledge of the conditions of events, and of relationships. They will not and must not regard this statement of fact as an insult, we for our part are in the last resort not so well informed on India or Egypt, not to speak of Palestine. But I could wish that these gentlemen would at this moment concentrate the prodigious knowledge which they possess and the infallible wisdom which is their peculiar property on, let us say, precisely Palestine. What is taking place there has a damnably strong smell of violence and precious little of democracy. But all that I merely cite as an example, in no way as criticism, for after all I am only the representative of my German people, not an advocate for the cause of others. And that is where I differ from Mr. Churchill and Mr. Eden, who are advocates for the entire world.

"I am only the representative of my people. As such I do everything I consider to be necessary, and if Mr. Churchill says to me: 'How can the Head of a State cross swords with a member of the British Parliament?' I answer: 'Mr. Churchill, you should feel only the more honored. From the fact that in Germany even the Head of the State is not afraid to cross swords with a member of the British Parliament you can judge how high is the prestige of a member of the British Parliament with the German people. And besides, *I am not the Head of the State in the sense of being either Dictator or Monarch: I am the Leader of the German People! I could have given to myself—of that folk may be convinced—quite other titles. I have kept my old title and I will keep it so long as I live, because I do not wish to be anything else and never think of becoming anything else.* The old title contents me. Mr. Churchill and these gentlemen are delegates of the English people and I am delegate of the German people—the only difference lies in the fact that only a fraction of the English votes were cast for Mr. Churchill, while I can say that I represent the whole German people.

"My old fellow-fighters, if I summon you and, together with you, the whole German people to watchfulness, I have a holy right to do so. During these few years I have won great successes for the nation. The nation must understand that I am always anxious for its security. I would not, at the end of my days, have to close my eyes with the same somber prophecies on my lips as was the case with Bismarck. . . ."

Press

Le Temps, November 10—This renewed insistence on the colonial problem, which in our opinion is not at issue and cannot be presented without involving grave complication, is perhaps not calculated to speed the conferences which everybody wishes to see proceed in the spirit of mutual understanding. . . .

SPEECH OF JANUARY 12, 1939

Berlin

Background

1938

November 10-12—In retaliation for assassination of a German diplomat in Paris, Nazis arrest thousands of Jews, burn synagogues and impose a fine of 1,000,000,000 marks on the Jews.

November 14—United States calls back Berlin Ambassador to report.

November 16—Britain recognizes Italy's conquest of Ethiopia.

November 18—Germany recalls Washington ambassador to report.

November 30—One-day general strike in France against longer working hours. Daladier breaks strike.

Italian deputies in Rome shout for return of Corsica, Tunisia, Savoy and Nice.

December 6—France and Germany sign pact of friendship in Paris.

December 24—Lima Conference adopts a declaration of American solidarity.

1939

January 4—President Roosevelt in message to Congress stresses need for increased armaments.

January 11—Chamberlain visits Mussolini in Rome. No settlement is arrived at concerning war in Spain or Italian claims against France.

January—Franco's troops capture Barcelona.

The Speech

"... THE German nation recalls with profound thankfulness that the year 1938 brought to our people too the realization of its right to self-determination—a right which none may bargain away. If this result was attained without breaking the peace of Europe for a single day, a large share in that achievement is due to the policy of a wise understanding on the part of the Powers, which found its expression in the Munich agreement. I have already taken the opportunity in another place on the occasion of this New Year to express the gratitude felt by the German people towards those statesmen who in the year 1938 undertook to co-operate with Germany in seeking to find the means for a peaceful settlement of urgent problems. That we succeeded in reaching the peaceful solution which we all desired, we owe not only to the will to peace and to the sense of responsibility of the Governments concerned, but above all to their recognition of the fact that necessities based on historical development and on the natural needs of the peoples must sooner or later be acknowledged; they cannot be brushed aside so as to damage any individual people or State, and still less can they be obstructed by violent means. The Powers concerned have from the recognition of this fact drawn the necessary conclusions for their political decisions and have thus made a genuine contribution not only towards the preservation of European peace, but also towards the creation of a healthier and a happier Europe."

SPEECH OF JANUARY 30, 1939

Berlin, Reichstag

Background

1939

January 21—Schacht removed from post of Reichsbank director. Funk becomes Minister of Economics and Reichsbank director.

January 22—SA takes over education of all men over seventeen who are not being given education elsewhere.

The Speech

"Members of the German Reichstag:

"When, six years ago this evening, tens of thousands of National Socialist fighters marched through the Brandenburg Gate to the light of their torches to express to me, who had just been appointed Chancellor of the Reich, their feeling of overwhelming joy and their vows as faithful followers countless anxious eyes all over Germany and in Berlin gazed upon the beginning of a development, the end of which still seemed unknown and unpredictable. . . . One thing remains unforgotten: It seemed that only a miracle in the twelfth hour could save Germany. We National Socialists believed in this miracle. Our opponents ridiculed our belief in it. The idea of redeeming the nation from a decline extending over fifteen years simply by the power of a new idea seemed to the non-National Socialists fantastic nonsense.

"To the Jews and the other enemies of the State, however, it appeared to be the last flicker of the national power of resistance. And they felt that when it had disappeared, then they would be able to destroy not only Germany but all Europe as well. Had the German Reich sunk into bolshevik chaos it would at that very moment have plunged the whole of Western civilization into a crisis of inconceivable magnitude. Only islanders with the most limited vision can imagine that the Red plague would have stopped of its own accord before the sacredness of the democratic idea or at the boundaries of disinterested States.

"The rescue of Europe began at one end of the Continent with Mussolini and Fascism. National Socialism continued this rescue in another part of Europe and at the present moment we are witnessing in still a third country the same drama of a brave triumph over the Jewish international attempt to destroy European civilization. . . ."

"On January 30, 1933, I moved into the Wilhelmstrasse filled with the deepest anxiety for the future of my people. Today—six years later—I am able to speak before the first Reichstag of Great Germany! We are, indeed, perhaps better able than other generations to realize the full meaning of those pious words: 'What a change by the grace of God.' . . ."

"As I today see you assembled before me as the representatives of our German people from all over the Reich and know that among you are the newly elected men of the Ostmark [Austria] and the Sudetenland I am once more overwhelmed by tremendous impressions of the events of a year which realized the dream of centuries.

"How much blood has been shed in vain for this goal! How many million Germans have consciously or unconsciously trodden the bitter path to sudden or painful death for the sake of this ideal! How many others have been condemned to drag out behind the walls of fortresses and prisons lives they would gladly have given for Great Germany! How many hundreds of thousands have been scattered over the wide world by the endless stream of German emigration, driven by misery and want! For many a year they still think of their unfortunate homeland, but as generations go by they forget it. And now in a single year it has been possible to realize this dream. . . ."

"I will now in a few sentences give you the facts of the historical events of the memorable year 1938. Among the fourteen points which President Wilson promised Germany in the name of all the Allies as the basis on which a new world peace was to be established when Germany laid down her arms was the fundamental principle of the self-determination of peoples. The proclamation of this principle might have been of fundamental importance. Actually during the following period the Allied Powers of the day also applied these theories when they could make them serve their own selfish purposes. Thus they refuse to return Germany's colonial possessions, alleging that it would be wrong to return the native inhabitants of the colonies to Germany against their will.

"But, of course, in 1918 no one took the trouble to find out what their will was. But while the Allies thus upheld the right of self-determination for primitive Negro tribes, they refused in 1918 to grant to a highly civilized nation like the Germans the rights of man which had previously been solemnly promised to them. All efforts to bring about a change in the situation to normal methods of reasonable revision have hitherto failed, and are bound to fail in the future, in view of the well-known attitude of the Versailles powers. Indeed, all the articles dealing with revision in the Covenant of the League of Nations had only a platonic significance.

"I myself, as a son of the Ostmark, was filled with a sacred wish to solve this problem and thus lead my homeland back to the Reich. In January, 1938, I finally resolved that in the course of that year, in one way or another, I would fight for and win the right of self-determination for the 6,500,000 Germans in Austria. I invited Herr Schuschnigg, then Chancellor of Austria, to an interview at Berchtesgaden and made it clear to him that the German Reich would no longer inactively tolerate any further oppression of these German comrades. . . . The result was an agreement which permitted me to hope for a solution of this difficult problem by means of a general understanding.

"In my Reichstag speech of February 22, I stated that the Reich could no longer be indifferent to the fate of the 10,-000,000 Germans in Central Europe who were separated from the motherland against their will. I stated that further oppression and mistreatment of these Germans would lead to the most energetic counter measures.

"A few days later, Herr Schuschnigg decided to violate in a glaring manner the agreement which he had entered into at Berchtesgaden. His idea was by means of a faked plebiscite to destroy the legal basis of the national right of self-determination and the will of these 6,500,000 Germans. On the evening of Wednesday, March 9, I learned of this intention through Schuschnigg's speech at Innsbruck. That night I ordered the mobilization of a certain number of infantry and mechanized divisions with orders to cross the frontier on Saturday, March 12, at 8 A.M. in order to liberate the Ostmark. On the morning of Friday, March 11, the mobilization of these army and SS units was completed. They took up their positions during the course of the day. Meanwhile in the afternoon, due to the pressure of all the events and the rising of the citizens in the Ostmark, Schuschnigg resigned.

"On Friday night I was asked to order the German troops to march into Austria to prevent grave internal disorders in that country. Toward 10 P.M. troops were already crossing the frontier at numerous points. At 6 P.M. the next morning the main body began to march in. They were greeted with tremendous enthusiasm by the population which was thus at last free. . . .

"The first election to the Greater German Reichstag, which took place on April 10, expressed the overwhelming approval of the German nation. . . . A few weeks later, influenced by the international campaign of hate carried on by certain newspapers and individual politicians, Czechoslovakia began an intensified oppression of the Germans within her borders.

"Close upon 3,500,000 of our fellow-countrymen lived there in self-contained settlements which for the most part adjoined the boundaries of the Reich. Together with the Germans who were driven out during twenty odd years by the Czech reign of terror, this makes a total of over 4,000,000 persons who were retained in this State against their will and were ill-treated to a greater or less degree. No world power with any sense of honor would have watched such a state of affairs permanently. The man responsible for this development which gradually made Czechoslovakia the exponent of all hostile intentions directed against the Reich, was Dr. Benes.

"Despite a declaration twice given to the Czechoslovakian President, Dr. Benes, in my name, that Germany had not mobilized a single soldier, despite the same assurances that it was possible to make to representatives of foreign powers, the fiction was maintained and disseminated that Czechoslovakia for her part had been forced to mobilize in consequence of the German mobilization and that Germany had thus had to countermand her own mobilization and to renounce her plans. . . ."

"I resolved to solve, once and for all, and this radically, the Sudeten German question. On May 28, I ordered:

"1. That preparations should be made for military action against this State by October 2;

"2. That the construction of our western defenses should be greatly extended and speeded up. . . .

"The immediate mobilization of ninety-six divisions was planned to begin with and arrangements were made whereby these could be supplemented in a short time by a larger number.

"Developments late in the summer and the plight of the Germans in Czechoslovakia showed that these preparations were justified. The various stages of the final settlement of this problem are a matter of history. . . .

"If certain newspapers and politicians in the rest of the world now allege that Germany thus threatened other nations by military blackmail it can only be as a result of crude distortion of the facts. Germany restored the rights of self-determination to 10,000,000 of her fellow-countrymen in a territory where neither the British nor any other Western nation have any business. . . ."

"And I need not assure you gentlemen that in the future as well we shall not tolerate the Western States' attempting to interfere in certain matters which concern nobody but ourselves in order to hinder natural and reasonable solutions by their intervention.

"We were all happy therefore when, thanks to the initiative of our good friend, Benito Mussolini, and thanks also to the highly appreciated readiness of Mr. Chamberlain and M. Daladier, it became possible to find the elements of an agreement which not only allowed of the peaceful settlement of a matter which admitted no further delay but could moreover be looked upon as an example of the possibility of a general and sensible treatment and settlement of certain vital problems. . . ."

"This unique event in the history of our nation represents for you, gentlemen, a sacred and everlasting obligation. You are not the deputies of a district or of a certain side, you are not the representatives of particular interests, but you are, first of all, the chosen delegates of the whole German nation. You are thus guarantors of that German Reich which National Socialism has made possible and created. You are therefore in duty bound to serve with the deepest loyalty the movement which paved the way for and realized the miracle of German history in the year 1938. In you must be incorporated in the most superlative form the virtues of the National Socialist party—loyalty, comradeship and obedience. . . ."

"The history of the last thirty years has taught us all one great lesson, namely, that the importance of nations in the world is proportionate to their strength at home. The number and value of a population determines the importance of a nation as a whole. The final decisive part played in the valuation of the real strength of a nation will always be found in the state of its internal order; that is, the organization of its national strength.

"The German of today is no different from that of ten, twenty or thirty years ago. Since then the number of Germans has not increased to any considerable extent. The capabilities of genius and energy cannot be considered more plentiful than in former times. The one thing which has changed considerably is the way in which these values are utilized to the full by the manner of their organization, and thanks to the formation of a new method of the selection of leaders. . . ."

"Gentlemen, we are faced with enormous and stupendous tasks. A new history of the leadership of our nation must be constructed. Its composition is dependent on race. It is, however, just as necessary to demand and make sure through the system and method of our education that above all bravery and the readiness to accept responsibility will be regarded as essential qualities in those about to assume public office of any kind.

"When appointing men to leading positions in the State and party, greater value should be placed on character than on purely academic or allegedly intellectual suitability. It is not abstract knowledge which must be considered as a decisive factor wherever a leader is required but rather a natural talent for leadership, and with it a highly developed sense of responsibility which brings with it determination, courage and endurance. It must be recognized on principle that the lack of a sense of responsibility can never be made up for by a supposedly first-class academic training, of which certificates may supply the fruit. Knowledge and qualities of leadership, which always imply energy, are not incompatible. But in doubtful cases knowledge can in no circumstances be a substitute for integrity, courage, bravery and determination. These are the qualities that are more important in a leader of the people in the State and party.

"And I say this to you now, gentlemen, looking back on

the one year in German history which has shown me more clearly than the whole of my previous life how vital and essential these very qualities are; *and how in time of crisis one single energetic man of action outweighs ten feeble intellectuals. But as a factor in society this new type, selected as embodying the qualities of leadership, must also be freed from numerous prejudices which I can really only describe as the untruthful and fundamentally nonsensical code of social morals. There is no attitude which cannot find its ultimate justification in the benefit which it brings to the community as a whole.*

"Anything that is obviously unimportant or even harmful to the existence of the community is not to be recognized as a moral code on which a social order can be built up. And most important of all, the national community is possible only when laws are recognized which are binding for all. It will not do to expect or demand that one man should act in accordance with principles which in the eyes of the others are absurd or harmful or even just unimportant. I fail to appreciate the efforts of social classes, which are dying out, to cut themselves off from real life and keep themselves artificially alive behind a hedge of dry, outlived class laws. . . ."

"So long as the idea is only to secure a peaceful burial place there is no objection. But if this is an attempt to place a barrier in the way of life's progressive march then the windstorm of youth will clear away the whole tangled growth in its downward sweep. In the German State of today, the people's State, there are no social prejudices. And consequently there is no special social code of morals. This State recognizes only the laws of life and the necessities at which man has arrived through reason and insight. National Socialism recognizes these laws of necessity and it is one of the concerns of National Socialism to have them respected. . . ."

"Gentlemen, we live in an age when the air is full of the cries of democratic defenders of morals and world reformers. Judging from the statements of these apostles one might almost conclude that the whole world is only waiting its chance to redeem the German nation from its unhappy plight, to lead it back to the blessed state of cosmopolitan brotherhood and mutual assistance in international affairs which we Germans were so thoroughly able to test during the fifteen years before the National Socialist assumption of power.

"Speeches and newspapers in these democracies tell us every day about the difficulties we Germans face. One difference is to be noted between the speeches of the statesmen and the leading articles of their journalists. The statesmen either pity us or else unctuously praise the tried recipes—which unfortunately, however, do not seem to be so successful in their own countries; the journalists on the other hand give expression to their true sentiments somewhat more candidly. They inform us confidently and with a feeling of malicious pleasure that we are either suffering a famine or that one is—God willing—about to descend upon us, that we are facing ruin as the result of a financial crisis, or else a production crisis or —if even that should not come to pass—a consumption crisis.

"The only thing is that the sagacity of these democratic world economic scholars, of which we have so much concrete proof, does not always produce quite uniform diagnosis. During the past week alone, in view of the increased concentration of German self-assertiveness, one could read at the same time:

"1. That although Germany had a surplus of production she would succumb as a result of the lack of consumption power;

"2. Although there was a huge consumers' demand, the shortage of production goods alone would bring the country to ruin;

"3. That we should certainly collapse under the terrific burden of our debts;

"4. That we wanted no debts, but by National Socialist policy in this field too we were acting contrary to the last sacred capitalist ideas, and consequently—please God—would ruin ourselves;

"5. That the German people were in revolt on account of the low standard of living;

"6. That the State could no longer maintain the high standard of living of the German people—and so on.

"All these and many similar theses of these democratic world economic dogmatists had their forerunners in countless statements made during the period of the National Socialist struggle and in particular during the last six years. In all these laments and prophecies there is only one sincere strain, and that is the single honest democratic wish that the German people, and particularly the National Socialist Germany of today, should finally perish. . . ."

"What is the root cause of all our economic difficulties? It is the overpopulation of our territory. And in this connection there is only one fact and one question which I can hold up to the Western and the extra-European democracies.

"The fact is this: In Germany there are 135 people to the square kilometer, living entirely without their former reserve; for fifteen years a prey to all the rest of the world, burdened with tremendous debts, without colonies, but the German people are nevertheless fed and clothed, and, moreover, there are no unemployed among them.

"While the question is this: Which of the so-called great democracies is capable of performing the same feat? If we chose particular methods, the reason was simply that we were forced into particular circumstances. And in fact, our position was so difficult that there can be no possible comparison with the position of the other great States. There are countries in the world where instead of 135 people to the square kilometer, as there are in Germany, there are only between five and eleven, where vast stretches of fertile land lie fallow, where all imaginable minerals are available. There are countries which have all this and the natural wealth of coal, iron and ore and yet are not even capable of solving their own social problems, of doing away with unemployment or overcoming their other difficulties.

"And now the representatives of these States swear by the wonderful qualities of their democracy. They are quite at liberty to do so as far as they are concerned. But as long as we still had an offshoot of this democracy in Germany we had 7,000,000 unemployed; trade and industry were faced with absolute ruin in town and country, and society was on the point of revolution. Now we have solved these problems in spite of our difficulties, and for this we have our regime and our internal organization to thank. The representatives of foreign democracies marvel that we now take the liberty of maintaining that our regime is better than the former one; above all they marvel that the German people acquiesce in the present regime and reject the former.

"But, after all, does not a regime which has the support of 99 per cent of the people represent quite a different kind of democracy from the solution which in some countries is possible only with the help of extremely doubtful methods of influencing election results? And above all, what is the meaning of this attempt to foist something onto us which—insofar as it is a question of government by the people—we already possess in a much clearer and better form? But as for the method that is so much recommended, it has proved absolutely useless in our country.

"In those other countries it is maintained that collaboration should be possible between democracies and what they term dictatorships. And what might that mean? The question of the form of government or of the organization of the national community is not a subject for international debate at all. It is a matter of absolute indifference to us in Germany what form of government other nations have. At the most, it is a matter of indifference to us whether National Socialism—which is our copyright, just as fascism is the Italian one—is exported or not. We are not in the least interested in this ourselves! We see no advantage in making shipments of

National Socialism as an idea, nor do we feel that we have any occasion to make war on other people because they are democrats.

"The assertion that National Socialism in Germany will soon attack North or South America, Australia, China, or even The Netherlands, because different systems of government are in control in these places, is on the same plane as the statement that we intend to follow it up with an immediate occupation of the full moon. . . ."

"If certain methods of our economic policy appear injurious to the rest of the world, it should recognize that a hatred on the part of the former victor States, which was irrational and purposeless from an economic point of view, was chiefly responsible for making these efforts necessary. On this occasion again, as so often before, I wish to make clear in a few words to you, gentlemen, and thus to the entire German people, an existing situation which we must either accept or alter.

"Before the war Germany was a flourishing economic power. She participated in international trade and observed the economic laws which had general validity at that time as well as the methods of that trade. I need say nothing here with regard to the compulsion to participate in this trade activity since it is presumptuous to assume that God created the world only for one or two peoples. Every people has the right to ensure its existence on this earth.

"The German people is one of the oldest civilized peoples of Europe. Its contribution to civilization is not based on a few phrases of politicians but on immortal achievements which have been of positive benefit to the world. It has exactly the same right as any other people to share in the opening up and development of the world. Nevertheless, even in pre-war years, English circles upheld the idea—which was utterly childish from an economic point of view—that the destruction of Germany would tremendously increase British profits from trade. In addition, there was the further fact that even then the Germany of that day was believed to be in the final analysis a not entirely amenable factor with regard to the domination of the world which the Jews were attempting to establish.

"Consequently, from this side all available means were utilized to incite to an attack upon Germany. The war in which Germany found herself involved, purely as a result of a mistaken interpretation of loyalty to an ally, ended after over four years with that fantastic proclamation of the famous American President Wilson. These fourteen points, which were then supplemented by four additional ones, represent the solemn commitments of the Allied powers, on the basis of which Germany laid down her arms. After the Armistice these undertakings were broken in the most infamous manner.

"There then began the insane efforts of the victor States to transform the sufferings of the war into a permanent state of warfare during times of peace. For the most part an end has been put to this condition today. This has not happened because the democratic statesmen have displayed insight or even merely a sense of equity but solely through the strength of the reawakened German nation.

"It is in any case a fact that at the end of the war any rational considerations would have shown that no State had visibly profited. The clever British writers of economic articles, who had formerly written that destruction of Germany would increase the wealth of every individual Englishman and benefit the welfare of their country, were forced—at least for a certain period, when reality too clearly showed the untruth of their statements—to remain silent. Similar brilliant discoveries have begun to crop up again in the speeches of British politicians and the leading articles of the same type of newspaper writers during the past few months. What was the war fought for? In order to destroy German seapower, which then occupied second place. . ."

"From the banks of the Pacific Ocean in the Far East to

the waters of the North Sea and the coast of the Mediterranean, other forms of government are spreading with great rapidity. Any benefits one can possibly imagine from this war have been completely canceled, not merely by the tremendous sacrifices of human lives and goods but also by the continuing burden on all production, and above all on the budgets of the States. This, however, was a fact which was evident and could be seen immediately after the war. If it had been taken into consideration, the peace treaties would certainly have been drawn up on a different basis.

"For example, proof for all time to come of an extraordinarily limited insight in judging economic possibilities was furnished by the sums proposed in the years 1919 and 1920 as possible reparations payments. They are so far beyond the bounds of any economic reason that one can only assume a general desire for world destruction as the sole intelligible cause for this procedure, which otherwise can only be characterized as insanity. . . ."

"But this was not all: in order to prevent or hamper any autarchic activity by Germany, the Reich was even deprived of its own colonial possessions which had been acquired by purchases and treaty. This means that the strongest people of Central Europe was forced through a series of truly brilliant maneuvers to work much harder than before as an exporting nation regardless of cost. For German exports had to be large enough not only to satisfy German requirements, but also to provide additional insanely high reparations, which, of course, meant that, in order to pay 1 mark, 3 or 4 marks' worth of goods had to be exported, since in the long run these gigantic sums could only be paid from profits and not from capital. Since Germany was not in a position to fulfill these obligations the victor nations by means of loans subsidized German trade competition on the world market, after ten or twelve million men had given their lives on the battlefield to eliminate the trade enemy from the world market.

"I will only mention parenthetically that this insane procedure finally led to exaggerated developments and in the end upset all national economies and caused serious currency crises. The entire conduct of the so-called victor powers after the end of the war was completely irrational and irresponsible. The theft of the German colonies was morally an injustice. Economically it was utter insanity! The political motives advanced were so mean that one is tempted merely to call them silly. . . ."

"In actual fact the problem at the end of the war had become still more critical than it was before the war. Quite briefly, the problem was as follows:

"How can a just and sensible share in the world's wealth be assured to all great nations? For surely no one can seriously assume that, as in the case of Germany, a mass of 80,000,000 intelligent persons, can be permanently condemned as pariahs, or be forced to remain passive forever by having some ridiculous legal title, based solely on former acts of force, held up before them. And this is true not only of Germany but of all nations in a similar position, *for it is quite clear that: either the wealth of the world is divided by force, in which case this division will be corrected from time to time by force, or else the division is based on the ground of equity and therefore, also, of common sense, in which case equity and common sense must also really serve the cause of justice and ultimately of expedience.*

"But to assume that God has permitted some nations first to acquire a world by force and then to defend this robbery with moralizing theories is perhaps comforting and above all comfortable for the 'haves,' but not for the 'have nots.' It is just as unimportant as it is uninteresting and lays no obligation upon them. Nor is the problem solved by the fact that a most important statesman simply declares with a scornful grin that there are nations which are 'haves' and that the others on that account must always be 'have nots.' . . ."

"As far as Germany is concerned the situation is very simple. The Reich has 80,000,000 inhabitants; that means over fifteen persons to the square kilometer. The great German colonial possessions, which the Reich once acquired peacefully by treaties and by paying for them, have been stolen—contrary indeed to the solemn assurance given by President Wilson, which was the basic condition on which Germany laid down her arms.

"The objection that these colonial possessions are of no importance in any case should only lead to their being returned to us with an easy mind. But the objection that this is not possible because Germany would not know what to do with them since she did not do anything with them before is ridiculous. Germany, which was late in acquiring her colonial possessions, was able to develop them in a relatively short time and before the war was not faced by the same acute needs as today. This objection is consequently just as foolish as if anybody were to question a nation's capacity to build a railway because it had no railway 100 years ago.

"The further objection that her colonial possessions cannot be returned to her because Germany would thus acquire a strategic position is a monstrous attempt to deny general rights to a nation and a people *a priori*. For this can be the only answer: Germany was in any case the only State which set up no colonial army since she trusted to the terms of the Congo Act which were afterward broken by the Allies.

"Germany does not require her colonial possessions at all in order to set up armies there—she has a sufficiently large German population for this purpose at home—but to relieve her economic difficulties. But even if this be not believed, it is wholly immaterial and in no way affects our rights. Such an objection would only be justified if the rest of the world wished to give up its military bases and were only forced to maintain them if Germany were to be given back her colonies. The fact remains that a nation of 80,000,000 will not be willing permanently to be assessed differently from other nations.

"The fallacy and poverty of these arguments clearly show that at bottom it is only a question of power, in which common sense and justice receive no consideration from the common standpoint of view. The very reason which could once be advanced against taking Germany's colonies from her can be used today for their return.

"As she lacks a sphere of economic development for herself, Germany is forced to satisfy her own requirements by an increasing participation in world trade and in exchanges of goods. For on one point those very nations must be agreed, which themselves have immense economic possibilities at their disposal, either because they themselves occupy large territories or because they have great additional colonial possessions—namely, that the economic existence of a nation cannot be maintained without a sufficient supply of foodstuffs or without independent raw materials. If both are lacking a nation is forced to participate in world trade under all circumstances and perhaps to an extent which may even be undesirable to other countries. Only a few years ago, when conditions forced Germany to adopt her Four-Year Plan, we could to our great astonishment hear from the lips of British politicians and statesmen the reproach—which at that time sounded so sincere—that Germany was withdrawing from the sphere of international economics, even from world economic contacts, and was thus retiring into regrettable isolation.

"I replied to Mr. Eden that this apprehension was perhaps a little exaggerated and if it was meant at all sincerely was not admissible. *Conditions today make it quite impossible for Germany to withdraw from world trade. They simply compel us by the mere force of necessity to participate in it under all circumstances even when the form of our participation perhaps does not suit one country or another. . .*"

"If certain countries combat the German system this is

done in the first instance because through this German method of trading the tricks of international currency and Bourse speculations have been abolished in favor of honest business transactions. Germany, moreover, does not force her trading methods upon anybody else, but neither does she let any parliamentary democrat lecture her on the principles on which she shall or may act. We are buyers of good foodstuffs and raw materials and suppliers of equally good commodities! It is clear that everything which an economic system cannot produce in the territory in which its own currency circulates can only be imported by an increased turnover in exports. But since, as I have already emphasized, a nation which has an insufficient freedom of movement economically is imperatively forced to import foreign raw materials and foodstuffs, its economic system by doing so is acting under the most imperious force which exists, namely, the force of necessity! . . ."

"If ever need makes humans see clearly it has made the German people do so. Under the compulsion of this need we have learned in the first place to take full account of the most essential capital of a nation, namely, its capacity to work. All thoughts of a gold reserve and foreign exchange fade before the industry and efficiency of well-planned national productive resources. *We can smile today at an age when economists were seriously of the opinion that the value of currency was determined by the reserves in gold and foreign exchange* lying in the vaults of the national banks and, above all, was guaranteed by them. *Instead of that we have learned to realize that the value of a currency lies in a nation's power of production,* that an increasing volume of production sustains a currency, and could possibly raise its value, whereas a decreasing production must, sooner or later, lead to a compulsory devaluation. . . ."

"At one point, however, nature sets the limit to any further intensification of effort. That means, if some change does not take place, that German consumption power would find its natural limitation in the maximum of production of food supplies. *The situation which would then arise could only be overcome in two ways:*

"*First, by means of additional imports of foodstuffs and increased exports of German products,* which would necessitate the importation of at least some of the raw materials necessary for their manufacture, with the result that only a proportion of imports received would be available for the purchase of foodstuffs, or,

"*Second, the extension of our nation's living space* so that in our domestic economy the problem of Germany's food supplies can be solved.

"*As the second solution is for the time being not yet feasible,* by reason of the continued blindness of the one-time victorious powers, we are forced to occupy ourselves with the first; in other words, we *have to export in order to buy foodstuffs* and, moreover, as these exports require raw materials, all of which we do not possess, we are forced to export still more in order to assure ourselves of these extra raw materials. This necessity is consequently not of a capitalistic kind, as perhaps may be the case in other countries, but arises out of the uttermost need a nation can meet with, namely, the need for its daily bread. And when in this matter statesmen of other countries threaten us with I do not know what kinds of economic counter-measures, I can only give the assurance that in such a case a desperate economic struggle would ensue, which would be easy for us to carry out, easier for us than for the ever-satiated nations because our leading idea would be a very simple one: *the German nation must live; that means export or die.* And I assure all the international skeptics that the German nation will not die, least of all for this reason, but that it will live. If need be it will place all the production resources of our new National Socialist community at the disposal of its leaders to begin such a struggle, and to see it through. . . ."

"In 1933 and 1934 I made one offer after another to set

reasonable limits to armaments. They were coldly rejected, as was the claim for the return of the stolen German colonial possessions. If these gifted statesmen and politicians in the other countries draw up an account of the net profits which have accrued to them from the military and colonial inequality, and therefore the general legal inequality for which they have so persistently contended, then they will perhaps hardly be able to contest that they have already paid far too much for their supposed military superiority, and the wonderful colonial possessions they took from Germany.

"Economically it would have been wiser to have reached a reasonable and prudent agreement with Germany in regard to the colonies and European politics, rather than to have taken a course, which perhaps yields enormous dividends to the international armament profiteers, but at the same time forces the gravest burdens on the nations. I estimate that the 3,000,000 square kilometers of the German colonial possessions which have fallen to England and France, together with the refusal to accept Germany on a basis of political and military equality, will in a short time have cost England alone 20,000,000,000 gold marks; and I am afraid that in the not too distant future this sum will increase at an even greater rate with the result that, far from yielding golden profits, the former German colonies will cost a great deal. The objection could be raised that this would also apply to Germany. Granted that it is no great pleasure for us either, there is one difference between us: We are struggling for a vital right, without which we cannot in the long run live, whereas the others are struggling to uphold an injustice which is only a burden to them and yields no profit whatsoever.

"Under the present circumstances the only way open to us is to continue our economic policy of trying to produce the utmost from the territory at our disposal. This compels us to intensify our efforts in all branches, in order to expand production. This, in turn, forces us to carry out the Four-

Year Plan more resolutely than ever. This means we must further utilize our labor resources, and here we are approaching a new period in Germany's economic policy. . . ."

"To this purpose, trade and industry, and finance must necessarily be more closely concentrated. In this connection I am resolved to complete the transformation of the Reichsbank, begun January 30, 1937, changing it from a bank under international influence to a purely German bank of issue. If some other countries complain that thereby another German undertaking would lose its international features and characteristics, then we can only reply that we are absolutely determined that every institution in our national life shall have primarily German, that is, National Socialist, features. . . ."

"Today, gentlemen, I regard it as the duty of every German to understand the economic policy which the Reich Government is pursuing and to give every possible support thereto. Above all, to remember, both in town and country, that it has its foundation not in some financial theory or other but in a very simple realization of the function of production; that is, in an understanding of the fact that it is the amount of goods produced that is decisive.

"The fact that we have other supplementary problems to face, that we are obliged to employ a large percentage of our national labor power for national armaments which are not in themselves productive, is to be regretted but cannot be helped. Ultimately the economic structure of present-day Germany is bound up for better or for worse with the political security of the State. It is better to realize this in good time. Therefore I regard it as the supreme duty of the National Socialist Government to do everything within human power to strengthen our national defenses.

"I rely here on the understanding of the German people and, above all, on its powers of recollection. For the period in which Germany was defenseless was not one in which we enjoyed any particular equality of right, whether internationally, politically or economically. It was rather one marked by the most humiliating treatment ever meted out to a great nation, and by the direst extortion.

"We have no reason to assume that if at any time in the future Germany were to suffer a second fit of weakness her fate would be different. On the contrary, some of those very men who once hurled the firebrands of war into the world are still at work today, as driving forces or driven instruments for the stirring up of the peoples, endeavoring to keep up enmities and so prepare the way for a new outbreak of strife.

"You in particular, gentlemen, should bear one thing in mind:

"In certain democracies it is apparently one of the special prerogatives of political-democratic life to cultivate an artificial hatred of the so-called totalitarian States. A flood of reports, partly misrepresentations of fact, partly pure inventions, are let loose, the aim being to stir up public opinion against nations which have done nothing to harm the other nations and have no desire to harm them, and which indeed have been for years the victims of harsh injustice. *When we defend ourselves against such agitators as Churchill, Duff Cooper, Eden or Ickes and the rest, our action is denounced as encroachment on the sacred rights of the democracies.* According to the way these agitators see things, they are entitled to attack other nations and their governments, but no one is entitled to defend himself against such attacks. I need hardly assure you that as long as the German Reich continues to be a sovereign State, no English or American politician will be able to forbid our Government to reply to such attacks. And the arms that we are forging are our guarantee for all time to come that we shall remain a sovereign State—our arms and our choice of friends.

"Actually the assertion that Germany is planning an attack on America could be disposed of with a mere laugh, as one

would prefer to pass over in silence that incessant agitation of certain British warmongers, but we must not forget this:

"First, owing to the political structure of these democratic States, it is possible that a few months later these warmongers might themselves be in the government. We, therefore, owe it to the security of the Reich to bring home to the German people in good time the truth about these men. *The German nation has no feeling of hatred toward England, America or France.* All it wants is peace and quiet.

"But these other nations are continually being stirred up to hatred of Germany and the German people by Jewish and non-Jewish agitators. And so, should the warmongers achieve what they are aiming at, our own people would be landed in a situation for which they would be psychologically quite unprepared and which they would thus fail to grasp. *I therefore consider it necessary that from now on our Propaganda Ministry and our press should always make a point of answering these attacks* and, above all, bring them to the notice of the German people. The German nation must know who the men are who want to bring about a war by hook or by crook.

"It is my conviction that these people are mistaken in their calculations, for when once National Socialist propaganda is devoted to the answering of attacks, we shall succeed just as we succeeded inside Germany herself in overcoming, through the convincing power of our propaganda, the Jewish world enemy.

"The nations will in a short time realize that National Socialist Germany wants no enmity with other nations, that all the assertions as to our intended attacks on other nations are lies—lies born out of morbid hysteria or of a mania for self-preservation on the part of certain politicians; and that in certain States these lies are being used by unscrupulous profiteers to salvage their own finances, that, above all, international Jewry may hope in this way to satisfy its thirst for revenge and gain, that on the other hand this is the grossest defamation that can be brought to bear on a great and peace-loving nation.

"*Never, for instance, have German soldiers fought on American soil unless it was in the cause of American independence and freedom;* but American soldiers were brought to Europe to help strangle a great nation that was striving for its freedom. *Germany did not attack America, but America attacked Germany, as the committee of investigation of the American Senate concluded,* from purely capitalist motives, without any other cause. But there is one thing that every one should realize: These attempts cannot influence Germany in the slightest in the way in which she settles her Jewish problem. On the contrary, in connection with the Jewish question, I have this to say: *It is a shameful spectacle to see how the whole democratic world is oozing sympathy for the poor tormented Jewish people, but remains hard-hearted and obdurate when it comes to helping them, which is surely, in view of its attitude, an obvious duty.* The arguments that are brought up as an excuse for not helping them actually speak for us Germans and Italians.

"For this is what they say:

"First, 'We'—that is, the democracies—'are not in a position to take in the Jews.' Yet in these empires there are not even ten people to the square kilometer. While Germany with her 140 inhabitants to the square kilometer is supposed to have room for them!

"Second, they assure us: 'We cannot take them unless Germany is prepared to allow them a certain amount of capital to bring with them as immigrants.'

"For hundreds of years Germany was good enough to receive these elements, although they possessed nothing except infectious political and physical diseases. What they possess today, they have to by far the largest extent gained at the cost of the less astute German nation by the most reprehensible manipulations.

"Today we are merely paying this people what they

deserve. When the German nation was, thanks to the inflation instigated and carried through by Jews, deprived of the entire savings that it had accumulated in years of honest work, when the rest of the world took away the German nation's foreign investments, when we were divested of the whole of our colonial possessions, these philanthropic considerations evidently carried little noticeable weight with democratic statesmen.

"Today I can only assure these gentlemen that, thanks to the brutal education with which the democracies favored us for fifteen years, we have completely hardened to all attacks of sentiment. After more than 800,000 children of the nation had died of hunger and undernourishment at the close of the war, we witnessed almost 1,000,000 head of milking cows being driven away from us in accordance with the cruel paragraphs of a dictate that the humane democratic apostles of the world forced upon us as a peace treaty.

"We witnessed over 1,000,000 German prisoners of war being retained in confinement for no reason at all for a whole year after the war was ended. We witnessed over one and a half million Germans being torn away from all that they possessed in the territories lying on our frontiers, and being whipped out with practically only what they wore on their backs. We had to endure having millions of our fellow-countrymen torn from us without their consent, and without their being afforded the slightest possibility of existence. I could supplement these examples with dozens of the most cruel kind. For this reason we asked to be spared all sentimental talk.

"The German nation does not wish its interests to be controlled by any foreign nation. France to the French, England to the English, America to the Americans, and Germany to the Germans. We are resolved to prevent the settlement in our country of a strange people that was capable of snatching for itself all the leading positions in the land, and to oust it. For it is our will to educate our own nation for these leading positions. We have hundreds of thousands of very intelligent children of peasants and of the working classes. We shall have them educated—in fact, we have already begun —and we wish that one day they, and not the representatives of an alien race, may hold the leading positions in the State altogether with our educated classes.

"Above all, German culture, as its name alone shows, is German and not Jewish, and therefore its management and care will be entrusted to members of our own nation. If the rest of the world cries out with a hypocritical mien against this barbaric expulsion from Germany of such an irreplaceable and culturally eminently valuable element, we can only be astonished at this reaction. For how thankful they must be that we are releasing apostles of culture and placing them at the disposal of the rest of the world. In accordance with their own declarations they cannot find a single reason to excuse themselves for refusing to receive this most valuable race in their own countries. Nor can I see a reason why the members of this race should be imposed upon the German nation, while in the States that are so enthusiastic about these 'splendid people' their settlement should suddenly be refused with every imaginable excuse. I think the sooner this problem is solved the better, *for Europe cannot settle down until the Jewish question is cleared up. It may very well be possible that sooner or later an agreement on this problem may be reached in Europe, even between those nations that otherwise do not so easily come together.*

"The world has sufficient space for settlement, but we must once and for all get rid of the opinion that the Jewish race was only created by God for the purpose of being in a certain percentage a parasite living on the body and the productive work of other nations. *The Jewish race will have to adapt itself to sound constructive activity as other nations do, or sooner or later it will succumb to a crisis of an inconceivable magnitude.*

"One thing I should like to say on this day, which may

be memorable for others as well as for us Germans: In the course of my life I have very often been a prophet and have usually been ridiculed for it. During the time of my struggle for power, it was in the first instance the Jewish race that only received my prophecies with laughter when I said that I would one day take over the leadership of the State and with it that of the whole nation and that I would then, among many other things, settle the Jewish problem. Their laughter was uproarious, but I think that for some time now they have been laughing on the other side of their face. Today *I will once more be a prophet. If the international Jewish financiers in and outside Europe should succeed in plunging the nations once more into a world war, then the result will not be the bolshevization of the earth, and thus the victory of Jewry, but the annihilation of the Jewish race in Europe!* For the time when the non-Jewish nations had no propaganda is at an end. National Socialist Germany and fascist Italy have institutions that enable them when necessary to enlighten the world about the nature of a question of which many nations are instinctively conscious, but which they have not yet clearly thought out. At the moment Jews in certain countries may be fomenting hatred under the protection of a press, of the film, of wireless propaganda, of the theater, of literature, etc., all of which they control. . . ."

"The nations are no longer willing to die on the battlefield that this unstable international race may profiteer from a war or satisfy its Old Testament vengeance. The Jewish watchword, 'Workers of the world, unite!' will be conquered by a higher realization, namely, 'Workers of all classes and of all nations, recognize your common enemy!'

"Among the outcries against Germany raised today in the so-called democracies is the assertion that National Socialist Germany is an anti-religious State. I therefore wish to make the following solemn declaration to the whole German nation:

"1. No one in Germany has hitherto been persecuted for

his religious views, nor will any one be persecuted on that account!

"2. The National Socialist State, since January 30, 1933, has, through its State organs, placed the following sums accruing from public taxes, at the disposal of both churches: . . ." [There follows a list of grants to the churches.]

"It is therefore a piece of impertinence—to put it mildly—for foreign politicians, of all people, to talk about hostility to religion in the Third Reich. If, however, the German churches really should regard this position as unbearable, the National Socialist State would be at any time prepared to make a clear separation between church and State such as prevails in France, America and other countries. I should only like to ask this question: what sums have France, England or America paid to their churches through the State within the same period of time?

"3. The National Socialist State has neither closed any church nor prevented any service from being held, nor has it ever influenced the form of a church service. It has neither interfered with the doctrinal teaching nor with the creed of any denomination.

"But the National Socialist State will ruthlessly make clear to those clergy who, instead of being God's ministers, regard it as their mission to speak insultingly of our present Reich, its organization or its leaders, that no one will tolerate a destruction of this State and that a clergy that places itself beyond the pale of the law will be called to account before the law like any other German citizen. Let it be mentioned, however, that there are tens of thousands of clergy of all Christian denominations who fulfill their ecclesiastical duties just as well or probably better than the political agitators, without ever coming into conflict with the laws of the State. The State considers their protection its task. The destruction of the enemies of the State is its duty.

"4. The National Socialist State is neither prudish nor deceitful. There are, however, certain moral principles adherence to which is in the interests of the biological health of a nation, and with which we tolerate no tampering. Pederasty and sexual offenses against children are punishable by law in this State, and no matter who commits such crimes.

"When, some five years ago, certain heads of the National Socialist party were found guilty of these crimes, they were shot. When other persons in public or private life, even priests, are guilty of such offenses, they are, according to law, sentenced to terms of imprisonment or hard labor. It is no concern of ours if priests break their other vows, such as chastity, etc. Not a single word about that has ever been published in our press. For the rest, this State has only once interfered in the inner organization of the churches. This happened in 1933, when I myself attempted to unite the hopelessly disrupted regional churches in Germany into one large and powerful Reich church. The attempt failed, owing to the opposition of some of the regional bishops. In consequence, no further efforts were made; after all, it is not our task to defend the Protestant Church or even to strengthen it by forcible means in face of the opposition of its own supporters!

"There can be only political reasons for other countries and for certain democratic statesmen in particular in taking up cudgels on behalf of individual German clergy, for these same statesmen were silent when hundreds of thousands of priests were butchered or burned in Russia; they were silent when in Spain tens of thousands of priests and nuns were massacred with bestial cruelty and burned alive. They could not, and cannot, deny these facts, that they were silent and are silent now.

"Meanwhile—I must mention this to the democratic statesmen—it was just because of such butchery that numerous National Socialist and fascist volunteers placed themselves at the disposal of General Franco in order to help him in his efforts to prevent bolshevist lust for blood from spreading over Europe and over the greater part of the civilized world.

It was anxiety for European culture and for real civilization that compelled Germany to take sides in the fight carried on in Nationalist Spain against the bolshevist destroyers. It does not say much for the mentality predominant in various countries that cannot conceive of such a step being taken for purely unselfish reasons. However, National Socialist Germany sympathized with General Franco's uprising out of a sincere desire to see him succeed in delivering his country from the dangers that at one time had threatened to engulf Germany herself. . . ."

"In view of the dangers that threaten all around us, *I appreciate it as a piece of great good fortune to have found in Europe and outside it States that, in the same way as the German nation, are compelled to carry on a hard struggle to safeguard their existence. I refer to Italy and Japan.* In the Western World of today the Italians, as the descendants of the ancient Romans, as we Germans, as the descendants of the Germanic peoples of those times, are the oldest peoples —and our relations with each other reach farther back than do those between any other nations. In my speech in the Palazzo Venezia on the occasion of my visit to Italy, I pointed out that it was indeed a calamity that the mightiest civilized nation of the ancient world and the young nation of a new world in process of formation should, owing to the absence of a natural dividing line and under the influence of many other circumstances, become involved in centuries of fruitless conflict.

"But out of the contacts of a thousand years there grew up a sense of community; and this community must only have its roots in countless racial ties, but it developed an immeasurable historical and cultural significance. The debt that the Germanic peoples owe to the ancient world as regards the organization of the State and, consequently, national development, as well as in the sphere of civilization in general, cannot be estimated in detail, and is in its sum total immense. Since then nearly 2,000 years have passed. And now we, too have made our own abundant contribution to civilization. But we have always maintained close spiritual ties with the Italian people and with its cultural and historical past.

"In the nineteenth century there was a strangely similar process of unification. The German peoples became united in the German Reich, and the Italian States were united in the Kingdom of Italy. In the same year—1866—both nations were fated to take up arms simultaneously for the new form that their State was to assume.

"Today we are experiencing this parallel development for the second time. A man of outstanding historic importance was the first to bring a new idea to oppose the democratic notions that had become barren in this people and to carry this idea to victory within a few years. It is hard to estimate the significance of fascism for Italy. What fascism has done for the preservation of civilization is as yet incalculable. Who can stroll through Rome or Florence without being moved at the thought of the fate that all these unique documents of human art and civilization would have suffered if Mussolini and his fascist movement had not succeeded in saving Italy from bolshevism? Germany was faced with this same danger. . ."

"Let no one in the world make any mistake as to the resolve that National Socialist Germany has made so far as this friend is concerned. It can only serve the cause of peace if it is quite clearly understood that *a war of rival ideologies waged against the Italy of today will, once it is launched and regardless of its motives, call Germany to the side of her friend*. Above all let no one be ill-advised by those isolated bourgeois weaklings who vegetate in every country and who cannot understand that in the life of nations it is not necessarily cowardice but also courage and honor that may prompt wisdom.

"As regards National Socialist Germany, she is well aware of the fate that awaits her if ever an international power, whatever its motive, should succeed in overcoming fascist

Italy. We realize the consequences that would follow upon such an event and face them unflinchingly. The fate of Prussia in 1805 and 1806 will not be repeated a second time in German history. Weaklings like the advisers of the King of Prussia in 1805 will not be asked their opinion in the Germany of today. The National Socialist State realizes the danger and is determined to take all steps to counteract it.

"I know, too, that not only our defense forces but also Italy's military power, are equal to the severest military requirements. Just as it is impossible to judge the present German Army by the standard of the army of the German Bund of, say, 1848, so it is likewise impossible for any evaluation of modern fascist Italy to be made by the standards of the days when the Italian State was not yet united. Only a hysterical, unteachable, tactless and extremely malicious press can forget in so short a time that only a few years ago it made a thorough fool of itself with its prophecies as to the probable outcome of the Italian campaign in Abyssinia, and it is not one whit better now in its judgment of Franco's national forces in the Spanish campaign.

"Men make history. But they also forge the instruments that are suited to the forming of history, and, above all, they give them spirit. *Great men, however, are themselves merely the strongest, most concentrated expression of a nation.*

"National Socialist Germany and fascist Italy are strong enough to safeguard peace against every one, and to end resolutely and successfully any conflict that irresponsible elements lightly start.

"This does not mean that we desire war, as is asserted in the irresponsible press day by day. It simply means that we take this stand because, first, we understand that other nations, too, desire to assure themselves of their share of the world's riches due them by virtue of their number, their courage and their worth; and that, second, in recognition of these rights, we are determined to give common support to common interests. Above all, however, that we shall never under any circumstances yield to any threats amounting to extortion! *Thus our relationship with Japan is determined by the recognition of the need to stem, as we are determined to do, the tide of the threatened bolshevization of a world gone blind, with all the resolution at our command.*

"The anti-Comintern pact will perhaps one day become the crystallization point of a group of powers whose ultimate aim is none other than to eliminate the menace to the peace and culture of the world instigated by a satanic apparition. The Japanese nation, which in the last two years has set us so many examples of glorious heroism, is undoubtedly fighting in the service of civilization at the other side of the world. Her collapse would not benefit the civilized nations of Europe or of other parts of the world, but would only lead to the certain triumph of bolshevism in the Far East. Apart from international Jewry, which is desirous of this development, no people in the world can wish to see this take place.

"The tremendous efforts made last year ultimately attained their end by peaceful means, and we would add to our thanks to Mussolini our unreserved expression of gratitude to the two other statesmen who during the critical hours attached greater value to peace than to the preservation of an injustice. Germany has no territorial demands against England and France apart from that for the return of our colonies. While the solution of this question would contribute greatly to the pacification of the world, it is in no sense a problem that could cause a war. If there is any tension in Europe today, it is primarily due to the irresponsible activity of an unscrupulous press that scarcely permits a day to go by without disturbing the peace of mankind through alarming news that is as stupid as it is mendacious. . . ."

"Announcements by American film companies that they intend to produce anti-Nazi—that is, anti-German—films can but induce us to produce anti-Semitic films in Germany. Here, too, our opponents should not permit themselves any delusions as to the effectiveness of what we can do. There will be very many States and peoples who will show great understanding for supplementary instruction of this kind on such an important subject! We believe that if the Jewish international campaign of hatred by press and propaganda could be checked, good understanding could very quickly be established between the peoples. It is only such elements that hope steadfastly for a war. I, however, believe in a long peace! For in what way do the interests of England and Germany, for example, conflict?

"*I have stated over and over again and again that there is no German, and, above all, no National Socialist, who even in his most secret thoughts has the intention of causing the British Empire any kind of difficulty*. From England, too, the voices of men who think reasonably and calmly express a similar attitude with regard to Germany. It would be a blessing for the whole world if mutual confidence and cooperation could be established between the two peoples. *The same is true of our relations with France. We have just celebrated the fifth anniversary of the conclusion of our nonaggression pact with Poland, There can scarcely be any difference of opinion today among the true friends of peace with regard to the value of this agreement. . . .*"

"*Our relations with Hungary are based on a long and well-proven friendship,* a common interest and on traditional mutual esteem. Germany has gladly undertaken to contribute to the redressing of the wrongs inflicted on that country.

"*Yugoslavia is a State that has increasingly attracted the attention of our people since the war.* The high regard that the German soldiers then felt for this brave people has since been deepened and has developed into genuine friendship. Our economic relations with this country are undergoing constant development and expansion, just as is the case with the friendly countries of *Bulgaria, Greece, Rumania, Turkey, Switzerland, Belgium, Holland, Denmark, Norway, Sweden, Finland, and the Baltic States.*

"The essential reason for this is to be found in the natural conditions that make it possible for these countries and Germany to complement each other's economic systems.

"Germany is happy today in the possession of peaceful frontiers in the west, south and north. Our relations with the western and northern States become all the more satisfactory with the increasing tendency in these countries to turn away from certain articles of the Covenant of the League of Nations that involve danger of war.

"The addition of Hungary and Manchukuo to the anti-Comintern pact is a welcome symptom of the consolidation of world-wide resistance to the Jewish-International-Bolshevist threat to the peoples of the world.

"The relations of the German Reich with the countries of South America are satisfactory, and economic relations with them continue to expand.

"Our relations with the United States are suffering from a campaign of defamation carried on to serve obvious political and financial interests, which, under the pretense that Germany threatens American independence, is endeavoring to mobilize the hatred of an entire continent against the European States that are nationally governed. We all believe, however, that this does not reflect the will of the millions of American citizens who, despite all that is said to the contrary by the gigantic Jewish-capitalistic propaganda through the press, the radio and the films, cannot fail to realize that there is not one word of truth in all these assertions. *Germany wishes to live in peace and on friendly terms with all countries, including America.* Germany refrains from any intervention in American affairs and likewise decisively repudiates any American intervention in German affairs. *The question, for instance, as to whether Germany maintains economic relations and does business with the countries of South and Central America, concerns nobody but them and ourselves.* Germany anyway is a great and sovereign country and is not subject to the supervision of American politicians.

"Quite apart from that, however, I feel that all States

today have so many domestic problems to solve that it would be a piece of good fortune for the nations if responsible statesmen were to confine their attentions to their own problems. . . ."

"We may now regard this process of growth of the German nation as virtually completed. The greater German Reich now embodies our people's entire struggle for existence over 2,000 years. All streams of German blood flow into the Reich, and there are united in it all past traditions, their symbols and standards, and above all the great men of whom Germans of past periods have reason to be proud. . . ."

"As we include them in this great Reich in grateful reverence, the wealth of German history is revealed in all its glory. Let us thank Almighty God that He has granted to our generation and to us the great blessing of experiencing this period of history and this hour."

Press

Le Temps, February 2—The Fuehrer's speech became more moderate in its terms when it dealt with problems directly affecting relations with the democratic powers. . . . As usual, he denounced communism, the influence of the Jews, and anything which hindered the totalitarian system. All this rather tended to produce the effect of a retrospective polemic. . . . In reference to the Munich settlement, the Fuehrer took pride in stating that last September an agreement had been reached which did more than provide a peaceable conclusion to an affair which to his mind could no longer be disputed. It was also "an example of the possibility of a reasonable general settlement and a reasonable liquidation of certain vital problems." If we understand him correctly, the Fuehrer assumes that the Western powers will not interfere in any problems of Central and Eastern Europe—problems, he states, which are the affair of Germany alone. While maintaining this, he also would establish a system whereby certain vital problems might be negotiated. What problems does he mean? This point ought to be clarified and defined. . . .

On the whole the speech is better than many had feared, for it raises no insurmountable barriers to a policy of co-operation.

New York Times, February 1—Why press so strongly the issue of colonies at this time? Various explanations may provide the answer. There is Hitler's debt to Mussolini, and Mussolini's more immediate interest in the colonial question. There is the "particularly difficult economic question" at home, of which Hitler speaks, and the convenience of an alibi (in the lost colonies) for the failure of six years of National Socialism to raise the living standards of the German people. There is the possibility of a later policy which could waive colonial demands for the time being, in exchange for a wholly free hand in Eastern Europe. There is the strategy of troubling the waters of European diplomacy in order to fish better in them.

London Times, January 31—The great risk which the other signatories of the Versailles settlement have taken in assenting to its revision is that their action should be attributed to weakness or fear rather than to the reluctance to resist actions and demands which . . . could not be rebutted with an easy conscience. The great question before Europe now is whether the experience of 1938 has been tragically misinterpreted . . . by those to whom they have brought the national gains celebrated yesterday . . . Hitler's review of events and policy . . . broke no new ground in that matter. It seemed to be addressed in the main to Britain and the United States. . . . There was perhaps no more audacious or more astonishing flight of dialectic in yesterday's speech than that in which the Fuehrer went on to reproach the nations with their ungenerous reception of the victims of German racial policy—a reproach which would still stagger the world even if the German Government had not deprived the exiles of the means of resuming their livelihood in new lands by stripping them of their positions. Nor was there a more sinister flourish in the speech than the suggestion that another war would mean the destruction of the Jewish race in Europe. . . . It is more than three years since the British Government took the lead in proposing international consultation upon the access to raw materials, the lack of which yesterday served Hitler as the foundation for his defence of the Four-Year-Plan and for his renewed claim to colonial territory . . . But . . . the basis for negotiation does not exist without the assurance of collaboration for common ends. . . . But no task lies nearer to hand, if war is to be laid aside as an instrument of policy, than that of a common exploitation of the ample means which exist of increasing the standard of life for people of every race and color. . . . However, Hitler has belied the more nervous prophets . . .

•

SPEECH OF FEBRUARY 24, 1939

Munich

To the Old Guard

Background

1939

February 1—In conference with U.S. Senators at the White House, President Roosevelt is reported to have said that "the frontiers of America are on the Rhine." This the President later denied having said.

February 6—Chamberlain pledges support to France against danger.

February 10—Pope Pius XI dies.

February 14—Battleship *Bismarck* launched.
February—France orders American planes.

The Speech

"THIS year the Reich has gained beautiful lands and true German men, and its growth in power is obvious to all. There is no doubt that this never could have happened if my Party had not been behind me: the great expression of the national will, the mighty organization which has kept the German people forthright and fearless. . . ."

"We have our problems also. But we shall solve them all by diligence, resoluteness, ingenuity, strength of will and close co-operation.

"In 1920 in this same hall I announced as the most important point in our program the demand for the unity of all Germans. That goal has now been reached.

"Tremendous, unbelievable events have taken place since then. . . . Many of the questions raised in our program have already been solved. Today the Jewish question is no longer a German problem, but a European one. National Socialist Germany has created a new economic doctrine which views capital as the servant of the economy and the economy as the servant of the people. We are the first nation to make the ingenuity and industry of our people the basis of prosperity. If the positive element of Christianity is love of one's neighbor, that is, caring for the sick, clothing the poor, feeding the hungry and quenching the thirst of the parched, then we are true Christians! For in these respects the people's community of National Socialist Germany has tremendous accomplishments to its credit.

"Naturally everyone cannot be converted. There are still a few opponents of National Socialism in Germany, though these are dying out. There are our familiar friends of the black-red-gold coalition—the same people who are today building a coalition against us throughout the world. . . ."

"Twenty years ago, nameless and alone, I began. Nineteen years ago I stood for the first time in this place, facing alone a shouting mob, many of whom still opposed me. *Together with a few dozen comrades I began the struggle to conquer a great nation, a struggle carried through under inconceivable difficulties. How can anyone expect that now when I have the power I should be afraid of threats.*

"I have never known fear, and I would be ashamed of myself and unworthy to be the leader of the German nation if I knew it today. The warmongers will not frighten us with threats! But if they should really succeed in throwing the nations into the madness of a war, we will not be the ones to capitulate. The year 1918 will never be repeated in German history!

"When I look back over this truly miraculous development, German folk-comrades, I am always compelled to reflect that the rise of the Party has been like a dream. You can imagine for yourselves what it means to me to return to those who once set out upon our road together with me. It is inspiring to return to those whom I know, not only since March, 1933, but since the times when it was *dangerous to be a National Socialist*. It is wonderful for me to return every year to the familiar group of my old comrades in battle. . ."

"The only thing that can trouble our rejoicing is the thought that some comrades did not live to see the final victory. This is the feeling I had last year. There is the old Austrian general who lived cleanly all his life, thought only of Greater Germany and fought for Greater Germany—old General Krauss. And then, a few days before I marched into his homeland—for he was a Sudeten German—the old man closed his eyes forever. Probably he would have been overcome by his joy. Perhaps it would have killed him. However, though we must regret that individuals, that so many comrades, have not been able to rejoice with us, there is one consolation. We know that their struggle was not in vain;

in the end they attained their goal, if only in that their spirit was with us and in us. . . ."

"Germany has fulfilled our dream at last, and it is our task to see that she becomes all that we outlined in our program nineteen years ago in this very hall. And that this will take place is as certain as that I stand here before you.

"Let us close our eyes a moment and look into the future. Those who come after us will receive something very different from what we received nineteen years ago!"

•

THE DISMEMBERMENT OF CZECHOSLOVAKIA

Background

1939

February 27—Britain and France recognize Franco.

March 2—Cardinal Pacelli is elected Pope under the name of Pius XII.

Marshal Pétain is appointed French Ambassador to Burgos, Franco's temporary capital.

March 10—Stalin tells Communist Party Congress that England and France tried to foment German-Soviet war.

March 14—President Hacha of "Czeckia" and his foreign Minister, Chvalkowsky, are summoned to Berlin by Hitler and made to accept Germany's protectorate.

Hungary invades Ruthenia.

PHASE V

The Road to War

March 15, 1939 — October 6, 1939

COMMENT

AFTER the occupation of Prague by the German armies on March 15, 1939, Hitler's strategy followed roughly the same general lines as that which led up to Munich.

His belief that the democracies were morally weak and internally divided and that they could still be confused, was strengthened by the persistence of the anti-war sentiment in these democracies, and by the obvious reluctance of their leaders to admit that the policy of appeasement had come to an end. He knew that they would go to the limit before facing war and he knew that as far as he was concerned, he was ready to face war if necessary.

Obviously the Fuehrer would not resort to war if he could obtain the same results by other means. Another Munich would have suited him just as well, and all his moves during that period, although increasingly reckless, show that he would have accepted a settlement provided he obtained what he wanted. At no point, however, did he consider the possibility of a compromise. If someone was to compromise it would have to be his opponents.

Although the situation as it took shape in the spring of 1939 was somewhat similar to the one that existed a year before, there were differences which forced Hitler to modify his strategy accordingly. These modifications were not very important, however, and the speeches and actions of Hitler which led him on the road to war are sufficiently similar to those that led him to Munich, to compel the conclusion that Hitler's grand strategy had been settled long before. At any moment after the successful reoccupation of the Rhineland, he was prepared to go to war and he could not be bluffed. This was not demonstrated until he attacked Poland, but it was equally true a year before when the democracies backed down and went to Munich.

In spite of this truth, there were many in the democracies who believed more firmly than ever that Hitler had been bluffing all along, and that the time had come to prove their contention. They unwittingly helped Hitler on the road to war by spreading the idea that the failure of the policy of appeasement made it imperative to renounce it altogether. The only way to prevent both another Munich and war, they argued, was to convince Hitler that 1939 was not 1938, and that the democracies had at last learned their lesson. Hitler's bluff should be called once and for all.

This theory was, of course, greatly facilitated by the fact that the annexation of Czechoslovakia had cost Hitler the good will of many appeasers. Chamberlain had to admit that all his faith in the sincerity and the pledges of Hitler had been finally dashed. Those who believed that if Hitler could not be trusted to keep his word to others, he would at least keep it to himself, were profoundly disillusioned. Hitler had repeated so many times that he was merely interested in reuniting all the Germans that he was believed; and many thought that this claim was just or at least defensible. The annexation of the Sudeten was accepted on that basis. But the Czechs were not Germans. Their integration into the Reich caused a wave of indignation among those who insisted on believing that Hitler was acting according to a certain set of principles and that he had a doctrine.

This disillusion precipitated the Allies into a new policy. Chamberlain having convinced himself that Hitler was dishonest and unprincipled, hastened to create what was called a "peace front." He hastily gave guarantees to Poland, Rumania and Greece that England and France would defend their independence in case of aggression. He also started to negotiate with Moscow in order to rally Stalin to the cause of peace.

This did not embarrass Hitler to any great extent. From the point of view of his political strategy, it even helped him. Like the Kaiser in 1914, he proclaimed that Germany was being "encircled," and this new *leit-motiv* enabled him to consolidate his fundamental thesis: That Germany was a victim, constantly threatened by the outside world, that his only intention was peace, but that he was gradually being pushed with his back to the wall and that he had to insure Germany's own defense against a brutal and aggressive world.

If Hitler lost the good will of the appeasers by occupying Prague, he nevertheless gained very positive advantages: Poland was nearly encircled and the Balkan States were at his mercy. He had gained a springboard for future conquests, important economic resources and the Skoda plant.

What his next step should be was clear when he denounced his ten-year pact of non-aggression with Poland. This pact had been made by Hitler himself in 1933 and it was his earliest diplomatic achievement. Speaking about it in 1938, Hitler had said:

"On this fifth anniversary of the first great international conference concluded by the Reich, we note with great admiration that our relations with the State with which we have perhaps the greatest antagonism . . . have become increasingly friendly. I know well that this is due to the fact that at this epoch it was not a western parliamentarian who resided in Warsaw, but a Polish Marshal, who being personally in command, had understood the importance for the whole of Europe of such an agreement between Germany and Poland. Many have asked what was the value of this pact. But it has been victoriously tested and I can say that since the League of Nations has ceased its continuous efforts to disturb Danzig and appointed a new high commissioner, this dangerous spot for European peace has completely lost its threatening character."

The cancellation of this pact by its own author was accompanied by a series of incidents and denunciations now all too familiar.

The well-known *leit-motiv* of the persecuted Germans was turned on with the full power of Goebbels' orchestra. The same propaganda had preceded the *Anschluss* and the "liberation" of the Sudeten. Hitler evidently thought that what had worked so well twice would work again. The newspaper and radio campaigns against the "barbarous" Poles were an exact repetition of those launched against the Austrians and the Czechs.

Once again the Fuehrer gave the impression that the reading of his own newspapers was making him so sick at heart and so indignant that he could hardly restrain his righteous wrath. He confided to anyone who would listen that he was a man of great patience but that the repetition of such atrocities by the neighbors of the peaceful Reich was more than any civilized man like himself could bear.

The build-up of the persecuted blood-brothers *leit-motiv* was elaborate and loud. From the point of view of strategy, it served—as it had served before—to convince many people in the outside world that the Danzig trouble was again a purely German affair. Naturally, it could not have happened without Versailles and this basic theme was not forgotten. In fact Hitler assumed that every one was now agreed with him that the question of Danzig and the Corridor had to be settled because it was the worst feature of the *Diktat*.

The democracies naturally held a totally different point of view. Their contention was that Hitler was once more creating and exploiting a series of local incidents in order to force an independent country (Poland) into submission. The memories of similar occurrences were too fresh in their minds to be forgotten, and although they could not but recognize that something should be done to settle the question of Danzig and the Corridor, they were resolved that it should be done through peaceful negotiations and that Poland should be treated on an equal footing with Germany. They did not want war but they did not want another Munich either.

It might be remarked in passing that this is one more instance when Hitler used the psychological advantages he had gained before by his strategy of threats further to push these advantages by the same methods. The so-called "war of nerves" is cumulative in its effects. The "campaign" of 1938 made the "campaign" of 1939 easier. Hitler could allow himself to be more daring and more ruthless. The world had become accustomed to many of his tricks. There was nothing new in the procedure which served to build up the Polish crisis. The insults hurled at the Poles, the accusations that they were maltreating the Germans, the building up to a climax which would finally force the Fuehrer to take matters into his own hands, even Hitler's fits of rage as reported by the diplomats who visited him—all this was too well known and too familiar to cause any surprise. But the mere fact that the world had grown used to being bullied by Hitler did not make the bullying less effective. The democratic governments were obsessed by their own previous inability to cope with Hitler's temper.

When, for instance, the question was raised of sending a Polish plenipotentiary (possibly Mr. Beck himself) to discuss a settlement with Hitler, M. Coulondre, the French Ambassador in Berlin, wrote to Georges Bonnet as follows:

> ". . . Nevertheless there would be serious objection to Mr. Beck coming to Berlin in the present circumstances. The journey would inevitably recall the unhappy precedents of Dr. Schuschnigg and Dr. Hacha. It would be exploited by the Reich with all the dramatic effects of which German propaganda is capable, as a moral victory and a sign of weakening. German demands would thereby be increased . . ."

Thus the democratic statesmen were perfectly aware of the mechanism of the crisis in which they were caught. They saw the traps opening before their eyes. But this vision did not help them much because the psychological setting created by Hitler never enabled them to gain control of the situation. During the whole development of the crisis which led up to the invasion of Poland, the French and British leaders (and those of the neutral countries as well) were pleading and appealing, but Hitler remained master of the events. He could increase the pressure or relax it as he saw fit because all his moves were determined by a definite strategic plan, while his opponents could do nothing but try to assuage him. He retained the offensive and forced them to remain on the defensive.

The only risk that Hitler ran was that the democracies and the neutrals might suddenly have been able to shake the fatal spell that held them, and themselves assume a definitely aggressive attitude. This would have meant that, at some point (and it did not much matter when) they would have taken a political offensive backed with force. It would have meant a co-ordinated *attack* against Hitler instead of a futile attempt at co-ordinated defense.

In the atmosphere that prevailed then—and which was to prevail for months after the war actually started—this was out of the question. The neutrals, to begin with, would not accept any policy other than the one which finally led them to their doom. They would not act, either singly or collectively. They preferred to believe the innumerable assurances given them by Hitler that he had no designs on them whatsoever. When President Roosevelt asked Hitler if he was prepared to respect the integrity of some thirty countries of which he gave a list, Hitler hastened to ask each of these countries if they felt themselves threatened by him. They, of course, assured him that they did not, and President Roosevelt thus unwittingly played into Hitler's hands by giving him this remarkable opportunity to get from the sheep assurance that they were not afraid of the wolf.

The inability of the democracies and of the neutrals to appraise Hitler's real purpose was never more clearly demonstrated than in the way they reacted to the "bombshell" of the German-Soviet pact, signed in Moscow on August 23.

Clearly enough this action showed only one thing: That Hitler placed strategy above all other considerations. In allying himself with Stalin or neutralizing him, he avoided a repetition of the mistake made by Imperial Germany in 1914 which he had condemned in *Mein Kampf*—the war on two fronts. He thus broke the "peace front" so painfully engineered by Chamberlain, and from then on it is notable that Hitler does not talk of "encirclement" any more. Thanks to this great *coup,* he could safely revert to his favorite theme —as exposed in his speech to the Reichstag on September 1— that he had no purpose other than to settle the question of Danzig and the Corridor. There was no question of a world war. Quite the contrary. All he asked was that the democracies should let him solve this painful German problem which was nobody's concern but his own. He had no intention of fighting either England or France or anyone else. He did not even intend to annihilate Poland, but merely find a new basis of understanding with that country. The invasion of Poland, as described by Hitler, was made necessary only because his efforts to settle the problem of Danzig and the Corridor peacefully had failed, because Germany had been attacked by the barbarous Poles and because the injustices of the Versailles Treaty had to be righted once and for all.

It is true that from the point of view of the National Socialist doctrine, the Russian pact was a total repudiation of Hitler's very *raison d'être.* He had risen to power on the anti-communist slogan. *Mein Kampf* is a long indictment of bolshevism, and the fight against it is Hitler's mission.

"Germany is today the next great battle aim of bolshe-

> vism," wrote Hitler in *Mein Kampf* (page 961). "It requires all the force of a young missionary idea once again to inspire our nation to break out of the coils of this international snake and internally to check the tainting of our blood, so that the nation's forces can thereby be devoted to the securing of our nationality, which may make it possible to prevent a reptition of the final catastrophe until the end of time. But if one pursues this goal, then it is insanity to ally oneself with a power which has as its rulers the mortal enemy of our own future. . . . The *struggle against Jewish bolshevization of the world requires a clear attitude toward Soviet Russia. You cannot drive out the Devil with Beelzebub*."

Thus Hitler repudiated himself, so to speak, and suddenly removed the main prop of the whole Nazi doctrine which he himself had preached with such ardor and had committed to eternity in his apocalyptic though slightly confused style.

This was indeed an astonishing event, as portentous as if Wagner had suddenly decided to scrap the *Götterdämmerung* and to end the *Nibelungen* in collaboration with Tchaikowsky.

The democracies, however, chose to be not only baffled but indignant when they heard of the Soviet-German pact. It appeared to them as the most catastrophic ideological betrayal that the world had seen. That Stalin, the head of world communism, should desert the cause of peace seemed to them incredible. That Hitler, who had built his National Socialist party on the idea of eradicating bolshevism from the world should ally himself with it, was no less fantastic. In the outside world, the moral shock was fearful. The conservatives who had some secret fondness for Hitler because he was leading the crusade against communism felt betrayed, but no less than the parties of the left who had remained faithful to the dream of the USSR as the last stronghold of antinazism.

But the ideological scandal thus created in the world only worked to Hitler's advantage. The real issue was befogged more than ever by irrelevant speculations. When Hitler made his Reichstag speech of September 1, he again pretended that his only objective was to settle the Danzig and the Corridor problem. He congratulated himself on the conclusion of a pact which ruled out all recourse to violence between Germany and Russia. He was vague as to the full implications of the pact. Was it a real alliance? Had Stalin offered more than economic and diplomatic support? Was there a precise deal between Moscow and Berlin? The world wondered. But while it wondered, the German armies marched into Poland from the West to meet the Russian armies moving in from the East.

On the twenty-sixth of September a new agreement was signed between the Soviets and the Reich the result of which was the Fourth Partition of Poland, its complete elimination from the map of Europe as an independent nation.

Hitler did not trouble to explain why the necessity of settling the question of Danzig and the Corridor should end up in the division of a nation of thirty-six million people between Stalin and himself. Even the annexation of Czechoslovakia had been "rationalized." But times had changed. It was more or less admitted that neither the democracies nor the neutrals could do anything to stop Hitler in the East. They were powerless.

But although the strategy of conquest was unfolding itself in such obvious manner, the British and the French still felt relatively secure. Hitler was reiterating his assurances that he had no claims against any of his western neighbors, and although they were sufficiently alarmed to have actually gone to war in fulfillment of their pledge to Poland, they were not alarmed enough to do anything but prepare to defend themselves against a possible turn of the wind.

Many were even secretly pleased to see Hitler moving East. They felt that there might still be some hope of localizing the conflict. Hitler and Stalin might dominate Eastern and Southern Europe. Perhaps they would eventually quarrel when it came to dividing the spoils. Although Hitler had just demonstrated that he could not be bluffed and that he would actually make war in spite of his love for peace, there might still be a chance of avoiding a "world war." London was not bombed, the Maginot Line was not attacked. This was surprising indeed. But in spite of so many disillusions concerning Hitler's pledges, it might be that he did intend, after all, to keep his last promises: not to attack France and England and the Western world. Perhaps it meant that if he was not bluffing as far as the East was concerned, he was still afraid of attacking the West.

Thus Hitler's whole strategy during the phase extending from the occupation of Prague to the end of the Polish campaign can be summarized as follows:

He actually succeeded in conquering Poland and destroying the last powerful ally of the democracies in the East. This he did without causing any more positive reaction on the part of England and France than to force them into declaring formal war on the Reich, but without any intention of attacking him.

France and England were lulled into the belief that, somehow or other, the war could be stopped before it came to them. The Blitzkrieg had worked against the Poles. It could obviously not work against the British Navy and the Maginot Line.

All the appeals of the neutrals, whether they came from the Pope, the King of the Belgians, or President Roosevelt, had proved totally ineffectual, but the sense of danger was not great enough to inspire any change of method. Hitler had broken all his pledges, but he had not attacked any neutral as yet. Provided one did not provoke him, one might escape. European neutrals reaffirmed their neutrality. The American isolationists went into high gear.

Hitler had decisively engaged himself on the road to war.

But as far as his enemies were concerned, i.e., the whole civilized world, they still hoped that defense would be enough.

Appeasement had failed. The Chamberlain peace front had been broken. The war front of Hitler, Stalin, Mussolini and Japan was immeasurably strengthened. The "phony war" was on.

•

SPEECH OF MARCH 23, 1939

Memel, Town Theater

Background

1939

March 15—German troops enter Prague. Bohemia and Moravia are made part of the Reich. Chamberlain, in comments, protests against this violation of the Munich agreement.

March 16—Slovakia becomes German protectorate.

March 17—Chamberlain recalls British Ambassador to Berlin for consultation.

March 18—French Chamber of Deputies votes dictatorial powers to Daladier.

March 19—Russia refuses to recognize seizure of Czechoslovakia.

March 20—Memel returns to the Reich.

The Speech

"Memel Germans! Fellow citizens!

"In the name of the entire German people I greet you today and am happy to receive you into our Great German Reich.

"I thereby lead you back into that home which you have not forgotten and which has never forgotten you. . . ."

"You had been left in the lurch at one time by a Germany that surrendered to disgrace and ignominy. Now, however, you have returned into a mighty new Germany that again knows the unshakable conceptions of honor, that does not want to and will not entrust its fate to strangers, but that is ready and determined to master its own fate and to give it form even if another world does not like it.

"For this new Germany today more than 80,000,000 Germans stand sponsor.

"You will now flow into this great stream of our national life, of our labor, our faith, our hopes and, if necessary, also our sacrifices.

"You will understand this better than other Germans who have the good fortune of being permitted to live in the heart of our great Reich. You are the frontier of the country and you will feel what it means not to be forsaken but to know that behind you is a powerful Reich, a consolidated nation.

Just as you were the sufferers from German impotence and disunion, so also were other Germans. From dire need and suffering, however, there has now sprung up for us a new community spirit. Let it be our will and our determination that it shall never again break asunder, and let it be our oath that no other power on earth shall ever break or bend it.

"Twenty years of suffering and misery should be a warning to us and a lesson for all future times."

"What we can expect from the other world we know. We do not have the intention to inflict suffering on this other world. But the suffering that it inflicted on us must come to and end. . . ."

[As delivered, this passage in Herr Hitler's speech read: "What we can expect from the other world we know. We do not have the intention to inflict suffering on this other world; however, those sufferings that it inflicted on us we had to make good again and I believe that in essentials we have already arrived at the conclusion of this unique restitution."]

Press

New York Times—Herr Hitler spoke about two minutes. He decorated Dr. Neumann with the Nazi badge of honor.

London Times, March 24, 1939—In an editorial called "Democracy and Defense," ". . . when Hitler tells the world again at Memel that his expansion is now substantially complete, who has any reason to accept his declaration?"

Le Temps, March 24, 1939—. . . The Fuehrer praised the new German spirit of community which he said no other Power could ever again forget or assail. . . .

•

SPEECH OF APRIL 1, 1939

Wilhelmshaven

Background

1939

March 28—Madrid surrenders to Franco, marking the end of the Civil War in Spain.

March 31—Chamberlain pledges Britain and France to guarantee the independence of Poland.

April 1—The United States recognizes Franco.

The Speech

"German Fellow-Citizens:—He who wants to have the deepest impression of the decay and resurrection of Germany most vividly must go and see the development of a city like Wilhelmshaven, which today reverberates with life and activity and which still a short time ago was a dead spot nearly without means of existence and without prospects of a future —it pays to revisualize this past.

"When this city experienced its first upward move it coincided with the rise of the German Reich after its unification. This Germany was in a state of peace.

"During the same time as the so-called peace-loving and Puritan nations led a great number of wars, Germany then knew only one aim: To maintain peace, to work in peace, to raise the prosperity of its inhabitants, and thereby to contribute to human culture and civilization.

"This Germany of peace times has attempted, with unending diligence, with geniality, and with steadiness, to form its life within and to safeguard outwardly—through participation in peaceful competition with the nations—its due place in the sun.

"Even though this Germany through the decades was the safest guarantor of peace, and even though she occupied herself with peaceful things, she was unable to prevent other nations, and especially their statesmen, from following this rise with envy and hatred and finally to answer with a war.

"Today we know from the documents of history how the encirclement policy of those times was carried on in a planned way by England.

"We know from numerous findings and publications that in that country the conception was that it would be necessary to bring down Germany militarily because its destruction would insure every British citizen a greater abundance of life's possessions.

"Certainly at that time Germany made mistakes. Its most serious mistake was to see this encirclement and not to stave it off in time.

"The only fault we can blame the regime of that time for is that the Reich had full knowledge of this devilish plan of a raid and yet it did not have the power of decision to ward it off in time and could only let this encirclement ripen until the beginning of the catastrophe.

"The result was the World War. In this war the German people, although it had by no means the best armaments, fought heroically. No people can claim the glory for itself to have forced us down—much less so that nation whose statesmen today speak the greatest words.

"Germany at that time remained undefeated and unconquered on land, at sea, and in the air—however, it was Germany.

"But there was the power of the lie and the poison of propaganda which did not balk at misinterpretation and untruth.

"This Germany faced the world in absolute defenselessness because it was unprepared.

"When [President Woodrow] Wilson's Fourteen Points were published, not only many German fellow-citizens but above all the 'leading' men saw in these Fourteen Points not only the possibility of ending the World War but also the pacification of the world at large.

"A peace of reconciliation and understanding was promised—a peace that was to know neither victor nor vanquished, a peace of equal justice for all, a peace of equal distribution of colonial domains and equal recognition of colonial desires, a peace that was to be finally crowned by a league of all free nations.

"It was to be a guarantor of equal rights that would make it seem superfluous in the future for peoples to bear the armaments that previously, so it was said, were so heavily burdensome.

"Therefore, disarmament—disarmament of all the nations.

"Germany was to go ahead as a good example. Everybody was obliged to follow this disarmament. Also the age of secret diplomacy was to be ended. All problems henceforth were to be discussed openly and freely.

"First of all, however, the right of self-determination of nations finally was to have been settled and raised to its proper importance.

"Germany believed in these assurances. With faith in these declarations it had dropped its weapons. And then a breach of a pledge began such as world history had never seen before.

"When our nation had dropped its weapons, a period of suppression, blackmailing, plundering, and slavery began. Not another word about peace without victor or vanquished, but an endless sentence of condemnation for the vanquished. Not another word about justice, but of justice on your side and injustice and illegality on the other.

"Robbery upon robbery, oppression upon oppression were the consequences.

"No one in this democratic world bothered himself any more about the sufferings of our people. Hundreds of thousands fell in the war, not from enemy weapons, but from the hunger blockade. And after the war ended, this blockade was continued for months in order to oppress our people still more.

"Even German war prisoners, after an endless time, had to remain in captivity. The German colonies were stolen from us, German foreign holdings were simply seized and our merchant marine taken away.

"Added to that was a financial plundering such as the world had never before seen. The monetary penalties which were imposed on the German people reached astronomical figures.

"Of these an English statesman said that they could only be fulfilled when the German standard of living was reduced to the lowest possible level and Germans worked fourteen hours daily. What German spirit, German alertness, and German labor through decades and decades had collected and saved was lost in a few years.

"Millions of Germans were either torn away from the Reich or were prevented from returning to the Reich. The

League of Nations was not an instrument of a just policy of understanding among nations, but is and was a guarantee of the meanest dictation man ever invented.

"So was a great people raped and led toward a misery that you all know. A great people through a broken pledge was cheated of its rights and its existence rendered practically impossible. A French statesman coined the following expression: 'There are 20,000,000 Germans too many in the world!'

"Germans ended their lives out of despair, others slid into lethargy and an inevitable destiny and still others were of the opinion that everything must be destroyed; still others set their teeth and clenched their fists in unconscious rage. Still others believed that the past should be restored—restored just as it was.

"Everyone had an idea of some sort. And I, as an unknown soldier of the World War, drew my conclusions.

"It was a very short and simple program. It ran: Removal of the internal enemies of the nation, termination of the divisions within Germany, the gathering up of the entire national strength of our people into a new community, and the breaking of the peace treaty—in one way or another!

"For as long as this dictate of Versailles weighed upon the German people it was actually damned to go to the ground. If, however, other statesmen now declare that right must rule on this earth, then they should be told that their crime is no right, that their dictate is neither right nor law but above this dictate stand the eternal rights of peoples to live.

"The German people were not created by providence in order to follow obediently a law which suits the English or the French, but rather in order to champion their right to live. That is why we are here! I was determined to take up this battle of advocating the German right to live.

"I took it up first within the nation.

"In place of a great number of parties, social ranks, and societies, a single community now has taken its place—the

German national community! To bring it to realization and to deepen it more and more is our task.

"I had to hurt many in this time. However, I believe that the good fortune in which the entire nation is participating today must richly compensate every single one for what he had to give up dearly on his own part.

"You all have sacrificed your parties, societies, and associations, but you have obtained in return a great strong Reich. And the Reich today, thank God, is strong enough to take your rights under its protection.

"We no longer are dependent on the good graces or disgraces of other States or their statesmen.

"When, more than six years ago, I obtained power, I took over a wretched inheritance. The Reich seemed to possess no more possibilities of existence for its citizens.

"I undertook the work at that time with the one single capital which I possessed. It was the capital of your strength to work.

"Your strength to work, my fellow-citizens, I now have begun to put to use. I had no foreign exchange. I had no gold reserve. I had only one thing—my faith and your work!

"Thus we began the gigantic work of rebuilding based upon the confidence of the nation, instilled with the belief and the confidence in its eternal values.

"Now we have found a new economic system, a system which is this: Capital is the power of labor and the coverage of money lies in our production.

"We have founded a system based on the most sincere foundation there is, namely: Form your life yourself! Work for your existence! Help yourself and God will help you!

"Within a few years we have wrenched Germany from despair. But the world did not help us. If today an English statesman says one can and must solve all problems through frank deliberations, I should like to tell this statesman just this: An opportunity has been open for fifteen years before our time.

"If the world says today that the nations must be divided into virtuous nations and into such as are not virtuous—and that the English and French belong to the first class, and the Germans and Italians belong to those not virtuous—we can only answer: The judgment whether a people is virtuous or not virtuous can hardly be passed by a human being. That should be left to God.

"Perhaps the same British statesman will retort: 'God has passed the verdict already, because He presented the virtuous nations with one quarter of the world and He took everything away from the nonvirtuous!'

"The question may be permitted: 'By what means have the virtuous nations obtained for themselves this quarter of the world.'

"And one must answer: 'They did not apply virtuous methods!'

"For 300 years this England acted without virtue in order now in maturity to speak of virtue. Thus it could appear that during this British period without virtue 46,000,000 Englishmen have subdued nearly one-quarter of the world while 80,000,000 Germans, because of their virtue, must live at a rate of 140 to one square kilometer.

"Indeed, twenty years ago, the question of virtue still was not entirely clear for the British statesmen insofar as it concerned conceptions of property. One still held it compatible with virtue simply to take away the colonies of another people that had acquired them through treaty or through purchase because one possessed the power—this very power which now, to be sure, should be deemed as something abominable and detestable.

"I have only one thing to ask the gentlemen here: whether they believe what they say or do not believe it. We do not know.

"We assume, however, that they do not believe what they say. For if we should assume that they themselves really believe it then we would lose every respect for them.

"For fifteen years Germany patiently bore its lot and fate. I also sought in the beginning to solve every problem through talks. I made an offer in the case of each problem and each time it was turned down!

"There can be no doubt that every people possesses sacred interests, simply because they are identical with their lives and their right to live.

"When, today, a British statesman demands that every problem which lies in the midst of Germany's life interest first should be discussed with England, then I, too, could demand just as well that every British problem first is to be discussed with us.

"Certainly, these Englishmen may give me the answer: 'The Germans have no business in Palestine!' I answer that we do not want anything in Palestine.

"Just as we Germans have little to do in Palestine, just as little business has England mixing in our German section of existence. And if they now declare that it involves general questions of law and justice I could approve of this opinion only if it was considered as binding to both of us.

"They say we have no right to do this or that. I should like to raise the counter-question: What right, for example, has England to shoot down Arabs in Palestine just because they defend their homeland; who gives them this right?

"Anyway, we have not slaughtered thousands in Central Europe but instead we have regulated our problems with law and order.

"However, I should like to say one thing here: The German people of today, the German Reich of today is not willing to surrender life interests, it also is not willing to face rising dangers without doing something about them.

"When the Allies, without regard or purpose, right, tradition, or even reasonableness, changed the map of Europe, we had not the power to prevent it. If, however, they expect the Germany of today to sit patiently by until the very last day when this same result would again be repeated—while they create satellite States and set them against Germany—then they are mistaking the Germany of today for the Germany of before the war.

"He who declares himself ready to pull the chestnuts out of the fire for these powers must realize he burns his fingers.

"Really, we feel no hatred against the Czech people. We have lived together for years. The English statesmen do not know this. They have no idea that Hradcany castle was not built by an Englishman but by a German and that the St. Vitus Cathedral likewise was not erected by Englishmen but that German hands did it.

"Even the French were not active there. They do not know that already at a time when England still was very small a German Kaiser was paid homage on this hill [Hradcany castle]—that one thousand years before me the first German King stood there and accepted the homage of this people.

"Englishmen do not know that. They could not know that and they do not have to know it. It is sufficient that we know it and that it is true that this territory lay in the living space of the German people for over a thousand years.

"Despite this, however, we would have had nothing against an independent Czech State if, first, it had not suppressed Germans, and, second, if it had not been intended as the instrument of a future attack on Germany. When, however, a former French Air Minister writes in a newspaper that on the basis of their prominent position it is the task of these Czechs to strike at the heart of German industry with air attacks during war, then one understands that this is not without interest to us and that we draw certain conclusions from it.

"It would have been up to England and France to defend this airbase. Upon us fell the task of preventing such an attack at all events. I sought to accomplish this by a natural and simple way.

"When I first saw that every effort of that kind was destined to be wrecked and that elements hostile to Germany again would win the upper hand, and as I further saw that this State had long since lost its inner vitality—indeed, that it already was broken to pieces—I again carried through the old German Reich. *And I joined together again what had to be united because of history and geographical positions, and according to all rules of reason.*

"Not to oppress the Czech people! It will enjoy more freedom than the suppressed people of the virtuous nations.

"I have, so I believe, thereby rendered peace a great service, because I have rendered innocuous in time an instrument which was destined to become effective in war against Germany. *If they now say that this is the signal that Germany now wants to attack the entire world, I do not believe that this is meant seriously: such could only be the expression of a bad conscience.*

"Perhaps it is rage over the failure of a farflung plan, perhaps it is an attempt to create tactical preconditions for a new policy of encirclement.

"Be that as it may: it is my conviction that thereby I have rendered peace a great service and out of this conviction I decided three weeks ago to name the coming party rally the 'Party Convention of Peace.'

"For Germany has no intention of attacking other people. What we, however, do not want to renounce is the building up of our economic relations. We have a right thereto and I do not accept any condition from a European or a non-European statesman.

"The German Reich is not only a great producer but also a gigantic consumer, just as we as a producer will be an irreplaceable trade partner, so as a consumer we are capable of honorably and fairly paying for what we consume.

"We are not thinking about making war on other peoples. However, our precondition is that they leave us in peace.

"In any case the German Reich is not ready everlastingly to accept intimidation or even a policy of encirclement.

"I once made an agreement with England—namely, the

Naval Treaty. It is based on the earnest desire which we all possess never to have to go to war against England. But this wish can only be a mutual one.

"*If this wish no longer exists in England, then the practical preconditions for this agreement therewith are removed* and Germany also would accept this very calmly. We are self-assured because we are strong, and we are strong because we are united and because in addition we are looking forward. And in this city, my fellow citizens, I can address the one exhortation to you: Look into the world and to all its happenings with open eyes. Do not deceive yourselves about the most important precondition in life—namely, the necessity to be strong.

"We have experienced this for fifteen years. Therefore I have made Germany strong again and erected an armed force, an army on land, at sea, and in the air.

"When they say in other countries that they will arm and will keep arming still more, I can tell those statesmen only this: They will not be able to tire me out. I am determined to proceed on this road and I have a conviction that we shall proceed faster than the others. No power on earth will ever again be able to entice the weapons from us through any phrase.

"Should, however, somebody be craving for measuring their strength with ours, then the German people also are ready at any time and I am ready and determined.

"Just as we think, our friends also think, especially the State with which we are bound most closely and with which we are marching now and will march under all circumstances forever.

"If hostile journalists do not know of anything else to write, then they write about rents or breaks in the Axis. They ought to hold their peace. This Axis is the most natural political instrument existing in this world.

"It is a political combination which owes its origin not

only to reasonable political deliberation and the desire for justice but also to the power of an ideal.

"This construction will be more durable than the momentary ties of nonhomogeneous bodies on the other side. For if some one tells me today that there are no philosophical or ideological differences of any kind between England and Soviet Russia, then I can only say:

" 'I congratulate you, gentlemen!'

"I believe that the time is not far distant in which the philosophical community between Fascist Italy and National Socialist Germany will prove essentially different than the one between democratic Great Britain and the bolshevist Russia of Stalin.

"However, if there really should be no ideological difference, then I can only say: How correct, indeed, is my position toward Marxism and communism and democracy! Why two phenomena if they possess the same contents?

"In these days we experience a very great triumph and a deep inner satisfaction. A country which also was devastated by bolshevism, where hundreds of thousands of human beings, women, men, children, and patriarchs have been slaughtered, has liberated itself, liberated despite all the ideological friends of bolshevism who sit in Great Britain, France and in other countries.

"We can understand this Spain only too well in its struggle and we greet and congratulate it for its success. We Germans of today can express this with special pride, since many German young men have done their duty there. They have helped as volunteers to break a tyrannic regime and to return to a nation the right of self-determination.

"We are pleased to note how fast, how extremely fast, the philosophical change came over the deliverers of war material on the Red side. We note how much they now, all of a sudden, understand this National Spain and how ready they are to conduct with this National Spain, if not philosophical, then at least economic business.

"This also is a sign showing the trend of development.

"My fellow-citizens, I believe that all States will be facing the same problem which we have faced.

"State after State will either fall under the Jewish bolshevist pest or it will defend itself.

"We have done it and have now erected a national German people's State. This people's State wants to live in peace and friendship with any other State but it will never again let itself be forced down by another State.

"I do not know whether the world will become fascist! But I am deeply convinced that this world in the end will defend itself against the most severe bolshevistic threat that exists.

"Therefore I believe that a final understanding between nations will come sooner or later. Only when this Jewish wedge among peoples is removed can the establishment of co-operation among nations—built on lasting understanding—be considered.

"Today we must rely upon our own strength! And we can be satisfied with the results of this trust in ourselves—inwardly and outwardly.

"When I came to power, my fellow-citizens, Germany was divided and impotent internally, and outwardly the sport of foreign designs. Today we are in order domestically. Our business is flourishing.

"Abroad perhaps we are not loved, but respected. Yet we receive attention! That is the decisive factor! Above all we have given the greatest possible good fortune to millions of our fellow-citizens—the return into our Greater German Reich.

"Second: We have given Central Europe a great piece of good fortune, namely, peace—peace that will be protected by German might. And this might can no longer be broken by any world power. That is our pledge!

"So we will show that over two million citizens did not fall in the Great War in vain. From their sacrifice came

Greater Germany. From their sacrifice was this strong young German people that the Reich called into being and that has now made itself felt. In the face of this sacrifice we shall not shy away from any sacrifice if it is ever necessary.

"Let the world understand that!

"It can make pacts and draw up declarations as much as it wishes. *I have no faith in paper, but I do have faith in you, my fellow-citizens!*

"The greatest breach of faith of all time was committed against us Germans. Let us take care that our people internally are never again in a position to be broken. Then no one in the world will threaten us. Then peace will either be maintained for our people or, if necessary, peace will be enforced.

"Then our people will bloom and flourish. Our people will be able to put their geniality, their ability, their diligence and steadfastness into the works of peace and human culture. This is our desire. We hope for it and we believe in it.

"Twenty years ago that party was founded—at that time a tiny organization. Consider the road from that time until today! Consider the wonders which have occurred about us.

"Believe, therefore, because of this wonderful road, also in the course of the German people in its coming great future!

"Germany—Sieg Heil! Sieg Heil! Sieg Heil!"

Press

New York Times, April 3—It is evident from the speech which Hitler made yesterday at Wilhelmshaven that Britain's warning of her willingness to go to war if Poland is attacked at this juncture of affairs of Europe has been read with care in Germany. It was a truculent speech, in the usual Hitler manner, filled with derision for the democracies and boasts of Germany's willingness to "measure her strength" with that of any other nation in war as well as in peace. But it proposed no immediate action other than a possible denunciation of Germany's naval treaty with Britain—which would amount merely to an empty gesture—and it refrained significantly from any ultimatum to Poland.

Le Temps, April 3—The Wilhelmshaven speech was distinguished by a reaffirmation of German's desire for peace, and at the same time a thinly disguised threat to Poland. . . . Chancellor Hitler declared that Germany did not dream of attacking other nations, and he offered as proof his decision to call the next Congress of the National Socialist Party the "Congress of Peace." He would do well to wait until that desire for peace is expressed clearly in the acts of the Berlin Government, before congratulating himself.

London Times, April 3—Although Hitler's speech at Wilhelmshaven was overshadowed by the British pledge to Poland, it was clearly bitter and threatening, particularly against Britain's efforts to protect Eastern European States from Germany.

•

SPEECH OF APRIL 28, 1939

Berlin, Reichstag

1939

April 5—Lebrun is re-elected President of the French Republic for seven years.

April 7—Italy invades Albania.

April 13—Britain and France extend pledge of guarantee to Rumania and Greece.

April 15—Roosevelt sends a message to Hitler and Mussolini inviting them to observe a ten-year truce and asking them to pledge themselves not to attack thirty-one nations of which he gives the list.

April 20—Mussolini denies having any aggressive aims.
April 23—British Ambassador returns to Berlin.
April 24—British Cabinet approves conscription.

The Speech

"Members of the German Reichstag! The President of the United States of America has addressed a telegram to me with the curious contents of which you are already familiar. Before I, the addressee, actually received the document the rest of the world had already been informed of it by radio and newspaper reports; and numerous commentaries in organs of the democratic world press had already generously enlightened us as to the fact that this telegram was a very skillful, tactful document destined to impose upon the States in which people govern, the responsibility for warlike measures adopted by the plutocratic countries.

"In view of these facts I decided to summon the German Reichstag so that you gentlemen might have the opportunity of hearing my answer first, and of either confirming that answer or rejecting it. In addition, I considered it desirable to keep to the method of procedure initiated by President Roosevelt and to inform the rest of the world on my part and by our means of my answer.

"But I should like also to take this opportunity of giving expression to feelings with which the tremendous historical happiness of the month of March inspires me. I can give vent to my deepest feelings only in the form of humble thanks to Providence, who called upon me and vouchsafed to me, once an unknown soldier of the great war, to rise to be the leader of my so dearly loved people. . . ."

"I have worked only to restore that which others once broke by force. I have desired only to make good that which satanic malice or human unreason destroyed or demolished. I have therefore taken no step which violated the rights of others, but have only restored that justice which was violated twenty years ago.

"The present Greater German Reich contains no territory which was not from the earliest times part of this Reich, not bound up with or subject to its sovereignty. Long before an American continent had been discovered—to say nothing of settled—by white people, this Reich existed, not merely in its present extent but with the addition of many regions and provinces which have since been lost.

"Twenty-one years ago, when the bloodshed of war came to an end, millions of minds were filled with the ardent hope that a peace of reason and justice would reward and bless the nations which had been visited by the fearful scourge of the Great War. I say 'reward' for all these men and women, whatever the conclusions arrived at by historians, bore no responsibility for these fearful happenings.

"And if in some countries there still were politicians who even at that time could be charged with responsibility for this, the most atrocious massacre of all time, yet vast numbers of combatant soldiers of every country and nation were at most deserving of pity but were by no means guilty.

"I myself, as you know, had never played a part in politics before the war, and only, like millions of others, performed such duties as I was called upon to fulfill as a decent citizen and soldier. It was therefore with an absolutely clear conscience that I was able to take up the cause of freedom and the future of my people, both during and after the war.

"And I can therefore speak in the name of millions and millions of others equally blameless when I declare that all those who had only fought for their nation in loyal fulfillment of their duty were entitled to a peace of reason and justice, so that mankind might at last set to work to make good by joint effort the losses which all had suffered.

"But the millions were cheated of this peace; for not only did the German people or other people fighting on our side suffer through the peace treaties, but these treaties had an annihilating effect on the victor countries.

"For the first time appeared the misfortune that politics should be controlled by men who had not fought in the war. The feeling of hatred was unknown to soldiers, but not to those elderly politicians who had carefully preserved their own precious lives from the horror of war and who now descended upon humanity in the guise of insane spirits of revenge.

"Hatred, malice and unreason were the intellectual forebears of the Treaty of Versailles. Living space and States with history going back a thousand years were arbitrarily broken up and dissolved. Since time immemorial men who belong together have been torn asunder; the economic conditions of life have been ignored, while the peoples themselves have been converted into victors and vanquished, into masters possessing all rights and slaves possessing none. . . ."

"However, when this new world order turned out to be a catastrophe, the democratic peace dictators of American and European origin were so cowardly that none of them ventured to take the responsibility for what occurred. Each put the blame on the others, thus endeavoring to save himself from the judgment of history.

"However, the people who were maltreated by their hatred and unreason were, unfortunately, not in a position to share with those who had injured them in this escape. . . ."

"One of the most shameful acts of oppression ever committed is the dismemberment of the German nation and the political disintegration of her living space—which has, after all, been hers for thousands of years—was provided for in the dictate of Versailles.

"I have never, gentlemen, left any doubt, that in point of fact it is scarcely possible anywhere in Europe to arrive at a harmony of State and national boundaries which will be satisfactory in every way.

"On one hand, migration of peoples which gradually came

to a standstill during the last few centuries and development of large communities, on the other, have brought about a situation which, whatever way they look at it, must necessarily be considered unsatisfactory by those concerned.

"It was, however, the very way in which these national and political developments were gradually stabilized in the last century which led many to consider themselves justified in cherishing hope that in the end a compromise would be found between respect for the national life of various European peoples and recognition of established political structures—a compromise by which, without destroying political order in Europe and within the existing economic basis, nationalities could nevertheless be preserved.

"This hope was abolished by the Great War. Peace—the dictate of Versailles—did justice neither to one principle nor to the other. Neither the right of self-determination nor yet political, let alone economic, necessities and conditions for European development, were respected.

"Nevertheless, I never left any doubt that—as I have already emphasized—even revision of the Treaty of Versailles would also find its limit somewhere. And I have always said so with utmost frankness—not for any tactical reasons but from my innermost conviction.

"As national leader of the German people, I have never left any doubt that whenever higher interests of the European comity were at stake, national interests must, if necessary, be relegated to second place in certain cases.

"And—as I have already emphasized—this is not for tactical reasons, for I have never left any doubt that I am absolutely earnest in this attitude of mine. For quite a number of territories which might possibly be disputed I have, therefore, come to final decisions which I have proclaimed not only to the outside world but also to my own people, and have seen to it that they should abide by them.

"I have not, as France did in 1870-71, described the cession of Alsace-Lorraine as intolerable for the future, but I have here drawn a difference between the Saar Territory and these two former imperial provinces. And I have never changed my attitude, nor will I ever do so.

"I have not allowed this attitude to be modified or jeopardized inside the country on any occasion, either in the press or in any other way. *Return of the Saar Territory has done away with all territorial problems in Europe between France and Germany. I have, however, always regarded it as regrettable that French statesmen should take this attitude for granted.*

"This is, however, not the way to look at the matter. It was not for fear of France that I preached this attitude. As a former soldier I see no reason whatever for such fear. Moreover, as regards the Saar Territory, I made it quite clear we would not countenance any refusal to return it to Germany.

"No, I have confirmed this attitude to France as an expression of appreciation of the necessity to attain peace in Europe, instead of sowing the seed of continual uncertainty and even tension by making unlimited demands and continually asking for revision. If this tension has nevertheless now arisen, the responsibility does not lie with Germany but with those international elements which systematically produce such tension in order to serve their capitalist interests.

"I have given binding declarations to a large number of States.

"None of these States can complain that even a trace of a demand contrary thereto has been made to them by Germany. *None of the Scandinavian statesmen, for example, can contend that a request has ever been put to them by the German Government or by German public opinion which was incompatible with the sovereignty and integrity of their State.*

"I was pleased that a number of European States availed themselves of these declarations by the German Government to express and emphasize their desire for absolute neutrality. This applies to Holland, Belgium, Switzerland, Denmark.

"I have already mentioned France. I need not mention

Italy, with whom we are united in the deepest and closest friendship, *or Hungary and Yugoslavia,* with whom we, as neighbors, have the fortune to be on very friendly terms.

"On the other hand, I have left no doubt from the first moment of my political activity that there existed other circumstances which represent such a mean and gross outrage of the right of self-determination of our people that we can never accept or endorse them.

"I have never written a single line or made a single speech displaying a different attitude toward the above-mentioned States. On the other hand, with reference to other cases, I have never written a single line or made a single speech in which I have expressed any attitude contrary to my actions.

"1. Austria! The oldest Eastern march of the German people, was once the buttress of the German nation on the southeast of the Reich.

"The Germans of this country are descended from settlers from all the German tribes, even though the Bavarian tribe did contribute a major portion. Later this Ostmark became the crown lands and nucleus of the five-century-old German Empire, with Vienna as the capital of the German Reich of that period.

"This German Reich was finally broken up in the course of a gradual dissolution by Napoleon the Corsican, but continued to exist as a German federation, and not so long ago fought and suffered in the greatest war of all time as an entity which was an expression of the national feelings of the people, even if it was no longer one united State. I myself am a child of this Ostmark.

"Not only was the German Reich destroyed and Austria split up into its component parts by the criminals of Versailles, but Germans also were forbidden to acknowledge that community which they had confessed for more than a thousand years. I have always regarded elimination of this state of affairs as the highest and most holy task of my life. I have never failed to proclaim this determination. And I have always been resolved to realize these ideas which haunted me day and night.

"I should have sinned against my call by Providence had I failed in my own endeavor to lead my native country and my German people of Ostmark back to the Reich and, thus, to the community of German people.

"In doing so, moreover, I have wiped out the most disgraceful side of the Treaty of Versailles. I have once more established the right of self-determination and done away with democratic oppression of seven and a half million Germans.

"I have removed the ban which prevented them from voting on their own fate, and carrying out this vote before the whole world. The result was not only what I expected but also precisely what had been anticipated by the Versailles democratic oppressors of the peoples. For why else did they stop a plebiscite on the question of Anschluss!

"2. When in the course of the migrations of peoples, the Germanic tribes began, for reasons inexplicable to us, to migrate out of the territory which is today Bohemia and Moravia, a foreign Slav people made its way into this territory and made a place for itself between the remaining Germans. Since that time the living space of this Slav people has been inclosed in the form of a horseshoe by Germans.

"From an economic point of view independent existence is, in the long run, impossible for these countries except on a basis of relationship with the German nation and German economy. But apart from this, nearly four million Germans lived in this territory of Bohemia and Moravia.

"The policy of national annihilation which set in, particularly after the Treaty of Versailles under pressure of the Czech majority, combined, too, with economic conditions and a rising tide of distress, led to emigration of these German elements so that Germans left in the territory were reduced to approximately 3,700,000.

"The population of the fringe of territory is uniformly

German, but there are also large German linguistic enclaves in the interior. The Czech nation is, in its origins, foreign to us, but in the thousand years in which the two peoples have lived side by side a Czech culture has, in the main, been formed and molded by German influences.

"Czech economy owes its existence to the fact of having been part of the great German economic system. The capital of this country was for a time a German imperial city, and it contains the oldest German university. Numerous cathedrals, town halls, and palaces of nobility and citizen class bear witness to the influence of German culture.

"The Czech people itself has in the course of centuries alternated between close and more distant contacts with the German people. Every close contact resulted in a period in which both the German and the Czech nations flourished: every estrangement was calamitous in its consequences.

"We are familiar with the merits and values of the German people, but the Czech nation, with the sum total of its skill and ability, its industry, its diligence, its love of its native soil and of its own national heritage, also deserves our respect.

"There were, in actual fact, periods in which this mutual respect for the qualities of the other nation were a matter of course.

"The democratic peacemakers of Versailles can take credit for having assigned to this Czech people the special rôle of a satellite State capable of being used against Germany. For this purpose they arbitrarily adjudicated foreign national property to the Czech State which was utterly incapable of survival on the strength of the Czech national unit alone; that is, they did violence to other nationalities in order to give a firm basis to a State which was to incorporate a latent threat to the German nation in Central Europe.

"For this State, in which the so-called predominant national element was actually in the minority, could be maintained only by means of brutal assault on national units which formed a major part of the population.

"This assault was possible only insofar as protection and assistance was granted by European democracies. This assistance could naturally be expected only on condition that this State was prepared loyally to take over and play the role which it had been assigned at birth, but the purpose of this role was none other than to prevent consolidation of Central Europe, to provide a bridge to Europe for bolshevik aggression, and, above all, to act as the mercenary of European democracies against Germany.

"Everything else followed automatically. The more this State tried to fulfill the task it had been set, the greater was the resistance put up by national minorities. And the greater the resistance, the more it became necessary to resort to oppression.

"This inevitable hardening of internal antitheses led, in its turn, to increased dependence on democratic European founders and benefactors of the State. For they alone were in position to maintain in the long run the economic existence of this unnatural and artificial creation.

"Germany was primarily interested in one thing only and that was to liberate nearly four million Germans in this country from their unbearable situation and make it possible for them to return to their home country and to the thousand-year-old Reich.

"It was only natural that this problem immediately brought up all other aspects of the nationalities problem. But it also was natural that removal of different national groups should deprive what was left of the State of all capacity to survive—a fact of which the founders of the State had been well aware when they planned it at Versailles, since it was for this very reason that they decided on assault on other minorities and had forced these against their will to become part of this amateurishly constructed State. . . ."

"What was expected from this State is shown most clearly by the observation of the French Air Minister, M. Pierre Cot, who calmly stated that the duty of this State in case of any conflict was to be an airdrome for the landing and taking off of bombers from which it would be possible to destroy the most important German industrial centers in a few hours.

"It is comprehensible, therefore, that the German Government in its turn decided to destroy this airdrome for bombing planes. They did not come to this decision because of hatred of the Czech people. Quite the contrary. For, in the course of a thousand years during which the German and Czech people had lived together, there had often been periods of close co-operation lasting hundreds of years and between these, it is true, only short periods of tension.

"In such periods of tension, the passions of people struggling together in the front trenches of national position can very easily dim the feeling of justice and thus lead to the wrong total impression. This is a feature of every war. It was solely in the long epochs of living together in harmony that the two peoples agreed they were both entitled to advance the holy claim to deference for and respect of their nationality.

"But in these years of struggle, my own attitude toward the Czech people was never anything else than that of guardian of the unilateral national and Reich interest, combined with feelings of respect for the Czech people.

"One thing is certain: If the democratic midwives of this State had succeeded in attaining their ultimate goal, the German Reich would certainly not have been destroyed, although we might have sustained heavy losses.

"No! The Czech people, by reason of its size and position, would presumably have had to put up with much more dreadful and—I am convinced—catastrophic consequences.

"I am happy it has proved possible, even to the annoyance of democratic interests, to avoid this catastrophe in Central Europe, thanks to our own moderation and also to the good judgment of the Czech people. That which the best and wisest Czechs have struggled for decades to attain is as a matter of course granted to this people in the National Socialist

German Reich, namely, the right to their own nationality and the right to foster this nationality and to revive it. National Socialist Germany has no notion of ever betraying the racial principles of which we are proud. They will be beneficial not only to the German nation but to the Czech people as well. . . ."

"As late as March, 1938, I believed that by means of gradual evolution it might prove possible to solve the problem of minorities in this State and, at one time or another, by means of mutual co-operation to achieve a common platform which would be advantageous to all interests concerned, politically as well as economically.

"It was not until M. Benes, who was completely in the hands of his democratic, international financiers, turned the problem into a military one and unleashed a wave of suppression over Germans, at the same time attempting, by that mobilization of which you all know, to inflict international defeat upon the German State and to damage its prestige, that it became clear to me that a solution by these means was no longer possible. For the false report of German mobilization was quite obviously inspired from abroad and suggested to the Czechs in order to cause the German Reich such loss of prestige.

"I do not need to repeat once more that in May of the past year Germany had not mobilized one single man, although we were all of the opinion that the very fate of Herr Schuschnigg should have shown all others the advisability of working for mutual understanding by means of more just treatment of national minorities.

"I for my part was, at any rate, prepared to attempt this kind of peaceful development with patience and, if need be, in a process lasting some years. However, it was exactly this peaceful solution which was a thorn in the flesh of agitators in the democracies.

"They hate us Germans and would prefer to eradicate us completely. What do the Czechs mean to them? They are nothing but a means to an end. And what do they care for the fate of a small and valiant nation? Why should they worry about the lives of hundreds of thousands of brave soldiers who would have been sacrificed for their policy? . . ."

"You are acquainted, gentlemen, with decisions I made at the time:

"1. Solution of this question, and what is more, by October 10, 1938, at the latest.

"2. Preparations of this solution with all means necessary to leave no doubt that any attempt at intervention would be met by the united force of the whole nation. . . . The decision of Munich led to the following result:

"1. The return of the most essential parts of the German border settlements in Bohemia and Moravia to the Reich.

"2. The keeping open of the possibility of solution of other problems of that State—that is, the return or separation of existing Hungarian and Slovak minorities.

"3. There still remained the question of guarantees. As far as Germany and Italy were concerned, a guarantee of this State had, from the first, been made dependent upon the consent of all interested parties bordering on Czechoslovakia; that is to say, the guarantee was coupled with actual solution of problems concerning the parties mentioned which were still unsolved.

"The following problems were still left open:

> "1. Return of Magyar districts to Hungary;
> "2. Return of Polish districts to Poland;
> "3. Solution of the Slovak question;
> "4. Solution of the Ukrainian question.

"As you know, negotiations between Hungary and Czechoslovakia had scarcely begun when both Czechoslovak and Hungarian negotiators requested Germany and Italy, the country which stands side by side with Germany, to act as arbitrators in defining new frontiers between Slovakia, Carpatho-Ukraine and Hungary. The countries concerned made no use themselves of the possibility of appealing to the four powers; on the contrary, they expressly renounced this possibility, that is, they declined it.

"And this was only natural. All people living in this territory desired peace and quiet. Italy and Germany were prepared to answer their call. Neither England nor France raised any objection to this arrangement, which actually constituted a formal departure from the Munich agreement.

"Nor was it possible for them to do so; it would have been madness for Paris or London to have protested against an action on the part of Germany or Italy which had been undertaken solely at the request of the countries concerned.

"The decision arrived at by Germany and Italy proved—as always in such cases—entirely satisfactory to neither party. From the very beginning the difficulty was that it had to be accepted voluntarily by both parties. Thus, when the decision came to be put into effect, violent protests were raised immediately following on the acceptance by the two States.

"Hungary, prompted by general and particular interests, demanded Carpatho-Ukraine, while Poland demanded direct means of communication with Hungary.

"It was clear that in such circumstances even the remnant of the State which Versailles had brought into being was predestined to extinction. It was a fact that perhaps only one single State was interested in preservation of the status quo, and that was Rumania; the man best authorized to speak on behalf of that country told me personally how desirable it would be to have a direct line of communication with Germany, perhaps via Carpatho-Ukraine and Slovakia.

"I mention this as an illustration of the feeling of being menaced by Germany from which the Rumanian Government—according to American clairvoyants—are supposed to be suffering. But it was now clear that it could not be Germany's task permanently to oppose the development or actually to fight for the maintenance of a state of affairs for which we could never have made ourselves responsible. The stage was thus reached at which, in the name of the German Government, I decided to make a declaration to the effect that we had no intention of any longer incurring the reprobation of opposing the common wishes of Poland and Hungary as regards their frontiers simply in order to keep an open road of approach for Germany to Rumania.

"Since, moreover, the Czech Government resorted once more to its old methods and Slovakia also gave expression to its desire for independence, further existence of the State was out of the question. The construction of Czechoslovakia worked out at Versailles had had its day.

"It broke up not because Germany desired its break-up, but because in the long run it was impossible to construct and uphold around a conference table artificial States which are incapable of survival. Consequently, in reply to the question regarding a guarantee which was submitted by England and France a few days before the dissolution of this State, Germany refused this guarantee since all conditions for it laid down at Munich were lacking.

"On the contrary, when, after the whole structure of the State had begun to break up and, practically speaking, had already dissolved itself—the German Government finally decided also to intervene. It did this only in fulfillment of an obvious duty, for the following point should be noted:

"On the occasion of the first visit of the Czech Foreign Minister, M. Chvalkovsky, to Munich, the German Government plainly expressed their views on the future of Czechoslovakia. I myself assured M. Chvalkovsky on that occasion that, provided loyal treatment was meted out to large German minorities remaining in Czech territory and provided general appeasement of the whole State was attained, we would guarantee a loyal attitude on the part of Germany and would, for our part, place no obstacles in the way of the State.

"But I also made it clear beyond all doubt that if the Czechs were to undertake any steps in line with the political tendencies of Dr. Benes, their former President, Germany would not put up with any development along such lines but would stifle it in its earliest stages. I also pointed out at that time that the maintenance of such a tremendous military arsenal in Central Europe for no reason or purpose could only be regarded as a focus of danger.

"Later developments proved how justified my warning had been. A continuous and rising tide of underground propaganda and a gradual tendency on the part of Czech newspapers to lapse into the old style of writing made it finally clear even to the greatest simpleton that the old state of affairs would soon be restored.

"The danger of military conflict was all the greater, as there was always the possibility that some madman or other might get control of the vast stores of munitions. This involved the danger of immense explosions. As proof of this, I cannot refrain, gentlemen, from giving you an idea of the truly gigantic amounts of this international store of explosives in Central Europe.

"Since occupation of this territory, the following have been confiscated and placed in safe-keeping:

"Air force: airplanes, 1,582; anti-aircraft guns, 501.

"Army: guns, light and heavy, 2,175; mine throwers, 785; tanks, 469; machine guns, 43,875; automatic pistols, 114,000; rifles, 1,090,000.

"Ammunition: infantry ammunition, over 1,000,000,000 rounds; shells, over 3,000,000 rounds; other implements of war of all kinds—for example, bridge-building equipment, aircraft detectors, searchlights, measuring instruments, motor vehicles, and special motor vehicles—in vast quantities!

"I believe it is a good thing for millions and millions of people that I, thanks to the last-minute insight of responsible men on the other side, succeeded in averting such an explosion and found a solution which I am convinced has finally abolished this problem of a source of danger in Central Europe.

"The contention that this solution is contrary to the Mu-

nich agreement can neither be supported nor confirmed. This agreement could, under no circumstances, be regarded as final because it admitted that other problems required and remained to be solved.

"We cannot really be reproached for the fact that the parties concerned—and this is the deciding factor—did not turn to the four powers but only to Italy and Germany; nor yet for the fact that the State as such finally split up of its own accord and there, consequently, is no longer any Czechoslovakia.

"It was, however, understandable that long after the ethnographic principle had been made invalid, Germany should take under her protection her interests dating back a thousand years, which are not only of a political but also of an economic nature.

"The future will show whether the solution which Germany has found is right or wrong. However, it is certain that the solution is not subject to English supervision or criticism. For Bohemia and Moravia as remnants of former Czechoslovakia have nothing more whatever to do with the Munich agreement. Just as English measures in, say Northern Ireland, whether they be right or wrong, are not subject to German supervision or criticism.

". . . During the whole of my political activity I have always expounded the idea of close friendship and collaboration between Germany and England. In my movement I found innumerable others of like mind. Perhaps they joined me because of my attitude in this matter. This desire for Anglo-German friendship and co-operation conforms not merely to sentiments which result from the racial origins of our two peoples but also to my realization of the importance for the whole of mankind of the existence of the British Empire.

"I have never left room for any doubt of my belief that the existence of this empire is an estimable factor of value for the whole of human cultural and economic life. By what-

ever means Great Britain has acquired her colonial territories —and I know that they were those of force and often brutality—nevertheless I know full well that no other empire has ever come into being in any other way and that, in the final resort, it is not so much the methods that are taken into account in history as the success, and not the success of the methods as such but rather the general good which the methods yield.

"Now, there is no doubt that the Anglo-Saxon people have accomplished immeasurable colonizing work in the world. For this work I have sincere admiration.

"The thought of destroying this labor appeared and still appears to me, seen from the higher human point of view, as nothing but a manifestation of human wanton destructiveness. However, this sincere respect of mine for achievement does not mean foregoing the securing of the life of my own people.

"I regard it as impossible to achieve lasting friendship between the German and Anglo-Saxon peoples if the other side does not recognize that there are German as well as British interests, that not only is preservation of the British Empire the meaning and purpose of the lives of Britishers, but also that for Germans freedom and preservation of the German Reich is their life and purpose.

"A genuine, lasting friendship between these two nations is conceivable only on the basis of mutual regards. The English people rule a great empire. They built up this empire at a time when the German states were divided and weak. . . ."

"Now, if England cannot understand our point of view, thinking, perchance, that she may look upon Germany as a vassal State, then our love and friendly feelings have indeed been wasted on England. We shall not despair or lose heart on that account, but—relying on the consciousness of our own strength and the strength of our friends—we shall then find ways and means to secure our independence without impairing our dignity.

"I have heard the statement of the British Prime Minister to the effect that he is not able to put any trust in German assurances. Under the circumstances, I consider it a matter of course that we no longer wish or expect him or the British people to bear the burden of a situation which is only conceivable in an atmosphere of mutual confidence.

"When Germany became National Socialist and thus paved the way for her national resurrection in pursuance of my unswerving policy of friendship with England, of my own accord I made the proposal for voluntary restriction of German naval armaments. That restriction was, however, based on one condition, namely, the will and conviction that war between England and Germany would never again be possible. This wish, this conviction, are alive in me today.

"I am now, however, compelled to state that the policy of England is both unofficially and officially leaving no doubt about the fact that such a conviction is no longer shared in London and that, on the contrary, opinion prevails there that no matter in what conflict Germany should some day be entangled, Great Britain would always have to take her stand against Germany. Thus war against Germany is taken for granted in that country.

"I most profoundly regret such a development, *for the only claim I have ever made and shall continue to make on England is that for return of our colonies.* But I always made it very clear that this would never become a cause of military conflict. I have always held that the English, to whom these colonies are of no value, would one day understand the German situation and would then value German friendship higher than the possession of territories which, while yielding no real profit whatever to them, are of vital importance to Germany.

"Apart from this, however, I have never advanced a claim which might in any way have interfered with British interests or have become a danger to the empire and thus have meant any damage to England. I have always kept within the limit of such demands as are intimately connected with Germany's living space, and thus the eternal property of the German nation.

"Since England today, by press and officially, upholds the view that Germany should be opposed under all circumstances and confirms this policy of encirclement known to us, the basis for the naval treaty has been removed. I have therefore resolved to send today a communication to this effect to the British Government.

"This is to us not a matter of practical material importance —for I still hope that we shall be able to avoid an armaments race with England—but an action of self-respect. *Should the British Government, however, wish to enter once more into negotiations with Germany on this problem, no one would be happier than I at the prospect of still being able to come to a clear and straightforward understanding.*

"Moreover, I know my people—and I rely on them. *We do not want anything that did not formerly belong to us, and no State will ever be robbed by us of its property;* but whoever believes that he is able to attack Germany will find himself confronted with a measure of power and resistance compared with which that of 1914 was negligible.

"In connection with this I wish to speak at once of that matter which was chosen by the same circles which caused the mobilization of Czechoslovakia as the starting point for a new campaign against the Reich.

"I have already assured you, gentlemen, at the beginning of my speech, that never either in the case of Austria or in the case of Czechoslovakia have I adopted in my political life any attitude which is not compatible with events which have now happened. I therefore pointed out in connection with the problem of Memel Germans that this question, if it was not solved by Lithuania herself in a dignified and generous manner, would one day have to be raised by Germany herself.

"You know that the Memel territory was also once torn

from the Reich quite arbitrarily by the dictate of Versailles and that finally in the year 1923, that is, already in the midst of a period of complete peace, this territory was occupied by Lithuania and thus more or less confiscated. The fate of Germans has since then been real martyrdom.

"In the course of the re-incorporation of Bohemia and Moravia within the framework of the German Reich it was also possible for me to come to an agreement with the Lithuanian Government which allowed return of this territory to Germany without any act of violence and without shedding blood. Also, in this instance, I have not demanded one square mile more than we formerly possessed and which was stolen from us.

"This means, therefore, only that territory has returned to the German Reich which had been torn from us by the madmen who dictated peace at Versailles. But this solution, I am convinced, will only prove advantageous to relations between Germany and Lithuania, seeing that Germany, as our behavior has proved, has no other interest than to live in peace and friendship with this State and to establish and foster economic relations with it. . . ."

"As far as Germany is concerned, she is, in any case, determined not to allow certain economically important markets to be stolen from her by terroristic intervention or threats.

"This, however, is not only in our own interest but also in the interest of our trade partner. Here, as in every business, it is not one-sided but mutual dependency.

"How often do we have the pleasure of reading in the amateurish economic articles of our democratic newspapers that Germany, because she maintains close economic relations with a country, makes that country dependent upon her? This is sheer, harassing, Jewish nonsense. For if Germany supplies an agrarian country today with machines and receives foodstuffs in payment, the Reich, as a consumer of foodstuffs, is at least as dependent, if not more dependent, on the agrarian country as the latter is dependent on us from whom it receives industrial products in payment.

"Germany regards the Baltic States as one of its most important trade partners. And for this reason it is in our interest that these countries should lead an independent, ordered national life of their own.

"This is, in our opinion, a necessary condition for that international economic development which is again the condition upon which exchange of goods depends.

"I am, therefore, happy that we have been able to dispose also of the point of dispute between Lithuania and Germany. For this does away with the only obstacle in the way of the policy of friendship which can prove its worth—as I am convinced it will—not in political compliments but in practical economic measures.

"The democratic world was, it is true, once more extremely sorry that there was no bloodshed—that 175,000 Germans were able to return to the homeland which they loved above everything else, without the few hundred thousands of others having to be shot for it!

"This grieved the apostles of humanitarianism deeply. It was, therefore, no wonder that they immediately began to look out for new possibilities of bringing about a thorough disturbance of the European atmosphere after all. And so, as in the case of Czechoslovakia, they again resorted to the assertion that Germany was taking military steps, that it was supposedly mobilizing. This mobilization was said to be directed against Poland.

"There is little to be said as regards German-Polish relations.

"Here, too, the peace treaty of Versailles—of course, intentionally—inflicted the most severe wound on Germany.

"The strange way in which the corridor giving Poland access to the sea was marked out was meant, above all, to prevent for all time the establishment of an understanding between Poland and Germany. This problem is, as I have already stressed, perhaps the most painful of all problems for Germany.

"Nevertheless, I have never ceased to uphold the view that the necessity of free access to the sea for the Polish State cannot be ignored and that is a general principle valid for this case, too. Nations which Providence has destined or, if you like, condemned to live side by side, would be well advised not to make life still harder for each other artificially and unnecessarily.

"The late Marshal Pilsudski, who was of the same opinion, was, therefore, prepared to go into the question of clarifying the atmosphere of German-Polish relations and finally to conclude an agreement whereby Germany and Poland expressed their intention of renouncing war altogether as a means of settling questions which concerned them both.

"This agreement contained one single exception which was in practice conceded to Poland. It was laid down that pacts of mutual assistance already entered into by Poland—this applied to a pact with France—should not be affected by the agreement. But it was obvious that this could apply only to a pact of mutual assistance already concluded beforehand, and not to whatever new pacts might be concluded in the future.

"It is a fact that the German-Polish agreement resulted in remarkable lessening of European tension. Nevertheless, there remained one open question between Germany and Poland which sooner or later quite naturally had to be solved —the question of the German City of Danzig.

"Danzig is a German city and wishes to belong to Germany. On the other hand this city has contracts with Poland which were admittedly forced upon it by the dictators of the peace of Versailles. But since, moreover, the League of Nations, formerly the greatest stirrer-up of trouble, is now represented by a high commissioner—incidentally a man of extraordinary tact—the problem of Danzig must in any case come up for discussion at the latest with the gradual extinction of this calamitous institution.

"I regarded peaceful settlement of this problem as a further contribution to the final loosening of European tension. For this loosening of tension is assuredly not to be achieved through agitations of insane warmongers, but through removal of real elements of danger.

"After the problem of Danzig had already been discussed several times some months ago, I made a concrete offer to the Polish Government. I now make this offer known to you, gentlemen, and you yourselves will judge whether this offer did not represent the greatest imaginable concession in the interests of European peace.

"As I have already pointed out, I have always seen the necessity of access to the sea for this country and have consequently taken this necessity into consideration. I am no democratic statesman, but National Socialist and realist.

"I considered it, however, necessary to make it clear to the government in Warsaw that just as they desire access to sea, so Germany needs access to her province in the East. Now, these are all difficult problems.

"It was not Germany who was responsible for them, however, but rather the jugglers of Versailles who, either in their maliciousness or their thoughtlessness, placed 100 powder barrels round about in Europe all equipped with hardly extinguishable lighted fuses.

"These problems cannot be solved according to old-fashioned ideas; I think rather that we should adopt new methods.

"Poland's access to the sea by way of the Corridor and, on the other hand, a German route through the Corridor have no kind of military importance whatsoever. Their importance is exclusively psychological and economic. To accord military importance to a traffic route of this kind would be to show one's self completely ignorant of military affairs. Consequently, I have had the following proposal submitted to the Polish Government:

"1. Danzig returns as a free State into the framework of the German Reich.

"2. Germany receives a route through the Corridor and a railway line at her own disposal possessing the same extra-territorial status for Germany as the Corridor itself has for Poland.

"In return, Germany is prepared:

"1. To recognize all Polish economic rights in Danzig.

"2. To insure for Poland a free harbor in Danzig of any size desired which would have completely free access to sea.

"3. To accept at the same time the present boundaries between Germany and to regard them as ultimate.

"4. To conclude a twenty-five-year non-aggression treaty with Poland, the treaty, therefore, which would extend far beyond the duration of my own life; and

"5. To guarantee the independence of the Slovak State by Germany, Poland, and Hungary jointly—which means, in practice, renunciation of any unilateral German hegemony in this territory.

"The Polish Government has rejected my one and only offer and has only declared it is prepared to:

"1. Negotiate concerning the question of a substitute for the Commissioner of the League of Nations, and

"2. To consider facilities for the transit of traffic through the Corridor.

"I have regretted dearly this incomprehensible attitude of the Polish Government, but that alone is not the decisive fact; the worst is that now Poland, like Czechoslovakia a year ago, believes, under pressure of a lying international campaign, that it must call up troops although Germany on her part has not called up a single man and had not thought of proceeding in any way against Poland.

"As I have said, this is in itself very regrettable, and posterity will one day decide whether it was really right to refuse this suggestion, made this once by me. This—as I have said—was an endeavor on my part to solve a question which ultimately affects the German people by a truly unique compromise and to solve it to the advantage of both countries.

"According to my conviction, Poland was not a giving party in this solution at all but only a receiving party because it should be beyond all doubt that Danzig will never become Polish.

"An intention to attack on the part of Germany, which was merely invented by the international press, led as you know, to a so-called guarantee offer and to the obligation on the part of the Polish Government for mutual assistance which would also, under certain circumstances, compel Poland to take military action against Germany in the event of conflict between Germany and any other power and in which England, in her turn, would be involved.

"This obligation is contradictory to the agreement which I made with Marshal Pilsudski some time ago, seeing that in this agreement reference is made exclusively to existing obligations, that is, at that time, namely, to obligations of Poland toward France of which we were aware. To extend this obligation subsequently is contrary to the terms of the German-Polish non-aggression pact.

"Under these circumstances I should not have entered into this pact at that time because what sense can non-aggression pacts have if one partner in practice leaves open an enormous number of exceptions?

"There is either collective security, that is, collective insecurity and continuous danger of war, or clear agreements which, however, exclude fundamentally any use of arms between contracting parties.

"Therefore I look upon the agreement which Marshal Pilsudski and I at one time concluded as having been unilaterally infringed by Poland and thereby no longer in existence!

"I have sent a communication to this effect to the Polish Government. However, I can only repeat at this point that my decision does not constitute modification of my attitude in principle with regard to problems mentioned above. Should the Polish Government wish to come to fresh contractual arrangements governing its relations with Germany, I can but welcome such an idea provided, of course, that these arrangements are based on an absolutely clear obligation binding both parties in equal measure. . . ."

"In past weeks Germany has experienced and celebrated the victory of Nationalist Spain with most fervent sympathy. As I resolved to answer the plea of General Franco to give him the assistance of National Socialist Germany in countering international support of bolshevik incendiaries, this step of Germany's was misinterpreted and abused in a most infamous way by these same international agitators.

"They declared at the time that Germany intended to establish herself in Spain and proposed taking Spanish colonies; indeed, the landing of 20,000 soldiers in Morocco was invented as an infamous lie. In short, nothing was omitted that could cast suspicion on the idealism of our and Italian support in order to find material for fresh warmongering. In a few weeks now, the victorious hero of Nationalist Spain will celebrate his festive entry into the capital of his country.

"The Spanish people will acclaim him as their deliverer from unspeakable horrors and as their liberator from bands of incendiaries who are estimated to have more than 775,000 human lives on their conscience through executions and murders alone.

"Inhabitants of whole villages and towns literally were butchered under the silent, benevolent patronage of West European and American democratic humanitarian apostles.

"In this, his triumphal procession, volunteers of our German legion will march together with their Italian comrades in the ranks of valiant Spanish soldiers. We hope to be able to welcome them home soon afterward. The German nation will then know how bravely its sons have played their part on that soil, too, in the struggle for liberty of a noble people and therewith for the salvation of European civilization; for if subhuman forces of bolshevism had proved victorious in Spain they might easily have spread across the whole of Europe. . . ."

"As mentioned at the beginning, the world on April 15, 1939, was informed of the contents of a telegram which I myself did not see until later. It is difficult to classify this document or to arrange it in any known scheme. I will therefore endeavor before you, gentlemen, and thus before the whole German people, to analyze necessary answers in your name and in that of the German people.

I

"Mr. Roosevelt is of the opinion that I, too, must realize that throughout the world hundreds of millions of human beings are living in constant fear of a new war or even a series of wars.

"This, he says, is of concern to the people of the United States for whom he speaks, as it must also be to the peoples of the other nations of the entire Western Hemisphere.

"In reply to this it must be said in the first place that this fear of war has undoubtedly existed among mankind from time immemorial, and justifiably so.

"For instance, after the peace treaty of Versailles fourteen wars were waged between 1919 and 1938 alone, in none of which Germany was concerned, but in which the States of the 'Western Hemisphere,' in whose name President Roosevelt also speaks, were indeed concerned.

"In addition, there were in the same period twenty-six violent interventions and sanctions carried through by means of bloodshed and force.

"Germany also played no part whatever in these. The United States alone has carried out military interventions in six cases since 1918. Since 1918 Soviet Russia has engaged in ten wars and military actions involving force and bloodshed.

"Again Germany was concerned in none of these, nor was she the cause of any of these events. It would, therefore, be a mistake in my eyes to assume that the fear of war inspiring European and non-European nations can at this present time be directly traced back to actual wars at all.

II

"The reason for this fear lies simply and solely in an unbridled agitation on the part of the press, an agitation as mendacious as it is base, in the circulation of vile pamphlets about the heads of foreign States, and in an artificial spreading of panic which in the end goes so far that interventions from another planet are believed possible and cause scenes of desperate alarm.

"I believe that as soon as the responsible governments impose upon themselves and their journalistic organs the necessary restraint and truthfulness as regards the relations of the various countries to one another, and in particular as regards internal happenings in other countries, the fear of war will disappear at once, and the tranquillity which we all desire so much will become possible.

"In his telegram Mr. Roosevelt expresses the belief that every major war, even if it were to be confined to other continents, must have serious consequences while it lasts, and also for generations to come.

"The answer: No one knows this better than the German people. For the peace treaty of Versailles imposed burdens on the German people which could not have been paid off even in a hundred years, although it has been proved precisely by American teachers of constitutional law, historians, and professors of history that Germany was no more to blame for the outbreak of the war than any other nation.

"But I do not believe that every conflict must have disastrous consequences for the whole surrounding world, that is for the whole globe, provided the whole world is not systematically drawn into such conflicts by means of a network of nebulous pact obligations.

"For, since in past centuries and—as I pointed out at the beginning of my answer—also in the course of the last decades, the world has experienced a continuous series of wars, if Mr. Roosevelt's assumption were correct humanity would already have a burden, in the sum total of the outcome of all these wars, which it would have to bear for millions of years to come.

III

"Mr. Roosevelt declared that he had already appealed to me on a former occasion on behalf of a peaceful settlement of political, economic and social problems and without resort to arms.

"The answer: I myself have always been an exponent of this view and, as history proves, have settled necessary political, economic, and social problems without force of arms, that is, without resort to arms.

"Unfortunately, however, this peaceful settlement has been made more difficult by the agitation of politicians, statesmen, and newspaper representatives who were neither directly concerned nor even affected by the problems in question.

IV

"Mr. Roosevelt believes that the 'tide of events' is once more bringing the threat of arms with it, and that if this threat continues a large part of the world is condemned to a common ruin.

"The answer: As far as Germany is concerned, I know nothing of this kind of threat to other nations, although I every day read in the democratic newspapers lies about such a threat.

"Every day I read of German mobilizations, of the landing of troops, of extortions—all this in regard to States with whom we are not only living in deepest peace but also with whom we are, in many cases, the closest friends.

V

"Mr. Roosevelt believes further that in case of war victorious, vanquished, and neutral nations will all suffer.

"The answer: As a politician I have been the exponent of this conviction for twenty years, at a time when unfortunately the responsible statesmen in America could not bring themselves to make the same admission as regards their participation in the Great War and its issue.

VI

"Mr. Roosevelt believes lastly that it lies with the leaders of the great nations to preserve their peoples from the impending disaster.

"The answer: If that is true, then it is a punishable neglect, to use no worse word, if the leaders of nations with corresponding powers are not capable of controlling their newspapers which are agitating for war, and so to save the world from the threatening calamity of an armed conflict.

"I am not able to understand, further, why these responsible leaders, instead of cultivating diplomatic relations between nations, make them more difficult and indeed disturb them by recalling ambassadors, etc., without any reason.

VII

"Mr. Roosevelt declared finally that three nations in Europe and one in Africa have seen their independent existence terminated.

"The answer: I do not know which three nations in Europe are meant. Should it be a question of the provinces reincorporated in the German Reich I must draw the attention of Mr. Roosevelt to a historical error.

"It is not now that these nations sacrificed their independent existence in Europe, but rather in 1918 when they, contrary to solemn promises, were separated from their communities and made into nations which they never wished to be and never were, and when they had forced upon them an independence which was no independence but at the most could only mean dependence upon an international foreign world which they hated.

"As for the fact, however, that one nation in Africa is alleged to have lost its freedom—that too, is but an error; for it is not a question of one nation in Africa having lost its freedom—on the contrary practically all the previous inhabitants of this continent have been made subject to the sovereignty of other nations by bloody force, thereby losing their freedom.

"Moroccans, Berbers, Arabs, Negroes, etcetera, have all fallen victim to foreign might, the swords of which, however, were inscribed not 'Made in Germany,' but 'Made by Democracies.'

VIII

"Mr. Roosevelt then speaks of the reports which admittedly he does not believe to be correct but which state that further acts of aggression are contemplated against still other independent nations.

"The answer: I consider every such unfounded insinuation as an offense against the tranquillity and consequently the peace of the world. I also see therein something which tends to frighten smaller nations or at least make them nervous.

"If Mr. Roosevelt really has any specific instances in mind in this connection I would ask him to name the States which are threatened with aggression and to name the aggressor in question. It will then be possible to refute these monstrous general accusations by brief statements.

IX

"Mr. Roosevelt states that the world is plainly moving toward the moment when this situation must end in catastrophe unless a rational way of guiding events is found.

"He also declares that I have repeatedly asserted that I and the German people have no desire for war and that if this is true there need be no war.

"The answer: I wish to point out first, that I have not conducted any war; second, that for years past I have expressed my abhorrence of war and, it is true, also my abhorrence of warmongers, and third, that I am not aware for what purpose I should wage a war at all. I should be thankful to Mr. Roosevelt if he would give me some explanation in this connection.

X

"Mr. Roosevelt is finally of the opinion that the peoples of the earth could not be persuaded that any governing power has any right or need to inflict the consequences of war on its own or any other people save in the cause of self-evident home defense.

"The answer: I should think that every reasonable human being is of this opinion; but it seems to me that in almost every war both sides claim a case of unquestionable home defense, and that there is no institution in this world, including the American President himself, which could clear up the problem unequivocally.

"There is hardly any possibility of doubt, for example, that America's entry into the Great War was not a case of unquestionable home defense. A research committee set up by President Roosevelt himself has examined the cause of America's entry into the Great War, and reached the conclusion that the entry ensued chiefly for exclusively capitalistic reasons. Nevertheless, no practical conclusions have been drawn from this fact.

"Let us hope, then, that at least the United States will in the future itself act according to this noble principle, and will not go to war against any country except in the case of unquestionable home defense.

XI

"Mr. Roosevelt says further that he does not speak from selfishness, nor fear, nor weakness, but with the voice of strength and friendship for mankind.

"The answer: If this voice of strength and friendship for mankind had been raised by America at the proper time, and if, above all, it had possessed some practical value, then at least there could have been prevented that treaty which has become the source of the direst derangement of humanity and history, namely, the dictate of Versailles.

XII

"Mr. Roosevelt declares, further, that it is clear to him that all international problems can be solved at the council table.

"The answer: Theoretically one ought to believe in this possibility, for common sense would correct demands on the one hand and show the compelling necessity of a compromise on the other.

"For example, according to all common-sense logic and the general principles of a higher human justice, indeed, according to the laws of a divine will, all peoples ought to have an equal share of the goods of this world.

"It ought not then to happen that one people needs so much living space that it cannot get along with fifteen inhabitants to the square kilometer, while others are forced to nourish 140, 150, or even 200 on the same area.

"But in no case should these fortunate peoples curtail the existing living space of those who are, as it is, suffering, by robbing them of their colonies, for instance. I would therefore be very happy if these problems could really find their solution at the council table.

"My skepticism, however, is based on the fact that it was America herself who gave sharpest expression to her mistrust in the effectiveness of conferences. For the greatest conference of all time was without any doubt the League of Nations.

"That authoritative body, representing all the peoples of the world, created in accordance with the will of an American President, was supposed to solve the problems of humanity at the council table.

"The first State, however, that shrank from this endeavor was the United States—the reason being that President Wilson himself even then nourished the greatest doubts of the possibility of really being able to solve decisive international problems at the conference table.

"We honor your well-meant opinion, Mr. Roosevelt, but opposed to your opinion stands the actual fact that in almost twenty years of the activity of the greatest conference in the world, namely, the League of Nations, it has proved impossible to solve one single decisive international problem.

"Contrary to Wilson's promise, Germany was hindered for many years by the peace treaty of Versailles from participating in this great world conference. In spite of the most bitter experience, one German Government believed that there was no need to follow the example of the United States, and that they should therefore take their seat at this conference table.

"It was not till after years of purposeless participation that I resolved to follow the example of America and likewise leave the largest conference in the world. Since then I have solved the problems concerning my people which, like all others, were, unfortunately, not solved at the conference table of the League of Nations—and, too, without recourse to war in any case.

"Apart from this, however, as already mentioned, numerous other problems have been brought before world conferences in recent years without any solution having been found.

"If, however, Mr. Roosevelt, your belief that every problem can be solved at the conference table is true, then all nations, including the United States, have been led in the past 700 or 800 years either by blind men or by criminals.

"For all of them, including the statesmen of the United States, and especially her greatest, did not make the chief part of their history at the conference table but with the aid of the strength of their people.

"The freedom of North America was not achieved at the conference table any more than the conflict between the North and the South was decided there. I will say nothing about the innumerable struggles which finally led to the subjugation of the North American Continent as a whole.

"I mention all this only in order to show that your view, Mr. Roosevelt, although undoubtedly deserving of all honor, finds no confirmation in the history either of your own country or of the rest of the world.

XIII

"Mr. Roosevelt continues that it is no answer to the plea for peaceful discussion for one side to plead that, unless they receive assurances beforehand that the verdict will be theirs, they will not lay aside their arms.

"The answer: Do you believe, Mr. Roosevelt, that when the final fate of nations is in the balance a government or the leaders of a people will lay down their arms or surrender them before a conference, simply in the blind hope that in their wisdom or, if you like, their discernment, the other members of the conference will arrive at the right conclusion?

"Mr. Roosevelt, there has been only one country and one government which has acted according to the recipe extolled in such glowing terms, and that country was Germany. The German nation once, trusting in the solemn assurances of President Wilson and in the confirmation of these assurances by the Allies, laid down its arms and thus went unarmed to the conference table.

"It is true that as soon as the German nation had laid down its arms it was not even invited to the conference table, but, in violation of all assurances, was made to suffer the worst breaking of a word that had ever been known.

"Then one day, instead of the greatest confusion known in history being resolved around the conference table, the cruelest dictated treaty in the world brought about a still more fearful confusion.

"But the representatives of the German nation, who, trusting to the solemn assurance of an American President, had laid down their arms and therefore appeared unarmed, were not received, even when they came to accept the terms of the dictated treaty, as the representatives of a nation which, at all events, had held out with infinite heroism against a whole world for four years in the struggle for its liberty and independence; they were subjected to even greater degradations than can ever have been inflicted on the chieftains of Sioux tribes.

"The German delegates were insulted by the mob, stones were thrown at them, and they were dragged like prisoners, not to the council table of the world but before the tribunal of the victors; and there, at the pistol's point, they were forced to undergo the most shameful subjection and plundering that the world had ever known.

"I can assure you, Mr. Roosevelt, that I am steadfastly determined to see to it that not only now, but for all future time, no German shall ever enter a conference defenseless. but that at all time and forever every German negotiator should and shall have behind him the united strength of the German nation, so help me God.

XIV

"The President of the United States believes that in conference rooms as in court it is necessary that both sides enter in good faith, assuming that substantial justice will accrue to both.

"The answer: German representatives will never again enter a conference that is for them a tribunal. For who is to be the judge there? At a conference there is no accused and no prosecutor, but two contending parties. And if their own good sense does not bring about a settlement between the two parties, they will never surrender themselves to the verdict of disinterested foreign powers.

"Incidentally, the United States itself declined to enter the League of Nations and to become the victim of a court which was able, by a majority vote, to give a verdict against individual interests. But I should be grateful to President Roosevelt if he would explain to the world what the new World Court is to be like.

"Who are the judges here, according to what procedure are they selected, and on what responsibility do they act? And above all, to whom can they be made to account for their decision?

XV

"Mr. Roosevelt believes that the cause of world peace would be greatly advanced if the nations of the world were to give a frank statement relating to the present and future policy of their governments.

"The answer: I have already done this, Mr. Roosevelt, in innnumerable public speeches. And in the course of this present meeting of the German Reichstag, I have again—as far as this is possible in the space of two hours—made a statement of this kind.

"I must, however, decline to give such an explanation to any one else than to the people for whose existence and life

I am responsible, and who, on the other hand, alone have the right to demand that I account to them. However, I give the aims of the German policy so openly that the entire world can hear it in any case.

"But these explanations are without significance for the outside world as long as it is possible for the press to falsify and suspect every statement, to question it or to cover it with fresh lying replies.

XVI

"Mr. Roosevelt believes that, because the United States as one of the nations of the Western Hemisphere is not involved in the immediate controversies which have arisen in Europe, I should therefore be willing to make such a statement of policy to him, as the head of a nation so far removed from Europe.

"The answer: Mr. Roosevelt therefore seriously believes that the cause of international peace would really be furthered if I were to make to the nations of the world a public statement on the present policy of the German Government.

"But how does Mr. Roosevelt come to expect of the head of the German State, above all, to make a statement without the other governments being invited to make such a statement of their policy as well?

"I certainly believe that it is not feasible to make such a statement to the head of any foreign State, but rather that such statements should preferably be made to the whole world, in accordance with the demand made at the time by President Wilson, for the abolition of secret diplomacy.

"Hitherto I was not only always prepared to do this but, as I have already said, I have done it only too often. Unfortunately, the most important statements concerning the aims and intentions of German policy have been in many so-called democratic States either withheld from the people or distorted by the press.

"If, however, President Roosevelt thinks that he is qualified to address such a request to Germany or Italy, of all nations, because America is so far removed from Europe, we on our side might, with the same right, address to the President of the American Republic the question as to what aim American foreign policy has in view in its turn.

"And on what intentions this policy is based—in the case of the Central and South American States, for instance. In this case Mr. Roosevelt would, rightly, I must admit, refer to the Monroe Doctrine and decline to comply with such a request as an interference in the internal affairs of the American continent. We Germans support a similar doctrine for Europe—and, above all, for the territory and the interests of the Greater German Reich.

"Moreover, I would obviously never presume to address such a request to the President of the United States of America, because I assume that he would probably rightly consider such a presumption tactless.

XVII

"The American President further declares that he would then communicate information received by him concerning the political aims of Germany to other nations now apprehensive as to the course of our policy.

"The answer: How has Mr. Roosevelt learned which nations consider themselves threatened by German policy and which do not?

"Or is Mr. Roosevelt in a position, in spite of the enormous amount of work which must rest upon him in his own country, to recognize of his own accord all these inner spiritual and mental impressions of other peoples and their governments?

XVIII

"Finally, Mr. Roosevelt asks that assurance be given him that the German armed forces will not attack, and above all, not invade, the territory or possessions of the following independent nations he then names as those coming into question: Finland, Latvia, Estonia, Norway, Sweden, Denmark, the Netherlands, Belgium, Great Britain, Ireland, France, Portugal, Spain, Switzerland, Liechtenstein, Luxemburg, Poland, Hungary, Turkey, Iraq, the Arabias, Syria, Palestine, Egypt, and Iran.

"The answer: I have first taken the trouble to ascertain from the States mentioned, firstly, whether they feel themselves threatened, and secondly and above all, whether this inquiry by the American President was addressed to us at their suggestion, or at any rate, with their consent.

"The reply was in all cases negative, in some instances strongly so. It is true that I could not cause inquiries to be made of certain of the States and nations mentioned because they themselves—as for example, Syria—are at present not in possession of their freedom, but are occupied and consequently deprived of their rights by the military agents of democratic States.

"Apart from this fact, however, all States bordering on Germany have received much more binding assurances and, above all, suggestions, than Mr. Roosevelt asked from me in his curious telegram.

"But should there be any doubt as to the value of these general and direct statements which I have so often made, then any further statement of this kind, even if addressed to the American President, would be equally worthless. For ultimately it is not the value which Mr. Roosevelt attaches to such statements which is decisive, but the value attached to these statements by the countries in question.

"But I must also draw Mr. Roosevelt's attention to one or two historical errors. He mentioned Ireland, for instance, and asks for a statement to the effect that Germany will not attack Ireland. Now, I have just read a speech delivered by de Valera, the Irish Taoiseach (Prime Minister), in which, strangely enough, and contrary to Mr. Roosevelt's opinion, he does not charge Germany with oppressing Ireland, but reproaches England with subjecting Ireland to continuous aggression at her hands.

"With all due respect to Mr. Roosevelt's insight into the needs and cares of other countries, he may nevertheless be assured that the Irish Taoiseach will be more familiar with the dangers which threaten his country than the President of the United States.

"In the same way, the fact has obviously escaped Mr. Roosevelt's notice that Palestine is at present occupied not by German troops but by the English; and that the country is having its liberty restricted by the most brutal resort to force, is being robbed of its independence, and is suffering the cruelest maltreatment for the benefit of Jewish interlopers.

"The Arabs living in that country will therefore certainly not have complained to Mr. Roosevelt of German aggression, but they do voice a continuous appeal to the world, deploring the barbarous methods with which England is attempting to suppress a people which loves its freedom and is but defending it.

"This, too, is perhaps a problem which would have to be solved at the conference table, that is, in the presence of a just judge, and not by physical force, military means, mass executions, burning down villages, blowing up houses and so on.

"For one fact is undoubtedly certain: In this case England is not defending herself against a threatened Arab attack, but as an interloper, and, without being called upon to do so, is endeavoring to establish her power in a foreign territory which does not belong to her.

"A whole series of similar errors which Mr. Roosevelt has made might be pointed out, quite apart from the difficulty of military operations on the part of Germany in States and countries, some of which are 2,000 and 5,000 kilometers away from us. In conclusion, however, I have the following statement to make:

"The German Government is nevertheless prepared to give each of the States named an assurance of the kind desired by Mr. Roosevelt on the condition of absolute reciprocity, provided that the State wishes it and itself addresses to Germany a request for such an assurance together with appropriate proprosals.

"As concerns a number of the States included in Mr. Roosevelt's list, this question can probably be regarded as settled from the very start, since we are already either allied with them or at least united by close ties of friendship.

"As for the duration of these agreements, Germany is willing to make terms with each individual State in accordance with the wishes of that State.

"But I should not like to let this opportunity pass without giving above all to the President of the United States an assurance regarding those territories which would, after all, give him most cause for apprehension, namely the United States itself and the other States of the American continent.

"And I here solemnly declare that all the assertions which have been circulated in any way concerning an intended German attack or invasion on or in American territory are rank frauds and gross untruths, quite apart from the fact that such assertions, as far as the military possibilities are concerned, could have their origin only in a stupid imagination.

XIX

"The American President then goes on to declare in this connection that he regards the discussion of the most effective and immediate manner in which the peoples of the world can obtain relief from the crushing burden of armaments as the most important factor of all.

"Mr. Roosevelt perhaps does not know that this problem, insofar as it concerns Germany, has already been completely solved on one occasion. Between 1919 and 1923 Germany had already completely disarmed—as was expressly confirmed by the allied commissions. . . ."

"In this point, as in all others where Germany believed that a promise would be kept, she was disgracefully deceived. All attempts to induce the other States to disarm, pursued in negotiations at the conference table over many years, came, as is well known, to nothing. This disarmament would have been but the execution of pledges already given and at the same time just and prudent.

"I myself, Mr. Roosevelt, have made any number of practical proposals for consultation and tried to bring about a discussion of them in order to make possible a general limitation of armaments to the lowest possible level.

"I proposed a maximum strength for all armies of 200,000, similarly the abolition of all offensive weapons, of bombing planes, of poison gas, etc. It was not possible, however, to carry out these plans in the face of the rest of the world although Germany herself was at the time completely disarmed. I then proposed a maximum of 300,000 for armies.

"The proposal met with the same negative reception. I then submitted a great number of detailed disarmament proposals—in each case before the forum of the German Reichstag and consequently before the whole world. It never occurred to anyone even to discuss the matter. The rest of the world began, instead, to increase still further their already enormous armaments.

"And not until 1934, when the last of my comprehensive proposals—that concerning 300,000 as the maximum size of the army—was ultimately turned down did I give the order for German rearmament which was now to be very thorough.

"Nevertheless, I do not want to be an obstacle in the way of disarmament discussions at which you, Mr. Roosevelt, intend to be present. I would ask you, however, not to appeal first to me and to Germany, but rather to the others; I have a long line of practical experience behind me and shall remain skeptically inclined until reality has taught me to know better.

"Mr. Roosevelt gives us his pledge, finally, that he is prepared to take part in discussions looking toward the most practical manner of opening up avenues of international trade to the end that every nation of the world may be enabled to buy and sell on equal terms in the world's market, as well as to possess assurances of obtaining the raw materials and products of peaceful economic life.

"The answer: It is my belief, Mr. Roosevelt, that it is not so much a question of discussing these problems theoretically as of removing in practice the barriers which exist in international trade. The worst barriers, however, lie in the individual States themselves.

"Experience so far shows at any rate that the greatest world economic conferences have come to nothing simply because various countries were not able to maintain order in their domestic economic systems; or else because they infected the international capital market with uncertainty by currency manipulation and above all by causing continual fluctuations in value of their currencies to one another.

"It is likewise an unbearable burden for world economic relations that it should be possible in some countries for some ideological reason or other to let loose a wild boycott of agitation against other countries and their goods and so practically to eliminate them from the market.

"It is my belief, Mr. Roosevelt, that it would be a great service if you, with your great influence, would remove these barriers genuinely to free world trade beginning with the United States. For it is my conviction that if the leaders of nations are not even capable of regulating production in their own countries or of removing boycotts pursued for ideological reasons which can damage trade relations between countries to so great an extent, there is much less prospect of achieving by means of international agreements any really fruitful step toward improvement of economic relations.

"An equal right for all of buying and selling in world markets can only be guaranteed in this way. Further, the German people has made in this regard very concrete claims and I would appreciate it very much if you, Mr. Roosevelt, as one of the successors to the late President Wilson, were to devote yourself to seeing that promises be at last redeemed on the basis of which Germany once laid down her arms and gave herself up to the so-called victors.

"I am thinking less of the innumerable millions extorted from Germany as so-called reparations than of territories stolen from Germany.

"In and outside Europe, Germany lost approximately 3,000,000 square kilometers of territory, and that in spite of the fact that the whole German colonial empire, in contrast to colonies of other nations, was not acquired by way of war but solely through treaties of purchase.

"President Wilson solemnly pledged his word that German colonial claims, like all others, would receive the same just examination. Instead of this, however, German possessions were given to nations that have always had the largest colonial empires, while our people were exposed to a great anxiety which is now—as it will continue to be in future—particularly pressing.

"It would be a noble act if President Franklin Roosevelt were to redeem the promises made by President Woodrow Wilson. This would, in the first place, be a practical contribution to the moral consolidation of the world and consequently to the improvement of its economic conditions.

"Mr. Roosevelt also stated in conclusion that the heads of all the great Governments are, in this hour, responsible for the fate of humanity.

"They cannot fail to hear the prayers of the peoples to be protected from the foreseeable chaos of war. And I, too, would be held accountable for this.

"Mr. Roosevelt! I fully understand that the vastness of your nation and the immense wealth of your country allow you to feel responsible for the history of the whole world and for the history of all nations. I, sir, am placed in a much more modest and smaller sphere. You have 130,000,000 people on 9,500,000 square kilometers.

"You possess a country with enormous riches in all mineral resources, fertile enough to feed a half-billion people and to provide them with all necessities.

"I once took over a State which was faced by complete ruin, thanks to its trust in the promises of the rest of the world and to the bad regime of democratic governments. In this State there are roughly 140 people to each square kilometer—not 15, as in America. The fertility of our country cannot be compared with that of yours.

"We lack numerous minerals which nature has placed at your disposal in unlimited quantities.

"Billions of German savings accumulated in gold and foreign exchange during many years of peace were squeezed out of us and taken from us. We lost our colonies. In 1933 I had in my country 7,000,000 unemployed, a few million workers on half-time, millions of peasants sinking into poverty, destroyed trade, ruined commerce; in short, general chaos.

"Since then, Mr. Roosevelt, I have only been able to fulfill one simple task. I cannot feel myself responsible for the fate of the world, as this world took no interest in the pitiful state of my own people.

"I have regarded myself as called upon by Providence to serve my own people alone and to deliver them from their frightful misery. Consequently, during the past six and one-half years, I have lived day and night for the single task of awakening the powers of my people, in view of our desertion by the whole of the rest of the world, of developing these powers to the utmost and of utilizing them for the salvation of our community.

"I have conquered chaos in Germany, re-established order and enormously increased production in all branches of our national economy, by strenuous efforts produced substitutes for numerous materials which we lack, smoothed the way for new inventions, developed traffic, caused mighty roads to be built and canals to be dug, called into being gigantic new factories and at the same time endeavored to further the education and culture of our people.

"I have succeeded in finding useful work once more for the whole of 7,000,000 unemployed, who so appeal to the hearts of us all, in keeping the German peasant on his soil in spite of all difficulties, and in saving the land itself for him, in once more bringing German trade to a peak and in assisting traffic to the utmost.

"As precaution against the threats of another world war, not only have I united the German people politically, but I have also re-armed them; I have also endeavored to destroy sheet by sheet that Treaty which in its 448 articles contains the vilest oppression which peoples and human beings have ever been expected to put up with.

"I have brought back to the Reich provinces stolen from us in 1919; I have led back to their native country millions of Germans who were torn away from us and were in misery; I have re-established the historic unity of German living space and, Mr. Roosevelt, I have endeavored to attain all this without spilling blood and without bringing to my people, and consequently to others, the misery of war.

"I, who twenty-one years ago was an unknown worker and soldier of my people, have attained this, Mr. Roosevelt, by my own energy, and can, therefore, in the face of history, claim a place among those men who have done the utmost which can be fairly and justly demanded from a single individual.

"You, Mr. Roosevelt, have a much easier task in comparison. You became President of the United States in 1933 when I became Chancellor of the Reich. In other words, from the very outset you stepped to the head of one of the largest and wealthiest States in the world.

"You have the good fortune to have to feed scarcely fifteen people per square kilometer in your country. You have at your disposal the most unlimited mineral resources in the world. As a result of the large area covered by your country and the fertility of your fields, you are enabled to insure for each individual American ten times the amount of commodities possible in Germany. Nature has in any case enabled you to do this.

"In spite of the fact that the population of your country is scarcely one-third greater than the number of inhabitants in Greater Germany, you possess more than fifteen times as much living space. Conditions prevailing in your country are on such a large scale that you can find time and leisure to give your attention to universal problems. Consequently, the world is undoubtedly so small for you that you perhaps believe that your intervention and action can be effective anywhere.

"In this sense, therefore, your concerns and suggestions cover a much larger and wider area than mine, because my world, Mr. Roosevelt, in which Providence has placed me and for which I am therefore obliged to work, is unfortunately much smaller, although for me it is more precious than anything else, for it is limited to my people!

"I believe, however, that this is the way in which I can be of the most service to that for which we are all concerned, namely, the justice, well-being, progress and peace of the whole human community."

Press

New York Times—Hitler has made and broken so many promises—he would never annex Austria, he would be satisfied with the Sudeten area of Czecho-Slovakia, he would never bring a non-Germanic people into the German Reich—that it has long since become necessary to look beyond his words and to attempt to gauge the temper, the strategy, and the larger purposes that lie behind them. It is a fair appraisal of the speech that was made to the Reichstag yesterday that it seems to foreshadow no immediate move on Germany's part, but that it offers no assurance whatever for the longer future. . . .

The whole of the Hitler speech makes it clear that, however short or long the present breathing-space, Germany under National Socialism is bent upon creating a new empire. Gone entirely (it would have to go after the seizure of Czecho-Slovakia) is the old Hitler slogan of racial unity and a Germany seeking only to bring German racial groups into the German fatherland. The new slogan is not racial unity but "living room" and power.

London Times, April 29— . . . Hitler would not be where he is if he were not a master of the democratic technique which he affects to despise. . . . Hitler is, in tone at least, on the defensive. Germany herself is represented once again on the defensive. . . . The errors of the Versailles Treaty are perfectly familiar. . . . The British have been foremost with the belief that certain German claims were grounded in justice. . . . For this reason Britain was unwilling to resist the reoccupation of the Rhineland, the *Anschluss,* and the recovery of the Sudeten Germans. It is well that that should be . . . understood.

Le Temps, April 30—This speech gives us the impression that the moral effect of President Roosevelt's appeal and the introduction of compulsory military service in England have really confronted the Reich government with an embarrassing situation. . . . Without doubt this accounts for certain peculiarities of the speech: the absence of any virulent and systematic attack on Soviet Russia, the difference in tone when he spoke to France, to England, and to Poland. This also accounts for the fact that the Chancellor, discussing the colonial question, devoted most of his venom to England. In fact, the Chancellor rejected President Roosevelt's suggestions.

The whole polemic section of his answer to Mr. Roosevelt sought to oppose certain elements of the American nation to the elected chief of that nation. . . . The denunciation of the Anglo-German naval accord is naturally a reply to the decision of the British Government to establish compulsory military service in the United Kingdom. . . . But the denunciation of the Polish-German pact of 1934 may have far more serious consequences.

•

SPEECH OF SEPTEMBER 1, 1939

Berlin, Reichstag

Background

1939

May 3—Maxim Litvinov, Russian Foreign Minister, is dismissed and replaced by Molotov.

May 5—In Milan, a military alliance is signed between Germany and Italy.

May 6—George VI and Queen Elizabeth sail for Canada and the United States.

May 11—Chamberlain says that German use of force in Danzig will mean war.

June 11—Britain sends William Strang to Moscow to negotiate a pact with Russia.

July 4—President Roosevelt asks for the repeal of the arms embargo.

August 5—French and British military missions go to Moscow to discuss military alliance.

August 10—In Danzig, Fuehrer Forster declares that Danzig must return to the Reich.

August 12—Ciano and Ribbentrop confer with Hitler at Berchtesgaden.

August 16—Germany demands return of Danzig.

Intensive press and radio campaign is launched in Germany, demanding settlement of Danzig question.

The Franco-British Peace Efforts:

August 22—The Soviet-German Pact is announced. On the same day Chamberlain addresses a letter to Hitler to tell him that the new agreement would not alter Great Britain's obligation to Poland, and asking for a truce to settle the German-Polish difficulties.

August 23—Sir Neville Henderson hands this letter to Hitler at Berchtesgaden. According to the Ambassador, Hitler was "excitable and uncompromising." He says that Britain had given Poland a blank check and that he could not tolerate further persecution of the Germans by the Poles.

At a second interview with Henderson, Hitler says he would attack Poland if another Polish atrocity were reported to him. The Fuehrer reiterates his desire for friendship with England. "Germany," he says, "never has intended nor intends in the future to attack either Great Britain or France," but adds that he was ordering immediate mobilization of the German Army.

August 24—Georges Bonnet instructs Noel, French Ambassador in Warsaw, to moderate, if possible, the impatience of the Poles.

The Neutrals Appeal:

August 23—King Leopold of Belgium, together with the rulers of the Oslo group, sends a worldwide appeal for peace.

Poland responds, accepting the idea of negotiations. The Pope, Pius XII, supports the appeal of the Oslo States.

August 24—President Roosevelt sends an appeal to Hitler and Mosciki, Polish President, urging both Chiefs of State to refrain from hostilities and to seek solution by impartial arbitration.

August 25—Mosciki, President of Poland, accepts any form of impartial mediation. Germany only replies on the thirty-first through a note handed to Secretary Hull by Chargé d'Affaires Hans Tomsen.

Hitler Offers to Protect the British Empire:

August 24—Chamberlain makes a report to Commons on the situation. Although pessimistic, the British Prime Minister says there is still hope of avoiding war.

August 25—Henderson sees Hitler who tells him that he "desired to take a step in regard to England which was to be as decisive as the steps taken in regard to Russia." He denies that Germany wants to conquer the world. "He himself was a man of great decisions and he would in this case also be capable of great action. He approved of the British Empire and was prepared to pledge himself personally to its existence and to devote the might of the German Reich to that end." He adds that Germany would never again enter into a conflict with Russia. Once the Polish question was settled he would guarantee the British Empire. If Britain did not accept these propositions, war would be inevitable.

August 26—Henderson flies to London to help prepare the British reply. (The previous day, August 25, a formal agreement of mutual assistance between England and Poland was signed.)

August 25—While waiting for the return of Henderson from London, Hitler writes a letter to Daladier telling him how reluctant he would be to fight France but saying that the decision did not rest with him.

August 26—Daladier replies to Hitler, appealing to him to prevent war but saying that France was bound by her engagement with Poland in case of aggression.

August 26—Warsaw expresses its willingness to an exchange of population between Germany and Poland as a possible solution of the dilemma, but complains that the Poles are being ill-treated by the Germans.

Coulondre, the French Ambassador to Berlin, reports that he had made a verbal appeal to Hitler supporting Daladier's, but remarked, "perhaps I moved him, but I did not prevail; his stand was taken." Hitler told Coulondre that it was useless to discuss with Poland and that the soldiers of that "barbarous country" were not controlled any more by their Government. "Poland will not cede Danzig and I desire that Danzig return to the Reich."

August 27—Hitler writes again to Daladier, saying, "No nation with a sense of honor can ever give up almost 2,000,000 people and see them maltreated on its own frontiers. I therefore formulated a clear demand: Danzig and the Corridor must return to Germany. The Macedonian conditions prevailing along our eastern frontiers must cease. I see no possibility of persuading Poland, who deems herself safe from attack by virtue of guarantees given to her to agree to a peaceful solution. . . . If fate decrees that our two peoples [the French and the Germans] should fight one another once more over this question it would be from different motives. I for my part, Mr. Daladier, would fight with my people for the reparation of an injustice while the others would fight for its retention. This is all the more tragic in view of the fact that many great men of your nation have long since recognized the folly of the solution found in 1919, and the impossibility of keeping it up forever. I am fully conscious of the grave consequences which such a conflict would involve. But I think that Poland would suffer most, for whatever the issue of such a war, the Polish State of today would in any case be lost."

August 28—Henderson flies back to Berlin. The British note accepted the idea of Anglo-German negotiations but insisted on the immediate solution of the German-Polish conflict. The British note said that the Polish Government was prepared to enter into discussions.

August 29—Hitler gives his reply to Henderson. The Fuehrer repeats his complaints against the Poles and reasserts that the German Government must have a settlement of the Danzig question at once. The German note suggests that a

Polish plenipotentiary should come to Berlin. Hitler and Ribbentrop deny this is an ultimatum.

The Poles Agree to Negotiate:

August 29—The Poles authorize Lipski, their Ambassador in Berlin, to undertake negotiations with the Reich. But simultaneously (on August 30) Poland orders "defensive military measures." This is interpreted by Berlin as general mobilization.

August 30—Halifax wires to Henderson saying that they could not advise the Polish Government to send a plenipotentiary, and recommending that they should accept Ambassador Lipski as a negotiator. Henderson sees Ribbentrop and has a very heated scene with him. Ribbentrop reads out to the British Ambassador in German a long document containing sixteen points which represent, according to Ribbentrop, the basis of negotiations with Poland. Henderson asks for a copy of this document but is refused, Ribbentrop saying that it is "outdated." Ribbentrop says he could not consider inviting the Polish Ambassador to come and see him.

August 31—The sixteen points are broadcast throughout the world, but there is no indication that they have been communicated to Warsaw. After leaving Ribbentrop, Henderson remarks that he returned to H. M. Embassy "convinced that the last hope for peace had vanished."

August 31—At 6:30 P.M. Lipski calls on Ribbentrop, who asks him if he has full powers to negotiate. Lipski replies negatively. The sixteen points are apparently not discussed in this interview.

September 1—Early in the morning the Reichstag is summoned and Hitler delivers the following speech:

The Speech

"FOR months we have been suffering under the torture of a problem which the Versailles *Diktat* created—a problem which has deteriorated until it becomes intolerable for us. Danzig was and is a German city. The Corridor was and is German. Both these territories owe their cultural development exclusively to the German people. Danzig was separated from us, the Corridor was annexed by Poland. As in other German territories of the East, all German minorities living there have been ill-treated in the most distressing manner. More than one million people of German blood had in the years 1919-20 to leave their homeland.

"As always, I attempted to bring about, by the peaceful method of making proposals for revision, an alteration of this intolerable position. It is a lie when the outside world says that we only tried to carry through our revisions by pressure. Fifteen years before the National Socialist party came to power there was the opportunity of carrying out these revisions by peaceful settlements and understanding. On my own initiative I have, not once but several times, made proposals for the revision of intolerable conditions. All these proposals, as you know, have been rejected—proposals for limitation of armaments and even, if necessary, disarmament; proposals for the limitation of warmaking; proposals for the elimination of certain methods of modern warfare. You know the proposals that I have made to fulfill the necessity of restoring German sovereignty over German territories. You know the endless attempts I made for a peaceful clarification and understanding of the problem of Austria, and later of the problems of the Sudetenland, Bohemia, and Moravia. It was all in vain.

"It is impossible to demand that an impossible situation should be cleared up by peaceful revision and at the same time constantly reject peaceful revision. It is also impossible to say that he who undertakes to carry out these revisions for himself transgresses a law, since the Versailles *Diktat* is not law to us. A signature was forced out of us with pistols at our head and with the threat of hunger for millions of people. And then this document, with our signature, obtained by force, was proclaimed as a solemn law.

"In the same way I have also tried to solve the problem of Danzig, the Corridor, etc., by proposing a peaceful discussion. That the problems had to be solved was clear. It is quite understandable to us that the time when the problem was to be solved had little interest for the Western Powers. But that time is not a matter of indifference to us. Moreover, it was not and could not be a matter of indifference to those who suffer most.

"In my talks with Polish statesmen I discussed the ideas which you recognize from my last speech to the Reichstag. No one could say that this was in any way an inadmissible procedure or undue pressure. I then naturally formulated at last the German proposals, and I must once more repeat that there is nothing more modest or loyal than these proposals. I should like to say this to the world. I alone was in the position to make such proposals, for I know very well that in doing so I brought myself into opposition to millions of Germans. These proposals have been refused. Not only were they answered first with mobilization, but with increased terror and pressure against our German compatriots and with a slow strangling of the Free City of Danzig—economically, politically, and in recent weeks by military and transport means.

"Poland has directed its attacks against the Free City of Danzig. Moreover, Poland was not prepared to settle the Corridor question in a reasonable way which would be equitable to both parties, and she did not think of keeping her obligations to minorities.

"I must here state something definitely: Germany has kept these obligations; the minorities who live in Germany are not persecuted. No Frenchman can stand up and say that any Frenchman living in the Saar territory is oppressed, tortured, or deprived of his rights. Nobody can say this.

"For four months I have calmly watched developments, although I never ceased to give warnings. I informed the Polish Ambassador three weeks ago that if Poland continued to send to Danzig notes in the form of ultimatums, if Poland continued its methods of oppression against the Germans, and if on the Polish side an end was not put to Customs measures destined to ruin Danzig's trade, then the Reich could not remain inactive. I left no doubt that people who wanted to compare the Germany of today with the former Germany would be deceiving themselves.

"An attempt was made to justify the oppression of the Germans by claiming that they had committed acts of provocation. I do not know in what these provocations on the part of women and children consist, if they themselves are maltreated, in some cases killed. One thing I do know—that no Great Power can with honor long stand by passively and watch such events.

"I made one more final effort to accept a proposal for mediation on the part of the British Government. They proposed, not that they themselves should carry on the negotiations, but rather that Poland and Germany should come into direct contact and once more pursue negotiations.

"I must declare that I accepted this proposal, and I worked out a basis for these negotiations which are known to you. For two whole days I sat with my Government and waited to see whether it was convenient for the Polish Government to send a plenipotentiary or not. Last night they did not send us a plenipotentiary, but instead informed us through their Ambassador that they were still considering whether and to what extent they were in a position to go into the British proposals. The Polish Government also said that they would inform Britain of their decision.

"Deputies, if the German Government and its Leader patiently endured such treatment, Germany would deserve only to disappear from the political stage. But I am wrongly judged if my love of peace and my patience are mistaken for weakness or even cowardice. I, therefore, decided last night and informed the British Government that in these circumstances I can no longer find any willingness on the part of the Polish Government to conduct serious negotiations with us.

"These proposals for mediation have failed, because in the meanwhile there first of all came as an answer the sudden Polish general mobilization, followed by more Polish atrocities. These were again repeated last night. Recently in one night there were as many as twenty-one frontier incidents; last night there were fourteen, of which three were quite serious. I have, therefore, resolved to speak to Poland in the same language that Poland for months past has used toward us. This attitude on the part of the Reich will not change.

"The other European States understand in part our attitude. I should like here above all to thank Italy, which throughout has supported us, but you will understand that for the carrying on of this struggle we do not intend to appeal to foreign help. We will carry out this task ourselves. *The neutral States have assured us of their neutrality, just as we had already guaranteed it to them.*

"When statesmen in the West declare that this affects their interests, I can only regret such a declaration. It cannot for a moment make me hesitate to fulfill my duty. What more is wanted? *I have solemnly assured them, and I repeat it, that we ask nothing of these western States and never will ask anything. I have declared that the frontier between France and Germany is a final one. I have repeatedly offered friendship and, if necessary, the closest co-operation to Britain, but this cannot be offered from one side only.* It must find response on the other side. *Germany has no interests in the West, and our western wall is for all time the frontier of the Reich on the West. Moreover, we have no aims of any kind there for the future. With this assurance we are in solemn earnest, and as long as others do not violate their neutrality we will likewise take every care to respect it.*

"I am happy particularly to be able to tell you of one event. *You know that Russia and Germany are governed by two different doctrines. There was only one question that had to be cleared up. Germany has no intention of exporting its doctrine. Given the fact that Soviet Russia has no intention of exporting its doctrine to Germany, I no longer see any reason why we should still oppose one another.* On both sides we are clear on that. Any struggle between our people would only be of advantage to others. *We have, therefore, resolved to conclude a pact which rules out forever any use of violence between us.* It imposes the obligation on us to consult together in certain European questions. It makes possible for us economic co-operation, and above all it assures that the powers of both these powerful States are not wasted against one another. Every attempt of the West to bring about any change in this will fail.

"At the same time I should like here to declare that this political decision means a tremendous departure for the future, and that it is a final one. Russia and Germany fought against one another in the World War. That shall and will not happen a second time. In Moscow, too, this pact was greeted exactly as you greet it. I can only endorse word for word the speech of the Russian Foreign Commissar, Molotov.

"I am determined to solve (1) the Danzig question; (2) the question of the Corridor; and (3) *to see to it that a change is made in the relationship between Germany and Poland that shall insure a peaceful co-existence.* In this I am resolved to continue to fight until either the present Polish Government is willing to bring about this change or until another Polish Government is ready to do so. I am resolved to remove from the German frontiers the element of uncertainty, the everlasting atmosphere of conditions resembling civil war. I will see to it that in the East there is, on the frontier, a peace precisely similar to that on our other frontiers.

"In this I will take the necessary measures to see that they do not contradict the proposals I have already made known in the Reichstag itself to the rest of the world, that is to say, *I will not war against women and children. I have ordered my air force to restrict itself to attacks on military objectives.* If, however, the enemy thinks he can from that draw *carte blanche* on his side to fight by the other methods, he will receive an answer that will deprive him of hearing and sight.

"This night for the first time Polish regular soldiers fired on our own territory. Since 5:45 A.M. we have been returning the fire, and from now on bombs will be met with bombs. Whoever fights with poison gas will be fought with poison gas. Whoever departs from the rules of humane warfare can only expect that we shall do the same. I will continue this struggle, no matter against whom, until the safety of the Reich and its rights are secured.

"For six years now I have been working on the building up of the German defenses. Over ninety milliards have in that time been spent on the building up of these defense forces. They are now the best equipped and are above all comparison with what they were in 1914. My trust in them is unshakeable. When I called up these forces, and when I now ask sacrifices of the German people and if necessary every sacrifice, then I have a right to do so, for I also am today absolutely ready, just as we were formerly, to make every personal sacrifice.

"I am asking of no German man more than I myself was ready throughout four years at any time to do. There will be no hardships for Germans to which I myself will not submit. My whole life henceforth belongs more than ever to my people. I am from now on just first soldier of the German Reich. *I have once more put on that coat that was the most sacred and dear to me. I will not take it off again until victory is secured, or I will not survive the outcome.*

"Should anything happen to me in the struggle, then *my first successor is Party Comrade Goering;* should anything happen to Party Commander Goering *my next successor is Party Comrade Hess.* You would then be under obligation to give to them as Fuehrer the same blind loyalty and obedience as to myself. *Should anything happen to Party Comrade Hess, then by law the Senate will be called, and will choose from its midst the most worthy—that is to say the bravest—successor.*

"As a National Socialist and as a German soldier I enter upon this struggle with a stout heart. My whole life has been nothing but one long struggle for my people, for its restoration, and for Germany. There was only one watchword for that struggle: faith in this people. One word I have never learned: that is, surrender.

"If, however, anyone thinks that we are facing a hard time, I should ask him to remember that once a Prussian king, with a ridiculously small State, opposed a stronger coalition, and in three wars finally came out successful because that State had that stout heart that we need in these times. I would, therefore, like to assure all the world that a November 1918 will never be repeated in German history. Just as I myself am ready at any time to stake my life—anyone can take it for my people and for Germany—so I ask the same of all others.

"Whoever, however, thinks he can oppose this national command, whether directly or indirectly, shall fall. We have nothing to do with traitors. We are all faithful to our old principle. It is quite unimportant whether we ourselves live, but it is essential that our people shall live, that Germany shall live. The sacrifice that is demanded of us is not greater than the sacrifice that many generations have made. If we form a community closely bound together by vows, ready for anything, resolved never to surrender, then our will will master every hardship and difficulty. And I would like to close with the declaration that I once made when I began the struggle for power in the Reich. I then said: "If our will is so strong that no hardship and suffering can subdue it, then our will and our German might shall prevail."

Press

London Times, September 2—The long period of international tension, never appreciably relaxed throughout the summer, was ended yesterday by an act of naked aggression, which by itself exposes the hollowness of all Nazi declarations of peaceful intent and Herr Hitler's clumsy sophistries. . . .

In coming to the help of Poland we have no material interest of our own to maintain. Nonetheless shall we be fighting for that which is vital to our life and to the life of all civilized peoples. For we know that, in a world where respect for the rights of the weak and for the plighted word can be overridden by the high hand of military power, there is no tolerable life for nations or for individuals, and they who must wholeheartedly repudiate the use of force, or the threat of force, as an instrument of policy have no choice but to answer force with force when it is invoked against the ideas by which they live. . . .

The sole object of British diplomacy has been to bring the dispute between Poland and Germany to discussion on terms of equality. For that discussion Poland was ready; the German autocrat rejected it. From all over the world—from the Holy See, from the President of the United States, from the Sovereigns of Belgium and the Netherlands—have come appeals for a peaceful settlement and offers to assist it. They have been rebuffed by the will of one man. He has not sought to deny his responsibility; in his harangue to his docile Reichstag yesterday he claimed it and gloried in it. The power for destruction that he has chosen to use has never in history been so completely concentrated in one man's hands.

Le Temps, September 2—Until the last moment France has been bent on maintaining peace. She has welcomed all suggestions, searched for all possible conciliations in order to keep away from the world this abominable scourge. While being resolved to fulfill her pledges, she has taken all the initiatives that might insure for Europe a secure life with dignity and honor. And as late as yesterday she still hoped that peaceful words and negotiations might prevail, that the aggression would not take place, that the disputes would be solved through negotiations, that an armistice would precede the attack. France has a clear conscience and her soul is at peace.

New York Times, September 3—Since he came to the leadership of Germany—to go no farther back—Adolf Hitler has built up a record of mendacity and duplicity which made it all but impossible for the statesmen of other countries to know how it was possible to negotiate with him. Regarding the specific issue of Poland, for example, Hitler has repeatedly declared since 1933 that the issue was in effect settled. In Nuremberg less than a year ago (September 12, 1938) he declared: "When in Poland a great statesman and patriot was ready to conclude a pact with us we immediately accepted the treaty recognizing our respective frontiers as inviolable. This treaty has done more for peace than all the chattering in Geneva put together."

In 1934 Hitler declared that Germany had no territorial ambition beyond the return of the Saar. In 1935 he declared that "The German Government will unconditionally respect the other articles of the Treaty of Versailles including territorial clauses, and will bring about revisions that are unavoidable as times change only by peaceful arrangement." He declared at the same time that "Germany has neither the wish nor the intention to mix in internal Austrian affairs or annex or unite with Austria." A year ago he twice asserted that if the Sudeten territories were ceded this would be the last territorial demand he would make in Europe. Hitler has broken each one of his pledges in turn. In turn he has made the new demands that he promised not to make. In turn he has used each capitulation on the part of other statesmen to demand further concessions and surrenders.

SPEECH OF SEPTEMBER 19, 1939

Danzig

Background

1939

September 1—German armies invade Poland.

September 3—Britain and France at war with Germany. President Roosevelt pledges effort to maintain United States at peace.

September 4—S.S. Athenia sunk. Australia and New Zealand at war with Germany. Cordell Hull proclaims American neutrality.

September 10—Canada declares war on Germany.

September 13—President Roosevelt calls Congress to revise Neutrality Law.

September 17—Russian troops march into eastern Poland.

The Speech

"My District Leader, My Dear Danzigers:

"Not only you experience this moment with deepest emotion; nay, the entire German nation experiences it with you, and I, too, am aware of the greatness of the hour when I, for the first time, tread on the soil which German settlers occupied five centuries ago and which for five centuries was German, and which—thereof you may rest assured—will remain German. . . . "

"The fact that a province was torn from the German Reich and that other German territories were given to the Polish State was explained on the grounds of national necessity. Later, plebiscites everywhere showed that no one wished to become a part of the Polish State—that Polish State which arose out of the blood of countless German regiments. It then expanded at the expense of old settlement areas and above all at the expense of intelligence and economic possibility.

"One thing has been clearly proved in the last twenty years; the Poles who had not founded that culture also were not able to maintain it. It has been shown again that only he who is himself culturally creative can permanently maintain real cultural performance.

"Thirty years would have been sufficient to reduce again to barbarism those territories which the Germans, painstakingly and with industry and thrift, had saved from barbarism. Everywhere traces of this retrogression and decay were visible.

"Poland itself was a 'nationalities State.' That very thing had been created here which had been held against the old Austrian State. At the same time Poland was never a democracy. One very thin anemic upper class here ruled not only foreign nationalities but also its so-called own people.

"It was a State built on force and governed by the truncheons of the police and the military. The fate of Germans in this State was horrible. *There is a difference whether people of lower cultural value has the misfortune to be governed by a culturally significant people or whether a people of high cultural significance has forced upon it the tragic fate of being oppressed by an inferior.*

"In this inferior people all its inferiority complexes will be compensated upon a higher culture-bearing people. This people will be horribly and barbarically mistreated and Germans have been evidence of this fate for twenty years.

"It was, as already emphasized, tragic and painful. Nevertheless, as everywhere else, I tried to find a solution here which might have led to a fair adjustment. I have tried in the West and then later in the South to maintain final frontier delineations in order thus to deliver region upon region from uncertainty and assure peace and justice for the future. I made the greatest efforts to attain the same thing here also. . . ."

"The world, which immediately sheds tears when Germany expels a Polish Jew who only a few decades ago came to Germany, remained dumb and deaf toward the misery of those who, numbering not thousands but millions, were forced to leave their home country on account of Versailles—that is, if these unfortunates were Germans.

"What was for us and also for me most depressing was the fact that we had to suffer all this from a State which was far inferior to us; for, after all, Germany is a Great Power, even though madmen believed the vital rights of a great nation could be wiped out by a crazy treaty or by dictation.

"Germany was a big power and had to look on while a far inferior people of a far inferior State maltreated these Germans. There were two especially unbearable conditions: First, this city whose German character nobody could deny was not only prevented from returning to the Reich but in addition an attempt was made to Polonize it by all kinds of devices; second, the province [East Prussia] severed from the German Reich had no direct contact with the Reich, but traffic with this province was dependent upon all kinds of chicanery or upon the good will of this Polish State.

"No power on earth would have borne this condition as long as Germany. I do not know what England would have said about a similar "peace solution" at its expense or how America or France would have accepted it. I attempted to find a solution—a tolerable solution—even for this problem. I submitted this attempt to the Polish rulers in the form of verbal proposals. You know these proposals. They were more than moderate. . . ."

"I do not know what mental condition the Polish Government was in when it refused these proposals. I know, however, that millions of Germans sighed with relief, since they felt I had gone too far. As an answer, Poland gave the order for the first mobilization. Thereupon wild terror was initiated, and my request to the Polish Foreign Minister to visit me in Berlin once more to discuss these questions was refused. Instead of going to Berlin, he went to London. For the next weeks and months there were heightened threats, threats which were hardly bearable for a small State but which were impossible for a Great Power to bear for any length of time.

"We could read in Polish publications that the issue at stake was not Danzig but the problem of East Prussia, which Poland was to incorporate in a short time. That increased. Other Polish newspapers stated that East Prussia would not solve the problem, but that Pomerania must, under all circumstances, come to Poland.

"Finally it became questionable in Poland whether the Oder would be enough as a boundary or whether Poland's natural boundary was not the Oder but the Elbe. It was debated whether our armies would be smashed before or behind Berlin.

The Polish Marshal, who miserably deserted his armies, said that he would hack the German Army to pieces. And martyrdom began for our German nationals. Tens of thousands were dragged off, mistreated, and murdered in the vilest fashion. Sadistic beasts gave vent to their perverse instincts, and this pious democratic world watched without blinking an eye.

"I have often asked myself: Who can have so blinded Poland? Does anyone really believe that the German nation will permanently stand that from such a ridiculous State? Does anyone seriously believe that? It must have been believed because certain quarters described it as possible to the Poles, certain quarters which general warmongers have occupied decades long, yes, hundreds of years long and which they occupy even today.

"These quarters declared that Germany was not even to be considered as a Power. The Poles were told that they would easily be able to resist Germany, and, going a step further, assurance was given that if their own resistance was not enough they could depend on the resistance and assistance of others. The guarantee was given which put it into the hands of a small State to begin a war, or again perhaps not to do so.

"For these men Poland, too, was only a means to an end. Because today it is being declared quite calmly that Poland was not the primary thing, but that the German regime is. I always warned against these men. You will recall my Saarbruecken and Wilhelmshaven speeches. In both these speeches I pointed out the danger that in a certain country such men could rise and unmolested preach the necessity of war—Herren Churchill, Eden, Duff-Cooper, etc.

"I pointed out how dangerous this is, especially in a country where one does not know whether these men may not be the Government in a short time. I was then told that that would never happen. In my opinion they are now the Government. It happened exactly as I then foresaw. I then decided for the first time to warn the German nation against them. But I also have left no doubt that Germany, under no circumstances, will capitulate to the threats or coercion of these people.

"On account of this answer I have been strongly attacked: because certain practices have gradually been developed in democracies: namely, in democracies war may be advocated. There foreign regimes and statesmen may be attacked, calumniated, insulted, sullied because there reign freedom of speech and the press. In authoritarian States, on the other hand, one may not defend one's self because there reigns discipline.

"You know, of course, of those August days. I believe it would have been possible in those last August days, without the British guarantee and without agitation by these warmongers, to have reached an understanding. At a certain moment England herself offered to bring us into direct discussion with Poland. I was ready. Of course it was the Poles who did not come.

"I came to Berlin with my Government and for two days waited and waited. Meanwhile, I had worked out a new pro-

posal. You know it. I had the British Ambassador informe
of it on the evening of the first day. It was read to him sen
tence by sentence and the Reich Foreign Minister gave hin
a supplementary explanation. Then came the next day an
nothing occurred except for Polish general mobilization, re
newed acts of terror, and finally attacks against Reich terri
tory.

"Now in the life of nations, patience must not always b
interpreted as weakness. For years I patiently looked on thes
continuous provocations. What keen suffering I underwen
in these years only few can imagine, because there was hardl
a month or week in which deputations from these district
did not come to me depicting unbearable conditions and im
ploring me to interfere.

"I have always begged them to try again. This continue
for years, but I have recently also warned that this could no
go on forever. After again waiting and even receiving nev
proposals I finally decided, as I declared in the Reichstag, t
talk with Poland in the same language as they talked to us
or believed they could talk to us—the language which alon
they seem to understand.

"Also, at this moment peace could have been saved
Friendly Italy and Il Duce came in and made a suggestio
for mediation. France agreed. I also expressed my agreement
Then England rejected also that suggestion and replied that
instead, Germany might be served with a two-hour ultima
tum with impossible demands. England erred in one thing
There once was a government in Germany in November
1918, that was kept by England, and they confound the pres
ent German regime with one they kept and confound th
present German nation with the misled and blinded natio
of that time.

"One does not send ultimatums to the Germany of today
May London make note!

"In the last six years I had to stand intolerable things fron
States like Poland—nevertheless I sent no ultimatum. Th

German Reich is not inclined and will not be addressed in such a tone. I knew if Poland chose war she chose it because others drove her into war, those others who believed they might make their biggest political and financial killing in this war. But it will not be their biggest killing, but their biggest disappointment.

"Poland chose to fight and she received a fight. She chose this fight light-heartedly because certain statesmen assured her they had detailed proof of the worthlessness of Germany and her armed forces, of the inferiority of our armament, of the poor morale of our troops, of defeatism within the Reich, of a discrepancy between the German people and its leadership.

"The Poles were persuaded that it would be easy not only to resist but also to throw our army back. Poland constructed her campaign on these assurances of the Western general staffs. Since then eighteen days have passed, and hardly elsewhere in history can the following be said with more truth: The Lord has struck them down with horse, with man and with wagon.

"As I speak to you our troops stand along a great line from Brest-Litovsk to Lwow, and at this moment endless columns of the smashed Polish Army have been marching as prisoners from that sector since yesterday afternoon. Yesterday morning there were 20,000; yesterday afternoon 50,000; this morning 70,000. I do not know how great the number is now, but I know one thing: what remains of the Polish Army west of that line will capitulate within a few days, they will lay down their arms or be crushed. At this moment, our thankful hearts fly to our men. The German Army gave those genius-statesmen, who were so well-informed as to conditions within the Reich, a necessary lesson. . . ."

"At this moment we want to give the Polish soldier absolute justice. At many points the Pole fought bravely. His lower leadership made desperate efforts, his middle-grade leadership was too unintelligent, his highest leadership was bad, judged by any standard. His organization was—Polish. . . ."

"I ordered the German Air Force to conduct humanitarian warfare—that is, to attack only fighting troops. The Polish Government and army leadership ordered the civilian population to carry on the war as francs-tireurs from ambush. It is very difficult under these circumstances to hold one's self back. I want to stress that the democratic States should not imagine it must be that way. If they want it otherwise, they can have it otherwise. My patience can have limits here also. . . ."

"So, we have beaten Poland within eighteen days and thus created a situation which perhaps makes it possible one day to speak to representatives of the Polish people calmly and reasonably.

"Meantime, Russia felt moved, on its part, to march in for the protection of the interests of the White Russian and Ukrainian people in Poland. *We realize now that in England and France this German and Russian co-operation is considered a terrible crime.* An Englishman even wrote that it is perfidious—well, the English ought to know. I believe England thinks this co-operation perfidious because the co-operation of democratic England with bolshevist Russia failed, while National Socialist Germany's attempt with Soviet Russia succeeded.

"I want to give here an explanation: *Russia remains what she is; Germany also remain what she is. About only one thing are both regimes clear: neither the German nor the Russian regime wants to sacrifice a single man for the interest of the Western democracies.* A lesson of four years was sufficient for both peoples. We know only too well that alternately, now one then the other, would be granted the honor to fill the breach for the ideals of the Western democracies.

"We therefore thank both peoples and both States for this task. We intend henceforth to look after our interests ourselves, and we have found that we best have been able to look after them when two of the largest peoples and States reconcile each other. *And this is made simpler by the fact that the British assertion as to the unlimited character of German foreign policy is a lie. I am happy now to be able to refute this lie for British statesmen. British statesmen, who continually maintain that Germany intends to dominate Europe to the Urals now will be pleased to learn the limits of German political intentions.* I believe this will deprive them of a reason for war because they profess to have to fight against the present regime because it today pursues unlimited political goals.

"Now, gentlemen of the great British Empire, *the aims of Germany are closely limited. We discussed the matter with Russia—they, after all, are the most immediately interested neighbor—and if you are of the opinion that we might come to a conflict on the subject—we will not.*

"Britain ought to welcome the fact that Germany and Soviet Russia have come to an understanding, for this understanding means the elimination of that nightmare which kept British statesmen from sleeping because they were so concerned over the ambitions of the present [German] *regime to conquer the world. It will calm you to learn that Germany does not, and did not, want to conquer the Ukraine.* We have very limited interests, but we are determined to maintain those interests despite all dangers, despite anyone.

"And that we did not permit ourselves to be trifled with in those past eighteen days may have been proved sufficiently. How a definite settlement of State conditions in this conflict will look depends first and foremost upon the two countries which there have their most important vital interests.

"Germany has there limited but unalterable claims, and she will realize those claims one way or another. *Germany and Russia will put in place the hotbed of conflict in the European situation which later will be valued only as a relaxation of tension.*

"If the Western Powers now declare that this must not be,

under any circumstances, and if especially England declares that she is determined to oppose this in a three- or five- or eight-year war, then I want to say something in reply:

"Firstly, *Germany, by extensive yielding and renunciation in the west and south of the Reich, has accepted definite boundaries.* Germany tried by these renunciations to attain lasting pacification. And we believe we would have succeeded were it not that certain warmongers could be interested in disturbing the European peace.

"I have neither toward England nor France any war claims, nor has the German nation since I assumed power. I tried gradually to establish confidence between Germany and especially its former war enemies. I attempted to eliminate all tensions which once existed between Germany and Italy, and I may state with satisfaction that I fully succeeded.

"That ever closer and more cordial relations were established was due also to personal and human relations between Il Duce and myself. I went still further, I tried to achieve the same between Germany and France. *Immediately after the settlement of the Saar question I solemnly renounced all further frontier revisions, not only in theory but in practice. I harnessed all German propaganda to this end in order to eliminate everything which might lead to doubt or anxiety in Paris.*

"You know of my offers to England. I had only in mind the great goal of attaining the sincere friendship of the British people. Since this now has been repulsed, and since England today thinks it must wage war against Germany, I would like to answer thus:

"Poland will never rise again in the form of the Versailles Treaty. That is guaranteed not only by Germany but also guaranteed by Russia.

"It is said in England that this war, of course, is not for Poland. That is only secondary. More important is the war against the regime in Germany. And I receive the honor of special mention as a representative of this regime. If that is now set up as a war aim, I will answer the gentlemen in London thus:

"It is for me the greatest honor to be thus classed. On principle I educated the German people so that any regime which is lauded by our enemies is poison for Germany and will therefore be rejected by us. If, therefore, a German regime would get the consent of Churchill, Duff-Cooper and Eden it would be paid and kept by these gentlemen and hence would be unbearable for Germany. That, certainly, is not true with us. It is, therefore, only honorable for us to be rejected by these gentlemen. I can assure these gentlemen only this: If they should praise, this would be a reason for me to be most crestfallen. I am proud to be attacked by them.

"But if they believe they can thereby alienate the German people from me, then they either think the German people are as lacking in character as themselves or as stupid as themselves. They err in both. National Socialism did not educate the German people in vain during the past twenty years. We are all men who, in their long struggle, have been nothing but attacked. That only tended to increase the love of our followers and created an inseparable union. And as the National Socialist party took upon itself this years-long struggle, finally to win it, thus the National Socialist Reich and the German people take up the fight and those gentlemen may be convinced: By their ridiculous propaganda the German people will not be undermined. *Those bunglers will have become our apprentices for many years before they can even attempt propaganda.*

"If peoples go to pieces it will not be the German people, who are fighting for justice, who have no war aims and who were attacked.

"Rather, those peoples will break when they gradually find out what their misleaders plan, and gradually grasp for what little reason they are fighting, and that the only reasons for war are the profits or political interests of a very small clique. *A part of it declared in Britain that this war will last three years. Then I can only say: My sympathies are with the French poilu. What he is fighting for he does not know.* He knows only that he has the honor to fight at least three years. But if it should last three years, then the word capitulation will not stand at the end of the third, and at the end of the fourth year the word capitulation also will not be, and not in the fifth either, and also not in the sixth or seventh year.

"These gentlemen should take note of the following: To-day you have the Germany of Frederick the Great before you. These gentlemen can believe this. The German people will not split up in this fight but become more unified. If anything splits up it will be those States that are not so homogeneous, those empires built on the oppression of peoples. We are fighting only for our naked beings. We are not able ourselves to be misled by propaganda.

"Just imagine! There are people who say there are those ruling in another land who do not please us, so now we have war with them. Naturally they do not carry on the war themselves, but look about for someone to conduct it for them. They provide cannon and grenades while others provide grenadiers and soldiers. Such an utter lack of conscience!

"What would be said if one of us should say that the present regime in France or Britain does not suit us and consequently we are conducting a war? What immeasurable lack of conscience. For that, millions of persons are whipped into death. These gentlemen can say that calmly, for they themselves never have been on the battlefield for even an hour.

"But we will see how long they keep nations at war. There can be no doubt of one thing, however. We will take up the gauntlet and we will fight as the enemy fights. England, with lies and hypocrisy, already has begun to fight against women and children. They found a weapon which they think is invincible: namely, sea power. And because they cannot be attacked with this weapon they think they are justified in making war with it against women and children—not only of enemies but also of neutrals if necessary.

"Let them make no mistake here, however. *The moment could come very suddenly in which we could use a weapon with which we cannot be attacked. I hope then they do not suddenly begin to think of humaneness and of the impossibility of waging war against women and children.* We Germans do not like that. It is not in our nature. In this campaign I gave an order to spare human beings. When columns cross a market-place it can occur that someone else becomes the victim of attack.

"In those places where insane or crazy people did not offer resistance not one windowpane was broken. In Cracow, except for the air field, railroads and the railroad station, which were military objectives, not one bomb fell. On the other hand, in Warsaw the war is carried on by civilian shootings in all streets and houses. There, of course, the war will take in the whole city. We followed these rules and would like to follow them in the future. It is entirely up to England to carry out her blockade in a form compatible with international law or incompatible with international law. We will adapt ourselves thereto.

"But there should be no doubt about one thing:

"England's goal is not 'a fight against the regime' but a fight against the German people, women and children. Our reaction will be compatible, and one thing will be certain: This Germany does not capitulate. We know too well what fate would be in store for Germany. Mr. King-Hall [Commander Stephen King-Hall, retired naval officer who writes a privately-circulated news letter] told us in the name of his masters: A second Versailles, only worse.

"What can be worse? The first Versailles Treaty was intended to exterminate 20,000,000 Germans. Thus the second can only realize this intention. We received more detailed illustrations of what has been intended, what Poland shall have, what crowns will be placed on what heads in France, etc. The German people take notice of this and shall fight accordingly. . . ."

"We are determined to carry on and stand this war one way or another. We have only this one wish, that the Almighty, who now has blessed our arms, will now perhaps make other peoples understand and give them comprehension of how useless this war, this débâcle of peoples, will be intrinsically, and that He may perhaps cause reflection on the blessings of peace which they are sacrificing because a handful of fanatic warmongers, persons who stand to gain by war, want to involve peoples in war. . . ."

Press

New York Times, September 20—The most noteworthy feature of Hitler's first speech as a military conqueror is that it contains nothing new. . . . Hitler is still explaining why he invaded Poland. Despite the pleas of President Roosevelt, the Pope and the Oslo Powers, the offers to mediate of King Leopold and Queen Wilhelmina, he is still shouting he sought everywhere for peace and nobody would give it to him. . . . Hitler scoffs at the folly of those who try to rupture the "unbreakable ties" between Germany and Italy, or rather between "myself and Mussolini." But he still clings to the idea that he can drive a wedge between France and Britain.

London Times, September 20— . . . some of it [the speech] reads like a rehash of "Mein Kampf" with its gibes at the so-called "Polish State.". . . Proposals which were never communicated in full to any of the Allied Governments . . . now masquerade . . . as the earnest efforts of a zealous seeker for peace. . . . Such a speech calls for a practical and not an argumentative reply. . . .

Le Temps, September 21— . . . In his speech in Danzig, M. Hitler, a prisoner of his own crimes, merely argued in his own defense against the evidence, merely dealt in falsehoods in order to conceal from the eyes of his people the tragic aspects of the situation created by the German resort to force, to conceal inescapable realities. He repeated for the hundredth time his charges against the "Diktat" of Versailles.

. . . M. Hitler limited himself to proclaiming that he has no war aims in regard to France and England. What was noteworthy about the Danzig speech was that he made no really constructive proposals, and that he did not explain the circumstances and the conditions of the collusion between Germany and Russia. . . .

PHASE VI

The "Phony" War

October 6, 1939 — April 9, 1940

COMMENT

BETWEEN the end of the Polish campaign on September 27, 1939, and the invasion of Denmark and Norway by the German armies on April 9, 1940, World War II, as the American newspapers liked to call it, was marked by no major military action. With the exception of the sinking of the pocket-battleship *Graf Spee* by the English, opposite Montevideo (December 17), and the Russian-Finnish War, there was practically no spectacular fighting anywhere.

The British tightened their blockade and the French, having manned the Maginot Line, occupied themselves unhurriedly to improve their defense system. Skirmishes took place from time to time along the line. The French who had advanced a few hundred yards in German territory, during the first weeks of the war, withdrew in the fall when the idea of a winter offensive—if it had ever been entertained—was given up. German and French guns remained silent. Factories on both sides of the line, and even between the lines, worked day and night, in perfect security and without blackout. It is said that on Christmas Eve, Hitler visited the Western Front, and that, for the first time since he was a corporal in World War I, he put his foot on French soil.

But if there was no military action to speak of, during these six months, the political and psychological warfare was carried on with relentless intensity. Poland having been lost, the Allies and the neutrals found themselves faced with a situation which was at once new and all too familiar.

It was new because, since September 3, England and

France were formally at war with Germany. But it was familiar in this sense that the absence of real fighting, the continuation of peace-time life and persistence of all the internal conflicts within the democracies made this period appear as a mere prolongation of the "war of nerves." Chamberlain had said that this war was necessary to put an end to the unbearable conditions under which the unfortunate people of Europe had been living for several years. *"Il faut en finir,"* he had said. But it so happened that even the state of war did not relieve the frightful nervous strain imposed on his neighbors by the devilish technique of Hitler. England and France had mobilized. They had done that before. But this time they meant business. They were resolved not to lay down their arms until Hitler had been defeated.

But to defeat Hitler it was necessary to be able to fight him. The Allies did not want to take the offensive because they were sure that whoever attacked was fated to meet disaster. They wanted Hitler to attack. Militarily and psychologically they were prepared for the worst, provided the worst followed more or less a predictable pattern. They had not been dismayed by the Blitzkrieg in Poland. The Poles had not listened to the advice of the Allied High Command. Their defeat was unfortunate, but it was not surprising. Besides, they had no Maginot Line.

But Hitler did not attack. Instead, and as soon as he had finished with Poland, he offered peace to the Allies.

It will never be possible to determine which of Hitler's numerous peace offers were sincere and which were merely destined to confuse his opponents and soften up their morale in order to better prepare the surprise of a new attack.

Human beings have a habit of judging a new situation by referring to precedents. The memory of Munich was vivid when the war started and there are many who believed—and still believe—that Hitler is always ready to accept a new Munich at any moment. On the other hand, it has sometimes been rumored that Hitler regretted Munich, because he felt at the time that he should have forced war upon the Allies, and therefore advanced more rapidly his program of conquest.

Be that as it may, the offers of peace which were made by Hitler in his speech of October 6, 1939, were directly in line with his usual strategy of appealing to the anti-war feeling of the world while at the same time threatening his opponents with utter destruction if they did not accept his proposals.

The kind of peace which Hitler offered at that moment was described in terms which were vague and general enough to be at once tempting and alarming. They were predicated on the recognition by his opponents that the affairs of the whole of Europe east of the Rhine were to be settled by the two largest continental powers: Germany and Russia, without any outside interference. He renewed his pledges to respect the independence of such states as Switzerland, Holland, Denmark, Belgium, the Scandinavian countries, Yugoslavia and Hungary. The frontiers of France were to remain unchanged. From England he asked nothing, apparently, but a return of the former German colonies.

In spite of his often-expressed scorn for international conferences, he suggested that one should be held to study such problems as disarmament and the economic reconstruction of the new Europe.

There is little reason to believe that Hitler expected his peace offers would be accepted. He knew that the democratic nations who had finally gone to war against him because they were tired of the "appeasement" policy, would not suddenly revert to it—demobilize their armies and fleet—and sit around a conference table to listen to Hitler telling them how he thought the peace of the world should be organized and the security of Europe guaranteed.

Nevertheless these "peace offers" of Hitler—which according to Hitler himself were to be the last—were carefully studied and discussed in the outside world which was unofficially informed that the Fuehrer would wait ten days for a reply.

Before that period had expired, Daladier and Chamberlain made it known that no peace could be envisaged as long as Hitler did not propose to repair the damage already done—as, for instance, the restoration of Poland and Czechoslovakia.

As this was obviously out of the question, the matter was officially dropped. The "peace offensive" was considered a failure. The war was to go on until ultimate victory.

But if such was the interpretation of the situation as expressed by the spokesmen of the Allies, it did not put an end to the confusion which existed in the minds of the democratic people. In fact Hitler's speech of October 6 only increased the atmosphere of doubt and hesitancy which had proved so useful to his purpose on many other occasions. It threw a smoke screen as to his real intentions, behind which he was able to prepare the spring offensive.

If he ever had an intention of achieving another Munich after the Polish conquest, he soon abandoned that idea. On January 30, 1940, he announced that the phase of political and military preparation was ended and that real war was going to break out soon. "In the last five months," he said, "we have not slept." Three months later, on March 10, he was even more explicit: he told the German people that he was ready to sacrifice his own life for their good, that the great final ordeal was near and that total victory was in sight.

Considering the speeches of Hitler during this six-month period, one cannot help but be struck by the persistent inability of his opponents to measure fully the tremendous advantage which Hitler was gaining over them by pursuing the dual strategy of terror and confusion of which his speeches are the continuous expression.

Although there was an increasing tendency to minimize the importance of what Hitler said, and to disregard his promises as much as his abuses, the resistance to the Hitlerian technique was nevertheless not definite enough to enable the belligerent democracies and the neutrals to counteract effectively the dissolving effect of Hitler's peace talk and of his renewed affirmations that he had no quarrel with any one of his neighbors—whether neutrals or enemies.

It may be said that the stratagem of the "peace offensive"—whether intended to be taken seriously or used as a mere blind to cover the preparation of the great offensive in the West—was to have an effect which Hitler himself could not possibly expect.

In fact, during the six months that followed the conquest of Poland, the behavior of the Allies, of the European neutrals, and of the United States could not have been very different if Nazi gauleiters had already been secretly in charge in Paris, London, Washington, Brussels. The Hague, etc. . . . Not that the patriotism of the democratic leaders of the time can be questioned. In most cases, even, they were perfectly aware of the extreme perils in which they found themselves. But their actions were subordinated to public opinions which, in all cases, were inclined to react precisely in the best way to serve Hitler's purposes.

Nothing illustrates this better than the manner in which the outside world behaved in presence of the Russian aggression against Finland. In America as well as in Europe there was for the first time a wave of genuine indignation and a semblance of unity. In spite of the fact that Hitler and Stalin had obviously concluded a series of preliminary agreements concerning the partition of Poland and the disposition of the Baltic States, the Russian invasion of Poland raised once more the hope that this aimless and "phony" war against Hitler could be redirected into a crusade against the Red Peril. For a while, the illusion that Hitler was in a precarious position and that that was the reason of his inactivity was powerfully stimulated. For a while, too, the fantastic concept that a deal could be achieved behind Hitler's back—preferably with Goering—was encouraged by several American and neutral go-betweens.

The mission of Mr. Sumner Welles who was sent to tour Europe with the avowed purpose of gathering information for President Roosevelt was seized upon—sometimes with hope, sometimes with suspicion—by those who persisted in believing that "appeasement" was still possible.

Hitler's peace offensive of the fall, although it had failed, was thus taken up by those against whom it had been directed. Unconsciously, perhaps, the hope that the war could be stopped before it started was still directing the policies and the actions of the very men who had pledged themselves to prosecute the war to ultimate victory. The general pattern of things, such as it had existed before the war actually started, was still the same: the Allies relying on their theory of the defensive were trying to convince themselves that Hitler was still hesitant and afraid of launching a suicidal attack. The neutrals of Europe, although they could have little illusion left as to their security in case Hitler did actually proceed with his program of European domination, still pretended to believe in pledges and treaties which they knew were invalid. America was engaged in the elaborate discussion of the lifting of the arms embargo with the intention of being better able to aid the Allies, while at the same time the newspaper writers and the cartoonists were jeering at the Allies and their "phony war." America wanted the defeat of Hitler as passionately as it had ever wanted anything. But at the same time it did not want to fight for this defeat. In the same way as twenty-two years before it had wanted "peace without victory," it now wanted "victory without war."

In the presence of such confusion and division, Hitler's confidence in himself had just reason to rise to a new high level.

Never inclined to modesty, his speeches of that period marked nevertheless a considerable progress in Hitler's assertion of his own power, and his conviction that he was the Man of Destiny showed itself in every word.

One of the most important and fundamental themes of the

National Socialist dogmas, i.e., the concept of German Justice, now expanded with a cynicism never equaled in the history of the world.

Hitler became completely frank concerning the problems of what is just or wrong, bad or evil. What is just had long ceased to be an intellectual problem in Nazi Germany. Justice is what is good for Germany, and what is good for Germany is determined by Hitler.

This simple principle was not new and the courts of Germany had been applying it for many years in dispensing justice inside Germany. But now Hitler was sufficiently sure of himself, and—as he said—his prestige was great enough, to enable him to speak to the world as the supreme judge of what is good or bad for all other nations. He could proclaim that he was responsible to no one except Destiny. For the first time, perhaps, since his advent to power, Hitler really felt that he could talk to the world as its recognized master. "The pacifist humane ideal might be a very good one," wrote Hitler in *Mein Kampf,* "if first one man had made himself master of the world."

His sense of superiority over all human beings, and more particularly over democratic statesmen, expressed itself through scorn, sarcasm, and sometimes through pity. He complained that it has always been "his bad luck to fight against a lot of zeros." In the course of one of his speeches he parodied Chamberlain whom he referred to as a "carrying-Bible hypocrite," by folding his manuscript and holding it up solemnly in a prayer-like attitude. On another occasion he justified certain rough decisions he had been obliged to take by explaining that the fait accompli method to which he had to resort sometimes saved a lot of trouble for the democratic leaders who were thus spared the pain of persuading their own public opinions of the necessity of accepting Hitler's concept of justice.

One of his favorite *leitmotivs*—the denunciation of the uncontrolled and irresponsible journalists in the democratic countries—was taken up with renewed vigor after the collapse of Poland. But an impartial observer is obliged to say that Hitler was ungrateful towards the free press which, during the whole period of the "phony war" and after, served his purposes so well in giving an honest running-account of the ups-and-downs of the various peace offensives which took place at the same time, and in describing the confusion which existed in the democracies and among the neutrals.

That Hitler felt he had reached a point where he could disregard completely his own doctrine was proved by two important departures. The first was the new treatment of the *Lebensraum* Theme.

The doctrine of the *Lebensraum* had always been fairly elastic. Hitler never clearly defined what the actual physical frontiers of the Third Reich should be. The arguments for more room were always based on comparisons between the land area controlled by other nations—and more particularly the British Empire and the United States—and the land area occupied by the Germans. The arguments were intended to convey the impression that other people had immense territories to live in—regardless of their productivity, the climate, or any other consideration—while the Germans were hemmed in to the narrow limits of their own frontiers.

How Hitler proposed to remedy this state of things was never made clear by him, but the outside world assumed for a long time that the *Lebensraum* theory was merely an extension of the doctrine of racial reunion by which all Germans should be gathered into one community.

The annexation of Czechoslovakia and the conquest of Poland dispelled this illusion. The *Lebensraum* theory now meant conquest and occupation of whatever territory Hitler thought he could grab, either by threat of violence or by actual war.

But it was soon to be seen that Hitler meant even more than that: A new theory—the principle of "resettlement of

German populations"—was put into practice immediately after the Polish conquest.

An experiment on this line had already been carried on when Tyrolians of German origin were invited to leave their native land and the flag of Mussolini to immigrate to the Reich. This immigration was not compulsory—at least in theory. Some Tyrolese immigrated to Germany and others stayed.

But in the case of the Polish resettlement, no choice was offered to the Germans who for centuries had been living in the Baltic States. They were forcibly uprooted and settled on Polish soil.

This method, as Hitler explained it, was the real solution to the problem which had baffled the makers of the Treaty of Versailles when they had tried to reconcile the principle of ethnological grouping and the demarcation of new national frontiers.

But if one considers the theory of "resettlement" of populations in the light of Hitler's grand strategy, the transfer of German populations from the Baltic States to Poland reveals once again with what ease Hitler is able to revise his doctrines, extend them, or shuffle them in order to further his program of domination.

First of all the principle of "resettlement" is in direct violation of the quasi-mystical concept—so dear to the Nazi ideologists—that there is some sort of sacred link between man and the land on which he and his ancestors were born. The Germans whom Hitler forced to leave the shores of the Baltic had their roots there. If the "blood and soil" doctrine had any meaning, the logical thing to do would have been to integrate the Baltic States into the Reich, not to uproot the Germans living there to transplant them into Poland. But the Baltic States had been turned over to Russia—at least for the time being—through a deal which was as much a violation of the ethnological principle as anything that the makers of the Treaty of Versailles had ever done.

But the Hitler solution had other far-reaching implications and gave a new meaning to the *Lebensraum* doctrine as a method of justifying conquest of any territory, anywhere in the world, by the simple process of settling these territories with people of German stock.

The procedure was to be further illustrated after the defeat of France when Alsatians and Lorrainers were expelled from their homes to make room for Germans. And it needs little imagination to foresee how the system can be further extended to any part of the world.

Thus—at the beginning of the war—Hitler had already demonstrated how the mystical dogma of "blood and soil" could be transformed into a method of pure German conquest. This dogma after giving birth to the theory of reuniting all Germans (which had justified the annexation of Austria and the Sudeten), then expanded into the mechanism of the *Lebensraum* (which was given as an explanation of the Czechoslovak conquest). The *Lebensraum,* in turn, found a new implementation in the procedure of settling Germans in foreign lands and thus proclaiming that these lands have, *ipso facto,* become German.

It may be noted that Hitler justified the resettlement of Poland with Germans by arguing that the Poles were an inferior race who had demonstrated over centuries their inability to develop and "civilize" their country. To replace them by members of the German Master-Race was obviously beneficial to humanity as a whole, and Hitler was quite confident that History, judging him by the results achieved and not by the methods employed, would bless him.

By the time the spring of 1940 came, Hitler was in an excellent position, both militarily and psychologically, to undertake what he thought would be the final operations which would force a decision by the end of the year.

The Allies and the European neutrals were bogged down in a state of confused demoralization which they themselves had chosen to call "the phony war." They were at once scared of Hitler's unpredictable next move, and hopeful that he, in turn, was too scared to move at all. They played with the prospect of future peace—a peace shaped by themselves, of course—and listened with secret eagerness to the reassuring voices of those who still said there might be no real war.

America was playing the dual and complicated role of the great protector of all neutrals and of the main backer of the Allies. Firmly opposed to going to war herself, America was openly impatient at the obvious reluctance of her champions to get going. Their inability or unwillingness to formulate their peace aims was equally irritating to American public opinion.

So on March 16, 1940, President Roosevelt, speaking before a Congress of Christian Missionaries, gave an outline of the future peace: "Today," said the President, "we seek a moral basis for peace. It cannot be a real peace if it fails to recognize brotherhood. It cannot be a lasting peace if the fruit of it is oppression, or starvation, or cruelty, or human life dominated by armed camps. It cannot be a sound peace if small nations must live in fear of powerful neighbors. It cannot be a moral peace if freedom from invasion is sold for tribute. . . ."

Three weeks later, on April 9, 1940, the German armies invaded Denmark and Norway. The "phony" war was over.

•

SPEECH OF OCTOBER 6, 1939

Berlin, Reichstag

Background

1939

September 21—United States Congress convenes in special session. President Roosevelt reads a message asking for an amendment of the Neutrality Act to provide for the lifting of the arms embargo.

September 24—Mussolini makes a speech stating that there is no reason to continue the war now that the Polish question has been settled.

September 27—Warsaw surrenders.

September 28—Germany and Russia divide Poland between them. Russia makes an agreement with Estonia, thus gaining naval bases on the Baltic.

October 2—Pan-American conference decides on the establishment of "a sea safety zone" around the Western Hemisphere.

October 5—Russia signs a mutual-aid pact with Latvia, obtaining naval bases on the Baltic.

The Speech

"IT WAS a fateful hour, on the first of September of this year, when you met here as representatives of the German people. I had to inform you then of serious decisions which had been forced upon us as a result of the intransigeant and provocative action of a certain State.

"Since then five weeks have gone by. I have asked you to come here today in order to give you an account of what has passed, the necessary insight into what is happening at present and, so far as that is possible, into the future as well.

"For the last two days our towns and villages have been decorated with flags and symbols of the new Reich. Bells are ringing to celebrate a great victory, which, of its kind, is unique in history. A State of no less than 36,000,000 inhabitants, with an army of almost fifty infantry and cavalry divisions, took up arms against us. Their arms were far-reaching, their confidence in their ability to crush Germany knew no bounds.

"After one week of fighting there could no longer be any doubt as to the outcome. Whenever Polish troops met German units, they were driven back or dispersed. Poland's ambitious strategy for a great offensive against the territory of the Reich collapsed within the first forty-eight hours of the campaign. Death-defying in attack, advancing at an unconquerable rate of progress, infantry, armored detachments, air force and units of the navy were soon dictating the course of events.

"They were masters of the situation throughout the campaign. In a fortnight's time the major part of the Polish Army was either scattered, captured, or surrounded. In the meantime, however, the German Army had covered distances and occupied regions which twenty-five years ago would have taken over fourteen months to conquer.

"Even though a number of peculiarly gifted newspaper strategists in other parts of the world attempted to describe the pace at which this campaign progressed as not coming up to Germany's expectations, we ourselves all know that in all history there has scarcely been a comparable military achievement.

"That the last remnants of the Polish Army were able to hold out in Warsaw, Modlin, and on Hela Peninsula until October 1 was not due to their prowess in arms, but only to our cool thinking and our sense of responsibility.

"I forbade the sacrifice of more human lives than was absolutely necessary. That is to say, I deliberately released the German Supreme Command from adherence to a principle still observed in the Great War demanding that for the sake of prestige certain objectives must under all circumstances be reached within a certain time limit.

"Everything which it is imperative to do will be done regardless of sacrifice, but what can be avoided will not be done.

"There would have been no difficulty for us in breaking the resistance of Warsaw between the 10th and 12th of September, just as we finally broke it September 25-27, only that in the first place I wanted to spare German lives and in the second place I still clung to the hope, misdirected though it was, that the Polish side might for once be guided by responsible common sense instead of by irresponsible lunacy. But in this instance we were once more confronted with the spectacle which we had witnessed before on the largest possible scale.

"The attempt to convince the responsible Polish command—in so far as it existed—that it was futile and in fact insane to attempt resistance, especially in a city of more than a million inhabitants, proved entirely fruitless. A "generalissimo," who himself took to inglorious flight, forced upon the capital of his country a resistance which could never lead to anything but its destruction.

"Since it was realized that Warsaw's fortifications alone were not likely to withstand the German attack, the entire city was converted into a fortress and barricaded in every direction. Batteries were mounted in every square and great courtyard, thousands of machine-gun posts manned and the whole population called up to take part in the fighting.

"Sheer sympathy for women and children caused me to make an offer to those in command of Warsaw at least to let civilian inhabitants leave the city. I declared a temporary armistice and safeguards necessary for evacuation, with the result that we all waited for emissaries just as fruitlessly as we had waited at the end of August for a Polish negotiator. The proud Polish commander of the city did not even condescend to reply.

"To make sure, I extended the time limit and ordered bombers and heavy artillery to attack only military objectives, repeating my proposal in vain. I thereupon made an offer that the whole suburb of Praga would not be bombarded at all, but should be reserved for the civilian population in order to make it possible for them to take refuge there.

"This proposal, too, was treated with contempt on the part of the Poles. Twice I attempted to evacuate at least the international colony from the city. In this I finally succeeded after great difficulties, in the case of the Russian colony, actually at the last moment. I then ordered a general attack on the city for September 25.

"The same defenders who at first considered it beneath their dignity even to reply to my humane proposals, made on grounds of humanity, then very rapidly changed face. The German attack opened on September 25, and Warsaw capitulated on the 27th.

"With 120,000 men the defenders did not even attempt to break through as our German General Litzmann once did at Brzesiny with a vastly inferior force, but, on the contrary, preferred to lay down arms.

"Any comparison with the Alcazar is entirely out of place. There for weeks on end Spanish heroes defied the bitterest attacks and earned a right to lasting fame. Here, on the other hand, a great city was unscrupulously exposed to destruction, only to capitulate after a forty-eight-hour assault.

"The Polish soldiers as individuals fought bravely on many occasions, but their officers, beginning with the command, can only be described as irresponsible, unconscientious and inefficient. Before the bombardment of Hela I had also given orders that not a single man should be sacrificed until the most careful preparation for action had been made. There, too, surrender came at the very moment when the Germans had at length announced their intention of attacking and had begun to do so.

"I have made these statements, gentlemen, with the object of forestalling the invention of historical legends, for if legend is to be woven around any who took part in this campaign, it should be woven around German soldiers who, during the attack and on the march, added yet another page to their immortal glorious record.

"Legends could be woven, too, around the heavy artillery which performed untold feats of endurance in rushing to the assistance of the infantry. Men of our armored mechanized units who, with dauntless courage and heedless of counter-attacks and numerical superiority of the enemy, attacked again and again are worthy of this legend.

"Such a legend should also immortalize the airmen who, fearless of death and knowing that if anti-aircraft fire did not kill them in the air, they would, if forced to make a parachute landing, inevitably suffer frightful death, continued with steadfast courage to carry out reconnoissance flights and attacks with bombs or machine-gun fire whenever they were commanded to do so and whenever they found objectives.

"The same is true of the brave men of our submarine fleet. If, within four weeks, we totally annihilated a State with a population of 36,000,000 and corresponding military strength, and if during this whole period our victorious arms have not suffered a single setback, this cannot be ascribed simply to good luck but constituted certain proof of fine training, excellent leadership, and indomitable courage. . . ."

"Our knowledge of the strength of our fighting forces fills us all with a well of confidence, for they have not only proved that they are strong in attack, but also that they are strong in retaining what they have won. The excellent training received by the individual officers and men has been amply justified. It is this training which is responsible for the extremely few casualties which—hard as they are for the individual to bear—are on the whole far less than we ventured to expect.

"Admittedly the total number of casualties gives no idea of the severity of the various encounters, for certain regiments and divisions suffered very heavy losses when they were attacked by Polish forces which were numerically superior or came into conflict with such forces when they themselves were attacking. . . ."

"As I am now about to make known to you the number of our dead and wounded, I request that you rise from your seats. Though owing to the training given our troops, the effectiveness of our weapons and the command of our forces the figures do not amount to even one-twentieth of what our apprehensions had been at the outset of the campaign, we will never forget that every soldier who fell fighting brought for his people and our Reich the greatest sacrifice that man can bring.

"According to the casualty list of up to September 30, 1939, which will not change materially, the total losses for the army, navy and air force, including officers, are as follows: 10,572 killed; 30,322 wounded; 3,404 missing. Unfortunately, of those missing a certain number who fell into Polish hands will probably be found to have been massacred and killed.

"All our gratitude is due to the victims of the campaign in Poland, while the wounded may be assured of our best attention and care, and the families of those killed of our sympathy and help.

"By the capitulation of the fortresses of Warsaw and Modlin and the surrender of Hela, the Polish campaign has come to an end. The task of safeguarding the country against vagabonding marauders, gangs of robbers and individual groups of terrorists will be carried through with all energy.

"The outcome of the war was the annihilation of all Polish armies, followed by the dissolution of the Polish State. Six hundred and ninety-four thousand prisoners have set out on their march to Berlin. The amount of war material captured cannot yet be estimated.

"Since the outbreak of the war, the German forces have at the same time in calm preparedness taken up positions in the West ready to meet the enemy.

"The naval forces of the Reich have fulfilled their duty in the attack on the Westerplatte, Gdynia, Oxhoeft and Hela, and in protecting the Baltic Sea and the German North Sea coast our submarines are fighting in a spirit worthy of the memory of our heroes in the last war.

"In the face of this historically unprecedented collapse of a structure purporting to be a State, the question in almost everybody's mind is as to the reason for such a phenomenon.

"Versailles was the cradle of a Polish State which had emerged from the untold sacrifice of blood—not of Polish but of German and Russian blood. Poland, who for centuries past had proved herself incapable of existence, was in 1916 artificially begotten and in 1919 no less artificially born by a German government just as incapable of existence.

"In utter disregard of almost 500 years of experience, without consideration for the lesson of historical development during many centuries, without appreciation for ethnographic conditions and with no regard for all economic expediencies, a State was constructed at Versailles which, according to its whole nature, was sooner or later bound to become the cause of a most serious crisis.

"A man who, I am sorry to say, now ranks among our fiercest enemies, at that time clearly foresaw all this. I mean Mr. Lloyd George. Like so many others he sounded warning, not only at the time of the creation of that structure but also in the course of its subsequent expansion which had taken place in utter disregard of reason and right.

"At that time he expressed apprehension that in that State an accumulation of conditions was being created containing the risk of conflicts which sooner or later might lead to great European complications.

"As a matter of fact, conditions surrounding the structure of this new so-called State, as far as its nationalities were concerned, could not be clarified until now. It requires some knowledge of Polish census methods to realize how utterly alien to truth, and therefore irrelevant, statistics on the national composition of that territory were and are.

"In 1919 the Poles laid claims to the territory where they pretended to have a majority of 95 per cent—in East Prussia, for instance—whereas a plebiscite later showed the Poles actually had reached a figure of 2 per cent.

"In the State finally created, which contained parts of former Russia, Austria, and Germany, non-Polish elements were so brutally ill-treated, suppressed, tyrannized and tortured that any plebiscite depended entirely on the good will of local administrative officials for producing such results as were desired or demanded.

"Nor did indisputable Polish elements receive much better recognition. And then, on top of all this, statesmen of our Western Hemisphere spoke of this kind of creation as of democracy of the fundamentals of their own system.

"In that country there ruled a minority of aristocratic or non-aristocratic large, vast estate-owners and wealthy intellectuals to whom under the most favorable circumstances their own Polish compatriots were nothing but mass man power. For that reason the regime was never backed by more than 15 per cent of the total population.

"The economic distress and low cultural level corresponded with these conditions. In 1919 this State took over from Prussia and also from Austria provinces which had been developed through hundreds of years of hard toil, some of them being in a most flourishing condition. Today, after the elapse of twenty years, they are at a point of gradually turning into steppes again.

"The Vistula, the river whose estuary has always been of such tremendous importance for the Polish Government. owing to the lack of any and all care is now already unsuitable for any real traffic and, depending on the season, is either an unruly stream or a dried-up rivulet.

"Towns as well as villages are in a state of neglect. The roads, with very few exceptions, are badly out of repair and in a terrible condition. Anyone who travels in that country for two or three weeks will get the proper idea of the classical German term '*Polnische Wirtschaft*,' meaning a 'Polish state of affairs!'

"In spite of the unbearable conditions prevailing in that country, Germany endeavored to establish peaceful relations with it. During the years 1933 and 1934 I endeavored to find some equitable compromise between our national interests and our desire for the maintenance of peace with that country. There was a time, when Marshal Pilsudski was still alive, when it seemed possible for this hope to materialize were it only to a modest extent.

"Unlimited patience and still greater self-restraint were called for because many of the regional Polish administrative officials took the understanding between Germany and Poland to be merely a license for the persecution and annihilation of the Germans in Poland with even less risk. In the few years up to 1922 more than one-and-a-half million Germans had been forced to leave their homes. They were hunted out, often without being able to take even their most necessary clothing.

"When, in 1938, the Olsa territory went to Poland, they used the same methods against the Czechs who lived there. Often within a few hours many thousands of these had to leave their working places, their homes, their villages and towns at the shortest notice without being allowed to take anything more with them than a suitcase or a little box with clothing.

"Things like this went on for years, and for years we looked on, always striving to attain some improvement in the lot of the unhappy Germans living there by establishing closer relations. It was, however, impossible to overlook the fact that every German attempt thereby to secure the removal of these intolerable conditions was taken by the Polish rulers to be nothing more than a sign of weakness, if not of stupidity.

"When the Polish Government proceeded in a thousand ways gradually to subjugate Danzig as well, I endeavored, by means of practical proposals, to secure a solution whereby Danzig, in accordance with the wishes of its population, could be nationally and politically united with Germany without impairing the economic needs and so-called rights of Poland. If today any one alleges that these were ultimative demands, that allegation is a lie.

"The proposals for a solution, as communicated to the

Polish Government in March, 1939, were nothing but the suggestions and the ideas already discussed long ago between myself and Polish Foreign Minister Beck, except for the fact that in the spring of 1939 I thought I would be able to facilitate the acceptance of these proposals by the Polish Government in the face of their own public opinion by the offer to concede to them an equivalent.

"The fact that the Polish Government at that time refused to consider a discussion of these proposals was due to two reasons: for one thing, the inflamed chauvinist powers behind the Government never intended to solve the problem of Danzig, but on the contrary already lived in the hope, expounded later in publications and speeches, of acquiring territory from the Reich far beyond the bounds of Danzig; in fact, they hoped to be in a position to attack and conquer.

"These aims, far from stopping at East Prussia, were climaxed by a flood of publications and a continuous sequence of speeches, addresses, resolutions, etc., in addition to the incorporation of East Prussia, for the annexation of Pomerania and Silesia. The Oder represented the minimum of frontier claims and finally even the Elbe was described as the natural dividing line between Germany and Poland.

"These demands, which today may appear crazy but which were then presented with fanatical seriousness, were based in a simply ridiculous manner on the assumption of a 'Polish mission of civilization' and declared justified because they were supposed to be capable of fulfillment in view of the strength of the Polish Army.

"While I was inviting the then Polish Foreign Minister to take part in a conference for the discussion of our proposals, the Polish military generals were already writing about the inefficiency of the German Army, the cowardice of the German soldiers, the inferiority of the German weapons, the obvious superiority of the Polish forces and the certainty, in case of war, of defeating the Germans at the gates of Berlin and of annihilating the Reich.

"The man, however, who intended, as he expressed it, to hack the German Army to pieces at the gates of Berlin, was not just an illiterate, insignificant Pole but their commander-in-chief, Rydz-Smigly, who at present resides in Rumania.

"Violations and insults which Germany and her armed forces had to put up with from these military dilettantes would never have been tolerated by any other State, just as they were not expected from any other nation. No French or English generals would ever have presumed to express a judgment of the German armed forces similar to that which we heard read from the Polish side for years, particularly since March, 1939; and on the other hand no German general would have spoken in that manner of English, French or Italian soldiers.

"A great deal of self-control was needed to keep calm in face of these simply shameless insults, in spite of the fact that we knew that the German armed forces could destroy and sweep away the whole of this ridiculous State and its army within a few weeks.

"But this attitude, for which the Polish leaders themselves were responsible, was the fundamental reason why the Polish Government refused even to discuss the German proposals.

"Another reason was that fatal promise of guarantee given to the State which, although not menaced at all, very rapidly became convinced it could afford to challenge a Great Power without risk once it was assured of the support of two Great Powers, perhaps even hoping this way to lay the foundation for realization of all its own insane ambitions.

"For, as soon as Poland felt certain of that guarantee, minorities living in that country had to suffer what amounted to a reign of terror. *I do not consider it my task to speak of the lot of the Ukrainians, or White Russian population, whose interests now lie in the hands of Russia.*

"However, I do feel it my duty to speak of the lot of those helpless thousands of Germans who carried on the tradition of those who first brought culture to that country centuries ago and whom the Poles now began to oppress and drive out. Since March, 1939, they had been victims of truly satanic terrorization. How many of them had been abducted and where they are cannot be stated even today.

"Villages with hundreds of German inhabitants are now left without men because they all have been killed. In others women were violated and murdered, girls and children outraged and killed. In 1598 an Englishman—Sir George Carew—wrote in his diplomatic reports to the English Government that the outstanding features of Polish character were cruelty and lack of moral restraint.

"Since that time this cruelty has not changed. Just as tens of thousands of Germans were slaughtered and sadistically tormented to death, so German soldiers captured in fighting were tortured and massacred.

"This pet lapdog of the Western democracies cannot be considered a cultured nation at all.

"For more than four years I fought in the great war on the Western Front, but such things did not happen on either side.

"Things that have occurred in Poland, in the past few months, and especially the last four weeks, constitute flaming accusations against those responsible for the creation of a so-called State lacking every national, historical, cultural, and moral foundation. Had only 1 per cent of these atrocities been committed in any part of the world against the English people, I should be interested to see the indignation of those gentlemen who today in hypocritical horror condemn the German or Russian procedure.

"No! To grant guarantees to this State and this Government as was done could only lead to appalling disasters. Neither the Polish Government, nor the small cliques supporting it, nor the Polish nation as such were capable of measuring the responsibilities which were implied in such guarantees in Poland's favor by half of Europe.

"The passionate sentiment thus aroused, together with the

sense of that security which had been unconditionally guaranteed to them, counted for the behavior of the Polish Government during the period between April and August this year.

"It was also the cause of the attitude they adopted toward my conciliatory proposals. The Government rejected these proposals because they felt themselves protected, or even encouraged, by public opinion and public opinion protected them and encouraged them on their way because it had been left in ignorance by its Government and particularly because in its every action it felt itself sufficiently protected from without.

"All this led to an increase in the number of appalling atrocities committed against German nationals in Poland and to the rejection of all proposals for a solution and in the end to the steadily growing encroachments on actual Reich territory. It was quite comprehensible that such a state of mind interpreted German longsuffering as a weakness, that is, that every concession on Germany's part was regarded as proof of the possibility of some further aggressive steps.

"A warning given Poland to refrain from sending Danzig any more notes amounting to ultimata and above all to desist from economic strangulation of that city did not ease the situation in the least; it resulted, in fact, in complete stoppage of all Danzig means of communication.

"The warning to suspend or at least to take steps against the unceasing cases of murder, ill treatment and torture of German nationals in Poland had the effect of increasing these atrocities and of calling for more bloodthirsty harangues and provocative speeches from the Polish local administrative officials and military authorities.

"The German proposals aiming at a last-minute agreement on a just and equitable basis were answered by a general mobilization. The German request that an intermediary should be sent, founded on a proposal made by Great Britain, was not complied with and on the second day was answered by an offensive declaration.

"Under these circumstances it was obvious that if further incursions into the Reich's territory occurred, Germany's patience would be at an end. What the Poles had erroneously interpreted as weakness was in reality our sense of responsibility and my firm determination to come to an understanding if that at all was possible.

"Since they believed that this patience and longsuffering was a sign of weakness which would allow them to do anything, no other course remained than to show them their mistake by striking back with the weapons which they themselves had used for years.

"Under these blows their State has crumbled to pieces in a few weeks and is now swept from the earth. One of the most senseless deeds perpetrated at Versailles is thus a thing of the past.

"If this step on Germany's part has resulted in a community of interests with Russia, that is due not only to the similarity of the problems affecting the two States, but also to that of the conclusions which both States had arrived at with regard to their future relationship.

"In my speech at Danzig I already declared that Russia was organized on principles which differ from those held in Germany. However, since it became clear that Stalin found nothing in the Russian-Soviet principles which should prevent him from cultivating friendly relations with States of a different political creed, National Socialist Germany sees no reason why she should adopt another criterion. The Soviet Union is the Soviet Union, National Socialist Germany is National Socialist Germany.

"But one thing is certain: from the moment when the two States mutually agreed to respect each other's distinctive regime and principles, every reason for any mutually hostile attitude had disappeared. *Long periods in the history of both nations have shown that the inhabitants of these two largest*

States in Europe were never happier than when they lived in friendship with each other. The Great War, which once made Germany and Russia enemies, was disastrous for both countries.

"It is easy to understand that the capitalist States of the West are interested today in playing off these two States and their principles against each other. For this purpose, and until it is realized, they certainly regard the Soviet Union as a sufficiently respectable partner for the conclusion of a useful military pact. But they regard it as perfidy that their honorable approaches were rejected and in their place rapprochement took place between those two very powers who had every reason for seeking happiness for their respective peoples in developing their economic relationship along the lines of peaceful co-operation.

"Months ago I stated in the Reichstag that the conclusion of the German-Russian non-aggression pact marked the turning point in the whole German foreign policy. The new pact of friendship and mutual interest since signed between Germany and the Soviet Union will insure not only peace but a constant satisfactory co-operation for both States.

"Germany and Russia together will relieve one of the most acute danger spots in Europe of its threatening character and will, each in her own sphere, contribute to the welfare of the peoples living there, thus aiding to European peace in general. If certain circles today see in this pact either the breakdown of Russia or Germany—as suits them best—I should like to give them my answer.

"For many years imaginary aims were attributed to Germany's foreign policy which at best might be taken to have arisen in the mind of a schoolboy.

"At a moment when Germany is struggling to consolidate her own living space, which only consists of a few hundred thousand square kilometers, *insolent journalists in countries which rule over 40,000,000 square kilometers state Germany is aspiring to world domination!*

"German-Russian agreements should prove immensely comforting to these worried sponsors of universal liberty, for do they not show most emphatically that their assertions as to Germany's aiming at domination of the Urals, the Ukraine, Rumania, etc., are only excrescences of their own unhealthy war-lord fantasy?

"In one respect it is true Germany's decision is irrevocable, namely in her intention to see peaceful, stable, and thus tolerable conditions introduced on her eastern frontiers; also it is precisely here that Germany's interests and desires correspond entirely with those of the Soviet Union. *The two States are resolved to prevent problematic conditions arising between them which contain germs of internal unrest and thus also of external disorder and which might perhaps in any way unfavorably affect the relationship of these two great States with one another.*

"Germany and the Soviet Union have therefore clearly defined the boundaries of their own spheres of interest with the intention of being singly responsible for law and order and preventing everything which might cause injury to the other partner.

"The aims and tasks which emerge from the collapse of the Polish State are, insofar as the German sphere of interest is concerned, roughly as follows:

"1. Demarcation of the boundary for the Reich, which will do justice to historical, ethnographical and economic facts.

"2. Pacification of the whole territory by restoring a tolerable measure of peace and order.

"3. Absolute guarantees of security not only as far as Reich territory is concerned but for the entire sphere of interest.

"4. Re-establishment and reorganization of economic life and of trade and transport, involving development of culture and civilization.

"5. As the most important task, however, to establish a new order of ethnographic conditions, that is to say, resettlement of nationalities in such a manner that the process ultimately results in the obtaining of better dividing lines than is the case at present. In this sense, however, it is not a case of the problem being restricted to this particular sphere, but of a task with far wider implications for the east and south of Europe are to a large extent filled with splinters of the German nationality, whose existence they cannot maintain.

"In their very existence lie the reason and cause for continual international disturbances. In this age of the principle of nationalities and of racial ideals, it is utopian to believe that members of a highly developed people can be assimilated without trouble.

"It is therefore essential for a far-sighted ordering of the life of Europe that a resettlement should be undertaken here so as to remove at least part of the material for European conflict. Germany and the Union of Soviet Republics have come to an agreement to support each other in this matter.

"The German Government will, therefore, never allow the residual Polish State of the future to become in any sense a disturbing factor for the Reich itself and still less a source of disturbance between the German Reich and Soviet Russia.

"As Germany and Soviet Russia undertake this work of re-establishment, the two States are entitled to point out that the attempt to solve this problem by the methods of Versailles has proved an utter failure. In fact it had to fail because these tasks cannot be settled sitting around a table or by simple decrees. Most of the statesmen who in Versailles had to decide on these complicated problems did not possess the slightest historical training, indeed they often had not even the vaguest idea of the nature of the task with which they were faced.

"Neither did they bear any responsibility for the consequences of their action. Recognition that their work might be faulty was of no significance because in practice there was no way for a real revision. It is true that in the Treaty of Versailles provision was made for keeping open the possibility of such revisions but in reality all attempts to attain such a revision miscarried and they were bound to miscarry because the League of Nations as the competent authority was no longer morally justified to carry out such a procedure.

"After America had been first to refuse to ratify the Treaty of Versailles, or to join the League of Nations, and later when other countries also felt they could no longer reconcile their presence in this organization with the interests of their respective countries, the League degenerated more and more into a clique of parties interested in the Versailles dictate.

"At any rate it is a fact that none of the revisions recognized from the outset as necessary had ever been effected by the League of Nations.

"Since in our time it became customary to regard a refugee government as still existing even if it consists of three members provided they have taken with them sufficient gold so as not to be an economic burden to the democratic country offering hospitality, it may be assumed that the League of Nations, too, will carry on bravely if but two nations sit there together. Perhaps even one will do!

"But according to the government of the League any revision of the Versailles clauses would still be adjudicated exclusively by this illustrious organization—that is, in other words, revision would be practically impossible.

"The League of Nations is not living but already a dead thing, nevertheless the peoples concerned are not dead but alive and they will uphold their vital interests, however incapable the League of Nations may be of seeing, grasping, or respecting those interests.

"National Socialism is not a phenomenon which has grown up in Germany with the malicious intent of thwarting League efforts at revision, but a movement which arose because for fifteen years the most natural human and social rights of a great nation had been suppressed and denied redress.

"And I personally take exception at seeing foreign states-

men stand up and call me guilty of having broken my word because I have now put these revisions through.

"On the contrary I pledged my sacred word to the German people to do away with the Treaty of Versailles and to restore to them their natural and vital rights as a great nation.

"The extent to which I am securing these vital rights is modest.

"This I ask: If forty-six million Englishmen claim the right to rule over forty million square kilometers of the earth, it cannot be wrong for eighty-two million Germans to demand the right to live on 800,000 square kilometers, to till their fields and to follow their trades and callings, and if they further demand the restitution of those colonial possessions which formerly were their property, which they had not taken away from anybody by robbery or war but honestly acquired by purchase, exchange and treaties. Moreover, in all my demands, I always first tried to obtain revisions by way of negotiation.

"I did, it is true, refuse to submit the question of German vital rights to some non-competent international body in the form of humble requests. Just as little as I suppose that Great Britain would plead for respect of her vital interests, so little ought one to expect the same of National Socialist Germany. I have, however, and I must emphasize this fact most solemnly, limited in the extreme the measure of these revisions of the Versailles Treaty.

"Notably in all those cases where I did not see any menace to the natural, vital interests of my people, I have myself advised the German nation to hold back. Yet these eighty million people must live somewhere. There exists a fact that not even the Versailles Treaty has been able to destroy; although it has in the most unreasonable manner dissolved States, torn asunder regions economically connected, cut communication lines, etc., yet the people, the living substance of flesh and blood, has remained and will forever remain in the future.

"It cannot be denied that since the German people has found its resurrection through National Socialism, the relation existing between Germany and the surrounding nations has been cleared up to a great extent.

"The uncertainty that today is weighing down the common life of nations is not due to German demands, but to the malignant insinuations published in the so-called democracies.

"The German demands themselves were formulated in a very clear and precise way. They have, it is true, found their fulfillment not thanks to the insight of the League of Nations but thanks to the dynamics of natural development.

"The aim of the German foreign policy as pursued by me has never been other than to guarantee the existence—that is to say, the life—of the German people, to remove the injustice and nonsense contained in a treaty which not only destroyed Germany economically but has drawn the victor nations into disaster as well.

"For the rest, however, our whole work of rebuilding was concerned with the home affairs of the Reich and no country in the world had a greater longing for peace than the German people. It was fortunate for humanity and no misfortune at all that I succeeded in removing the craziest, most impossible clauses of the Versailles Treaty by peaceful methods and without compromising foreign statesmen in the internal politics of their countries.

"That some details of this action may have been painful to certain interested parties is comprehensible. But the merit is all the greater for the fact that this reorganization was brought about without bloodshed in all cases but the last one.

"The last revision of this treaty could have been brought about in exactly the same peaceful way had not two circumstances I have mentioned had the contrary effect. That is chiefly the fault of those who not only took no pleasure in the former peaceful revision, but on the contrary complained of the fact that by peaceful methods a new Central Europe was being built up; that is to say, a Central Europe that was able once more to give its inhabitants work and bread.

"As I have already mentioned, it was one of the aims of the Government of the Reich to clear up the relation between ourselves and our neighbors. Allow me to point out some facts that cannot be refuted by the scribblings of international press liars.

"First. *Germany has concluded non-aggression pacts with the Baltic States.* Her interests there are of an exclusively economic nature.

"Second. *In former times Germany never had any conflict of interests or indeed litigation points with the Northern States and she has none today either.*

"Third. Germany has taken no steps in regard to the German territory handed over to Denmark under the terms of the Treaty of Versailles; she has, on the contrary, established local and friendly relations with Denmark. *We have claimed no revision, but we have concluded a non-aggression pact with Denmark. Our relations with that country are thus directed toward unswervingly loyal and friendly co-operation.*

"Fourth. *Holland: the new Reich has endeavored to continue the traditional friendship with Holland; it did not take over any differences between the two States nor did it create new ones.*

"Fifth. *Belgium: immediately after I had taken over the Government I tried to establish friendly relations with Belgium. I renounced any revision as well as any desire for revision. The Reich has put forward no claim which might in any way have been regarded as a threat to Belgium.*

"Sixth. Switzerland: Germany adopted the same attitude toward Switzerland. The Reich Government has never given the slightest cause for doubt regarding their desires to establish friendly relations with the country. Moreover, they themselves have never brought forward any complaint regarding the relations between the two countries.

"Seventh. Immediately after the Anschluss [with Austria] became an accomplished fact *I informed Yugoslavia that the frontier in common with that country would henceforth be regarded as unalterable by Germany and that we wished only to live in peace and friendship with that country.*

"Eighth. *The bond which binds us to Hungary is old and traditional, one of close and sincere friendship.* In this instance, too, our frontiers are unalterable.

"Ninth. *Slovakia appealed to Germany of her own accord for assistance in connection with her establishment as a State.* Her independence is recognized and not infringed upon by the Reich.

"Tenth. However, it is not only with these states but also with the Great Powers that Germany has improved and settled those relations which to a certain extent had been adversely affected by the Treaty of Versailles.

"My first step was to bring about an alteration in the relations between Italy and the Reich. *The existing frontiers between these two States have been formally recognized as unalterable by both countries. Any possibility of a clash of interests of a territorial nature has been removed.* One-time enemies during the World War, they have in the meantime become sincere friends.

"Establishment of friendly relations was not the final development, but, in the periods which followed, this led to the signing of a cordial pact based on our mutual philosophies and political interests which has proved itself to be an important factor in European co-operation.

"My chief endeavor, however, has been to rid our relations with France of all trace of ill will and render them tolerable for both nations. I once set forth with the utmost clarity Germany's claims in this domain and have never gone back on that declaration. Return of the Saar territory was one demand

which I regarded as an indispensable pre-condition of Franco-German understandings.

"After France herself had found a just solution of this problem, Germany had no further claims against France. No such *claim exists any longer and no such claim shall ever be put forward. That is to say, I have refused even to mention the problem of Alsace-Lorraine* not because I was forced to keep silent, but because this matter does not constitute a problem which could ever interfere with Franco-German relations.

"I accepted the decision made in 1919 and refused to consider ever embarking upon war for the sake of a question which, comparatively speaking, is of slight importance for Germany's vital interests, but which is certainly likely to involve every second generation in a deadly war fear. France realized this.

"It is impossible for any French statesman to get up and declare I have ever made any demands upon France the fulfillment of which would be incompatible with French honor or French interest. It is, however, true that instead of demands I have always expressed to France my desire to bury forever our ancient enmity and bring together these two nations, both of which have such glorious pasts.

"Among the German people, I have done my utmost to eradicate the idea of everlasting enmity and to inculcate in its place a respect for the great achievements of the French nation and for its history, just as every German soldier has the greatest respect for the feats of the French Army. I have devoted no less effort to the achievement of an Anglo-German understanding, nay, more than that, of an Anglo-German friendship.

"At no time and in no place have I ever acted contrary to British interests. Unfortunately I have only too often been forced to guard against instances of British interference in German affairs, even in cases which did not concern Great Britain in the least. I actually considered it as one of my life aims to reconcile these two peoples, not only through mutual understanding but through inner sympathy.

"The German nation has gladly followed my lead in this respect. If my endeavors have been unsuccessful, it is only because of an animosity on the part of certain British statesmen and journalists, which has deeply affected me personally.

"They made no secret of the fact that—for reasons which are unfathomable to us—their sole aim was to seize the first opportunity in order to resume the fight with Germany. The fewer reasons of substantial nature these men have for their schemes, the more they attempt to motivate their actions with empty phrases and assertions.

"But I believe even today that there can only be real peace in Europe and throughout the world if Germany and England come to an understanding. Because of this conviction I have often shown the way to an understanding. If in the end there was not the desired result, it was really not my fault.

"Finally, *I now also attempted to bring the relations between the Reich and Soviet Russia to a normal and, in the end, to a friendly basis. Thanks to a similar trend of thought on the part of Mr. Stalin these endeavors have now been realized. Now with that State lasting and friendly relations have been established,* the effect of which will be a blessing to both nations.

"Thus the revision of the Versailles Treaty carried through by me did not cause any chaos in Europe, but on the contrary produced the prerequisite of clear, stable and bearable conditions.

"Only those who detest this order of things in Europe and wish for disorder can feel hostile to these actions. *If, however, certain people think themselves obliged to reject with a hypocritical air the method by which a tolerable order of things was established in Central Europe, then my only reply to them is that in the end it is not so much the method but the useful result that counts.*

"Before I came into power Central Europe, that is to say

not only Germany but also the surrounding States, was sinking into the hopeless distress of unemployment and production had decreased, involving an automatic jump in commodity consumption. The standard of living went down. Distress and misery were the result.

"No criticizing foreign statesman can deny that not only in the old Reich but also in all the territory now merged with it, it has become possible to remove these indications of decay in the face of the most adverse conditions.

"It has thus been proved that only as an entity is this Central European space capable of existence and that whoever breaks up that entity commits a crime against millions of people.

"To have wiped out that crime does not amount to a breach of my word, but to me is honor itself; I am proud of it as my deed before history.

"Neither the German people nor myself has taken an oath on the Treaty of Versailles; I have merely taken an oath on the welfare of my people, who gave me my mandate and on the welfare of those whom destiny has placed within our living space, thus inseparably binding them to our own welfare.

"To guarantee the existence and thus the life of all of them is my sole concern.

"Any attempt to criticize, judge or reject my actions from the rostrum of international presumption has no foundation before history and personally leaves me stone-cold. I was called to my post by the confidence vested in me by the German people, whose attitude toward me is only strengthened by any such attempt at criticism or interference from abroad.

"Moreover, previous to each single revision I have put forward proposals. I had attempted, by means of negotiations, to achieve and secure what was absolutely indispensable. In a certain number of cases I was successful. In other cases, I am sorry to say, my readiness to negotiate and perhaps also the small extent of my demands and the modesty of my proposals were interpreted as a sign of weakness and therefore rejected. Nobody could have regretted this more than I did.

"There are, however, in the life of nations certain necessities which, if they are not brought about by peaceful methods, must be realized by force, however regrettable this appears, not only to the life of the individual citizen but also to the life of the community. It is undeniable that the greater interests common to all must never be impaired by the stubbornness or ill will of individuals and communities. To Poland, too, I made the most moderate proposals.

"They were not only rejected, but on the contrary brought forth the general mobilization of that State, for which reasons were advanced which proved conclusively exactly that it was the very modesty of my proposals which was considered a confirmation of my weakness, nay, even of my fear. Really, such an experience is apt to make anyone shrink from ever again making any reasonable and moderate proposals.

"Also at present I once more read in certain newspapers that every attempt to bring about a peaceful settlement of relations between Germany on the one hand and France and England on the other was doomed to failure, and that any proposal in that direction only proved that I, filled with apprehension, anticipated Germany's collapse and that I only made such a proposal out of cowardice, or from a bad conscience.

"When, irrespective of all this, I have expressed my ideas on this problem, I am prepared to appear in the eyes of these people as a coward or a finished man. I can afford to run that risk, because the judgment to be passed upon me by history will not, thank God, be written by these miserable scribblers, but is established by my life's work, and because I do not care very much about any judgment that may be passed upon me by these people at the time.

"My prestige is sufficient for me to allow myself such an attitude, because the question of whether my following thoughts are actually dictated by fear or desperation will in

any case be settled by the future course of events. Today I can only regret that those people, whose bloodthirstiness cannot have enough of war, unfortunately are not where the war is actually being fought, and never were at such places where people were shooting it out.

"I can very well understand that there are interested parties who profit more from war than from peace, and I also understand that for a certain variety of international journalist it is more interesting to report on war than on peaceful activities or cultural achievements, which they are incapable of either judging or understanding. And finally it is clear to me that there is a certain Jewish international capitalism and journalism that has no feeling at all in common with the people whose interests they pretend to represent, but who, like Herostrates of old, regard incendiarism as the greatest success of their lives. But there is still another reason why I feel obliged to voice my opinion.

"When reading certain international press publications, or listening to speeches of various capitalist glorifiers of war, I consider myself entitled to speak and reply in the name of those who are forced to serve as the living substance for the mental activities of these formulators of war aims, that living substance to which I myself belonged as an unknown soldier for more than four years during the Great War.

"It is, perhaps, a magnificent effect when a statesman or a journalist stands up and in enthusiastic words announces the necessity of removing the regime of another country in the name of democracy or something similar. Practical execution of these glorious slogans, however, has quite a different aspect.

"Newspaper articles are being written today which are sure of an enthusiastic reception by the distinguished public. Realization of demands therein contained, however, is apt to arouse much less enthusiasm. I shall not deal with the powers of judgment or the gifts of such people. Whatever they may write has no bearing on the real nature of such a struggle.

"These scribblers announced before the Polish campaign that German infantry perhaps was not bad, but that tanks and mechanized units in general were inferior and would be sure to break down in action.

"Now, after the defeat of Poland, the same people brazenly assert that the Polish armies have collapsed only because of German tank formations and other mechanized troops, but that, on the other hand, German infantry had deteriorated most remarkably and had got the worst of it in every clash with the Polish.

" 'In this fact,' so one such writer actually says, 'one has the free right to see a favorable symptom for the course of the war in the West, and the French soldier will know how to take advantage of this.'

"I think so, too, provided he has read that article and can remember it later on. He will then probably box the ears of these military soothsayers. But unfortunately that will be impossible, since these people never will put their theories on inferiority of the German infantry to a personal test on the battlefields, but will merely describe these qualities from their editorial sanctums.

"Six weeks—let us say fourteen days—of concentrated shell-fire, and these war propagandists would soon think differently. They always are talking of the necessities of world politics, but they have no knowledge of military realities.

"I do know them and for that reason I consider it my duty to speak here, even at risk of the warmonger again seeing in my speech evidence of my anxiety and symptoms of the degree of my despair.

"Why should this war in the West be fought? For restoration of Poland? Poland of the Versailles Treaty will never rise again. This is guaranteed by two of the largest States in the world. Final re-organization of this territory and the question of re-establishment of the Polish State are problems which will not be solved by a war in the West but exclusively by Russia on the one hand and Germany on the other. Furthermore, the elimination of the influence of these two Powers within the territories concerned would not produce a new State but utter chaos.

"The problems awaiting solution there will never be solved either at the conference table or in editorial offices, but by the work of decades. It is not enough that a few statesmen who are not really concerned with the fate of the people affected get together and pass resolutions. It is necessary that someone who has himself a share in the life of these territories takes over the task of restoring really enduring conditions there. The ability of the Western democracies to restore such ordered conditions has at least in recent times not been proved.

"The example of Palestine shows it would be better to concentrate on the tasks at hand and solve these in a reasonable manner instead of meddling with problems which lie within the vital spheres of interest of other nations and could certainly be better solved by them. At any rate, Germany has in her Protectorate of Bohemia and Moravia not only established peace and order but, above all, has laid the foundation for a new economic prosperity and increasing understanding between the two nations. England still has much to accomplish before she can point to similar results in her Protectorate in Palestine.

"One also realizes that it would be senseless to annihilate millions of men and to destroy property worth millions in order to reconstruct a State which at its very birth was termed an abortion by all those not of Polish extraction.

"What other reason exists? Has Germany made any demands of England which might threaten the British Empire or endanger its existence? On the contrary, Germany has made no such demands on either France or England.

"But if this war is really to be waged only in order to give Germany a new regime, that is to say, in order to destroy the present Reich once more and thus to create a new Treaty of Versailles, then millions of human lives will be sacrificed in vain, for neither will the German Reich go to pieces nor will a second Treaty of Versailles be made. And even should this come to pass after three, four, or even eight years of war, then this second Versailles would once more become the source of fresh conflict in the future.

"In any event, a settlement of the world's problems carried out without consideration of the vital interests of its most powerful nations could not possibly, after the lapse of from five to ten years, end in any other way than that attempt made twenty years ago which is now ended. No, this war in the West cannot settle any problems except perhaps the ruined finances of certain armament manufacturers, newspaper owners, or other international war profiteers.

"Two problems are ripe for discussion today.

"First, the settlement of the problems arising from the disintegration of Poland and, second, the problem of eliminating those international difficulties which endanger the political and economic existence of the nations.

"What then are the aims of the Reich Government as regards the adjustment of conditions within the territory to the west of the German-Soviet line of demarcation which has been recognized as Germany's sphere of influence?

"First, the creation of a Reich frontier which, as has already been emphasized, shall be in accordance with existing historical, ethnographical and economic conditions.

"Second, the disposition of the entire living space according to the various nationalities; that is to say, the solution of the problems affecting the minorities which concern not only this area but nearly all the States in the Southwest of Europe.

"Third, in this connection: An attempt to reach a solution and settlement of the Jewish problem.

"Fourth, reconstruction of transport facilities and economic life in the interest of all those living in this area.

"Fifth, a guarantee for the security of this entire territory, and sixth, formation of a Polish State so constituted and governed as to prevent its becoming once again either a hotbed of anti-German activity or a center of intrigue against Germany and Russia.

"In addition to this, an attempt must immediately be made to wipe out or at least to mitigate the ill effects of war; that is to say, the adoption of practical measures for alleviation of the terrible distress prevailing there.

"These problems can, as I have already emphasized, perhaps be discussed but never solved at the conference table.

"If Europe is really sincere in her desire for peace, then the States in Europe ought to be grateful that Russia and Germany are prepared to transform this hotbed into a zone of peaceful development and that these two countries will assume the responsibility and bear the burdens inevitably involved.

"For the Reich this project, since it cannot be undertaken in an imperialistic spirit, is a task which will take fifty to a hundred years to perform.

"Justification for this activity on Germany's part lies in the political organizing of this territory as well as in its economic development. In the long run, of course, all Europe will benefit from it. Second, and in my opinion by far the most important task, is the creation of not only a belief in, but also a sense of, European security.

"For this it is necessary first that aims in the foreign policy of European States should be made perfectly clear.

"As far as Germany is concerned the Reich Government is ready to give a thorough and exhaustive exposition of the aims of its foreign policy.

"In so doing, they begin by stating that the Treaty of Versailles is now regarded by them as obsolete; in other words, that the government of the German Reich, and with them the whole German people, no longer see cause or reason for any further revision of the Treaty, apart from the demand for adequate colonial possessions justly due to the Reich, namely, in the first instance, for the return of German colonies.

"This demand for colonies is based not only on Germany's historical claim to German colonies but above all on her elementary right to a share of the world's resources of raw materials. This demand does not take the form of an ultimatum, nor is it a demand backed by force, but a demand based on political justice and sane economic principles.

"Secondly, the demand for a real revival of international economic life, coupled with an extension of trade and commerce, presupposes a reorganization of the international economic system; in other words, of production in the individual States. In order to facilitate the exchange of goods thus produced, however, markets must be organized and a final currency regulation arrived at so that the obstacles in the way of unrestriced trade can be gradually removed.

"Thirdly, the most important condition, however, for a real revival of economic life in and outside of Europe is the establishment of an unconditionally guaranteed peace and of a sense of security on the part of the individual nations.

"This security will not only be rendered possible by the final sanctioning of the European status, but above all by the reduction of armaments to a reasonable and economically tolerable level. An essential part of this necessary sense of security, however, is a clear definition of the legitimate use of an application of certain modern armaments which can, at any given moment, have such a devastating effect on the pulsating life of every nation and hence create a permanent sense of insecurity.

"In my previous speeches in the Reichstag I made proposals with this end in view. At that time they were rejected —maybe for the simple reason that they were made by me. I believe, however, that a sense of national security will not return to Europe until clear and binding international agreements have provided a comprehensive definition of the legitimate and illegitimate use of armaments.

"A Geneva convention once succeeded in prohibiting, in civilized countries at least, the killing of wounded, ill treatment of prisoners, war against noncombatants, etc., and just as it was possible gradually to achieve universal observance of this statute, a way must surely be found to regulate aerial warfare, use of poison gas and submarines, etc., and also so to define contraband that war will lose its terrible character of conflict waged against women and children and against noncombatants in general. A growing horror of certain methods of warfare will of its own accord lead to their abolition and thus they will become obsolete.

"In the war with Poland I endeavored to restrict aerial warfare to objectives of so-called military importance, or only to employ it to combat active resistance at a given point. But it must surely be possible to emulate the Red Cross and to draw up some universally valid international regulations. It is only when this is achieved that peace can reign, particularly in our densely populated continent—a peace which, uncontaminated by suspicion and fear, will provide the only possible condition for real economic prosperity.

"I do not believe that there is any responsible statesman in Europe who does not in his heart desire prosperity for his people. But such a desire can only be realized if all the nations inhabiting this continent decide to go to work together. To assist in assuring this co-operation must be the aim of every man who is sincerely struggling for the future of his own people.

"To achieve this great end, the leading nations of this continent will one day have to come together in order to draw up, accept, and guarantee a statute on a comprehensive basis which will insure for them all a sense of security, of calm—in short, of peace.

"Such a conference could not possibly be held without the most thorough preparation; this is, without exact elucidation of every point at issue.

"It is equally impossible that such a conference, which is to determine the fate of this continent for many years to come, could carry on its deliberations while cannon are

thundering or mobilized armies are bringing pressure to bear upon it.

"If, however, these problems must be solved sooner or later, then it would be more sensible to tackle the solution before millions of men are first uselessly sent to death and milliards of riches destroyed.

"Continuation of the present state of affairs in the West is unthinkable. Each day will soon demand increasing sacrifices.

"Perhaps the day will come when France will begin to bombard and demolish Saarbruecken. German artillery will in turn lay Mulhouse in ruins. France will retaliate by bombarding Karlsruhe and Germany in her turn will shell Strasbourg.

"Then the French artillery will fire at Freiburg, and the German at Kolmar or Schlettstadt. Long-range guns will then be set up and from both sides will strike deeper and deeper and whatever cannot be reached by the long-distance guns will be destroyed from the air.

"And that will be very interesting for certain international journalists and very profitable for the airplane, arms, and munitions manufacturers, but appalling for the victims.

"And this battle of destruction will not be confined to the land. No, it will reach far out over the sea.

"Today there are no longer any islands. And the national wealth of Europe will be scattered in the form of shells and the vigor of every nation will be sapped on the battlefields.

"One day, however, there will again be a frontier between Germany and France, but instead of flourishing towns there will be ruins and endless graveyards.

"Mr. Churchill and his companions may interpret these opinions of mine as weakness or cowardice if they like. I need not occupy myself with what they think; I make these statements simply because it goes without saying that I wish to spare my own people this suffering.

"If, however, the opinions of Messrs. Churchill and followers should prevail, this statement will have been my last.

"Then we shall fight. Neither force of arms nor lapse of time will conquer Germany. There never will be another November 1918 in German history. It is infantile to hope for the disintegration of our people.

"Mr. Churchill may be convinced that Great Britain will win. I do not doubt for a single moment that Germany will be victorious.

"Destiny will decide who is right.

"One thing only is certain. In the course of world history, there have never been two victors, but very often only losers. This seems to me to have been the case in the last war.

"May those peoples and their leaders who are of the same mind now make their reply. And let those who consider war to be the better solution reject my outstretched hand.

"As Fuehrer of the German people and Chancellor of the Reich, I can thank God at this moment that he has so wonderfully blessed us in our hard struggle for what is our right, and beg Him that we and all other nations may find the right way, so that not only the German people but all Europe may once more be granted the blessing of peace.

Press

New York Times, October 7—Those who had expected Hitler to make the dramatic gesture yesterday of announcing his resignation to the Reichstag were not successful prophets. He did not announce his resignation. Instead he asked by implication for the resignation of Mr. Chamberlain and M. Daladier. . . .

Le Temps, October 8—M. Hitler tried to get out of the dilemma into which his policies have driven him by savagely attacking Poland and by buying the alliance of bolshevik Russia at an exorbitant price. In short, M. Hitler, while affirming his desire to see the end of hostilities, continues to demand that the world bow before the fait accompli of the annihilation of Poland. He continues to show his determination to exclude all the other powers from the East, where Germany, allied with Soviet Russia, wishes to exercise absolute rule. He calls for the end of hostilities and suggests a conference. But he begins by advancing the principle that Germany must obtain not only her old colonies, but colonies commensurable "to the interests and the greatness of the Reich." Such impudence leaves one stunned, and we ask ourselves how he can dare to make such grandiose claims in the face of powers which have put him in such a critical position; for the speech reveals clearly that he has only slight confidence in the developments of the war which he has unleashed and which he is now unable to curb, even though he wishes to. . . .

•

SPEECH OF OCTOBER 10, 1939

Berlin, Sportpalast

Background

1939

October 7—Daladier, answering Hitler's speech of October 6, declares that France will not lay down her arms until guarantees for a real peace and general security are obtained.

October 9—Russian troops mass along the frontier of Finland. The Finnish Government sends a delegation to Moscow.

The Speech

". . . NOW fate has forced us for the defense of the Reich to take up arms. Within a few weeks that State which most insolently presumed to threaten German interests has been conquered, and that by virtue of a military achievement that stands alone in history, thanks to the valiant heroism of our soldiers and their brilliant leadership.

"We know not what the future has in store, but we are convinced of one thing: No power in the world will be able again to force us to our knees. They will neither defeat us militarily, destroy us economically, nor spiritually wear us down. Under no circumstances will they experience any kind of German capitulation.

"I have given expression to our readiness for peace. Germany has no cause for war against the Western Powers. They have recklessly provoked a war on the flimsiest grounds. If they reject our readiness for peace, then Germany is determined to take up the battle and fight it out—this way or that.

"Neither terror of the moment nor the proclamation of the duration of the war will intimidate us or make us waver. Ahead of us stands the eternal life of our people and nothing can shake us, perplex us, or drive us to despair. Quite the opposite, what the other world chooses, it may have.

"The path I had to take to rescue Germany from destruction through the Versailles Treaty was a thorny path. Since then almost twenty years have elapsed, but today the Reich stands more powerful than ever. The road ahead of us cannot be any more trying than that we have left behind. Since we never lost courage along the path from the past to the present, we will much less lose courage striding along the path to the future. . . ."

"Perhaps it will also be an answer to the stupidity of those in the world who believe they will be able internally to disrupt the solidarity of the German people. We want to show them the effects of these imbecilic attempts. We want to show them how, through them, the German people are bound and welded more strongly and more solidly together. We can perhaps thus best disperse their hopes, which consist in believing one can interfere in the internal German Constitution just as it pleases any outsider.

"We want to suggest to them it is necessary to respect the inner constitution of other peoples.

"What we must suffer jointly the world can be sure we will be able to take. I hope they will be able to take it as well as we. Now, more than ever before, the time is coming when National Socialism will develop the full scope of its power in the creation, development, and bearing of the nation.

"We National Socialists once came from war, from the experience of war. Our world ideal developed in war; now, if necessary, it will prove itself.

"The decision for that no longer rests with us but with the other world. With us lies only a grim determination to receive the decision one way or another and then certainly to fight to the bitter end. Thus the War Winter Relief must now above all help to join the German national community more firmly than ever.

"A community for battle, a community for victory and in the end for peace.

"For the more determinedly we accept the sacrifices that such a war may bring, the harder they are, the more certain we are that we will win the peace for which our nation is striving. For it is my conviction that some day the time will come when uncertainty must end. It must be possible that the German nation can live its life within the limits of its living space according to its own desires without being constantly molested by others, when the German people will have that share of the world's riches which because of their numbers and worth they can claim."

Press

New York Times, October 11—Four days having passed since he made his "final" peace offer to the Western Powers before the Reichstag and no official reaction from Great Britain or France resulting, Chancellor Hitler this afternoon mounted the rostrum again and reiterated that "if they reject our readiness for peace, then Germany is determined to take up the battle and fight it out—this way or that."

Le Temps, October 12—The Chancellor exhorted his people to penitence. The tone of the speech was that of a man visibly irritated to the extreme by the repulse of his peace offensive.

•

THE SPEECH OF NOVEMBER 8, 1939

Munich

Background

1939

October 12—Replying to Hitler's peace offers, Chamberlain declares that no peace is possible until Czechoslovakia and Poland are restored.

In America, Colonel Lindbergh, speaking on the radio, attacks the proposed revision of the Neutrality Law. He suggests that a distinction be made between offensive and defensive weapons.

October 16—Russia obtains new naval bases on the Baltic through a pact signed with Lithuania.

October 19—Turkey signs a treaty of mutual assistance with England and France.

October 21—The French High Command announces that French troops which had occupied German territory, in front of the Maginot Line, have been withdrawn.

November 4—Roosevelt signs amended Neutrality Act repealing the arms embargo and instituting the "cash and carry" system.

November—Queen Wilhelmina of Holland and King Leopold of Belgium address an appeal for peace to Germany, England, and France, offering their services as mediators.

November 8—A bomb explosion wrecks the Munich Beer Hall shortly after Hitler has left it. Eight persons are killed and sixty wounded.

The Speech

"I HAVE come to you only for a few hours in order in your midst to commemorate a day which for ourselves, for the party, and thus for the whole German people is of great significance.

"It was a difficult decision which we had to take at the time. Our apparent failure nevertheless became the hour of the birth of the National Socialist Movement, for in its wake came the great trial which gave us the opportunity to make our aims public and thus acquaint the masses of our people with the ideas of National Socialism.

"That in the four years from 1919 till 1923 the National Socialist Movement grew to such an extent that it succeeded in mobilizing the whole nation was due to the general situation which then existed. A terrible catastrophe had come over Germany. After forty-five years of peace Germany was driven into war.

"Much has been said about war guilt. The German Government of the old Reich was 'guilty' only of one thing: that was that it allowed many favorable opportunities for war to slip away. There had been many such opportunities if Germany had really wanted to start a war.

"The same Powers as before have driven Germany into war today; and they have done this while using the same phrases and the same lies as before. Britain and France did not defeat us on the battlefield. That was a great lie.

"Many people abroad are amazed at my great self-confidence. I gained it at the front; for never had I the feeling when I was in the fighting line that our enemies were superior to us.

"No Briton and no Frenchman ever showed more courage than our German soldiers. We were beaten only by lies, and it was then as it is today: Churchill and his companions drove us into war. But in those days they had to face only a weak German Government.

"The British lies at that time were the same as they are today.

"What were the aims of Britain in the last war?

"Britain said that she was fighting for justice. Britain has been fighting for justice for 300 years. As a reward God gave her 40,000,000 square kilometers of the world and 480,000,000 people to dominate. That is how God rewards the people who fight for freedom; and, be it noted, those who also fight for self-determination. For Britain fought this fight as well.

"Britain has also been fighting for civilization. Civilization exists in Britain alone—in the British mining districts, in the distressed areas, in Whitechapel, and in the other sloughs of mass misery and destitution.

"It has been said that the British are not fighting the German people at all, but only the régime which speaks for the German people. It is Britain's task, they say, to liberate the German people from this régime and to make it happy. Britain is fighting to free the German people from militarism. In fact she wants to free Germany to such an extent that it would not be necessary for Germany to carry arms, and even if Germany desired to do so Britain wants to prevent her and thus make her liberation complete.

"For 300 years Britain has conquered people after people. Now she is satisfied; now there must be peace. . . .

"Today a British Minister appears and says:

" 'We would only be too glad to come to an agreement with Germany if only we could trust the words of the German Government.'

"I could say exactly the same myself. How gladly we would come to an understanding with Britain if only we could trust the word of her leaders. Has ever an enemy been deceived in a more infamous manner than the German people by British statesmen during the last 20 years?

"Our colonies were taken away, our trade was destroyed, our Navy was taken from us. Millions of Germans were torn from Germany and maltreated. The German people were plundered. Reparations were imposed upon them which could not have been paid in 100 years and which threw the German people into the deepest misery. . . .

"Since then Germany has become a World Power, thanks to our movement. . . ."

"But it was, of course, understood that the ancient foe would stand forth again. There are two kinds of Britons, for even in Britain there are many men who hate this hypocrisy and these lies. But they have been silenced or else they keep quiet.

"You know the efforts that I have made for many years to come to an understanding with Great Britain. We have renounced a great deal, but there is no government which can renounce the right to live, and the National-Socialist Government naturally does not think of making such a renunciation.

"It is my intention to safeguard the life and security of the German people. I have not the slightest intention of making such renunciation.

"Germany of today, at any rate, is ready and determined to defend and re-establish her frontiers and her *Lebensraum*.

"If Halifax declared yesterday that he stands for *Kultur,* then I reply we had a *Kultur* at a time when the British had not the slightest idea of *Kultur*. And in these last six years more has been done for *Kultur* in Germany than in the last 100 years in Britain. Wherever we went, whether Prague, Posen, or Vienna, in fact everywhere, we did not find monuments of British *Kultur,* but of German *Kultur*. Perhaps monuments of British *Kultur* stand in Egypt or India.

"We have built up an army of which there is no equal in the world, and this army is backed by a people of such compact unity as is unparalleled in history; and above this army and this people there is a Government with fanatical will power similarly without precedent.

"This new German Reich had no war aims whatsoever against Britain and France. I defined my attitude on this matter in my last speech, when for the last time I held out my hand to Britain and France.

"The case of Poland has shown how little the British are really interested in the existence of that State. Otherwise Britain should have declared war also on Soviet Russia, which has taken possession of half that country. But now the British declare that they have new war aims. They say they are fighting Nazidom and will go on waging war until they find someone who is ready to sacrifice himself to them.

"If the British declare that they are fighting for freedom, then the British might have given a wonderful example by granting their own Empire full liberty.

"There is only war because the British wanted war. We are convinced that the war will last until the wealth of this world is distributed justly. . . ."

"We also believe that this war must end without a new war having to follow every few years. For this reason we consider it obvious that a state of affairs from which such an event can emerge must come to an end; and that state of affairs is one in which a single people claims for itself the right to play the part of a world police.

"As far as Germany is concerned, Britain will have to recognize this time that the attempt to establish a police dictatorship is bound to fail.

"But at the bottom of this matter there is really nothing except their profound hatred of National-Socialist Germany.

"What they hate is the Germany which constitutes a bad example. They hate a *soziales* [communal] Germany. They hate the Germany of Social Welfare. They hate the Germany of the abolition of class distinction. They hate the Germany which has achieved all this. They hate the Germany which during the past seven years has made every effort to create for her nationals an adequate standard of living. They hate that Germany. They hate the Germany which provides her sailors with decent accommodation in ships. They hate it because they feel that their own people might be infected by it. They hate the Germany of social legislation.

"They hate the Germany which celebrates May 1 as a Labor Day. They hate the Germany which washes her children so that they need not run about covered with lice, as is the case in their own country. And who hates us? Their capitalists. Their Jewish and non-Jewish barons. It is they who hate us because they see in all these activities a bad example which is apt to stir up the British people.

"They hate the Germany of welfare for the younger generation. They hate the strong Germany which marches forward. They hate the Germany of the Four-Year Plan. We started the Four-Year Plan to help ourselves. We have not taken anything from them by this activity. But they fought against the Four-Year Plan, maintaining that it must be stopped. And why? Because it makes Germany sound.

"Their struggle is a struggle against a free and sound Germany, and our struggle is a struggle for the establishment of a sound and strong community of people and for the security of this community against the rest of the world. . . ."

"They have compared this war with the Second Punic War. It is clear who is Rome and who is Carthage. In any case Britain was not Rome in the first World War, and in the second Britain will certainly not be victorious. This time the British face a different Germany, and they will find this out at no distant date. . . ."

"We have forgotten nothing, but we have learned much. Each British balloon which drops a few intellectual leaflets proves that nothing has changed there in the past 20 years, but every reaction from Germany ought to demonstrate to them that things are moving here.

"But Britain does not want peace. We heard it again yesterday. I said everything in my Reichstag speech and I will not add anything else to it. *What now remains to be said will be addressed to the British in a language they will understand.*

"We regret that France has allowed herself to be taken into the services of these British warmongers and is now marching side by side with them. *We were never afraid of a one-front war, and today we have only one front and we shall maintain ourselves there. I have never regarded the fact that we succeeded in reaching an understanding with Russia as a success for German policy, but as a success for reason.*

"There was a time when both peoples bled white in a mutual struggle without gaining anything thereby. Now we have agreed that we will not do this favor a second time for London and Paris.

"Today we are standing at the crossroads of history. Germany has changed completely. Germany of today, Germany of 1940, of 1941, and of 1942 is not to be compared with the Germany of 1915, 1916, 1917, and 1918. There were things in Germany which confronted us when we were only a party, and which as a mere party we succeeded in overcoming. Today we are in power. Our will today is as unshakable in the struggle against the outside world as it was in the struggle which we carried on as a party at home.

"Anything is conceivably possible except our capitulation. When it is said that this war will last three years I reply that however long it may last Germany will never capitulate.

"Britain has stated that she is prepared for a three-years' war. At the outbreak of the war I gave orders to Field-Marshal Goering that he should plan everything for a five-years' war."

Press

New York Times, November 10— . . . The denunciation of British policy which Herr Hitler delivered tonight may have been motivated by the apparent failure of the monarchs' joint offer to evoke in the Western capitals the affirmative response which had perhaps been anticipated here—and in which response the Reich was not disinterested. . . .

Le Temps, November 10— . . . Chancellor Hitler's speech proves that he rejects any possibility of any sort of negotiation. M. Hitler declared chiefly that Germany could not sacrifice her own life, which, of course, no one had ever demanded. . . . All this is merely the impression of the confusion, the disorder, and the rage of a delirious mind confronted with difficulties which it had not anticipated. . . .

•

SPEECH OF JANUARY 30, 1940

Sportpalast, Berlin

Background

1939

November 29—Soviet troops invade Finland and bomb Helsinki.

December 1—Daladier, in a speech broadcast to America, denounces the Communists in France.

December 5—Ex-President Hoover takes the leadership in a Finnish relief fund drive.

December 10—The United States Government grants Finland a credit of $10,000,000 for agricultural supplies.

December 14—The League of Nations, meeting in Geneva, expels Russia for invading Finland.

December 17—The German battleship "Graf Spee" is scuttled in the harbor of Montevideo.

December 23—Roosevelt appoints Myron C. Taylor as his personal representative to the Vatican.

1940

January 20—Winston Churchill vigorously warns the neutral countries that they cannot keep out of the war and advises them to join the Allies.

The Speech

"GERMAN men and women, seven years is a short period. It is a reflection only of the normal lifetime of a man and only a second in the life of a nation. And yet these seven years appear to us to have been longer than many decades of the past. A great historical experience is concentrated in this period—the resurrection of a nation which was threatened by destruction. It was a period tremendously rich in events, which are difficult to forget for us, who not only were allowed to witness them but who also took part in their making.

"There is much talk today about the democratic ideal. That is, there is much talk of it, not in Germany but in the rest of the world. We in Germany have had a sufficient experience of the democratic ideal in the past. If the rest of the world today is again praising this ideal we can reply that the German people had no less than fifteen years' opportunity for coming to know the democratic ideal in its pure form. We are only the successor of democracy.

"We are presented now with the most marvelous war aims. Britain is in fact very experienced in the production of war aims, since she is the country which has waged the most wars in the world. These war aims say that a new Europe will arise—a Europe full of justice—and this general justice will make armaments superfluous and therefore general disarmament will follow; and since disarmament has as its consequence flourishing economics, trade will then begin to flow—trade above all, much trade, free trade. Culture then will flourish, and religion too. Put in a nutshell, at last the Golden Age will come.

"But, most unfortunately, we have been promised this Golden Age a good many times before, and it is the same people who describe it anew today.

"These are old, worn-out records, which have been played before, and we can only be very sorry for these gentlemen who are not capable of finding one new idea to lure our people. We were promised this in 1918, that the new Europe and the new justice would come; containing as their most essential element the self-determination of the people. At the time also the program of disarmament, of general disarmament, was set before us—a general disarmament which would be crowned by a union of disarmed nations determined to talk away, discuss away, all differences by means of free speech. It was maintained that general disarmament, carried out by a world parliament, should lead to great prosperity, not only in industry but more particularly in trade, especially free trade—so they never grew tired of saying.

"As for religion—well, at the end of the last war they talked less about religion than at the beginning of this war. Nevertheless, in 1918 they said that the coming era would be very wonderful and pleasing in the sight of God.

"We have experienced what happened in reality. They smashed old States to pieces without asking their peoples whether they agreed to what was intended to be their destiny. Not in a single instance was the will of the nation really considered. Not only political bodies, but also excellent economic structures were destroyed. Those who were responsible for these acts were unable to put anything better in the place of what they destroyed because they looked upon European history with unparalleled arrogance.

"In one word, Europe was broken up. Nations were deprived of their rights after having been deprived of their art, and a system was set up which divided the world into victors and vanquished. There was much talk about disarmament, but the other States continued to arm—and they also continued to have their wars as before. And the nations which disarmed were unable to defend themselves against the arrogance of the others.

"The same madness reigned in the field of economics, where the crazy system of reparation resulted in the misery not only of the vanquished but also of the victors.

"No nation suffered more severely from the economic depression than Germany. At the same time culture was decaying and religion was being neglected. There was not one Englishman during all those fifteen years who remembered Christian charity and mercy. Now they are wallowing in the Bible; but in those days their real Bible was the Treaty of Versailles. There are hundreds of paragraphs in the Treaty of Versailles, and each one is blackmail and oppression; and this Treaty of Versailles rested on the League of Nations, which was built only for the one reason—to compel Germany to obey the dictates of the Treaty.

"Foreign politicians nowadays pretend that it is impossible to trust the German nation; but this indeed could not fit in with the democratic Germany of the past. For that Germany was built by them, and there was no reason why they should not have trusted the Germany which was their own work.

"You all remember the misery of the breakdown of 1918, the tragedy of 1919, and all those years of economic decay, of the enslavement and impoverishment of our people, but most of all that complete sense of hopelessness. It is depressing to recall that time, when a great nation had lost all confidence, not only in itself but also in all justice in this world.

"Throughout all this time democratic Germany hoped in vain. She also tried in vain to bring about an improvement, and she protested in vain. International finance remained brutal and ruthless. It squeezed the German people as much as it could. An Allied statement even said sarcastically that there were 20,000,000 Germans too many in the world. They remained deaf to misery and unemployment. They did not care about the ruin of our agriculture, of our industry, and our commerce.

"We all remember how the mood of depression spread in Germany. At this time when all hopes, all pleas, and all protests had failed, the Nationalist Socialist Movement was born. It was born out of the realization that in this world one must not hope, nor protest, nor plead, but one must first of all help oneself. For fifteen years democratic Germany had preached reliance upon the outside world and its institutions. Each faction in Germany had its own international patron saint. Some relied on the solidarity of the international proletariat, others on international democracy with its League of Nations. Others again relied on the conscience of the world and on civilization. But all their hopes were vain. We have replaced this hoping by another kind of reliance—reliance on the only help of which one can be sure—namely, one's own strength. Their hopes were replaced by the faith of the people and the mobilization of its own inherent internal values.

"We had but few real means at our disposal. What we regarded as the stones with which to build the new Reich was: First, the working power of our people; secondly, its intelligence; and thirdly, what our vital space and our soil were able to produce. On this we based our work, and on this initiated Germany's resurrection, which never threatened the world, which was a purely domestic reform, but which nevertheless called forth the hatred of others.

"This tragic development became especially evident when we proclaimed the Four-Year Plan. Our idea was one which should have created enthusiasm in the world. A people wanted to help itself. It did not appeal for outside help nor for charity from others. It decided to rely upon its own creative abilities, upon its diligence, and upon its intelligence. But nevertheless the outside world began to roar.

"British statesmen shouted: 'What do you think you are doing? Your Four-Year Plan does not fit in with our world economy.' As if they ever had given Germany an opportunity of taking a place in world economy! They were envious of the resurrection of the German people, and because we foresaw this we simultaneously proceeded with the mobilization of our strength.

"We were not able to get justice, in spite of having begged for it for many years. So, in 1934, Germany started her general rearmament to her greatest capacity. In 1935 I introduced general conscription. In 1936 I ordered the occupation of the Rhineland. In 1937 the Four-Year Plan began to function. In 1938 Austria and the Sudetenland were incorporated in the Reich. And in 1939 we started to fence in the Reich against its foes, who had already unmasked themselves.

"All this could have come about in another way if the rest of the world had only come to an understanding about Germany's claims. Some people say we ought to have negotiated. But have I not more than once brought forward Germany's colonial aims as a basis for negotiation, and have I not received nothing but a severe 'No' and even had to face fresh hostility? Britain and France were determined from the moment of the reawakening of the Reich to take up the cudgels against her. For 300 years Britain has pursued a plan to prevent a real consolidation of Europe. In the same way France has striven for many centuries to prevent a consolidation of Germany. When, therefore, Chamberlain stands up today and pronounces his war aims, the history of his own nation refutes them.

"For 300 years his people have spoken like him. They have always fought for God and religion. Never have they fought for the sake of material aims, but because they have only had ethical aims God has rewarded them with much riches.

"Britain always pretended to be a fighter for truth and justice and the protagonist of all virtues. God has proved His gratitude for this. Within three centuries Britain conquered fifteen and a half million square miles of the globe, not for reasons of selfishness or lust for power. No! On the contrary, it was only in the execution of a mission entrusted to her by the Lord and for the sake of holy religion.

"Of course, Britain did not want to be alone as the fighter for God. On the contrary, she always invited others to take part in such struggles. Today, too, they are trying to find others to share the struggle with them. Indeed, this policy has proved very profitable for Britain.

"The story of the conqueror of 15,500,000 square miles is a long chapter of oppression, tyranny, subjugation, and plunder. Things happened in the course of this great conquest which would have been impossible in any other State or in the case of any other nation. Britain waged war for any cause, be it to extend her trade or to make others smoke opium, or else because she wanted to obtain gold mines or diamond fields. It was also thus in the case of the Great War. She pretended to fight for ideals, but the fact that she stole the German colonies, took the German Navy, and confiscated Germany's investments abroad was characteristic of her methods. When Chamberlain today walks about with the Bible in his hands and preaches about war aims, it strikes me that this picture resembles the devil walking about with a prayer-book and stalking a human soul.

"All this is neither new nor original. It is obsolete, stale stuffing which nobody can believe any longer. Moreover, no nation will burn its fingers twice. The trick of the Pied Piper of Hamelin works only once. Likewise the apostles of international understanding cannot again betray the German nation.

"Compared with this attitude I must really praise Mr. Churchill. He publicly uttered what Chamberlain only secretly thinks. He admitted that it is his aim to annihilate and disintegrate the German nation as a whole.

"The French generals, too, quite openly admit these aims. I really think that this way we can understand each other better. Why not publicly admit it? Indeed, we prefer them when they say all this in public. Their real aims are to restore the Germany of 1648, a Germany dismembered and disintegrated.

"There are 80,000,000 Germans living in Central Europe. For the past three centuries these Germans have been deprived of their most privileged right of living because they have not been united. When these 80,000,000 Germans are united they are a power. When they are dismembered they are completely powerless, for it means nothing when small nations try to press their rights or protest against injustice.

"That is the real reason why the British have always been opposed to the unification of Germany or Italy. They used to speak of the 'precipitate' formation of the German 'Kaiserreich.' Yes, naturally, they would like once again to have a Germany consisting of 200, 300, or 400 provinces or even dynasties.

"Such a Germany, they say, could easily be again a country of poets and thinkers. Thinkers and poets, they believe, do not eat so much as laborers, and that in their view is another advantage. This, indeed, is a problem of the day. But now these nations have to face a united and young German nation. They will soon experience on a large scale what we have experienced on a smaller scale in Germany.

"In Germany, too, there were people who were of the opinion that those who have should go on having, and that those who have nothing should go on having nothing. This condition, they said, should remain unchanged. These powers in Germany were opposed by contrary forces. Some of them were striving only to destroy everything. 'If we can't have our portion,' they thought, 'let us destroy everything anyway.' National Socialists, on the other hand, were striving gradually and slowly to change these conditions and to give those who have nothing a fair share.

"A parallel development is proceeding on a large scale, on an international scale. *It cannot be tolerated any longer that the British nation of 44,000,000 souls should remain in possession of fifteen and a half million square miles of the world's surface.* They pretend to have obtained it from God and are not prepared to give it away. *Likewise the French nation owns more than three and a half million square miles, while the German nation with 80,000,000 souls only possesses about 230,000 square miles.*

"This is a problem which has got to be solved, and which will be solved in the same way in which the social problem will be solved. We are experiencing now on an international scale what we have been experiencing inside Germany in the past. When National Socialism was striving for power, its opponents, the Liberal and Democratic parties, clamored for the compulsory dissolution of the National Socialist party. In the same way the world is now striving to dissolve the German nation. By dismembering the nation they think they can deprive it of its power. That is really the aim of Great Britain and France in the present struggle.

"The reply of the German nation will be the same reply that the German nation has given in its internal struggle. You are all well aware that we did not gain our victory internally by doing nothing. This victory, you remember, was preceded by a heavy struggle, going on practically for fifteen years. We have not gained our power internally as a present from heaven, but we had to fight for it toughly and bravely.

"When eventually in 1933 we came to power, and I took upon my shoulders the responsibility for the future of the German nation, it was clear to me that the real struggle was still before me. The aim of this struggle, I knew, was the liberation of the German nation.

"Whatever I have created since then has been created with this in view. The party, the SA, the SS, the German Labor Front, the Army, the Navy, and the Air Force, they have all been created with one object and one only—the liberation of the German people. For a long time I tried to reach this goal by means of persuasion and negotiation, and in some cases I must admit I have been successful.

"The German people do not feel any hate against France

or Britain. The German people only want to live in friendship with these two peoples. The German people have no claims whatsoever which could hurt these peoples. The German people do not want to take anything away from these peoples.

"But when they started on their campaign of hatred, it went so far that I had to say:

" 'This cannot go on. I cannot remain a passive spectator.' I had to answer these hatemongers. We had educated the German people in no sort of hatred, but one day the hatemongers abroad, as we knew, would sit in the governments of their respective countries and start to realize their aims; and the German people would not know what it was all about.

"Therefore I gave the order to enlighten the German people. I was also determined from this moment on to safeguard the defense of the Reich against any event. Today the hatemongers admit they wanted the war. Yes, Poland would probably have come to an agreement, but they did not want it. They confess that they did not want to come to an understanding. They wanted war."

"Well, then, they have started the war and I can only say to France and Britain that they, too, will get all the war they want. The first phase of the struggle was a political one. For many years Germany pursued, together with Italy, a common policy. So far this has not undergone any changes. An intimate friendship exists between both States. They have common interests and are determined to bring them to a common denominator.

"The pious and Bible-believing Mr. Chamberlain tried hard last year to conclude an alliance with Russia, but he did not succeed. Now I understand very well how furious the British are that I have done what Mr. Chamberlain tried to do, and I also understand that what in Mr. Chamberlain would have been a God-pleasing action is a Godless one on my part. But the Almighty will be well pleased, I am sure, that in one large area at least a senseless struggle has been avoided.

"For centuries past Germany and Russia lived in friendship side by side. Why should that not be possible in the future too? I say it will be possible because both people wish it so; and each attempt to make it impossible will be frustrated because the motives of such an attempt will be clearly understood by every one. *Thus in the first place Germany became politically free at her back door and our second task was to make her militarily free also.*

"The British war experts hoped that the struggle with Poland would in no circumstances be decided before six or twelve months, but they were frustrated by the strength of our Army. The State to which Britain had given her guarantee was brushed off the map within eighteen days without this guarantee having been fulfilled.

"The first phase of the struggle is over—the second phase can start. Mr. Churchill is itching for this second phase. Both he and his satellites have pronounced the hope that at last the war with bombs is to start, and they write that this war with bombs will not exclude women and children—as if Britain had ever left women and children out of her wars. The whole blockade is nothing but a fight against women and children. Remember the Boer War and its concentration camps for women and children. The idea of concentration camps was born in British brains. I have looked this subject up in the encyclopedia and have copied the relevant passage. The British put women and children into the concentration camps and 20,000 Boer women perished. Why should Britain's methods of warfare be any different today?

"We thought of all this and we made our preparations. Herr Churchill may be convinced that by now we know what he has achieved in these five months. We also know what France has done. *But he does not seem to know what Germany has done in these five months. Those gentlemen seem to think that we have slept for five months. Since I entered the political arena I have hardly slept a single day of any importance, not to speak of the past five months.*

"There is one assurance I can give the German people—a tremendous task has been carried out in these five months. In fact, all that was created in Germany in the previous seven years fades in comparison with it. Our arms factories are working according to plan. Our plans have been a success, and our foresight begins to bear fruit in all respects—such big fruit in fact that our enemies are gradually beginning to copy our methods.

"But their copying is only on a small scale. The British wireless, of course, knows better. To judge by British broadcasts, there can be no sunshine in England now as the sky must be darkened by countless squadrons of airplanes. The whole world, according to these British broadcasts, seems to be one great storehouse of munitions working for Britain in order to equip vast British armies.

"Germany, on the contrary, seems to face a complete breakdown. Today I learned that we had only three U-boats left. This is a bad state of affairs indeed, but only for British propaganda, if you ask me, because once the U-boats are sunk—which I am sure will happen tonight or tomorrow—what will be left for them to sink? All they will be able to do then will be to destroy the U-boats which we have not yet built. British propaganda will then have to invent some theory about the resurrection of U-boats, since British ships will continue to be sunk. Once we possess no more U-boats these sinkings can only be the work of boats that the British have already once destroyed.

"We have also read that I am deeply grieved and downcast as I had expected that we would build U-boats at the rate of two a day, but that instead we are building only two a week—they say. I can only reply to this that it is not good for war reports, and especially broadcast speeches, to be made by members of a race which has not fought for several thousand years. It seems to me that the last war of the Maccabees must by now have lost its value as military education.

"When I look at this foreign propaganda my confidence in our victory grows immeasurably, for I have gone through this experience before. The propaganda which was staged against us for fifteen years by our adversaries in Germany made use of the same slogans and phrases. Nay, it was even thought out by the same kind of brain and used the same jargon. Such people I overcame—one single man, who had gathered round him a small group of collaborators.

"But today it is Germany, a great world Power, which has to deal with it. If age makes one venerable it does not necessarily make one intelligent, and he who has once been struck with blindness is still blind today. Those whom the gods would destroy they first make blind. Today they are confronted with the might of the German Army, which is the first in the world, and by the German nation, which is united by understanding and discipline, the result of the glorious National Socialist education.

"This is not a mere fantasy. Parties have been liquidated, trends wiped out, and one Union has been put in their place. We are not going to repeat the state of 1918. If Daladier doubts the solidity of this unity, if he thinks that my own countrymen are not behind me, then I answer him:—

" 'M. Daladier, perhaps you will make the acquaintance of my Austrians, who will teach you a lesson. You will make the acquaintance of Austrian divisions and their regiments, just as you are going to make the acquaintance of other German divisions and regiments. For let me tell you, you are not facing different German tribes. No, M. Daladier, you are facing the German people, and a National Socialist people at that. This German nation has been cured of all the temptations of international ideologies, and it will remain cured because the National Socialist party is pledged to watch over it.'

"If my adversaries think that there might be antagonism between the Army, the Party, the State, and myself, then I would remind them that my former foes placed their hopes in such possibilities over a period of fifteen years. As a National Socialist I have learned to work, to fight, and to deal with worries. Indeed, it almost seems that Providence has nothing but worries in store for this generation. But we are not going to be ungrateful to Providence.

"Twenty-five years ago we learned a warning lesson. Then the German nation went into a struggle which was forced upon it without being adequately prepared. France had then made much better use of her man-power, Russia, too, was against us, and, finally, it was possible to mobilize against us the whole world. Germany went into this struggle and performed a miracle. The year 1914 saved our German land from a foreign invasion. The year 1915 improved the position of the Reich. The years 1916-17 brought struggle after struggle. Often there seemed to be the danger of a defeat, but, as if by a miracle, the German Reich was saved again and again.

"The blessing of Providence was evidently with her. It was at that turning point that the German people began to be ungrateful. They ceased to trust their own strength and began to trust the Providence of others. In the end they even began to rise up against their own Reich and their own leaders, and it was at that moment that Providence turned away from the German people.

"At that time I held the view that this catastrophe did not fall upon us without our having deserved it. On the contrary I was of the opinion that we only got from Providence what we deserved. The German nation had been ungrateful, and victory was denied to it. This mistake will not be repeated a second time. The National Socialist party never failed to fight against its foes in days of adversity, and today it is the task of the German nation to fight against its enemies.

"Eighty million people are now stepping to the front. The number of our enemies is about the same. But these 80,000,000 Germans have the best domestic organization conceivable. They have a strong faith and I may say not the worst leadership. Indeed I am convinced that the best leadership is theirs. Both nation and leadership are united in one conviction—there can be no reconciliation until our clear rights are realized and assured.

"We have no wish to see in two, three, or five years another struggle about our rights. Those rights are not a matter of party. I myself am merely the spokesman of the German nation. It is not my person which is at stake, but I am certainly not one of those who ever lower the flag. The German nation has given me its confidence, and I shall be worthy of it. I turn my eyes to the past and to the future and I am determined to be worthy of them. The German nation too must prove worthy of its past and its future.

"The present generation is the bearer of Germany's destiny. Our enemies shout today: 'Germany must perish.' The answer which Germany gives them is: 'Germany will live, and she will be victorious.'

"At the beginning of the eighth year of the National Socialist revolution our hearts turn to the German nation and to the future of Germany, which we shall serve, for which we shall fight, and, if necessary, die—but never capitulate. Germany, *Sieg Heil!*"

Press

London Times, January 31— . . . Last night's tirade . . . is interesting only as an example of the systematic mendacity upon which German morale is apparently built. . . . It would certainly be the greatest mistake to suppose that there has been any measurable breakaway from allegiance to him [among the German people].

New York Times, January 31—Versailles is Hitler's stock in trade. If it did not exist he would have to invent it. For Versailles is the only argument with which he can attempt to justify the utter recklessness of a policy that has once more led the German people into war. . . . This constantly reiterated denunciation of Versailles as the source of all evil in postwar Europe serves Hitler's purpose, but it is not good history. Admittedly, the Versailles Treaty was not as far-sighted in some respects as it should have been. Its reparation sections were fantastic. But there is this to be remembered of the reparation sections: that they were abandoned before Hitler himself entered office; that even before they were abandoned a vast amount of capital flowed into Germany in the form of foreign loans; that to a great extent Germany used these foreign loans to make reparation payments, and then defaulted on the foreign loans. . . .

Le Temps, February 1—Chancellor Hitler found it proper to mock at the war aims that the Allies had enunciated, to sum up with heavy irony the hope of seeing a new Europe organized on the basis of law, liberty, and justice. He chose to discard any hope of a return of economic prosperity, of the development of culture, and the rebirth of religious feeling and spiritual forces. All this M. Hitler deplored and he took pains to contrast to these ideas what he himself had accomplished in seven years of National Socialist rule.

•

SPEECH OF FEBRUARY 24, 1940

Munich

Background

1940

February 9—Roosevelt announces that he is sending Sumner Welles, Under-Secretary of State, to confer with the leaders of Italy, Germany, England, and France for the purpose of gathering information.

Cordell Hull announces that conversations have already

been engaged with several neutral countries to study the conditions of the future peace.

February 10—Roosevelt, speaking before the Youth Congress, denounces the Soviet aggression on Finland which he compares to similar acts of the Nazis.

February 16—Sweden rejects a Finnish demand for military aid.

February 17—The British raid a German prison ship, the *Altmark,* in a Norwegian fjord and rescue 326 prisoners.

The Speech

"MY GERMAN Comrades: Twenty years ago I appeared for the first time before the German public. That was the hardest and most dramatic decision of my life.

"Now again I stand among you. That in itself is remarkable. When I appeared before at that time I was not a pacifist; I am still a soldier.

"Our nation at that time had collapsed, which was unexampled in history. We were the victims of an enormous world deception, but we were not alone; the others were also deceived.

"They cheated the Arabs, but, incidentally, they also cheated the Jews. In their own States the victorious nations did not get what they expected.

"To be sure, most of all, our own German people were deceived. A world of equality, a world in which no arms would be needed and in which, therefore, eternal peace would rule.

"Germany laid down her arms because of the fourteen points. The German people at that time were deceived in their hope for a new organization of the world.

"Germany was without rights because she was defenseless. Germany at that time was a paradise but not for the German people, but for the Jews, the speculators, the exploiters, for the gangsters.

"We had at that time the rule of the victors as opposed to

the vanquished. We were, of course, not in a position to ask what we thought was due us. We had a democratic regime at that time, but this regime of ours was treated, perhaps, as it should have been treated, because it did not have the means to back up its words.

"We had approximately forty-six political parties, all trying to do their best to work in the interest of the German nation. Financial burdens were assumed by the regime for the purpose of rebuilding our nation; but these financial obligations were slowly turning into economic obligations.

"As far as I was concerned, at that time, I was of a strictly different opinion. I was of the opinion that things could not continue in that fashion. I decided that our political arena was nothing but the fighting arena for the various political factions. I realized that our government structure at that time was absolutely untenable, and that it could not be maintained.

"I realized above all, that bourgeois nationalist ideals were confronted and opposed by socialist principles. I realized that compromise in itself was impossible. I realized that only the victory of one side or the other could bring about a solution.

"But in all these internal upheavals of that period, in all the readjustments we were facing, I realized that there was one thing which was indestructible. And that one thing was the individual German, in other words, the German character.

"The German nation and the German character had proved their mettle during the four years of the World War. Proceeding from this point, I realized that out of all these political parties there had to arise the one, united German Reich, the one Reich of one unified will. It was necessary to call forth the best that is, and has always been, in the German nation.

"And that force, that strength inherent in the German people, was called forth at that memorable occasion twenty years ago. A great many things had to be brought about in order to assert this power. At that time, of course, it was principally a question of fighting our internal enemies.

"You all know that I had to face these battles in a fighting spirit. I was always willing to accomplish our ends through peaceful means, but force was essential whenever force was the only means by which our aims could have been accomplished.

"You all remember how we proceeded, step by step, starting here in this place, spreading over Bavaria, and from then on gradually extending over the nation as a whole. It was a fight which took us roughly thirteen years—thirteen years of struggle, crowned by ultimate success.

"After that time we were faced with the necessity of translating our initial success into wider results. You all know the things we accomplished in the fields of rebuilding the national character, in rebuilding our cities, in rehabilitating our unemployed. But then our democratic enemies began to tell us what to do.

"These people who tell us what to do are those who possess half the world, and they cannot even solve their own problems. Our reconstruction, on the other hand, has been accomplished entirely with our small resources, and we shall eventually and completely succeed without their help.

"It seems that these people, who rule half the world, believe that they are called upon by God to continue this rule, and as soon as anybody else lays claim to what they are honestly entitled they raise the cry that tyranny is the issue. God Almighty has not created the world for the English to dominate.

"We Germans lay no claim to world domination. We only ask to be left alone in our own living space. But, as far as this living space is concerned, we permit no interference. Of course, we also insist on our just share of our own colonies.

"At the time when the Arabs are protesting, Chamberlain steps up and says Germany is fighting for the supremacy of the world. This capitalistic, plutocratic conception, that there are only two kinds of people, the haves and the have-nots, will also be destroyed.

"The influence of England has not been perceptible in Central Europe. Central Europe has been built up by Germany and we won't suffer any threats in this Lebensraum of ours.

"Already during the Great War Churchill was one of the great warmongers, and at that time I was a very small man without political influence. We have therefore come from entirely different worlds.

"After the war these people carried on their business and made enormous profits through rearmament. Now these people have begun again with their warmongering. They again have the hopes that other people will fight for them and these hopes are in part well founded. So they have prepared this war in their own peculiar manner.

"One thing we know: Neither in a military nor in an economic way can Germany be defeated. Today we have nothing but leaders of the German people up to the very top. Today Germans achieve their standing through energy and not through birth. The German nation has regained confidence in itself. . . ."

"Is it not natural that they should hate me? If Eden or Chamberlain does not trust me, then I am proud of that fact, because to be respected and honored by them would mean that I am a traitor to the German nation.

"The hatred of my enemies does not concern me in the least. As I have fought inside Germany for a period of thirteen years in order to achieve harmony, so will I now fight our external enemies. Of course, they think that the affair of 1918 can be repeated. But little do they know what the present-day Germany is like.

"We are traveling along parallel lines with Italy because our interests are mutual. Likewise do we have a complete understanding with Russia. Of course, it is only natural that the English should feel horrible at not having been able to accomplish what we have done.

"But even Japan is today not on the side of our enemies. We can definitely say that, at least, they are friendly neutrals. . . ."

"It is the leadership of the German nation that counts. It is the leadership which must display the same courage as is expected to be displayed by the common soldier. And I am happy to say that, thank God, today we do have just such leadership.

"We are able to say at this time, with the utmost assurance, that militarily and economically, Germany today is invincible. As far as I am concerned, *I am nothing but the flint that strikes the spark out of the German nation.*

"Let us not forget that in our national effort, as we have exerted it in all these years, we have mobilized every ounce of energy there is within the total capacity of the Reich. We are a nation that is led by innumerable men, by innumerable leaders who, individually, do all in their power to maintain the Reich at the level of the might it displays today.

"The German nation has traversed a strenuous school of political education and it has emerged strong and purified. How sorrowful is the spectacle of English propaganda, trying to bring about the downfall of the German nation through sowing the seed of distrust. When these English propaganda voices are taking to the air their German accent sounds as peculiar as perhaps their own English sounds.

"They have got their war because they wanted it. Think of it, these people, these plutocratic warmongers, are the ones who believe that perhaps every twenty years they should be in a position to tell others how far they can develop. But now things are different this time; we are prepared to wage this war as long as it may last, to the bitter end.

"Furthermore, these people forget that during the World War they faced us in outspoken numerical superiority. But today everything is vastly changed. We are at the peak of our efficiency.

"But there is something else I believe, and that is that there is a God. This God has given the same right to all nations. And this God again has blessed our efforts during the past thirteen years.

"Some people, of course, call it luck; others, Providence. And others again speak of it as coincidence.

"I, however, believe that we are here dealing with divine justice. If you deal with people who have given everything they have, who have worked in the belief that they are right, then it cannot be but that Providence, our God, as I prefer to say, will not abandon such a nation.

"This God of whom I speak will not abandon us. He will guide us further along the path we have set our foot upon, and in this feeling of righteousness and justice we shall continue our efforts as we have begun them, certain that victory will be ours, because it is so ordained."

Press

Le Temps, February 26— . . . The speech of Chancellor Hitler said nothing new. The master of the Third Reich persists in his old mistakes, in the old crimes committed by him against the German people, against Europe, against humanity. His argument is the pretense that the "capitalist" powers wanted the war. . . . What is important from the political point of view is that Mr. Hitler has proclaimed that Germany needs Central Europe for her living space, and that in that living space which has been created by the Germans the Reich will permit no outside interference. . . .

New York Times— . . . Herr Hitler spoke for an hour, and while his speech was chiefly retrospective it was punctuated with fervent professions of faith in his people, which he said issued from the loyalty with which they followed him and accepted his policies. There was no reference to Germany's war aims or foreign policies except the recurring warning that Germany would no longer tolerate dictation and intimidations from abroad.

London Times, February 26— . . . Except of the accident that it was delivered on the same day (as a Chamberlain speech) there would be no reason whatever to take any notice of Hitler's latest speech . . . a feebler rehash of the speech he has already delivered fifty times. . . .

•

SPEECH OF MARCH 10, 1940

Berlin

Background

1940

February 25–March 21—Sumner Welles visits Rome, Berlin, Paris, London, and sails back for home.

March 11—Allies offer full aid to Finland.

March 12—Soviet-Finnish peace treaty is signed. Russia acquires Karelian Isthmus and a naval base at Hangoe.

The Speech

". . . THE power of decision and the daring, reckless courage of the great statesmen and army leaders of the past were no greater achievements than those expected of us today. In those days, too, statesmen and generals were loved by the gods only because they often dared and demanded the seemingly impossible.

"Scarcely one of the great battles of history bore visible evidence of its success or failure within itself at the outset.

Many an action that, judged from the point of view of numbers and material, should have led to victory ended in defeat because its leaders lacked the spirit to win and many others that, according to all human calculations, were foredoomed to destruction were later entered in history as most glorious victories.

"Nations are weighed in the spirit of their soldiers and are either found wanting and stricken from the book of life and history or found to be worthy of bearing new life. Our nation, with its difficult geo-political situation, was saved again and again only through the heroic actions of its men.

"We have lived for 2,000 years only because there were always men ready to stake all and, if necessary, sacrifice all for the common weal. But these heroes did not give their lives thinking thereby to free later generations of a like obligation. The achievements of the past would all be in vain if a single generation were lacking in strength or the will to make equal sacrifices.

"As a former soldier in the World War, I have only one humble boon to ask of Providence: May we be granted that the final chapter in the great conflict of nations be concluded with honor for our German nation."

Press

London Times, March 11, news article called "Hitler's melancholy mood"—The speech was suitable to the occasion, solemn in tone, and free from the Fuehrer's usual ranting. . . . Politically the speech was innocuous. . . .

PHASE VII

Blitzkrieg in the West

April, 1940 — October, 1940

COMMENT

"I HAVE already assured you, and all of you, my friends, know that if a long time elapses without my speaking, or if things seem quiet, this does not mean that I am doing nothing."

Thus spoke Adolf Hitler in the year 1940, and with ample justification. The soapbox orator of the early days has indeed little time to indulge in the art which enabled him to establish his domination over the German people and to lead them on the path of war and conquest. It would be too much to say that Hitler had given up speechmaking. He still knew that his voice was one of his strongest weapons, and that in an honest inventory of Germany's formidable war machine, his vocal chords should be listed as Item No. I.

But the extraordinary series of campaigns which, in less than four months, had brought the German armies to the northernmost tip of Norway and to the Spanish frontier, to Warsaw in Poland and to Brest in Britanny, are military exploits unequaled since Napoleon. And Hitler, the conqueror, was now too busy with military strategy and the actual battle to have much time left for oratory.

It cannot be shown as yet whether Hitler himself planned the military operations which brought about the conquest of Norway, Holland, Belgium, and the total defeat of what had —up to then—been considered the best fighting force in the world: the French Army. He himself, while rendering homage to his generals and his soldiers, claimed the credit for the timing of the operations and for their planning. In his war speeches, and particularly in the one of July 19, 1940, he dwelt with obvious satisfaction on a detailed and technical description of the military strategy which produced victory for his arms, without allowing anyone to doubt that he personally planned it all.

This new role of Hitler as the Supreme Commander was accepted and confirmed by all his subordinates and propagandists. Field Marshal Goering, speaking to the press on May 20, likened Hitler to Frederick the Great and said that he was wholly responsible for the plan of campaign. All phases of the offensive were worked out by him in advance, asserted Goering, even to the outlines of minor actions.

By the time France capitulated, Hitler's estimation of himself made him an equal to the greatest conquerors of the world, and when he gazed on the tomb of Napoleon, in the Invalides in Paris, there was little reason for him to be overawed by this silent confrontation. He had certainly done at least as well as that other "Little Corporal."

In fact he was doing even better and his ambition was greater. Because whereas Napoleon had not attempted to change the people he conquered nor their way of life, Hitler was now bent on revolutionizing not only Europe but the whole world. His purpose, or mission, was not only to extend the frontiers of the German Reich, but to spread the new doctrine of National Socialism—a dream which could not be achieved except by transforming the very nature of man.

This has always been implicit in the National Socialist ideology, but after the defeat of France the universality of National Socialism was openly proclaimed as an aim.

Writing in the *Angriff* on May 14, Robert Ley, head of the German Labor Front, said that "Hitler's God-given natural mission" was to make the world happy and reasonable. "He brought Germany to reason," wrote Robert Ley, "and thereby made us happy. We are convinced he will bring Europe and the world to reason and thereby make Europe and the world happy. That is his irrevocable mission."

But if Hitler was different from Napoleon—and much more like Mahomet—in his messianic conception of himself, he was to meet a problem not unlike the one that confronted the Emperor of the French after he failed to cross the Channel and had to carry on the war on the continent without the mastery of the seas.

The question of sea power against land power has never been solved conclusively, but history seems to have demonstrated, up to now, that the control of a continent such as Europe cannot be maintained successfully and for any length of time if the seas are dominated by another power.

This theory has been challenged several times in European history, the last time by Napoleon, and it is being challenged again by Hitler.

Naturally it would be foolish to assume that historical events can be fitted into any particular theory, and that if a theory has proved right several times, it will always prove right. But it is true that different nations have an implicit faith that the theory to which their nation is committed—for geographic and historical reasons—is the right one, and they usually will try over and over again to demonstrate that fact.

England being an island and dependent on her Empire *must* put her faith in the predominance of sea power. Continental powers, like France in the past or Germany today, *must* believe that land forces will assure their success whenever one of their leaders gets it into his mind that his mission is to go out and conquer the world.

Under modern conditions, these two basic theories have undergone profound modifications. The possibilities of regimented economy, such as conceived by the Nazis, and especially the potentialities of aerial warfare, have increased considerably the apparent chances of success of a continental power. Admiral Mahan's demonstration of the ultimate superiority of sea power is still considered valid by such nations as England and the United States (the doctrine of the "freedom of the seas" is its practical application), but contemporary German theorists, and among them Haushofer, the apostle of Geopolitik and the friend of Rudolf Hess, have perfected the contrary theory that continental domination must ultimately mean control of the seas also.

To use a familiar image, in the fight between the elephant and the whale the elephant has the final advantage—according to the modern German theorists.

Hitler has contributed greatly in perfecting the weapons which would permit a land power to establish its domination over the world without actually mastering the seas. Leaving aside the improvements of submarine warfare and the extensive possibilities of modern air warfare (bombing planes, parachutists, etc.), the use of propaganda and of psychological weapons have nullified, to a great extent, the sea defenses of his most distant enemies. Battleships may be able to stop an actual invasion if they control a body of water as large as the Atlantic. They cannot stop words and ideas which spread disunity and weaken a nation from the inside. The whale is powerless against the Trojan Horse.

Nevertheless, and in spite of the astounding success of Hitler's technique of conquest, in spite of the careful planning which helped him to defeat or outwit all his opponents one by one, it is obvious that from the earliest days of his career he showed doubt and hesitancy whenever he tried to define his attitude toward England and the British Empire.

Leaving aside the hypocritical pledges given time and time again in his speeches, the lies and the trickery of his strategic maneuvers, the program of Hitler insofar as it concerned continental Europe had followed a fairly clearly comprehensive pattern. The program was laid down in *Mein Kampf* and can be summed up in one sentence: Hitler was resolved that no other strong military power should exist on the continent of Europe, except Germany. This meant the destruction of the French Army and the elimination of France as a strong nation. It meant the reduction or the annexation of all other smaller countries, from the Arctic Circle to the Black Sea. It meant checking Russian expansion westward and eventually the control of its industrial and agricultural resources.

All this, in terms of Geopolitik, was plain sailing. Even the extension of German domination to Africa could be foreseen and achieved with the proper use of the "continental" methods of conquest. Hitler had plans for all these moves or contingencies and *Mein Kampf,* as well as his speeches, gives the impression that he is at ease—so to speak—in this kind of land strategy.

But when it comes to dealing with England and her Empire, one cannot escape the impression that, from the earliest days of his writing and speechmaking, Hitler had no clear idea as to the way to meet that problem.

According to *Mein Kampf,* Germany could have only two allies: Italy and Britain. Italy, of course, was brought into the Axis, but it is obvious that Hitler never understood why England resisted all his entreaties and his threats, nor why finally the British Empire made war upon him.

In innumerable speeches, the same refrain comes back: "I want to live on friendly terms with England. I want nothing from England (except the return of German colonies). I will even protect England against anyone. Why should England be concerned with what I am doing in Europe? Why am I forced to make war on England?" But another refrain is no less frequent: "England is the tyrant of the world. England is too rich. The British Empire must be destroyed. England is run by Jews and democrats. There can be no peace until England is defeated."

As late as July 19, 1940, after the conquest of France, Hitler expressed again—in one self-contradictory sentence—the predicament in which he found himself toward England—this queer ambivalent attitude of "wanting to be friends" and "wanting to kill." "Mr. Churchill ought, perhaps, for once to believe me when I prophesy that a great Empire will be destroyed"—said Hitler—"an Empire which it never was my intention to destroy or even to harm." But then Hitler, as a man who realizes that there is no other way out of his own dilemma, concludes: "I do, however, realize that this great struggle, if it continues, can only end with the complete annihilation of one or the other of the two adversaries."

Thus, at the height of his power, the conqueror of Europe had to admit that he could not dominate Europe as long as the mightiest maritime power, England and her Empire, still refused to recognize him as master of the continent. Whether Hitler did not intend originally to dominate the whole world—as he has frequently asserted—or whether he hoped to do so indirectly by forcing England into partnership with him, the fact remains that the refusal of England to lay down her arms, after the defeat of France, forced him to accept a challenge for which he had not fully prepared. The resistance of England compelled Hitler to extend his war effort indefinitely, "until the complete annihilation of one or the other of the adversaries."

If one keeps in mind this general aspect of the conflict, it becomes apparent that, for the first time perhaps, the grand strategy of Hitler went wrong precisely at the moment when he seemed to have achieved his most spectacular triumphs.

The conquest of Poland, the invasion of the Scandinavian peninsula, and the destruction of the French armies were part of a coherent program aimed at obtaining a rapid and total victory and finishing the war. To fulfill this program, all the plans had been carefully made a long time in advance—not only by Hitler but by the German High Command. Within the limits of that program everything worked like clockwork, including the psychological weapons. In fact, the effectiveness of Hitler's strategy proved even greater than he himself, perhaps, expected. Not only did the mechanized divisions and the Luftwaffe assert their irresistible superiority over the old-fashioned methods of the French system of defense, but the moral disintegration of the French people was found to be infinitely more advanced than could have been suspected. Years of "war of nerves," ten months of "phony war," treason, disunity, and "fifth column" activity of all kinds had done their work. France, under the attack, collapsed in forty-five days. And it is difficult to say whether that unprecedented result is to be attributed more to the actual power of the invading armies or to the internal forces of disruption, which—like time-bombs—had been set years in advance.

The occupation of Paris on June 14, 1940, followed by the armistice of June 22, should—according to all historic precedents—have put an end to the whole war. There is little doubt that all the participants in this drama were firmly convinced that England would not and could not carry on the war after the defeat of her main ally. The occupation of two-thirds of France, and particularly of the whole coast, completed the encirclement of the British Isles. England had no army left on the continent and no visible means of building up her home defenses in time. Under such circumstances, further resistance was hopeless.

Such was the judgment of Mussolini, for instance, who entered the war on June 10 completely unprepared—as proved later—to fight for more than a few weeks. Such was the conviction of the French generals and politicians, who could not possibly have signed the fateful armistice of Compiègne had they not been convinced that the defeat of France meant the end of the war.

And such apparently was also the opinion of Hitler, who having finally reached the Channel and the Atlantic, had good reason to believe that England, recognizing the senselessness of further resistance, would surrender. The prodigious rapidity with which Hitler had conquered the continent should establish once for all the principle of his invincibility. If he had been able to defeat in less than a month the strongest army of Europe, what chance had England? If he had entered Paris on June 14—as predicted—why shouldn't he be in London before the summer was over?

The psychological effect of announcing in advance his schedule which had worked so well—up to now—was tried once more. German propaganda announced that Hitler would be in London on August 15, and then on September 15. But after that, no date was set. In his speech of September 4, Hitler said that he had no timetable any longer. "Britain is preparing for a three-year war," he said, "and I have told the Reich Marshal: 'Goering, we must be prepared for a five-year war.' "

The last effort made by Hitler to bring the war to a quick end was the massive air raids over London of August and September. Their purpose was apparently to break the British morale and destroy the R.A.F. If this had succeeded, an invasion might have been fairly easy, even with the limited supply of transport ships that Hitler then possessed. From the point of view of military strategy, this was the last attempt to conquer a sea power with the same technique by which continental countries had been conquered. The Luftwaffe had been used once more as the spearhead of the tanks and motorized divisions. But the land forces could not follow through. Hitler's boast that "there were no more islands" proved wrong—at least for the time being—and from then on he had to revise completely his plan of conquest. The unforeseen stubbornness of England brought Hitler rather abruptly to face a new phase of the war and forced him to try his own hand at solving one of the oldest riddles of history: can one conquer and hold the land without ruling the seas?

The reasons why England refused to surrender to Hitler—thus upsetting the predictions of all concerned—are not all to be found in the opposition of land strategy against sea power. Far from it. It is true that the Channel is wider than the Meuse or the Somme, and that to cross it presented technical problems for which the German High Command had made no adequate preparations. But the real reasons for Hitler's failure to end the war on schedule are of a totally different order. They are psychological, and can be summed up quite simply: For the first time since he came to power, Hitler found himself face to face with a people who were actually ready to die rather than surrender, and who were led by a man whom Hitler could hate but could not despise and who could not, by any stretch of the imagination, be included in the collection of "zeros" which Hitler so scathingly denounced as being his usual opponents.

There are really no points of comparison between Adolf Hitler, the son of an obscure Austrian customs official, and Winston Churchill, the grandson of the seventh Duke of Marlborough. One is an adventurer whose extraordinary rise to power is due as much to the accidents of a historic world crisis as to his own fanatical belief in his mission as the redeemer of his country and of the world. The other is the most perfect product of British aristocratic training, a man who was born to greatness and whose whole life is dedicated to the study of politics, history, and military affairs. While Hitler was nothing but an obscure corporal in the war of 1914-18, Churchill was already running that war. Hitler is without learning, uncouth and untraveled. However effective his eloquence, his vocabulary is more than ordinary, his grammar incorrect, and his accent unpleasant to cultured Germans' ears. Churchill has traveled all over the world. He is a great scholar and his speeches will remain as models of English oratory. Hitler is the incarnation of the irrational spirit of the masses. Churchill is the product of twenty centuries of what we recognize as "civilization." They are poles apart.

And yet they have one strange point in common: their absolute faith in the greatness of their respective people and their will to fight until victory is achieved.

No doubt there is a complete difference in the quality of Churchill's faith in his people and that of Hitler's. The two men are inspired by motives which cannot possibly be compared. But there is a certain similarity in their ability to create courage out of despair, strength out of weakness, the will to conquer out of defeat.

Hitler has laughed at the English because they said that each new defeat strengthened them and therefore brought them nearer to ultimate victory. Hitler said he preferred successes. But Hitler himself started from a deeper abyss than Churchill found himself in the spring of 1940, and he, too, when he began to rouse the Germans with his party of seven men, could have said, "I have nothing to offer you but blood, tears, sweat, and toil."

The transformation of the British people was as sudden as it was incomprehensible to Hitler and his advisers. This certainly had not been foreseen by the Fuehrer. It has often been said that the strength of the British resides in the fact that they do not know when they are beaten. This may be so, but the peculiar quality of the British morale, as it manifested itself after Dunkirk, was of a kind to upset completely the Hitlerian technique of conquest. Their new unity was real, and it seemed that intimidation and the strategy of terror could not prevail against it. Ribbentrop's prophecy that England would not fight, and that of all the prey it was the easiest, had not been fulfilled.

At the height of his glory, and after the futile attempt to cow the English with the terror from the air, Hitler made up his mind—reluctantly—that he would have to carry on the war until one of the two Empires—his own or the British—was destroyed.

The conquest of continental Europe was practically achieved with the downfall of France. Nothing was left but to mop up the Balkans. But the real Second World War started then.

This first important setback of Hitler, which can now be judged in retrospect, was not clearly visible at the time. The conviction that England could not resist more than a few weeks or months at the best persisted all through the fall and winter. In many quarters this conviction gave a new impetus to the defeatist and appeasement spirit both in Europe and in America.

The American isolationists found in the probable—if not certain—downfall of England new arguments to slow up or stop altogether the help given to England. It was useless to back a loser, they said, and the only hope of salvation for America was to build her home defenses and wait.

Simultaneously the appeasers found a new and subtle ally in the Government of Marshal Pétain which, after having signed the armistice, moved to Vichy.

As has been indicated before, the chief reason why the French generals and politicians asked for an armistice was because they were convinced that the end of the war in France meant the end of the war everywhere. They hoped that France would be favorably treated by the German victor because she had been so prompt to recognize Hitler as the master of Europe.

The unforeseen resistance of England upset these calculations, and after a period during which the Pétain Government assumed an attitude of neutrality, they were gradually forced to transform the defeat into a reversal of alliance. The Vichy Government embarked on the policy of so-called "collaboration" which was ultimately to mean a policy of helping Germany against England, with the purpose of hastening the peace as the only means of saving France.

The fact that the great majority of the French people were still placing all their hopes in a British victory could not offset the psychological effect of having the Vichy Government accept and work for a German victory. France, tied as it was by traditional friendship with America, became a kind of broker for the appeasers and defeatists of both continents. Marshal Pétain and his associates re-echoed Hitler's words when he said "I cannot see why this war must go on."

The men of Vichy could not see why the war should go on because their own decision to capitulate had no justification if the war did go on.

Thus, in spite of the necessity for Hitler to reorganize all his plans on the basis of a long war, he remained faithful to his favorite strategy of utilizing every sign of weakness in his opponents, every vestige of the old errors to spread confusion, doubt, and division.

His speeches are less frequent, and the world is less interested in what he has to say, but through all the changing events and the varying fortunes of a mortal struggle, one senses in Hitler the same urge to move forward, to break all obstacles because there is no other solution left for him now than to conquer the world.

•

SPEECH OF JULY 19, 1940

Berlin, Reichstag

Background

1940

March 20—French Premier Daladier resigns after receiving only 239 votes against 300 abstentions on a vote of confidence.

March 22—Paul Reynaud becomes premier and forms a cabinet composed of thirty-three ministers and secretaries of state. The Chamber gives Paul Reynaud an effective majority of only one vote.

March 28—Sumner Welles returns to America.

The Interallied Supreme War Council meets in London and decides 1.) that there shall be no separate peace; 2.) that the Franco-British agreements will continue after the war and as long as they are necessary for the security of the world.

March 30—President Roosevelt declares that the reports brought back by Sumner Welles show that there is no possibility of peace for the moment.

The Germans publish a White Book containing sixteen documents, allegedly seized in the archives of Warsaw, and showing that several American ambassadors (particularly William Bullitt and Joseph Kennedy) have encouraged the Allies and the Poles to go to war. President Roosevelt says that these documents are forgeries.

April 4—Winston Churchill gets general supervision over the British fighting forces.

The Scandinavian Campaign

April 8—The Allies announce laying mine field off Norway to close a loophole in the blockade.

April 9—German armed forces invade Denmark and Norway. King Christian of Denmark offers no resistance and the whole country is occupied in one day.

The Norwegians resist and succeed in sinking several German battleships in the Oslofjord. Nevertheless the Germans enter Oslo. Simultaneously several Norwegian ports fall into German hands, either through treason or direct occupation by German forces.

King Haakon of Norway flees from his capital after having rejected a German ultimatum presented to him at the same moment as the attack.

A puppet government under Quisling is set up in Oslo.

April 12—British fleet tries to intercept German communications in the Skagerrak.

April 15—A small British force lands in Namsos, Norway.

April 19—More British landings in Namsos, Aandalsnes and Narvik.

April 30—Germans capture Dombas, enabling the German forces coming down from Trondheim to join with those coming up from Oslo, and forcing the Allies to retreat North.

May 2-3—Chamberlain announces the evacuation of Aandalsnes and Namsos, thus admitting the loss of the whole of central and southern Norway. The Allies will try to maintain their foothold in Narvik where the Germans are still resisting. (Narvik was finally occupied by the Allies on May 28 but abandoned on June 9. The remnants of the Norwegian Army surrendered and King Haakon took refuge in London.)

Interlude

May 7-8—Chamberlain defends his policy before the Commons. He is violently attacked by the Opposition. Critics cry: "*You* missed the bus!" Leopold S. Amery, a Conservative, quotes Oliver Cromwell, saying: "You have sat too long here for any good you have been doing. Depart, I say. Let us have done with you. In the name of God, go!" Lloyd George speaks out: "The Prime Minister must remember that he has met this foe of ours in peace and in war, and he has always been worsted." Winston Churchill, First Lord of the Admiralty, attempts to defend the Cabinet. The vote for support of the Cabinet shows 281 for, 200 against.

May 10—Neville Chamberlain tenders his resignation to the King. Winston Churchill heads a coalition Cabinet.

Collapse in the West

May 10—Holland, Belgium and Luxembourg are invaded by the German armies. The Belgians and the Dutch appeal for help from the Allies. French and British troops are rushed into the Lowlands.

President Roosevelt, answering an appeal of King Leopold, speaks of "American anger" and denounces isolationism.

May 13—German troops reach Rotterdam cutting the Netherlands in two. Rotterdam has been submitted to a terrific air bombarment.

May 14—The Dutch armies give up resistance.

May 15—Battle of the Meuse. The French Ninth Army is defeated.

May 16—President Roosevelt, addressing Congress, requests an additional credit of $1,182,000,000 for defense.

May 17—The Germans occupy Brussels. In France the advance continues. General Gamelin issues an order reminiscent of the one issued by General Joffre just before the battle of the Marne.

May 18—Premier Reynaud brings Marshal Pétain into his Cabinet, as Vice-Premier. In a broadcast to the nation he says the situation is "serious but not desperate."

The 21 American Republics publish a statement protesting against the German invasion of the Low countries.

Mussolini replies in a non-committal way to a message that President Roosevelt had addressed to him a few days before.

May 19—General Maxime Weygand replaces General Gamelin as generalissimo of the Allied armies.

The allied forces are in retreat on the whole front.

Winston Churchill in a world broadcast summons the British people to total war. He announces that Paul Reynaud has given him assurances that, whatever happens, France will fight to the end.

Charles Lindbergh, in a speech, declares that the United States "must stop this hysterical chatter of calamity and invasion." He says that the United States cannot be invaded.

May 21—The Germans reach the Channel at Abbéville, cutting off the Allied armies in Flanders.

Paul Reynaud, speaking before the French Senate, says that "the country is in danger" and accuses certain army chiefs of having committed "unbelievable errors." He denounces "traitors, defeatists and cowards."

The Fall of Paris

May 22—The British Parliament passes the "Emergency Powers Act, 1940" giving the Government right to conscript every person and every piece of property in the realm.

May 28—Belgian armies surrender on King Leopold's orders.

May 29-June 4—Evacuation of Dunkirk by British troops.

June 3—German planes bomb Paris.

June 4—Speaking in Commons, Winston Churchill admits that the Belgian campaign was "a colossal military disaster" but states that the war is going on until victory.

June 5—The Germans attack the French on the Somme.

June 10—Italy declares war on the Allies.

The Germans cross the Seine, West of Paris.

President Roosevelt, speaking on the radio, reviews the efforts made by America to keep Italy out of the war and refers to Mussolini's decision as "a stab in the back."

In a message to Roosevelt, Paul Reynaud asks the President to send more aid and to declare publicly that he will support the Allies by all means "short of an expeditionary force."

June 11—The French Government moves to Tours.

June 12—Meeting in a chateau near Tours, the French Cabinet hears a report from General Weygand who says that the situation is desperate. The question of an armistice arises.

June 13—Another appeal for more help (particularly planes) is sent to Roosevelt by Paul Reynaud.

June 14—Paris falls.

June 16—The French Government moves to Bordeaux.

The British propose the creation of an "Anglo-French Union."

The French Cabinet votes by thirteen to eleven for an armistice. Paul Reynaud resigns.

June 17—Marshal Pétain heads the new Cabinet. In a broadcast, he announces that he has asked for an armistice.

June 18—Speaking from London, General de Gaulle asks the French people to continue the fight and denounces the new French Government.

June 20—Marshal Pétain, in a broadcast, states that his government will not leave the soil of France.

June 22—A Franco-German armistice is signed in the forest of Compiègne in the presence of Hitler.

June 24—A Franco-Italian armistice is signed. Hostilities cease.

After the Defeat of France

June 27—Rumania cedes Bessarabia and Northern Bukovina to Russia.

July 4—The British fleet attacks the French fleet in Oran and sinks several ships, damaging others.

July 6—France breaks diplomatic relations with England.

July 10—Roosevelt submits to Congress a $4,800,000,000 defense program.

July 14—Churchill declares that Britain will carry on the fight for years.

The Speech

"MEMBERS of the Reichstag! I have summoned you to this meeting in the midst of our tremendous struggle for the freedom and the future of the German nation.

"I have done so, firstly, because I consider it imperative to give our own people an insight into the events, unique in history, that lie behind us; secondly, because I wish to express my gratitude to our magnificent soldiers, and thirdly, with the intention of appealing once more, and for the last time, to common sense in general.

"If we compare the causes which prompted this historic struggle, and the magnitude and the far-reaching effects of military events, we are forced to the conclusion that its general course and the sacrifices it has entailed are out of all proportion to the alleged reasons for its outbreak, unless they were nothing but a pretext for underlying intentions.

"The program of the National Socialist Movement, insofar as it affected the future development of the Reich's relations with the rest of the world, is simply an attempt to bring about a definite revision of the Treaty of Versailles, though as far as at all possible this was to be accomplished by peaceful means. This revision was absolutely essential.

"The conditions imposed at Versailles were intolerable, not only because of their humiliating discrimination and because the disarmament which they insured deprived the German nation of all its rights, but far more so because of the consequent destruction of the material existence of one of the great civilized nations of the world and the proposed annihilation of its future, the utterly senseless accumulation of immense tracts of territory under the domination of a number of states, the theft of all the irreparable foundations of life and indispensable vital necessities from a conquered nation.

"Even while this Dictate was being drawn up, men of insight, even among our foes, were uttering warnings about the terrible consequences which the ruthless application of its insane conditions would entail, a proof that even among them the conviction predominated that such a Dictate could not possibly be upheld in days to come. Their objections and protests were silenced by the assurance that the Statutes of the newly created League of Nations provided for the revision of these conditions. In fact, the League was supposed to be the competent authority. The hope of revision was thus at no time regarded as presumption but as something natural.

"Unfortunately, the Geneva institution, as those responsible for Versailles had intended, never looked upon itself as a body competent to undertake any sensible revision, but from the very outset as nothing more than the guarantor of the ruthless enforcement and maintenance of the conditions imposed at Versailles. All attempts made by democratic Germany to obtain equality for the German people by revision of the Treaty proved unavailing.

"It is always in the interest of the conqueror to represent stipulations that are to his advantage as sacrosanct, while the instinct of self-preservation in the vanquished leads him to acquire the common human rights that he has lost. For him, the dictate of an overbearing conqueror has all the less legal force since he has never been honorably conquered. Owing to a rare misfortune, the German Empire between 1914-1918 lacked good leadership. To this, and to the as yet unenlightened faith and trust placed by the German people in the words of democratic statesmen our downfall was due.

"Hence, the Franco-British claim that the Dictate of Versailles was a sort of international, holy, supreme code of laws appeared to be nothing more than a piece of insolent arrogance to every honest German. The assumption, however, that British or French statesmen should actually claim to be the guardians of justice, and even of human culture, is mere stupid effrontery—a piece of effrontery that is thrown into a sufficiently glaring light by their own extremely negligible achievements in this direction.

"Seldom have any countries in the world been ruled with a lesser degree of wisdom, morality and culture than those which are at this moment exposed to the ragings of certain democratic statesmen.

"The program of the National Socialist Movement, besides freeing the Reich from the innermost fetters of a small substratum of Jewish, capitalistic and pluto-democratic profiteers, proclaimed to the world our resolution to shake off the shackles of the Versailles Dictate. Germany's demands for this revision were a vital necessity and essential to the existence and honor of every great nation. They will probably one day be regarded by posterity as extremely reasonable.

"In practice, all these demands had to be carried through contrary to the will of the Franco-British rulers. We all regarded it as a sure sign of successful leadership in the Third Reich, that for years we were able to effect this revision without a war. Not that, as the British and French demagogues asserted, we were at that time incapable of fighting. When, thanks to growing common sense, it finally appeared as though international co-operation might lead to a peaceful solution of the remaining problems, the agreement to this end signed in Munich on September 29, 1938, by the four leading interested States was not only not welcomed in London and Paris but was actually condemned as a sign of abominable weakness.

"Now that peaceful revision threatened to be crowned with success the Jewish, capitalist warmongers, their hands stained with blood, saw their tangible pretext for realizing their diabolical plans vanish into thin air. Once again we witness the conspiracy of wretched, corruptible, political creatures and money-grabbing financial magnates, for whom war was a welcome means of furthering their business. ends. The poison scattered by the Jews throughout the nations began to exercise its disintegrating influence on sound common sense. Scribblers concentrated upon decrying honest men who wanted peace, as weaklings and traitors, and upon denouncing the opposition parties as the 'fifth column,' thus breaking all internal resistance to their criminal war policy.

"Jews and Freemasons, armaments manufacturers and war profiteers, international business men, stock exchange jobbers seized upon political hirelings of the desperado type who described war as something infinitely desirable. It was the work of these criminal persons that the Polish state was spurred on to adopt an attitude that was out of all proportion to Germany's demands, still less with the attendant consequences.

"For Pre-eminently in its dealings with Poland, the German Reich had exercised genuine self-restraint since the National Socialist regime came into power.

"One of the most despicable and foolish measures of the Versailles Dictate, namely the severance of an old German province from the Reich, was crying out aloud for revision. But what were my requests? I name myself in this connection because no other statesman might have dared to propose a solution such as mine to the German nation. It merely required the return of Danzig, an ancient and purely-German city, to the Reich and the creation of a means of communication between the Reich and its severed province. Even this was to be decided by a plebiscite, subject to the control of an international body. If Mr. Churchill and the rest of the war-mongers had felt a fraction of the responsibility toward Europe that inspired me they could never have begun their infamous game.

"It was only due to these other European and non-European powers and their war interests that Poland rejected my proposals which in no way affected either her honor or existence, and in their stead had recourse to terror and to the sword.

"In this case we once more showed unexampled and truly superhuman self-control, since for months, despite murderous attacks on minority Germans, and even despite the slaughter of tens of thousands of our German fellow-countrymen, we still sought for an understanding by peaceful means.

"What was the situation? One of the most unnatural creations of the Dictate of Versailles, puffed up with political and military pomp, insults another state for months on end and threatens to grind it to powder, to fight battles on the outskirts of Berlin, to hack the German armies to pieces, to extend its frontiers to the Oder or the Elbe and so forth. Meanwhile the other State, Germany, watches this tumult in patient silence, although a single movement of her arms would have sufficed to prick this bubble, inflated with folly and hatred.

"On September 2, the conflict might still have been averted. Mussolini proposed a plan for the immediate cessation of all hostilities and for peaceful negotiations. Though Germany saw her armies storming to victory, I nevertheless accepted this proposal. It was only the Franco-British war-mongers who desired war—not peace. More than that, as Mr. Chamberlain said, they needed a long war because they had now invested their capital in armament shares, had purchased machinery, and required time for the development of their business interests and the amortization of their investments. For, after all, what do these citizens of the world care about Poles, Czechs or such-like people?

"On June 19, 1940, a German soldier found a curious document when searching some railway trucks standing in the station of La Charité. As the document bore a distinctive inscription, he immediately handed it over to his commanding officer. It was then passed on to other quarters, where it was soon realized that we had lighted on an important discovery.

"The station was subjected to another, more thoroughgoing search. Thus it was that the German High Command gained possession of a collection of documents of unique historical significance. They were the secret documents of the Allied Supreme War Council, and included the minutes of every meeting held by this illustrious body.

"This time Mr. Churchill will not succeed in contesting or lying about the veracity of these documents as he tried to do when documents were discovered in Warsaw.

"These documents bear marginal notes inscribed by Messrs. Gamelin, Daladier, Weygand and others. They can, thus, at any time, be confirmed or refuted by these very gentlemen. They further give remarkable evidence of the machinations of the warmongers and war-extenders. Above all, they show that those stony-hearted politicians regarded all the small nations as a means to their ends; that they had attempted to use Finland in their own interest; that they had determined to turn Norway and Sweden into a theater of war; that they had planned to fan a conflagration in the Balkans in order to gain the assistance of a hundred divisions from those countries; that they had planned the bombardment of Batum and Baku by ruthless and unscrupluous interpretation of Turkey's neutrality, who was not unfavorable to them; that they inveigled Belgium and the Netherlands more and more completely, until they finally entrapped them into binding General Staff agreements, and so on and so forth.

"The documents further give a picture of the dilettante measures by which these political warmongers tried to quench the blaze which they had lighted; of their democratic militarism, which is in part to blame for the appalling fate that they have inflicted on hundreds of thousands, even millions, of their own soldiers; of their barbarous unscrupulousness, which caused them callously to force mass evacuation of their peoples which brought them no military advantages, though the effects on the population were outrageously cruel. These same criminals are responsible for having driven Poland into war. Eighteen days later this campaign was to all intents and purposes at an end.

"On October 6, 1939, at this very place, I addressed the German nation for the second time during this war. I was able to inform them of our glorious military victory over the Polish State. At the same time I appealed to the insight of the responsible men in the enemy states, and to the nations themselves. *I warned them not to continue this war, the consequences of which could only be devastating. I particularly warned the French of embarking on a war which would forcibly eat its way across the frontier, and which, irrespective of its outcome, would have appalling consequences.* At the same time, I addressed this appeal to the rest of the world, although I feared as I expressly stated, that my words would not be heard, and would more than ever arouse the fury of the interested warmongers.

"*Everything happened as I predicted.* Responsible elements in Britain and France scented, in any appeal, a dangerous attack on their war profits. They therefore immediately began to declare that every thought of a conciliation was out of the question, nay even a crime, that the war had to be pursued in the name of civilization, of humanity, of happiness, of progress and, to leave no stone unturned, in the name of religion itself. For this purpose Negroes and bushmen were to be mobilized. Victory, they then said, would come of its own accord. It was in fact within their easy reach, as I myself must know very well, and have known for a long time since, or I should not have broadcast my appeal for peace throughout the world. For if I had had any justification for believing in victory, I should never have proposed an understanding with Britain and France without making any demands.

"In a very few days these agitators had succeeded in representing me to the rest of the world as a veritable coward. For this peace proposal of mine I was abused, and personally insulted. Mr. Chamberlain, in fact, spat upon me before the eyes of the world, and following the instructions of the instigators and warmongers in the background,—men such as Churchill, Duff Cooper, Eden, Hore-Belisha and others—declined even to mention peace, let alone to work for it. Thus this ultra-capitalistic clique of people with a personal interest in the war clamored out for its continuance. This is now taking place.

"I have already assured you, and all of you, my friends, know that if a long time elapses without my speaking or if things seem quiet this does not mean that I am doing nothing. With us it is not necessary, as it is in the democracies, to multiply every airplane that is built by five or by twelve, and then broadcast it to the world. Even for a hen it is not clever to announce in a loud voice every egg she is about to lay. However, it is very much more stupid for statesmen to babble to the world of projects which they have in mind, thereby informing them in good time. It is thanks to the excited chattering of two of these great democratic statesmen that we have been kept informed as to our enemy's plans for extending the war and their concentration on Norway and Sweden.

"While this Anglo-French war fleet was looking around to find new possibilities of extending the war or roping in new victims, I was working to complete the reorganization of the German forces, to form new units, to accelerate production of war material and to complete the training of the entire naval, military and air forces for their new tasks. Apart from that, the bad weather in late autumn and the winter necessitated the postponement of military operations. During March, however, we received information about Anglo-French intentions of intervening in the Russo-Finnish conflict, presumably not so much for the sake of helping the Finns, as in order to damage Russia which was regarded as a power working with Germany. These intentions developed into the decision to take an active part, if at all possible, in the Finnish war in order to obtain a base for carrying the war into the Baltic. At the same time, however, the proposals of the Allied Supreme War Council became more and more insistent, either to set the Balkans and Asia Minor on fire in order to cut off Germany's supply of oil from Russia and Rumania, or to obtain possession of the Swedish iron ore. With this object in view, a landing was to have been made in Norway with the main object of occupying the iron ore railway leading from Narvik across Sweden to the port of Lulea.

"The conclusion of peace between Russia and Finland caused the contemplated action in the Northern States to be withheld at the last moment; but a few days later these intentions again became more definite and a final decision was reached. Britain and France had agreed to carry out an immediate occupation of a number of the most important points in Norway under the pretext of preventing Germany from benefiting from further war supplies of Swedish ore. In order to secure this Swedish ore entirely, they intended to march into Sweden and to deal with the small forces which Sweden was in a position to assemble, if possible in a friendly way, but with force if necessary.

"That this danger was imminent we learned through the uncontrollable verbosity of no less a person than the First Lord of the Admiralty. We received further confirmation of this through a hint given by the French Premier, Mr. Reynaud, to a foreign diplomat. Until a short time ago, however, we were unaware that the date for this action had already been twice postponed before the 8th of April and that the occupation was to have taken place on the 8th, this being the third and final date. In fact, this was not definitely confirmed until the finding of the records of the Allied Supreme War Council. As soon as the danger of the Northern States being dragged into the war became apparent, I gave the necessary orders to the German forces. The case of the *Altmark* showed, at the time, that the Norwegian Government were not prepared to safeguard their neutrality. Reports from observers made it clear, moreover, that there was complete agreement, at least between the leading men of the Norwegian Government and the Allies.

"Finally the reaction of Norway to the penetration of British minelayers into Norwegian territorial waters dispelled the last shadow of doubt. This was the signal for the commencement of the German operation which had been prepared in every detail.

"Actually the position was different from what we believed it to be on April 9. Whereas at that time we believed that we had anticipated the British occupation by a few hours, today we know that the landing of the British troops had been planned for the 8th, and that the embarkation of the British units had already commenced on the 5th and 6th. However, at the same moment, the first news of the German action, or rather of the departure of the German fleet, was received at the British Admiralty and in view of this fact, Mr. Churchill decided to order the disembarkation of the units which were already on board ship so that the British fleet could first seek out and attack the German vessels. This attempt failed; only a single British destroyer came into contact with German naval vessels and was sunk before it could convey any information to the British Admiralty or to the British fleet. Thus followed the landing of the first German detachments on the 9th in an area stretching from Oslo northwards to Narvik. When information of this was received in London, Mr.

Churchill had already been anxiously waiting for some hours to hear of the successes of his fleet.

"This blow, gentlemen, is the boldest undertaking in the history of the German forces.

"The successful execution became possible, only thanks to the command and conduct of all German soldiers taking part. The achievements of our three services, Army, Navy and Air Force in this fight for Norway are expressive of the highest military qualities. The Navy carried out the operations assigned to it, and, later on, the transport of troops, against an enemy who, altogether, possessed ten-fold superiority. All the units of our young German Navy have covered themselves, in this action, with imperishable glory. Not until after the war will it be possible to disclose the difficulties encountered in this campaign in the way of setbacks, losses and accidents. That they finally overcame all difficulties is due to the conduct of both officers and men. The Air Force, which was often the only means of transport and communication in this enormous area, surpassed itself in every respect. The daring attacks on the enemy, on ships, and on disembarked troops can hardly be more highly praised than the tenacity and courage displayed by those transport pilots who, in spite of dirty weather, kept on flying in the Land of the Midnight Sun in order to land soldiers and throw down supplies, often in blinding snow-storms.

"The Norwegian fjords have become the graveyard of many a British warship. The British fleet was finally obliged to yield before the incessant, violent attacks of German dive-bombers and evacuate those territories of which it had been stated, with excellent taste, in a British paper a few weeks previously, that it would be a pleasure for Britain to take up the German challenge.

"Great demands were made of the soldiers already during transport. Air-landing troops provided the first foothold at many places. Division after division followed in a stream and commenced war operations in a territory which provided exceptional facilities for resistance on account of its natural characteristics and, so far as Norwegian units were concerned, was very bravely defended. As regards the British troops landed in Norway, the only remarkable fact worth mentioning was the unscrupulousness with which troops, so poorly equipped and trained and under such inadequate leadership, were put ashore as an expeditionary force. They were definitely inferior from the very outset. On the other hand, the achievements of the German infantry, the engineers, of our artillery, our signallers and other units will go down in history as a proud example of heroism. The word "Narvik" will forever be immortalized as a magnificent testimony to the spirit of the armed forces of the National Socialist Reich.

"Messrs. Churchill, Chamberlain and Daladier were, until recently, very badly informed in regard to the nature of German unity. I announced at the time that the future would probably teach them a lesson, and I may with safety assume that more than anything else the action of mountain troops from Austria on this, the most northerly front of our struggle for freedom, will have furnished them with the necessary information in regard to the Reich and its sons. . . ."

"Before the campaign in Norway had come to an end, the news from the West became more and more threatening. Though actually before the outbreak of war plans had been made to break through the Maginot Line in the event of an unavoidable conflict with France and Britain—an undertaking for which the German troops had been trained, and for which they were equipped with the necessary arms—the necessity became evident, in the course of the first months of the war, of envisaging some action against Belgium or Holland if need be. Whereas Germany, at first, had hardly concentrated any forces near the frontiers of Holland and Belgium —apart from the troops necessary for her security—while otherwise extending her system of fortifications, noticeable concentration of French forces was taking place along the Franco-Belgian frontier. The massing of practically all the tank divisions and mechanized divisions in this sector in particular, indicated the intention—in any case, however, the possibility—of their being thrown forward in a lightning dash through Belgium to the German frontier. The following facts, however, now made the matter definite.

"Whereas, given a fair and proper interpretation of Belgian and Dutch neutrality, both countries would have been compelled to turn their attention towards the West in view of the concentration of very powerful Anglo-French forces on their frontier, they both commenced to reduce their own forces there in order to man the German frontier. At the same time the news of the General Staff conversations that were proceeding, threw a peculiar light on Belgian and Dutch neutrality. There is no need for me to emphasize that these conversations should have been carried on with both sides if they had been really neutral. For the rest, there was such an accumulation of signs pointing to an advance of Anglo-French troops through Holland and Belgium against the German industrial districts, that this threat now had to be regarded by us as a most serious danger.

"I therefore acquainted the German forces with the possibility of such a development and gave them the necessary, detailed instructions. In numerous discussions in the Army High Command with the Commanders-in-Chief of the three services, the group of army commanders, down to the chiefs of important individual units, the various tasks were allotted and discussed and applied with every understanding as a basis for special training of the troops. The whole German plan of advance was accordingly altered. The careful observations which had been made everywhere, gradually compelled us to realize that an Anglo-French thrust was to be expected at any moment after the beginning of May. Between May 6 and 7 fears that the advance of the Allies into Holland and Belgium could be expected any moment were multiplied, particularly on account of telephone messages between London and Paris which had come to our knowledge. The following day, on the 8th, I therefore gave orders for immediate attack at 5:35 in the morning, on May 10.

"The basic idea for these operations was, disregarding small unimportant successes, so to dispose the entire forces, principally the Army and the Air Force, that the total destruction of the Anglo-French Armies would be the inevitable consequence, so long as the operations provided for in the plan were correctly executed.

"In contradiction to the Schlieffen Plan of 1914, I arranged for the operations to bear mainly on the left wing of the front, where the break-through was to be made, though ostensibly retaining the principles of the opposite plan. This strategy succeeded. The establishment of the entire plan of operations was made easier for me, of course, by the measures adopted by the enemy himself. For the concentration of the entire Anglo-French mechanized forces along the Belgian frontier, made it appear certain that the High Command of the Allied Armies had resolved to proceed into this area as rapidly as possible. Relying upon the powers of resistance of all the German infantry divisions employed in the operation, a blow directed at the right flank of the Anglo-French Motorized Army Corps must, in these circumstances, lead to the complete destruction and breaking up, in fact, probably to the surrounding, of the enemy forces. As a second operation, I had planned to aim for the Seine and LeHavre and also to secure a position on the Somme and the Aisne, from which a third attack could be made, this attack being intended to advance across the plateau of Langres to the Swiss frontier with the heaviest forces. At the conclusion of the operations, it was intended to reach the coast south of Bordeaux. The operations were carried out in accordance with this plan and in this order.

"The success of this—the most tremendous series of battles in the history of the world—is due, above all, to the German soldier himself. He has again proved his worth in the most convincing way on every battlefield on which he fought. And all the branches of the German people take an equal share in this glorious achievement. The soldiers of the new Provinces, incorporated since 1938, have also fought magnificently, and have made their contribution of blood. By reason of this heroic effort on the part of all Germans, the National Socialist German Reich will, at the conclusion of the war, forever be sacred and dear to the hearts, not only of those living today, but also to coming generations.

"As I come to express my appreciation of the forces whose efforts have made this most glorious victory possible, my first words of praise are due to the Command, which was equal to the highest demands made upon it during this campaign.

"The Army has carried out the duties allotted to it under the command of its Commander-in-Chief, Gen. von Brauchitsch and his Chief-of-General Staff, Halder, in a truly glorious manner.

"If the Command of the German Army of yesterday is considered to be the best in the world, then today it is worthy of at least the same admiration. In fact, success being the deciding factor in the final evaluation, the Command of the new Germany Army must be accounted still better. The Army in the West was under the command of Generals Ritter von Leeb, von Rundstedt and von Bock, divided into three Army groups. The army group of General Ritter von Leeb had the primary duty of holding, at all cost, the left wing of the German Western Front, from the Swiss frontier as far as the Moselle. Not until a further stage in the operation was it intended to give this front an active share in the battle of destruction, with two armies under the command of Generals von Witzleben and Dollmann.

"On the 10th of May, at 5:35 in the morning, the two army groups under the command of General von Rundstedt and General von Bock were ready for the attack. Their allotted task was to force their way through the enemy positions at the frontier, along the whole front from the Moselle to the North Sea, to occupy Holland, to advance against Antwerp and the Dyle position, to take Liège; above all to reach the Meuse with the massed defensive forces of the left wing, to carry the crossing between Namur and Craignan near Sedan, with the main body of the tank and mechanized divisions, as these operations proceeded, to force their way to the sea, closely following the canal and river system of the Aisne and the Somme and connecting together all available tank and mechanized divisions.

"The southern army group of General von Rundstedt was also allotted the important task, as the break-through proceeded, to insure the covering of the left flank according to plan, in order totally to exclude the possibility of a repetition of the miracle of the Marne in 1914. This tremendous operation which already decided the further course of the war and led, as had been planned, to the destruction of the main body of the French army and also of the whole British Expeditionary Force, threw a glorious light upon German leadership. . . ."

"The continuation of the operations in the general direction of the Aisne and the Seine were not undertaken, in the first place, with a view to taking Paris, but in order to obtain or secure suitable points for the commencement of operations, with the object of forcing a way through as far as the Swiss frontier. This enormous offensive operation was carried out according to plan, thanks to the brilliant conduct of all ranks. The change in the High Command of the French Army which took place in the meantime was intended to reinforce the French powers of resistance and to turn the battle, which had commenced so unfortunately for the Allies, in the direction in which they desired. As a matter of fact it was found possible to proceed at many places with the new offensive of the German Army, only after the most desperate resistance had been overcome.

"Not only the courage but also the training of the German soldier was here given an opportunity of demonstrating its value. Encouraged by the example of innumerable officers and non-commissioned officers, and also of individual soldiers, the infantry itself was carried forward, time after time, even in the most difficult situations. Paris fell. The crushing of the enemy resistance on the Aisne cleared the way for a break-through to the Swiss frontier. In a tremendous encircling movement, the armies forced a passage behind the Maginot Line which was itself being attacked at two points west of Saarbruecken and Neubreisach, by the Leeb Army Group which had previously been in reserve, and was penetrated under the command of Generals von Witzleben and Dollmann. Thus we were successful, not only in completely encircling the tremendous front of French resistance, but also in breaking it up into small units and enforcing France's capitulation.

"These operations were crowned by the general advance of all German armies, the foremost place again being taken by the unconquerable tank divisions and motorized divisions of the army. With the object of destroying the broken-up remnants of the French Army or of occupying French territory, the left wing pushed forward for this purpose, towards the mouth of the Rhone and the direction of Marseille, and the right wing across the Loire in the direction of Bordeaux and the Spanish frontier. I shall render a special report elsewhere in regard to the entry of our Ally into the war, which had meanwhile taken place. When Marshal Pétain made an offer to the effect that France would lay down her arms he was not relinquishing any forces which still remained intact, but was ending a situation which, in the view of every soldier, was quite untenable. Only the bloodthirsty dilettantism of Mr. Churchill enabled him either not to comprehend this or to deny it against his better knowledge. . . ."

"At dawn on May the 10th, thousands of fighter planes and dive-bombers, covered by chaser planes, swept down upon the enemy air bases. In the course of a few days, complete mastery of the air had been achieved, and not for one moment during the struggle was it surrendered. Only in places where no German airmen were present, for the time being, were enemy chasers or bombers able to make even a fleeting appearance. Apart from this, their activities were confined to night work.

"The Air Force in this war was under the command of the Field Marshal. Its duties were: to annihilate the enemy air force or to make it impossible for them to carry out flights; second, to afford direct and indirect support to the troops in action and indirectly, by continuous attacks, to destroy the enemy's lines of communication and to weaken and to break the enemy's morale and powers of resistance, and to land parachute troops. The broad lines of the plan according to which the Air Force was employed and the manner in which it adapted itself to the tactical demands of the moment were outstanding. It is true that the successes achieved would have been impossible without the bravery of the Army; but any bravery of the Army would have been in vain without the heroic efforts of the Air Force. Both Army and Air Force deserve the highest praise.

"The Air Force carried out its operations in the West under the personal command of Field Marshal Goering. . . ."

"In concluding these purely military observations on the events, the traditional love of truth compels me to pay due honor to the fact that all this would not have been possible had it not been for the attitude of the home front, and more particularly without the founding, the achievements and the activity of the National Socialist party. At the time of the greatest disaster, in the year 1919, it already proclaimed in its program, the re-establishment of the German National Army, and for decades has pursued this ideal with fanatical determination. Without its achievements, all the preliminaries for a rebirth of Germany would have disappeared, and with them the possibility of a creation of a German Army.

"It has, above all, provided the ideological foundation for

our struggle. In opposition of the senseless sacrifice of human life practiced by our democratic adversaries for their plutocratic interests, it championed a truly social community of the people. Thus it created that close unity between the front-line soldiers and the home front which was so sorely lacking in the World War. From its ranks, therefore, I should like to name four men, who, among innumerable others, have won the greatest merit in the struggle to make it possible for the new Germany to celebrate victory.

"Reichminister Hess, himself an ex-serviceman who fought in the Great War, has from the earliest foundation of the movement been a most faithful comrade in the struggle for the establishment of our present State and its Army.

"Lutze, Chief-of-Staff of the Storm Troopers, who has organized the millions of Storm Troopers in the spirit of the greatest sacrifice to the State and assured their preliminary training and their subsequent careers after leaving the army;

"Himmler, Chief of the German Police and creator of the SS units on active service;

"Hierl, the founder and leader of the Labor Service of the Reich;

"Reichminister Major-General Dr. Todt, the organizer of munitions supplies and the builder of our mighty network of strategical roads and of the line of fortifications in the West;

"Reichminister Dr. Goebbels, the organizer of a propaganda, the efficiency of which is best gauged by comparison with that of the World War. . . ."

"I cannot conclude these tributes without, finally, thanking the man who for years has been realizing my aims of foreign policy in unceasing loyalty and self-sacrificing service. The name of von Ribbentrop, as Foreign Minister, will for all time be connected with the political rebirth of the German Nation.

"Members of the Reichstag! As Fuehrer and Commander-in-Chief of the German Army I have determined to honor the most distinguished Generals before that forum which is in truth the most representative of the entire German people. At their head I must place that man for whom I find it difficult to express sufficient thanks for his services which bind his name to the movement, the State and, above all, the German Air Force. My party colleague Goering has, since the foundation of the Storm Troopers, been connected with the development and the progress of the Movement. Since the assumption of power, his work and his readiness to shoulder responsibility have accomplished tasks, in innumerable spheres, which will never be forgotten in the history of our people.

"Since the re-establishment of the German Army, he has been the creator of the German Air Force. It is granted to but a few mortals, in the course of their lives, to create a military instrument from nothing, and to develop it until it becomes the mightiest weapon of its kind. *Field Marshal Goering, as creator of the German Air Force has, individually, made the highest contribution to the reconstruction of the German Army.* As Commander of the German Air Force he has contributed to the creation of the prerequisites for the victory gained so far in this war. *Goering's merits are unique.* I therefore confer on him the rank of 'Marshal of the Reich,' and award to him the Grand Cross of the Iron Cross. . . ."

"I cannot conclude my survey of this struggle, without at this time making mention of our ally. Ever since the commencement of the National Socialist regime two points were prominent in the program of its foreign policy: the achievement of a real understanding and friendship with Italy, and second, the achievement of the same relationship with England.

"You are aware, gentlemen, that these ideals inspired me twenty years ago to the same extent as they did later. I have expressed and defended these ideals in print and in speeches on innumerable occasions, even when I was only a member of the Opposition in the democratic Republic.

"As soon as the German people entrusted me with its leadership, I immediately attempted to realize in practical form, this, the oldest of the ideals of National Socialist foreign policy. *Even today, I still regret that in spite of all my efforts I have not succeeded in achieving that friendship with England which, as I believe, would have been a blessing for both peoples. I was not successful, in spite of determined and honest efforts.*

"But I am all the more happy, that the first point in the program of ideals in my foreign policy could be realized. *Thanks for this are due, chiefly, to the genius who today stands at the head of the Italian people. It is entirely due to his success, the effects of which will endure for centuries to come, that it was possible to establish contact between the two revolutions which spiritually are so nearly related and now, finally, to establish a bond of blood which is destined to grant Europe new life.* That I personally have the honor to be the friend of this man is a great joy to me in view of the unique nature of his destiny, which has just as much in common with mine as our two revolutions and, moreover, as the history of the unification and the rise of our two nations.

"*Since the rebirth of the German people, it has been only from Italy that any voice of human understanding has reached us.* A lively community of interests arose from this reciprocal understanding. It was finally sealed by a Treaty. When, last year, this war was thrust upon Germany, against my wish and desire, the continued action of our two States was decided upon in discussion between Mussolini and myself. The advantages accruing to Germany from the attitude of Italy were exceptional.

"It is not only economically that the situation and attitude of Italy were of advantage to us, but also from a military point of view. From the very commencement of the war,

Italy held strong units of our enemy occupied, and above all, diminished the freedom of their strategical dispositions. When, however, the Duce considered that the right moment had come to take up arms against the continued and intolerable violations represented by French and British acts of interference and the King declared war, he did so of his own accord. Our feeling of gratitude must, therefore, be all the deeper.

"Italy's entry into the war played a part in hastening France's recognition of the fact that further resistance would be completely unavailing. Since then, our Ally has fought, first, on the ridges and peaks of the Alps, and is now fighting in the wide regions which form her sphere of interest. The air attacks and the naval engagements now being carried out by our Ally are being followed up in that spirit which is typical of the Fascist revolution, and are being watched by us in that spirit which is inspired in National Socialism by Fascist Italy.

"The anguish felt by Italy so recently at the death of Marshal Balbo is also Germany's anguish. Her every joy is also shared by us. Our co-operation in both the political and military spheres is complete. It will extinguish the injustice done to the German and Italian peoples in the course of centuries. For our efforts will be crowned by a common victory.

"If now, gentlemen, I speak of the future, it is in no spirit of boastful vainglory. That I can confidently leave to others who probably need it more than I, for example, Mr. Churchill. I would like, without any exaggeration, to provide you with a view of the situation, as it is, and as I see it.

"The course of the war during the last ten months has proved that I was right and that the opinions of our opponents were wrong. When British statesmen declare that their country has always emerged stronger from every defeat and every disaster, then it is at least not conceit when I inform

you that we should emerge, similarly, all the stronger from our successes.

"As far back as September 3, last year, I told you that come what may, neither force of arms nor time would get Germany down. In military power the Reich is stronger than ever before. You have learned of the losses, admittedly heavy for the individual but slight in their total, which the German Army has suffered in action during the last three months. When you consider that during this period we have established a front stretching from the North Cape to the Spanish frontier, you will realize that these losses, especially as compared with those during the Great War, are amazingly slight. This is due, apart from the brilliant standard of the army leaders, to the excellent tactical training of the individual soldier and units, and the co-operation of the various fighting services.

"It is due secondly, to the quality and efficiency of our new armaments, and, thirdly, to our deliberate renunciation of any so-called successes merely for reasons of prestige. I myself have, on principle, endeavored to avoid making an attack or carrying out any operations not actually essential in connection with the annihilation of our enemies, but undertaken merely for the sake of fancy prestige.

"Nevertheless we had naturally prepared for very much heavier losses. The man-power of our nation, thus spared, will strengthen our struggle for our freedom which has been forced upon us. At present many of our divisions are being withdrawn from France and are returning to their headquarters. Many are being given leave. Arms and equipment are being overhauled and replaced by fresh supplies. Taking all in all, the Army today is stronger than ever.

"The loss in arms in Norway, and especially during the campaign against Holland, Belgium and France is entirely negligible. The output is out of proportion to the loss. The Army and Air Force are, at this moment, more perfectly equipped and stronger than before our advances in the West.

"Ammunition was manufactured on so large a scale and the existing supplies are so enormous that either a limitation or change of production is becoming necessary in numerous sections, since many of the existing depots and stores, in spite of huge extensions, are no longer in a position to accommodate further supplies.

"The consumption of munitions as during the Polish campaign was small beyond all expectations and is negligible compared to the supplies. The total amount of supplies for the Army and Air Force and all services is considerably greater than before our attack in the West.

"*Thanks to the Four Year Plan, Germany was admirably prepared for the most severe trial.* No Army in the world has adapted itself to the use of such materials essential for the conduct of war, as were produced within the country in place of those which had to be imported, to anything like the extent to which this had been achieved in Germany. Thanks to the efforts of the Marshal of the Reich, the adaptation of the German economic system to an autarchic war economy had been accomplished even in peacetime. We possessed the two most vital raw materials, coal and iron, in what I may, today, term unlimited quantities. The supply of fuel we have in storage is plentiful and our productive capacity is on the increase, and will, within a short time, be sufficient for our requirements, even if our imported supply should cease. Thanks to our system of collecting old metal, our reserve supplies of metal have increased to such a degree that we can carry on, even for any length of time, and will not be at the mercy of any contingency.

"*In addition, there are the tremendous possibilities presented by the acquisition of inestimable spoils and the exploitation of the territories occupied by us.* In the spheres of economic interest controlled by them, *Germany and Italy have at their disposal 200 million persons, among whom they can draw on 130 million for military man-power, whilst over 70 million are engaged in purely economic activities.*

"I told you on September 3, gentlemen, that in order to carry on this war I had promulgated a new Five Year Plan. Today, I am in a position to assure you that the necessary measures have been taken, so that come what may, I do not now anticipate any contingency of a threatening nature. Thanks to measures adopted in time, food supplies are likewise guaranteed, however long the war may last.

"Thanks to their National Socialist training, *the people of Germany did not enter this war in a spirit of superficial and blatant patriotism, but with the fanatical grimness of a nation aware of the fate that awaits it should it be defeated.* The efforts of our enemies to shatter this unity by means of propaganda, were as stupid as they were futile. Ten months of war have only served to strengthen our fanaticism. It is a great misfortune that world opinion is not formed by men who see things as they are, but only by men who see them as they wish to see them.

"I have recently perused innumerable documents from the Ark of the Covenant which stood in the Allied headquarters, containing, among other things, reports on conditions in Germany and memoranda on the morale of the German people. These reports were made by diplomats but, on reading them, one can merely ask oneself whether the authors were blind, stupid, or low scoundrels.

"I readily admit that there naturally were, and probably still are, people in Germany who watch almost with regret while the Third Reich marches on to victory.

"Incorrigible reactionaries and unseeing nihilists may well learn that things have gone very differently from what they had hoped. But their number is negligible, and their significance still more so. Unfortunately, however, it would appear that when judgment is passed upon the German people abroad, the scum of the nation is chosen as a criterion. The result is that the diseased imagination of shipwrecked statesmen fastens upon these last reasons for renewed hope. Thus,

British Generals alternately choose 'General Hunger' or 'Threatening Revolution' as their ally.

"There is nothing, however far-fetched, which these men would not hold out as a hope to their own people, in order to be able to survive for a few weeks longer. The German nation has given proof of its morale, in the shape of its sons, fighting on the field of battle, who within the space of a few weeks overthrew and annihilated that adversary who ranked next to Germany in military power. Their spirit was and is the spirit of the German homeland.

"In the opinion of British politicians their last hopes, apart from Allied peoples consisting of a number of kings without a throne, statesmen without a nation and generals without an army, seem to be based on fresh complications which they hope to bring about, thanks to their proven skill in such matters.

"A veritable 'Wandering Jew' among these hopes is the belief in the possibility of a fresh estrangement between Germany and Russia. German-Russian relations have been finally established. The reason for this is that Britain and France, authorized by certain lesser powers, continually credited Germany with the desire to conquer territory which lay outside the sphere of German interest. *It was said, at one time, that Germany wanted to possess the Ukraine; again, that she intended to invade Finland; yet again, that she had threatened Rumania, and finally, fears were entertained for the safety of Turkey.*

"In these circumstances, I conceived it right to enter into straightforward discussions with Russia, in order to define clearly, once and for all, what Germany believes she must regard as her sphere of interests vital to her future, and which Russia, on the other hand, considered essential for her existence. This clear definition of their several spheres of interest was followed by a new basis for German-Russian relations. *All hope that the completion of this might give rise to fresh tension between Germany and Russia is futile.*

Neither has Germany undertaken any steps which would have led her to exceed the limits of her sphere of interest, nor has Russia done anything of the kind. Britain's hope that she could, by bringing about a new European crisis, better her own position, amounts, insofar as this concerns Germany's relation with Russia, to a false conclusion. British statesmen are always somewhat slow in grasping facts but they will learn to see this in time.

"In my speech of October 6, I prophesied correctly the further development of this war. I assured you, gentlemen, that never for one moment did I doubt in our victory. As long as one does not insist on regarding defeat as the visible sign and guarantee of ultimate victory, I would appear to have been justified by the course which events have taken so far.

"Although I was convinced of the course they would take, I nevertheless, at the time, held out my hand in an endeavor to reach an understanding with France and Britain. You will remember the answer which I received. All my arguments as to the folly of continuing the struggle and pointing to the certainty that, at best, there is nothing to gain, but all to lose, were either received with derison or completely ignored.

"I told you at the time that on account of my peace proposals I expected even to be branded as a coward who did not want to fight on because he could not. That is exactly what did happen. I believe, however, that the French,—of course not so much the guilty statesmen as the people,—are beginning to think very differently about that 6th of October. Indescribable misery has overtaken that great country and people since that day.

"I have no desire to dwell on the sufferings brought on the soldiers in this war. Even greater is the misery caused by the unscrupulousness of those who drove millions from their homes without reason, merely in the hope of obstructing German military operations,—an assumption which it is truly difficult to understand. As it turned out, the evacuation proved disastrous for Allied operations, though far more terrible for the unfortunate evacuees. Neither in this world nor in the next, can Messrs. Churchill and Reynaud answer for the suffering they have caused by their councils and decrees to millions of people. All this, as I said once before, need never have happened. For, even in October, I asked nothing from either France or Britain but peace. But the men behind the armaments industries wanted to go on with the war at all costs—and now they've got it.

"I am too much of a soldier myself not to understand the misery caused by such a development. *From Britain I now hear only a single cry—the cry, not of the people but of the politicians, that the war must go on!*

"I do not know whether these politicians already have a correct idea of what the continuation of this struggle will be like. They do, it is true, declare that they will carry on with the war and that, even if Great Britain should perish, they would carry on from Canada. I can hardly believe that they mean by this that the people of Britain are to go to Canada. Presumably only those gentlemen interested in the continuation of their war will go there. The people, I am afraid, will have to remain in Britain and the people in London will certainly regard the war with other eyes than their so-called leaders in Canada.

"Believe me, gentlemen, I feel a deep disgust for this type of unscrupulous politician who wrecks whole nations and states. *It almost causes me pain to think that I should have been selected by Fate to deal the final blow to the structure which these men have already set tottering. It never has been my intention to wage wars, but rather to build up a state with a new social order and the finest possible standard of culture. Every year that this war drags on is keeping me away from this work,* and the causes of this are nothing but ridiculous nonentities,—as it were 'Nature's political misfits,' unless their corruptibility labels them as something worse.

"Only a few days ago Mr. Churchill reiterated his declaration that he wants war. Some six weeks ago he began to wage war in a field where he apparently considers himself particularly strong, namely air raids on the civil population, although under the pretense that the raids are directed against so-called military objectives. Since the bombardment of Freiburg these objectives are open towns, market-places and villages, burning houses, hospitals, schools, kindergartens and whatever else may come their way. Until now I have ordered hardly any reprisals, but that does not mean that this is, or will be, my only reply.

"I have often said that our answer, which will come one day, will bring upon the people unending suffering and misery. Of course, not upon Mr. Churchill for he, no doubt, will already be in Canada, where the money and children of those principally interested in the war have already been sent. For millions of other people, however, great suffering will begin. *Mr. Churchill ought perhaps, for once, to believe me when I prophesy that a great Empire will be destroyed—an Empire which it was never my intention to destroy or even to harm. I do, however, realize that this struggle, if it continues, can end only with the complete annihilation of one or the other of the two adversaries.* Mr. Churchill may believe that this will be Germany. I know that it will be different.

"In this hour, I feel it to be my duty before my own conscience to appeal once more to reason and common sense in Great Britain as much as elsewhere. I consider myself in a position to make this appeal since I am not the vanquished, begging favors, but the victor speaking in the name of reason.

"I can see no reason why this war must go on.

"I am grieved to think of the sacrifices which it will claim. I should like to avert them, also from my own people. I know that millions of German men, young and old alike, are burning with the desire at last to settle accounts with the enemy who, for the second time, has declared war upon us for no reason whatever. But I also know that at home there are many women and mothers who, ready as they are to sacrifice all they have in life, are yet bound to it by their very heartstrings.

"Possibly, Mr. Churchill will again brush aside this statement of mine by saying that it is merely born of fear and of doubt in our final victory. In that case, I shall have relieved my conscience in regard to the things to come.

"Deputies and Members of the German Reichstag: In looking back upon the last ten months we are all struck by the grace of Providence which has allowed us to succeed in our great work. Providence has blessed our resolve and guided us in our difficult task. As for myself, I am deeply moved, realizing that Providence has called upon me to restore to my people their freedom and honor. The humiliation and disgrace which originated twenty-two years ago in the forest of Compiègne, have forever been obliterated in the same place. Today I have named before history the men who made it possible for me to accomplish this great task. All of them have given their best and have devoted all their faculties and energy to the German people.

"Let me conclude by mentioning those unknown heroes who have fulfilled their duty in no less a degree. Millions of them risked life and limb, and were at every moment prepared, as true German officers and soldiers, to bring for their people the greatest sacrifice of which man is capable. Many of them now lie buried side by side with their fathers who fell in the Great War. They bear witness to a silent heroism. They are the symbol of those hundreds of thousands of infantrymen, tank corps men, engineers and gunners, sailors and airmen and SS men and of all those other soldiers who joined in the fight of the German forces for the freedom and future of our people and for the eternal greatness of the National Socialist Reich.

Press

New York Times— . . . In form and in substance, Hitler's ultimatum yesterday was "the mixture as before." It bristled with arrogance and with the worship of brute force. It contained the same falsifications of history which have come from Hitler on past occasions. It professed the same sweet reasonableness, the same "disgust" with a continuance of the bloodshed and suffering which he deliberately loosed upon the world last September. It was another attempt to undermine the morale of the enemy, to weaken his willpower, to provoke a revolution of opinion in Britain which would give victory to Germany without a long and costly struggle. The British know what the rejection of this ultimatum will mean. They know that it will subject their island, their homes, their lives and their children's lives to the most fiendish assault which the mind of man has ever contrived. But they know, too, what it would mean to accept any peace which deprived them of their strong weapons of defense and forced them to rely upon the word of a man in whom there is no honor. . . .

London Times, July 20,— . . . Perhaps the most unexpected feature of Hitler's speech to the Reichstag last night . . . was the new emphasis laid on the possibility of a long war. He made no further allusion to the dictation of peace in London on August 15. . . .

The Fuehrer showed himself anxious rather to reassure the audience about the capacity of the Reich to endure the blockade, however long the war might last. . . . It is curious that the speech contained no reference whatever to America, notwithstanding the vigorous words in which Mr. Roosevelt . . . had pledged the resources of the United States more uncompromisingly than ever to sustain the cause of freedom. [Speaking of the invaded neutral nations:] Hitler scoffed at the suggestion that other small countries, still independent, might have cause for anxiety; he declared that he had reached final accord on all points with Russia—which does not explain the present massing of troops and strengthening of fortifications on his eastern frontier—and he strove to reassure such states as Finland, Rumania and Turkey. The speech culminated, as was generally expected, in an appeal to Great Britain, in the name of reason, to avert the calamities of a war *à outrance* by making peace now. The rulers and people of this country . . . understand the responsibility they bear in declaring that it must go on to the end. . . . Hitler in effect admits that his offer of peace is purely perfunctory by attaching to it no indication whatever of the terms on which peace is possible. Presumably any terms that he would now propose would be based on acquiescence and co-operation in the so-called "new order" for Europe . . . the reduction of most of Europe to serfdom in the interest of the hegemony of the self-chosen German race. . . .

•

SPEECH OF SEPTEMBER 4, 1940
WARTIME WINTER RELIEF CAMPAIGN

Berlin, Sportpalast

Background

1940

July 29—Germany launches mass air raids over Britain. From then on, until the end of September, these raids are to increase in intensity. They constitute the first attempt of Germany to break the resistance of England by air-power alone.

August 17—Germany announces total blockade of waters around Britain.

August 18—President Roosevelt and Prime Minister Mackenzie King set up a joint board of defense for the U.S.A. and Canada.

August 19—Italy conquers British Somaliland.

August 21—Rumania cedes the Dobruja to Bulgaria.

August 25—First British air raid over Berlin.

August 28—U.S. Senate passes the Selective Service Bill.

August 30—Under pressure of Germany and Italy, Rumania cedes part of Transylvania to Hungary.

September 5—Fifty American destroyers are exchanged with England for British bases in the western hemisphere.

The Speech

"THE first year of war came to its end a few days ago. The second has begun, and we are opening a new Winter Relief Campaign.

"The successes of the first year, my countrymen, are unique —so unique that our enemies could not anticipate the course of events and that even many Germans have scarcely been able to grasp their magnitude and speed.

"We cannot draw a comparison with the first year of the World War, for at that time, in spite of utmost bravery and tremendously greater sacrifices, only partial results were attained and not a single important decision won. As for today, we need only cast a glance at the huge triangle now protected by German arms: in the East, the river Bug; in the North, the North Cape, Kirkenes and Narvik; in the South, the Spanish border. A number of our foes have been eliminated. And it is only thanks to her fortunate geographic location and to her extraordinary speed at withdrawing that England has not yet suffered the same fate. For things are not as some British politicians describe them; namely, that the British Army is like a spirited horse, eager for battle and burning with the desire to be let loose at last to fight the Germans. The British were close enough to us at one time to satisfy any such 'desire' without difficulty, but they withdrew from our vicinity and described their sorry retreats as great victories. All their 'successes' are of this nature. Besides the vast territory at present dominated by German troops, our Italian ally has undertaken an offensive in East Africa; he has strengthened his position there and has thrown the English back.

"Naturally, the British have had 'successes,' too. However, their successes are of a kind which people in their normal senses cannot understand. Time and again we have seen British propaganda pass from one extreme to the other—from the greatest heights to the lowest depths—only to achieve even greater heights a few days later. For instance, at one time the following appeared in their papers: 'The die is now being cast. If the Germans do not get to Paris—and they will not—they have lost the war. Should they nevertheless get there, England will win the war.' In this fashion, England has won many 'victories' since September third. Her most magnificent victory—or as we see it, her most shameful failure—was the flight from Dunkirk.

"But what won't a man do in a pinch! We need only read the British war communiqués to know the nature of these 'successes.' We find such phrases as 'we are told that . . .,' or 'it is stated in well-informed circles . . .,' or 'it is to be gathered from the statement of experts . . .,' or 'there is serious basis for the assumption that . . .' Once they even used this formula: 'It is believed that there are reasons for the assumption that, etc.'

"Any defeat can be transformed into a success in this way. Just as we were entering Poland, the British propagandists declared that they had learned from well-informed circles that the Germans had already suffered a considerable number of grave defeats and that the Poles were victoriously pushing towards Berlin. Only a few days later, 'well-informed circles' stated emphatically that events in the East had definitely taken a 'new turn.'

"Equally well-informed 'experts' remarked that, even should Germany be successful—which was, of course, impossible—this success would be a failure in the light of higher strategic values. After we had reached the very gates of Warsaw, British reports stated that 'there was justification for the belief that the Allied attack in the West had won its first decisive success.'

"This sort of thing went on until the day when Poland was no more. The comment elicited by these events was something like this: 'This is a great relief. Poland in the East has always been our weakest spot. Now, at last, we can concentrate on the theater of war in which we are superior to the Germans—and that they will soon find out.'

"Then things were quiet for quite a while. Of course, this period was a colossal, continuous success for British forces and an equally constant defeat for the Germans. It is inconceivable how much the English achieved during those months and how much we missed! What all didn't British politicians see clearly and calculate correctly; what right moments didn't they seize during that time!—And how many busses didn't we miss! And then came Norway!

"When operations began, British war-news makers rejoiced over the 'frightful mistake' the Germans had made. 'The Germans have at last made a mistake, and now they will suffer for it' was the comment, and the British were happy that at last an opportunity had come of measuring their strength against ours. Of course, they could have done this at any time, for after all, on the Western front only a few hundred yards had separated our positions. But there they had acted as if we were invisible to them.

"And now in Norway, thanks to our stupidity, and particularly my own, a kindly fate for the first time gave them the opportunity of pitting their military might against ours. And they *got* their fight.

"It is really an irony of fate that the blow which was probably the hardest the British suffered at the time was due to their own propaganda. For long after we had thrown the Norwegians back beyond Hamar and Lillehammer, a British brigade came marching along, innocent and unsuspecting, towards Hamar. They had no communications with their rear—our 'Stukas' and fighting bombers had seen to that. So they listened to the British Broadcasting System. And from the British Broadcasting System, the brigadier learned that we were still a long way from Lillehammer and that we had been badly beaten. So the brigadier marched into Lillehammer at the head of the brigade and peacefully went to bed, a box filled with documents labelled 'strictly secret' and 'not to be abandoned to the enemy' at his side. And here, during the night, our troops captured him and his precious treasure chest. That is what happens when a man relies on that noted war correspondent, Mr. Churchill.

"It was the same thing everywhere: they lied and lied. When they were thrown into the sea, they called it a 'tremendous victory.' When they saved a few shattered remnants from Andalsnes and Namsos, they told the world that this was 'the most stupendous success in modern British military history.' Of course, we cannot beat that: but we have a few facts to confront it with. Militarily, Norway ceased to exist within a few weeks and the British forces had to evacuate. Then came the battle of the West—and we did not miss that bus either. This last campaign, in particular, was an uninterrupted series of defeats for the Allied coalition. The facts—the historical facts—prove it conclusively. And yet this campaign, too, ended in a spectacular British victory—the magnificent, glorious feat of arms at Dunkirk. I have seen with my own eyes what they left behind; it looked rather untidy.

"Now French resistance, too, has been broken. How do they explain that away? After Norway had been thoroughly cleared of the Allies, the explanation was: 'But that is what we wanted. All we wanted was to get the Germans up here. This is a victory, an outstanding victory for us; it shortens our front.'

"And now, after the French collapse, the text was: 'Now, for the first time, England can really concentrate her forces.

We are no longer compelled to scatter and waste our troops. Now we have reached the strategic position we have wished and hoped for all the time. The dead weight of France has been dropped. All it did was cost us valuable British blood. But now we'll show them!'

"From the very beginning, definite predictions were made as to how long the war would last. 'The war will last three years. Britain is preparing for three years of war,' said London. This had to be done, for the wealthy people who own stock in munitions factories are intelligent enough to know that their new plants could not possibly pay inside of six months or a year. The thing simply has to last longer than that.

"However, I was just as careful, *and immediately said to the Reich Marshal: 'Goering, we must be prepared for a five-year war.' Not that I thought that the war would last five years. But no matter what happens, England will be broken, one way or another. That is the only timetable I have.* Of course, everything will be prepared wisely, carefully and conscientiously. Of that, you are aware. And if today, in England, people are very inquisitive and are asking: 'But why doesn't he come?' they may rest assured; he'll come all right. One shouldn't be so inquisitive. This world will be set free. The possibility of one nation blockading a continent whenever it feels like it must be done away with once and for all. It must be made impossible in the future for a pirate state to deliver four hundred and fifty million people to poverty and misery whenever it feels so inclined. As Germans we are sick and tired, for all time, of having England tell us what to do, even, whether we may drink coffee or not. When the British feel like it, they simply stop our coffee imports. I, myself, do not drink coffee, but it angers me that others should not be allowed to drink it.

"It is simply unbearable that a nation of eighty-five million people can be penalized by another nation whenever it suits some plutocrat in London. I have offered the English people the hand of friendship time and again. You know yourselves: that was my foreign program. The other day I made that offer for the last time. *I now prefer to fight until, finally, a perfectly clear decision is reached.* This clear decision can only consist in the elimination of the regime of vile and miserable warmongers and the creation of a situation in which it will, in the future, be impossible for one nation to play tyrant over all Europe. Germany and Italy will see to it that history will never repeat itself.

"All Britain's Allies will avail her nothing, neither Haile Selassie nor Mr. Benes, nor any of the others; not even King Haakon or Queen Wilhelmina or the French General de Gaulle. Whatever other plans they may have, whatever they may be scheming in the deepest recesses of their minds, we are on our guard, we are prepared for anything, we are resolved and ready to act at any time. We cannot be frightened by anything. The German National Socialists have been tempered and toughened by hard experience. First, we were soldiers in the Great War; later, fighters for German resurrection. What we suffered in those years has hardened us. We cannot be intimidated nor taken by surprise.

"When the British entered the war a year ago, they said they had an ally. We were curious as to who that might be. They said: 'He is a General, his name is "General Revolution."' How little they know the German people and their new National Socialist State! London waited for 'General Revolution' to do something. Nothing happened on September 6 and 7, and disappointment came on September 8. They were so sure that 'General Revolution' would take the offensive within a week—but he was nowhere to be found.

"Then they said: 'We have an alliance with another general; his name is "General Hunger."' Right from the start we had expected that these great humanitarians would try to starve millions of women and children as they did in the World War, and we were prepared. This General was another blank, a phantom—another one of Mr. Churchill's 'jacko'-lanterns.' They have now discovered a third Ally, 'General Winter.' He was here once before. He failed then and he will fail again.

"As long as the English have such obscure foreign generals they should not forget to promote their own most prominent native general to the rank of, say, a marshal of the empire. I refer to 'General Bluff.' He is their one reliable ally and thoroughly deserves promotion to the most exalted rank. As far as we are concerned, that general cannot beat us. Maybe the British people can be fooled by him; but the German people know England too well to be duped. The babbling of Mr. Churchill or of Mr. Eden—reverence for old age forbids the mention of Mr. Chamberlain—doesn't mean a thing to the German people. At best, it makes them laugh. For a character like Mr. Duff Cooper there is no word in conventional German. Only the Bavarians have a word that adequately describes this type of man, and that is: *Krampfhenne.** The gentlemen may set their minds at rest. They will not win the war by such means. The other means, thank God, are in our hands, and they will remain in our hands. When the hour has struck, in place of Generals Hunger, Revolution, Winter and Bluff, we shall again appoint General Action. And then we shall see who is the best of them!

"The gratitude of the German nation to its soldiers I have already conveyed in my Reichstag speech.† In these days we are particularly grateful to the Air Force, to those courageous men who fly to England day after day to deliver our answer to what the clever Mr. Churchill invented. I shall have more to say about that later. But the thanks which I wish above all to voice today are addressed to the home front. They are thanks for the year which has just passed, thanks to the entire German nation for the conduct it displayed in this year, in situations which were not always easy.

"For perhaps some of us do not realize what it meant to

* An excitable hen.

† July 19, 1940.

evacuate 700,000 people within a few weeks last year. It was done without a hitch. Of course, as compared with some other peoples, everything had been well prepared. But what these people had to shoulder was often very hard and they put up with it admirably. We are happy that they have now been able to go home.

". . . It is wonderful to witness the splendid discipline of our people in this war. We see it particularly well just now, while Mr. Churchill is demonstrating his new brain-child, the night air raid. Mr. Churchill is carrying out these raids, not because they promise to be highly effective, but because his air force cannot fly over Germany in daylight. Whereas German fliers and German planes are over English soil every day, the Englishman, in daylight, can scarcely manage to get across the North Sea. That is why he comes at night and, as you know, drops his bombs indiscriminately on residential districts, farms and villages. Wherever he sees a light, he drops a bomb. For three months I did not answer, because I believed that such madness would be stopped. Mr. Churchill took this for a sign of weakness. No doubt you know that we are now answering it every night to an ever-increasing extent.

"*If the British Air Force drops two or three or four thousand kilograms of bombs, we will drop a hundred and fifty, a hundred and eighty, two hundred thousand, three hundred thousand, four hundred thousand kilograms and more in a single night.* If they say that they will carry out large-scale attacks on our cities, we will blot out theirs. We will stop the handiwork of these night pirates, so help us God. *The hour will come when one of us will crack—and it will not be National Socialist Germany.*

"Once before in my life, I carried out such a fight to the bitter end. My foe was broken—that foe who now, in England, finds his last European refuge. In view of this, it is essential to realize how important is the shaping and development of our German National community. We could not have achieved all this if out there on the front lines there stood a German soldier, lost and unable to count on any one but himself—out of touch with kindred souls at home.

"The strength of the German soldier at the front is founded upon the knowledge and certainty that he is backed by the entire nation, in iron unity and fanatical in purpose. Our people have high aims, far higher than merely winning the war. What we want to do is build a new State. And that is why others hate us so. They have said it often enough. They say: 'But your social experiments are very dangerous. If that kind of thing begins to spread, and if our workers see it, it will be bad. It costs billions and earns nothing. There is no profit and no dividend to be gotten out of it. What good is it? We are not interested in such a development. We welcome everything that helps the materialistic progress of humanity—provided that such progress nets a profit. But social experiments—all the things you are doing—can only serve to awaken the greed of the masses and to pull us off our pedestal. You can hardly expect that of us.'

"We have been looked upon as the bad example; whatever we tried was no good because it was meant for the people. We have taken the road to truly social legislation and towards a sociological development which is hated in other countries. For they are plutocracies in which a very small clique of capitalists rules the masses and, naturally, co-operates closely with the international Jews and the Freemasons. We have known these enemies from the days of our inner struggle; it is the dear old coalition of the Weimar system.

"They hate us on account of our social principles, and everything that we plan and carry out in that direction looks dangerous to them. They are convinced that this development must be destroyed. But I am convinced that the future belongs to this development, and that those states which do not follow it will sooner or later collapse. Unless they find a solution dictated by reason, the states which have social problems remaining unsolved will sooner or later end in chaos. National Socialism has prevented chaos in Germany.

"You know our aims, and you know that we defend them persistently and with fixity of purpose—and that we shall achieve them. That is why all these international plutocracies, the Jewish newspapers, the Stock Exchanges of the world, hate us; that is why all the countries whose attitude is identical or similar, are in sympathy with those democracies. It is precisely because we know that the fight is a struggle for the entire social foundation of our nation and is directed against the very substance of our life that, while we are fighting for these ideals, we must profess them again and again.

"Our Winter Relief Campaign, the most magnificent relief organization in the world, is a powerful demonstration of this spirit.

"No one will doubt that we could easily have found other ways of solving the financial problem involved in relief. The simplest way would have been taxation. It would not have been necessary to build up this gigantic organization; we could have had it all done by civil servants. But while the financial result might have been the same or even better, spiritually it would have fallen far short of what has been achieved, for in its present form it is a voluntary organization of the German national community, applied to a practical end.

"The people have been educated not only to give, but also to do voluntary charity work themselves. For there are two who do their share: the one who gives his offering and the other who administers it—without pay. Every little girl who helps in the street collections, all the occupational groups, up to the leaders of government, business, art and so forth, who carry out this work—all undergo a practical education in the community spirit.

"And that, my countrymen, is the decisive point. We are all of us burdened by traditions of the past, of origin, of social status, or of a profession. We must either renounce the co-operation of millions of people, whose activities as citizens and whose professional work are indispensable but who are not yet awake to such a spirit of community or we must educate them in that spirit. National Socialism has always taken the stand that every attitude is to be understood as a product of education, habit and heredity, and that it can be influenced by education.

"The child growing up in our country did not at birth have prejudices of caste or class; such prejudices are created by education. The differences are artificially forced upon the child, and unless we wish to renounce our desire to form a truly organic, well-built human society we must remove those differences. We have undertaken this task of rebuilding human society, and we are beginning to carry it through in every field. As soon as the child has reached the age at which, formerly, it was educated to the differences in life, we begin to educate it in the things we all have in common.

"And if one person or another asks about the results:— Well, we have been at our task for little more than a few years; first, in building the sense of community in our party, and, second, for nearly eight years in the German nation. That is a short time, but the results are tremendous if we consider that for centuries every effort had been headed in the opposite direction. These tremendous demonstrations of our community sense show what has been achieved.

"Twenty years ago, all this would have been impossible; thirty years ago, unimaginable; forty years ago it would even have been wholly unwanted; today it is a reality. *We educate people toward a uniform view of the fundamentals of life, towards a uniform, equal sense of duty. We are convinced that after this kind of education has gone on for some time people will be the products of that education. In other words, they will then be as representative of the new ideas as they are still, in part, representative of older views.* It is a long, hard road of refinement and education. That progress is being made is best illustrated by the Winter Relief Campaign.

"When the first campaign was started, there were many people in Germany who said: 'Why, what's this? A man with a collection box? Avoid him'—or perhaps made some silly remark.

"That this has changed, one can can easily see from the fact that the amounts have increased from year to year. Perseverance did the trick. The most hide-bound conservative realized after a while, first, that since the collectors always came back, it did him no good to refuse, second, that he really should do his part and, third, that after all, a real job was being done.

"How many wounds we have healed in Germany with this fund! We have helped human reconstruction everywhere. What huge social facilities we have created!

"Believe me, the opposition of many people to such innovation is merely due to inertia and congenital slowness of mind. But once they see what a job is being done, they say: 'Well, if that's what my money helps do, there is no reason why I should not do my bit.'

"I would never have hoped or imagined that this thing would become so great or that it might ever do so much good. What is being done is simply magnificent. And when once a man comes to realize this, even if he is a bull-headed believer in the old order, he is well along on the road towards understanding the new Germany.

"On the other hand, if we had said to a man, thirty years ago: 'Sir, here's a collection box. Now, you go and stand at the street corner and ask people to give you a coin for their fellow men,'—what would his answer have been?

" 'Now, now, I'll contribute myself. But you cannot ask me to do that. After all, I'm Mr. So-and-So, I'm not going to do that. What would people say? How do I know that some fellow won't come along with some fool remark?'

"That man would have been no better than the one who

might have made the remark to him. Education is mutual. It is excellent if people see what silly things some people will say to others. But within a very few years, the Winter Relief Work has shown how easy it is for a great idea to influence the people of a nation.

"All it requires is a little time. We attack them from all sides. This education is being carried on everywhere. I don't know how often Napoleon's words about a Marshal's baton in every soldier's knapsack used to be quoted in bygone days. They were not to be taken literally for normally it was impossible for a soldier even to think of such possibilities.

"All that has been changed today. Where formerly the highest decorations were awarded only to officers, every brave private can earn them today. A world of prejudice has been done away with,—a whole world of prejudice—and, believe me, in decades to come, life in our State will become more and more fine. The tasks become greater and greater. They help us to bring our people closer and closer together and to create an ever more genuine community. And if there are some who simply will not co-operate, we'll give them a state funeral at the end of their days. For they will be the last vestiges of a past age, almost of historic interest. But the future belongs to the young nations which solve this problem. We have undertaken its solution and we'll carry it through.

"The more the world realizes that this great nation is one single community, the more it will realize how hopeless is England's fight. The enemy may be able to break a people who are divided, but eighty-five millions united in one will, one resolve and one readiness to act cannot be broken by any power on earth."

Press

New York Times— . . . Hitler's humor is rare, but his patience has even stricter limits. A dozen times it has reached "the end"—in Czecho-Slovakia, in Poland, in France, in Rumania, over and over again in the past two months with those stubborn British—and now once more he has come to the last limit of his forbearance. Why, then, does he hold his hand? Threats as definite as last night's he has made many times before; yet in no case have they been the prelude to immediate action. Before his former coups, on the contrary, he was at pains to reassure the victim. France was worn down by a winter of waiting. Belgium, the Netherlands and Norway, after many alarms, were lulled into a sense of security before the sudden pounce. . . .

The British cannot afford to discount by a decimal the chances of invasion, as Anthony Eden warned on the anniversary of Britain's declaration of war. But the contrast between Hitler's conduct before previous invasions and his present tactics, the loud warnings that he is surely coming, give rise to questions as to why "General Action" is stalled, and why Hitler overstrains his well-worn patience. Even for that laughing audience it could have been no joke when he broke the news that the British spoke of a three-year war but that Germany was preparing for five years. . . .

PHASE VIII

War on the British Empire

October, 1940 — June, 1941

COMMENT

HITLER'S attempt to destroy the R.A.F. and break the English will by massive air attacks having failed in September 1940, a new phase of the war opened which was to last through the winter and the spring of 1941. This phase was to be different from the preceding ones in two essential respects: for the first time, the war machine which Hitler has built seemed to be inadequate for the immediate fulfillment of its objective, the defeat of England. And for the first time also, Hitler gave the impression of losing the initiative and of being forced into a series of moves which he might have wanted to make at another time, or to avoid altogether.

It should be noted, however, that to follow Hitler's plans during this period became increasingly difficult. The whole of the continent of Europe was under the strictest censorship. The last sources of information were places like Berne in Switzerland, Ankara in Turkey, but the American correspondents in these cities had to limit their activity to relaying news which was, more often than not, rumor, the accuracy of which was difficult to check. Switzerland, Sweden, Turkey and Portugal were the last so-called neutrals from which some measure of objectivity could be expected. But if they were not under a complete black-out like the rest of Europe, they were nevertheless living under a constant threat. They could not give out news freely, and to know what was going on in Europe, one had to resort to the most primitive means: the grape-vine system and the reports of travelers.

Thus the basis of information was official or semi-official

news handed out by the governments. And as far as continental Europe was concerned, all such news was directly or indirectly controlled by Berlin and the propaganda services of Dr. Goebbels.

To try to interpret the motives and projects of Hitler, under such circumstances, can therefore be only a tentative job, especially as Hitler himself spoke less often and, when he did, solely for the purpose of immediate effect.

It is no speculation to state, however, that from the moment he reached the shores of the Atlantic and was confronted with the problem of fighting sea power with land forces, Hitler's whole political and military strategy became less clear in its visible outline.

Up to then—i.e., up to the downfall of France—the lines of this strategy were easily discernible: Hitler's program was to destroy the main military power which opposed him on the continent, and he hoped, having done this, that England would surrender and make peace. He had no reason to be concerned with America because he believed that his mastery over Europe would be firmly established long before the United States could be of any positive help to his opponents.

But this plan failed because England refused to admit defeat and because the resistance of the British Isles enabled America to launch a program of armament and defense which could not even have been started had Hitler's initial plan of a quick victory come true.

This check to Hitler's calculations and timetable left him in the awkward position of having achieved the most remarkable series of military triumphs since Napoleon but with no tangible result to show for them except the undeniable fact that the German armies had established their supremacy.

But military supremacy, even for the Germans, who had for so long sought to achieve it, is not an end in itself. Even Hitler, who now fancied himself as a great military commander, would have liked to be able to offer his people a tangible reward for the years of sacrifice and effort he had imposed on them. Therefore the main problem for Hitler, at the beginning of this second year of the war, was either to propose a peace that would be acceptable to Britain, or to devise some means by which Britain could be forced to surrender.

The first choice was out of the question. The British had made it clear that they would go on fighting until they themselves were victorious. Hitler's ancient and persistent dream of an alliance with England had never been less likely to come true.

As for the second alternative, the defeat of England presented difficulties of such an order that all of Hitler's ideas on the subject and all his past experience seemed to be of little use. New plans and new techniques—both military and political—had to be devised, but as they were devised and tried out, it became apparent that to carry them out successfully implied considerably more time and more effort than had been foreseen.

Far from being able to bring back peace to his people and allow them to enjoy the earthly paradise he had promised them, Hitler was compelled to extend the theater of war and to give up any idea of fixing any time limit to his effort. This very change of strategy was forced upon him. And from then on his choice was limited to where and when he should extend the war, but that he had to extend it was a necessity.

It is for this reason that, from then on, all his moves gave the impression of being somewhat uncoordinated and, at times, erratic. No doubt there was no change in the technique of the German Army: the Blitzkrieg worked as well in the Balkans or in Libya as it had in Poland or France. Hitler remained the master of the strategy of terror and blackmail, and he found no difficulty in compelling Bulgaria, Rumania or even the Vichy Government to obey his will. Everywhere there were Quislings and Darlans to act as his puppets. He even reached new heights in political cunning when he induced Marshal Pétain to become his ally under the guise of being the heroic savior of France. But while Hitler's mastery over continental Europe went unchallenged, while there seemed to be no limit to his freedom of movement, the fact remains that all his actions during these nine or ten months were conditioned by forces which he did not control. One of these forces was the pressure of the German people themselves who desired peace; the other was the determination of England to go on with the war.

The result was that he had to pursue two objectives which were mutually exclusive: the first was to defeat England and the second to impose his New Order in Europe.

The idea of defeating England by invasion having proved impracticable, there remained the slow process of besieging the British Isles. This implied cutting England's life line in the Atlantic and in the Mediterranean.

This in itself meant abandoning the idea of a short war. To starve England would be a long undertaking. Moreover there was the ever-increasing risk of bringing America actively into the war. In spite of Hitler's boast that he could defeat any coalition of nations, the prospect of American participation could not possibly be re-assuring to the Germans who remembered the last war.

Nevertheless it became apparent that Hitler was prepared to take the dual risk of a long war and of America's entry into the war—or rather, that there was nothing that he could do which would surely remove these risks.

The growing importance of the American factor was one of the major reasons why Hitler was compelled to revise his plans, and although he has been careful not to defy the United States too openly—in order to slow up as much as possible the American intervention—America had to be included in his calculations from the moment President Roosevelt was re-elected for a third term in November, 1940.

The reason for this is not that President Roosevelt had, as his ultimate purpose, to plunge his country into the war, but rather that his re-election was interpreted throughout the world as a proof that the majority of the American people were resolved to resist Hitlerism at home, and, if possible, help to defeat it abroad. The re-election of President Roosevelt gave the forces of resistance to Hitlerism a leader whose prestige was great enough to match that of Hitler himself. With Churchill in London and Roosevelt in Washington, a fighting front was established potentially strong enough not only to "stop Hitler" but eventually to defeat him. For the first time since Hitler came to power in 1933, he met two adversaries whose vision was sufficiently broad and whose understanding of the situation sufficiently clear to make his usual strategy of intimidation, threats, blackmail and deceit largely ineffectual.

Ever since October 5, 1937, when President Roosevelt had delivered his famous Chicago speech on the necessity of placing the aggressor nations "in quarantine," American public opinion had been subjected to a "campaign of education" carried on perseveringly by the President himself and by Secretary of State Cordell Hull. In spite of isolationist and pacifist opposition, Franklin Roosevelt succeeded in gaining the confidence of an increasing majority of his compatriots. His pessimistic views of the situation were amply vindicated by events, and after his third election, his foreign policy was constantly supported by at least seventy-five per cent of public opinion.

This policy pursued one single objective: to prevent the domination of Hitlerism both as a military hegemony and as a political, economic and philosophical tyranny. Under the guidance of President Roosevelt, the American people gradually became convinced that American security itself was being threatened by Hitler's victories and that, if he succeeded in destroying British sea power, America's chance of survival as an independent nation would be endangered.

Thus America gradually awoke to the realization that the control of the seas should not pass to Hitler. As soon as this principle became clear to American consciousness, its application became a question of method and expediency. The Lend-Lease Bill which President Roosevelt signed on March 11, 1941, marks the definite alignment of American power against Hitler. By committing themselves to support England without any limit except those of practical production, the United States compelled Hitler to include them in his program of conquest. Whether Hitler ever intended to subjugate the whole world, he was now compelled to do so. The peace which he had promised his people and the New Order which he planned to establish could not be achieved as long as the British Empire and America stood in the way.

Hitler himself became conscious of this fact and his speeches of this period contain many allusions to it. Although always careful not to attack America directly in order both to encourage hesitancy in the United States and to reassure German opinion at home, he frequently admitted that the conflict had now become a war between two fundamentally hostile systems, his own and that of Roosevelt and Churchill. "We are involved in a conflict in which more than the victory of only one country or the other is at stake," said Hitler on December 10, 1940, "it is rather a war of two opposing worlds." And in the same speech, after comparing the decadence of England under the leadership of "Etonian and Harrovian" aristocracy with the unity and equality of the National Socialist system, Hitler concluded: "These are the two worlds. I grant that one of the two must succumb."

It may be noted in passing that in spite of his avowed resolution to defeat England, Hitler continued to refer to his lifelong dream of coming to an understanding with that country. His attitude had always been curiously ambivalent in that respect, a mixture of hatred and admiration which led him into queer apologies and protests whenever he mentioned Britain. "I have offered her my hand again and again. It was the very essence of my program to come to an understanding with her." And in the speech of December 10, 1940, he made this curious protest: "Only a madman can say that I have ever had an inferiority complex with respect to the British. I have never had any such feeling of inferiority." As if he still hoped that the great dream formulated in *Mein Kampf* of an alliance with England could be made palatable to the English under Churchill as the dream of an alliance with Italy had been realized through Mussolini. . . .

Furthermore, the backing of England by America made this dream of alliance even more improbable. Because whereas Hitler could exert his sarcasm against the traditional class system of England, America did represent the nearest thing to a true democracy that history had seen. Two worlds were indeed opposed and Hitler for once had to agree with Roosevelt in admitting that the two could not live side by side.

In order to force British surrender, Hitler carried on two series of military and naval operations during the period September, 1940–June, 1941 which, however spectacular and dangerous, brought no conclusive results.

The first one was called the battle of the Atlantic. In the eyes of Winston Churchill himself it was the main battle. The destruction of shipping was intense and if sustained at the same rate was bound to cut the line of supplies coming from America and to reduce England to starvation.

The second battle was that of the Mediterranean. The conquest of the Balkans was carried on with the usual speed and efficiency of the *Blitzkrieg* methods. Its purpose, according to Hitler, was to prevent the Allies from establishing a secondary front in southern Europe and to close the Near East and the Mediterranean to the British. The remarkable conquest of Crete by air transports and parachutists gave Germany apparent domination over the eastern Mediterranean. But these successes, however rapid and spectacular—

however demoralizing for the British and their allies—had brought no decisive solution by the end of the Spring, 1941. Those who had predicted that the whole of the Mediterranean would be under Axis domination by that time were proved wrong. Gibraltar, Suez and the oil fields of Iraq were still in British hands.

Similarly, in the political field no durable progress was achieved. The efforts to bring France into active participation in the war against England met with the resistance of the French public opinion, which in spite of Marshal Pétain's and Admiral Darlan's appeals for increased "collaboration" with Germany and the New Order, remained hopeful in the ultimate victory of England.

No positive progress was made with Spain either. Unable to recover from the aftermath of the Civil War, this country gave little more than moral support to Hitler. Nothing apparently could have stopped a German army from marching through Franco's Spain to attack Gibraltar from the rear—nothing except, perhaps, the poverty of the country itself which was starving and incapable of feeding a foreign army.

As for Italy, the loss of Ethiopia, defeats in Libya and heavy losses at sea practically eliminated her from the war. Not only could the Italians not be counted as military allies any longer, but they had to be rescued by German divisions both in Greece and in Africa. The imperial ambitions of Mussolini had vanished. His position in relation to Hitler was not very different from that of a Nazi *gauleiter.* Italy, for all intents and purposes, had become a German province like Holland and Norway.

Thus, although the German Army was in effective control of the whole of Europe, from Warsaw to Brest and from Narvik to Salonika, all the operations conducted during the first half of the second year of the war were characterized by an apparent lack of planning and by inconclusiveness. Much was undertaken and many projects were talked about, but few were carried through.

In fact the most positive result of these first eighteen months of Hitlerian rule was that the whole of continental Europe was returning rapidly to a state of chaos. National boundaries had ceased to exist. Two-thirds of France remained under German military control and the Vichy Government was just as ignorant on June 22, 1941, of what the future status of France would be as it was a year before when the armistice was signed.

Belgium, Holland, Denmark, Norway had become German colonies and were treated as such. In Poland, it was stated that eighteen per cent of the population had already been eliminated by the Germans. The Balkans had returned to a condition of anarchy and turmoil reminiscent of the early years of the century. Nazi agents had revived hatred and jealousy between races who had but recently learned to live at peace together. Moslems turned against Christians. Croats, Dalmatians, Serbians were once again engaged in fratricidal warfare and persecutions. The puppet governments ruling in Budapest, Bucharest and Sofia were nevertheless given enough liberty by their German rulers to revive ancient hatreds and stir up nationalistic feuds.

The brutal oppression of the Czechs had gradually broken down their silent and sturdy resistance. The grain from the rich fields of Bohemia was moved northward while the factories were turning out guns and tanks for the armies of the conqueror.

The whole of Europe had been plundered with ruthless German efficiency. The methods employed varied according to the region, but the result was always the same: the products of the conquered lands, whatever they might be, were used up by the German Army or served to replenish the stocks of the Reich. Everywhere the conquered people were made to feel the oppressive tyranny of their new masters, and everywhere also these new masters forced the people into varying degrees of slavery.

It mattered little whether this new form of subjection assumed the disguised form of so-called voluntary "collaboration" as in France, or whether it took the shape of conscript labor, as in Poland or Czechoslovakia. The consequence was the same: with amazing rapidity the whole standard of living fell throughout Europe to a level which had not been known for centuries. In less than a year, it seemed as if one hundred and fifty years of civilization had been wiped out. Near-famine in certain regions, want and scarcity everywhere became the norm. Culture receded. Only a few books were published in countries which, like France, Holland, Belgium and Norway had led the way in art and literature. The freedom of the press disappeared. Such newspapers as survived were only allowed to express the views of the conquerors or of their puppet governments. Seldom had Europe as a whole been subjected to such physical and spiritual degradation. Seldom had a whole form of civilization been so quickly and radically menaced by the destructiveness of tyranny.

But no echo of this disaster can be found in Hitler's speeches. Quite the contrary; and if future historians had nothing to base their judgment on except these speeches, their conclusion would be that Europe had never been so close to the millennium nor so anxious to hasten the final triumph of its new Messiah.

It had always been Hitler's conviction, ever since he started to unite Germany under the flag of National Socialism, that the condition of success was the possibility of maintaining himself and the German nation in a state of fanatical devotion towards the mystical aim which he had set for the German people. His belief that victory would automatically ensue never left him, and it may well be that the messianic conception he had of himself is what enabled him so consistently to disregard the ruins and misery which his conquests spread and to assert that out of these ruins and sufferings, in spite of all evidence to the contrary, a New European Order was being born.

The *leitmotiv* of the New Order was not new. For several

years the theorists of National Socialism, as well as Hitler himself, had made it clear that the purpose of Nazism was to transform radically the political, social and spiritual complexion of Europe. The fundamental idea of the Nazi New Order was that all European nations should be integrated into one vast economic and political unit under the direction of Berlin. Europe was to be Germanized, in the sense that no culture or political form hostile to Germany would be tolerated. Europe would be organized into a field of exploitation for the master-race and the people of Europe reduced to a state of total dependency, which, in practice, meant varying degrees of serfdom.

Although there had been a great deal of disagreement within Germany itself as to the methods necessary to achieve this end, there was unanimity as to the objective, and there is little reason to doubt that the vast majority of the Germans were united behind Hitler in this major purpose.

But it is interesting to note that the *leitmotiv* of the New Order and the expression itself had now become a substitute for the final victory which he had promised and could not obtain. To the Germans as well as to the conquered people he had to offer something more than the indefinite continuation of military triumphs and the enforcement of the laws of military occupation. But at the same time, it had become apparent that Hitler's New Order was indistinguishable from domination supported by force and that as long as other powerful groups of nations such as the Anglo-American block refused to recognize Hitler's rule, there could be no New Order and no peace.

"I am convinced that 1941 will be the crucial year of a great new order in Europe" said Hitler on January 30. "The world shall open up for everyone. Privileges for individuals, the tyranny of certain nations and their financial rulers shall fall. And last of all, this year will help to provide the foundations of a real understanding among peoples, and with it the certainty of conciliation among nations."

Thus, in the midst of European chaos, Hitler had to prophesy, as he had always done, that the end was near and that peace, order and happiness would reign on earth. And one is led to wonder whether these hopeful words are intended to deceive those who hear them or whether they are not the expression of a man who tries to evade the reality such as he had himself created.

There is little new in Hitler's strategy during this period as reflected in his speeches. One finds the same persistent effort to exonerate himself from all responsibility for the prolongation of the war, the same accusations hurled at his opponents, the same glorification of his own achievements. The effect of his speeches on the outside world, however, is much reduced, and one senses, from time to time, that he himself is aware that his opponents have to a great extent shaken off the morbid spell produced by his oratory. His appeals for peace fall on deaf ears and this may be why he has to resort to more spectacular and, at the same time, more dangerous methods, such as the alleged peace mission of Rudolph Hess.

But in stabilizing his conquests, no progress had been accomplished. On the contrary, the picture offered an increasingly sharper contrast between Hitler's dream of a regenerated and peaceful world and the frightful reality. Europe was changed indeed, but what that change meant was a tragic regression, an accumulation of ruins and untold suffering.

The German people, the *Herrenvolk,* were surrounded by a vast and ever-expanding rim of devastation where hatred and rebellion brewed. The plundering of these borderlands and the enslavement of the conquered nations were the basis of Hitler's New Order. And what this New Order actually meant in practice could now be seen: it was nothing but the system by which Hitler's armies could be maintained at the expense of the conquered.

The New Order in fact was only an attractive word to designate the rule of military occupation.

If no one could question the fact that Hitler was now the master of Europe thanks to the power of his army, no one could doubt either that Hitler had now become the prisoner of his own war machine and that there was no choice for him except to keep it going. In his early days, he had said that to regain her place in the sun, Germany should be strong and armed. But the means had become an end in themselves. The whole German nation and all the people of Europe were now employed in one huge single task, in one monolithic industry: the industry of war. War for Hitler had become a necessity. Only through the continuation of war could he hope to keep himself in power and he saw clearly that there was no alternative left for him and his people than total victory or total disaster.

"We know perfectly well that if we are defeated in this war it would not only be the end of our National Socialist work of reconstruction, but the end of the German people as a whole. For without its power of co-ordination, the German people would starve. Today the masses dependent on us number 120 or 130 millions, of which 85 millions alone are our own people. We remain aware of this fact."

Thus spoke Hitler at the end of 1940, which meant in plain language that Germany from now on could survive only as long as her "power of co-ordination," i.e., her domination over other people, could be maintained and extended.

But by June 22, 1941, exactly one year after the signature of the armistice with France, Hitler's "work of reconstruction" was far from completion. All he had to show was one year of unfinished business. His major effort, the subjugation of England, by either force or persuasion, had failed. The life-lines of the Empire, though threatened, were still secure. As long as there were people outside the "power of co-ordination" of Germany, Hitler had to fight on.

But to fight on, Hitler needed more food, more oil and

more raw materials of all kinds than even the whole resources of Western Europe could provide. The resistance of England and the growing power of America were creating the kind of situation most dreaded by Hitler's generals: a stalemate. And the experience of the last war had shown how such a stalemate would end if allowed to endure. Although Germany's domination now extended to the shores of the Atlantic and of the Mediterranean, Germany was still encircled. To break this circle before it was too late became an imperative necessity.

•

SPEECH OF NOVEMBER 8, 1940

Munich

Background

September 20—Ribbentrop confers with Mussolini in Rome.

September 25—General de Gaulle, head of the Free French forces, tries to land in Dakar, supported by the British. The attempt fails.

September 27—Germany, Italy, and Japan sign a pact of alliance in case one of them should be attacked by a country not yet participating in the war. This is admittedly aimed at the United States.

October 4—Hitler and Mussolini confer at Brenner Pass.

October 8—German troops begin occupation of Rumania, "to protect oil fields."

October 10—Luftwaffe attacks more than fifty London districts.

October 13—President Roosevelt denounces policy of appeasement which he considers as a weapon of the totalitarian States.

October 18—Vichy promulgates decree barring Jews from certain professions.

October 22—Hitler confers with Laval in France.

October 23—Hitler confers with Franco on Franco-Spanish border.

October 24—Hitler confers with Pétain at Montoire (France).

October 28—Italy invades Greece. Hitler and Mussolini meet at Florence.

November 5—Franklin Roosevelt elected President of the United States for third term.

The Speech

"I AM one of the hardest men Germany has had for decades, perhaps for centuries, equipped with the greatest authority of any German leader.

"But above all, I believe in my success. I believe in it unconditionally. I am firmly convinced that this struggle will not end differently by a single hair than the struggle that I once waged in Germany itself.

"I am convinced that providence has brought me this far and has spared me from all the dangers in order to let me lead the German people in this battle. . . ."

"I participated in the great war, I belong to those who then were cheated of their success. It is therefore my unshakable determination that this struggle shall not end as did that one. . . ."

Germany was "poorly armed" when that war broke out, "but she held for four years."

"For four year they [the Allies] strained themselves, and then they had to get the American magician-priest, who found a formula that took in the German nation, trusting in the word of honor of a foreign President. . . ."

"You know the foreign political conception I had in those days. I wanted the closest friendship with England. I thought the Germanic races should go together.

"I wanted the same relationship with Italy. I also thought of Japan as a power with whose interests our own could coincide. . . ."

"If England had agreed, good. They did not agree. Also good.

"But then no compromises; nothing done by halves. I decided that either we were no soldiers or else we were the best in the world. . . ."

"Then came the moment when it was no longer a question of whether war could be avoided entirely, but only if it could be avoided for one or two or three years by means of very serious German humiliations. At the moment when I realized that England wanted only to gain time, that over there they were determined under any circumstances to wage war with us, in that same moment I had only one wish:

"If they were determined to declare war on us, then I hoped they would do it while I was still alive. . . ."

"If England says that the war will continue, that is all the same to me. But it will end with our victory. You may believe me in that. . . ."

"As far as American production figures are concerned, they cannot even be formulated in astronomical figures. In this field, therefore, I do not want to be a competitor. But I can assure you of one thing: German production capacity is the highest in the world. And we will not climb down from it, *because we are in a position today to mobilize the power of almost all Europe—and that I shall do so industrially you may well believe. . . ."*

"Germany today, in any case, is, together with her Allies, strong enough to oppose any combination of powers in the world. There is no coalition of powers that could equal ours. . . ."

"As to peace, it is my unalterable determination to carry the conflict on to a clear decision.

"Just as I, as a National Socialist, declined all compromise in the battle for Germany, I today refuse all compromise. Some one must break, and under no circumstances will it be Germany."

Press

New York Times, November 9—Hitler delivered his speech with fire and vigor and was unsparing in his caustic denunciation of Great Britain as the seeker of war. It was a warlike pronouncement. . . .

•

SPEECH OF DECEMBER 10, 1940

Berlin, Rheinmetall-Borsig Works

Background

November 9—Chamberlain dies.

November 12—Molotov received in Berlin.

November 13—British seaplanes attack Italian ships in Taranto.

November 14—Coventry devastated by Luftwaffe.

November 20—Admiral Leahy appointed United States Ambassador at Vichy.

November 23—Rumania signs Berlin-Tokyo-Rome pact.

December 3—Italian defense lines crumble in Albania.

December 9—British open offensive against Italians in Egypt.

The Speech

"FELLOW-COUNTRYMEN, workers of Germany:

"Nowadays I do not speak very often. In the first place I

have little time for speaking, and in the second place I believe that this is a time for action rather than speech. We are involved in a conflict in which more than the victory of only one country or the other is at stake; *it is rather a war of two opposing worlds*. I shall try to give you, as far as possible in the time at my disposal, an insight into the essential reasons underlying this conflict. I shall, however, confine myself to Western Europe only. The peoples who are primarily affected—85 million Germans, 46 million Britishers, 45 million Italians, and about 37 million Frenchmen—are the cores of the States who were or still are opposed in war. If I make a comparison between the living conditions of these peoples the following facts become evident:

"Forty-six million Britishers dominate and govern approximately 16 million square miles of the surface of the earth. Thirty-seven million Frenchmen dominate and govern a combined area of approximately 4 million square miles. Forty-five million Italians possess, taking into consideration only those territories in any way capable of being utilized, an area of scarcely 190,000 square miles. Eighty-five million Germans possess as their living space scarcely 232,000 square miles. That is to say: 85 million Germans own only 232,000 square miles on which they must live their lives and 46 million Britishers possess 16 million square miles.

"Now, my fellow-countrymen, this world has not been so divided up by providence or Almighty God. This allocation has been made by man himself. The land was parcelled out for the most part during the last 300 years, that is, during the period in which, unfortunately, the German people were helpless and torn by internal dissension. Split up into hundreds of small states in consequence of the Treaty of Muenster at the end of the Thirty Years' War, our people frittered away their entire strength in internal strife. . . . While during this period the Germans, notwithstanding their particular ability among the people of Western Europe, dissipated their powers in vain internal struggles, the division of the world proceeded beyond their borders. It was not by treaties or by binding agreements, but exclusively by the use of force that Britain forged her gigantic Empire.

"The second people that failed to receive their fair share in this distribution, namely the Italians, experienced and suffered a similar fate. Torn by internal conflicts, devoid of unity, split up into numerous small states, this people also dissipated all their energy in internal strife. Nor was Italy able to obtain even the natural position in the Mediterranean which was her due.

"Thus in comparison with others, these two powerful peoples have received much less than their fair share. The objection might be raised: Is this really of decisive importance?

"My fellow-countrymen, man does not exist on theories and phrases, on declarations or on systems of political philosophy; he lives on what he can gain from the soil by his own labor in the form of food and raw materials. This is what he can eat, this is what he can use for manufacture and production. If a man's own living conditions offer him too little, his life will be wretched. We see that within the countries themselves, fruitful areas afford better living conditions than poor barren lands. In the one case there are flourishing villages; in the other poverty-stricken communities. A man may live in a stony desert or in a fruitful land of plenty. This handicap can never be fully overcome by theories, nor even by the will to work.

"We see that the primary cause for the existing tensions lies in the unfair distribution of the riches of the earth. And it is only natural that evolution follows the same rule in the larger framework as it does in the case of individuals. Just as the tension existing between rich and poor within a country must be compensated for either by reason or often, if reason fails, by force, so in the life of a nation one cannot claim everything and leave nothing to others. . . ."

"The great task which I set myself in internal affairs was to bring reason to bear on the problems, to eliminate dangerous tensions by invoking the common sense of all, to bridge the gulf between excessive riches and excessive poverty. I recognized, of course, that such processes cannot be consummated overnight. It is always preferable to bring together widely separated classes gradually and by the exercise of reason, rather than to resort to a solution based on force. . . ."

"Therefore, the right to live is at the same time a just claim to the soil which alone is the source of life. When unreasonableness threatened to choke their development, nations fought for this sacred claim. No other course was open to them and they realized that even bloodshed and sacrifice are better than the gradual extinction of a nation. Thus, at the beginning of our National Socialist Revolution in 1933, we set forth two demands. The first of these was the unification of our people, for without this unification it would not have been possible to mobilize the forces required to formulate and, particularly, to secure Germany's essential claims. . . ."

"For us, therefore, national unity was one of the essential conditions if we were to co-ordinate the powers inherent in the German nation properly, to make the German people conscious of their own greatness, realize their strength, recognize and present their vital claims, and seek national unity by an appeal to reason.

"I know that I have not been successful everywhere. For nearly fifteen years of my struggle I was the target of two opposing sides. One side reproached me: 'You want to drag us who belong to the intelligentsia and to the upper classes down to the level of the others. That is impossible. We are educated people. In addition to that, we are wealthy and cultured. We cannot accept this.'

"These people were incapable of listening to reason; even today there are some who cannot be converted. However, on the whole the number of those who realize that the lack of unity in our national structure would sooner or later lead to the destruction of all classes has become greater and greater.

"I also met with opposition from the other side. They said: 'We have our class consciousness.' However, I was obliged to take the stand that in the existing situation we could not afford to make experiments. It certainly would have been simple to eliminate the intelligentsia. Such a process could be carried out at once. But we would have to wait fifty or perhaps a hundred years for the gap to refill—and such a period would mean the destruction of the nation. For how can our people, its 360 per square mile, exist at all if they do not employ every ounce of brain power and physical strength to wrest from their soil what they need? This distinguishes us from the others. In Canada, for example, there are 2.6 persons per square mile; in other countries perhaps 16, 18, 20 or 26 persons. Well, my fellow-countrymen, no matter how stupidly one managed one's affairs in such a country, a decent living would still be possible.

"Here in Germany, however, there are 360 persons per square mile. The others cannot manage with 26 persons per square mile, but we must manage with 360. This is the task we face. That is why I expressed this view in 1933: 'We *must* solve these problems and, therefore, we *shall* solve them.' Of course that was not easy; everything could not be done immediately. Human beings are the product of their education, and, unfortunately, this begins practically at birth. Infants are clothed in different ways. After this has been going on for centuries, someone suddenly comes along and says:—'I want to unwrap the child and remove all its clothing so that I may discover its true nature'—which is, of course, the same in every case. You have only created the difference by the external wrappings; underneath these they are all alike.

"However, it is not so easy to do this. Everyone resists being unwrapped. Everyone wishes to retain the habits he has acquired through his upbringing. But we will carry out our task just the same. We have enormous patience. I know that what has been done for three, four, or five centuries cannot be undone in two, three, or five years. The decisive point is to make a start. . . ."

"It has been a tremendous task. The establishment of a German community was the first item on the program in 1933. The second item was the elimination of foreign oppression as expressed in the Treaty of Versailles, which also prevented our attaining national unity, forbade large sections of our people to unite, and robbed us of our possessions in the world, our German colonies.

"The second item on the program was, therefore, the struggle against Versailles. No one can say that I express this opinion for the first time today. I expressed it, my fellow-countrymen, in the days following the Great War when, still a soldier, I made my first appearance in the political arena. My first address was a speech against the collapse, against the Treaty of Versailles, and for the re-establishment of a powerful German Reich. That was the beginning of my work. What I have brought about since then does not represent a new aim but the oldest aim. It is the primary reason for the conflict in which we find ourselves today. The rest of the world did not want our inner unity, because they knew that, once it was achieved, the vital claim of our masses could be realized. They wanted to maintain the Dictate of Versailles in which they saw a second peace of Westphalia. However, there is still another reason. I have stated that the world was unequally divided. American observers and Englishmen have found a wonderful expression for this fact: They say there are two kinds of peoples—the 'haves' and the 'have-nots.' We, the British, are the 'haves.' It is a fact that we possess sixteen million square miles. And we Americans are also 'haves,' and so are we Frenchmen. The others—they are simply the 'have-nots.' He who *has* nothing *receives* nothing. He shall remain what he is. He who has is not willing to share it.

"All my life I have been a 'have-not.' At home I was a

'have-not.' I regard myself as belonging to them and have always fought exclusively for them. *I defended them and, therefore, I stand before the world as their representative. I shall never recognize the claim of the others to that which they have taken by force.* Under no circumstances can I acknowledge this claim with regard to that which has been taken from us. It is interesting to examine the life of these rich people. In this Anglo-French world there exists, as it were, democracy, which means the rule of the people by the people. Now the people must possess some means of giving expression to their thoughts or their wishes. Examining this problem more closely, *we see that the people themselves have originally no convictions of their own. Their convictions are formed, of course, just as everywhere else. The decisive question is who enlightens the people, who educates them? In those countries, it is actually capital that rules;* that is, nothing more than a clique of a few hundred men who possess untold wealth and, as a consequence of the peculiar structure of their national life, are more or less independent and free. They say: 'Here we have liberty.' By this they mean, above all, an uncontrolled economy, and by an uncontrolled economy, the freedom not only to acquire capital but to make absolutely free use of it. That means freedom from national control or control by the people both in the acquisition of capital and in its employment. This is really what they mean when they speak of liberty. These capitalists create their own press and then speak of the 'freedom of the press.'

"In reality, every one of the newspapers has a master, and in every case this master is the capitalist, the owner. This master, not the editor, is the one who directs the policy of the paper. If the editor tries to write other than what suits the master, he is ousted the next day. This press, which is the absolutely submissive and characterless slave of the owners, molds public opinion. Public opinion thus mobilized by them is, in its turn, split up into political parties. The difference between these parties is as small as it formerly was in Germany. You know them, of course—the old parties. They were always one and the same. In Britain matters are usually so arranged that families are divided up, one member being a conservative, another a liberal, and a third belonging to the labor party. Actually, all three sit together as members of the family, decide upon their common attitude and determine it. A further point is that the 'elected people' actually form a community which operates and controls all these organizations. For this reason, the opposition in England is really always the same, for on all essential matters in which the opposition has to make itself felt, the parties are always in agreement. They have one and the same conviction and through the medium of the press mold public opinion along corresponding lines. One might well believe that in these countries of liberty and riches, the people must possess an unlimited degree of prosperity. But no! On the contrary, it is precisely in these countries that the distress of the masses is greater than anywhere else. Such is the case in 'rich Britain.'

"She controls sixteen million square miles. In India, for example, a hundred million colonial workers with a wretched standard of living must labor for her. One might think, perhaps, that at least in England itself every person must have his share of these riches. By no means! In that country class distinction is the crassest imaginable. There is poverty —incredible poverty—on the one side, and equally incredible wealth on the other. They have not solved a single problem. The workmen of that country which possesses more than one-sixth of the globe and of the world's natural resources dwell in misery, and the masses of the people are poorly clad. In a country which ought to have more than enough bread and every sort of fruit, we find millions of the lower classes who have not even enough to fill their stomachs, and go about hungry. A nation which could provide work for the whole world must acknowledge the fact that it cannot even abolish unemployment at home. For decades this rich Britain has had two and a half million unemployed; rich America, ten to thirteen millions, year after year; France, six, seven, and eight hundred thousand. Well, my fellow-countrymen—what then are we to say about ourselves?

"It is self-evident that where this democracy rules, the people as such are not taken into consideration at all. The only thing that matters is the existence of a few hundred gigantic capitalists who own all the factories and their stock and, through them, control the people. The masses of the people do not interest them in the least. They are interested in them just as were our bourgeois parties in former times—only when elections are being held, when they need votes. Otherwise, the life of the masses is a matter of complete indifference to them.

"To this must be added the difference in education. Is it not ludicrous to hear a member of the British Labor Party—who, of course, as a member of the Opposition is officially paid by the government—say: 'When the war is over, we will do something in social respects'?

"It is the members of Parliament who are the directors of the business concerns—just as used to be the case with us. But we have abolished all that. A member of the Reichstag cannot belong to a Board of Directors, except as a purely honorary member. He is prohibited from accepting any emolument, financial or otherwise. This is not the case in other countries.

"They reply: 'That is why our form of government is sacred to us.' I can well believe it, for that form of government certainly pays very well. But whether it is sacred to the mass of the people as well is another matter.

"The people as a whole definitely suffer. I do not consider it possible in the long run for one man to work and toil for a whole year in return for ridiculous wages, while another jumps into an express train once a year and pockets enormous sums. Such conditions are a disgrace. On the other hand, we National Socialists equally oppose the theory that all men are equals. Today, when a man of genius makes some astounding invention and enormously benefits his country by his brains, we pay him his due, for he has really accomplished something and been of use to his country. However, we hope to make it impossible for idle drones to inhabit this country.

"I could continue to cite examples indefinitely. *The fact remains that two worlds are face to face with one another.* Our opponents are quite right when they say: 'Nothing can reconcile us to the National Socialist world.' How could a narrow-minded capitalist ever agree to my principles? It would be easier for the Devil to go to church and cross himself with holy water than for these people to comprehend the ideas which are accepted facts to us today. But we have solved our problems.

"To take another instance where we are condemned: They claim to be fighting for the maintenance of the gold standard as the currency basis. That I can well believe, for the gold is in their hands. We, too, once had gold, but it was stolen and extorted from us. When I came to power, it was not malice which made me abandon the gold standard. Germany simply had no gold left. Consequently, quitting the gold standard presented no difficulties, for it is always easy to part with what one does not have. We had no gold. We had no foreign exchange. They had all been stolen and extorted from us during the previous fifteen years. But, my fellow-countrymen, I did not regret it, for we have constructed our economic system on a wholly different basis. In our eyes, gold is not of value in itself. It is only an agent by which nations can be suppressed and dominated.

"When I took over the government, I had only one hope on which to build, namely, the efficiency and ability of the German nation and the German workingman; the intelligence of our inventors, engineers, technicians, chemists, and so forth. I built on the strength which animates our economic system. One simple question faced me: Are we to perish because we have no gold; am I to believe in a phantom which spells our destruction? I championed the opposite opinion: Even though we have no gold, we have capacity for work.

"*The German capacity for work is our gold and our capital, and with this gold I can compete successfully with any power in the world.* We want to live in houses which have to be built. Hence, the workers must build them, and the raw materials required must be procured by work. My whole economic system has been built up on the conception of work. We have solved our problems while, amazingly enough, the capitalist countries and their currencies have suffered bankruptcy.

"Sterling can find no market today. Throw it at any one and he will step aside to avoid being hit. But our Reichsmark, which is backed by no gold, has remained stable. Why? It has no gold cover; it is backed by you and by your work. You have helped me to keep the mark stable. German currency, with no gold coverage, is worth more today than gold itself. It signifies unceasing production. This we owe to the German farmer, who has worked from daybreak till nightfall. This we owe to the German worker, who has given us his whole strength. The whole problem has been solved in one instant, as if by magic.

"My dear friends, if I had stated publicly eight or nine years ago: 'In seven or eight years the problem of how to provide work for the unemployed will be solved, and the problem then will be where to find workers,' I should have harmed my cause. Every one would have declared: 'The man is mad. It is useless to talk to him, much less to support him. Nobody should vote for him. He is a fantastic creature.' Today, however, all this has come true. Today, the only question for us is where to find workers. That, my fellow-countrymen, is the blessing which work brings.

"Work alone can create new work; money cannot create

work. Work alone can create values, values with which to reward those who work. The work of one man makes it possible for another to live and continue to work. And when we have mobilized the working capacity of our people to its utmost, each individual worker will receive more and more of the world's goods.

"We have incorporated seven million unemployed into our economic system; we have transformed another six millions from part-time into full-time workers; we are even working overtime. And all this is paid for in cash in Reichsmarks which maintained their value in peacetime. In wartime we had to ration its purchasing capacity, not in order to devalue it, but simply to earmark a portion of our industry for war production to guide us to victory in the struggle for the future of Germany.

"My fellow-countrymen, we are also building a world here, a world of mutual work, a world of mutual effort, and a world of mutual anxieties and mutual duties. It did not surprise me that other countries started rationing only after two, three, five, and seven months, and in some cases only after a year. Believe me, in all these countries, this was not due to chance but to policy. Many a German may have been surprised that food cards appeared on the first morning of the war. Yet, there are, of course, two sides to this food card system. Some people may say: 'Wouldn't it be better to exclude this or that commodity from rationing? What use are a few grams of coffee when nobody gets much anyway? Without rationing, at least a few would get more.' Now that is exactly what we want to avoid. We want to avoid one person having more of the most vital commodities than another. There are other things—a valuable painting, for instance. Not everybody is in a position to buy a Titian, even if he had the money. Because Titian painted only a few pictures, only a few can afford his work. This or that man can buy one if he has enough money. He spends it, and it circulates through the country. But in the case of food, everybody must be served alike.

"The other countries waited to see how things would develop. The question was asked: 'Will meat be rationed?' That was the first sounding of a warning. In other words: 'If you are a capitalist, cover your requirements, buy yourself a refrigerator and hoard up a few sides of bacon.'

" 'Shall we ration coffee? There are two opinions as to whether it should be rationed or not. It might be possible that in the end those who think that coffee should be rationed might triumph.' They devote four whole weeks to the discussion and everybody who has a spark of egotism—as they have in the democracies—says to himself: 'Aha, so coffee is to be rationed in the near future; let us hoard it.' Then, when the supplies are exhausting themselves, it is at last rationed.

"It was just this that we wanted to avoid. That is why in order to ensure equal distribution, we have had to impose certain restrictions from the very start. And we are not well-disposed toward those who do not observe regulations.

"One thing is certain, my fellow-countrymen: *All in all, we have today a state with a different economic and political orientation from that of the Western democracies.*

"Well, it must now be made possible for the British worker to travel. It is remarkable that they should at last hit upon the idea that traveling should be something not for millionaires alone, but for the people too. In this country, the problem was solved some time ago. In the other countries—as is shown by their whole economic structure—the selfishness of a relatively small stratum rules under the mask of democracy. This stratum is neither checked nor controlled by anyone.

"It is therefore understandable if an Englishman says: 'We do not want our world to be subject to any sort of collapse.' Quite so. The English know full well that their Empire is not menaced by us. But they say quite truthfully: 'If the ideas that are popular in Germany are not completely eliminated, they might become popular among our own people, and that is the danger. We do not want this.' It would do no harm if they did become popular there, but these people are just as narrow-minded as many once were in Germany. In this respect they prefer to remain bound to their conservative methods. They do not wish to depart from them, and do not conceal the fact.

"They say, 'The German methods do not suit us at all.'

"And what are these methods? You know, my comrades, that I have destroyed nothing in Germany. I have always proceeded very carefully, because I believe—as I have already said—that we cannot afford to wreck anything. I am proud that the Revolution of 1933 was brought to pass without breaking a single windowpane. Nevertheless, we have wrought enormous changes.

"I wish to put before you a few basic facts: The first is that in the capitalistic democratic world the most important principle of economy is that the people exist for trade and industry, and that these in turn exist for capital. We have reversed this principle by making capital exist for trade and industry, and trade and industry exist for the people. In other words, the people come first. Everything else is but a means to this end. When an economic system is not capable of feeding and clothing a people, then it is bad, regardless of whether a few hundred people say: 'As far as I am concerned it is good, excellent; my dividends are splendid.'

"However, the dividends do not interest me at all. Here we have drawn the line. They may then retort: 'Well, look here, that is just what we mean. You jeopardize liberty.'

"Yes, certainly, we jeopardize the liberty to profiteer at the expense of the community, and, if necessary, we even abolish it. British capitalists, to mention only one instance, can pocket dividends of 76, 80, 95, 140, and even 160 per cent from their armament industry. Naturally they say: 'If the German methods grow apace and should prove victorious, this sort of thing will stop.'

"They are perfectly right. I should never tolerate such a state of affairs. In my eyes, a 6 per cent dividend is sufficient. Even from this 6 per cent we deduct one-half and, as for the rest, we must have definite proof that it is invested in the interest of the country as a whole. In other words, no individual has the right to dispose arbitrarily of money which ought to be invested for the good of the country. If he disposes of it sensibly, well and good; if not, the National Socialist state will intervene.

"To take another instance, besides dividends there are the so-called directors' fees. You probably have no idea how appallingly active a board of directors is. Once a year its members have to make a journey. They have to go to the station, get into a first-class compartment and travel to some place or other. They arrive at an appointed office at about 10 or 11 A.M. There they must listen to a report. When the report has been read, they must listen to a few comments on it. They may be kept in their seats until 1 P.M. or even 2. Shortly after 2 o'clock they rise from their chairs and set out on their homeward journey, again, of course, traveling first class. It is hardly surprising that they claim 3,000, 4,000, or even 5,000 as compensation for this. Our directors formerly did the same—for what a lot of time it costs them! Such effort had to be made worth while! Of course, we have got rid of all this nonsense, which was merely veiled profiteering and even bribery.

"In Germany, the people, without any doubt, decide their existence. They determine the principles of their government. In fact it has been possible in this country to incorporate many of the broad masses into the National Socialist party, that gigantic organization embracing millions and having millions of officials drawn from the people themselves. This principle is extended to the highest ranks.

"For the first time in German history, we have a state which has absolutely abolished all social prejudices in regard to political appointments as well as in private life. I myself am the best proof of this. *Just imagine: I am not even a lawyer, and yet I am your Fuehrer!*

"It is not only in ordinary life that we have succeeded in appointing the best among the people for every position. We have Reichsstatthalters who were formerly agricultural laborers or locksmiths. Yes, we have even succeeded in breaking down prejudice in a place where it was most deep-seated —in the fighting forces. Thousands of officers are being promoted from the ranks today. We have done away with prejudice. We have generals who were ordinary soldiers and noncommissioned officers twenty-two and twenty-three years ago. In this instance, too, we have overcome all social obstacles. Thus, we are building up our life for the future.

"As you know we have countless schools, national political educational establishments, Adolf Hitler schools, and so on. To these schools we send gifted children of the broad masses, children of working men, farmers' sons whose parents could never have afforded a higher education for their children. We take them in gradually. They are educated here, sent to the *Ordensburgen,* to the Party, later to take their place in the State where they will some day fill the highest posts. . . ."

"Opposed to this there stands a completely different world. In the world the highest ideal is the struggle for wealth, for capital, for family possessions, for personal egoism; everything else is merely a means to such ends. Two worlds confront each other today. *We know perfectly well that if we are defeated in this war it would not only be the end of our National Socialist work of reconstruction, but the end of the German people as a whole.* For without its powers of coordination, the German people would starve. *Today the masses dependent on us number 120 or 130 millions, of which 85 millions alone are our own people.* We remain ever aware of this fact.

"On the other hand, that other world says: 'If we lose, our world-wide capitalistic system will collapse. For it is we who save hoarded gold. It is lying in our cellars and will lose its value. If the idea that work is the decisive factor spreads abroad, what will happen to us? We shall have bought our gold in vain. Our whole claim to world dominion can then no longer be maintained. The people will do away with their dynasties of high finance. They will present their social claims, and the whole world system will be overthrown.'

"I can well understand that they declare: 'Let us prevent this at all costs; it must be prevented.' They can see exactly how our nation has been reconstructed. You see it clearly. For instance, there we see a state ruled by a numerically small upper class. They send their sons to their own schools, to Eton. We have Adolf Hitler schools or national political educational establishments. On the one hand, the sons of plutocrats, financial magnates; on the other, the children of the people. Etonians and Harrovians exclusively in leading positions over there; in this country, men of the people in charge of the State.

"These are the two worlds. I grant that one of the two must succumb. Yes, one or the other. But if we were to succumb, the German people would succumb with us. If the other were to succumb, I am convinced that the nations will become free for the first time. We are not fighting individual Englishmen or Frenchmen. We have nothing against them. For years I proclaimed this as the aim of my foreign policy. We demanded nothing of them, nothing at all. When they started the war they could not say: 'We are doing so because the Germans asked this or that of us.' They said, on the contrary: 'We are declaring war on you because the German system of Government does not suit us; because we fear it might spread to our own people.' For that reason they are carrying on this war. They wanted to blast the German nation back to the time of Versailles, to the indescribable misery of those days. But they have made a great mistake.

"If in this war everything points to the fact that gold is fighting against work, capitalism against peoples, and reaction against the progress of humanity, then work, the peoples, and progress will be victorious. Even the support of the Jewish race will not avail the others.

"I have seen all this coming for years. What did I ask of the other world? Nothing but the right for Germans to reunite and the restoration of all that had been taken from them—nothing which would have meant a loss to the other nations. How often have I stretched out my hand to them? Ever since I came into power. *I had not the slightest wish to rearm.*

"For what do armaments mean? They absorb so much labor. It was I who regarded work as being of decisive importance, who wished to employ the working capacity of Germany for other plans. I think the news is already out that, after all, I have some fairly important plans in my mind, vast and splendid plans for my people. It is my ambition to make the German people rich and to make the German homeland beautiful. I want the standard of living of the individual raised. I want us to have the most beautiful and the finest civilization. I should like the theater—in fact, the whole of German civilization—to benefit all the people and not to exist only for the upper ten thousand, as is the case in England.

"The plans which we had in mind were tremendous, and I needed workers in order to realize them. Armament only deprives me of workers. I made proposals to limit armaments. I was ridiculed. The only answer I received was 'No.' I proposed the limitation of certain types of armament. That was refused. I proposed that airplanes should be altogether eliminated from warfare. That also was refused. I suggested that bombers should be limited. That was refused. They said: 'That is just how we wish to force our regime upon you.'

"I am not a man who does things by halves. If it becomes necessary for me to defend myself, I defend myself with unlimited zeal. When I saw that the same old warmongers of the World War in Britain were mobilizing once more against the great new German revival, I realized that this struggle would have to be fought once more, that the other side did not want peace.

"It was quite obvious: Who was I before the Great War? An unknown, nameless individual. What was I during the war? A quite inconspicuous, ordinary soldier. I was in no way responsible for the Great War. However, who are the rulers of Britain today? They are the same people who were warmongering before the Great War, the same Churchill who was the vilest agitator among them during the Great War; Chamberlain, who recently died and who at that time agitated in exactly the same way. It was the whole gang, members of the same group, who believe that they can annihilate nations with the blast of the trumpets of Jericho.

"The old spirits have once more come to life, and it is against them that I have armed the German people. I, too, had convictions: I myself served as a soldier during the Great War and know what it means to be fired at by others without being able to shoot back. *I know what it means not to have any ammunition or to have too little, what it means always to be beaten by the other side.* I gained my wholehearted faith in the German people and in the future during those years, from my knowledge of the German soldier, of the ordinary man in the trenches. He was the great hero in my opinion. Of course, the other classes also did everything they could. But there was a difference.

"The Germany of that time certainly seemed quite a tolerable country to anybody living at home amid wealth and luxury. One could have his share of everything, of culture, of the pleasures of life, and so on. He could enjoy German art and many other things; he could travel through the German countryside; he could visit German towns and so forth. What more could he wish for? Naturally, he defended it all.

"On the other hand, however, there was the ordinary common soldier. This unimportant proletarian, who scarcely had sufficient to eat, who always had to slave for his existence, nevertheless fought at the front like a hero for four long years. *It was in him that I placed my trust, and it is with his help that I won back confidence in myself.* When the others had lost their faith in Germany, I regained mine, never losing sight of the ordinary man in the street. I knew that Germany could not perish.

"Germany will not perish so long as she possesses such men. I have also seen how these combatants, these soldiers again and again faced an enemy who could annihilate them simply by his superior material. I was not of the opinion at that time that the British were personally superior to us. *Only a madman can say that I have ever had any inferiority complex with respect to the British. I have never had any such feeling of inferiority.*

"The problem of the individual German against the individual Englishman did not present itself at all at that time. Even at that time they went whining round the whole world until they found support. *This time I was determined to make preparations throughout the world to extend our position, and secondly, to arm at home in such a manner that the German soldier would no longer be obliged to stand alone at the front, exposed to superior forces.*

"The trouble has come. I did everything humanly possible —going almost to the point of self-abasement—to avoid it. I repeatedly made offers to the British. I had discussions with their diplomats here and entreated them to be sensible. But it was all in vain. They wanted war, and they made no secret of it. For seven years Churchill had been saying: 'I want war.' Now he has got it.

"It was regrettable to me that nations whom I wished to bring together and who, in my opinion, could have cooperated to such good purpose, should now be at war with one another. But these gentlemen are aiming at destroying the National Socialist State, at disrupting the German people and dividing them again into their component parts. Such were the war aims they proclaimed in the past and such are their war aims today. However, this time they will be surprised, and I believe that they have already had a foretaste of it.

"There are among you, my fellow-countrymen, many old soldiers who went through the Great War and who know perfectly well what space and time mean. Many of you fought in the East during that war, and all the names which you read about in 1939 were still quite familiar to you. Perhaps many of you marched in bad weather or under the burning sun at that time. The roads were endless. And how desperate was the struggle for every inch of ground. How much blood it cost merely to advance slowly, mile by mile. Think of the pace at which we covered these distances this time. Eighteen days, and the state which wished to cut us to pieces at the gates of Berlin was crushed.

"Then came the British attack on Norway. As a matter of fact, I was told by those Englishmen who always know everything that we had slept through the winter. One great statesman even assured me that I had missed the bus. Yet we arrived just in time to get into it before the British. We had suddenly reawakened. In a few days we made sure of this. We took Norwegian positions as far north as Kirkenes, and I need not tell you that no one will take the soil on which a German soldier stands.

"And then they wanted to be cleverer and speedier in the West—in Holland and Belgium. It led to an offensive that many, especially among our older men, envisaged with fear and anxiety. I am perfectly well aware of what many were thinking at that time. They had experienced the Great War on the Western Front, all the battles in Flanders, in Artois, and around Verdun. They all imagined: 'Today the Maginot line is there. How can it be taken? Above all, how much blood will it cost; what sacrifices will it call for; how long will it take?' Within six weeks this campaign too, had been concluded.

"Belgium, Holland, and France were vanquished; the Channel Coast was occupied; our batteries were brought into position there and our bases established. Of these positions, too, do I say: 'No power in the world can drive us out of this region against our will.'

"And now my fellow-countrymen, let us think of the sacrifices. For the individual, they are very great. The woman who has lost her husband has lost her all, and the same is true of the child that has lost its father. The mother who has sacrificed her child, and the betrothed or the sweetheart who have been parted from loved ones never to see them again have all made great sacrifices. However, if we add all these losses together and compare them with the sacrifices of the Great War, then—however great they may be for the individual—they are incomparably small. Consider that we have not nearly so many dead as Germany had in 1870-71 in the struggle against France. We have broken the ring encircling Germany by these sacrifices. The number of wounded is also extremely small, merely a fraction of what was expected.

"For all this, our thanks are due to our magnificent army, inspired by a new spirit and into which the spirit of our national community has also penetrated. The army now really knows for what it is fighting. We owe thanks to our soldiers for their tremendous achievements. But the German soldier gives thanks to you, the munitions workers, for forging the weapons for his use. For this is the first time that he has gone into battle without feeling that he was inferior to the enemy in numbers or that his weapons were of poorer quality. Our weapons were better in every respect.

"That is your doing; the result of your workmanship, of your industry, your capacity, your devotion. Millions of German families still have their breadwinners today and will have them in the future, innumerable fathers and mothers still have their sons—and their thanks are due to *you,* my munitions workers. You have forged for them the weapons with which they were able to go forward to victory, weapons which today give them so much confidence that everyone knows we are not only the best soldiers in the world but that we also have the best weapons in the world. Not only is this true today; it will be more so in the future.

"That is the difference between today and the Great War. But not only that. Above all, this time the German soldier is not short of ammunition. I do not know, my fellow-countrymen, but it may be that when exact calculations are made after the war, people will perhaps say: 'Sir, you were a spendthrift. You had ammunition made which was never used. It is still lying about.' Yes, my fellow-countrymen, I have had ammunition made because I went through the Great War, because I wished to avoid what happened then and because shells are replaceable and bombs are replaceable but men are not.

"And thus the problem of ammunition in this struggle was no problem at all; perhaps only a supply problem. When the struggle was over we had scarcely used a month's production. Today we are armed for any eventuality, whatever Britain may do. *Every week that passes Britain will be dealt heavier blows, and if she wishes to set foot anywhere on the Continent she will find us ready once more.* I know that we are not out of practice. I hope that the British have also forgotten nothing.

"As far as the war in the air is concerned, this too, I hoped to avert. We accepted it. We shall fight it to the finish. I did not want it. I always struggled against it. We did not wage such a war during the whole of the Polish campaign. I did not allow any night attacks to be carried out. In London they said: 'Yes, because you couldn't fly by night.'

"In the meantime, they have noticed whether we can fly by night or not. Naturally, it is not possible to aim so well at night and I wanted to attack military objects only, to attack at the front only, to fight against soldiers, not against women and children. That is why we refrained from night attacks. We did not use this method in France. We carried out no night attacks from the air. When we attacked Paris, only the munitions factories were our objectives. Our airmen aimed with wonderful precision. Anybody who saw it could convince himself of that.

"Then it occurred to that great strategist, Churchill, to commence unrestricted war from the air by night. He began it in Freiburg im Breisgau and has continued it. Not one munitions plant has been demolished. Yet according to British news reports, the one in which we are at present assembled is nothing but a mass of craters. They have not even caused a single munitions factory to cease production. On the other hand, they have unfortunately hit many families, helpless women and children. Hospitals have been one of their favorite objectives. Why? It is inexplainable. You yourselves, here in Berlin, know how often they have bombed our hospitals.

"Very well, I waited for a month, because I thought that after the conclusion of the campaign in France the British would give up this method of warfare. I was mistaken. I waited for a second month and a third month. If bombs were to be dropped I could not assume the responsibility before the German people of allowing my own countrymen to be destroyed while sparing foreigners. Now, this war, too, had to be fought to its end. And it is being fought; fought with all the determination, with all the materials, with all the means and all the courage at our disposal. *The time for the decisive conflict will arrive. You may be sure it will take place. However, I should like to tell these gentlemen one thing: It is we who shall determine the time for it.* And on this point I am cautious. We might perhaps have been able to attack in the West during the autumn of last year, but I wanted to wait for good weather. And I think it was worth while waiting.

"We ourselves are so convinced that our weapons will be successful that we can allow ourselves time. The German people will certainly hold out. I believe that they will be grateful to me if I bide my time and thus save them untold sacrifices.

"It is one of the characteristics of the National Socialist State that even in warfare, at times when it is not absolutely necessary, it is sparing of human life. After all, the lives of our fellow-citizens are at stake.

"In the campaign in Poland we forbade many attacks or rapid advances, because we were convinced that a week or a fortnight later the problem would solve itself.

"We have gained many great successes without sacrificing a single man. That was also the case in the West. It must remain so in the future. We have no desire to gain any successes or to make any attacks for the sake of prestige. We never wish to act expect in accordance with sober military principles. What has to happen must happen. We wish to avoid everything else. As for the rest, all of us hope that reason will again be victorious and peace will return. The world must realize one thing, however: Neither military force, economic pressure, nor the time factor will ever force Germany to surrender. Whatever else may happen, Germany will be the victor in this struggle.

"I am not the man to give up, to my own disadvantage, a struggle already begun. I have proved this by my life in the past and I shall prove to those gentlemen—whose knowledge of my life until now has been gathered from the *emigré* press —that I have remained unchanged in this respect.

"When I began my political career, I declared to my supporters—they were then only a small number of soldiers and workers—'There is no such word as capitulation in your vocabulary or mine.'

"I do not desire war, but when it is forced upon me I shall wage it as long as I have breath in my body. And I can wage it today, because I know that the whole German nation is behind me. I am the guardian of its future and I act accordingly.

"I could have made my own life much more easy. I have been fighting for twenty years, and I have assumed the burden of all these anxieties and of this never-ceasing work, convinced that it must be done for the German people. My own life and my own health are of no importance. I know that, above all, the German Army, every man and every officer of it, supports me in the same spirit. All those fools who imagined that there could ever be any disruption here have forgotten that the Third Reich is not the same as the Second. The German people stand behind me to a man. And at this point I thank, above all, the German workman and the German peasant. They made it possible for me to prepare for this struggle and to create, as far as armaments were concerned, the necessary conditions for resistance. They also provide me with the possibility of continuing the war, however long it may last.

"I also give special thanks to the women of Germany—to those numberless women, who must now perform part of the heavy work of men, who have adapted themselves to their war duties with devotion and fanaticism and who are replacing men in so many positions. I thank you all—you who are making this personal sacrifice, who are bearing the many restrictions that are necessary. I thank you in the name of all those who represent the German people today and who will be the German people of the future.

"This struggle is not a struggle for the present but primarily a struggle for the future. I stated on September 3, 1939, that time would not conquer us, that no economic difficulties would bring us to our knees, and that we could still less be defeated by force of arms. The morale of the German people guarantees this.

"The German people will be richly rewarded in the future for all that they are doing. When we have won this war it will not have been won by a few industrialists or millionaires, or by a few capitalists or aristocrats, or by a few bourgeois, or by anyone else.

"Workers, you must look upon me as your guarantor. I was born a son of the people; I have spent all my life struggling for the German people, and when this hardest struggle of my life is over there will be new tasks for the German people.

"We have already projected great plans. All of our plans have but one aim: to develop still further the great German State, to make that great German nation more and more conscious of its existence and, at the same time, to give it everything which makes life worth living.

"We have decided to break down to an ever-increasing degree the barriers preventing individuals from developing their faculties and from attaining their just due. We are firmly determined to build up a social state which must and shall be a model of perfection in every sphere of life. . . ."

"When this war is ended, Germany will set to work in earnest. A great 'Awake!' will sound throughout the country. Then the German nation will stop manufacturing cannon and will embark on peaceful occupations and the new work of reconstruction for the millions. Then we shall show the world for the first time who is the real master, capitalism or work. Out of this work will grow the great German Reich of which great poets have dreamed. It will be the Germany to which every one of her sons will cling with fanatical devotion, because she will provide a home even for the poorest. She will teach everyone the meaning of life.

"Should anyone say to me: 'These are mere fantastic dreams, mere visions,' I can only reply that when I set out on my course in 1919 as an unknown, nameless soldier I built my hopes of the future upon a most vivid imagination. Yet all has come true.

"What I am planning or aiming at today is nothing compared to what I have already accomplished and achieved. It will be achieved sooner and more definitely than everything already achieved. *The road from an unknown and nameless person to Fuehrer of the German nation was harder than will be the way from Fuehrer of the German nation to creator of the coming peace.*

Press

New York Times, December 11— . . . He spoke in moderate tones. . . . Hitler's remarks seem to have been designed chiefly for home consumption. . . . There was no indication in his remarks today how long he expected the war to last. At the same time there was no indication that he expected it to be concluded in the immediate future. . . .

London Times, December 11—Instead of once more threatening Britain with annihilation by Nazi bombs, Hitler was at pains to emphasize the dire consequences to her "should she attempt to again set foot on the continent" . . . the first time that he has publicly contemplated such a contingency. . . . Few people in this country will quarrel with the statement that more is at stake in this struggle than victory of one country over another. . . . It can only be because Hitler reads British policy in the light of his own designs that he predicts that the loss of the war by Germany will mean "the end of the German people. . . ."

•

SPEECH OF JANUARY 30, 1941

Berlin, Sportpalast

Background

1940

December 11—British take Sidi Barrani and thousands of Italian prisoners.

December 12—Marquess of Lothian, British Ambassador in Washington, dies.

December 14—Pétain ousts Laval from French Cabinet.

December 15—British, pressing offensive, invade Libya.

December 29—In fireside chat, President Roosevelt asks for increased aid to Britain to defeat totalitarianism.

1941

January 3—British capture Tobruk (Libya).

January 6—In message to Congress, President Roosevelt reiterates pledge to bring aid to the Allies, and asserts that America will never accept a peace dictated by the totalitarian countries.

January 10—Lend-Lease-Bill introduced in Congress: it proposes to abolish financial compensations for purchase of war material in America by the Allies, and gives the President power to furnish them with all necessary weapons to fight the Axis Powers.

Germany and USSR sign a pact of friendship extending their trade agreements.

January 24—Lord Halifax, new British Ambassador to Washington, arrives on board British battleship George V. President Roosevelt greets him in Chesapeake Bay.

The Speech

"WHAT were the underlying causes of the Great War? Too many treatises have already been written on the subject. American professors were commissioned by the President to investigate the causes of the Great War, and they came to the conclusion that there was no question of Germany's 'war guilt.' At moments of historic importance, only those personalities count who stand out among their contemporaries as individuals of eminent ability. At the outbreak of the war, there were no outstanding personalities on either side. The basic reasons could not, therefore, lie in the failure or intentions of individuals. The causes were deeper ones.

"In the first place, the German form of government could

not have caused that war. Germany was already a democracy. And what a democracy she was! A slavish copy of foreign Western models, a compromise between monarchy and parliamentary democracy; that is to say, a so-called constitutional monarchy, in which Parliament practically held the reins. The form of government in itself could in no way have been the cause of the war of the so-called democracies against the Reich. It might be nearer the truth to say that Germany, as a political factor in relation to the rest of the world, furnished some cause for the Great War because the German peoples and States, after centuries of dissension and impotence, had finally combined, if only in appearance, to form a new State, a new Reich. This introduced a new element in the so-called European 'balance of power,' one which was regarded, of course, as 'disturbing.' Perhaps a still more cogent reason was the dislike of Germany as a commercial competitor. Germany had for centuries attempted to relieve her economic distress by condemning her people to starve or emigrate. While consolidating her political power, the Germany of those days began to develop in an increasing degree as a commercial power. She exported goods instead of human beings and secured essential world markets for herself. From our point of view, this process was natural and fair; but others regarded it as an incursion into their most cherished domains.

"This leads us straight to Britain, the State which considered this to be an intolerable encroachment. For three hundred years, Britain had gradually formed her so-called Empire—not through the free choice of the peoples concerned, or through spontaneous demonstrations and aspirations on their part, but by force. Thus the Empire was built up. War after war was waged; people after people were robbed of their liberty; State after State was crushed to create the structure called the British Empire. Democracy was merely used as a mask in this process. Behind this mask lurked the enslavement of peoples, the oppression and gagging of individuals. Even today this State does not dare to allow its various components to decide by popular vote whether, after centuries of British influence and infiltration, they want to remain voluntary members of the British domain. On the contrary! By the thousands, Egyptians and Indian Nationalists find their way into dungeons and prisons. Concentration camps were not invented in Germany. They are British inventions. It was the intention of the British overlords, by such means, gradually to break the spirit of other peoples, to crush their national resistance until they willingly accepted the British yoke.

"With this end in view, Britain employed yet another mighty weapon: that of lies and propagandistic phrases. There is a saying that 'when the Briton speaks of God, he means calico.' This is still true today. How piously these people behave on the surface! Yet they have no compunction in involving nation after nation in conflicts for their own material interests. We can only say: Seldom has human hypocrisy attained such a level as in the case of the Britain of today.

"In any event, after 300 blood-stained years of British history, today 46 million Britons in the home country dominate approximately one-quarter of the earth, in area and in population. About 15,400,000 square miles is the share of 46 million persons. It is important, my fellow-countrymen, that we should constantly reiterate this fact, because shameless democratic liars stand up and maintain that the so-called totalitarian States wish to conquer the world. In reality, it is our old enemies who have always been the conquerors and aggressors.

"In the course of its evolution, the British Empire has left nothing but a stream of blood and tears in its wake. Today, without doubt, Britain rules over a huge part of the earth's surface. But even now this world domination is not carried out by the strength of an idea, but essentially by brute force, and where this fails to suffice, by the power of capitalistic or commercial interests. The singular origin and development of the British Empire was possible only because the European Continent never once united to react against it. This was shown very clearly by the elimination of the German Reich.

"For 300 years, there was practically no Germany. While the British spoke of God but considered their business interests alone, the German people were waging long and bloody internal wars over matters of religious beliefs and differences. This was one of the reasons which made the growth of the British Empire possible. In exactly the same proportion as the German people spent their strength in internal struggles, and so disappeared as a factor in world affairs, Britain was able to form her Empire by robbing others.

"However, it was not only Germany that was to all intents and purposes excluded from world competition during these three centuries. The same is true of Italy. Conditions there were similar to those in Germany, although it was not so much religious controversy as affairs of state and the various dynasties that prevented unity. The elimination of other great nations in the Far East, who similarly withdrew from the rest of the world and, without considering their own living space, sank into a voluntary isolation 400 years ago, took place for other reasons. In this way a political distribution of forces came into being, which Britain described as the 'balance of power,' but which in reality meant a disorganized Europe for the benefit of Great Britain.

"For centuries it has been the object of British policy to maintain this state of disorganization, not, of course, under its real name, but under a more pleasant appellation. They spoke, not of calico or the disorganization of peoples, but of God and the 'balance of power.' In reality, the 'balance of power' is a circumlocution for the helplessness of the European Continent which enabled Britain to play off one State against another, time after time, as it suited her. It enabled her to keep nations involved in internal strife and to push herself forward without hindrance in those parts of the world that could muster relatively little resistance.

"And yet if we still speak of Britain as a world Power or as master of the world today, we are laboring under a delusion. In spite of her conquest of the world, Britain is socially the most backward state in Europe, a state managed solely for the benefit of a relatively small upper class, closely associated with Jewish interests. The interests of the masses receive no consideration whatever in the affairs of the State. Here, too, phrases disguise the truth. They may prate of 'liberty,' of 'democracy,' of 'the achievements of a liberal system,' but they mean only the stabilization of the ruling class which, by virtue of its investments, controls and directs the press and formulates public opinion.

"Thus it is possible that—in an Empire so blessed by Nature, in a State which has the greatest riches of the earth at its disposal, together with immense expanses of land with perhaps two inhabitants per square mile—millions of human beings in no way share these blessings, but live more miserably than the masses of overpopulated Central Europe. The land which is a paradise for the few, offers the masses only untold misery—miserable food, miserable clothing and, above all, miserable housing, insecurity in employment and in the whole field of social legislation.

"And if a British Labor Secretary who, however, receives a salary from the State as a member of the opposition, gets up and says that after the war and victory Britain must begin to deal with social questions, to solve social problems and to care for the masses, I can only tell him his remarks are of interest solely because they confirm our statement that Britain is sociologically the most backward country in the world; in Germany these things were done long ago. The tremendous riches reveal themselves as unfruitful when we look beneath the surface and consider not merely a few individuals, but the condition of the people as a whole.

"British world domination is also an illusion from an

external point of view. There are new centers in the world. Giant States have grown up outside this European Continent, or have extended far beyond it; States which cannot be attacked nor even menaced by Britain. *The entire conception of British world domination is now based on the one principle of receiving aid from others against the Continent.* Outside the European Continent, British diplomacy can at most attempt to maintain its position by trying to play one Power off against another in order to maintain at least some measure of its world might.

"In Europe, the awakening of the nations has already swept away the theory of the 'balance of power,' which is the principle of disorganization. The Germans have begun to grow into a single nation and in the midst of this disorganized Continent the formation of the new Reich has started. South of us, Italy has gone the same way. New elements have come into being and have made the balance of power a chimera. And it is this that is the real and deeper cause for the Great War.

"Since 1871, when the German peoples began to organize and formed a Reich under the genius of a great statesman—when the national renaissance of the German people, already slowly beginning to manifest itself, was realized in the form of national unity—it was Britain who began to make us the object of her hate. As early as 1871, or even in 1870, immediately after the battle of Sedan, British newspapers began to point out that this new structure was more dangerous to Britain than the old France had been. They hoped that Prussia might succeed in overcoming France in a long war, but they did not deem desirable a national German renaissance, or the evolution of a new German Reich built around Prussia.

"Thus came the period from 1871 to 1914. Britain unswervingly agitated for war against Germany. She displayed her enmity toward Germany at every opportunity, until finally the Great War broke out, the work of a very small group of unscrupulous international rogues. Britain could carry on this world war only with the help of other countries.

"In this connection it is interesting to trace the whole course of British world power policy for the last 400 years. First, war with Spain with the aid of the Dutch; then, war with the Dutch with the aid of other European States, including France; then, war with France with the aid of Europe; finally, war with Germany with the aid of Europe and the rest of the world.

"The Great War which shook Europe from 1914 to 1918 was exclusively the deliberate work of British politicians. In spite of the fact that the whole world was mobilized against her, Germany was not actually conquered. We do not hesitate to say that today. I did not wish to criticize the past until I had done something better myself. Today, however, as one of the men who have done better, I am in a position to judge and to criticize the past.

"I can only say that the disaster of 1918 was nothing but the result of a rare conglomeration of personal incompetence in the leadership of our people—an unparalleled conglomeration such as never occurred in the past and will, I assure you, never be repeated in the future. Nevertheless, the German soldier withstood the onslaught of the world in arms for over four years. And he would have held out still longer, had it not been for a further factor, namely, the belief of the German people in the honor of the 'democratic' world and its politicians. The faith which the German people had in that world's promises at the time caused them terrible suffering.

"If the British believe that it is sufficient today to play the old propaganda gramophone records of 1917-18 with the object of producing new effects, I can only say that they have forgotten nothing, nor, unfortunately for them, have they learned anything. That is where they differ from the German people. The German people have learned since that time, and have forgotten nothing. We do not wish to be petty.

"There have been other breaches of faith in history. But what took place in the years 1918, 1919, 1920, and 1921 was not one breach of faith but a whole series of such breaches. It was not a matter of breaking one promise; indeed, not a single promise was kept. Never has a great nation been deceived as Germany was then. What did they promise us, this credulous people, and what did they do to us? We were plundered and exploited. They used foreign statesmen from America to induce greater credulity in the German people. Perhaps that was the reason why the German people let themselves be deceived by the maneuver. Now the German people are for all time immune against similar attempts.

"Year after year the German people had the opportunity for reflecting on the value of 'democratic' assurances and promises, 'democratic' words and 'democratic' statesmen. They could make comparisons and speak from their own experience. And as a result of this, the National Socialist Movement arose. *If we are asked, 'Why have you seized upon an entirely new ideology?' the answer is: 'Because the old ideology failed miserably; and not only at home.'*

"Democracy was certainly a poor affair in our country, when forty or fifty parties competed with one another in their *Weltanschauung* and other interests. Some started out with capitalistic ideas; others possessed no more mental vision than bicycle clubs. Still others again represented the interests of small home owners. It was a sorry state of affairs.

"But apart from that—If our foreign relations had been improved by this wretched internal democratic malformation of our national life, we might have said, it has certainly failed at home, but it has at least secured for us decent treatment from other countries. At home, the whole system was a failure. But abroad, at any rate, peoples seemed to take us seriously. A mite, but only a mite, of what has been promised was fulfilled.

"Was the National Socialist State robbed, duped, and blackmailed for fifteen years? No, it was 'democratic' Germany. When, upon leaving a hospital in 1918, I returned home and lived through the winter of 1918-19 I realized, as did others, that no new life could be expected from the political setup existing in Germany at the time. And therefore I, like others, began to seek a way out.

"It was then that I formulated the idea that later, as National Socialism, took hold of the German people. It was based on the recognition that the German nation had collapsed because it permitted itself the luxury of dissipating its strength at home. According to an unimpeachable law, this dissipation of energy at home made us ineffective abroad. The German democracy of those days naturally hoped to obtain the good will of other countries. It found nothing but the crude selfishness of base and callous financial interests which set out to rob wherever a victim could be found. Nothing else could have been expected. But the die had been cast. One thing seemed clear to me: True reconstruction could not begin from without, but must come from within.

"First, there must be a reformation of the internal political life of the German nation, enabling Germany's full strength and, above all, her idealism to be mustered anew. This idealistic force, as things stood at that time, was centered in two camps: the socialist and the nationalist. *These were the two camps which, although violently opposed to each other, simply had to be welded together into a new unity.* Today, my fellow-countrymen, when millions and millions are marching in the spirit of this unity, you look upon the evolution of the National Socialist State as a matter of course. In the years 1918 and 1919, however, it was considered the figment of a diseased imagination. At best they thought: 'Poor stupid fellow!'

"Perhaps that was a good thing, my fellow-countrymen. *If I had been taken seriously in those days, I should probably have been done away with.* The Movement was much too small to be able to offer resistance. *So, perhaps, it was natural destiny or the working of providence that we were laughed at, ridiculed, and made the butt of a campaign of derision.* Gradually we became successful in disseminating the seeds of a new national community. The success of the Movement was an almost incredible historical phenomenon, achieved by the efforts of completely unknown men who enrolled the support of the people.

"Only in one other State was this process similarly successful: in Italy, and nowhere else in Europe. A beginning can perhaps be seen in many other States. In some democracies the significance of such an evolution is probably recognized. It is thought that something similar can be arrived at by trickery. However, one thing is overlooked: *such a renaissance of a people is really a miraculous process that calls for faith rather than abstract intellectualism.*

"In 1918, 1919, 1920, and 1921 this primitive faith of the masses was gradually vouchsafed to us. It became the true basis of our Movement. It led the simple people from factories, mines, farms and offices to come forward and fight for the future of the idea, the Movement, and its ultimate victory. At that time we maintained that if the German nation did not re-establish its position in the world and become a powerful factor in world politics, our population would shortly shrink by 20 million people.

"Unemployment reached a higher figure from year to year. This brought real aimlessness into national ideas and economic planning. The ever recurring changes of Government prevented any provision for the future. Projects lasting more than three months were to no purpose because those in power knew when they started that in three months' time they would no longer be in office.

"One politician would say: 'Why should I clear up another man's mess?' Another would say: 'Why should I do better if another is soon to succeed me?' There was no longer any reason to seek a really effective solution of any problem. In this way, national impotence increased, ruin spread, the number of unemployed grew. As the number of the employed diminished, the load on their shoulders became unavoidably heavier, while their ability to bear it decreased. Finally there was nothing left but collapse, the extent of which could not be foreseen. And so it seemed probable that the warm-hearted and humane prophecy of the great French democrat, Clemenceau, that there were 20 million Germans too many, would be realized.

"To counteract this development, a program to concentrate Germany's strength, to protect our right to live free of all dangers, came into being. In so doing we chose a course which lay between two extremes. In the first place, we had fallen into one extreme, the liberal and individualistic, which made the individual the center, not only of speculation, but of action. On the other side stood the theory of humanitarianism as a universal doctrine. Between these two extremes lay our ideal, a national community in body and in spirit, designed and founded by providence into the midst of which man is set to achieve the purpose of his life.

"Fully conscious of what we were doing, we subordinated all our thoughts to this end; we adapted all our interests and measures to it. *Out of this arose the ideology of National Socialism. In itself it represents the conquest of individualism—not in the sense of curtailing individual faculties or paralyzing individual initiative, but in the sense of setting the interest of the community above the liberty and the initiative of the individual.* The interests of the community became the regulating and, if necessary, the commanding factor.

"Thus we started our struggle against them all, against the followers of individualistic principles as much as against the adherents of so-called humanitarianism. . . ."

"There now arose perhaps the greatest spiritual struggle that German history has ever known. I could not compel anyone to walk by my side or to enter my organization: they had to be personally convinced. Personal conviction alone enabled them to make the great sacrifices demanded. My struggle was intended to be a spiritual struggle only, fought with the aid of the spoken and the written word—in short, with the aid of conviction. Only when a malicious opponent said: 'I cannot withstand your spirit, but I am stronger than you are and will oppose you by force,' then, as an ex-service man, I chose the only reply with which force can be answered. I opposed force by force. . . ."

"Today I am justified in saying that we were victorious all along the line in this spiritual struggle. When I finally came to power, I did so legally under Field Marshal von Hindenburg, the Reich President, as a result of the overwhelming strength of the Movement behind me. In other words, *the so-called National Socialist Revolution defeated 'democracy' in the days of democracy by means of democracy. It ensured power for itself by perfectly legal means. I stand before you today on the basis of the mandate entrusted to me by the German people, a mandate which is far more complete than those held at this moment by any so-called 'democratic' statesmen.*

"When I came to power in 1933, our path lay unmistakably before us. Our internal policy had been exactly defined by our fifteen-year-old struggle. Our program, repeated a thousand times, obligated us to the German people. I should be a man without honor, worthy of being stoned, had I retracted a single step of the program I then enunciated. . . ."

"My foreign policy had identical aims. My program was to abolish the Treaty of Versailles. It is futile nonsense for the rest of the world to pretend today that I did not reveal this program until 1933, or 1935, or 1937. Instead of listening to the foolish chatter of *émigrés,* these gentlemen would have been wiser to read what I have written—and written thousands of times.

"No human being has declared or recorded what he wanted

more than I. Again and again I wrote these words: 'The abolition of the Treaty of Versailles.' Not because it was a quixotic idea of my own, but because the Treaty of Versailles was the greatest injustice and the most infamous maltreatment of a great nation in recorded history, and because it was impossible for our nation to continue to exist in the future unless Germany was free of this stranglehold.

"I first put this program forward and defended it as a soldier in 1919. It is this same program that I carried before me unswervingly as my solemn obligation during the long years of my struggle for power. When I came to power, I did not say to myself, as a democratic politician would: 'The Moor has done his duty; the Moor can go.' At that very moment I thanked God, who has brought me so far, that I could at last carry my program out. However, I did not wish to carry out my program by force. Instead, I did my utmost to accomplish my purpose by persuasion alone.

"My Reichstag speeches, which no democratic statesman can delete from the pages of history, are a proof of this. What offers I made to them! How earnestly I begged them to be sensible and not to curtail the vital requirements of a great nation. How often I proved to them that they were acting senselessly and against their own advantage, that they were only harming themselves. What did I not do during those long years to pave the way for an understanding with them? It would never have been necessary to embark on an armament race if the others had not wanted to do so. I made one proposal after another. But every proposal that came from me immediately excited a certain international Jewish capitalistic clique, just as had been the case in Germany, my fellow-countrymen, where every sensible proposal made by National Socialists was immediately turned down simply because of its origin.

"In my Reichstag speech of May 17, 1933, and in those which followed, in my innumerable proclamations at public meetings, in all the memoranda which I drew up, one thought was prevalent: to find, under all circumstances, a way by which this Treaty could be revised along peaceful lines. That this Treaty was a despicable document was finally admitted even by those who drew it up. They even admitted that the possibilities of revision should be examined.

"They elected the League of Nations for this purpose; in other words, they put the cart before the horse. This League of Nations, which had been devised to insure the fulfillment of the Treaty, was to see to its revision. In the first place, we were not originally members of the League, and when we did join, it only meant the delivery of annual payments by us. That was the only positive result for Germany of membership in the League. Yet Germany was a democracy, and her democrats went a-begging in Geneva. They groveled on their knees before the international forum in Geneva, vainly pleading for revision. As a National Socialist, I realized before many months had passed that nothing could be gained from this forum. And I drew my conclusions. Apparently our opponents confused us with the persons with whom they dealt after November, 1918. But neither the German nation nor we ourselves have anything in common with those people. They were not Germany. They were a few miserable creatures paid by Englishmen and Frenchmen, and hired by the Jews. They were not the German people. Far from it. It is an insult to confuse us with them.

"Consequently, if they believed that they could employ the same methods with us that had been employed with the men of November, 1918, they were gravely mistaken. Theirs was a complete misconception of the situation. For that could not be expected of us—to go begging to Geneva, to have our petitions kicked about, and to go begging again.

"That would have meant confusing a German ex-serviceman with the traitors of 1918. These men of November, 1918, knew no course but submission, for they were caught in the financial trammels of the other world. But we had no reason to bow to the rest of the world. *Does England think I have an inferiority complex with regard to her?* They swindled and duped us in those days, but we were never defeated by British soldiers. Nor does the situation seem to have changed today. It was clear to me that if nothing could be done in Geneva by means of voluntary negotiations it was best to quit. I have never in my life forced my company upon anyone. Those who do not wish to speak to me need not do so. I shall not be the loser. There are 85 million Germans, and we Germans need not force ourselves upon others. We were a world empire for more than 300 years while Great Britain was nothing but a little island.

"We were forced to take the path we have trodden. The League of Nations had nothing for us but scorn and contempt. That was why we left it. The same applies to the Disarmament Conference. We have continued along the course that was forced upon us, always still trying, whenever opportunity arises, to come to an understanding. And allow me to point out that in one instance I almost seemed to succeed, namely, with regard to France. When the Saar plebiscite had taken place and the Saar territory rejoined us, we drew our conclusions. I thereupon renounced any further revision of Germany's western frontiers.

"The French accepted this as a matter of course. I pointed out to the French Ambassador, however, that this was not the matter of course that they imagined. I told him that we were making a sacrifice for the sake of peace. We made the sacrifice; in return we expected at least peace. But the ruthlessness of the capitalistic plutocrats again rapidly came to the fore in these countries. It was promoted by *émigrés* who painted a ludicrous picture of the German situation, which one's opponent believed because it was pleasant to believe it, and it was fed by the Jewish hatred.

"This coalition of plutocratic interests, on the one hand, and instinctive Jewish hatred and *émigré* lust for revenge on the other, succeeded in confusing the world more and more by weaving webs of fine phrases and by agitating against the new German Reich with exactly the same devices they had employed against its predecessor. In those days, it was Imperial Germany to which they objected; today it is National Socialist Germany. In reality, it is whatever Germany happens to be.

"I am resolved on no account to surrender one whit of our rights. That would not be the sacrifice of a theory, but the sacrifice of millions of lives in days to come. Neither will I sacrifice one point of my Party program; for I will not sacrifice the future of our race. No man can do so unless he has to stand before his people and confess that he can no longer defend their interests. Then another would shoulder his responsibilities.

"We did not assume power with the intention of surrendering the interests of the German people. On the contrary, we did so with the determination to defend Germany's interests at all costs. My fellow-countrymen, you must not think that the surrendering of interest at a certain point would bring peace for all time.

"We saw that in the old German Reich, beginning with the surrender of its western provinces. This was followed by fresh surrenders and by new sacrifices every few years, until Germany was finally demolished and our people became powerless for many centuries. I was determined at the outset not to yield one inch. Therefore, when I began to see that the old warmongers of the Great War—old men such as Messrs. Churchill, Eden, Duff Cooper, Hore-Belisha, Vansittart, Chamberlain, Halifax, and others were beginning to incite war, as they had done before, I began to realize that they did not care in the least for a just settlement with Germany, but that they believed that they could easily overthrow Germany again—the quicker, the better.

"You know what happened during the years after that. During those years, beginning with 1934, I rearmed. *When I announced the extent of Germany's rearmament in the Reichstag in September, 1939, the rest of the world did not believe me.* That was perhaps understandable. Those who live on bluff think that others do likewise. We have witnessed that in Germany itself. *Even here, my opponents never believed a word I said. Every prophecy was ridiculed, every declaration made ludicrous, every picture of the future described as a fantastic chimera.*

"And now we are experiencing the same thing once more abroad. I, for my part, can only tell the world I have rearmed—and mightily so. The German nation knows this today, although it does not know all by far. It is not necessary to talk about everything. Accomplishment alone is decisive.

"We demanded nothing of others. *When France entered this war, there was no reason for her to do so. It was only that she wanted to fight Germany again.* She said: 'We want the Rhineland. We want to tear Germany apart; tear Austria away and dissolve Germany.' With such wild fantasies, simply impossible in the twentieth century with its nationalist ideals, they pictured the overthrow of the Reich. It was all utterly childish.

"And Britain? I have offered her my hand again and again. *It was the very essence of my program to come to an understanding with her.* There was only one question: the return of the German colonies. I stated that we were willing to discuss the matter. Time was of no importance, and I fixed no limit. These colonies are useless to Britain. She possesses 15 million square miles, and what does she do with them? Nothing. It is nothing but the avarice of old usurers who are unwilling to part with anything they possess. They are morbid characters who watch their neighbors starve. Though they have no use for what they hold, they would rather cast it into the sea than give it up. The idea that they might lose something nauseates them.

"For this reason I demanded nothing that belonged to the British, but only that which had been robbed and stolen from us in 1918 and 1919—robbed and stolen contrary to the solemn assurances of the American President Wilson.

We have never demanded anything from them and we have never insisted on anything. I repeatedly offered them my hand, but always in vain. The reasons are quite clear to us. First of all, there is the German unity in itself. They hate our State, regardless of its Constitution, Imperial or National Socialist, democratic or dictatorial. To this they are quite indifferent. Secondly, they hate, above all, the social progress of this Reich. . . ."

"British labor leaders suddenly appear with 'new' social ideas, as stale and out of date as any I can imagine. Gentlemen, put them back into their coffin. They are matters that we cast aside long ago. If you wish to know how to proceed along such lines you must not take a program that was modern with us in the eighties and nineties. You must come to us and study, gentlemen, if you want to learn how to go about your task. But even then, the very fact that now, suddenly, something of this kind should be proposed is sufficient. What then are these gentlemen actually waging war for? First of all, they say, to fight against National Socialism. The nations of the world must shed blood—so that the British can suddenly fish out the details of a program that lies in our ancestors' bottom-most dresser drawers.

"What is their reason? They could have had social gains much more cheaply. But it is proof that even there the people are beginning to stir. Trouble arose because someone—I think he was a colonel—declared that 'socially advanced' Britain has no use for officers from the 'lower classes.' Officers can be selected only from the 'upper classes.' 'The lower strata' are of no use in this respect.

"Why, I ask, are they perturbed because he said such a thing? They should be annoyed that the fact exists, and not merely because someone has at last been indiscreet enough to say so. It is interesting to note that nobody was shocked that he represented actual facts. In England, only men of the upper crust can play important roles. That is what should annoy them; not the fact that someone has been silly enough to let the truth slip out in wartime.

"If they want to know something, this class prejudice was abolished long ago in our country. Only a short time ago these people 'proved' to us that our officers and generals were of no use because they were young and contaminated by National Socialism. In other words, they were in some way connected with the broad masses. Developments have shown where the best generals may be found, over there or over here.

"If the war lasts much longer, it will be a great misfortune for Britain. The British will experience all sorts of things. And, perhaps, some day they will dispatch a commission to take over our program. It is this social Germany which this clique of Jews, financiers, and business czars hates the most. Regarding these people, our foreign policy and our internal and economic policies are absolutely clear and determined. . . ."

"Even after the war had begun, there were possibilities for an agreement. Immediately after the Polish campaign, I again offered my hand. I demanded nothing from France or Britain. Still, all was in vain. Immediately after the collapse in the West, I again offered my hand to Britain. Howls and shouts were my only reception. They literally spat on me. They were outraged. Very well, it is all in vain. . . ."

"Looking back on the past, I must say that *to all intents and purposes the year just ended and part of the previous year decided this war.* First of all the adversary they mobilized against us in the East was eliminated in a few weeks. The attempt to cut off our northern ore supplies and to gain bases for an attack against northeast Germany was wiped out within a month and a half. The attempt to reach the Ruhr district via Holland and Belgium collapsed in a few days. France suffered the same fate. Britain was chased off the Continent.

"I have often read that the British intend to start a great

offensive somewhere. My only desire is that they let me know beforehand, for I would be only too glad to evacuate the area. I would spare them all the difficulties of landing. Then we could come forth and discuss matters once more—but this time in the only language that they are capable of understanding. They hope—for, after all, they must hope some time or other—but what do they expect?

"*We are established on this continent; and where we are established no one will ever dislodge us.* We have created impregnable bases. *When the time comes, we shall strike decisively.* History will prove to these gentlemen in 1941 that we have made full use of our time.

"What are they hoping for? New help? America? I can only say that from the very outset, we have acted with reserve. *It is obvious to everyone who has any respect for the truth that the German nation has no quarrel with the American people. Germany has never claimed any interests on the American continent, apart from the fact that Germans took part in the struggle for the liberation of that continent. If States of that continent try to enter the European conflict, the situation will quickly alter.* Then Europe will defend itself. Let there be no mistake—whoever believes that he can help Britain must realize one thing above all: *Every ship, with or without convoy, that comes within range of our torpedo tubes, will be torpedoed.*

"We have been drawn into war against our will. No man can offer his hand more often than I have. But if they want to fight to exterminate the German nation, then they will get the surprise of their lives. This time they will not meet a worn-out Germany, as in the Great War. They will encounter a Germany mobilized in the highest sense of the word, capable of fighting, and determined to fight. If there are hopes to the contrary, I do not understand them.

"They say Italy will drop out. It would be better for these gentlemen not to invent revolutions in Milan, but to guard against outbreaks in their own countries. They regard relations between Germany and Italy in the same way as they are accustomed to behave towards their own friends. When one of the democracies helps another it always ask for something in exchange: bases or something of that sort. And these bases are promptly occupied.

"When Italian air squadrons were transferred to the Atlantic coast, British newspapers said that the Italians would direct our air wars and in future would demand a base on the Atlantic. Now that German squadrons are in Sicily, they say that Germany will probably seize Sicily. I assure these gentlemen that such tales will not have the slightest influence on anyone, either in Germany or in Italy. They merely show the morbid senselessness of the Britons who imagine these things.

"Above all, it shows that they do not understand the slogan of the war: 'Wherever we can beat England, we shall beat England.' If they foresee victory in the few reverses our ally has suffered, I do not understand the British. Up to now, they have always looked upon their own lack of success as proof of victory. They may rest assured. This account is a total account. It will be settled at the end of the war, item by item, square mile by square mile.

"There is still another fact they must observe: The Duce and I are neither Jews nor opportunists. When we two shake hands, it is with the firm grasp of men of honor. I hope that this will dawn upon these gentlemen and be clear to them through the course of the year.

"Perhaps they base their hopes on the Balkans. I should not pay much attention to that, because one thing is certain: *Wherever Britain puts in an appearance we shall attack her,* and we are strong enough to do so. Perhaps they place their hopes in other nations, whom they believe they can persuade to come in. I do not know.

"But, my fellow-countrymen and fellow-countrywomen, I assure you, who have known me for so many years as a careful far-sighted man, that every conceivable possibility has been soberly considered and carefully calculated. Victory will be ours. Perhaps they still have another hope, but it is not quite so strong—and that is *hunger*. We have organized our life. We knew from the very beginning that there could be no surplus in wartime. But the German people will never starve, never. The British will come closer to it than we. As for raw materials, all provisions have been made by us in this respect. This was the purpose of the Four-Year Plan. Perhaps a few Britons realize this by now.

"There is only one other aspect worth noting: they really believe that they can again throw dust into the eyes of the German people with their lies and catch phrases. Here, too, I can only say that they should not have slept so long. They should have taken a little more interest in the internal development of the German people. They attempt to estrange the Italian people from the Duce in the same idiotic way.

"A British Lord stands up and appeals to the Italian people no longer to follow the Duce, but rather his Lordship. What an ass! Another Lord stands up and advises the German nation to follow his Lordship, to turn away from me. Many different people have tried to do that, people who had no idea of the German nation, of the National Socialist State, of our community or of the marching columns of our army.

"*They have not the slightest notion of propaganda.* They have just borrowed a few people from Germany because they are apparently not quite sure of the effect of their ideas. The people they borrowed are the emigrants, the ones who failed so miserably in Germany. They are their advisers, as we can tell by their leaflets.

"We know exactly who has done what: This man has done this, that man has done that—just as senselessly as when they were among us. Only in those days their mouthpiece was the *Vossische Zeitung*. Now it is the [London] *Times* or a similar organ. And these people imagine that tales so old and so out of date, which lost their attractiveness even in the

Vossiche Zeitung, will now create interest because they are suddenly printed in the *Times* or the *Daily Telegraph. Verily, softening of the brain seems to prevail in that 'democracy.'*

"You can rest assured that the German nation will do everything essential to its interests. It will follow its leaders. It knows that its leadership has only one aim. It realizes fully that at the head of the Reich stands a man who neither has a bundle of shares in his pocket, nor pursues his way for personal gain. I am proud to say that the German nation follows its leadership through thick and thin. A spirit has sprung to life in this nation—a spirit which accompanied us for a long time once before, a whole-hearted willingness to accept every responsibility.

"We shall repay every blow with interest—compound interest. The combat will strengthen us more and more. No matter what force they mobilize against us, no matter if the world were full of devils, we shall succeed.

"When they finally say: 'Yes, but what about the mistakes they make?' I answer: 'Good Lord, who does not make mistakes?' Early this morning I read that a British Minister—I do not know who—had in some way or other calculated that I had made seven mistakes in 1940—seven whole mistakes. The man errs. I totaled them up myself; *I did not make seven mistakes—but 724. I made further calculations and found that my adversaries had made 4,385,000 mistakes.* And he can believe me. I have calculated them exactly. But even with our mistakes, we shall manage to carry on. If we make only as many mistakes this year as last, I shall thank God upon my knees. If our adversaries are just as clever as they were last year, I shall also be satisfied.

"And so we enter the new year with armed forces equipped as never before in German history. The number of land divisions has been tremendously increased. Their composition has been improved. The vast and unique experience of warfare has been utilized and applied to officers and men alike. Work has been done and work continues to be done unceasingly. Equipment is improving. Our adversaries will discover to what extent.

"At sea, submarine warfare will begin in the spring, and you will find we have not been idle. The Air Force will introduce itself similarly. Our whole Army will force a decision one way or another. Production has been vastly increased in every respect. What others are merely planning is reality with us. The German nation stands calmly behind its leaders, with confidence in its Army and ready to bear what fate demands of it.

"I am convinced that 1941 will be the crucial year of a great new order in Europe. The world shall open up for everyone. Privileges for individuals, the tyranny of certain nations and their financial rulers shall fall. And last of all, this year will help to provide the foundations of a real understanding among peoples, and with it the certainty of conciliation among nations.

"At the same time, I do not want to forget the directions I gave to the German Reichstag on the first of September, 1939—directions to the effect that when the other world has been delivered from the Jews, Judaism will have ceased to play a part in Europe. They may still laugh today, just as they laughed over my prophecies in the past. The coming months and years will prove that what I foresaw was right.

"Even now our racial creed is penetrating nation after nation and I hope that those nations who are still opposed to us will some day recognize the greater enemy within them. Then they will join us in a combined front, a front against international Jewish exploitation and racial degeneration. . . ."

Press

New York Times, January 31—Hitler tells us not to interfere; will torpedo aid ships, he says. . . . Adolf Hitler directly challenged the United States yesterday on the question of aid to Britain. . . . Exactly what Herr Hitler meant by that must await further elucidation to be fully clear, for on August 17, 1940, Germany declared a total blockade of the British Isles. Since then Germany has always claimed and exercised the right to sink all vessels possible within the zone about the British Isles as delineated in the blockade proclamation. Hitler today, however, did not specifically mention the blockade zone as being the exclusive danger zone for such ships, nor did he specify whether merely those ships transporting assistance to the British or all ships of nations extending such aid would be the targets of German torpedoes.

London Times, January 31— . . . Hitler, who was evidently feeling "on top of the world," promised that 1941 would be a historic year in the creation of the new order in Europe. . . .

Le Temps (Edition de Lyon), February 2—Chancellor Hitler's speech in Berlin on Thursday, on the occasion of the eighth anniversary of the triumph of National Socialism, undoubtedly is of great importance at this time, when the war is entering on its decisive phase. It proceeds strictly along the well-known line of Hitler's doctrine, which should not surprise us since the National Socialist power, in the pride of its military victories, occupies a large part of Europe and fights its battle with England with heightened energy. It is quite natural, too, for the Fuehrer to put emphasis upon what he calls "the liberation of the German people," since this is in the eyes of his people the justification of all his actions.

The part of the speech which, from a political point of view, is most significant of the present turn the war is taking is, first of all, the direct attack upon England. This is ultimately the meaning of the new order in Europe which Germany wishes to establish. . . . M. Hitler is of the opinion that the existence of the British Empire inevitably excludes other European nations, particularly Germany; he believes that Great Britain has tried to direct the energies of Europe along certain channels that are favorable to herself, and that she has used every means to keep Europe in a state of disorganization, to further her own aims. . . . And so the positions are clearly defined; they exclude any prospect of compromise.

It is the British power which Germany and Italy, bound in close unity, propose to destroy. The Fuehrer has given warning that wherever England shows herself, there will the Axis Powers attack, for they possess the strength to do so.

•

SPEECH OF FEBRUARY 24, 1941

Munich

Background

1941

February 7—British capture Bengazi in Lybia.

February 9—Admiral Darlan appointed as Vice-Premier and successor to Marshal Pétain.

February 21—Franco confers with Mussolini in Bordighierra, then meets Pétain in Montpellier.

The Speech

"Fellow Party Members:

"The twenty-fourth of February is always, and rightly so, a day of vivid memories for us. On this date and from this very hall began the Movement's amazing march to victory, which bore it to the helm of the Reich, to leadership of the nation and its destiny. This day is a great day for me too.

Surely, it is seldom that a political leader can stand before the same band of followers that hailed his first great public appearance twenty-one years before, and repeat the same program. Seldom can a man proclaim the same doctrines and put them into practice for twenty-one years without at any time having had to relinquish a single part of his original program. In 1920, when we met for the first time in this hall, many of you must have asked yourselves: 'Dear me, a new party, another new party! Why do we want a new party? Don't we have parties enough? . . .'

"Thus began a heroic struggle, opposed at its inception by nearly all. Nevertheless, the essential objects of the Movement embraced the decisive element. Its clear and unambiguous aim did not allow the Movement to become the tool of definite and limited individual interests, but raised it above all special obligations to the particular obligation of serving the German nation in its entirety, of safeguarding its interests regardless of momentary dissensions or confused thoughts. Thus, today, after twenty-one years, I again stand before you. . . ."

"It was in this very town that I began my struggle, my political struggle against Versailles. You know this, you old members of my party. How often did I speak against Versailles! I probably studied this treaty more than any other man. To this day, I have not forgotten it. The treaty could not be abolished by humility, by submission. It could only be abolished by reliance upon ourselves, by the strength of the German nation.

"The days of bitter struggle necessarily led to a selection of leaders. When today I appear before the nation and look at the ranks that surround me, I look at a band of men, real men who stand for something. On the other hand when I regard the cabinets of my opponents, I can only say: 'Quite incapable of being put in charge even of one of my smallest groups.' Hard times resulted in a selection of first class men who naturally caused us a little anxiety now and then. Everybody who is worth his salt is sometimes difficult to handle. In normal times it is not always easy to get divergent elements to work together instead of against one another. But as soon as danger threatens, they form the most resolute body of men. Just as selection is a natural consequence of war and brings real leaders to the fore among soldiers, so in the world of politics selection is the outcome of struggle. It was a result of this slow development, this eternal struggle against opposition, that we gradually acquired leaders with whose aid we can today achieve anything.

"When, on the other hand, I look at the rest of the world, I am obliged to say: They were simply asleep while this miracle was taking place. Even today they refuse to grasp it. They do not realize what we are, nor do they realize what they themselves are. They go on like a figure of 'Justice'—with blindfolded eyes. They reject what does not suit them. They do not realize that two revolutions in Europe have created something new and tremendous. We are fully conscious of the fact that a second revolution, where the assumption of power occurred earlier than it did in our country, proceeded parallel with ours. The fascist Revolution, too, yielded the same results. Complete identity exists between our two revolutions, not only as regards aims, but also as regards methods. Over and above this there is our friendship, which is more than co-operation with a purpose in view. Nor do our opponents realize yet, that once I regard a man as my friend, I shall stand by him. . . ."

". . . I wish to display no faltering in this matter. *There cannot be the slightest doubt that the bond uniting the two revolutions, and especially the bond uniting their two leaders, is indissoluble, and that one will always support the other*. Moreover, it is a common enemy whom we shall defeat.

"There was a time when Italy, fascist Italy, which is engaged in the same struggle as we are, which is shut in in the same way as we are, which is as over-populated as we are and, up until now, has been given no better chance of living than we, kept powerful enemies engaged in our behalf. Numerous British ships were engaged in the Mediterranean; numerous British airplanes were engaged in the African colonies. This was a very good thing for us, for, as I told you the other day, *our warfare at sea is just beginning.* The reason for this is that we first wanted to train new crews for the new submarines which will now make their appearance on the scene. Let no one doubt that they are about to appear.

"Just two hours ago I received a communiqué from the Commander-in-Chief of the Navy stating that the reports of the last two days from our ships and submarines on the high seas reveal that another 215,000 tons have been sunk; that of this total 190,000 tons were sunk by submarines alone, and that this figure includes a single convoy of 125,000 tons which was destroyed yesterday.

"From March and April on, those gentlemen will have to be prepared for something very different. They will see whether we have been asleep during the winter, or whether we have made good use of our time. During the long months when we had so few submarines to fight our battles, Italy kept large forces engaged. It does not matter to us whether our Stukas attack British ships in the North Sea or in the Mediterranean; the result is always the same. One thing is certain: Wherever Britain touches the Continent she will immediately have to reckon with us, and wherever British ships appear, our submarines will attack them until the hour of decision comes. Thus, except for Germany, only Italy has had a revolution which, in the long run, will lead, must lead and has led to the construction of a new national community.

"We had to exercise patience for many a long year, and I can only say: My opponents may believe that they can terrify me with the threat of time, but I have learned to wait.

and I have never been idle while waiting. We had to wait ten years after 1923 until we at last came into power. But you old members of the Party know that we accomplished much in those ten years. . . . We were never in the habit of setting ourselves a limit and saying: This must be done on March 1, or June 15, or September 7. . . ."

"These sharp-witted journalists who are now in England —they are no longer among us—knew all about it. Now they said: 'August 13 is the turning point; National Socialism is done for.' August 13 came—and National Socialism was not done for. A few months later they had to fix a new date. Finally came January 30, 1933. Then they said: 'Well, now they have made their mistake! They have gained power, and in six weeks they will be finished—three months at the most. Three months, and that will be the end of them.' The six weeks and the three months passed, and still we were not finished.

"And so they kept on fixing new dates for our downfall, and now, in wartime, they are doing exactly the same thing. And why not? They are the same people, the same prophets, the same political diviners who prophesied the future so wonderfully when they were here. Now they are employed as assistants in the British Ministry of Information and the British Foreign Office. They always know exactly that on such and such a date the Germans will be finished. We have experienced that more than once. You all know what they said. I need only refer to the celebrated utterance of a great British statesman whom you in Munich know by sight—Mr. Chamberlain. A few days before April 9, of last year, he said: 'Thank God, he has missed the bus.' I can remind you of another—the British Commander-in-Chief—who said: 'A few months ago I was afraid, now I am afraid no longer. They have missed their opportunity. Besides, they only have young generals. That is their mistake and their misfortune; it is the same with all their leaders. They have lost their opportunity. It is all over.' A few weeks later this general had departed. Probably he, too, was too young.

"Today they are doing exactly the same thing. They always fix final dates. In the autumn they said: 'If they don't land now, all is well. In the spring of 1941 Britain will transfer the offensive to the Continent.' I am still waiting for the British offensive. They have transferred the offensive elsewhere, and now, unfortunately, we must run after them wherever they happen to be. But we shall find them wherever they run. And we shall strike them where they are most vulnerable.

"Thus, twenty-one years of a dauntless struggle for our Movement have passed. After thirteen years we at last came to power. Then came years of preparation of our foreign policy, of gigantic work at home. You know that it is all an exact repetition of what happened in the Party. We asked nothing of the world but equal rights, just as we asked for the same rights at home. At home we demanded the right to meet freely, the right which the others possessed. We demanded the right of free speech, the same right as a parliamentary party as the others held. We were refused and persecuted with terrorism. Nevertheless, we built up our organization and won the day. . . ."

"Of course, a fundamental social principle was necessary to achieve this. It is today no longer possible to build up a state on a capitalistic basis. The peoples eventually begin to stir. The awakening of the peoples cannot be prevented by wars. On the contrary, war will only hasten it. Such states will be ruined by financial catastrophes which will destroy the foundations of their own former financial policy.

"The gold standard will not emerge victorious from this war. Rather, the national economic systems will conquer. And these will carry on among themselves the trade that is necessary for them. . . ."

"In this respect we can look to the future with confidence. Germany is an immense factor in world economy, not only as a producer but also as a consumer. We certainly have a great market for our goods. But we are not only seeking markets; we are also the greatest buyers. The Western world wants, on the one hand, to live upon its empires and, on the other hand, to export from its empires as well. That is impossible because in the long run the nations cannot carry on one-sided trade. They not only have to buy, but also have to *sell.* They can sell nothing to these empires. The peoples will therefore trade with us in the future, regardless of whether this happens to suit certain bankers or not. Therefore we will not establish our economic policy to suit the conceptions or desires of bankers in New York or London. . . ."

"Our economic policy, I repeat, is determined solely by the interests of the German people. From this principle we shall never depart. If the rest of the world says: 'War,' I can only say: 'Very well. I do not want war, but no one, however peaceable, can live in peace if his neighbor intends to force a quarrel.'

"I am not one of those who see such a war coming and start whining about it. I have said and done all that I could; I have made proposal after proposal to Britain; likewise to France. These proposals were always ridiculed—rejected with scorn. However, when I saw that the other side intended to fight, I naturally did that which as a National Socialist of the early days, I did once before: I forged a powerful weapon of defense. And, just as of old, I proclaimed that we should be not merely strong enough to stand the blows of others but strong enough to deal blows in return. I built up the German armed forces as a military instrument of State policy, so that if war were inevitable, these forces could deliver crushing blows.

"Only a few days ago, an American general declared before an investigating committee in the House of Representatives that in 1936 Churchill had personally assured him, 'Germany is becoming too strong for us. She must be destroyed, and I will do everything in my power to bring about her destruction.'

"A little later than 1936, I publicly issued a warning against this man and his activities for the first time. When I noticed that a certain British clique, incited by the Jews—who are, of course, the fellows who kindle the flames everywhere—was intentionally provoking war, I immediately made all preparations on my part to arm the nation. And you, my old Party comrades, know that when I speak it is not a mere matter of words, for I act accordingly. We worked like Titans. The armaments we have manufactured in the past few years are really the proudest achievement that the world has ever seen. If the rest of the world tells us: 'We are doing likewise now,' I can only reply: 'By all means do so, for I have already done it. But above all, don't tell me any of your tales. I am an expert, a specialist in rearmament. I know exactly what can be made from steel and what can be made of aluminum. I know what achievements can be expected of men and what cannot be expected. Your tales do not impress me in the least. I enlisted the strength of the whole German nation in good time to assist in our arming and, if necessary, I shall enlist that of half Europe. I am prepared for all impending conflicts and consequently face them calmly.' Let the others face them with equal calm.

"I place my confidence in the best army in the world, in the best army which the German nation has ever possessed. It is numerically strong, it has the finest weapons and is better led than ever before. We have a body of young leaders who have not merely proved their worth in the present war but, I can well say, have covered themselves with glory. Wherever we look today, we see a bodyguard of chosen men to whom the German soldiers have been entrusted. They in their turn are the leaders of soldiers who are the best trained in the world, who are armed with the finest weapons on earth. Behind these soldiers and their leaders stands the German nation, the whole German people. In the midst of this people, forming its very core, is the National Socialist Movement which began its existence in this room twenty-one years ago,—this Movement the like of which does not exist in the democratic countries, this Movement whose only pendant is fascism. Nation and Army, Party and State are today one indivisible whole. No power in the world can loosen what is so firmly welded together. Only fools can imagine that the year 1918 can be repeated.

"We encountered the same ideas among our plutocrats at home. They, too, always hoped for internal disruption, dissolution, civil war of German against German. Exactly the same ideas are encountered today. They say: 'There will be a revolution in Germany in six weeks.' They do not know who is going to make the revolution. There are no revolutionaries among us. Thomas Mann and others like him went to England. Some have already left England for America, because England is too close to their revolution's future field of operations. They are establishing their headquarters far from their future field of battle. Nevertheless, they assert that the revolution will come. Who will make it? I do not know. How it will be made, I do not know either. All I know is that in Germany there can be, at the most, only a few fools who might think of revolution, and that they are all behind iron bars.

"Then they said: 'Winter, General Winter is coming, and he will force Germany to her knees.' But, unfortunately, the German people are 'winter-proof.' German history has passed through I do not know how many tens of thousands of winters. We will get through this one, too.

"Then they say: 'Starvation will come.' We are prepared against this, too. We know the humanitarian sentiments of our British opponents and so have made our preparations. I believe that starvation will reach them before it reaches us.

"Then they said: 'Time is on our side.' But time is only on the side of those who work. No one has been harder at work than we. Of that I can assure them. In fact, all these vague hopes which they are building up are absolutely childish and ridiculous. . . ."

"And so, in all due modesty, I have just one more thing to say to my opponents: I have taken up the challenge of many democratic adversaries and up to now I have always emerged the victor from the conflict. I do not believe that this struggle is being carried on under different conditions. That is to say, the relation of the forces involved is exactly the same as before. In any case *I am grateful to Providence that this struggle, having become inevitable, broke out in my lifetime and at a time when I still feel young and vigorous. Just now I am feeling particularly vigorous.* Spring is coming, the spring which we all welcome. The season is approaching in which one can measure forces. I know that, although they realize the terrible hardships of the struggle, millions of German soldiers are at this moment thinking exactly the same thing. . . ."

"If fate should once more call us to the battlefield, the blessing of Providence will be with those who have merited it by years of hard work. When I compare myself and my opponents in other countries in the light of history, I do not fear the verdict on our respective mentalities. Who are these egoists? Each one of them merely defends the interests of his class. Behind them all stands either the Jew or their own moneybags. They are all nothing but money-grubbers, living on the profits of this war. No blessing can come of that. I oppose these people merely as the champion of my country. I am convinced that our struggle will in the future be blessed by Providence, as it has been blessed up to now.

"When I first entered this hall twenty-one years ago, I was an unknown, nameless soldier. I had nothing behind me but my own conviction. During the twenty-one years since, a new world has been created. The road leading into the future will be easier than the road from February 24, 1920, to the present. I look to the future with fanatical confidence. The whole nation has answered the call. I know that when the command is given: 'Forward march!' Germany will march."

Press

London Times, February 25— . . . His address, both in form and substance, differed little from past utterances . . . delivered at the top of his voice. . . . Hitler's claim that 215,000 tons of shipping had been sunk during the forty-eight hours preceding his speech was only another of the fantasies which are so frequently voiced in German communiqués. It was learned in London . . . that there was no truth whatsoever in the claim.

New York Times, February 25— . . . It was considered significant, however, that he did not mention the Balkans or an invasion of Britain; that he made no promise to end the war this year and that he refrained from attacking the United States for its aid to Britain. . . . Hitler's utterances contained nothing truly programmatic. He merely repeated what he had announced on January 30, namely, that this war would gather momentum in the Spring. . . .

Le Temps (Edition de Lyon), February 26—The most interesting passages in regard to the development and the outcome of the war are those which concern the alliance with Italy, submarine warfare, and the new phase of the struggle. His attitude on Italo-German co-operation is identical with that of Il Duce. The Chancellor pointed to the solidarity of the German people, the army, the Party and the State. He left this subject to point out that there lies before the Reich a new year which must bring grave decisions. This obviously means that the heavy fighting which has been threatened for weeks and months past can no longer be delayed. What form will it take? We can be sure that Chancellor Hitler took care not to furnish details on the matter, since the element of surprise is one of the chief factors in any large-scale military or naval venture.

SPEECH OF MARCH 16, 1941

Berlin Zeughaus

Background

March 1—German troops enter Sofia. Bulgaria joins the Axis.

March 11—President Roosevelt signs Lend-Lease Bill.

March 16—German troops are reported massed in the Balkans, especially along the Yugoslav frontiers.

The Speech

"FOR the second time we enter this room for a memorial service to our people. For more than a year we have appreciated how inadequate are words to express the nation's thankfulness to its heroes. In times of long peace the memory of the terrible experiences of war, out of which rises heroism, gradually grows dim. It even happens that a whole generation knows nothing of war as such and honors its heroes without being in the least worthy of them.

"In such a circumstance the greatest sacrifice of man is acknowledged with superficial phrases. There is even danger that, while remembering heroes of times past, the men of the present regard themselves as free of the obligation to conduct themselves with a similar spirit of heroism.

"But if the German people in the year 1941 honors its heroes, it does so at a time and under circumstances that give it a right to hold up its head with pride as it pays tribute to men of the near and distant past who sacrificed their lives for the State.

"As twelve months ago in this consecrated hall we turned our thoughts to our heroes, there lay behind us the thoroughly successful beginning of a war that Germany did not want, but that was forced on us by the same forces that were responsible before in history for the great war of the peoples in 1914 to 1918.

"They were the elements whose goal that time was to rob the German nation of the most primitive right of life, who in the years of the Versailles Dictate raised as the dogma of the new world order political enslavement and economic impotence, and now are opposed to the revival of our people with the same hatred with which they once pursued the Second Reich.

"In complete misjudgment of the situation, in a sadly false estimate of their own and Germany's power, and in complete ignorance of the will and determination of the new German leadership, they expected a second crushing of our people would be as easy as the first attempt.

"The fact that the American General Wood, before the investigation committee of the American Senate, testified that as early as 1936 Churchill told him Germany was getting too strong again and must be destroyed in a new war established firmly in history the real responsibility for present developments.

"England and France alone wanted war—not so much the people as a thin stratum of political and financial leadership behind which, wielding its last power, stood international Jewry and its world conspiracies of democracy and Freemasonry.

"But it was the hope of these responsible warmakers that thrust Poland forward not only to attain outward justification for war but also to make sure in advance that Poland would play its World War role of dividing German strength.

"The eighteen-day campaign in Poland was but the precipitous end of these hopes. Under these circumstances the German people were able to enter the year 1940 with proud confidence. But our people did not deceive themselves as to the year lying ahead. The battle in the West, which remains in the memory of every living German World War soldier as an episode of suffering without end, had to be decided.

"In exact knowledge of our preparations and plans, in boundless confidence in the German soldier, his armament and leadership and ability and before all in his attitude, I dared on Memorial Day, 1940, to predict that the battle before us would end in the most glorious victory in our history. Eight weeks later this battle started.

"But before the defense forces struck in the West, what was probably the most important decision of the war was taken. On April 9, with just a few hours to spare, a dangerous British attempt to strike German defense powers in the heart from the north was anticipated. At dawn on May 10 this perhaps most dangerous threat to our military and political position had been swept aside. So the battle to a decision in the West could begin. It followed a course previously mapped out.

"What could not be done in four years of indescribable sacrifice in the World War was accomplished in a few weeks: the crushing of the British-French front.

"Despite the conclusion of the guilty British Prime Minister of that time, the year 1940 will go down in history as one of the most decisive and significant, because in this year there was a shift of power of truly historic importance. If in the year 1918 we could have had only a portion of this success the World War would have been won.

"Today German forces stand throughout the world, men and material strengthened to an inconceivable degree, ready to complete joyfully and confidently what was begun in the epochal year 1940. . . ."

"The German people have recovered everything that once was sacrificed in a foolish delusion. So today we can recall with lightened hearts the sacrifice of life in the World War. But in the illustrious events of the present we must not overlook the vast spiritual powers for which the German people and its soldiers must thank the heroism of their ancestors.

"The soldiers of the World War did not fall in vain. If at that time the sacrifice was not immediately crowned by success, their heroic conduct left a heritage that an ever worthy German generation will prize with deepest emotion and that paralyzes the memories of our enemies.

"It is perhaps this consciousness of strength that enabled the German people today to achieve such greatness. The people feel they are carrying out the will of heroic ancestors.

"Beside the dead of the World War lie now the fallen in continuation of this battle. And again, as then, the sons of our people lie in distant places, in the sea, everywhere as courageous fighters for their great German home. It is the same German man—be it in World War work or in the present fight that has been thrust upon us—who risks and gives his life to win for his people a greater future, a surer peace, a better organization and human comradeship than that given us by the dictators of Versailles.

"But we think also of the Italian soldiers, who as allies also must give up their lives in distant parts of the world. Their ideals and objectives are the same as ours: The world is not here for a few people, and an order based eternally on the distinction between the haves and the have-nots does not exist any more because the have-nots have determined to lay claim to their portion of God's earth.

"The home front, too, in this war must make a greater sacrifice than formerly. The heroism of the home front contributes its bit to the most decisive battle in German history. And here it is not only the man who must show the power of his resistance but the woman, too. The nation has become a battling unity. And not because they sought this fight but because it was forced on them.

"Behind us lies a winter of work. What remained to be improved has been done. The German Army is now the strongest military instrument in our history. In the months of this winter our allies bore the brunt of the whole power of the British attack, but from now on German forces again will resume their share of this load.

"No power and no support coming from any part of the world can change the outcome of this battle in any respect. England will fall. The everlasting providence will not give victory to him who, merely with the object of ruling through his gold, is willing to spill the blood of men.

"Germany demanded nothing of England and France. All the Reich's denunciations, its disarmament and peace suggestions, were vain. International finance and plutocracy want to fight this war to the finish. So the end of this war will and must be their destruction. Then may providence find a way to lead their people, from whom the chains will be struck, into a better order!

"When England and France declared this war, England immediately began a fight against civil life. To the blockade of the World War, that war against women and children, it added this time air and fire war against peaceful villages and cities. In both of these modes of war England will be defeated. The air war that Churchill started will destroy not Germany but England itself. Just so, the blockade will not strike Germany but its inventor.

"While the coming of winter limited battle actions on land, the fight in the air and on the sea continued. The heroism of submarine and ship crews goes hand in hand with that of our fliers. . . ."

"So we enter the year 1941, cool and determined to end what started the year before. It is quite immaterial what part of the earth or in which sea or in what air space our German soldiers fight. They will know they battle for fate and freedom and the future of our people forever.

"But while we end this battle victoriously we thank our heroes of the past, for we are saving that for which they fell: Germany, our people, and its great German Empire."

Press

London Times, March 17—Hitler spoke yesterday at a commemoration in the Berlin Zeughaus of the German war dead. He repeated the old assertions of Nazi propaganda and once more prophesied that "England will fall" and that Germany would "complete in 1941 what she had begun in the past."

New York Times, March 17—Neutral quarters profess to see in this a declaration by Herr Hitler that the pause in decisive military activity that has prevailed since the armistice of Compiègne is now to be broken and that the German land forces are again to be set in motion. Where, however, naturally remains a German secret.

•

HITLER'S ORDER OF THE DAY, APRIL 6, 1941

Berlin

Background

March 23—Japanese Foreign Minister Matsuoka visits Moscow.

March 25—Yugoslav Government signs pact with Axis in Vienna.

March 26—Matsuoka visits Berlin and is received by Hitler.

March 27—A popular revolt in Yugoslavia forces resignation of Regent Prince Paul's Government. Seventeen-year old King Peter II assumes power with General Simovitch as Premier. Nazi agencies in Serbia are wrecked by the people. German "tourists" and colonists leave the country.

In Lybia, German motorized divisions reinforce the Italians.

Conquest of Italian East Africa is practically completed by the British.

March 28—British fleet inflicts serious defeat on Italian Navy in Ionian sea.

April 6—A pact of non-aggression between Russia and Yugoslavia is made public.

Germany declares war on Yugoslavia and attacks both Yugoslavia and Greece.

From Berlin, Propaganda Minister Goebbels reads the following Order of the Day to the German Army of the East, in the name of the Fuehrer:

Order of the Day

"Soldiers of the Southeast Front:

"Since early this morning the German people are at war with the Belgrade Government of intrigue. We shall only lay down arms when this band of ruffians has been definitely and most emphatically eliminated, and the last Briton has left this part of the European Continent. These misled people realize that they must thank Britain for this situation, they must thank England, the greatest warmonger of all time.

"The German people can enter into this new struggle with the inner satisfaction that its leaders have done everything to bring about a peaceful settlement.

"We pray to God that He may lead our soldiers on the path and bless them as hitherto.

"In accordance with the policy of letting others fight for her, as she did in the case of Poland, Britain again tried to involve Germany in the struggle in which Britain hoped that she would finish off the German people once and for all, to win the war, and if possible to destroy the entire German Army.

"In a few weeks, long ago, the German soldiers on the Eastern Front swept aside Poland, the instrument of British policy. On April 9, 1940, Britain again attempted to reach its goal by a thrust on the German north flank, the thrust at Norway.

"In an unforgettable struggle the German soldiers in Norway eliminated the British within a period of a few weeks.

"What the world did not deem possible the German people have achieved. Again, only a few weeks later, Churchill thought the moment right to make a renewed thrust through the British Allies, France and Belgium, into the German region of the Ruhr. The victorious hour of our soldiers on the West Front began.

"It is already war history how the German Armies defeated the legions of capitalism and plutocracy. After forty-five days this campaign in the West was equally and emphatically terminated.

"Then Churchill concentrated the strength of his Empire against our ally, Italy, in Africa. Now the danger has also been banned from the African theater of the war through the co-operation of Italian and German units.

"The new aim of the British warmongers now consists of the realization of a plan that they had already hatched at the outbreak of the war and only postponed because of the gigantic victories of the German Army. The memory of the landing of British troops at Salonika in the course of the first World War also caught little Greece in the spider web of British intrigue.

"I have repeatedly warned of the attempt by the British to land troops in Southeastern Europe, and I have said that this constitutes a threat to the German Reich. Unfortunately this warning went unheeded by the Yugoslav nation. I have further tried, always with the same patience, to convince Yugoslav statesmen of the absolute necessity for their co-operation with the German Reich for restoration of lasting peace and order within Yugoslavia.

"After long effort we finally succeeded in securing the co-operation of Yugoslavia by its adherence to the Tripartite Pact without having demanded anything whatsoever of the Yugoslav nation except that it take its part in the reconstruction of a new order in Europe.

"At this point the criminal usurpers of the new Belgrade Government took the power of the State unto themselves, which is a result of being in the pay of Churchill and Britain. As in the case of Poland, this new Belgrade Government has mobilized decrepit and old people into their inner Cabinet. Under these circumstances I was forced immediately to recall the German national colony within Yugoslav territory.

"Members and officers of the German Embassy, employees of our consulates in Yugoslavia were daily being subjected to the most humiliating attacks. The German schools, exactly as in Poland, were laid in ruins by bandits. Innumerable German nationals were kidnaped and attacked by Yugoslavs and some even were killed.

"In addition, Yugoslavia for weeks has planned a general mobilization of its army in great secrecy. This is the answer to my eight-year-long effort to bring about closer co-operation and friendship with the Yugoslav people, a task that I have pursued most fastidiously.

"When British divisions were landed in Greece, just as in World War days, the Serbs thought the time was ripe for taking advantage of the situation for new assassinations against Germany and her allies.

"Soldiers of the Southeast Front: Now your zero hour has arrived. You will now take the interests of the German Reich under your protection as your comrades did a year ago in Norway and on the West Front. You will do just as well on the Southeast Front.

"In doing this, your duty, you will not be less courageous than the men of those German divisions who in 1915, on the same Balkan soil, fought so victoriously. You will be humane only in those places where the enemy is humane toward you. Where the enemy confronts you with utter brutality you will beat them back with the same weapon.

"The fight on Greek soil is not a battle against the Greek people, but against that archenemy, England, which is again trying to extend the war far into the Southeast Balkans, the same as he tried far in the north last year. For this reason, on this very spot in the Balkans, we shall fight shoulder to shoulder with our ally until the last Briton has found his Dunkerque in Greece.

"If any Greeks support this British course, then those Greeks will fall at the same time as the British.

"When the German soldier shall have proved himself, shall have proved that he is capable of beating the British in the Balkans, in the midst of snow and mountains, then also he will have proved that he can beat the British in the heat of the desert in Africa.

"However, *we will pursue no other ultimate aim than to win freedom for our German people and to secure a living-space for the German family*.

"The prayers and thoughts, the very life of all Germans, are again in the heart of every German soldier."

Press

New York Times, April 7—In the early hours of Palm Sunday morning, praying God "to lead the German Armies on their path," Adolf Hitler struck at two more small nations that wanted only to live their own lives in peace and freedom. The attack was begun in characteristic German fashion, with massed air assaults by Stuka bombers on a capital which had previously been declared an open city. It was followed, as all German attacks are followed, by an equally characteristic performance to which the foreign correspondents in Berlin were summoned, in order that they might hear from those in high authority how blameless is the German case, how shamefully the little German Reich had been bullied by big Yugoslovia and giant Greece, how noble the German nation felt, on this Palm Sunday morning, because "its leaders had done everything to bring about a peaceful settlement."

•

SPEECH OF MAY 4, 1941

Berlin, Reichstag

Background

1941

April 9—Yugoslav armies are crushed by German Blitzkrieg. German troops enter Salonika.

In a speech, Winston Churchill justifies the necessity of answering Greece's appeal for help, calls to America for increased help, saying that main battle is that of the Atlantic.

April 13—Japanese Foreign Minister Matsuoka, in Moscow, signs pact of friendship with Stalin.

April 18—Remnants of Yugoslav armies capitulate.

Germans pursue offensive in Greece against Anglo-Greek armies.

In Libya, German motorized divisions reach Egyptian border.

April 20—It is estimated that Germans have sunk well over 5,000,000 tons of Allied shipping since the beginning of the war.

April 23—Charles Lindbergh makes his first speech under the auspices of the "America First Committee," expressing the belief that England cannot be saved and that America should concentrate exclusively on hemispheric defense.

April 27—Germans enter Athens. The King of Greece and Government have fled to Crete.

Churchill, in speech, reviews recent events, reasserts importance of the battle of the Atlantic. Thanking America for increased help, implies that it is not sufficient.

May 2—Following a coup d'état in Iraq, a pro-Nazi Government is formed. British airport in Habbania is attacked by Iraq troops.

May 4—In Iraq, a British force quells revolt.

May 4-11—Heavy German air raids over Liverpool, Glasgow, and Hull.

The Speech

"Deputies. Men of the German Reichstag:

"At a time when only deeds count and words are of little importance, it is not my intention to appear before you, the elected representatives of the German people, more often than absolutely necessary. The first time I spoke to you was at the outbreak of the war when, thanks to the Anglo-French conspiracy against peace, every attempt at an understanding with Poland, which otherwise would have been possible, had been frustrated.

"The most unscrupulous men of the present time had, as they admit today, decided as early as 1936 to involve the Reich, which in its peaceful work of reconstruction was becoming too powerful for them, in a new and bloody war and, if possible, to destroy it. They had finally succeeded in finding a State that was prepared for their interests and aims, and that State was Poland.

"All my endeavors to come to an understanding with Britain were wrecked by the determination of a small clique which, whether from motives of hate or for the sake of material gain, rejected every German proposal for an understanding due to their resolve, which they never concealed, to resort to war, whatever happened.

"The man behind this fanatical and diabolical plan to

bring about war at whatever cost was Mr. Churchill. His associates were the men who now form the British Government.

"These endeavors received most powerful support, both openly and secretly, from the so-called great democracies on both sides of the Atlantic. At a time when the people were more and more dissatisfied with their deficient statesmanship, the responsible men over there believed that a successful war would be the most likely means of solving problems that otherwise would be beyond their power to solve.

"Behind these men there stood the great international Jewish financial interests that control the banks and the Stock Exchange as well as the armament industry. And now, just as before, they scented the opportunity of doing their unsavory business. And so, just as before, there was no scruple about sacrificing the blood of the peoples. That was the beginning of this war. A few weeks later the State that was the third country in Europe, Poland, but had been reckless enough to allow herself to be used for the financial interests of these warmongers, was annihilated and destroyed.

"In these circumstances I considered that I owed it to our German people and countless men and women in the opposite camps, who as individuals were as decent as they were innocent of blame, to make yet another appeal to the common sense and the conscience of these statesmen. On October 6, 1939, I therefore once more publicly stated that Germany had neither demanded nor intended to demand anything either from Britain or from France, that it was madness to continue the war and, above all, that the scourge of modern weapons of warfare, once they were brought into action, would inevitably ravage vast territories.

"But just as the appeal I made on September 1, 1939, proved to be in vain, this renewed appeal met with indignant rejection. The British and their Jewish capitalist backers could find no other explanation for this appeal, which I had made on humanitarian grounds, than the assumption of weakness on the part of Germany.

"They assured the people of Britain and France that Germany dreaded the clash to be expected in the spring of 1940 and was eager to make peace for fear of the annihilation that would then inevitably result.

"Already at that time the Norwegian Government, misled by the stubborn insistence of Mr. Churchill's false prophecies, began to toy with the idea of a British landing on their soil, thereby contributing to the destruction of Germany by permitting their harbors and Swedish iron ore fields to be seized.

"So sure were Mr. Churchill and Paul Reynaud of the success of their new scheme that finally, whether from sheer recklessness or perhaps under the influence of drink, they deemed it no longer necessary to make a secret of their intentions.

"It was thanks to these two gentlemen's tendency to gossip that the German Government at that time gained cognizance of the plans being made against the Reich. A few weeks later this danger to Germany was eliminated. One of the boldest deeds of arms in the whole history of warfare frustrated the attack of the British and French armies against the right flank of our line of defense.

"Immediately after the failure of these plans, increased pressure was exerted by the British warmongers upon Belgium and Holland. Now that the attack upon our sources for the supply of iron ore had proved unsuccessful, they aimed to advance the front to the Rhine by involving the Belgian and Dutch States and thus to threaten and paralyze our production centers for iron and steel.

"On May 10 of last year perhaps the most memorable struggle in all German history commenced. The enemy front was broken up in a few days and the stage was then set for the operation that culminated in the greatest battle of annihilation in the history of the world. Thus France collapsed, Belgium and Holland were already occupied, and the battered remnants of the British expeditionary force were driven from the Eurpoean continent, leaving their arms behind.

"On July 19, 1940, I then convened the German Reichstag for the third time in order to render that great account which you all still remember. The meeting provided me with the opportunity of expressing the thanks of the nation to its soldiers in a form suited to the uniqueness of the event. Once again I seized the opportunity of urging the world to make peace. And what I foresaw and prophesied at that time happened. My offer of peace was misconstrued as a symptom of fear and cowardice.

"The European and American warmongers succeeded once again in befogging the sound common sense of the masses, who can never hope to profit from this war, by conjuring up false pictures of new hope. Thus, finally, under pressure of public opinion, as formed by their press, they once more managed to induce the nation to continue this struggle.

"Even my warnings against night bombings of the civilian population, as advocated by Mr. Churchill, were interpreted as a sign of German impotence. He, the most bloodthirsty or amateurish strategist that history has ever known, actually saw fit to believe that the reserve displayed for months by the German Air Force could be looked upon only as proof of their incapacity to fly by night.

"So this man for months ordered his paid scribblers to deceive the British people into believing that the Royal Air Force alone—and no others—was in a position to wage war in this way, and that thus ways and means had been found to force the Reich to its knees by the ruthless onslaught of the British Air Force on the German civilian population in conjunction with the starvation blockade.

"Again and again I uttered these warnings against this specific type of aerial warfare, and I did so for over three and a half months. That these warnings failed to impress Mr. Churchill does not surprise me in the least. For what does this man care for the lives of others? What does he care for culture or for architecture. When war broke out he stated clearly that he wanted to have his war, even though the cities of England might be reduced to ruins. So now he has got his war.

"My assurances that from a given moment every one of his bombs would be returned if necessary a hundredfold failed to induce this man to consider even for an instant the criminal nature of his action. He professes not to be in the least depressed and he even assures us that the British people, too, after such bombing raids, greeted him with a joyous serenity, causing him to return to London refreshed by his visits to the stricken areas.

"It is possible that this sight strengthened Mr. Churchill in his firm determination to continue the war in this way, and we are no less determined to continue to retaliate, if necessary, a hundred bombs for every one of his and to go on doing so until the British nation at last gets rid of this criminal and his methods.

"The appeal to forsake me, made to the German nation by this fool and his satellites on May Day, of all days, are only to be explained either as symptomatic of a paralytic disease or of a drunkard's ravings. His abnormal state of mind also gave birth to a decision to transform the Balkans into a theater of war.

"For over five years this man has been chasing around Europe like a madman in search of something that he could set on fire. Unfortunately, he again and again finds hirelings who open the gates of their country to this international incendiary.

"After he had succeeded in the course of the past winter in persuading the British people by a wave of false assertions and pretensions that the German Reich, exhausted by the campaign in the preceding months, was completely spent, he saw himself obliged, in order to prevent an awakening of the truth, to create a fresh conflagration in Europe.

"In so doing he returned to the project that had been in his mind as early as the autumn of 1939 and the spring of 1940. It was thought possible at the time to mobilize about 100 divisions in Britain's interest.

"The sudden collapse which we witnessed in May and June of the past year forced these plans to be abandoned for the moment. But by the autumn of last year Mr. Churchill began to tackle this problem once again.

"In the meantime, however, certain difficulties had arisen. As a result, Rumania, owing to internal changes, dropped out of England's political scheme.

"In dealing with these conditions, I shall begin by giving you a brief outline of the aims of Germany's policy in the Balkans. *As in the past, the Reich never pursued any territorial or any other selfish political interest in the Balkans.* In other words, the Reich has never taken the slightest interest in territorial problems and internal conditions in these States for any selfish reason whatsoever.

"On the other hand, the Reich has always endeavored to build up and to strengthen close economic ties with these States in particular. This, however, not only served the interests of the Reich but equally the interests of these countries themselves.

"If any two national economic systems ever effectively complemented one another, that is especially the case regarding the Balkan States and Germany. Germany is an industrial country and requires foodstuffs and raw materials. The Balkan States are agrarian countries and are short of these raw materials. At the same time, they require industrial products.

"It was therefore hardly surprising when Germany thus became the main business partner of the Balkan States. Nor was this in Germany's interest alone, but also in that of the Balkan peoples themselves.

"And none but our Jew-ridden democracies, which can think only in terms of capitalism, can maintain that if one State delivers machinery to another State it thereby dominates that other State. In acual fact such domination, if it occurs, can be only a reciprocal domination.

"It is presumably easier to be without machinery than without food and raw materials. Consequently, the partner in need of raw material and foodstuffs would appear to be more tied down than the recipient of industrial products. *In this transaction there was neither conqueror nor conquered. There were only partners.*

"The German Reich of the National Socialist revolution has prided itself on being a fair and decent partner, offering in exchange high-quality products instead of worthless democratic paper money. For these reasons the Reich was interested in only one thing if, indeed, there was any question of political interest, namely, in seeing that internally the business partner was firmly established on a sound and healthy basis.

"The application of this idea led in fact not only to increasing prosperity in these countries but also to the beginning of mutual confidence. All the greater, however, became the endeavor of that world incendiary, Churchill, to put an end to this peaceful development and by shamelessly imposing upon these States utterly worthless British guarantees and promises of assistance to introduce into this peaceable European territory elements of unrest, uncertainty, distrust, and, finally, conflict.

"Originally, Rumania was first won over by these guarantees and later, of course, Greece. It has, meanwhile, probably been sufficiently demonstrated that he had absolutely no power of any kind to provide real help and that these guarantees were merely intended to rope these States in to follow the dangerous trend of filthy British politics.

"Rumania has had to pay bitterly for the guarantees, which were calculated to estrange her from the Axis powers.

Greece, which least of all required such a guarantee, was offered her share to link her destiny to that of the country that provided her King with cash and orders.

"Even today I feel that I must, as I believe in the interest of historical accuracy, distinguish between the Greek people and that thin top layer of corrupt leaders who, inspired by a King who had no eyes for the duty of true leadership, preferred instead to further the aims of British war politics. To me this is a subject of profound regret.

"Germany, with the faint hope of still being able to contribute in some way to a solution of the problem, had not severed relations with Greece. But even then I was bound in duty to point out before the whole world that we would not tacitly allow a revival of the old Salonika scheme of the Great War.

"Unfortunately, my warning was not taken seriously enough. That we were determined, if the British tried to gain another foothold in Europe, to drive them back into the sea was not taken seriously enough.

"The result was that the British began in an increasing degree to establish bases for the formation of a new Salonika army. They began by laying out airdromes and by establishing the necessary ground organization in the firm conviction that the occupation of the airdromes themselves could afterward be carried out very speedily.

"Finally a continuous stream of transports brought equipment for an army which, according to Mr. Churchill's idea and plans, was to be landed in Greece. As I have said, already we were aware of this. For months we watched this entire strange procedure with attention, if with restraint.

"The reverses suffered by the Italian Army in North Africa, owing to a certain material inferiority of their tanks and anti-tank guns, finally led Mr. Churchill to believe that the time was ripe to transfer the theater of war from Libya to Greece. He ordered the transport of the remaining tanks and of the infantry division, composed mainly of Anzacs, and was convinced that he could now complete his scheme, which was to set the Balkans aflame.

"*Thus did Mr. Churchill commit one of the greatest strategic blunders of this war.* As soon as there could be no further doubt regarding Britain's intentions of gaining a foothold in the Balkans, I took the necessary steps.

"Germany, by keeping pace with these moves, assembled the necessary forces for the purpose of counteracting any possible tricks of that gentleman. In this connection *I must state categorically that this action was not directed against Greece.*

"The Duce did not even request me to place one single German division at his disposal for this purpose. He was convinced that with the advent of good weather his stand against Greece would have been brought to a successful conclusion. I was of the same opinion.

"The concentration of German forces was therefore not made for the purpose of assisting the Italians against Greece. It was a precautionary measure against the British attempt under cover of the clamor caused by the Italo-Greek war to intrench themselves secretly in the Balkans in order to force the issue from that quarter on the model of the Salonika army during the World War, and, above all, to draw other elements into the whirlpool.

"This hope was founded principally on two States, namely, Turkey and Yugoslavia. But with these very States I have striven during the years since I came into power to establish close co-operation.

"The World War actually started from Belgrade. Nevertheless, the German people, who are by nature so ready to forgive and forget, felt no animosity toward that country. Turkey was our ally in the World War. The unfortunate outcome of that struggle weighed upon that country just as heavily as it did upon us.

"The great genius who created the new Turkey was the first to set a wonderful example of recovery to our allies whom fortune had at that time deserted and whom fate had dealt so terrible a blow. *Whereas Turkey, thanks to the practical attitude of her leaders, preserved her independence in carrying out her own resolutions, Yugolsavia fell a victim to British intrigue.*

"Most of you, especially my old Party comrades among you, know what efforts I have made to establish a straightforward understanding and indeed friendly relations between Germany and Yugoslavia. In pursuance of this aim Herr von Ribbentrop, our Minister of Foreign Affairs, submitted to the Yugoslav Government proposals that were so outstanding and so fair that at least even the Yugoslav State of that time seemed to become increasingly eager for such close co-operation.

"Germany had no intention of starting a war in the Balkans. On the contrary, it was our honest intention as far as possible to contribute to a settlement of the conflict with Greece by means that would be tolerable to the legitimate wishes of Italy.

"The Duce not only consented to but lent his full support to our efforts to bring Yugoslavia into a close community of interests with our peace aims. Thus it finally became possible to induce the Yugoslav Government to join the Three-power Pact, which made no demands whatever on Yugoslavia but only offered that country advantages.

"Thus on March 26 of this year a pact was signed in Vienna that offered the Yugoslav State the greatest future conceivable and could have assured peace for the Balkans. Believe me, gentlemen, on that day I left the beautiful city of the Danube truly happy not only because it seemed as though almost eight years of foreign policies had received their reward but also because I believed that perhaps at the last moment German intervention in the Balkans might not be necessary.

"We were all stunned by the news of that coup, carried through by a handful of bribed conspirators who had brought about the event that caused the British Prime Minister to

declare in joyous words that at last he had something good to report.

"You will surely understand, gentlemen, that when I heard this I at once gave orders to attack Yugoslavia. To treat the German Reich in this way is impossible. One cannot spend years in concluding a treaty that is in the interest of the other party merely to discover that this treaty has not only been broken overnight but also that it has been answered by the insulting of the representative of the German Reich, by the threatening of his military attaché, by the injuring of the aide de camp of this attaché, by the maltreating of numerous other Germans, by demolishing property, by laying waste the homes of German citizens and by terrorizing.

"God knows that I wanted peace. But I can do nothing but protect the interests of the Reich with those means which, thank God, are at our disposal. I made my decision at that moment all the more calmly because I knew that I was in accord with Bulgaria, who had always remained unshaken in her loyalty to the German Reich, and with the equally justified indignation of Hungary.

"Both of our old allies in the World War were bound to regard this action as a provocation emanating from the State that once before had set the whole of Europe on fire and had been guilty of the indescribable sufferings that befell Germany, Hungary, and Bulgaria in consequence.

"The general directions of operations issued by me through the Supreme Command of the German forces on March 27 confronted the Army and the Air Force with a formidable task. By a mere turn of the hand an additional campaign had to be prepared. Units that had already arrived had to be moved about. Supplies of armaments had to be assured and the air force had to take over numerous improvised airports, part of which were still under water.

"Without the sympathetic assistance of Hungary and the extremely loyal attitude of Rumania it would have been very difficult to carry out my orders in the short time envisaged.

"I fixed April 6 as the day on which the attack was to begin. The main plan of operation was: First to proceed with an army coming from Bulgaria against Thrace in Greece in the direction of the Aegean Sea.

"The main striking strength of this army lay in its right wing, which was to force a passage through to Salonika by using mountain divisions and a division of tanks; second, to thrust forward with a second army with the object of establishing connection as speedily as possible with the Italian forces advancing from Albania. These two operations were to begin on April 6.

"Third, a further operation, beginning on the eighth, provided for the break-through of an army from Bulgaria with the object of reaching the neighborhood of Belgrade. In conjunction with this, a German army corps was to occupy the Banat on the tenth.

"In connection with these operations general agreement had been made with our allies, Italy and Hungary. Agreements as to co-operation had also been reached between the two air forces. The command of the German Armies operating against Macedonia and Greece was placed in the hands of Field Marshal von List, who had already particularly distinguished himself in the previous campaigns. Once more and under the most exacting conditions he carried out the task confronting him in truly superior fashion.

"The forces advancing against Yugoslavia from the southwest and from Hungary were commanded by Col. Gen. von Weick. He, too, in a very short time with the forces under his command reached his objective.

"The Army and SS detachments operating under Field Marshal von Brauchitsch, as Commander in Chief, and the Chief of the General Staff, Col. Gen. Halder, forced the Greek Army in Thrace to capitulate after only five days, established contact with the Italian forces advancing from Albania, occupied Salonika, and thus generally prepared the way for the difficult and glorious break-through via Larissa to Athens.

"These operations were crowned by the occupation of the Peloponnesus and numerous Greek islands. A detailed appreciation of the achievements will be given by the German High Command.

"The Air Force under the personal command of Reich Marshal Goering was divided into two main groups commanded by Col. Gen. Loehr and General von Richthofen. It was their task, first, to shatter the enemy air force and to smash its ground organization; second, to attack every important military objective in the conspirators' headquarters at Belgrade, thus eliminating it from the very outset; third, by every manner of active co-operation everywhere with the fighting German troops to break the enemy's resistance, to impede the enemy's flight, to prevent as far as possible his embarkation.

"The German armed forces have truly surpassed themselves in this campaign. There is only one way of characterizing that campaign:

"Nothing is impossible for the German soldier. Historical justice, however, obliges me to say that of the opponents that have taken up arms against us, *most particularly the Greek soldiers, have fought with the greatest bravery and contempt of death.* He only capitulated when further resistance became impossible and therefore useless.

"But I am now compelled to speak of the enemy who is the main cause of this conflict. As a German and as a soldier I consider it unworthy ever to revile a fallen enemy. But it seems to me to be necessary to defend the truth from the wild exaggerations of a man who as a soldier is a bad politician and as a politician is an equally bad soldier.

"Mr. Churchill, who started this struggle, is endeavoring, as with regard to Norway or Dunkerque, to say something that sooner or later might perhaps be twisted around to resemble success. I do not consider that honorable but in his case it is understandable.

"The gift Mr. Churchill possesses is the gift to lie with a pious expression on his face and to distort the truth until finally glorious victories are made out of the most terrible defeats.

"A British Army of 60,000 to 70,000 men landed in Greece. Before the catastrophe the same man maintained, moreover, that it consisted of 240,000 men. The object of this army was to attack Germany from the south, inflict a defeat upon her, and from this point as in 1918 turn the tide of the war.

"I prophesied more correctly than Mr. Churchill in my last speech, in which I announced that wherever the British might set foot on the Continent they would be attacked by us and driven into the sea.

"Now, with his brazen effrontery, he asserts that this war has cost us 75,000 lives. He causes his presumably not over-intelligent fellow-countrymen to be informed by one of his paid creatures that the British, after having slain enormous masses of Germans, finally turned away from sheer abhorrence of the slaughter and, strictly speaking, withdrew for this reason alone.

"I will now present to you the results of this campaign in a few short figures. In the course of the operations against Yugoslavia there were the following numbers of purely Serbian prisoners, leaving out soldiers of German origin and some other groups, 6,198 officers, 313,864 men.

"The number of Greek prisoners, 8,000 officers and 210,000 men, has not the same significance. The number of Englishmen, New Zealanders and Australians taken prisoner exceeds 9,000 officers and men.

"The German share of the booty alone, according to the estimates at present available, amounts to more than half a million rifles, far more than 1,000 guns, many thousand machine-guns and anti-aircraft machine-guns, vehicles, and large amounts of ammunition. . . ."

"The losses of the German Army and the German Air Force as well as those of the SS troops in this campaign are the smallest that we have ever suffered so far. The German armed forces have in fighting against Yugoslavia and Greece as well as against the British in Greece lost:

"Army and SS Troops—Fifty-seven officers and 1,042 noncommissioned officers and men killed, 181 officers and 3,571 noncommissioned officers and men wounded, and 13 officers and 372 noncommissioned officers and men missing.

"Air Force—Ten officers and 42 noncommissioned officers and men killed and 36 officers and 104 noncommissioned officers and men missing.

"Once more I can only repeat that we feel the hardship of the sacrifice borne by the families concerned. The entire German nation expresses to them its heartfelt gratitude.

"Taking the measures as a whole, however, the losses suffered are so small that they constitute supreme justification, first, for the planning and timing of this campaign; second, for the conduct of operations; third, for the manner in which they were carried through.

"The training of our officers is excellent beyond comparison. The high standard of efficiency of our soldiers, the superiority of our equipment, the quality of our munitions and the indomitable courage of all ranks have combined to lead at such small sacrifice to a success of truly decisive historical importance.

"Churchill, one of the most hopeless dabblers in strategy, thus managed to lose two theaters of war at one single blow. The fact that this man, who in any other country would be court-martialed, gained fresh admiration as Prime Minister cannot be construed as an expression of magnanimity such as was accorded by Roman senators to generals honorably defeated in battle. It is merely proof of that perpetual blindness with which the gods afflict those whom they are about to destroy.

"The consequences of this campaign are extraordinary. In

view of the fact that a small set of conspirators in Belgrade again were able to foment trouble in the service of extra-continental interests, the radical elimination of this danger means the removal of an element of tension for the whole of Europe.

"The Danube as an important waterway is thus safeguarded against any further act of sabotage. Traffic has been resumed in full.

"Apart from the modest correction of its frontiers, which were infringed as a result of the outcome of the World War, the Reich has no special territorial interests in these parts. As far as politics are concerned we are merely interested in safeguarding peace in this region, while in the realm of economics we wish to see an order that will allow the production of goods to be developed and the exchange of products to be resumed in the interests of all.

"It is, however, only in accordance with supreme justice if those interests are also taken into account that are founded upon ethnographical, historical, or economic conditions.

"I can assure you that I look into the future with perfect tranquillity and great confidence. The German Reich and its allies represent power, military, economic and, above all, in moral respects, which is superior to any possible coalition in the world. The German armed forces will always do their part whenever it may be necessary. The confidence of the German people will always accompany their soldiers."

Press

New York Times, May 5—Herr Hitler's latest address to a complacent Reichstag is notable only for new perversions of history, further misrepresentation of facts, and a parade of statistics as worthless as they are incredible. . . . These Reichstag deliverances may serve their purpose within Germany, for the time at least. In the free world they arouse only contempt.

PHASE IX

Blitzkrieg in the East

June 22, 1941

COMMENT

"THE two contracting parties (Germany and Russia) obligate themselves to refrain from every act of force, every aggressive action and every action against one another. . . ."

The Russo-German pact of August 1939, from which these words are quoted, was considered at the time both as the most ignominious and masterly diplomatic stroke of Hitler. Ignominious, because by allying himself with the Soviets, Hitler repudiated the most fundamental doctrine of National Socialism which was the crusade against bolshevism; masterly, because it freed Germany from the nightmare of a war on two fronts and enabled the German High Command to concentrate all its efforts in the west. The war, in fact, was born out of that pact. The astounding military successes of Hitler and the establishment of his domination over Europe were due to it.

Less than two years later, on June 22, 1941, Hitler broke this pact. Without any warning, his armies invaded Russia on a front extending from the Baltic to the Black Sea. It was, according to Hitler himself, "the greatest march that the world hitherto had seen." It was also the greatest apparent reversal of policy, a complete strategic and ideological turn around.

The world was astounded.

Many observers had predicted that the day would be seen when Germany and Russia would come to grips. It was generally recognized that there could be no true alliance between the two totalitarian States. Berlin and Moscow were the capitals of two world-embracing revolutionary movements, whose methods and results were in many ways similar, but whose inspiration and ultimate aims were diametrically opposed. Hitler and Stalin were rivals. Their alliance was a matter of pure expediency by which both hoped to gain finally the upper hand.

From Hitler's point of view, the neutralisation of Russia in August, 1939, had been a strategic necessity. It allowed him freedom to make war. From Stalin's point of view, the war between Nazi Germany and the Western democracies could only result in weakening both, in spreading ruin and anarchy all over Europe, thus increasing tremendously his relative strength and preparing the way for world communism.

But the calculations of both dictators went wrong. The French Army—the strength of which Stalin had over-estimated like everybody else—was crushed in a month, and Hitler, far from being weakened by his effort, was more formidable than ever and the undisputed master of Europe. On the other hand, the resistance of England and the growing power of the United States prevented Hitler from ending the war with the democratic world. By the end of the Spring, 1941, Hitler was facing a dangerous stalemate.

Under these circumstances the temporary usefulness of the Russo-German pact of 1939 had run out. Whatever secret arrangements had been made between Moscow and Berlin concerning the division of their respective "spheres of influence" in Eastern and Southern Europe were now viewed under another light. There is no reason to disbelieve Hitler when he explained, in his proclamation of June 22, how painful it had been for him to send Ribbentrop to Moscow. Ribbentrop had had to make concessions to Stalin—the first that the Fuehrer's Foreign Minister or Hitler himself had ever had to make to anyone. But they were deemed worth while at the time. Any concession was worth while to break the "British encirclement policy."

A year later, however, Hitler began to realize that the

price he had paid to keep Russia quiet was too high. Stalin, seeing that the prospects of a long war of mutual attrition in the West were frustrated, began to reinforce his defenses against his ally and future enemy. By extending the "protection" of the Soviets over the Baltic States, by securing bases in Finland, by annexing Bessarabia and offering tentative support to Yugoslavia, he showed clearly that he understood the peril that faced him thanks to his own miscalculations. Far from giving assistance to his ally, either economically or otherwise, Stalin began to use the August, 1939, pact and the "concessions" he had obtained as a cover to reinforce his own defenses against Hitler and to create between Germany and Russia a chain of buffer states and annexed territories.

While all this was going on, Hitler, as he says himself with rare candor in his proclamation, had to keep silent. And the reason for this silence is clear: as long as Hitler entertained hope of defeating England either by invasion or by winning the battles of the Atlantic and the Mediterranean, he could afford to let Stalin wait. Once he had finished the war with the democracies, settling his account with Stalin would be easy and could be done at leisure.

But as was shown in the previous comment (Phase VIII), such hope of a rapid victory over England and America had to be abandoned some time between the fall of 1940 and the spring of 1941. By June, Hitler had the choice between waiting in a state of relative impotency while the British and American power developed or take some action which might enhance still further his prestige, increase his resources and show once more the might of his arms.

He chose the latter course, and when that choice was made he acted with even greater promptitude than he had ever done before. Russia was invaded without any ultimatum and no warning.

It is true that for weeks and months rumors had been rife that the relations between Moscow and Berlin were fast deteriorating, and it was the consensus of opinion that a showdown was near. Most observers believed that when the showdown came, Stalin would give in. But Hitler was too pressed by time to make any demands on Stalin. He had no intention of involving himself in negotiations with his ally. There had been a "Czech crisis," a "Polish crisis" and many others. There was to be no "Russian crisis." Hitler had no time for that. Besides his *demands* on Russia were not of a nature that could be discussed. Only the sword, a new Blitzkrieg, could settle the Russian account.

Contrary to most of Hitler's speeches, his proclamation of June 22 contained a number of admissions—besides many lies and hypocritical protests—which give plausible explanations of his decision to attack Russia.

The most important one is the admission that "the German High Command could no longer vouch for a radical conclusion of the war in the West, particularly as regards aircraft," as long as so much of Germany's forces were tied up in the east. In other words, Hitler recognized that he could not defeat England for the moment. There is little reason to believe him when he spoke of a threatened attack by Russia. The likeliness of the Soviet Army taking the offensive against Germany was small, to say the most. But the fact remains that, according to Hitler, the German High Command preferred to eliminate completely the Russian armies before undertaking any final operation in the West.

The second interesting point in this proclamation was the somewhat embarrassed confession that the reason why he had concluded a pact with "Jewish bolshevist rulers" in August, 1939, was one of sheer expediency—to prevent a war on two fronts. It might be noted in passing that this admission throws a strange light, retrospectively, on Hitler's numerous past assertions that he never intended to make war in the West.

What the proclamation did not mention were three other possible motives for the attack on Russia.

The first was the necessity of obtaining raw materials from the Ukraine, the Caucasus and elsewhere in order to supplement the food rations of the Germans and to keep the war machine going. Obviously the resources of Western Europe were not enough to match the potential production of America and Hitler needed to prepare for the prospect of a very long war.

The second is a question of principle, so to speak, the application of a doctrine expressed in *Mein Kampf* (page 963) and which is formulated as follows: "The political testament of the German nation for its dealings with the outside world should and must always read substantially: Never tolerate the establishment of two continental powers in Europe." After the elimination of the French Army, there still remained "two continental powers in Europe," Germany and Russia. Russia therefore had to be destroyed, as a matter of principle.

The third motive was the hope of spreading confusion all over the world by this sudden reversal to the fundamental National Socialist doctrine of fighting bolshevism. In fact, the war on Russia was immediately presented by Nazi propaganda as the crusade of civilization and Christianity against the forces of darkness and paganism. Hitler, in his new role of champion of Christianity, was to lead the whole of Europe against Moscow and destroy communism once and for all. This was a new war aim and a new and convenient ideological basis for the European New Order.

This new line of propaganda had a certain effect in Europe, particularly in the Catholic countries. Italy immediately declared war on the Soviets. Spain offered a contingent of volunteers and the Vichy Government encouraged the same idea. Finland and Rumania were fighting side by side with the German armies obviously anxious to recover the provinces they had lost through the collusion of Hitler and Stalin. For the first time, Hitler could boast that he had allies and that he was heading a coalition. . . . But the propaganda of the crusade against bolshevism had less effect in the countries where it was intended to have the most: namely in England and in America.

On the very day that Hitler marched into Russia, Winston Churchill made it clear that, whereas he certainly could not be suspected of communistic leanings, he nevertheless considered that the Russian people were the victims of an unjustifiable attack, that they should be helped by England as well as by her friends and that the entrance of the Russian armies into the war against Hitler was a great help to England. If there were English tories or ex-appeasers to fall for Hitler's appeal to call off the war against Germany and to join him in his holy crusade against the Red peril, their voices were not heard. England had apparently become adamant to Hitlerian trickery.

The Roosevelt administration took about the same stand. It was made known that America, while repudiating with equal vigor communism and nazism, was nevertheless satisfied to see the red and brown armies locked in a struggle which—it was hoped—would be long and costly. Most newspapers made it clear that the new turn of events did not mean that America was now committed to rescuing Stalin, but that every force which served to defeat Hitlerism should be welcomed and encouraged.

The isolationists, however, seized avidly the new bait tendered to them by Hitler. Senator Wheeler, ex-President Hoover and Charles A. Lindbergh did their best to prove that the new re-alignment of forces in Europe only demonstrated the soundness of their main argument: that it was folly for America to take sides in a war in which such reversals of alliances and ideological upturns occurred overnight. As Hitler had hoped, a campaign was launched to prove that helping England was helping Communism. But the confusion thus created was apparently superficial and of no long duration. Production of armaments and aid to Britain were not slowed down, and when President Roosevelt announced the occupation of Iceland by American forces, there was no protest, although no other step had as yet been taken which most clearly marked America's resolve to risk everything, including a "shooting war," in order to defeat Hitlerism.

Hitler and the whole of Nazi propaganda performed the abrupt somersault of denouncing their ally as the arch-enemy of humanity with as much ease as Stalin on his part executed similar acrobatics. At no point did Hitler appear conscious of the inconsistencies of his behavior, and the reasons for this may be that, as usual, his sincerity and the necessities of strategy could be kept apart in his mind in two separate compartments.

It is probable however that Hitler felt a certain satisfaction in being able to revert to his early theories, as expressed in *Mein Kampf,* when he had written such passages as these:

"I confess openly that in pre-war times I already held it better had Germany, at the sacrifice of the senseless colonial policy and at the sacrifice of the merchant and naval fleet, stood in alliance with England against Russia and thus switched from the feeble world-wide policy to a determined European policy of continental territorial acquisition. . . . I do not forget the constant impudent threat which the pan-Slav Russia dared level against Germany; I do not forget the constant practise mobilization whose sole point was to offend Germany. . . ." *(Mein Kampf,* p. 962.) Or again:

"The present rulers of Russia do not at all think of entering an alliance sincerely or of keeping one. . . . We must never forget that the regents of present-day Russia are common blood-stained criminals; that here is the scum of humanity. . . . We must not forget that the international Jew, who today rules Russia absolutely, sees in Germany, not an ally, but a State marked for the same destiny. But one does not conclude a treaty with someone whose sole interest is the destruction of his partner. . . . If anybody thinks of going into treaty ties with parasites, this resembles a tree's efforts to conclude to its own advantage an agreement with a mistletoe." (*Mein Kampf*, p. 959-960.)

The war against Russia had been forced on Hitler by many factors beyond his control and it was the beginning of an adventure with unpredictable consequences. It offered him however the satisfaction of being able to tell the world that, after all, he had never really changed his mind, and that all the prophecies contained in *Mein Kampf*—save one: the friendship with England—were being dutifully fulfilled.

•

PROCLAMATION OF JUNE 22, 1941

Background

1941

May 6—Stalin succeeds Molotov as premier of the USSR.

May 10—Rudolph Hess, Nazi leader, lands in Scotland by parachute from a plane. The news is given out in England on May 12, after the German news agency has announced that Hess had disappeared.

Air raid over London: Westminster Abbey, House of Parliament and British Museum badly damaged.

May 16—Marshal Pétain, in a broadcast, approves the policy of "collaboration" with Germany.

President Roosevelt warns France against this policy which he considers as a menace to the Western hemisphere.

In his press conference, President Roosevelt announces that twenty-four cargo ships are ready to depart for the Red Sea in spite of Germany's statement that this area is still a war zone.

May 19—In Syria, General Dentz, commander of the French troops, protests to the British against the bombing of Syrian airdromes where German planes, en route to Iraq, had landed.

May 20—The Germans attack Crete by air.

May 23—Admiral Darlan, vice-premier of the Vichy Government, broadcasts an appeal to the French asking for support in the policy of "collaboration" with Germany.

May 24—German battleship *Bismarck* sinks British battleship *Hood* off Greenland.

May 27—British sink *Bismarck* after long pursuit.

President Roosevelt, in nation-wide broadcast, proclaims a state of "unlimited emergency." The main points of his speech are: 1.) The domination of Europe by Hitler is a step towards the domination of the world. 2.) For the safety of the Western hemisphere, Hitler must be stopped. 3.) The Nazis threaten certain points vital for the defense of America. America should be ready to forestall the occupation of such places as the Azores, the Cape Verde Islands, Dakar and Iceland. 4.) Aid to Britain and to all those resisting Hitlerism must be assured. 5.) The freedom of the seas must be maintained. 6.) American sea patrols are now extended in the North and South Atlantic. 7.) America must decide for herself when and where her interests are threatened. 8.) America will not accept a Hitler-dominated world.

May 31—Crete falls to the Germans. After heavy losses, remnants of British forces are evacuated.

Bagdad is occupied by the British.

Admiral Darlan issues violent attack against England and announces that France's destiny is now linked with the New Order in Europe. Expresses conviction that England cannot win the war.

June 2—Hitler and Mussolini confer at the Brenner Pass.

USSR withdraws recognition from Greece owing to "her loss of sovereignty."

June 5—Cordell Hull issues statement denouncing the Vichy policy of "collaboration" as tantamount to aligning France with the powers of aggression.

June 6—Berlin denies as "absolutely silly" stories of Russian and German troop concentrations.

June 8—British and Free French forces march into Syria.

June 11—Sir Stafford Cripps, British Ambassador to Moscow, returns to London, intimating that his efforts to get to an understanding with Stalin have failed.

June 12—News breaks that an American ship, the *Robin Moor,* has been sunk by a German submarine in the South Atlantic on May 21.

June 14—Cordell Hull issues second note denouncing vigorously the Vichy policy of "collaboration." Calls new status "preposterous."

German and Italian funds in America are "frozen."

June 15—Increasing rumors of Germans massing troops on Russian border.

June 16—President Roosevelt orders closing of all German consulates and agencies in America.

June 18—Germany and Italy order closing of American consulates and "freezing" of American funds in both countries.

Turkey signs non-aggression pact with Germany.

Finland mobilizes.

June 20—In strongly-worded message to Congress, President Roosevelt denounces Germany for sinking the *Robin Moor,* and states that the United States will not be intimidated by such acts.

From Berne, Ankara, Stockholm, rumors persist concerning growing tension between Moscow and Berlin.

June 22—English and Free French take Damas in Syria.

German armies attack Russia on 2,500-mile front, from the Baltic to the Black sea.

Hitler issues the following proclamation:

Proclamation

"German people!

"National Socialists!

"Weighted down with heavy cares, condemned to months-long silence, the hour has now come *when at last I can speak frankly.*

"When on September 3, 1939, the German Reich received the English declaration of war there was repeated anew a British attempt to render impossible every beginning of a consolidation and thereby of Europe's rise, by fighting whatever power on the Continent was strongest at any given time.

"That is how of yore England ruined Spain in many wars. That is how she conducted her wars against Holland. That is how later she fought France with the aid of all Europe and that is how at the turn of the century she began the encirclement of the then German Reich and in 1914 the World War. Only on account of its internal dissension was Germany defeated in 1918. The consequences were terrible.

"After hypocritical declarations that the fight was solely against the Kaiser and his regime, the annihilation of the German Reich began according to plan after the German Army had laid down its arms.

"While the prophecies of the French statement, that there were 20,000,000 Germans too many—in other words, that this number would have to be exterminated by hunger, disease or emigration—were apparently being fulfilled to the letter, the National Socialist movement began its work of unifying the German people and thereby initiating resurgence of the Reich. This rise of our people from distress, misery and shameful disregard bore all the signs of a purely internal renaissance. Britain especially was not in any way affected or threatened thereby.

"Nevertheless, a new policy of encirclement against Germany, born as it was of hatred, recommenced immediately. Internally and externally there resulted that plot familiar to us all between Jews and democrats, Bolshevists and reactionaries, with the sole aim of inhibiting the establishment of the new German people's State, and of plunging the Reich anew into impotence and misery.

"Apart from us the hatred of this international world conspiracy was directed against those peoples which like ourselves were neglected by fortune and were obliged to earn their daily bread in the hardest struggle for existence.

"Above all, the right of Italy and Japan to share in the goods of this world was contested just as much as that of Germany and in fact was formally denied.

"The coalition of these nations was, therefore, only an act of self-protection in the face of the egoistic world combination of wealth and power threatening them. As early as 1936 Prime Minister Churchill, according to statements by the American General Wood before a committee of the American House of Representatives, declared Germany was once again becoming too powerful and must therefore be destroyed. In the Summer of 1939 the time seemed to have come for England to begin to realize its intended annihilation by repetition of a comprehensive policy of encirclement of Germany.

"The plan of the campaign of lies staged for this purpose consisted in declaring that other people were threatened, in tricking them with British promises of guarantees and assistance, and of making them march against Germany just as it did preceding the Great War. Thus Britain from May to August, 1939, succeeded in broadcasting to the world that Lithuania, Estonia, Latvia, Finland and Bessarabia as well as the Ukraine were being directly threatened by Germany.

"A number of these States allowed themselves to be misled into accepting the promise of guarantee proffered with these assertions, thus joining the new encirclement front against Germany. *Under these circumstances I considered myself entitled to assume responsibility before my own conscience and before the history of the German people not only of assuring these countries or their governments of the falseness of Brit-*

ish assertions, but also of setting the strongest power in the east, by especially solemn declarations, at rest concerning the limits of our interests.

"National Socialists! At that time you probably all felt that this step was bitter and difficult for me. Never did the German people harbor hostile feeling against the peoples of Russia. However, for over ten years Jewish Bolshevist rulers had been endeavoring from Moscow to set not only Germany but all Europe aflame. At no time ever did Germany attempt to carry her National Socialist *Weltanschauung* into Russia, but on the contrary Jewish Bolshevist rulers in Moscow unswervingly endeavored to foist their domination upon us and other European peoples, not only by ideological means but above all with military force.

"The consequences of the activity of this regime were nothing but chaos, misery and starvation in all countries. I, on the other hand, have been striving for twenty years with a minimum of intervention and without destroying our production, to arrive at a new socialist order in Germany which not only eliminates unemployment but also permits the worker to receive an ever greater share of the fruits of his labor.

"The success of this policy of economic and social reconstruction of our people, consisting of systematically eliminating differences of rank and class, has a true peoples' community as the final aim of the world.

"It was therefore only with extreme difficulty that I brought myself in August, 1939, to send my foreign minister to Moscow in an endeavor there to oppose the British encirclement policy against Germany. I did this only from a sense of all responsibility toward the German people, but above all in the hope after all of achieving permanent relief of tension and of being able to reduce sacrifices which might otherwise have been demanded of us.

"While Germany solemnly affirmed in Moscow that the territories and countries enumerated—with the exception of

Lithuania—lay outside all German political interests, a special agreement was concluded in case Britain were to succeed in inciting Poland actually into war with Germany. In this case, too, German claims were subject to limitations entirely out of proportion to the achievement of German forces.

"National Socialists! The consequences of this treaty which I myself desired and which was concluded in the interests of the German nation were very severe, particularly for Germans living in the countries concerned.

"Far more than 500,000 German men and women, all small farmers, artisans and workmen, were forced to leave their former homeland practically overnight in order to escape from a new regime which at first threatened them with boundless misery and sooner or later with complete extermination.

"Nevertheless, thousands of Germans disappeared. It was impossible ever to determine their fate, let alone their whereabouts. Among them were no fewer than 160 men of German citizenship. *To all this I remained silent because I had to.* For, after all, it was my one desire to achieve final relief of tension and, if possible, a permanent settlement with this State.

"However, already during our advance in Poland, Soviet rulers suddenly, contrary to the treaty, also claimed Lithuania.

"The German Reich never had any intention of occupying Lithuania and not only failed to present any such demand to the Lithuanian Government, but on the contrary refused the request of the then Lithuania to send German troops to Lithuania for that purpose as inconsistent with the aims of German policy.

"Despite all this I complied also with this fresh Russian demand. However, this was only the beginning of continually renewed extortions which kept on repeating ever since.

"Victory in Poland which was won by German troops exclusively caused me to address yet another peace offer to the

Western Powers. It was refused owing to efforts of international and Jewish warmongers.

"At that time already the reason for such refusal lay in the fact that Britain still had hopes of being able to mobilize a European coalition against Germany which was to include the Balkans and Soviet Russia. It was therefore decided in London to send Mr. Cripps as ambassador to Moscow. He received clear instructions under all circumstances to resume relations between the English and Soviet Russia and develop them in a pro-British direction. The British press reported on the progress of this mission as long as tactical reasons did not impose silence.

"In the autumn of 1939 and spring of 1940 the first results actually made themselves felt. As Russia undertook to subjugate by armed force not only Finland but also the Baltic States she suddenly motivated this action by the assertion, as ridiculous as it was false, that she must protect these countries from an outside menace or forestall it. *This could only be meant to apply to Germany, for no other power could even gain entrance into the Baltic area, let alone go to war there. Still I had to be silent.* However, those in power in the Kremlin immediately went further.

"Whereas in the spring of 1940 Germany, in accordance with the so-called pact of friendship, withdrew her forces from the Far Eastern frontier and, in fact, for the most part cleared these areas entirely of German troops, a concentration of Russian forces at that time was already beginning in a measure which could only be regarded as a deliberate threat to Germany.

"According to a statement that Molotov personally made at that time, there were twenty-two Russian divisions in the Baltic States alone already in the spring of 1940. Since the Russian Government itself always claimed it was called in by the local population, the purpose of their presence there could only be a demonstration against Germany.

"While our soldiers from May 5, 1940, on had been breaking Franco-British power in the west, Russian military deployment on our eastern frontier was being continued to a more and more menacing extent. From August, 1940, on I therefore considered it to be in the interest of the Reich no longer to permit our eastern provinces, which moreover had already been laid waste so often, to remain unprotected in the face of this tremendous concentration of Bolshevist divisions.

"*Thus there resulted British-Soviet Russian co-operation intended mainly at the tying up of such powerful forces in the east that radical conclusion of the war in the west, particularly as regards aircraft, could no longer be vouched for by the German High Command.* This, however, was in line with the objects not only of the British but also of the Soviet Russian policy, for both England and Soviet Russia intended to let this war go on for as long as possible in order to weaken all Europe and render it progressively more impotent.

"Russia's threatened attack on Rumania was in the last analysis equally intended to gain possession of an important base, not only of Germany's but also of Europe's, economic life, or at least destroy it. The Reich, especially since 1933, sought with unending patience to gain States in Southeast Europe as trading partners. We therefore also had the greatest interest in their internal constitutional consolidation and organization. Russia's advance into Rumania and Greece's tie-up with England threatened to turn these regions, too, within a short time into a general theater of war.

"Contrary to our principles and customs, and at the urgent request of the then Rumanian Government, which was itself responsible for this development, I advised acquiescence to the Soviet Russian demands for the sake of peace and the cession of Bessarabia. The Rumanian Government believed, however, that it could answer for this before its own people only if Germany and Italy in compensation would at least guarantee the integrity of what still remained of Rumania. *I did so with heavy heart, principally because when the Ger-*

man Reich gives a guarantee, that means it also abides by it. We are neither Englishmen nor Jews.

"I still believe at this late hour to have served the cause of peace in that region, albeit by assuming serious personal obligation. In order, however, finally to solve these problems and achieve clarity concerning the Russian attitude toward Germany, as well as under pressure of continually increasing mobilization on our Eastern frontier, I invited Mr. Molotov to come to Berlin.

"The Soviet Minister for Foreign Affairs then demanded Germany's clarification of or agreement to the following four questions:

"Point one was Molotov's question: Was the German guarantee for Rumania also directed against Soviet Russia in case of attack by Soviet Russia on Rumania?

"My answer: The German guarantee is a general one and is unconditionally binding upon us. Russia, however, never declared to us that she had other interests in Rumania beyond Bessarabia. The occupation of Northern Bukovina had already been a violation of this assurance. I did not therefore think that Russia could now suddenly have more far-reaching intentions against Rumania.

"Molotov's second question: That Russia again felt menaced by Finland. Russia was determined not to tolerate this. Was Germany ready not to give any aid to Finland and above all immediately to withdraw German relief troops marching through to Kirkenes?

"My answer: Germany continued to have absolutely no political interests in Finland. A fresh war by Russia against the small Finnish people could not, however, be regarded any longer by the German Government as tolerable, all the more so as we could never believe Russia to be threatened by Finland. Under no circumstances did we want another theater of war to arise in the Baltic.

"Molotov's third question: Was Germany prepared to agree that Russia give a guarantee to Bulgaria and send Soviet

Russian troops to Bulgaria for this purpose in connection with which he—Molotov—was prepared to state that the Soviets did not intend on that account, for example, to depose the King?

"My answer: Bulgaria was a sovereign State and I had no knowledge that Bulgaria had ever asked Soviet Russia for any kind of guarantee such as Rumania had requested from Germany. Moreover, I would have to discuss the matter with my allies.

"Molotov's fourth question: Soviet Russia required free passage through the Dardanelles under all circumstances and for her protection also demanded occupation of a number of important bases on the Dardanelles and Bosphorus. Was Germany in agreement with this or not?

"My answer: Germany was prepared at all times to agree to alteration of the Statute of Montreux in favor of the Black Sea States. Germany was not prepared to agree to Russia's taking possession of bases on the Straits.

"National Socialists! Here I adopted the only attitude that I could adopt *as the responsible leader of the German Reich but also as the representative of European culture and civilization and conscious of my responsibility*. The consequence was to increase in Soviet Russia the activity directed against the Reich, above all, however, the immediate commencement of undermining the new Rumanian state from within and an attempt to remove the Bulgarian Government by propaganda.

"With the help of the confused and immature leaders of the Rumanian Legion (Iron Guard) a coup d'état was staged in Rumania whose aim was to overthrow Chief of State General Antonescu and produce chaos in the country so as to remove all legal power of the government and thus the precondition for an implement of the German guarantee. *I nevertheless still believed it best to remain silent.*

"Immediately after the failure of this undertaking, renewed reinforcement of concentrations of Russian troops on Germany's eastern frontier took place. Panzer detachments and parachutists were transferred in continually increasing numbers to dangerous proximity to the German frontier. German fighting forces and the German nation know that until a few weeks ago not a single tank or mechanized division was stationed on our eastern frontier.

"If any final proof was required for the coalition meanwhile formed between England and Soviet Russia despite all diversion and camouflage, the Yugoslav conflict provided it. While I made every effort to undertake a final attempt to pacify the Balkans and in sympathetic co-operation with Il Duce invited Yugoslavia to join the Tripartite Pact, England and Soviet Russia in a joint conspiracy organized that coup d'état which in one night removed the then government which had been ready to come to agreement.

"For we can today inform the German nation that the Serb putsch against Germany did not take place merely under the British, but primarily under Soviet Russian auspices. As we remained silent on this matter also, the Soviet leaders now went still one step further. They not only organized the putsch, but a few days later also concluded that well-known friendship pact with the Serbs in their will to resist pacification of the Balkans and incite them against Germany. And this was no platonic intention: Moscow demanded mobilization of the Serb Army.

"Since even now I still believed it better not to speak, those in power in the Kremlin went still further: The Government of the German Reich today possesses documentary evidence which proves that Russia, in order finally to bring Serbia into the war, gave her a promise to supply her via Salonika with arms, aircraft, munitions and other war materials against Germany. And this happened almost at the very moment when I myself advised Japanese Foreign Minister Matsuoka that eased tension with Russia always was in hope, thereby to serve the cause of peace.

"Only the rapid advance of our incomparable divisions to

Skoplje as well as the capture of Salonika itself frustrated the aims of this Soviet Russian-Anglo-Saxon plot. Officers of the Serb air force, however, fled to Russia and were there immediately received as allies.

"The victory of the Axis Powers in the Balkans in the first instance thwarted the plan to involve Germany this Summer in months-long battles in Southeastern Europe while meantime steadily completing the alignment of Soviet Russian armies and increasing their readiness for war in order, finally, together with England and supported by American supplies anticipated, to crush the German Reich and Italy.

"*Thus Moscow not only broke but miserably betrayed the stipulations of our friendly agreement.* All this was done while the rulers in the Kremlin, exactly as in the case of Finland and Rumania, up to the last moment pretended peace and friendship and drew up an ostensibly innocent *démenti.*

"Although until now I was forced by circumstances to keep silent again and again, *the moment has now come when to continue as a mere observer would not only be a sin of omission but a crime against the German people—yes, even against the whole of Europe.*

"Today something like 160 Russian divisions are standing at our frontiers. For weeks constant violations of this frontier have taken place, not only affecting us but from the far north down to Rumania. Russian airmen consider it sport nonchalantly to overlook these frontiers, presumably to prove to us that they already feel themselves masters of these territories. During the night of June 17 to June 18 Russian patrols again penetrated into the Reich's territory and could only be driven back after prolonged firing. This has brought us to the hour when it is necessary for us to take steps against this plot devised by the Jewish-Anglo-Saxon warmongers and equally the Jewish rulers of the Bolshevist center in Moscow.

"German people! *At this moment a march is taking place that, as regards extent, compares with the greatest the world hitherto has seen.* United with their Finnish comrades, the fighters of the victory of Narvik are standing in the Northern Arctic. German divisions commanded by the conqueror of Norway, in co-operation with the heroes of Finnish freedom, under their marshal, are protecting Finnish soil. Formations of the German eastern front extend from East Prussia to the Carpathians. German and Rumanian soldiers are united under Chief of State Antonescu from the banks of the Pruth along the lower reaches of the Danube to the shores of the Black Sea. *The task of this front, therefore, no longer is the protection of single countries, but the safeguarding of Europe and thereby the salvation of all.*

"I therefore decided today again to lay the fate and future of the German Reich and our people in the hands of our soldiers.

"May God help us especially in this fight!"

SPECIAL INDEX TO HITLER'S MAJOR POLICIES AND IDEAS

(Italicized items in this special index are subordinate to the preceding item set in capitals).

I. DOCTRINES AND IDEAS

II. TREATIES, PACTS AND PLEDGES

III. ARGUMENTS AND JUSTIFICATIONS

IV. SPEECHES IN CRUCIAL MOMENTS

(Set in chronological order)

GENERAL INDEX

C

N

V

W

Y

Z